Reading for Thinking

Fourth Edition

Laraine E. Flemming

**Ann Marie Radaskiewicz,
Contributing Writer**

HOUGHTON MIFFLIN COMPANY
Boston   New York

Editor in Chief: Patricia A. Coryell
Senior Sponsoring Editor: Mary Jo Southern
Development Editor: Kellie Cardone
Editorial Assistant: Peter Mooney
Associate Project Editor: Christian Downey
Senior Manufacturing Coordinator: Marie Barnes
Marketing Manager: Annamarie Rice

Cover image: Tim Lewis

Printed in the U.S.A.

Library of Congress Control Number: 2001133257

ISBN: 0-618-21431-3

23456789-DOC-06 05 04 03

CONTENTS

Chapter 2   Power Tools for Learning: Annotating and Paraphrasing   *50*

Chapter 3   Reviewing Paragraph Essentials   *75*

Chapter 4   Understanding and Outlining Longer Readings   135

Chapter 5   Summarizing and Synthesizing: Two More Strategies for In-Depth Learning   *176*

 Chapter 6   Reading Between the Lines: Drawing the Right Inferences   *228*

Chapter 7 Defining the Terms *Fact* and *Opinion* 270

Chapter 8 Identifying Purpose and Tone 301

Chapter 11   Understanding and Evaluating Arguments   *422*

Chapter 12   Reading and Responding to Essay Questions   *496*

 **PREFACE**

To Instructors

Long-time users of *Reading for Thinking* will, I hope, be pleased to hear that the fourth edition bears a strong resemblance to previous editions. As in the past, the emphasis is on showing students that critical reading, rather than requiring a whole new set of skills, is a deeper and more analytical form of comprehension. Chapter by chapter, *Reading for Thinking* expands the notion of comprehension to include not just understanding the main idea but also recognizing how the writer's purpose can affect selection of evidence, choice of tone, degree of bias, and use of imagery.

Although almost half the readings in the fourth edition are new, the criteria by which they were selected have not changed. The readings were chosen to engage students' interest while adding to their store of general knowledge about current events and cultural allusions. Among the many topics addressed are the controversy surrounding Truman's decision to drop the atomic bomb, the changing technology of modern warfare, the evolution of the Barbie doll, and the short and brilliant life of Mexican artist Frida Kahlo. Like previous editions, this one offers numerous and carefully sequenced exercises. The number and the sequence are both important because they fulfill an essential objective of the text: The exercises in *Reading for Thinking* show students, in a clear, step-by-step fashion, how to push the boundaries of comprehension into the realm of critical reading.

Having assured previous users that much in this edition remains the same, let me now point out what's new.

New to the Fourth Edition

Digging Deeper Readings Each chapter now ends with an extended reading selection that picks up on a topic already introduced in the chapter. For example, after reading a brief passage hinting that President Polk purposely encouraged war with Mexico in order to expand U.S. borders, students now encounter a longer, more detailed reading, which makes a similar point. Each of the Digging

Deeper readings is accompanied by questions focusing on the skills introduced in the chapter.

Concept and Terminology Reviews Every chapter in *Reading for Thinking* now concludes with a test titled "Reviewing the Key Points." The purpose of these tests is to determine how well students have mastered the terminology and concepts explained in the chapter.

Skills Test Each chapter concludes with two to seven skills tests. Carefully sequenced according to degree of difficulty, the tests will help teachers precisely identify where more instruction and practice might be needed.

More Textbook Selections Because textbooks make up the bulk of student reading, it seemed wise to double the number of textbook selections included in previous editions. The fourth edition of *Reading for Thinking* offers numerous excerpts from a variety of disciplines, ranging from history to criminology.

A New Section on Rhetorical Questions Rhetorical questions are an important tool of persuasion. They also sometimes turn up in unlikely places, for example, in textbook writing that would otherwise seem intended mainly to inform. For this reason, a discussion of and practice with rhetorical questions have been added to the fourth edition.

More Work with Extended Arguments As reviewers of the third edition pointed out, even students who have an easy time analyzing and evaluating arguments in short passages sometimes get confused when an argument extends beyond a single paragraph. In response to that concern, this edition of *Reading for Thinking* has doubled the number of multiparagraph arguments.

New Topics for Arguments Aware that students may view analyzing arguments with something less than enthusiasm, I purposely selected real-world arguments that are bound to excite student interest and encourage heated discussion. Among the topics addressed in the chapter on arguments are the following: teaching creationism in the schools, the use of computerized cameras to catch speeders, El Al's controversial airline security precautions, and the dangers inherent in using reproductive technology to fashion the perfect child.

More Practice with Longer Reading Selections Although it's probably true that students who can pull the key points out of a paragraph are well on their way to doing the same with longer, multiparagraph readings, it's also true that students are constantly confronted with readings considerably longer than a single paragraph. It follows, then, that they need to hone their skills on longer reading selections. In this edition of *Reading for Thinking,* the number of extended readings—like the number of textbook selections—has doubled.

A New Section on Plagiarism Because many students don't realize that paraphrasing someone else's idea does not necessarily free a writer from providing attribution, a discussion of the relationship between paraphrasing and plagiarizing seemed a necessary and useful addition.

A New Explanation of Analogies in Arguments Arguing by analogy is common strategy in persuasive writing. Thus, it seemed important to include a discussion of how analogies are used and why they are never completely effective as evidence.

More Practice with Errors in Arguments It's often difficult to ferret out the irrelevant reason or circular logic tucked away in an otherwise sound argument. For that reason, the fourth edition offers students additional practice with locating errors in arguments.

More Exercises on Drawing Inferences The previous edition included an entire chapter on drawing inferences, and so, too, does this edition. However, students have more chances to create their own inferences. In particular, they get additional practice with inferring the main ideas of longer, multiparagraph readings.

A Completely Revised Section on Synthesizing In the fourth edition, students learn how to create synthesis statements that will help them review for exams.

A Revised Discussion of Using Summaries to Review The explanation of how summaries can serve as a tool for review has been revised and expanded so that students now get considerably more practice summarizing extended textbook selections.

A New Section on Adapting SQ3R *Reading for Thinking* now explains how SQ3R can be used to get the most from journal or magazine-length articles.

To My Reviewers

Because I had a great group of reviewers, revising *Reading for Thinking* was a relatively easy task. Although it certainly required time and work, I had a clear-cut blueprint to follow, one that was based on the astute suggestions offered by the following reviewers: Marilyn Burke of Austin Community College; Joan Hellman of Catonsville Community College; Ted Ridout of Bunker Hill Community College; Dawn Sedik of Valencia Community College; Deborah Spradlin of Tyler Junior College; and Jane Weber of Camden County College.

To My Editors

In addition, I have to thank my acquisitions editor, Mary Jo Southern, whose hard work on my behalf aided me throughout the process of revision. As always, I value Mary Jo as both my friend and my colleague. A very special thanks goes to senior editor Kellie Cardone, who, despite her numerous other responsibilities, always paid close and careful attention to both the manuscript and my concerns. I can't imagine being able to complete a revision without her. Thanks, too, go to Nancy Benjamin and her staff at Books By Design. Given the number of books Nancy packages, I am always amazed by and grateful for the close attention she and her staff give my books. And finally, what would I do without Mary Schnabel, who not only types my manuscripts, but also edits them, makes design suggestions, and just generally tells me when I am not making sense. She is a treasure, and may she never, ever retire.

Throughout the revising of this text, I have tried hard to respond to all the suggestions and comments I have received from both instructors and students. However, each new revision is bound to engender new thoughts on what works and what could be better, and that is as it should be. My hope, then, is that users of this new edition will feel free to send their comments, both positive and negative, along with suggestions for additional topics and materials to my e-mail address: laflemm@attglobal.net.

Laraine Flemming

Also Available in the Same Series

Reading for Thinking is the third and highest-level text in a three-part series. The two lower-level texts available offer the same step-by-step approach combined with lively readings and clear explanations. *Reading for Results* concentrates mainly on comprehension skills and includes one chapter on critical thinking. The perfect precursor to *Reading for Thinking, Reading for Results* lays the groundwork for all of the skills introduced in its more advanced sister text. Instructors teaching a basic reading course, however, might prefer to start with *Reading Keys.* This text offers more basic and abbreviated explanations along with greater repetition. It also lets students master both concepts and skills in small, incremental bites.

Created by Ulrich and Laraine Flemming to accompany this series, *Getting Focused* is a CD-ROM that introduces both comprehension and critical reading skills in a carefully sequenced program of tutorials and tests. Like the books, the software features the author's twin trademarks: lively readings and lucid explanations. In addition to this easy-to-navigate and graphically engaging software—free to a user of any Flemming text—instructors can find vocabulary, comprehension, and critical reading exercises on the author's personal website (http://users.dhp.com/~laflemm). Instructors can also go to Houghton Mifflin's developmental English website (http://college.hmco.com/devenglish/flemming/reading_results/8e/students/ace/). There you will find a variety of tests that cover vocabulary and comprehension skills.

C H A P T E R 1

Getting a Head Start: Strategies for Success

In this chapter, you'll learn

- **how to use a study technique called *SQ3R*.**
- **how to adapt *SQ3R* to shorter readings.**
- **how to underline while you read.**
- **how to acquire an academic vocabulary.**
- **how to take multiple-choice exams.**

By the time you finish this book, you'll possess all the reading skills necessary to achieve academic success. Still, like most students, you probably want to improve your academic performance immediately. The good news is that you can. If you put into practice all the pointers and tips introduced in Chapter 1, you'll be a better student in just a few weeks.

SQ3R: A System for Reading Textbooks

Textbooks aren't the same as novels. You can't just open up your textbook and start reading. Well, technically you can. But if you do, you won't understand and remember as much as you could if you used a study system like *SQ3R*.

Developed over fifty years ago by teacher and researcher Francis Robinson, *SQ3R* has stood the test of time, with numerous studies indicating that it improves comprehension. The letters *S-Q-R-R-R* stand for *survey, question, read, recite,* and *review.* Following each of these five steps when you read your textbooks will help you learn with greater speed and efficiency. So, without further ado, here's a brief explanation of each step.

S: Survey Before You Begin Reading

Survey a chapter before you begin reading it. Read only the title, the introduction, and the last page. Look carefully at all headings, captions, illustrations, and anything printed in the margins. Pay special attention to words printed in boldface or italics. Use this step to get a general sense of the chapter's content and to gauge how long it should take you to read it.

Q: Questions Help You Get Focused

To give your reading focus or purpose, use words like *why, what,* and *how* to transform headings into questions, such as "Why do glaciers grow and then retreat?" or "How do fossils of sea creatures end up on mountaintops?"

In addition to turning headings into questions, be sure to draw on your own personal knowledge and ask questions like "What do I know about this topic?" and "Do I agree with the author's point of view?" Questions like these also will help you focus your attention and maintain concentration while you read.

Raising and answering questions strengthens your motivation. Each time you can answer one of your own questions, you'll feel a sense of accomplishment. The more successful you feel, the more likely you are to keep reading.

R-1: Read the Chapter Section by Section

The first *R* in *SQ3R* stands for *read*. But here again, be systematic. Don't read a chapter straight through from beginning to end. Instead, read it in chunks or bites, going from chapter section to chapter section and pausing to review after each one.

Each time you begin a chapter section, raise questions based on the heading. Whenever possible, predict how you think the author's train of thought will continue. For example, if you see the heading *Differences Between Broadcast and Print Media*, mentally make a prediction and pose a question: "The author will probably point out several differences between television journalists and newspaper journalists. What exactly could those differences be?"

Even if you have to revise your questions and predictions when you finish reading a chapter section, those questions and predictions will serve their purpose. They will keep you focused on the material and alert you to differences between what you expected to read and what the author actually said.

Underline and Write While You Read

Want to make sure that you are really reading your assignment and not just letting your eyes glide across the page? Then get into the habit of underlining and writing while reading. While you are reading, underline key words in pencil, and jot key points and questions in the margins. When you go back for review, you can erase whatever seems less important the second time around and rewrite or add the rest in pen. Underlining and writing while reading forces you to maintain your concentration and really dig into the material. The close attention required to underline and write is what makes the difference between real reading and just letting your eyes drift across the page.

Annotate Pages

Like underlining, annotating (making marginal notes) while reading has a twofold reward. It will help you stay focused on the task at hand. It will also help you remember what you read, particularly if you are careful to **paraphrase** the author's language, using your own words whenever you can. By forcing you to re-create meaning in new and original language, paraphrasing gives your mind a chance to mull over the material. That's the real key to remembering.

R-2: Recite at the End of Each Chapter Section

Each time you finish a chapter section, you should recite the key points and any answers to questions you posed while surveying. Reciting will help you monitor, or check, your understanding of what you've read. Then you can decide if you need to reread the section. To recite, just ask yourself: "What were the key points in this reading?" Then see if you can come up with some or all of those points. Next, try to answer your original questions. If you can't recite any key points or answer your own questions, reread the entire chapter section immediately or mark it for a later rereading with the letters **RR.**

Write Out the Answers

If the reading assignment is especially difficult or particularly important, it's a good idea to write out the answers to your questions. When you write your answers, you can't fool yourself into thinking you've understood material that is actually vague or unclear in your mind.

R-3: Review After You Finish Reading the Chapter

When you finish your assignment, go back over the chapter and look at the headings. For each heading, try to mentally recite a few of the author's key points. Even better, ask a friend to quiz you on each of the headings.

Yes, using *SQ3R* will take extra time. Simply reading a chapter straight through without surveying or reciting, for example, is a quicker method of studying. Unfortunately, it's not particularly effective. Thus, it's very much worth your while to make *SQ3R*—or some similar method—a regular study habit.

CHECK YOUR UNDERSTANDING

Describe each step in *SQ3R* without looking back at the chapter. When you finish, compare what you've written with the actual descriptions to see how complete your answers are. *Note:* You probably won't remember all of the steps. Don't get discouraged. You will in time.

S: _____

_____

_____

Q: _____

R: _____

R: _____

R: _____

Adapting to Shorter Readings

SQ3R can be adapted to all kinds of reading. If, for example, an author uses questions between chapter sections, those questions can easily become part of your survey as well as part of your reading. Similarly, if you are assigned a much shorter reading in a magazine or a journal, you don't have to abandon *SQ3R*. Merely adapt your survey, making it include some or all of the following:

1. Read the title. If you can, turn it into a question. If a brief overview appears right underneath the title, as is often the case in journal articles, read that as well. Notice, too, if the title expresses a complete thought. If it does, that thought may be the main idea of the reading. Assume that it is until the reading proves your prediction incorrect.

2. Read the first paragraph. If the article seems technical or complicated, read the second paragraph as well.

3. Pose a question or two about the author's main point.

4. Read the first line of every paragraph. If the writing style is difficult or the content is unfamiliar, read the first and last sentence of every paragraph.

5. Look at any visual aids.

6. Read the last two paragraphs.

7. Ask yourself why your instructor assigned the reading. Try to figure out how it connects to your textbook assignments and classroom lectures.

Purpose Is the Key

Generally speaking, the steps in your survey depend mainly on your reading purpose. If you need to get a detailed understanding of the ideas or events mentioned in your text, you will include more steps in your survey. If, however, you want only a general understanding of the author's argument, you are likely to pare down the steps you use.

The following exercise will give you a chance to adapt *SQ3R* to a reading shorter than a chapter.

EXERCISE 1

DIRECTIONS Using the steps listed below, *survey* the selection entitled "Wartime Hawaii." When you finish, answer the questions in Part A on page 10. Then go back and *read* the excerpt from beginning to end, making sure to underline and annotate. When you finish your reading, answer the questions in Part B.

Survey Steps

1. Read the title and ask yourself, What does the author want to tell readers about wartime Hawaii?
2. Read the first paragraph and ask yourself, What point does the author want to make in the reading?
3. Read the headings and turn them into questions.
4. Read the first sentence of every paragraph.
5. Read the last paragraph.
6. Ask yourself if you already know anything about wartime Hawaii that might enhance your understanding of this reading.

Wartime Hawaii

Much as the war came to the United States initially and most dramatically at Pearl Harbor, the outlines of an increasingly multicultural United States emerging from the Second World War could be seen first and most clearly in Hawaii. The nearly one million soldiers, sailors, and marines stopping in Hawaii on their way to the battlefront, as well as the more than one hundred thousand men and women who left the mainland to find war work on the islands, expected the Hollywood image of a simple Pacific paradise: blue sky, green sea, and white sand; palm trees and tropical sunsets; exotic women with flowers in their hair. They found instead a complex multiracial and multiethnic society. The experience would change them, as they in turn would change the islands.

Hawaii's Multiracial Society

Before December 7, 1941, few Americans knew where Pearl Harbor was or even that Hawaii was a part of their country, a colonial possession, a territory annexed by the U.S. government in

1898. Few realized that Honolulu, a tiny fishing village when Captain James Cook sailed by the difficult entrance to its harbor in 1778, had subsequently become the major maritime center of a kingdom, the seat of a territorial government, and a gritty port city that would serve as the major staging ground for the war to be waged in the Pacific. And few knew that this American outpost, as a result of successive waves of immigration beginning in the 1870s by Chinese, Portuguese, Japanese, and Filipinos, had a population in 1940 in which native Hawaiians and white Americans (called *haoles*, which in Hawaiian means "strangers") each constituted only 15 percent of the islands' inhabitants.

The Nisei and Issei

The approximately 160,000 Hawaiians of Japanese ancestry—including some 100,000 second-generation Japanese, or *Nisei*, who had been born in Hawaii and were therefore U.S. citizens—composed Hawaii's largest ethnic group, more than a third of the population. Japan's attack on Pearl Harbor immediately raised fears of sabotage or espionage by Hawaiians of Japanese descent. Rumors flew of arrow-shaped signs cut in the sugarcane fields to direct Japanese planes to military targets and of *Nisei* women waving kimonos to signal Japanese pilots.

But in stark contrast to the wholesale incarceration of the Japanese in the Pacific coast states, where the dangers of subversive activities were slight in comparison to Hawaii, official military and administrative policy in the islands was to maintain traditional interracial harmony throughout the war, and to treat all law-abiding inhabitants of Japanese ancestry justly and humanely. "This is America and we must do things the American way," announced Hawaii's military governor. "We must distinguish between loyalty and disloyalty among our people." There was no mass internment of the *Nisei* and *Issei* (those who emigrated from Japan) as there was on the mainland.

For the *Issei*, loyalty to the United States had become an obligation, a matter of honor. To eliminate potential associations with the enemy, they destroyed old books, photographs of relatives, and brocaded *obi* (kimono sashes) and replaced portraits of the Japanese emperor with pictures of President Roosevelt. A burning desire to prove that they were true Americans prompted many of their Hawaiian-born children, often referred to as AJAs (Americans of Japanese ancestry), to become "superpatriots." AJAs contributed heavily to war-bond drives and sponsored their own "Bombs on Tokyo" campaign; they cleared areas for new military camps; and they converted the halls of Buddhist temples,

Shinto* shrines, and Japanese-language schools (all closed for the duration and reopened after the war) into manufactories of bandages, knit socks, sweaters, and hospital gowns (the latter sewn for the Red Cross and Office of Civil Defense). Their newly expanded contact with other Hawaiians, including *haoles,* hastened their assimilation into the larger Hawaiian society. In addition, AJAs served in the military campaigns in the Pacific as interpreters—translating, interrogating, intercepting transmissions, and cracking enemy codes; and they fought in Europe with the all-*Nisei* 442d Regimental Combat Team, the most highly decorated organization in the U.S. Army. These contributions gave the Japanese in Hawaii, as it did other ethnic groups, a new sense of their worth and dignity. The war experience aroused expectations of equal opportunity and treatment, of full participation in island politics, of no longer accepting a subordinate status to *haoles.*

Changing Attitudes Toward Haoles

Additionally, the attitudes of many Hawaiians toward *haoles* changed as native islanders witnessed a large number of whites doing manual labor for the first time. Their view that whites would always hold superior positions in society—as bosses, plantation owners, business leaders, and politicians—was turned topsy-turvy by the flood of Caucasian mainland war workers. The hordes of white servicemen crowding into Honolulu's Hotel Street vice district for liquor, for tattoos, for posed pictures with hula girls in grass skirts, for three-dollar sex at the many brothels,* and then for treatment at prophylaxis* stations to ward off venereal diseases also tarnished traditional notions of white superiority.

The Majority Becomes a Minority

Most of the whites who had come to Hawaii had never lived where whites did not constitute a majority and where *they* were the ones who were different. Most had never before encountered or conversed with those of African or Asian ancestry. Suddenly, they were in the midst of a mixture of ethnic and racial groups unmatched anywhere in the United States, in the midst of a society of people of diverse cultures working together for a common cause. So also were the nearly thirty thousand African-American servicemen and workers who arrived in the islands before the

---

*Shinto: a religion native to Japan characterized by worship of nature and ancestors.
*brothels: houses of prostitution.
*prophylaxis: preventive treatment for diseases.

war's end. Having experienced nothing like the fluid and relaxed racial relations of Hawaii's multiethnic society, blacks discovered an alternative to the racist America they knew. Some chose never to go back to the mainland. Others returned home to the States to press for the rights and freedoms they had first tasted in Hawaii. In so many ways, wartime Hawaii, termed "the first strange place" by historians Beth Bailey and David Farber, would anticipate the "strangeness" of U.S. society today. (Adapted from Boyer et al., *Enduring Vision*, pp. 779a and b.)

Part A: Surveying

DIRECTIONS Answer the following questions by filling in the blanks or circling the correct response.

1. The soldiers and wartime workers who came to Hawaii expected to find _____. But instead, they found _____.

2. Who composed Hawaii's largest ethnic group? _____

3. *True* or *False.* Unlike the mainland, Hawaii maintained interracial harmony throughout the war.

4. In wartime Hawaii, whites who lived there suddenly discovered what it was like to be _____.

5. In wartime Hawaii, African-Americans discovered _____

_____.

> **Stop!** Now go back and read the article from beginning to end. When you finish, answer the questions below.

Part B: Reading

DIRECTIONS Answer the following questions by filling in the blanks.

6. What general point about wartime Hawaii does the author make?

_____

7. The Nisei had been born in _____, whereas the Issei were born in _____.

8. Why did the Hawaiian-born Japanese become superpatriots?

   _____

9. Explain how the Hawaiian attitude toward *haoles* changed during wartime.

   _____

10. Give two reasons for that change.

   _____

   _____

 # Underlining While Reading

Underlining during the reading step of *SQ3R* is extremely important. Underlining while reading helps you concentrate. It also helps you think more deeply about the material. As a result, you'll remember more.

Yet despite the obvious benefits of underlining, many students don't know how to do it effectively. Either because they are afraid of leaving out something important or because they are not paying enough attention, students underline too much. (Although underlining too little can be a problem, it's much less common than underlining too much.) As a result, when exams roll around, students find themselves reviewing entire chapters rather than selected portions. To underline effectively, keep the following pointers in mind. (*Note:* To be completely effective, underlining should be combined with annotating, which is discussed on pages 50–54.)

Be Selective

Underline only the words necessary to explain the central or main point of the paragraph. You can figure out which words are central by asking yourself, "What words are essential to the author's meaning?" The answer to that question tells you the words that need to be underlined.

Here is a sample in which only the key words are underlined. Read just the underlined words and see how they convey the message of the paragraph.

Tornadoes

A **tornado** is a storm with a very intense low-pressure center. Tornadoes are short-lived and local in extent, but they can be extremely violent. They typically follow a very narrow, sharply defined path, usually in the range of 300–400 m wide. U.S. National Weather Service records show that tornadoes have the strength to drive 2 × 4 wooden boards through brick walls, lift an 83-ton railroad car, and carry a home freezer over a distance of 2 km. (Murck, Skinner, and Porter, *Environmental Geology*, p. 238.)

If you read just the underlined words in this passage, you can still re-create most of the original meaning. That's the true test of effective underlining.

You may be wondering why only one of the examples in the last sentence is underlined. Although all three are helpful in describing the intensity of a tornado, with a series of examples like this it's usually a good idea to underline the first item and then annotate the others in the margin, using words like *examples, reasons, consequences,* and so on.

Find a Balance Between Underlining Too Much and Underlining Too Little

Here are two more underlined passages. In the first one, the reader has underlined too much; in the second, too little.

Adaptive strategies are the unique cultural patterns ethnic minorities use to promote the survival and well-being of the community, families, and individual members of the group. Adaptive strategies help them gain access to educational, medical, political, and legal services, employment, housing, and other important resources and services. These strategies are reflected in the childrearing goals and practices found in these groups (Harrison et al., 1990). Three of the most important adaptive strategies are (1) the extended family, (2) biculturalism, and (3) ancestral world views. (Seifert, Hoffnung, and Hoffnung, *Lifespan Development*, p. 390.)

If you buy your textbooks in a used-book store, you'll notice that the excessive underlining shown above is very typical in used textbooks—at least in the first chapter. After that opening chapter, the underlining usually dribbles off to nothing. Students who underline every sentence often realize they are wasting their time and stop underlining. Unfortunately, they don't always take the time to figure out what they are doing wrong. Instead, they give up on underlining altogether.

Just as ineffective as too much underlining is underlining too little. To understand why, read just the underlined words in the following passage. See if you can figure out what the paragraph is about. Don't be surprised if you can't.

> The _extended family_ includes parents, children, and other relatives such as aunts, uncles, grandparents, and cousins, as well as some individuals not biologically related. In African-American extended families, for example, the high degree of interdependence among three or more generations of kin (child, parent, grandparent), as well as nonbiological family members, helps to provide the material aid such as food, shelter, clothing, money, child care, household maintenance, and social and emotional support that are critical for effective family functioning (Harrison et al., 1990; Stack, 1981). Hispanic-American families also show high degrees of connectedness, loyalty, and solidarity with parents and other relatives and of interdependence and mutual support (McGoldrick et al., 1982). (Seifert et al., _Lifespan Development_, p. 390.)

The person who underlined this passage correctly understood that the term _extended family_ was important. But beyond underlining that term, the reader hasn't even tried to highlight the definition or indicate its relationship to the two minority groups mentioned. As a result, the phrases that are underlined are all but useless for later reviews.

Use Pencil Rather Than Pen

While you are still learning how to underline efficiently, use a pencil rather than a pen or a felt-tip marker. That way, if you change your mind, you can always erase. After you review and further refine your understanding of what's essential, you can go back and underline again, this time with a pen or marker.

Check for Accuracy

Every once in a while, test your underlining to see if it makes sense. When you read over the underlined words, you should be able to fill in the gaps and come up with the general meaning of the passage. If reading only the underlined words doesn't make any sense, erase and start over.

EXERCISE 2

DIRECTIONS Circle the letter of the passage that best fits the guidelines for selective underlining described on pages 11–12.

EXAMPLE

a. Leadership Styles

Participative leaders share decision making with group members. Participative leadership encompasses so many behaviors that it can be divided into three subtypes: consultative, consensus, and democratic. **Consultative leaders** confer with group members before making a decision. However, they retain the final authority to make decisions. **Consensus leaders** are called that because they strive for consensus. They encourage group discussion about an issue and then make a decision that reflects general agreement and will be supported by group members. All workers who will be involved in the consequences of a decision have an opportunity to provide input. A decision is not considered final until all parties involved agree with the decision. Another criterion of consensus is that the group members are willing to support the final decision even if they do not agree with it totally. **Democratic leaders** confer final authority on the group. They function as collectors of group opinion and take a vote before making a decision. Some observers see very little differentiation between democratic leadership and free-rein leadership. (Adapted from DuBrin, *Leadership*, p. 110.)

b. Leadership Styles

Participative leaders share decision making with group members. Participative leadership encompasses so many behaviors that it can be divided into three subtypes: consultative, consensus, and democratic. **Consultative leaders** confer with group members before making a decision. However, they retain the final authority to make decisions. **Consensus leaders** are called that because they strive for consensus: They encourage group discussion about an issue and then make a decision that reflects general agreement and will be supported by group members. All workers who will be involved in the consequences of a decision have an opportunity to provide input. A decision is not considered final until all parties involved agree with the decision. Another criterion of consensus is that the group members are willing to support the final decision even if they do not agree with it totally. **Democratic leaders** confer final authority on the group. They function as collectors of group opinion and take a vote before making a decision. Some observers see very little differentiation between democratic leadership and free-rein leadership. (Adapted from DuBrin, *Leadership,* p. 110.)

c. **Leadership Styles**

Participative leaders share decision making with group members. Participative leadership encompasses so many behaviors that it can be divided into three subtypes: consultative, consensus, and democratic. **Consultative leaders** confer with group members before making a decision. However, they retain the final authority to make decisions. **Consensus leaders** are called that because they strive for consensus. They encourage group discussion about an issue and then make a decision that reflects general agreement and will be supported by group members. All workers who will be involved in the consequences of a decision have an opportunity to provide input. A decision is not considered final until all parties involved agree with the decision. Another criterion of consensus is that the group members are willing to support the final decision even if they do not agree with it totally. **Democratic leaders** confer final authority on the group. They function as collectors of group opinion and take a vote before making a decision. Some observers see very little differentiation between democratic leadership and free-rein leadership. (Adapted from DuBrin, *Leadership,* p. 110.)

EXPLANATION The correct answer is *b.* If you read over only the underlined words, you can still make sense of the paragraph without feeling that something crucial has been left out or that too much has been left in, forcing you to reread the entire paragraph.

a. **Hispanic Americans**

A new minority group has emerged in the United States—Hispanic Americans, also called Latinos. Today the category actually includes several groups. Besides Mexican Americans and Puerto Ricans, there are Cuban immigrants who began to flock to the Miami area when their country became communist in 1959. There are also the "other Hispanics"—immigrants from other Central and South American countries who have come here as political refugees and job seekers. By 1996, the members of all these groups totaled about 28 million, constituting nearly 11 percent of the U.S. population, the second largest minority. Because of high birth rates and the continuing influx of immigrants, Hispanic Americans are expected to outnumber African Americans in the next decade.

The Spanish language is the unifying force among Hispanic Americans. Another source of common identity is religion: at least 85 percent are Roman Catholic. There are, however, significant differences within the Hispanic community. Mexican Americans are by far the largest group, accounting for 64 percent of Hispanics. They are heavily concentrated in the Southwest and West. Puerto Ricans make up 11 percent and live mostly in the Northeast, especially in New York City. . . . Cubans constitute 5 percent of the U.S. Hispanic population. (Thio, *Sociology,* p. 299.)

b. **Hispanic Americans**

A new minority group has emerged in the United States—Hispanic Americans, also called Latinos. Today the category actually includes several groups. Besides Mexican Americans and Puerto Ricans, there are Cuban immigrants who began to flock to the Miami area when their country became communist in 1959. There are also the "other Hispanics"—immigrants from other Central and South American countries who have come here as political refugees and job seekers. By 1996, the members of all these groups totaled about 28 million, constituting nearly 11 percent of the U.S. population, the second largest minority. Because of high birth rates and the continuing influx of immigrants, Hispanic Americans are expected to outnumber African Americans in the next decade.

The Spanish language is the unifying force among Hispanic Americans. Another source of common identity is religion: at least 85 percent are Roman Catholic. There are, however, significant differences within the Hispanic community. Mexican Americans are by far the largest group, accounting for 64 percent of Hispanics. They are heavily concentrated in the Southwest and West. Puerto Ricans make up 11 percent and live mostly in the Northeast, especially in New York City. . . . Cubans constitute 5 percent of the U.S. Hispanic population. (Thio, *Sociology,* p. 299.)

c. **Hispanic Americans**

A new minority group has emerged in the United States—Hispanic Americans, also called Latinos. Today the category actually includes several groups. Besides Mexican Americans and Puerto

Ricans, there are Cuban immigrants who began to flock to the Miami area when their country became communist in 1959. There are also the "other Hispanics"—immigrants from other Central and South American countries who have come here as political refugees and job seekers. By 1996, the members of all these groups totaled about 28 million, constituting nearly 11 percent of the U.S. population, the second largest minority. Because of high birth rates and the continuing influx of immigrants, Hispanic Americans are expected to outnumber African Americans in the next decade.

The Spanish language is the unifying force among Hispanic Americans. Another source of common identity is religion: at least 85 percent are Roman Catholic. There are, however, significant differences within the Hispanic community. Mexican Americans are by far the largest group, accounting for 64 percent of Hispanics. They are heavily concentrated in the Southwest and West. Puerto Ricans make up 11 percent and live mostly in the Northeast, especially in New York City. . . . Cubans constitute 5 percent of the U.S. Hispanic population. (Thio, *Sociology*, p. 299.)

 ## Acquiring an Academic Vocabulary

In addition to a system for reading your academic assignments, you also need a system for mastering the academic vocabulary of college textbooks, readings, and lectures. As you might guess, the first step toward mastery is making sure you recognize the right words. So let's start there.

Recognizing Key Terms

Anxious for you to learn the specialized vocabulary of their subject matter, authors of textbooks usually provide an explicit definition right before or right after they introduce a key term. Thus, you need to pay close attention to any words that are highlighted in boldface, italics, or colored ink *and* followed or preceded by a definition. Such words are bound to belong to the specialized vocabulary of the subject you're studying. Look, for example, at the way the author of a textbook on management defines the term *corporate culture.*

Organizations develop unique internal cultures. Within the last decade, much attention has been focused on the relationship be-

Corporate culture is made up of shared values, symbols, myths, rituals, and language that shape the world of work.

tween a corporation's culture and its success. **Corporate culture** consists of the shared values, symbols, stories or myths, rituals, and language that shape an organization's work patterns. (Bulin, *Supervision*, p. 5.)

With a passage like this one, you should pause a moment to study the boldface term and its definition, both of which appear within the text itself as well as in the margin. Write the word and definition on an index card or in a vocabulary notebook so you can file it away for later review.

Boldface, colored ink, and marginal annotations are the most popular methods of highlighting textbook vocabulary, but italics, brackets, parentheses, and dashes are also widely used. Whenever you start an assignment, take a second or two to determine the method or methods an author uses to make specialized vocabulary jump out at the reader. These are the words that should become part of your vocabulary.

Breaking Words into Parts

Many English words—particularly those in your textbooks—include parts of other words drawn from Greek and Latin. Thus, if you learn some of the frequently appearing Greek and Latin prefixes and roots,* you can unlock the meanings of many, many different words.

While the meaning you derive from analyzing word parts may not be the exact same meaning you'd find in a dictionary, it will be close enough so that you can keep reading and not lose sight of the author's meaning. Take, for example, the word *intervention*. It's made up of the Latin prefix *inter* meaning "between" and the Latin root *ven* meaning "come." If you didn't know what the word *intervention* meant in the following sentence, you could figure it out from your knowledge of the two words parts, *inter* and *ven:* "The intervention of Swedish diplomat Raoul Wallenberg saved thousands of Hungary's Jews from certain death at the hands of Hitler's supporters." According to this sentence, Raoul Wallenberg came between or interfered with plans to execute Hungary's Jews.

A knowledge of Greek prefixes and roots is particularly valuable when taking science courses. For example, the Greek prefix *peri* means "around." Armed with that information, you can probably figure out definitions for the italicized word in this sentence: "The *periphery* of the volcano clearly showed signs of a recent eruption."

---

*roots: the core parts that carry a word's meaning.

If you guessed that *periphery* means "area around," you would be absolutely right.

In addition to figuring out word meanings, you can also usually remember a word's meaning more easily if you know something about its prefix or root. For example, if you know that *cardia* comes from *kardia,* the Greek word for "heart," you should have no trouble remembering that the *pericardium* is a fluid sac that encloses, or goes around, the heart.

The exercise that follows includes some useful prefixes and roots, along with one suffix.* A list of prefixes and roots is also included in the instructor's manual accompanying this textbook. Ask your instructor for a copy of that list and use it to expand your knowledge of frequently appearing word parts.

EXERCISE 3

DIRECTIONS Read over the list of word parts and their meanings. Then use your knowledge of word parts to determine the meanings of the italicized words.

mer:	Latin root	deserve, achieve
port:	Latin root	carry
pend, pond:	Latin root	hang, weigh
cracy:	Greek suffix	rule
pluto:	Greek prefix	wealth
philo:	Greek prefix	love
anthrop:	Greek root	human, humanity
miso:	Greek prefix	hatred

1. Next time you visit the office of a doctor or a lawyer, look at the awards, diplomas, or trophies on the wall. They have been placed there intentionally to indicate that the person inhabiting the office has accomplished tasks that *merit* approval or establish worth.

   Merit means _____.

2. There are those who claim that what we have in the United States is not a democracy but rather a *plutocracy.*

   Plutocracy means _____.

---

*suffix: suffixes, or word endings, usually tell you more about word function than word meaning.

3. Nowadays, the great industrialists and oil barons of the late nineteenth century are famous for their *philanthropy;* but there was a time when they were considered immoral plutocrats, consumed by the pursuit of money, not the love of humankind.

   Philanthropy means _____.

4. Some philosophers have argued that we would all be better off if we were led by a *meritocracy.*

   Meritocracy means _____.

5. The heavy, *pendulous* leaves of the plant were covered in a dark, slimy mold.

   Pendulous means _____.

6. The antihero of the French play is a *misanthrope* whose mean-spirited nature is only made tolerable by wit.

   Misanthrope means _____.

7. Her *deportment* during the funeral of her slain husband was incredibly brave.

   Deportment means _____.

8. As a scholar, she had written many *ponderous* articles about English morals and manners, but she made her fortune as a best-selling novelist writing lightweight mysteries.

   Ponderous means _____.

9. A long-time *Francophile,* he finally decided to return to the United States, but he was surprised to find that he was speaking English with just the hint of a French accent.

   Francophile means _____.

10. Try to *comport* yourself with a little more dignity when the queen arrives. This is a serious occasion.

    Comport means _____.

Using Context Clues

Like word parts, **context**—the sentence or passage in which a word appears—can give you an *approximate meaning* for an unfamiliar word. Although that meaning may not be exactly the same as the one in the dictionary, it will be close enough so that you can continue reading without interruption.

The following pages illustrate four of the most common context clues: contrast, restatement, example, and general knowledge.

Contrast Clues

Sentences containing contrast clues include **antonyms,** words or phrases opposite in meaning to the words you don't know. For example, suppose you were asked what the word *ostentatious* meant. You might not be able to define it. After all, the word doesn't turn up that often in everyday conversation. But suppose that word had a context, or setting, as in the following passage:

> Contrary to what many of us assume, the very rich are seldom *ostentatious* in their dress; they do not need to wear showy clothes to impress others. Secure in their wealth, they can afford to look plain and unimpressive.

In this case, the context of the word *ostentatious* provides contrast clues to its meaning. The words *plain* and *unimpressive* are antonyms for *ostentatious*. Using those contrast clues, you could **infer,** or read between the lines and figure out, that *ostentatious* means being showy or trying to impress.

Restatement Clues

For emphasis, authors sometimes deliberately say the same thing two different ways. Look, for example, at the following passage:

> Caffeine may well be bad for you. But without a cup of coffee in the morning, I get very *cantankerous*. My son says that on coffeeless days, I give new meaning to the words *cranky* and *ill-tempered*.

Here, the author announces that she becomes *cantankerous* in the morning if she doesn't have a cup of coffee. Then, to emphasize that point, she offers a restatement clue—two **synonyms,** or words similar in meaning, to the word *cantankerous: cranky* and *ill-tempered*. Thanks to that restatement, you can easily infer the meaning of *cantankerous*—"to be cranky and ill-tempered."

Example Clues

Be alert to passages in which the author supplies an example or an illustration of an unfamiliar word. Examples of the behavior or

thinking associated with a word can often give you enough information to infer a good approximate definition.

> The captain had a *dour* personality. He never laughed or smiled.
> He always prepared for the worst and seemed disappointed if the
> worst didn't happen.

You might infer from the examples in the above passage that
dour means "gloomy and depressed," and you would be absolutely
correct.

General Knowledge Clues

Although contrast, restatement, and examples are common context
clues, not all context clues are so obvious. Sometimes you have to
base your inference solely on your familiarity with the experience or
situation described in the text, as in the following example:

> As soon as I asked Magdalena to drive, I knew I had made a mis-
> take. She was an excellent driver but always took the most *circu-
> itous* route in order to enjoy the scenery. By the time we arrived at
> the restaurant, waiters were clearing the tables, and the restaurant
> was closed until dinnertime.

This passage does not contain any contrasts, restatements, or examples. But you can still figure out that *circuitous* means "indirect
or roundabout." After all, the driver *chose* to take the route, so *circuitous* cannot mean "wrong." Because they arrived too late for lunch,
the word must mean that the route was not direct.

CHECK YOUR UNDERSTANDING

Make up your own example of each context clue.

Contrast: _____

_____

Restatement: _____

_____

Example: _____

_____

General knowledge: _____

_____

Turning to the Dictionary

As the examples show, it's possible to infer a definition of an unfamiliar word from its context. Sometimes, however, context does not give you a definition that seems appropriate, and you won't be able to make sense of the passage without knowing what the word means. In a case like this, you should look up the word before you continue reading.

Using context to derive meaning is valuable because it allows you to read without constantly referring to a dictionary. However, after you finish reading, you should still compare the definitions you inferred with those in the dictionary. That way, you will be sure your definitions are correct.

EXERCISE 4

DIRECTIONS Use context to define the italicized words in the following sentences. Then identify the type of context clue that helped you infer your definition: *C* (contrast), *R* (restatement), *E* (example), or *G* (general knowledge).

EXAMPLE In *flagrant* disregard of the rules, she passed on the right and exceeded the speed limit by at least twenty miles an hour.

Definition *open, obvious*

Type of Clue *E*

EXPLANATION The examples of flagrant disregard—speeding, passing on the right—both suggest definitions like "open" and "obvious."

1. The surprise party was a complete *fiasco;* she had never before given a party that was such a failure.

Definition _____

Type of Clue _____

2. As a child he had been the most *gregarious* kid on the block, but as an adult he became a loner who found it difficult to bear the company of others.

Definition _____

Type of Clue _____

3. When the author stood at the podium to speak, there were no signs of her previous *trepidation*. In contrast to her earlier mood, she was remarkably relaxed and calm. Her voice did not break, her hands did not shake, and she seemed totally in command of the situation.

Definition _____

Type of Clue _____

4. That kind of *vituperation* has no place in a political campaign; he should be explaining his positions, not spewing insults.

Definition _____

Type of Clue _____

5. When it comes to publicity, the *incumbent* president obviously has more access to the press than other candidates. As the person already holding the office, the president is automatically followed everywhere by the press.

Definition _____

Type of Clue _____

6. He had come from an extremely *affluent* home where money was no object. But he gave it all up to live a life of poverty and serve those needier than himself.

Definition _____

Type of Clue _____

7. Although she wanted to, there was no way to *mitigate* the harshness of her criticism.

Definition _____

Type of Clue _____

8. The bulldog was remarkably *tenacious*. He wouldn't let go of the robber's leg even when the man rained blows down on his head. He only let go when his master yelled, "Stop!"

Definition _____

Type of Clue _____

9. Books on time management are popular primarily because *procrastination* is so common. After all, how many of us can honestly say we have never put off or postponed something we didn't want to do—washing the dog, writing a paper, cleaning the house—until the very last possible minute?

Definition _____

Type of Clue _____

10. After saving his mother from drowning, the twelve-year-old boy was *inundated* with letters praising him for his heroism.

Definition _____

Type of Clue _____

 # Reading and Responding to Multiple Choice

Currently, multiple-choice questions are the most popular type of exam question. Easy to correct, they also let teachers test a wide range of knowledge. It makes sense, therefore, for you to learn how skillful test takers read and respond to multiple-choice questions.

Understand the Purpose and Prepare Accordingly

For the most part, multiple-choice questions directly or indirectly rely on seven words: *who, what, where, why, when, which,* and *how.* These words readily lend themselves to brief questions that can be easily incorporated into multiple-choice answers, or options, like the ones listed below:

*1. Which of the following British colonies was founded last?
   a. Plymouth
   b. Pennsylvania
   c. Georgia
   d. Massachusetts Bay Colony
   e. Jamestown, Virginia

_____

*(*Answers:* 1.*c;* 2.*b*)

2. Who discovered the law of universal gravitation?

a. Johannes Kepler

b. Sir Isaac Newton

c. Galileo

d. Aristotle

e. Tycho Brahe

To study for multiple-choice tests, scour your textbook and lecture notes for references to famous figures, significant dates, crucial events, and major theories. Then review and reduce your notes until you have a collection of 3×5 index cards that show the name, date, event, or theory on one side with a brief description or explanation on the other. In the last day or two before the exam, rely primarily on your index cards for reviews.

Be Familiar with the Format

Just as understanding the structure of a paragraph makes you a better reader, understanding how multiple-choice questions are set up can make you a better test taker.

Type 1: Incomplete Sentence

The most common type of multiple-choice question starts with a partial or incomplete statement called the "stem." The test taker's job is to circle the letter of the ending that correctly completes the stem. Here's an example:

One of the chief reasons Americans were willing to join the peace-time North Atlantic Treaty Organization was because of the

a. Cuban Missile Crisis.

b. Hungarian Revolution.

c. Berlin Blockade.

d. Berlin Wall.

e. Bay of Pigs.

From a test-taking perspective, multiple-choice questions that open with an incomplete sentence can sometimes help you eliminate an option. When you're stuck on a multiple-choice question, you should always read the stem followed by each possible answer. If you're lucky, one or even two options might not grammatically fit the opening portion of the sentence as well as the other answers, and you can cross them out as potential answers. Look, for example, at the following:

Johannes Kepler was an

a. astronomer.

b. astrologer.

c. physicist.

d. anthropologist.

e. paleontologist.

In this case, you could immediately eliminate options *c* and *e* because the article *an* is almost always followed by words beginning with the vowels *a, e, i, o, u.* Although grammatical errors that make an option and the stem incompatible are not likely to appear in standardized tests created by an organization, they are possible in teacher-made tests. Your poor, overworked instructor has to create three different exams in one week. Under this type of pressure, it's easy for grammatical incompatibility to creep into a multiple-choice question and answer.

Type 2: Complete Sentence

Less common but still popular is a complete question followed by several answers:

From what source did the American Transcendentalists* find inspiration?[1]

a. the Bible

b. political leaders

(c.) nature

d. Buddhism

If you're stuck on a multiple-choice question with this format, start by reading the question with each separate answer. Sometimes one of the answers will jog your memory and help you make the correct choice.

---

*Transcendentalists: people like Henry David Thoreau, Margaret Fuller, and Ralph Waldo Emerson who turned to nature for inspiration.
[1]Adapted from William O. Kellogg, *AP United States History.* New York: Barron's Educational Service, 1996, p. 198.

Do the Easy Ones First

Whatever the format used on a multiple-choice exam, your first response should be to quickly read through all the questions, looking for those you can answer immediately. But even this first quick reading needs a method, so here's one that works for many successful test takers.

Anticipate the Answer, Then Read the Options

In your first reading of the whole exam, read each stem or question and see if an answer comes to mind. Then quickly skim the options, checking to see if an answer that closely resembles yours is there. *Make sure you read all the options.* You don't want to circle *a* without looking at *b* and then discover when you get the test back that *b* was really the better answer.

At this stage, it's important not to dawdle. If the options provided don't resemble the answer you came up with, don't try to make one fit by reading into the question and forcing words to assume meanings they don't normally possess. Instead, mark the question and go back to it once you have looked over the entire exam. After you have circled the answers you knew immediately, it's time to return to those questions that weren't quite as easy to answer.

Look for Key Words

If, on your second reading of a multiple-choice question, the answer still doesn't spring to mind, try to identify the names, events, or terms that are essential to the meaning of the stem or question. Then underline or circle them. Often, these key words or phrases will help you eliminate wrong answers and make it easier for you to determine the right one. Take, for example, the following test question. What word or phrase do you think might help you select an answer? Put a circle around it.

In what century did the Protestant Reformation begin?

a. sixteenth

b. nineteenth

c. eighteenth

d. seventeenth

If you circled the phrase "Protestant Reformation," you are on the right track and ready to start the process of elimination.

Use What You Know to Eliminate Wrong Answers

Let's say you studied hard but still drew a blank on the above question about the Protestant Reformation. Is it time to give up and go on to the next question? Absolutely not. Instead, try to call up what you know about the Protestant Reformation and test each option in the light of that knowledge.

For example, you may not know exactly when the Protestant Reformation began. However, when you look at each possible answer, you might know immediately that it occurred way before the eighteenth or nineteenth centuries. Good, now there are only two answers to choose from.

At this point, you may remember that Martin Luther, the leader of the Protestant Reformation, was born in 1483. Based on common sense, you wouldn't assume that Luther led a religious revolution before the 1500s. After all, he was still a teenager. And if Luther led the Reformation as an older adult, then—thanks to the process of elimination—you have your answer: The Protestant Reformation began in the sixteenth century, also known as the 1500s.

Look for the Option "All of the Above"

Sometimes when you look over the options, you'll notice that two or even three answers seem to be correct. Study those choices carefully to see if there is a word or phrase that might eliminate one of them. If there isn't and one option says "all of the above," that's probably the correct answer.

Watch Out for the Words *Not* and *Except*

Whenever you see the word *not* or *except* in the stem of a question, circle it to make it stand out. That way you'll be sure to take the word into consideration when choosing your answer. Consider, for example, the following question. Ignore the word *not* and you are bound to choose the wrong answer.

Which scientist was not involved in the making of the hydrogen bomb?

a. J. Robert Oppenheimer
b. Edward Teller
c. Werner von Braun
d. John von Neumann

Be Willing to Guess

Unless there's a penalty for a wrong answer, don't be afraid to guess as a last resort. If you are really stumped and just aren't sure which answer is right, circle the one you think most plausible, keeping in mind the following pointers. They sometimes apply and can help you make an "educated" guess.

Making an Educated Guess

1. The correct answer is sometimes longer and more detailed than the wrong answer.

2. The incorrect options are sometimes very similar and the correct answer is the one option that is quite different.

3. Words like *all, never,* and *always* frequently signal wrong answers, whereas words like *sometimes, usually,* and *generally* are more likely to be included in correct answers.

4. If two options seem equally correct and there's no option for "all of the above," choose the option that comes later in the list of answers. Test makers frequently put the wrong answer first because they know that some students are quick to choose the first seemingly correct answer they see.

5. Silly or foolish answers are not there to trick you. They really are wrong.

Don't Get Bogged Down

When you get your test, figure out generally how much time you can spend on each question. If you don't know the answer to a question and find yourself going way over your time limit, circle the question number and go back to it after you have answered all the other questions.

Avoid Overanalyzing

When answering multiple-choice questions, don't overinterpret or overanalyze either the stem or the options. Assign words their conventional, or common, meanings, and don't assume unlikely or rare meanings in an effort to discover where the instructor is trying to dupe you into choosing the wrong answer. Yes, your instructor wants to test your knowledge *and* your ability to read closely and carefully. But he or she does not want to mislead you with impossibly tricky questions or answers. So relax and take the language of the exam at its face value. There are no complicated, hidden meanings requiring you to wrench the language from its usual context.

EXERCISE 5

DIRECTIONS For each question, circle the letter of the correct response.

1. Multiple-choice questions are
   a. used primarily in science and history tests.
   b. not as popular as they once were.
   c. inferior to essay questions.
   d. the most popular type of test question.
   e. never used to test mathematical knowledge.

2. Multiple-choice questions rely heavily on the
   a. words *define, explain,* and *illustrate.*
   b. reader's ability to read between the lines.
   c. words *who, what, why, where, when, which,* and *how.*
   d. test taker's vocabulary.
   e. words *analyze, evaluate, annotate, synthesize, compare,* and *contrast.*

3. The incomplete portion of a multiple-choice test is called the
   a. stalk.
   b. stem.
   c. base.
   d. root.
   e. core.

4. When you first read the exam, you should read
   a. every second question.
   b. only the answers.
   c. only the questions that look hard.
   d. all the questions.
   e. only the questions that look easy.

5. When answering multiple-choice questions, you should
   a. never assume that words refer to their usual meanings.
   b. assume the instructor will try to trick you.
   c. avoid overinterpreting or overanalyzing.
   d. interpret the stem more carefully than the options.
   e. interpret the options more carefully than the stem.

■ **DIGGING DEEPER**

LOOKING AHEAD Earlier in this chapter, you learned how important it was for college students to learn some Greek and Latin word parts. The following reading suggests that Latin, in particular, should make a comeback—not just in college, but already in elementary school.

THE NEW CASE FOR LATIN

1 Amy High is decked out in the traditional pink dress and golden stole of ancient Rome. She bursts into a third-grade classroom and greets her students: "Salvete, omnes!" (Hello, everyone!) The kids respond in kind, and soon they are studying derivatives. "How many people are in a duet?" High asks. All the kids know the answer, and when she asks how they know, a boy responds, "Because duo is 'two' in Latin." High replies, "Plaudite!" and the fourteen kids erupt in applause. They learn the Latin root *later,* or side, and construct such English words as *bilateral* and *quadrilateral.* "Latin's going to open up so many doors for you," High says. "You're going to be able to figure out the meaning of words you've never seen before."

2   High teaches at Providence Elementary School in Fairfax City, Virginia, which has a lot riding on the success of her efforts. As part of Virginia's high-stakes testing program, schools that don't boost their scores by the year 2007 could lose state funding. So Fairfax City, just eighteen miles southwest of the White House, has upgraded its two crumbling elementary schools with new high-tech television studios, computer labs, and one very old feature—mandatory Latin.

3   Here lies one of the more counterintuitive developments of the standardized-testing movement: Though some critics complain that teachers are forced to dumb down their lessons and "teach to the test," some schools are offering more challenging course work as a way of engaging students. In the past three years, scores of elementary schools in high-stakes-testing states such as Texas, Virginia, and Massachusetts have added Latin programs. Says Allen Griffith, a member of the Fairfax City school board: "If we're trying to improve English skills, teaching Latin is an awfully effective, proved method."

4   This is not your father's Latin, which was taught to elite college-bound high schoolers and drilled into them through memorization. Its tedium and perceived irrelevance almost drove Latin

from public schools. Today's growth in elementary school Latin has been spurred by new, interactive oral curriculums, enlivened by lessons in Roman mythology and culture. "One thing that makes it engaging for kids is the goofy fun of investigating these guys in togas," says Marion Polsky, author of *First Latin: A Language Discovery Program,* the textbook used in Fairfax City.

5   Latin enthusiasts believe that if young students learn word roots, they will be able to decipher unfamiliar words. (By some estimates, 65 percent of all English words have Latin roots.) Latin is an almost purely phonetic language. There are no silent letters, and each letter represents a single sound. That makes it useful in teaching reading. And once kids master the grammatical structure of Latin—which is simple, logical, and consistent—they will more easily grasp the many grammatical exceptions in English.

6   In the 1970s and '80s, the U.S. government funded Latin classes in underperforming urban school districts. The results were dramatic. Children who were given a full year of Latin performed five months to a year ahead of control groups in reading comprehension and vocabulary. The Latin students also showed outsize gains in math, history, and geography. But Congress cut the funding, and nearly all the districts discontinued Latin.

7   Some curriculum experts have examined the evidence and still favor modern languages instead of Latin. John Chubb, chief executive of the Edison charter schools, said the company decided to make Spanish, not Latin, mandatory in its elementary schools because "we want our kids to be socialized to the outside world."

8   Still, Griffith, the Fairfax City school board member, believes that "so far, the Latin looks like a good investment." He took encouragement from the confident smiles of Amy High's students each time they correctly responded to a question. "They're so receptive," says High. "They don't even know they're learning." (Mike Eskenazi, "Education/Special Report: The New Case for Latin," *Time,* 12 December 2000, p. 61.)

Sharpening Your Skills

DIRECTIONS Answer the following questions by filling in the blanks or circling the letter of the correct response.

1. Which of the following statements sums up the author's message?

   a. In Virginia, a lot is riding on the elementary schools' new Latin program.

   b. Although a few teachers think Latin should make a comeback, most believe that Spanish should be the mandatory language in elementary schools.

c. In the hopes of improving vocabulary and language skills, many elementary schools have begun to add Latin to their curriculums.

d. Latin should be taught in elementary school because kids at that age will be receptive to it.

2. Supporters of Latin instruction claim that once students learn the simple, logical, and consistent grammar of Latin, they will have an

easier time learning _____.

3. In paragraph 5, the author says, "Latin is an almost purely phonetic language." Based on the context, what's a good approximate definition of the word *phonetic*?

_____

_____

4. At the core of the word *mandatory*, which appears in paragraph 2, is the root *mand*, meaning "to order." Based on context and your knowledge of that root, what's a good approximate meaning for *mandatory*?

_____

_____

5. In paragraph 3, the author calls the offering of challenging courses a "counterintuitive" development. Based on context and the fact that "counter" means against, how would you define this word?

_____

_____

WORD NOTES: ONE PREFIX, MANY MEANINGS

Mal is a prefix meaning "bad" or "badly." Use that knowledge along with the context to write definitions for the italicized words below.

1. In an attempt to win the election, each opponent *maligned* the other.

Maligned means _____.

2. The vampire's *malevolent* smile sent chills up and down her spine; she felt as if she had looked into the face of evil.

Malevolent means _____.

3. On her death bed, she issued a *malediction* against all who had defamed her.

Malediction means _____.

4. My aunt is a chronic *malcontent;* nothing ever pleases her.

Malcontent means _____.

5. The ancient Persians treated all *malefactors* harshly, assigning them severe punishments for small crimes like stealing fruit from the market.

Malefactors means _____.

Test 1: Reviewing the Key Points

> DIRECTIONS Answer the following questions by filling in the blanks or circling the correct response.

1. *True* or *False.* A good survey always has six separate steps.

2. What words will help you transform headings into questions?

   _____

3. How can you make sure that you are really reading and not just letting your eyes glide across the page?

   _____

4. What are the benefits of underlining and paraphrasing while you read?

   _____

   _____

5. Why is recitation an important part of reading?

   _____

6. What are the ways authors make specialized vocabulary stand out?

   _____

7. Identify the four common types of context clues.

   _____

8. *True* or *False.* An approximate definition should exactly match the dictionary definition of a word.

9. The most common multiple-choice questions start with _____

   _____.

10. What two words should you watch for and circle when taking multiple-choice exams?

    _____

Test 2: Using *SQ3R*

DIRECTIONS Survey the following selection using the steps listed below. When you finish, answer the questions in Part A on page 40. Then go back and read the selection from beginning to end. When you are done, answer the questions in Part B on page 41.

Survey Steps

---

1. Read the first and last paragraphs.
2. Use the title to pose a question.
3. Read the headings and the marginal note.
4. Read the first sentence of every paragraph.
5. Read through the questions on pages 40–41.

How the Need for Achievement Spurs Motivation

need achievement A motive influenced by the degree to which a person establishes specific goals, cares about meeting those goals, and experiences feelings of satisfaction by doing so.

Many athletes who hold world records still train intensely; many people who have built multimillion-dollar businesses still work fourteen-hour days. What motivates these people? A possible answer is a motive called **need achievement** (H. A. Murray, 1938). People with a high need for achievement seek to master tasks—such as sports, business ventures, intellectual puzzles, or artistic creations—and feel intense satisfaction from doing so. They work hard at striving for excellence, enjoy themselves in the process, take great pride in achieving at a high level, and often experience success.

Individual Differences How do people with strong achievement motivation differ from others? To find out, researchers gave children a test to measure their need for achievement and then asked them to play a ring-toss game. Children scoring low on the need-for-achievement test usually stood so close or so far away from the ring-toss target that they either could not fail or could not succeed. In contrast, children scoring high on the need-for-achievement test stood at a moderate distance from the target, making the game challenging but not impossible (McLelland, 1958).

Experiments with adults and children suggest that people with high achievement needs tend to set challenging, but realistic, goals. They actively seek success, take risks as needed, and are intensely satisfied with success. Yet if they feel they have tried their best, people with high achievement motivation are not too upset by failure. Those with low achievement motivation also like to succeed, but success tends to bring them not joy but relief at having avoided failure (Winter, 1996).

People with strong achievement motivation tend to be preoccupied with their performance and level of ability (Harackiewicz & Elliot, 1993). They select tasks with clear outcomes, and they prefer feedback from a harsh but competent critic rather than from one who is friendlier but less competent (Klich & Feldman, 1992). They like to struggle with a problem rather than get help. They can wait for delayed rewards, and they make careful plans for the future (F. S. Mayer & Sutton, 1996). In contrast, people who are less motivated to achieve are less likely to seek or enjoy feedback, and they tend to quit in response to failure (Graham & Weiner, 1996).

Development of Achievement Motivation Achievement motivation tends to be learned in early childhood, especially from parents. For example, in one study young boys were given a very hard task, at which they were sure to fail. Fathers whose sons scored low on achievement motivation tests often became annoyed as they watched their boys work on the task, discouraged them from continuing, and interfered or even completed the task themselves (B. C. Rosen & D'Andrade, 1959). A different pattern of behavior emerged among parents of children who scored high on tests of achievement motivation. Those parents tended to (1) encourage the child to try difficult tasks, especially new ones; (2) give praise and other rewards for success; (3) encourage the child to find ways to succeed rather than merely complaining about failure; and (4) prompt the child to go on to the next, more difficult challenge (McClelland, 1985).

Cultural influences also affect achievement motivation. Subtle messages about a culture's view of the importance of achievement often appear in the books children read and the stories they hear. Does the story's main character work hard and overcome obstacles, thus creating expectations of a payoff for persistence? Or does the main character loaf around and then win the lottery, suggesting that rewards come randomly, regardless of effort? And if the main character succeeds, is it the result of personal initiative, as is typical of stories in individualist cultures? Or is success based on ties to a cooperative and supportive group, as is typical of stories in collectivist cultures? Such themes appear to act as blueprints for reaching one's goals. It is not surprising, then, that ideas about achievement motivation differ from culture to culture. In one study, individuals from Saudi Arabia and from the United States were asked to comment on short stories describing people succeeding at various tasks. Saudis tended to see the people in the stories as having succeeded because of the help they got from others, whereas Americans tended to attribute success to the internal characteristics of each story's main character (Zahrani & Kaplowitz, 1993).

Achievement motivation can be increased in people whose cultural training did not encourage it in childhood (McClelland, 1985). For example, high school and college students with low achievement motivation were helped to develop fantasies about their own success. They imagined setting goals that were difficult but not impossible. Then they imagined themselves concentrating on breaking a complex problem into small, manageable steps. They fantasized about working hard, failing but not being discouraged, continuing to work, and finally feeling great about achieving success. Afterward, the students' grades and academic success improved, suggesting an increase in their achievement motivation (McClelland, 1985). In short, achievement motivation is strongly influenced by social and cultural learning experiences and by the beliefs about oneself that these experiences help to create. People who come to believe in their ability to achieve are more likely to do so than those who expect to fail (Butler, 1998; Dweck, 1998; Wigfield & Eccles, 2000). (Bernstein and Nash, *Essentials of Psychology*, pp. 274–276.)

Part A: Surveying

DIRECTIONS Answer the following questions by filling in the blanks or circling the correct response.

1. Throughout the reading, what question is the author trying to answer?

    _____

2. *True* or *False*. People with high achievement needs tend to set themselves impossible goals.

3. *True* or *False*. Achievement motivation is learned in adolescence.

4. *True* or *False*. Culture affects achievement motivation.

5. *True* or *False*. Once established, a person's level or degree of achievement motivation cannot be changed or altered in any way.

Part B: Reading

DIRECTIONS Answer the following questions by filling in the blanks or circling the letter of the correct response.

6. How do people with high achievement motivation respond to failure?

a. They get outraged and give up.

b. They criticize the person in charge for causing their failure.

c. If they've tried their best, they don't get too upset by failure.

d. They refuse to quit even when everything is against them.

7. Which of the following does *not* characterize people with high achievement motivation?

a. They prefer to get feedback from someone who won't hurt their feelings.

b. They like to struggle with a problem.

c. They tend to make careful plans for the future.

d. They select tasks with clear outcomes.

8. What was the difference when individuals from Saudi Arabia and the United States were asked to comment about people in stories succeeding at various tasks?

_____

_____

9. Which of the following does *not* characterize the parents of children with high achievement motivation?

a. They encourage their children to try difficult tasks, especially new ones.

b. Even if their children performed a task poorly, the parents give high praise in an effort to bolster their children's self-esteem.

c. They encourage their children to find ways to succeed rather than merely complaining about failure.

d. Once their children succeed at a task, the parents encourage them to go on to the next, more difficult challenge.

10. *True* or *False.* People who believe in their ability to achieve are more likely to succeed than people who expect to fail.

Test 3: Underlining Efficiently

DIRECTIONS For each pair of passages, circle the letter of the passage that has been more efficiently underlined.

1. a. Within each region of the United States, there are many unique influences and variations too numerous to mention. The key point, however, is that these **regional differences** may affect consumption patterns. To illustrate, due to a strong Mexican influence, consumers in the Southwest have a stronger preference for spicy foods as well as for foods such as tortillas, salsa, and pinto beans. Beef barbecue is particularly popular in Texas due to a large cattle industry, whereas parts of the Deep South lean toward pork barbecue. California has developed a reputation for health consciousness and health foods. There are even regional differences in the type of stuffing used at Thanksgiving. Cornbread stuffing tends to be more popular in the South, in contrast to oyster stuffing in the North. Asian families on the West Coast, on the other hand, are more likely to substitute rice for stuffing.

Styles of music may also differ across regions. The Deep South developed a distinct style of southern rock (e.g., the Allman Brothers and Lynyrd Skynrd). Nashville and Texas have traditionally been strongholds of country music, and Kentucky is known as the home of bluegrass. Seattle was once recognized as the capital of the "grunge sound," with bands such as Pearl Jam, Soundgarden, and Nirvana.

b. Within each region of the United States, there are many unique influences and variations too numerous to mention. The key point, however, is that these **regional differences** may affect consumption patterns. To illustrate, due to a strong Mexican influence, consumers in the Southwest have a stronger preference for spicy foods as well as for foods such as tortillas, salsa, and pinto beans. Beef barbecue is particularly popular in Texas due to a large cattle industry, whereas parts of the Deep South lean toward pork barbecue. California has developed a reputation for health consciousness and health foods. There are even regional differences in the type of stuffing used at Thanksgiving. Cornbread stuffing tends to be more popular in the South, in contrast to oyster stuffing in the North. Asian families on the West Coast, on the other hand, are more likely to substitute rice for stuffing.

Styles of music may also differ across regions. <u>The Deep South developed a distinct style of southern rock</u> (e.g., the Allman Brothers and Lynyrd Skynrd). Nashville and Texas have traditionally been strongholds of country music, and Kentucky is known as the home of bluegrass. <u>Seattle was once recognized as the capital of the "grunge sound," with bands such as Pearl Jam</u>, Soundgarden, and Nirvana.

2. a. Canada: A Harm-Based Approach to Obscenity

In February 1992, the Supreme Court of Canada <u>ruled that obscenity was to be defined by the harm it does to women's pursuit of equality.</u> In *Butler v. Her Majesty the Queen*, the Court unanimously <u>redefined obscenity</u> as sexually <u>explicit material that involves violence</u> or <u>degradation</u>.* According to the Canadian Court, <u>violent and degrading sexual material will almost always constitute an undue exploitation of sex</u> and <u>interferes with progress</u> toward gender equality.

The Court's ruling sets out clear guidelines. Adult erotica,* no matter how explicit, <u>is</u> not <u>considered obscene</u>. Erotic material that <u>contains violence</u>, <u>degradation</u>, <u>bondage</u>, or <u>children is considered illicit obscenity</u>. In effect, the Court decided that a threat to <u>women's equality is an acceptable ground</u> for some limitation of free speech. <u>As of this writing, Canada is</u> the only nation that has redefined obscenity in terms of <u>harm to women rather than as material that offends moral values</u>. (Allgeier and Allgeier, *Sexual Interactions*, p. 530.)

b. Canada: A Harm-Based Approach to Obscenity

In February <u>1992</u>, the <u>Supreme Court of Canada ruled</u> that <u>obscenity</u> was to be <u>defined by</u> the <u>harm</u> it does <u>to women's pursuit of equality.</u> In *Butler v. Her Majesty the Queen*, the <u>Court</u> unanimously <u>redefined obscenity as sexually explicit material</u> that <u>involves violence</u> or <u>degradation</u>. <u>According to</u> the Canadian <u>Court</u>, violent and <u>degrading sexual material</u> will almost always constitute an undue <u>exploitation of sex</u> and <u>interferes with progress</u> toward <u>gender equality</u>.

---

*degradation: the act of reducing to a lower condition.
*erotica: literature or art that focuses on sexual desire.

The Court's ruling sets out clear guidelines. Adult erotica, no matter how explicit, is not considered obscene. Erotic material that contains violence, degradation, bondage, or children is considered illicit obscenity. In effect, the Court decided that a threat to women's equality is an acceptable ground for some limitation of free speech. As of this writing, Canada is the only nation that has redefined obscenity in terms of harm to women rather than as material that offends moral values. (Allgeier and Allgeier, *Sexual Interactions*, p. 530.)

Test 4: Using Context Clues

DIRECTIONS Use context to define the italicized word in each sentence. Then circle the letter of the context clue you used to derive your definition.

1. When the storm began, we decided to wait for a more *auspicious* moment; no one in the group wanted to go on a picnic under such unfavorable conditions.

   Auspicious means _____

   _____.

   Context Clue a. contrast

                            b. example

                            c. restatement

                            d. general knowledge

2. I can't accept that *spurious* hundred dollar bill; it has George Washington's face where Benjamin Franklin's should be.

   Spurious means _____

   _____.

   Context Clue a. contrast

                            b. example

                            c. restatement

                            d. general knowledge

3. Because of its harsh policies, the government is in a very *precarious* position; and because it is so insecure, the World Bank is unwilling to extend the term of the country's loans.

   Precarious means _____

   _____.

   Context Clue a. contrast

                            b. example

                            c. restatement

                            d. general knowledge

4. The expression "Have a nice day" has been repeated so often, it has become *perfunctory.*

Perfunctory means _____

_____.

Context Clue   a. contrast

b. example

c. restatement

d. general knowledge

5. As a result of the high altitude, his brain had been deprived of oxygen and he was *incoherent*. Because he wasn't making any sense, his fellow climbers couldn't understand his warnings.

Incoherent means _____

_____.

Context Clue   a. contrast

b. example

c. restatement

d. general knowledge

6. The snowstorm *obliterated* all traces of the wolf's tracks.

Obliterated means _____

_____.

Context Clue   a. contrast

b. example

c. restatement

d. general knowledge

7. For half a semester, her professor had preached about the importance of *cohesion*. But in her haste, the student still managed to produce a paper that was poorly organized and lacking in unity.

Cohesion means _____

_____.

Context Clue   a. contrast

b. example

c. restatement

d. general knowledge

8. Having discovered that he had invented the details of his past, Frank's friends were appalled by his *duplicity*.

    Duplicity means _____

    _____.

Context Clue a. contrast

    b. example

    c. restatement

    d. general knowledge

9. Try as she might, she couldn't get any *purchase* on the mountain. Every time she tried to take a step, she would slide backwards.

    Purchase means _____

    _____.

Context Clue a. contrast

    b. example

    c. restatement

    d. general knowledge

10. Having been a hard-working, no-nonsense realist all his life, he decided it was time to indulge in some more *quixotic* pursuits.

    Quixotic means _____

    _____.

Context Clue a. contrast

    b. example

    c. restatement

    d. general knowledge

Test 5: Using Context Clues and Word Parts

DIRECTIONS Use context clues and the word parts in the list below to define the italicized words.

cred	belief
string, strict	draw or bind
solv	loosen, free
clam, claim	cry out

1. The *clamorous* crowd suddenly grew quiet once the speaker appeared.

   Clamorous means _____

   _____.

2. The rules of behavior in the nursery school were far too *stringent* for such young children.

   Stringent means _____

   _____.

3. You can't give any *credence* to her story; she has a hard time knowing the difference between fact and fiction.

   Credence means _____

   _____.

4. In all that *clamor*, it was hard to follow the conversation for more than a few minutes.

   Clamor means _____

   _____.

5. He's innocent and somewhat *credulous*, but he's nobody's fool.

   Credulous means _____

   _____.

6. She followed all of the religion's *strictures* faithfully, but she did so more out of fear than belief.

   Strictures means _____

   _____.

7. His financial *insolvency* made him a bad risk to most mortgage officers.

   Insolvency means _____

   _____.

8. The look of *incredulity* on her face spoke volumes. She didn't believe a word he said.

   Incredulity means _____

   _____.

9. After years of being in debt, he had finally become financially *solvent.*

   Solvent means _____

   _____.

10. The *constricted* feeling in her throat only grew stronger as the airplane rose higher, and she knew it would not go away until the plane landed.

    Constricted means _____

    _____.

C H A P T E R   2

Power Tools for Learning: Annotating and Paraphrasing

 In this chapter, you'll learn

- **how to effectively annotate pages while you read.**
- **how to paraphrase with accuracy and completeness.**

Chapter 1 emphasized the importance of annotating and paraphrasing while reading. Chapter 2 looks more closely at these two reading strategies so critical to academic success.

Annotating Pages

When done right, annotating pages—making notes in the margins—can improve both concentration and comprehension. Marginal annotations can also ensure that you remember more of what you read. However, annotations are only useful if you make the right kind. Comments like "Boy, this is boring" or "Say what?" won't produce a big learning bonus. When you annotate, you shouldn't waste space on trivial comments. Instead, do the following: (1) identify key points, (2) connect the author's words to your own experience, and (3) predict test questions.

Identify Key Points

To check your understanding, get a head start on your notes, or prepare for exam reviews, it's a good idea to jot in the margin the main point of a chapter section or article. If there's enough space, you should add some of the reasons, studies, or examples used to clarify or prove that point. Still, if there are several different reasons, examples, studies, or statistics cited in support of the author's main idea, you can't possibly note them all in the margins. The result would be a cluttered, hard-to-read page. A better idea is to use lines, arrows, numbers, or any other symbols you choose to indicate how the author explains and supports the central or key point of the passage.

Compare the following selections. Both are correctly underlined and annotated but in different ways. Still, each set of annotations makes the main idea and the supporting details stand out for easy access. The two excerpts illustrate a key point about annotating pages: We all have our own individual method or style.

Long Prison Terms

Some scholars think long prison sentences aren't effective or fair.

How many times have you heard the expression "Lock 'em up and throw away the key"? It captures the frustration law-abiding people feel about the problem of crime in America. It reflects a belief that society is best off when criminals are housed in prisons for long periods. This strategy has an obvious appeal—locking up offenders prevents them from committing additional crimes in the community, at least during the course of their confinement. Yet, <u>according to some</u> <u>scholars, long prison sentences may be unjust</u>, unnecessary, <u>counterproductive,*</u> <u>and inappropriate.</u>

• <u>Unjust</u> if <u>other offenders</u> who have <u>committed</u> the <u>same crime</u> receive shorter sentences.

*counterproductive: tending to hurt rather than help.

reasons why

- Unnecessary if the offender is not likely to offend again.
- Counterproductive whenever prison increases the risk of subsequent or habitual criminal behavior.
- Inappropriate if the offender has committed an offense entailing insignificant harm to the community. (Adler, Mueller, and Laufer, *Criminal Justice*, p. 349.)

In this case, the main idea—"Some scholars think long prison sentences aren't effective or fair"—is identified in the margin. The major details—the reasons why scholars don't think long sentences are effective—are highlighted by means of an arrow and the annotation "reasons why." The key words in each reason are also underlined, paving the way for later note taking.

Look now at another example of how the passage might be annotated.

Long Prison Terms

Some scholars think long prison sentences are unfair and don't work.

How many times have you heard the expression "Lock 'em up and throw away the key"? It captures the frustration law-abiding people feel about the problem of crime in America. It reflects a belief that society is best off when criminals are housed in prisons for long periods. This strategy has an obvious appeal—locking up offenders prevents them from committing additional crimes in the community, at least during the course of their confinement. Yet, according to some scholars, long prison sentences may be unjust, unnecessary, counterproductive, and inappropriate.

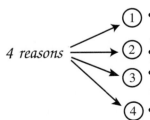

4 reasons

1. - Unjust if other offenders who have committed the same crime receive shorter sentences.
2. - Unnecessary if the offender is not likely to offend again.
3. - Counterproductive whenever prison increases the risk of subsequent or habitual criminal behavior.
4. - Inappropriate if the offender has committed an offense entailing insignificant harm to the community. (Adler et al., *Criminal Justice*, p. 349.)

In this instance, a slightly different paraphrase of the main idea appears in the margin. The four reasons that support the main idea get both a label and numbered arrows.

Exactly how you annotate is up to you. Each person has his or her own method. Also, different kinds of textbook material require different kinds of annotations. You might use more arrows or even diagrams in a science text or circle more dates in a history book. What's important is that you make annotating a habit. Once you do, you'll be surprised at your increased ability to concentrate, understand, and remember.

Symbols for Underlining and Annotating

The following chart shows symbols you can use to underline and annotate pages. Feel free to adapt the symbols listed here to better suit your particular needs. You can even make up your own symbols if you wish. Whatever symbols you decide on, just be sure to use them consistently, so you know exactly what each one represents.

Symbols for Underlining and Annotating Pages	
══ ══ ══	**Double underlining** to highlight the main idea of the entire reading
── ── ──	**Single underlining** to highlight main ideas in paragraphs
=	**Equal sign** used to signal a definition
1, 2, 3, 4	**Numbers** to itemize and separate a series of supporting details
(1830)	**Circles** to highlight key points, specialized vocabulary, key terms, statistics, and dates
?	**Question marks** to indicate confusion
!	**Exclamation points** to indicate your surprise at the author's statements
∿∿∿	**Squiggly lines** under words you need to look up in a dictionary

⟨↗ ↘	**Arrows** to identify cause and effect relationships
‖	**Vertical lines** to emphasize passages longer than a sentence or two
:	**Colon** to signal restatement
★★★	**Stars** to identify a crucial piece of information
RR	Symbol to indicate passages in need of a second reading
RP	Symbol to identify ideas for research papers
TQ	Symbol to identify the possible source of a test question
See p. 27 or Compare p. 27	**Cross-reference notes** to compare closely related statements in the text
Charles Darwin	**Boxes** to highlight names you need to remember

EXERCISE 1

DIRECTIONS Read, underline, and annotate the following passage. *Note:* Try your hand at using some of the symbols introduced in the chart on pages 53–54.

Rebellion in a Small Texas Town

The Mexican-American movement was a local one, born of poverty and oppressive segregation. Reflecting the grassroots character of the movement was the important role that youths played. Many Mexican-American teens and young adults adopted the term **Chicano** to stress their unwillingness to accept the dictates of Anglo society and to distinguish themselves from the more **accommodationist*** Mexican-Americans they called *Tio Tacos.*

In the small south Texas town of Ed Couch-Elsa, where the av-

*accommodationist: someone ready to adapt to existing conditions.

erage education level for Mexican-Americans was 3.5 years of schooling, Mexican-American students walked out of the high school in November 1968. Supported by their parents and most of the Mexican-American community, the students demanded dignity, respect, and an end to "blatant discrimination against Mexican-American students in the schools." For one thing, corporal punishment in the form of spankings was common for speaking Spanish on school grounds outside of Spanish class, and students wanted it stopped. The school board, blaming "outside agitators" for the unrest, suspended over 150 students and finally expelled 20. But changes took place. The board agreed not to discourage the speaking of Spanish and to incorporate a Mexican-American heritage program into the curriculum.

An extremely poor school district, Ed Couch-Elsa was limited in its efforts to improve the curriculum or educational environment, but under pressure from the Mexican-American community, other school districts, including Los Angeles, implemented Mexican-American studies and bilingual programs, hired more Mexican-American teachers and counselors, and adopted programs to meet the special needs of migrant farm worker children who moved from one school to another during picking season. By the 1970s, calls for bilingual education had become an important educational reform focus for the Latino community. (Berkin et al., *Making America,* p. 945.)

Make Connections

Research on learning shows that reading scores improve when students make connections between what they already know and what they read. For an illustration of how to create such links, look at the following passage. Yes, the paraphrased main idea appears in the margin along with one or two supporting details, but so too do some comments based on the reader's personal experience. Those comments appear in boldface.

Cancer Quackery

When cancer attacks, people do risky things like turn to quacks—multimillion-dollar business.

Aunt Mary

May be prof. educated, but also may not.

Cancer quackery is a multimillion-dollar industry in the U.S. alone each year. When cancer strikes, many people do foolish, irresponsible, or dangerous things. One of the things they do is turn to "quacks." These practitioners offer the cancer patient friendly attentiveness, hope, or "secret" cures. The person with cancer may be desperate, so the practitioner who can make these offers has appeal. Quacks may be professionally educated physicians; however, many times they have no degree and no medical education whatsoever.

Quack treatments are particularly risky in cancer's early stages.

Aunt Mary almost died because she went to a quack who treated her with apricot pits.

Quacks aren't easy to recognize.

Aunt Mary's doctor seemed like an old sweetheart—Ha!

Responsible physicians do not offer secret cures or make guarantees about treatment interventions. Quack treatments can be especially dangerous to the patient who has cancer in its early stages. Trying useless gadgets or therapeutically worthless drugs is costly and wastes valuable time. Quacks may have no conscience about telling patients that they have cancer when in fact they do not. After a series of worthless but expensive "treatments," the patient is declared "cured." The practitioner takes the credit, which opens the door for the testimonial and exploitation of more people. Quacks cannot be recognized by their appearance alone. They are smart, friendly, and impressively attired. They provide warmth, act concerned, and give assurance to patients who are filled with anxiety. (Mullen et al., *Connections for Health*, p. 380.)

As the example shows, this reader does not confine her marginal annotations to rephrasing the author's main idea and supporting details. She also includes personal comments that echo the author's thoughts. These comments anchor the author's ideas in memory by connecting them to a personal experience.

Record Potential Test Questions

In addition to taking notes and jotting comments in the margins of your text, you should also note possible test questions (TQ).

As you read, give special attention to words and sentences that stand out because of repetition, italics, boldface, or colored ink. All of these devices are used to emphasize key points and essential vocabulary. This is the kind of material likely to make its way into an exam. Once you've identified potentially test-rich material, use the words introduced in Chapter 1—*how, who, why, when, where, which,* and *what*—to formulate possible test questions. If you happen to know that your instructor favors essay exams, become familiar with the words likely to be used in essay exams (see the chart on pp. 499–500). Then you can use them to create test questions.

To illustrate, here's a sample passage accompanied by two test questions.

TQ: What is the function of the sympathetic nervous system?

TQ: Explain how the sympathetic nervous system prepares the body for fight or flight.

The sympathetic nervous system prepares the body to deal with emergency situations. It prepares us for "fight or flight." The system speeds up the heart, sends blood to the muscles, and releases sugar from the liver for quick energy. It can be activated by threat or by sexual arousal. (Allgeier and Allgeier, *Sexual Interactions,* p. 143.)

The test questions you predict may well appear on the exam. Even if they don't, writing potential exam questions in the margins is always worth the effort. When you finish a chapter section, you can test your understanding and review what you've read by trying to answer your own questions. When you try to answer potential test questions, you are simultaneously checking comprehension, aiding memory, and reviewing for exams—all of which make jotting test questions in the margins a highly effective study strategy.

EXERCISE 2

DIRECTIONS Read, underline, and annotate the following selection. Then circle the letters of the two test questions (p. 58) that you think would be appropriate to jot in the margins.

Ethics in Journalism

Two studies, both published in 1996, give us some idea of the importance of the study of ethics to students in journalism and mass communications programs. A survey of seventy-three free-standing media ethics courses at universities across the country revealed that "classes are full. The number of courses, students, teachers, and material are all on the growth curve." Another study noted that 44 percent of all the schools responding to its survey required students to take a journalism/mass communication ethics course. Media organizations have told educators that they value students who can think critically, solve problems, and who have developed a keen sense of ethics.

However, there are reasons for studying ethics that go beyond what potential employers want or expect. Proper behavior is a necessity for growth and order. If it is one of the objectives of an education to promote the growth and development of the individual, then the place to start is with one's own behavior. Developing a sense of what is right and wrong, or appropriate and inappropriate, will promote order, not only in the life of the individual but also in the structure of society at large. Think, for example, of the order required to move traffic on roads and highways. Speed limits are set, proper directions are indicated, and numerous suggestions are made—seat belts, for example—so that travel by automobile will be reasonably safe and efficient. Without the "rules" of the road, travel would be chaotic. Order is required if we are ever going to get anywhere. The same could be said of ethical behavior. It sets "rules" for proper human activity and as a result promotes growth, development, and order in our lives.

It should be noted, however, that ethics is not a panacea for every problem one encounters in the world. Not every problem is an ethical one, and even when an ethical problem does present itself, we sometimes make the wrong ethical decision, or we make the right ethical decision and it results in unforeseen negative consequences. Nevertheless, we must realize that without a large number of individuals "doing the right thing," most of us would not be doing much at all except fighting for survival and trying to figure out an increasingly chaotic world. Things are bad enough with ethics; think how bad they might be without them.

"Rather than accept the way things are, the ethical person asks how things ought to be." Ethics promotes not only a better individual but also a better society. Idealists might suggest that doing the right thing is a valuable end in itself, regardless of the degree to which it contributes to life or to the culture. Others see ethics as more practical, as a tool that can lead to positive personal and social outcomes.

The real test of ethics may be in "how we treat the stranger— whether we are able to recognize the humanity and dignity of the stranger. We are all prepared to acknowledge the dignity of those we think of as like ourselves and to treat them with respect. It is those we perceive as different that we are tempted to treat differently." (Leslie, *Mass Communication*, pp. 18–19.)

Test Questions

a. Give at least two reasons why the study of ethics is valuable.

b. Explain the origins of the word *ethics*.

c. Describe the "real test" of ethics.

d. Explain the difference between morality and ethics.

 # Good and Bad Paraphrasing

Like annotating, paraphrasing is a learned skill. It can be done well or poorly, and you need to know exactly what makes the difference. To begin that discussion, study the three passages below. The first is the original text, and it's followed by two possible paraphrases. Look over each paraphrase and decide which one is better.

Original   Video rental stores started out in the 1970s as locally owned mom-and-pop stores. But these small-scale operations didn't last very long after big national chains emerged and gobbled up most of the local markets.

Paraphrase   a. In the 1970s, video rental stores were frequently small and locally owned. But many of these stores lost their market and went out of business when the huge national chains came to town.

Paraphrase   b. In the late 1970s, video rental stores were wildly successful as small, locally owned businesses, but they couldn't compete with the huge national chains that charged less and drove smaller stores out of business.

Did you circle paraphrase *a?* If you did, you clearly know the difference between good and bad paraphrasing. *A good paraphrase finds new words to express the original meaning.* It changes the words but not the message. A bad paraphrase, like passage *b,* distorts the original meaning, adding (or deleting) details that never appeared in the original text. For instance, the original text never suggests the degree of success experienced by early video stores. We don't know if initially they were or were not "wildly successful." But paraphrase *b* suggests that we do.

The original text also doesn't say exactly why the locally owned video stores went out of business. Yet paraphrase *b* assumes price cutting was a factor. Maybe it was, but we don't know that from the original. In other words, paraphrase *b* distorts the original meaning—the last thing you want to do when you paraphrase.

EXERCISE 3

DIRECTIONS Identify the more accurate paraphrase by circling the appropriate letter.

Original **EXAMPLE** Political campaigns vary in the effectiveness with which they transmit their messages via the news media. Effective tactics recognize the limitations of both the audience and the media. The typical voter is not deeply interested in politics and has trouble keeping track of multiple themes supported with details. By the same token, television is not willing to air lengthy statements from candidates. (Janda et al., *The Challenge of Democracy,* p. 305.)

Paraphrase a. Most political campaigns simply do not take into account voter limitations. Instead, candidates assume that the typical voter is deeply interested in political issues. The truth is that the typical voter cares more about a candidate's image than about the candidate's political positions.

(b.) Not all political campaigns use the news media with equal effectiveness. Those that are successful recognize that television is not willing to air long, detailed explanations and that the typical voter neither understands nor cares much about political issues.

EXPLANATION In this case, paraphrase *a* is not correct. It says candidates assume that the typical voter is deeply interested in political issues. Yet the original says only that the typical voter is not deeply interested in politics. It makes no mention of what candidates do or do not assume. Paraphrase *a* also leaves out a key component, or element, of the original, which points out that "television is not willing to air lengthy statements." *Remember:* Accurate paraphrases retain all parts of the original meaning without adding new information.

Original **1.** Most Americans were taken by surprise when the second wave* of feminism swept the nation in the 1960s. Women's rights had been considered a dead issue—in the words of *Life* magazine, feminism seemed "as quaint as linen dusters* and high-button shoes." Supposedly, it lost its relevance once women won the vote. (Davis, *Moving the Mountain*, p. 26.)

Paraphrase   a. By the 1960s, feminism was again a hot topic, and most people were taken by surprise. Many people thought that the battle for women's rights was over when women won the right to vote.

  b. In the 1960s, to almost everyone's surprise, the feminist movement reappeared and became a force to be reckoned with. Surprisingly, no one realized at the time what consequences would result from the second wave of feminism.

Original **2.** You may have heard that colds come from being chilled, from getting your feet wet, from sleeping in a draft, or from not wearing a hat on cold, rainy, or windy days. Sound familiar? In fact, these so-called mechanisms do not explain the acquisition of colds whatsoever. (Mullen et al., *Connections for Health*, p. 403.)

Paraphrase   a. The old myths about catching colds are untrue. People catch colds from coming into contact with one of the two hundred different viruses that cause colds.

---

*wave: new trend or movement.
*dusters: long coats worn around the end of the nineteenth and beginning of the twentieth century.

b. Claims that catching colds from getting chilled or wet are not based on fact.

EXERCISE 4

DIRECTIONS Paraphrase each of the following statements.

Original **EXAMPLE** About 25 percent of people are primarily *auditory*, learning and thinking through hearing; another 15 percent are primarily *kinesthetic*, learning by feeling, touch, and movement. (Adapted from Lofland, *Powerlearning*, p. 13.)

Paraphrase *Around 25 percent of the population learns mainly through listening, whereas another 15 percent learns largely by touch or movement.*

EXPLANATION As it should, the paraphrase replaces most of the original language but retains the original meaning. *Note:* There may be times when there is no substitute for the original language; for example, in this case, *percent* would be a difficult word to replace.

Original **1.** Divorce lawyers all over the country are noticing a brand-new phenomenon: Internet-sparked divorces. In other words, marriages are breaking up when one spouse or the other meets someone online in a chatroom and decides that that someone is a true soulmate. There actually have been cases of spouses abandoning their marriage and running off with people they had met only online and never even seen.

Paraphrase _____

_____

_____

Original **2.** University of Tulsa psychologist Judy Berry studied seventy-three Oklahoma eighth graders who had taken a parenting course. For ten days, the children had to care for a ten-pound sack of flour as if it were a baby. Berry's research on her young subjects suggests the course worked: The teenagers in the study had a sounder sense of parental responsibility than they did before they took the course.

Paraphrase _____

_____

_____

When Should You Paraphrase?

At this point, you know the purpose of paraphrasing. However, you may not be quite sure *when* to paraphrase. Actually, the answer to that question varies. If, for example, you are reading material that is both difficult and unfamiliar—say, chemistry or philosophy—then paraphrasing the key points of every paragraph—the main idea and major supporting details—may be your best bet. It will be slow going, but there's a bonus. You will probably need to read the material only once rather than over and over again.

If you are reading a sociology or health textbook, where you are familiar with some of the concepts, or ideas, then paraphrase only the passages you don't readily understand. If you finish a paragraph and aren't quite sure of the author's meaning, it's the time to check your understanding by paraphrasing. If you can't paraphrase, mark the paragraph for rereading (RR). Paraphrasing chapter sections when you finish them is also an excellent way to test your understanding and ensure long-term remembering.

Paraphrasing and Plagiarism

When students write papers, they are often confused about the relationship between paraphrasing (rewording someone else's ideas) and plagiarizing (using someone else's ideas without attributing them, or mentioning their source). Some students assume they are not plagiarizing someone else's work if they change the wording while leaving the meaning intact. Yet this assumption is dead wrong. *Original ideas belong to the people who had them first.* If you use someone else's discovery or reinterpretation in a paper, you have to cite your source.

For instance, let's say you had read the following passage while you were researching a paper on the nineteenth-century brothers William and Henry James.

Studies of the brothers William and Henry James usually highlight the obvious differences. William, the philosopher-psychologist, is portrayed as clever, eloquent, and athletic, eager to explore the world around him. Henry, in contrast, is painted as the reclusive novelist—timid, watchful, sickly, and easily intimidated by his adventurous older brother. Yet, because they are wrapped up in pointing out the easy-to-see differences, authors of traditional studies have repeatedly missed an essential similarity: These famous nineteenth-century siblings chose to explore the same subject matter—the relationship between imagination and reality.

Having read that new interpretation, imagine now that you decided to paraphrase the author's point about the brothers' essential similarity in the introduction to your paper. The introduction might read like this:

Paraphrase
On the surface, William and Henry were the most opposite of brothers. William loved sports, people, and ideas. Articulate and brilliant, he drew both men and women to him like a magnet. Henry—shy, nervous, and uncomfortable with people—could only view William with admiration. Yet to focus on the differences between the brothers is to miss a more essential similarity. Both were fascinated by the same subject matter: They wanted to explore the relationship between what we actually experience and how we imagine it in our minds.

This second passage includes a solid paraphrase of the first author's key point. As it should, the paraphrase changes the author's words yet maintains the original idea. Unfortunately, that careful paraphrase still represents an act of plagiarism. It's clear in the original passage that the author has come up with a new insight, one that differs from already existing points of view. Thus it can't be absorbed into a paper without attribution. You need to cite your source. If you don't, you're plagiarizing. Ideas original to the person who first put them on paper cannot and must not find their way into your work without a reference to where those ideas came from.

Paraphrasing Common Knowledge

Unfortunately, warning students about the danger of plagiarism often leads to another problem. Anxious about plagiarizing, they cite sources for information that is **common knowledge,** or found in any number of reference works or studies. For example, if you looked up William James in five different biographies and reference works, you would find information very similar to the following:

William James (1842–1910) American philosopher and psychologist of the late nineteenth and early twentieth centuries. James was one of the first to suggest that humans, like other animals, possess instincts. He also argued that any view of the world is a compromise between the external reality and personal desires. Turning away from abstract theories, verbal solutions, fixed principles, and pretended absolutes, he looked at concrete experience, facts, and actions. The *Principles of Psychology* is the most complete expression of his theories about the mind and its workings. James's focus on the "stream of thought" also had a profound influence on fiction and helped inspire the writing technique "stream of consciousness," which revolutionized modern literature.

Read about William James in several different sources and you are bound to find descriptions similar to the one above. That means the information is common or general knowledge, and it can be paraphrased without a footnote. For the most part, anything expressed in a reference work is going to be common knowledge. In addition, any time you find the same point made in several different works, you can assume it falls under the heading of common knowledge.

To help you decide when you can or can't paraphrase without citing a source, keep in mind this rule of thumb: When a writer signals that he or she is offering a new opinion, reinterpreting existing facts, or challenging long-held opinions—as does the writer of the first passage on the James brothers (p. 63)—these ideas are not yours to freely paraphrase without mentioning where you got them. You need to cite your source.

CHECK YOUR UNDERSTANDING

1. Explain when it is acceptable to use information from an outside source without mentioning where it came from.

   _____

   _____

2. Describe the kind of information that requires you to cite your source.

   _____

   _____

■ DIGGING DEEPER

LOOKING AHEAD On pages 51–52, you learned that long prison sentences aren't a particularly good way of dealing with crime. Judges, however, can consider another option: innovative or alternative sentencing. Look over the innovative sentences described below and decide if you think they are a good alternative to prison sentences.

INNOVATIVE SENTENCING

1 Innovative sentences reflect a movement to reform the criminal justice system from the inside. Perhaps underlying most such sentences is the belief that sending an offender to jail pushes people toward a permanent life of crime. Innovative sentencing gives them a chance to change their lives outside prison.

2 Many judges fashion sentences, usually within the framework of probation, that stretch from handing out candy bars to onerous* conditions just short of prison bars. Consider these recent American sentences:

- Florida Circuit Court Judge Harry Lee Coe III ordered a person convicted of trying to "ram" a friend with her car to stay home for a year.

- The same judge sentenced a drug offender to one year in college without the right to leave campus.

- Tennessee Judge Joseph Brown Jr. invites the victims of a burglary to enter the homes of their burglars and take equivalent loot. According to Judge Brown, "The victims really get into it. They stalk the house, really look around." The burglars' reaction? "Their mouths just drop."

- Houston District Court Judge Michael McSpadden agreed to a request from an accused rapist that surgical castration be substituted for facing trial and the possibility of a thirty-five-year prison term. (McSpadden later withdrew his support for the plea and the rapist was sentenced to life in prison.)

- A Tulane County superior court judge (California) ordered a convicted child abuser to have an innovative birth control device implanted in her arm as a condition of probation.

- The same judge ordered a man who had stolen beer to wear a T-shirt proclaiming "on felony probation."

---

*onerous: troublesome, burdensome.

- A federal judge (New York) banished a reputed organized crime figure from entering the eastern and southern districts of New York State during the time of his probation.
- A Duval County circuit court judge (Florida) sentenced a seventeen-year-old woman convicted of smothering her newborn daughter to death to two years in prison and a ten-year probation term that would include finishing high school, receiving psychological and birth control counseling, and using birth control.
- A superior court judge in Arizona sentenced a seventeen-year-old mother convicted of child abuse to a lifetime use of contraception.
- A thirty-year-old woman who pleaded guilty to felony child neglect agreed to be sterilized as part of a plea agreement.
- A Suffolk County superior court judge (Massachusetts) ordered a teenager convicted of robbery, assault, and car theft to finish high school, maintain a job, and stay out of trouble for five years.
- An Alexandria judge (Virginia) sentenced a drunk driver to witness an autopsy.
- A circuit judge in Tennessee confined a man convicted of voluntary manslaughter to his home or yard for five years except for going to work each day and to the grocery store with his mother once a week.

Cruel and Unusual Punishment?

3 Are there any boundaries constraining a judge's sentencing practices? The Eighth Amendment to the U.S. Constitution does prohibit cruel and unusual punishment. Most of the innovative sentences are probation conditions and are not particularly cruel—but they are certainly unusual. For this reason alone, many such sentences have been overthrown on appeal.

4   But it is not a desire to be "unusual" that drives most judges to mete* out such punishments as finishing high school, going to college, watching an autopsy, or staying home. Motives vary from case to case and from judge to judge. For some, cost is an important consideration. The teenager who was ordered to finish high school and get a job would have cost the state $80,000 had he been imprisoned for two years. Overcrowding in prisons motivates others to come up with innovative sentences.

---

*mete: distribute, give.

5 The safety of a defendant can be a factor as well; there are times when a prison sentence is, in effect, a death sentence, as with the organized crime figure exiled from New York State. "He just knows too much," said the judge in that case, explaining that he was certain the defendant would have died at his own hands or someone else's in prison. Other judges are attempting to make more of an impact on a serious problem than can be made with fines or jail terms; the judge who sentenced the drunk driver to view an autopsy also has considered forcing convicted drunk drivers to ride with rescue squads or sit in emergency rooms so that they can see firsthand the problems that driving "under the influence" causes. (Adapted from Freda Adler, Gerhard O. W. Mueller, and William S. Haufer, *Criminal Justice.* New York: McGraw-Hill, 1994, pp. 352–353.)

Sharpening Your Skills

DIRECTIONS Answer the following questions by filling in the blanks or circling the letter of the correct response.

1. What belief underlies innovative sentencing?

_____

_____

2. In your own words, what are some of the reasons judges choose innovative sentencing?

_____

_____

3. Based on what you know about plagiarism, would you need to cite the author of this reading if you paraphrased his reference to the Eighth Amendment in paragraph 3? _____

Explain.

_____

_____

4. Based on your reading, which one of the following do you think would *not* appear on an exam?

   a. Explain why many innovative sentences have been overthrown on appeal.

   b. What are some of the factors that determine a judge's decision to use innovative sentencing?

   c. Why do more judges favor long jail terms over innovative sentencing?

5. What do you think of innovative sentencing? Are you for or against it? Whatever your opinion, please provide at least one reason.

_____

_____

WORD NOTES: ENLARGING VOCABULARY THROUGH HOMONYMS

The reading on pages 65–66 introduced the word "mete," which you may already know is a homonym. *Homonyms* are words that sound the same but have different meanings. In this instance, the homonyms are "mete," "meat," and "meet."

Now at this point, you may be wondering how homonyms can enhance your vocabulary. You probably learned about them in the fifth grade and the ones you learned—"two," "to," and "too," for example—are already very familiar. But in fact, there are other homonyms that are not as well known even though they make frequent appearances in both speech and writing. For example, there's "team," and "teem." You certainly know what a team is, but are you as clear on the word "teem"? After all, it's not used much in everyday speech. Still, it appears often enough in writing that it pays for you to learn its meaning—"to be full of or to swarm." Here's an example of the word in context: "Under the microscope, it was clear that the tissue was *teeming* with bacteria."

Because the human brain likes connected pieces of information, learning homonyms in pairs or groups of three makes their meanings easier to retain. You can, for example, tell yourself that the word "teem" suggests greater numbers than its homonym "team." Or you can create sentences that emphasize the different meanings of two homonyms as in "A brooch is a piece of jewelry pinned on a blouse or sweater, but 'to broach' is to approach, not to pin." Remember the sentence, and you have the meanings of both words at instant recall.

To get a complete list of homonyms, go to http://www.

finifter.com/tracy/pers/homonym. If that Web site has disappeared, just tell your search engine to head for "homonyms," and several other sites will pop up on your screen. Browse the various lists on the Web looking for unfamiliar homonyms. Once you find some you don't know at a glance, add them to your vocabulary. Meanwhile, here are two to get you started:

1. discreet (careful in speech and behavior)

Although he wanted to know her name, he tried to be *discreet* about his interest.

discrete (separate, individual)

He couldn't crack the code because he kept on combining the numbers when they should have remained *discrete.*

2. vial (small container)

Dr. Frankenstein handed her a *vial* of green liquid and ordered her to drink it.

vile (disgusting)

The liquid had a *vile* taste that burned her throat.

Test 1: Reviewing the Key Points

DIRECTIONS Answer the following questions by circling the correct response or filling in the blanks.

1. Annotating pages while you are reading can help you improve

   _____ and _____.

2. *True* or *False*. All marginal comments are useful.

3. When you annotate, you should try to do the following:

   (a) _____

   (b) _____

   (c) _____

4. *True* or *False*. Readers vary in the way they annotate pages.

5. Annotation should make the _____ stand out for easy access.

6. The goal of paraphrasing is to _____

   _____.

7. With difficult material, you should paraphrase _____

   _____.

8. If the material is fairly familiar, then paraphrase _____

   _____.

9. Plagiarizing means _____.

10. Information considered common knowledge can be _____

   _____.

Test 2: Recognizing an Accurate Paraphrase

DIRECTIONS Circle the letter of the more accurate paraphrase.

1. A *dialect* is a language use—including vocabulary, grammar, and pronunciation—unique to a particular group or region. Audiences sometimes make negative judgments about a speaker based on his or her dialect. Such negative judgments are called *vocal stereotypes*. (Gronbeck et al., *Principles of Speech Communication*, p. 100.)

Paraphrase a. A dialect is a particular way of speaking. Unfortunately, people sometimes judge others based on the way they speak. Southerners, for example, rightfully complain about being stereotyped because of their accent.

b. The term *vocal stereotypes* refers to the negative judgments people sometimes make based on a person's dialect. A dialect is speech unique to a group or region, and it includes vocabulary, grammar, and pronunciation.

2. Because China has banned them from selling their products door-to-door, vendors* for companies like Amway, Mary Kay, and Avon are not very happy with the Chinese government. According to the Chinese press, such door-to-door marketing tends to foster "excess hugging" and "weird cults."[1]

Paraphrase a. The Chinese government has given an odd reason for its ban on door-to-door salespeople from companies like Avon and Amway: they give rise to "weird cults" and "excess hugging."

b. Amway, Mary Kay, and Avon have decided to stop selling their products in China because their salespeople have become the victims of too much hugging.

3. During World War II, movies about Japan made little effort to develop a Japanese character or explain what Japan hoped to accomplish in the war. The Japanese remained nameless, faceless, and almost totally speechless. No attempt was made to show a Japanese soldier trapped by circumstances beyond his control, or a family man who longed for home, or an officer who despised the militarists* even if he supported the military campaign. This stands in sharp contrast to the portrayal of the German soldiers, who

---

*vendors: people who sell products.
[1]"China Slams the Door on the Avon Lady," *Newsweek*, May 4, 1998, p. 49.
*militarists: people devoted to war.

were often shown as decent human beings distinct from the Nazis. (Adapted from Clayton R. Koppes and Gregory D. Black, *Hollywood Goes to War.* Berkeley: University of California Press, 1998, p. 254.)

Paraphrase a. During World War II, Hollywood filmmakers were applauded for engaging in propaganda that was openly racist. The 1942 film *Wake Island,* for example, with its story of 377 Marines who resisted Japanese invasion, was a smash hit despite its use of racial stereotypes to characterize Japanese soldiers. Today, however, such cinematic practices, even during wartime, would be sharply criticized.

b. During World War II, Hollywood filmmakers made propaganda movies that failed to distinguish between the Japanese government's war machine and the Japanese soldier caught up in that machine. Oddly enough, they did not do the same in propaganda films about Germany. In these films, Hollywood filmmakers made a distinction between the Nazi government and the German people.

4. Disco became the biggest commercial pop genre* of the 1970s— actually, the biggest pop music movement of all time—and in the end, its single-minded, booming beat proved to be the most resilient and enduring stylistic breakthrough of the last twenty years or so. (Mikal Gilmore, *Night Beat.* New York: Doubleday, 1998, p. 241.)

Paraphrase a. In the 1970s, disco challenged rock and roll's position as the music of the young. But thankfully, following the success of *Saturday Night Fever,* disco died a fast and well-deserved death.

b. In the 1970s, disco was the hottest dance music around; over the last two decades, its pulsing beat has proved to have real staying power.

5. In the nineteenth and early twentieth centuries, the South American countries of Argentina, Uruguay, and Brazil had their own home-grown cowboys, called gauchos. Derived from the Spanish word *wáhcha,* the word *gaucho* usually referred to cowhands or horse handlers, but it could also refer to horse thieves and mercenaries.*

Paraphrase a. In the South American countries of Argentina, Uruguay, and Brazil, gauchos were considered romantic figures, and much like

---

*genre: type or class; a category of literature, music, or art.
*mercenaries: soldiers for hire, soldiers of fortune.

America's cowboys, they were the heroes of countless movies and novels. Among the most famous of these novels was *The Four Horsemen of the Apocalypse,* which also became a movie.

b. During the nineteenth and beginning of the twentieth centuries, American-like cowboys called gauchos worked the ranches of Uruguay, Argentina, and Brazil. Although the term *gaucho*—which comes from the Spanish word *wáhcha*—meant "cowboy" or "horse handler," it could also be a term that referred to horse thieves and soldiers of fortune.

Test 3: Paraphrasing with Accuracy

DIRECTIONS Paraphrase each of the following statements.

1. When things go wrong in a society, in a way and to a degree that can no longer be denied or concealed, there are various questions one can ask. A common one . . . is "Who did this to us?" (Bernard Lewis, *What Went Wrong?* New York: Oxford University Press, 2000, p. 94.)

   _____

   _____

   _____

2. In Colonial America, reading was not regarded as an elitist activity, and printed matter was spread among all kinds of people. (Neil Postman, *Amusing Ourselves to Death.* New York: Penguin Books, 1985, p. 35.)

   _____

   _____

   _____

3. Years ago, if there was major news, the public might see pictures of the event in their movie theaters a week or so later. But since we now expect to see live pictures from the scene almost immediately on TV, news departments compete with one another to be first in delivering pictures. (Neil Postman, *How to Watch TV News.* New York: Penguin Books, 1992, p. 45.)

   _____

   _____

   _____

4. In the late 1950s, union leaders Walter Reuther and George Meany battled over how to define American labor's role in the world. The liberal Reuther wanted unions to think of themselves as part of an international labor movement. The more conservative Meany insisted that American union members should concentrate on their own interests and let workers in other countries take care of themselves.

   _____

   _____

   _____

C H A P T E R 3

Reviewing Paragraph Essentials

 In this chapter, you'll learn

- **how to identify topics.**
- **how to recognize main ideas.**
- **how to locate topic sentences.**
- **how to identify major and minor details.**
- **how to recognize organizational patterns.**

Overall, *Reading for Thinking* assumes you have a solid knowledge of how to read a paragraph. Still, it doesn't hurt to do a quick review of paragraph essentials, and that is precisely what this chapter offers.

 ## Starting with the Topic

Finding the topic is the first step toward discovering the main idea of a paragraph. The **topic** of a paragraph is the subject the author

75

chooses to discuss or explore. It's the person, place, object, event, or idea most frequently mentioned or referred to by the author. Usually, you can find the topic by posing one key question: Who or what is most frequently mentioned or referred to in the paragraph? To illustrate, let's use the following example:

> The use of animals in scientific research is a controversial subject that provokes strong emotions on both sides. Animal rights activists define animals as sentient* beings who can think, feel, and suffer. They insist, therefore, that the rights of animals be acknowledged and respected. The more conservative animal rights activists argue that the use of animals in research should be strictly monitored, while the more radical activists insist that research using animals should be banned altogether. In response to these objections, research scientists who experiment on animals have reorganized their research to take better care of the animals involved. They argue, however, that research on animals is ethical and necessary because it saves human lives and alleviates* human suffering.

What's the topic of this paragraph? Is it "animal rights activists" or the "use of animals in research"? If you said it was the "use of animals in research" you are right on target. That is, indeed, the subject most frequently mentioned or referred to in the paragraph. The phrase "animal rights activists" is mentioned or referred to several times but not as frequently as the phrase "use of animals in research."

Another thing you should notice about the topic of the above paragraph is the number of words needed to express it; five, to be exact. Occasionally, you will be able to express the topic of a paragraph in a single word. However, much of the time you will need a phrase of two or more words to zero in on the precise topic. Look, for example, at the following paragraph. What's the topic?

> Although the fighting took place far from the United States, the Vietnam War deeply affected the way Americans lived their lives. Military service became an important, life-changing experience for more than 2 million Americans. In the typical tour of duty, they encountered racial tensions, boredom, drugs, and a widespread brutality against the Vietnamese. Even those Americans who did not fight were changed by the war. Millions of young men spent a

---

*sentient: aware, possessed of consciousness.
*alleviates: relieves, eliminates.

substantial part of their late adolescence or young adulthood wondering whether they would be drafted or seeking ways to avoid participation in the fighting. Far more men did not go to Vietnam than went, but the war created deep divisions among people of an entire generation. Those who fought in the war often resented those who did not, and people who did not go to Vietnam sometimes treated those who did with scorn, pity, or condescension. (Adapted from Schaller, Scharf, and Schulzinger, *Present Tense,* p. 301.)

Here again, no one single word could effectively sum up the topic. The word *Americans* won't do. Nor will the phrase "Vietnam War." To express the focus of the paragraph, we need a phrase like "the effect of the Vietnam War on American life." Note, too, that the words in the topic don't appear next to each other. This topic was created by combining words from different parts of the paragraph and adding the word *life.* The point here is that identifying the topic often requires you to do a good deal more than simply look for a word or two. On the contrary, frequently you have to figure out how to piece together a topic that will most effectively help you unlock paragraph meaning. To be effective, the topic you create should be general enough to include everything discussed in the paragraph and specific enough to exclude what isn't.

■ EXERCISE 1

DIRECTIONS Read each paragraph. Then circle the letter of the correct topic.

1. According to the attachment theory of love, adults are characterized, in their romantic relationships, by one of three styles. *Secure lovers* are happy when others feel close to them. Mutual dependency in a relationship (depending on the partner and the partner's depending on you) feels right to them. Secure lovers do not fear abandonment. In contrast, *avoidant lovers* are uncomfortable feeling close to another person or having that person feel close to them. It is difficult for avoidant lovers to trust or depend on a partner. The third type, *anxious-ambivalent lovers*, want desperately to get close to a partner but often find that the partner does not reciprocate the feeling, perhaps because anxious-ambivalent lovers scare away others. They are insecure in the relationship, worrying that the partner does not really love them. Research on the attachment theory shows that about 53 percent of adults are secure, 26 percent are avoidant, and 20 percent are anxious-ambivalent.

Topic a. mutual dependency in a relationship

         b. attachment theory of love

         c. secure lovers

2. Among the explanations of our nation's high divorce rate and high degree of dissatisfaction in many marriages is that we have such strong expectations of marriage. We expect our spouse to simultaneously be a lover, a friend, a confidant, a counselor, a career person, and a parent, for example. In one research investigation, unhappily married couples expressed unrealistic expectations about marriage (Epstein and Eidelson, 1981). Underlying unrealistic expectations about marriage are numerous myths about marriage. A myth is a widely held belief unsupported by facts. (Santrock, *Life-Span Development*, p. 445.)

Topic a. marriage

         b. expectations about marriage

         c. myths about marriage

3. Surveys show that about three out of four U.S. corporations have **ethics codes**. The purpose of these codes is to provide guidance to managers and employees when they encounter an ethical dilemma. A typical code discusses conflicts of interest that can harm the company (for example, guidelines for accepting or refusing gifts from suppliers, hiring relatives, or having an interest in a competitor's firm). Rules for complying with various laws, such as antitrust, environmental, and consumer protection laws, also are popular code provisions. The most effective codes are those drawn up with the cooperation and widespread participation of employees. An internal enforcement mechanism, including penalties for violating the code, puts teeth into the code. A shortcoming of many codes is that they tend to provide more protection for the company than for employees and the general public. They do so by emphasizing narrow legal compliance*—rather than taking a positive and broad view of ethical responsibility toward all company stockholders—and by focusing on conflicts of interest that will harm the company. (Frederick et al., *Business and Society*, p. 94.)

Topic a. U.S. corporations

         b. ethics codes

         c. penalties for violations of ethics codes

———————

*compliance: obedience.

4. Throughout the seventeenth and eighteenth centuries, the rulers of Russia allowed most Russians to live in miserable poverty. But in 1855 a new emperor, Alexander II, came to the throne. Unlike his predecessors, he was determined to improve the lot of the Russian people. Alexander II relaxed press censorship and permitted the Russians to travel abroad more freely. Under his rule, minorities in the empire were treated better, and the courts were reorganized so that criminals might have a trial by jury. Alexander's greatest achievement was his decision to free the serfs, the poor men and women who had been the slaves of the rich landowners.

Topic a. the suffering of the Russian people

      b. the achievements of Alexander II

      c. the rulers of Russia

5. Conjoined twins are usually classified into three basic categories depending on the point where they are joined. Twins of the first type are conjoined in a way that never involves the heart or the midline of the body. For example, about 2 percent of all conjoined twins are attached at the head only, and about 19 percent are joined at the buttocks. Twins of the second type are always joined in a way that involves the midline of the body. Many twins joined at the midline share a heart. Around 35 percent are fused together at the upper half of the trunk. Another 30 percent are joined at the lower half of their bodies. Finally, the third major type of conjoined twins includes the very rare forms. In this category are those in which one twin is smaller, less formed, and dependent upon the other, as well as the cases involving one twin born completely within the body of his or her sibling.

Topic a. twins who share a heart

      b. twins

      c. conjoined twins

 # From Topic to Main Idea

Once you know the topic of a paragraph, the next logical step is to determine the main idea. The **main idea** is the central point or message of the paragraph. The main idea is what unites, or ties together, all the sentences in the paragraph.

To discover the main idea of a paragraph, you need to ask two key questions: (1) What does the author want to say *about* the topic? and (2) What idea or thought is developed throughout most of the paragraph?

To illustrate how these questions can help you determine the main idea, let's look at two different paragraphs. Here's the first one.

> For a period of about seventy-five years (1765–1840), the Gothic novel, an early relative of the modern horror story, was popular throughout Europe. Many of the most popular novels—those written by Horace Walpole, Ann Radcliffe, and Monk Lewis—were sold by the thousands, quickly translated, and frequently plagiarized. The stories were the object of fascination because they described a world where mysterious happenings were a matter of course, and ghostly, hooded figures flitted through the night. Gothic novels were read and discussed by men and women of the upper classes, and publishers, ever alert to a ready market, made sure that copies of the books were available at bargain prices. Thus, even the poorest members of the working class could afford to pay a penny to enter the Gothic world of terror, and they paid their pennies in astonishing numbers.

In this example, the opening sentence announces that the Gothic novel enjoyed great popularity for almost a century. The remaining sentences either give specific examples of how popular the novels were or explain the source of their popularity. Because the author repeatedly returns to the idea that the Gothic novel was very popular, we can say that this is the main idea of the paragraph.

Now, try to determine the main idea in another paragraph. As you read the following example, look for the topic—the subject repeatedly mentioned or referred to—and keep asking yourself, "What does the author want to say about that topic?" and "What one idea is developed throughout most of the paragraph?"

> In the very near future, the world will face an energy shortage of extraordinary proportions. By the year 2040, the total population on Earth is expected to double to about 10 billion people. With the continued industrialization of Asia, Africa, and the Americas, world energy consumption is expected to triple. At that rate of consumption, the world's known oil supply will be depleted in about sixty years. The supply of gas will be depleted in about 100 years. If we are to maintain an acceptable quality of life, we must find new sources of energy that will make up for the shortages that are bound to occur in the coming decades.

The topic of this paragraph is "the energy shortage." That's the subject repeatedly mentioned or referred to. However, we still need to figure out what the author wants to say about that topic. We need to discover the one idea that is developed, not just in a single sentence, but throughout the paragraph.

If you go through the paragraph sentence by sentence, you'll see that each one further develops the point made in the first sentence: We're facing an energy shortage that's likely to arrive very soon. This main idea is developed not just in the opening sentence but throughout the entire paragraph.

CHECK YOUR UNDERSTANDING

Explain the difference between the topic and the main idea of a paragraph.

_____

_____

_____

■ EXERCISE 2

DIRECTIONS Read each paragraph. Then circle the appropriate letter to identify the topic and the main idea.

1. Impatient for victory as World War II dragged on, American leaders began to plan a fall invasion of the Japanese islands, an expedition that was sure to incur high casualties. But the successful development of an atomic bomb by American scientists provided another route to victory in World War II. The secret atomic program, known as the Manhattan Project, began in August 1942 and cost $2 billion. The first bomb was exploded in the desert near Alamogordo, New Mexico, on July 16, 1945. Only three weeks later, on August 6, the Japanese city of Hiroshima was destroyed by a bomb dropped from an American B-29 airplane called the *Enola Gay*. A flash of dazzling light shot across the sky; then, a huge purplish mushroom cloud boiled 40,000 feet into the atmosphere. Dense smoke, swirling fires, and suffocating dust soon engulfed the ground for miles. Much of the city was leveled almost instantly. Approximately 130,000 people were killed; tens of thousands more suffered severe burns and nuclear poisoning. On August 9, another atomic bomb flattened the

city of Nagasaki, killing at least 60,000 people. Four days later, the Japanese, who had been sending out peace feelers since June, surrendered. Formal surrender ceremonies were held September 2 on the battleship *Missouri*. (Norton et al., *A People and a Nation*, p. 827.)

Topic a. the invasion of Japan

   b. the atomic bomb

   c. World War II

Main Idea a. Desperate for a victory, American leaders planned an invasion of the Japanese islands.

   b. The atomic bomb gave the American forces another way to bring World War II to an end.

   c. The question of whether or not the United States had to use the atomic bomb to end World War II is still the subject of debate.

   d. Rather than dropping the atomic bomb, the United States should have invaded Japan.

2. People have many different reasons for wanting children. Some really like children and want an opportunity to be involved with their care. Some women strongly desire the experience of pregnancy and childbirth. Many young adults see parenthood as a way to demonstrate their adult status. For people coming from happy families, having children is a means of recreating their earlier happiness. For those from unhappy families, it can be a means of doing better than their parents did. Some people have children simply because it's expected of them. Because society places so much emphasis on the fulfillment motherhood is supposed to bring, some women who are unsure of what they want to do with their lives use having a child as a way to create an identity. (Seifert et al., *Lifespan Development*, p. 484.)

Topic a. childhood

   b. reasons for having children

   c. parenting and past experience

Main Idea a. Some people have children in order to recreate the happiness they themselves experienced growing up.

   b. There are many different reasons why people have children.

   c. Most people don't know why they have children; they just do what's expected of them.

d. Society places too much emphasis on the fulfillment motherhood is supposed to bring.

3. *Fiber* is generally defined as that part of plants (cell wall material) that is essentially indigestible. Though not a direct source of nutrition, dietary fiber serves at least two vital functions in the body. It speeds the passage of food waste through the colon, allowing less time for absorption of dietary cholesterol and less tissue exposure to potential cancer-producing substances in the feces. In addition, some high-fiber foods (especially vegetables such as cabbage, cauliflower, and broccoli) may stimulate the production of cancer-fighting enzymes in the intestinal tract. (Williams and Long, *Manage Your Life*, p. 70.)

Topic a. nutrition

b. cancer-producing substances

c. fiber

Main Idea a. Fiber is the indigestible portion of plants.

b. Fiber has no nutritional value.

c. Fiber serves the body in two important ways.

d. Fiber in the diet speeds up digestion.

4. Almost half the world's population speaks an Indo-European language. The various languages in this family, which developed largely in the area from Europe to India, hence the name, share some characteristics in vocabulary and grammar, so linguists believe they all descended from one common tongue. Indo-European languages are further classified into different subfamilies, among them the Germanic, Indo-Iranian, Italic, and Slavic subfamilies. The Germanic subfamily includes Danish, Swedish, German, Yiddish, and English, among others. The Indo-Iranian subfamily includes languages such as Sanskrit, Hindi, Punjabi, and Persian. The Italic languages include Latin, Italian, French, and Spanish. The Slavic languages are those such as Russian, Czech, and Polish.

Topic a. Indo-European languages

b. Germanic languages

c. language study

Main Idea a. The Germanic languages include Danish, Swedish, German, Yiddish, and English.

b. The Indo-European languages share a common vocabulary.

    c. Millions of people in the world speak an Indo-European language.

    d. Linguists now know that all languages descended from one common tongue.

5. Sports have become an increasingly integral part of American culture. Thus, it is not surprising that more and more children become involved in sports every year. Yet participation in sports can have both positive and negative consequences for children. Children's participation in sports can provide exercise, opportunities to learn how to compete, increased self-esteem, and a setting for developing peer relations and friendships. However, sports can also have negative consequences for children: too much pressure to achieve and win, physical injuries, a distraction from academic work, and unrealistic expectations for an athlete. Few people challenge the value of sports for children when conducted as part of a school education or intramural program, but some question the appropriateness of highly competitive, win-oriented sports teams in schools. (Adapted from Santrock, *Life-Span Development,* p. 276.)

Topic a. sports and self-esteem

    b. the benefits of school intramural sports programs

    c. positive and negative effects of sports in schools

Main Idea a. For children, participating in sports can have both drawbacks and advantages.

    b. School sports programs should not put so much emphasis on competition.

    c. Playing sports can teach children important lessons about life.

    d. Playing sports builds character.

 # Recognizing Topic Sentences

Topic sentences are general sentences that put into words the main idea or central thought of a paragraph. If someone were to ask you what a paragraph was about, you could use the topic sentence as explanation. Although not all paragraphs contain topic sentences, a good many do. Particularly in textbooks, writers favor topic sentences because they speed up communication between reader and writer, making it easier for the reader to follow the writer's train of thought without getting confused.

As you might guess, experienced readers are always on the lookout for topic sentences. They consciously search, that is, for general sentences that (1) are explained in more specific detail and (2) could be used to sum up the paragraph. Be forewarned, however: The first sentence of a paragraph is not always the topic sentence. Yes, topic sentences are more likely to open than to close a paragraph, but they can and do appear anywhere—beginning, middle, or end.

Topic Sentence in First Position

Authors often like to begin a paragraph with a topic sentence that sums up the main idea. The sentences that follow then go on to develop or prove the main idea expressed in the opening topic sentence. Here's an example of a paragraph with the topic sentence in first position:

Topic Sentence In the last few years, Judge Howard Broadman has become the center of controversy over what supporters and critics alike have come to call "creative sentencing." The term refers to the judge's penchant* for offering defendants what he considers acceptable alternatives to a jail sentence. For example, one defendant had to wear a T-shirt that announced his status as a criminal on probation. In another case, an abusive husband had to donate his car to a shelter for battered women. In perhaps his most publicized case, Judge Broadman gave a woman found guilty of child abuse a chance to avoid four years in jail if she would voluntarily allow Norplant, a form of birth control, to be implanted in her arm.

In this example, the topic sentence introduces the term "creative sentencing," and the rest of the paragraph gives examples of what that means.

Topic Sentence in Second Position

Sometimes an author will begin a paragraph with one or two introductory sentences and then follow with a topic sentence. For an illustration, read the following paragraph.

Topic Sentence [1]The letters and journals of America's early Pilgrims are filled with complaints about food or, more precisely, about the lack of it. [2]The first settlers, so adventurous when it came to travel, were amaz-

_____

*penchant: leaning, tendency.

ingly slow to recognize that seventeenth-century America offered almost every kind of food imaginable; it just wasn't the exact same food they were used to eating at home. [3]No, there wasn't much mutton, or lamb, to be had, but there were lobsters in abundance, along with oysters, duck, salmon, scallops, clams, and mussels. [4]There were also sweet and white potatoes, peanuts, squash, green beans, strawberries, and tomatoes. [5]Luckily for the settlers, the Indians in the New World grew and relished all of these foods, and they taught the Pilgrims to do the same. [6]But it took a while for the Pilgrims to catch on. [7]For example, during their first years in New England, the English settlers refused to eat clams or mussels. [8]They hadn't eaten them in the Old World, so in the new one, they fed them to the pigs. [9]No wonder their Indian neighbors often looked on in amazement or maybe even amusement.

In this paragraph, the first sentence is an **introductory sentence.** The sentence is not developed in the remainder of the paragraph. Instead, it offers a partial introduction to the topic: the early Pilgrims and their attitude toward food in the New World. The real point of the paragraph comes in the second sentence, where we learn that the early Pilgrims took an incredibly long time to recognize the wonderful selection of foods at their disposal. The second sentence is the topic sentence because it expresses an idea developed by the remaining sentences in the paragraph.

Here now is a variation on paragraphs that open with an introductory sentence or two. Once again, the introductory sentence helps introduce the topic but is not developed by any of the remaining sentences. The main difference between the paragraph that follows and the previous one is that the topic sentence begins with the contrast transition *however.*

Topic Sentence   [1]Most of us, males and females alike, love weddings. [2]However, a good deal of evidence in the English language implies that weddings are more important to women than to men. [3]A woman cherishes the wedding and is considered a bride for a whole year, but a man is referred to as a groom only on the day of the wedding. [4]The word *bride* appears in *bridal attendant, bridal gown, bridesmaid, bridal shower,* and even *bridegroom.* [5]Groom comes from the Middle English *grom,* meaning "man," but that meaning of the word is seldom used outside of the context of the wedding. [6]With most pairs of male/female words, people habitually put the masculine word first—*Mr. and Mrs., his and hers, boys and girls, men and women, kings and queens, brothers and sisters, guys and dolls,* and *host and hostess*—but it is the *bride and groom* who are talked about, not the *groom and bride.* (Adapted from Nilsen, *About Language,* p. 251.)

As you probably guessed, **contrast transitions** are words and phrases such as *but, however,* and *yet in reality.* These transitions signal to the reader that the author is about to contradict or modify a point previously made. Although contrast transitions don't always introduce topic sentences that follow on the heels of introductory sentences, they are quite common in this type of paragraph. As a matter of fact, if you spot one of the transitions listed below opening the second or third sentence of a paragraph, check to see if the next sentence and the topic sentence aren't one and the same.

Common Contrast Transitions	
however	in opposition
unfortunately	in contradiction
but	on the other hand
even so	nevertheless
yet	despite the fact
still	nonetheless
on the contrary	yet in fact
just the opposite	yet in reality

Topic Sentence in the Middle

Sometimes authors postpone the topic sentence until the middle of the paragraph. Look, for instance, at the paragraph that follows. The topic sentence appears smack in the middle. Notice, too, the use of a contrast transition. Here again, the transition signals that the author is about to change direction.

Topic Sentence

[1]In general, bats have a varied diet. [2]Flowers, insects, and fish are among their favorite foods. [3]Some bats, however, really are like the bats in horror movies. [4]They do, indeed, dine on blood. [5]<u>Contrary to their on-screen image, however, these so-called vampire bats don't attack and kill humans.</u> [6]They get their dinner from sleeping livestock. [7]Under the cover of darkness, they make small, pinprick incisions with their razor-sharp teeth. [8]Then they drink their fill from their sleeping prey. [9]Vampire bats are so skillful at getting their dinner they usually don't even wake the sleeping animals.

In this paragraph, the author uses several sentences to introduce the topic—vampire bats—and the real point of the paragraph comes in the fifth sentence.

Topic Sentence at the End

Sometimes authors develop a paragraph with a series of specific facts, examples, or studies. Then, in the last sentence, they state the main idea. To be sure, it's not the most common pattern, but it certainly does exist, as the following paragraph illustrates.

Topic Sentence   Advised about the sad plight of pandas who have been driven out of their homes, thousands of people will contribute money to save the pandas' natural habitat.* Similarly, "Save the Whale" campaigns have been in progress for years, and millions of dollars have been spent to help ailing or hunted whales. Currently, in many areas, bats are endangered, but don't expect a campaign to save them from extinction. Bats just don't have the appeal of ancient whales and cuddly pandas. <u>Most people are so repulsed by bats that wildlife organizations have been reluctant to mount a campaign to help them; they are convinced that no one would be interested.</u>

Topic Sentence in Two Steps

Much of the time, the main idea in a paragraph can be summed up in a single sentence. Still, you need to be prepared for a fairly common alternative: the two-step topic sentence. Here's an illustration of one.

[1]Movie director George Romero has made a number of horror films. [2]But none of his films has ever matched the fame won by *The Night of the Living Dead*. [3]Made on a low budget with inexperienced actors, the film tells the story of technology gone wrong. [4]Radiation in the atmosphere has caused the dead to come back to life and attack the living. [5]Not only have the dead come back to life, they have become cannibals as well. [6]Even worse, the living corpses are practically indestructible. [7]Only a bullet through the head can stop them, a discovery not made until the film is half over and the audience has been properly horrified. [8]Not surprisingly, Romero's film has become a cult classic, and true horror fans know the dialogue by heart.

---

*habitat: living environment.

In this paragraph, sentences 3 through 8 tell readers more about a film called *The Night of the Living Dead*. So at first glance, it would seem likely that sentence 2 is the topic sentence. But sentence 2, with its reference to "his films," requires the help of sentence 1 to effectively sum up the paragraph: "None of movie director George Romero's films has ever matched the fame won by his classic horror film, *The Night of the Living Dead*." Yes, writers do usually sum up main ideas in a single sentence, but not always. So be prepared to give them a little help by **synthesizing,*** or combining, two sentences into one complete topic sentence.

Question-and-Answer Topic Sentence

Particularly in textbooks, authors are likely to make the first or second sentence the topic sentence. However, they are also fond of opening a paragraph with a question. The answer that follows is usually the topic sentence.

Topic Sentence   What is genetics? In its simplest form, genetics is the study of heredity. It explains how certain characteristics are passed on from parents to children. Much of what we know about genetics was discovered by the monk Gregor Mendel in the nineteenth century. Since then, the field of genetics has vastly expanded. As scientists study the workings of genetics, they've developed new ways of manipulating genes. For example, scientists have isolated the gene that makes insulin, a human hormone, and now use bacteria to make quantities of it. (Kim Magliore, *Cracking the AP Biology Exam.* New York: Random House, 1998, p. 105.)

Questions for Analyzing Paragraphs

1. **To find the topic,** ask "Who or what is repeatedly mentioned or referred to here?"
2. **To discover the main idea,** ask "What does the author want to say *about* the topic? What idea is developed throughout most of the paragraph?"
3. **To locate the topic sentence,** ask "Which sentence or sentences could I use to sum up, in general terms, the content of the paragraph?"

---

*For more on synthesizing, see pp. 194–197.

EXERCISE 3

DIRECTIONS In the blank following each paragraph, write the number (or numbers) of the topic sentence.

1. ¹Compared with a corporate executive or a military officer, a teacher may not appear to have a great deal of power. ²But teachers have a special type of power. ³Henry Adams* caught the sense of the teacher's *long-term* power in the words "A teacher affects eternity: no one can tell where his influence stops." ⁴The teacher's powerful influence arises from the fact that he or she has an impact on people when they are still at a very impressionable stage. ⁵Teachers take "a piece of living clay and gently form it, day by day." ⁶Many careers are open to you, but few offer such truly inspiring power. (Adapted from Ryan and Cooper, *Those Who Can, Teach,* p. 148.)

Topic Sentence ——

2. ¹Before the collapse of the Communist party in Eastern Europe, the East German secret police, the *Staatsicherheit* (or Stasi), was an enormous bureaucracy that reached into every part of society. ²It had 85,000 full-time employees, including 6,000 people whose sole task was to listen in on telephone conversations. ³Another 2,000 steamed open mail, read it, resealed the letters, and sent them on to the intended recipients. ⁴The Stasi also employed 150,000 active informers and hundreds of thousands of part-time snitches. ⁵Files were kept on an estimated 4 to 5 million people in a country that had a total population, including children, of just 17 million. ⁶Although East Germany had a large standing army, the Stasi kept its own arsenal of 250,000 weapons. (Adapted from Janda et al., *The Challenge of Democracy,* p. 452.)

Topic Sentence ——

3. ¹What causes plants to bloom? ²Although you may think that plants flower based on the amount of sunlight they receive, they actually bloom according to the amount of uninterrupted darkness; this principle of plant bloom is called *photoperiodism.* ³Plants that bloom in late summer and fall, like asters and sedum, are called short-day plants. ⁴They require long periods of darkness and only short periods of light. ⁵Plants that flower in late spring and early summer,

---

*Henry Adams: (1838–1918) American historian.

such as daisies and poppies, are called long-day plants. ⁶They need only short periods of darkness to blossom.

Topic Sentence ____

4. ¹When most of us consider where to go on a vacation, outer space is not one of the obvious places that comes to mind. ²Yet in 2001, 60-year-old California multimillionaire Dennis Tito became the very first space tourist. ³Tito paid the Russians $20 million for a seat aboard their Soyuz spacecraft. ⁴Then, he prepared for the trip by spending eight months at a Russian cosmonaut training facility. ⁵On April 28, 2001, Tito and other cosmonauts blasted off from a launch pad in Kazakhstan. ⁶On April 30, the spacecraft docked with the International Space Station. ⁷They spent five days aboard the station, where Tito spent most of his time gazing out the windows and taking photographs. ⁸On May 6, the Soyuz capsule returned Tito and the rest of the crew back to Earth. Tito said he was happy he had achieved a life-long dream of visiting outer space.

Topic Sentence ____

5. ¹On the surface, effective listening might seem to require little more than an acute sense of hearing. ²But, in fact, there's a big difference between hearing and listening. ³*Hearing* occurs when sound waves travel through the air, enter your ears, and are transmitted by the auditory nerve to your brain. ⁴As long as neither your brain nor your ears are impaired, hearing is involuntary. ⁵It occurs spontaneously with little conscious effort on your part. ⁶*Listening*, in contrast, is a voluntary act that includes attending to, understanding, and evaluating the words or sounds you hear. ⁷If you sit through a lecture without making an effort to listen, there's a good chance that the speaker's words will become just so much background noise. (Flemming and Leet, *Becoming a Successful Student*, p. 93.)

Topic Sentence ____

6. ¹When we are extremely fearful or angry, our heartbeat speeds up, our pulse races, and our breathing rate tends to increase. ²The body's metabolism accelerates, burning up sugar in the bloodstream and fats in the tissues at a faster rate. ³The salivary glands become less active, making the mouth feel dry. ⁴The sweat glands may overreact, producing a dripping forehead, clammy hands, and "cold sweat." ⁵Finally, the pupils may enlarge, producing the wide-eyed look that is characteristic of both terror and rage. ⁶In effect,

strong emotions are not without consequences. [7]They bring about powerful changes in our bodies. (Rubin et al., *Psychology*, p. 370.)

Topic Sentence _____

7. [1]Every human body ages over time. [2]Scientists believe that the probable maximum human life span is about 150 years; the record of the oldest person to date is Shigechiyo Izumi (1865–1986) of Japan, who lived to be 120 years and 237 days. [3]There are two theories as to why all living things grow old and die. [4]The *free-radical theory* states that free radicals, certain chemicals produced as a by-product of biological activity, are particularly harmful to healthy cells. [5]As a person ages, free radicals gradually destroy cells until they can no longer function properly, causing the entire body (especially whole organ systems such as the kidneys or heart) to break down and die. [6]The *programmed senescence theory* suggests that the rate at which we age is predetermined, and that our genetic makeup controls the aging and death of the cells. [7]After enough of the cells die, the organs cease to function and death occurs. (Patricia Barnes-Svarney, ed., "Theories on Aging," *New York Public Library Science Desk Reference.* New York: Macmillan, 1995, p. 161.)

Topic Sentence _____

8. [1]On May 28, 1934, Elzire Dionne gave birth to five daughters who became famous as the Dionne Quintuplets. [2]Their birth made immediate headlines and was celebrated as a medical and maternal miracle. [3]Unfortunately, the little girls' fame was their downfall; almost from the moment of their birth, they were exploited by everyone around them. [4]Their parents were poor and didn't know how to support their family, which already included six children. [5]Confused and desperate, they agreed to put their five daughters on display at the Chicago World's Fair. [6]For a brief moment, it seemed as if the girls were saved from a miserable fate when the family physician, Dr. Allan Roy Dafoe, stepped in and insisted the girls were too frail to be on exhibit. [7]But after Dafoe took control of the girls' lives, he made himself rich by displaying the quintuplets to tourists and collecting fees for product endorsements.

Topic Sentence _____

9. [1]George W. Bush is only the second man in history who served as president of the United States just as his father did. [2]The first was John Quincy Adams, America's sixth president and the son of second president John Adams. [3]As a matter of fact, the elder George

Bush calls his son "Quincy." [4]George W. Bush and John Quincy Adams share other similarities, too. [5]Both men are their fathers' oldest sons. [6]Both men held public office before being elected president. [7]Adams was a United States senator and served as secretary of state, while Bush was governor of Texas. [8]Both men were in their fifties when they successfully ran for president. [9]Both men also achieved the presidency in a contested election because neither of them had won the popular vote. [10]Perhaps more than any other pair of presidents, George W. Bush and John Quincy Adams share a remarkable number of similarities.

Topic Sentence _____

10. [1]First Lady Edith Wilson has been called the "secret president," the "first woman president," and the "28th and a half president." [2]In 1919, her husband, President Woodrow Wilson, was serving his second term in office. [3]In September of that year, he suffered a near-fatal stroke, which left him partially paralyzed and nearly blind. [4]The president's doctors told Edith that her husband would recover faster if he stayed in office rather than resigning. [5]For over six months, Edith concealed the seriousness of his condition by running the country for him. [6]She read all of his documents and made decisions about which matters would be brought to his attention. [7]When the president seemed too ill to concentrate, she made decisions for him and communicated those decisions to his staff. [8]Wilson never fully recovered, and in 1921, at the end of his presidential term, Woodrow and Edith retired. [9]In 1924, after living three more years in virtual seclusion, President Wilson died. [10]Edith lived to be 89 years old and died in 1961.

Topic Sentence _____

CHECK YOUR UNDERSTANDING

Define the terms *topic, main idea*, and *topic sentence*.

Topic: _____

Main idea: _____

_____

Topic sentence: _____

_____

The Function of Supporting Details

Once you've found the main idea of a paragraph, you've identified the author's reason for writing the paragraph. However, there's more to a paragraph than the main idea. To clarify their ideas and make them convincing, authors use major and minor supporting details. The **major supporting details** are the examples, reasons, studies, statistics, facts, and figures that explain, develop, or prove an author's main idea or point. **Minor supporting details** further explain major details, add an interesting fact or story, or provide repetition for emphasis.

Because topic sentences are general sentences that sum up or interpret a variety of events, facts, examples, or experiences, they cover a good deal of ground and thus are subject to misunderstanding. Authors, therefore, use supporting details to avoid being misinterpreted, or misunderstood. Supporting details are the author's way of saying to readers, "I mean this, not that."

For an illustration of supporting details at work, look at the following sentence: "Most people who have survived near-fatal automobile accidents tend to behave in the same fashion." Given only this one sentence, could you be sure you understood the author's message? After all, that sentence could mean different things to different people. Perhaps survivors have nightmares or fears about their health. Maybe they are just very slow and careful drivers.

Look now at the following paragraph. Note how the addition of supporting details clarifies the author's meaning.

> Most people who have survived near-fatal automobile accidents tend to behave in the same fashion. They are fearful about driving even a mile or two over the speed limit and flatly refuse to go faster than the law allows. If they are not at the wheel, their terror increases. As passengers, they are extremely anxious and are prone to offering advice about how to take a curve or when to stop for a light.

In this instance, the supporting details illustrate the three types of behavior that the author has in mind. Those illustrations are the author's way of answering questions such as "What does 'behave in the same fashion' mean?"

Supporting details can range from reasons and examples to statistics and definitions. The form they take depends on the main idea they serve. Look, for example, at the following paragraph. Here the writer wants to convince readers that a book defending the right to be fat is very much worth reading:

[1]Marilyn Wann's book *Fat! So?* deserves a large and appreciative audience, one that does not consist solely of those who are overweight. [2]For starters, Wann is refreshingly unembarrassed about being fat (she tips the scales at 270), and that takes courage in a culture as obsessed as ours is with being thin. [3]If anything, the author encourages her readers—in the chapter titled "You, Too, Can Be Flabulous"—to embrace the word *fat* and use it in favorable contexts, such as "You're getting fat; you look great." [4]Still, despite her lively, and often humorous, style, Wann is good at describing the real misery our society inflicts on fat people. [5]Her chapters on the suffering endured by overweight teenagers are particularly moving, and they make a strong case for the need to attack, and attack hard, the tendency to treat the overweight as second-class citizens. [6]The book is also filled with sound advice about healthy eating habits. [7]Clearly, the author is not encouraging her readers to go out and gorge themselves on pizza and beer. [8]What she is suggesting is that they eat right in order to get fit, rather than thin. [9]Insisting that some people can, because of heredity, never be anything but overweight, Wann argues that they should not suffer for the genetic hand they've been dealt. [10]On the contrary, they should learn how to flaunt* their excess poundage and make society accept them just as they are.

In this paragraph, the major details all give reasons why Marilyn Wann's book deserves a wide audience. The minor details, in turn, flesh out and emphasize the major ones. Note, too, that at least two of the minor details are as important as the major detail they develop. In sentence 6, the author suggests that Wann's book is good because it offers sound advice about healthy eating. But without the presence of the minor details that follow, it would be hard to understand how a book celebrating fat could also provide tips on healthy eating. Minor details 7 and 8 help explain this seeming contradiction: Wann's advice focuses on eating to be fit rather than thin.

This illustration of major and minor details working together raises a key point: Don't be fooled by the labels *major* and *minor*. Sometimes minor details can be as meaningful as major ones, so you need to judge them in terms of what they contribute to the major details they modify. If a minor detail simply adds a personal note or provides repetition for emphasis, you don't need to think about it much, and you certainly don't need to include it in your notes. But if a major detail doesn't make much sense without the minor one that follows, then both details are equally important.

---

*flaunt: to show off.

CHECK YOUR UNDERSTANDING

Explain the difference between major and minor details.

_____

_____

EXERCISE 4

DIRECTIONS Read each paragraph and fill in the first blank with the number (or numbers) of the topic sentence. Answer the questions that follow by circling the correct response or filling in the blanks.

EXAMPLE

[1]What makes an effective leader? [2]To be sure, no one characteristic or trait defines an effective leader. [3]It is true, however, that the most effective leaders hold group members to very high standards of performance. [4]Setting such standards increases productivity because people tend to live up to the expectations set for them by superiors. [5]This is called the *Pygmalion** effect, and it works in a subtle, almost unconscious way. [6]When a managerial leader believes that a group member will succeed, the manager communicates this belief without realizing that he or she is doing so. [7]Conversely, when a leader expects a group member to fail, that person will not usually disappoint the manager. [8]The manager's expectation of success or failure becomes a self-fulfilling prophecy. [9]The manager's perceptions contribute to the success or failure. (DuBrin, *Leadership*, p. 85.)

a. Topic sentence: _3_

b. The major details help answer what question or questions about the topic sentence? *Why do effective leaders set such high standards?*

---

*Pygmalion: According to myth, Pygmalion, the king of Cyprus, carved and then fell in love with the statue of a woman who was transformed into a human being. The phrase *Pygmalion effect* reflects the myth's suggestion that wishing or believing something can make it happen.

c. *True* or *False:* Sentence 5 is a major supporting detail. Explain your answer. *This supporting detail further explains the previous one, making it a minor but far from unimportant detail.*

d. *True* or *False:* Sentence 9 is also a major supporting detail. Explain your answer. *The point made in Sentence 9 was already clear from previous statements in the paragraph, so the supporting detail adds little more than repetition.*

EXPLANATION Sentence 3 is the only sentence that can effectively sum up the paragraph. Explanations for the *true* and *false* answers already appear in the blanks above.

1. ¹Despite its rapid spread, Islam is not a religion for those who are casual about regulations. ²On the contrary, adhering to its rules takes effort and discipline. ³One must rise before dawn to observe the first of five prayers required daily, none of which can take place without first ritually cleansing oneself. ⁴Sleep, work, and recreational activities take second place to prayer. ⁵Fasting for the month of Ramadan,* undertaking the pilgrimage to Mecca at least once in a lifetime, paying tax for relief of the Muslim poor, and accepting Islam's creed require a serious and energetic commitment. ⁶On the whole, the vast majority of Muslims worldwide do observe those tenets.* (Adapted from Jan Goodwin, *Price of Honor*. New York: Penguin Books, 1994, p. 29.)

   a. Topic sentence: _____

   b. The major details help answer what question or questions about the topic sentence?

   _____

   _____

   c. *True* or *False:* Sentence 4 is a major supporting detail.

      Explain your answer. _____

      _____

   _____

   *Ramadan: Muslim holy month.
   *tenets: rules; principles.

d. *True* or *False:* Sentence 5 is also a major supporting detail.

Explain your answer. _____

_____

2. ¹The orchestra conductor Arturo Toscanini was born with a phenomenal memory that served him well throughout his career. ²For example, Toscanini could remember every single note of every musical score he had ever studied. ³Once, when he couldn't find a musical score for a performance, he simply wrote it down from memory. ⁴When the score was finally found, it was clear that Toscanini had not made one single error. ⁵When late in life his eyesight failed him, Toscanini conducted all of his concerts from memory. ⁶Audiences agreed that his blindness did not in any way hinder the conductor's performance.

a. Topic sentence: _____

b. The major details help answer what question or questions about the topic sentence?

_____

_____

c. *True* or *False:* Sentence 3 is a major detail.

Explain your answer. _____

_____

d. *True* or *False:* Sentence 6 is a minor detail.

Explain your answer. _____

_____

3. ¹Those cuddly toys known as teddy bears seem to have been around forever. ²But actually the first teddy bears came into being when President Theodore "Teddy" Roosevelt showed himself too much of a sportsman to shoot a staked bear cub. ³In 1902 Roosevelt visited Mississippi to settle a border dispute, and his hosts organized a hunting expedition. ⁴To make sure that the president would remain in a good mood, they staked a bear cub to the ground so that Roosevelt couldn't miss. ⁵To his credit, Roosevelt declined the offer to shoot the bear. ⁶When the incident was publicized, largely through a political cartoon by cartoonist Clifford Berryman, a Russian candy store owner named Morris Mitchom made up a toy bear out of soft,

fuzzy cloth and placed it in his shop window with a sign reading "Teddy's Bear." [7]The bear was a hit with passersby, and teddy bear mania spread rapidly throughout the country.

a. Topic sentence: _____

b. The major details help answer what question or questions about the topic sentence?

_____

_____

c. *True* or *False:* Sentence 4 is a minor detail.

Explain your answer. _____

_____

d. *True* or *False:* Sentence 6 is a major detail.

Explain your answer. _____

_____

4. [1]Did you ever ask yourself just how much truth there is to the eerie legend of Count Dracula? [2]You may be surprised to discover that centuries ago there did exist a Prince Vlad, said to be the source of the Dracula legends. [3]Prince Vlad, however, did not spend his time seeking out fresh young victims; instead, he had disobedient members of the villages he ruled brought to his castle, where they would be executed before his eyes. [4]On one occasion, Vlad became furious because some visiting Turkish diplomats failed to remove their turbans. [5]They meant no disobedience; it was simply not their custom to do so. [6]As punishment for this supposed insult, Vlad had the turbans nailed to their heads.

a. Topic sentence: _____

b. The major details help answer what question or questions about the topic sentence?

_____

_____

c. *True* or *False:* Sentence 4 is a minor detail.

Explain your answer. _____

_____

d. *True* or *False:* Sentence 5 is a major detail.

Explain your answer. _____

_____

5. ¹Many people don't know the difference between a patent and a trademark. ²But there is a difference. ³Usually granted for seventeen years, a patent protects both the name of a product and its method of manufacture. ⁴In 1928, for example, Jacob Schick invented and then patented the electric razor in an effort to have complete control over his creation. ⁵Similarly, between 1895 and 1912, no one but the Shredded Wheat company could make shredded wheat, because the company had the patent. ⁶A trademark is a name, symbol, or other device that identifies a product and makes it memorable in the minds of consumers. ⁷*Kleenex, Jell-O,* and *Sanka* are all examples of trademarks, as is the lion that introduces MGM pictures. ⁸Aware of the power that trademarks possess, companies fight to protect them and do not allow anyone else to use one without permission. ⁹Occasionally, however, a company gets careless and loses control of a trademark. ¹⁰*Aspirin,* for example, is no longer considered a trademark, and any company can call a pain-reducing tablet an aspirin.

a. Topic sentence: _____

b. The major details help answer what question or questions about the topic sentence?

_____

_____

c. *True* or *False:* Sentence 3 is a minor detail.

Explain your answer. _____

_____

d. *True* or *False:* Sentence 5 is a major detail.

Explain your answer. _____

_____

 # Recognizing Patterns of Organization

Discovering the topic and main idea of a paragraph will most definitely help you understand the author's message or meaning. But you can deepen and enhance that understanding by checking to see if the paragraph is organized according to one of the following patterns: (1) definition, (2) classification, (3) process, (4) sequence of dates and events, (5) comparison and contrast, or (6) cause and effect. Each of these patterns has specific characteristics, and knowing these characteristics can help you decide what to underline or what to include in your notes. As an additional bonus, your knowledge of paragraph patterns can help you to formulate potential test questions. In other words, the ability to spot organizational patterns is a reading skill definitely worth having.

Pattern 1: Definition

Textbook authors are fully aware that their student readers need to master the specialized vocabularies of their various courses. Thus, they frequently employ the definition pattern of organization in order to make sure that students get the full meaning of a key term. Ninety percent of the time, the definition pattern begins with an explanation of the term. As you learned in chapter 2, the term is usually highlighted in some way—boldface, italics, or colored ink—and it's followed by a detailed definition. Often, the author may also give a bit of the word's history, contrast it with a similar term, offer an example of the activity or behavior associated with the word, describe the conditions under which it comes into play, or define related terms.

Once they recognize the definition pattern, skillful readers know they have to make its key characteristics stand out for future review. Look, for example, at the way the following definition paragraph has been underlined and annotated to make the central characteristics of the pattern as visible as possible.

TQ: What is product modification?

TQ: What conditions must be met for product modification to take place?

Product modification refers to changing one or more of a product's characteristics. For this approach to be effective, several conditions must be met. First, the product must be modifiable. Second, existing customers must be able to perceive that a modification has been made. Third, the modification should make the product more consistent with customers' desires. (Pride et al., *Business,* p. 396.)

When you see an entire paragraph devoted to defining a key term, your best bet is a test question that asks you to recall some aspect of the definition. As you can see, that's the focus of the test questions shown above in the marginal annotations.

Pattern 2: Classification

Particularly in business and science textbooks, authors frequently explain a system of classification. They begin by explaining how some large group can be divided into smaller categories or subgroups. Then they identify and describe the specific characteristics of each subgroup. Here's an example. Again, check out the underlining and annotations that accompany the paragraph.

Hippocrates classified people according to the four fluids in their body.

TQ: Explain Hippocrates' system of classification.

Like his contemporaries,* the Greek physician Hippocrates believed that the human body consisted of four *humors,* or fluids: black bile, yellow bile, blood, and phlegm. Hippocrates' contribution was to classify human beings according to the fluid that predominated in their bodies. Persons with an excess of black bile were classified as ① *melancholic* and were presumed to be depressed and pessimistic. The ② *choleric,* possessing excess yellow bile, were considered quick-tempered and irritable. Persons with a predominance of blood were ③ *sanguine.* They were usually cheerful and optimistic. The ④ *phlegmatic,* possessing excess phlegm, were thought to be slow, unemotional, and uninvolved with the world at large. While the theory has long since been discarded, the meanings of some of these terms persist.

As soon as you realize that an author is intent on outlining a system of classification, jot a test question like the one above in the margin.

Pattern 3: Process

Like the classification paragraph, the process paragraph frequently turns up in both business and science texts, where authors need to explain, step by step, how something works or develops: Here, for example, is a paragraph that outlines the stages in digestion. Note how each step in the process of digestion is carefully explained.

Digestive system prepares food to be turned into energy.

TQ: Explain the process of digestion.

In the human body, the digestive system breaks down food so it can be used for energy. ① As food enters the mouth, chewing, along with enzymes in the saliva, break it down into small pieces. ② Next the esophagus contracts and pushes the food into the stomach, where muscles, enzymes, and digestive acids turn the food into a thick liquid. ③ That liquid is emptied into the small intestine, where most of its nutrients are absorbed. ④ What remains travels to the

*contemporaries: people living at the same time.

large intestine, where water is removed from digested food and turned into waste. (Adapted from Barnes-Svarney, *The New York Public Library Science Desk Reference*, p. 166.)

Anytime you recognize the process pattern, you would do well to jot down a test question that asks you to remember the sequence of stages or steps in the process described. Not only is this a likely test question, but answering it is also a sure-fire means of review.

Words like *steps, stages, phases,* and *process* are all signs that you are reading a process paragraph, but so too are the transitions listed below:

Transitions That Identify a Sequence of Steps

First, second, third	Toward the end
Finally	By the time
Then	At this point
Next	In this stage
Afterward	In the final stage

Pattern 4: Sequence of Dates and Events

Authors who write about history and government frequently use a **sequence of dates and events** to explain or argue their claims. In this pattern, the supporting details present a series of dates and events listed according to the order in which they occurred. Here's an example:

TQ: What are the dates of the Mexican-American War?

The Democrat James Polk became president of the United States in (1844) From the very beginning of his presidency, Polk made it clear that he intended to expand the boundaries of the United States. In (1846) he ordered General Zachary Taylor to take troops into Mexican territory. On (April 25) of the same year, the Mexican military fired on Taylor's troops and war between the United States and Mexico began, even though Congress had not yet officially declared it. By (1847) U.S. troops had arrived in Mexico City and were claiming victory. (The opening phrase in the Marines' anthem— "From the Halls of Montezuma"—is a reference to the arrival of

TG: What was the name of the treaty that ended the Mexican-American War?

those troops in Mexico's capital.) In (1848) Mexico and the United States signed the Treaty of Guadalupe Hidalgo, which ceded a portion of Mexican land that today includes Arizona, Utah, Nevada, and New Mexico to the United States. Polk had his wish: He had expanded and redefined U.S. borders. But in an effort to assuage* the war's critics—and there were many who considered the war with Mexico unjust—the United States government paid the Mexican government $15 million.

If you recognize a sequence of dates and events pattern in a paragraph, use your knowledge of the pattern to create test questions that focus on the significance of particular dates or the sequence of events that led up to some important happening or achievement.

Although the presence of several dates and events organized in a sequence is an obvious clue to this pattern, so too are the following transitions:

Transitions That Mark Dates and Events

After	Then
From _____ to _____	Finally
In _____	Before
In the years	Previously
During the years	A year later
In the years that followed	Following
In the following years	At that point
Between the years _____ and _____	

Pattern 5: Comparison and Contrast

In all kinds of textbooks, authors are likely to compare (mention similarities) and contrast (cite differences). Sometimes they devote an entire chapter section to pointing out the similarities and differences between two topics, but they are more likely to confine the

---

*assuage: calm, soothe.

comparison and contrast pattern to a single paragraph. Here is an example.

TG: Explain the difference between assertive and aggressive behavior. Give examples for each type.

My uncle Ralph always keeps cool.

My ex-wife is a good example.

Assertive behavior involves standing up for your rights and expressing your thoughts and feelings in a direct, appropriate way that does not violate the rights of others. It is a matter of getting the other person to understand your viewpoint. People who exhibit assertive behavior skills are able to handle their conflict situations with ease and assurance while maintaining good interpersonal relations. In contrast, aggressive behavior involves expressing your thoughts and feelings and defending your rights in a way that openly violates the rights of others. Those exhibiting aggressive behavior believe that others' rights must be subservient to theirs, and they have a difficult time maintaining good interpersonal relations. They are likely to interrupt, talk fast, ignore others, and use sarcasm or other forms of verbal abuse to maintain control. (Adapted from Reece and Brandt, *Effective Human Relations in Organizations,* pp. 350–353.)

A paragraph like the above with its two topics—assertive and aggressive behavior—and its emphasis on the differences between them has comparison and contrast written all over it. Thus, it all but cries out for you to predict a test question that asks for a description of how the two topics are similar or different.

Topic sentences such as "Spartan society was very different from the society of Athens" or "In the old West, there wasn't all that much difference between cowboys and cowgirls" are strong indications of the comparison and contrast pattern of development, particularly if they are accompanied by transitions like those listed in the box below.

Transitions That Signal Comparison or Similarity

Similarly	In like manner
Likewise	Along the same lines
In much the same vein	Just as
By the same token	Just like
In the same manner	

Transitions That Signal Contrast or Difference		
However	Nevertheless	In reality
But	Unfortunately	On the contrary
And yet	Whereas	In opposition
On the one hand	In contrast	Conversely
On the other hand	Nonetheless	
Still	Despite that fact	

Pattern 6: Cause and Effect

Because relating cause to effect is so basic to our thinking, you will encounter cause and effect paragraphs in every type of textbook. No matter what the discipline, or subject matter, authors need to explain how one event (the cause) produced another event (the effect).

Ultraviolet radiation is harmful.

TQ: What are some of the effects of ultraviolet radiation?

Effects

The ultraviolet radiation from the sun that reaches the earth's surface is a health threat. At the very least, it causes ① aging and wrinkling of the skin. At the very worst, it is responsible for ② cataracts, ③ sunburn, ④ snowblindness, and ⑤ skin cancer, which claims around 15,000 lives each year in the United States alone. Exposure to UV radiation also ⑥ suppresses the immune system, enabling cancers to become established and grow. In addition, ⑦ radiation slows plant growth, ⑧ delays seed germination, and ⑨ interferes with photosynthesis.* (Adapted from Kaufman and Franz, *Biosphere 2000*, p. 266.)

Cause and effect paragraphs are a likely source of test questions. When you encounter them in your reading, make sure you can easily identify both cause (or causes) and effect (or effects). Then turn that information into a question like the one that appears above.

---

*photosynthesis: process by which plants use sunlight to create food.

Transitions That Signal Cause and Effect

Consequently	Therefore
As a result	Thus
In response	In the aftermath
In reaction	Hence

Verbs That Connect Cause and Effect

Produces	Engenders
Brings about	Creates
Generates	Sets off
Initiates	Leads to
Causes	Results in
Fosters	Stimulates
Evokes	Triggers

Mixed Patterns

As you might expect, writers don't restrict themselves to a single paragraph pattern. If their material calls for it, they combine patterns. When you recognize two or more patterns in a paragraph or reading, see if you can generate a test question for each pattern. For an illustration, see the annotations that follow.

TQ: Define the term "scientific method."

All research studies of human development follow some form of **scientific method,** or set of procedures designed to ensure objective observations and interpretations of observations. Even though it is not always possible to follow these procedures perfectly, they form an ideal to which psychological research tends to aspire (Cherry, 1995; Levine & Parkinson, 1994). The procedures or

TQ: Explain each step in the scientific method.

steps in the scientific method are as follows: (1) *Formulating research questions.* Sometimes these questions refer to previous studies, such as when a developmental psychologist asks, "Are

Examples of research questions.

Professor Deepthought's studies of thinking consistent with studies of thinking from less developed countries?" Other times they refer to issues important to society, such as "Does preschool education make children more socially skilled later in childhood?" (2) *Stating questions as hypotheses.* A **hypothesis** is a statement that expresses a research question precisely. In making a hypothesis out of the preschool education question above, a psychologist

Example of hypothesis.

would further define the terms *preschool education* and *socially skilled:* "Do children in day care learn to share toys with other children at an earlier age than children cared for at home?" (3) *Testing the hypothesis.* Having phrased a research question as a hypothesis, researchers can conduct an actual study of it. The choice of study method usually depends on convenience, ethics, and scientific appropriateness. (Seifert and Hoffnung, *Child and Adolescent Development,* pp. 16–17.)

In this paragraph, the authors combine two patterns—definition and process—to make their point. What are two likely test questions based on this passage? Well, the two in the margins (p. 107) are definite possibilities.

Common Combinations

The previous example combines definition and process patterns. This is not unusual. These two patterns often work together because an author needs to define the key terms essential to understanding a particular process, or sequence of steps. Some of the other patterns likely to combine are process with cause and effect, classification with comparison and contrast, and definition with classification. All of which suggests one simple tip: If you recognize one member of a common combination, make it a point to check for its likely companion.

Common Combinations

Process with Cause and Effect and/or Definition
Classification with Definition and/or Cause and Effect
Sequence of Dates and Events with Cause and Effect

EXERCISE 5

DIRECTIONS Identify the pattern or patterns by circling the appropriate letter or letters.

1. The ethnic and racial classifications differed in the 1990 and 2000 United States Census questionnaires. In the 1990 census, Americans were asked to identify themselves as one of two ethnic categories. One category was Hispanic Origin; the other was Not of Hispanic Origin. In the 2000 census, there were again just two ethnic categories, but the categories were slightly expanded. The first category was Hispanic or Latino, and the second was Not Hispanic or Latino. The racial classifications underwent a more significant change. In the 1990 census, Americans were asked to identify themselves as belonging to one of five different racial categories. They could choose from: American Indian or Alaska Native; Asian or Pacific Islander; Black; White; or Some Other Race. The 2000 census expanded and reorganized this classification to include six categories: American Indian or Alaska Native; Asian; Black or African American; Native Hawaiian or Other Pacific Islander; White; or Some Other Race. Furthermore, respondents were permitted to select more than one category if they self-identified with two or more different races.

Topic Sentence a. definition

  b. classification

  c. process

  d. sequence of dates and events

  e. comparison and contrast

  f. cause and effect

2. Economists have classified resources into three general categories: land, labor, and capital. **Land** includes all natural resources, such as minerals, timber, and water, as well as the land itself. **Labor** refers to the physical and intellectual services of people and includes the training, education, and abilities of the individuals in a society. **Capital** refers to products such as machinery and buildings that are used to produce other goods and services. You will often hear the term *capital* used to describe the financial backing for some project to finance some business. Economists refer to funds used to purchase capital as **financial capital.** (Boyes and Melvin, *Fundamentals of Economics,* p. 4.)

Patterns   a. definition

b. classification

c. process

d. sequence of dates and events

e. comparison and contrast

f. cause and effect

3. On April 26, 1986, the worst accident in the history of nuclear power took place at the Chernobyl plant about 110 km north of Kiev in the Ukraine. At Chernobyl, the uranium was contained in fuel rods surrounded by graphite bricks, which served to moderate the nuclear reaction. (In the United States, commercial generating plants do not use graphite and have a containment dome.) The accident occurred when engineers turned off most of the reactor's automatic safety and warning systems to keep them from interfering with an unauthorized safety experiment. At this point, cooling water was one of the safety systems turned off. Unfortunately, the remaining water in the reactor then turned to steam, and the steam reacted with the nuclear fuel and the graphite bricks. An explosive mixture of gases formed and was ignited. The reactor was destroyed, the roof blew off the building, and the graphite bricks caught fire. Soviet officials claimed the fire was extinguished on April 29. According to Soviet reports, 500 people were hospitalized and the acknowledged death count stood at 31. Incidences of thyroid cancer, leukemia, and other radiation-related illnesses are high among people living near the power plant. More ominously, the radioactive particles produced by the explosion have been dispersed all over the planet by the natural circulation of air. It will be years before all of the effects of the Chernobyl disaster can be assessed. (Adapted from Sherman et al., *Basic Concepts of Chemistry,* p. 484.)

Patterns   a. definition

b. classification

c. process

d. sequence of dates and events

e. comparison and contrast

f. cause and effect

4. Viral marketing* is a highly successful sales technique that sold $7.7 billion of merchandise in 1999. Using this strategy, companies actually get their customers to sell products via word-of-mouth ad-

---

*Yes, the name does come from the expression "It spreads like a virus," which suggests speed.

vertising. In exchange for products, a current customer agrees to host a home party. This host or hostess then invites his or her friends, relatives, neighbors, and coworkers to come to the party to see the products, watch demonstrations, and tell stories about how the products are or can be used. In this friendly, fun, and sociable atmosphere, people are eager to buy and sell the products to one another. For instance, viral marketing has been used to sell millions of dollars of Tupperware plastic containers, Pampered Chef kitchenware, and Longaberger baskets.

Patterns a. definition

          b. classification

          c. process

          d. sequence of dates and events

          e. comparison and contrast

          f. cause and effect

5. During the process of labor, the mother's uterus contracts rhythmically and automatically to force the baby downward through the vaginal canal. The contractions occur in relatively predictable stages. The **first stage of labor** usually begins with relatively mild and irregular contractions of the uterus. As contractions become stronger and more regular, the *cervix* (the opening of the uterus) dilates, or widens, enough for the baby's head to fit through. Toward the end of this stage, which may take from eight to twenty-four hours for a first-time mother, a period of **transition** begins. The cervix nears full dilation, contractions become more rapid, and the baby's head begins to move into the birth canal. Although this period generally lasts for only a few minutes, it can be extremely painful because of the increasing pressure of the contractions. The **second stage of labor** includes complete dilation of the cervix to the actual birth. It usually lasts between one and one-and-one-half hours. During the **third stage of labor,** which lasts only a few minutes, the afterbirth (the placenta and umbilical cord) is expelled. (Adapted from Seifert and Hoffnung, *Childhood and Adolescent Development,* pp. 131–132.)

Patterns a. definition

          b. classification

          c. process

          d. sequence of dates and events

          e. comparison and contrast

          f. cause and effect

EXERCISE 6

DIRECTIONS Identify the paragraph pattern or patterns by circling the appropriate letter or letters. Then circle the letter of the one test question you would *not* be likely to predict, based on the paragraph.

1. Two small lakes in a remote part of Cameroon, a small country in central Africa, made international news in the mid-1980s when deadly clouds of carbon dioxide (CO_2) gas from deep beneath the surface of the lakes escaped into the surrounding atmosphere, killing animal and human populations far downwind. The first gas discharge, which occurred at Lake Monoun in 1984, asphyxiated* thirty-seven people. The second, which occurred at Lake Nyos in 1986, released a highly concentrated cloud of CO_2 that killed more than 1700 people. The two events have similarities other than location: Both occurred at night during the rainy season; both involved volcanic crater lakes; and both are likely to recur unless there is some type of technologic intervention.*

Patterns a. definition

b. classification

c. process

d. sequence of dates and events

e. comparison and contrast

f. cause and effect

Test Questions a. What caused the two disasters at Lake Monoun and Lake Nyos?

b. In what ways were the disasters at Lake Monoun and Lake Nyos similar?

c. How did the people of Cameroon react to the disasters at Lake Monoun and Lake Nyos?

2. In 1862 Congress passed the **Homestead Act.** This measure offered 160 acres of land free to any American citizen who was a family head and over twenty-one. The only conditions were that the settler live on the land for five years and make improvements to it. In the well-watered East, 160 acres was a sizable farm. Yet in the semi-arid West, it was barely enough to support a family. To prosper, a farmer needed at least twice that amount. Despite these risks, the Homestead Act produced an explosion of settlement. Within a

---

*asphyxiated: killed by loss of air.
*intervention: interference.

half century after the passage, all western territories had gained enough settlers—at least 60,000—to become states. As a result of the Homestead Act, most western areas experienced enormous population growth. (DiBacco et al., *History of the United States,* p. 315.)

Patterns a. definition

b. classification

c. process

d. sequence of dates and events

e. comparison and contrast

f. cause and effect

Test Questions a. In what year did Congress pass the Homestead Act?

b. What was the Homestead Act and what effect did it have?

c. Explain why the Homestead Act was considered a failure.

3. A **tsunami** is a very long ocean wave that is generated by a sudden displacement of the sea floor. The term is derived from a Japanese word meaning "harbor wave." Tsunamis are sometimes referred to as **seismic sea waves** because submarine and near-coast earthquakes are their primary cause. They are also popularly called "tidal waves," but this is a misnomer;* tsunamis have nothing to do with tides. Tsunamis can occur with little or no warning, bringing death and massive destruction to coastal communities. (Murck et al., *Environmental Geology,* p. 131.)

Patterns a. definition

b. classification

c. process

d. sequence of dates and events

e. comparison and contrast

f. cause and effect

Test Questions a. Tsunamis are caused by _____.

b. Describe how a tsunami affects ocean life.

c. What is the meaning of the word *tsunami* and what is its origin?

———————
*misnomer: inappropriate name.

4. Watergate,* the scandal that rocked the nation, began on June 17, 1972, when five men were caught trying to burglarize the offices of the Democratic National Committee. The arrest of the five men led to an investigation that uncovered a White House plan of systematic espionage* against political opponents. Deeply involved in that plan were the two top aides to President Richard Nixon, John Erlichman and H. R. Haldeman. On April 30, 1973, Attorney General Elliot Richardson appointed a special prosecutor, Harvard Law School professor Archibald Cox, to conduct a full-scale investigation of the Watergate break-in. On May 20, 1973, the Senate Committee on Presidential Activities opened hearings, and on July 16 White House aide Alexander Butterfield told the committee that President Nixon had taped all the conversations that occurred in his office. However, President Nixon refused to turn the tapes over to the investigating committee, and on October 20 he ordered the dismissal of prosecutor Cox. After a storm of public protest, Nixon agreed in June of 1974 to turn over the tapes. Once members of the committee had examined the tapes closely, they discovered that eighteen-and-one-half minutes had been mysteriously erased. By July 30 the House Judiciary Committee had approved three articles of impeachment. Rather than face almost certain disgrace, Richard Milhous Nixon resigned as president on August 9, 1974.

Patterns a. definition

b. classification

c. process

d. sequence of dates and events

e. comparison and contrast

f. cause and effect

Test Questions a. What was the public's response to the resignation of Richard Nixon?

b. Outline the chain of events that began with the break-in at the Watergate and ended with the resignation of Richard Nixon.

c. How did the scandal known as Watergate affect the U.S. government?

5. Manners and morals are terms that overlap, sometimes confusingly, but here I am using the two words in senses that are easier to distin-

---

*The Watergate is a hotel-apartment-office complex in Washington, D.C., where the committee's offices were located.
*espionage: spying.

guish. *Manners* would be the standards of conduct that prevail in a group, large or small, and hence they would change from group to group and year to year. *Morals* would be defined as the standards that determine the relations of individuals with other individuals, one with one—a child with each of its parents, a husband with his wife, a rich man with a poor man (not *the* rich with *the* poor)—and also the relations of any man with himself, his destiny, and his God. They are answers found by individuals to the old problems of faith, hope, charity or love, art, duty, submission to one's fate . . . and hence they are relatively universal; they can be illustrated from the lives of any individuals, in any place, at any time since the beginning of time. (Malcolm Cowley, *New England Writers and Writing*, p. 238.)

Patterns
a. definition
b. classification
c. process
d. sequence of dates and events
e. comparison and contrast
f. cause and effect

Test Questions
a. How does Malcolm Cowley apply the distinction between manners and morals to the work of Nathaniel Hawthorne?
b. According to Malcolm Cowley, morals are _____.
c. Explain the difference between manners and morals.

CHECK YOUR UNDERSTANDING
Name and describe each of the patterns introduced on pages 101–106.
1. _____
2. _____
3. _____
4. _____
5. _____
6. _____

■ **DIGGING DEEPER**

LOOKING AHEAD The paragraph on page 103 suggests that U.S. President James Polk encouraged a war with Mexico in an effort to expand U.S. boundaries. What's the first tip-off that the authors of the following reading seem to agree wholeheartedly with this point of view?

MR. POLK'S WAR

1 In early 1846, President James K. Polk ordered American troops under "Old Rough and Ready," General Zachary Taylor, to march south into Mexico and defend the contested border of the Rio Grande across from the town of Matamoros. Polk especially desired California as the prize in his expansionist strategy, and to that end he attempted to buy from the angry Mexicans a huge tract of land extending to the Pacific. When the effort failed, Polk waited for war. Negotiations between troops on the Rio Grande were awkwardly conducted in French because no American officer spoke Spanish and no Mexican spoke English. After a three-week standoff, the tense situation came to a head. On April 24, 1846, Mexican cavalry ambushed a U.S. cavalry unit on the north side of the river; eleven Americans were killed and sixty-three taken captive. On April 26 Taylor sent a dispatch overland to Washington, D.C., which took two weeks to arrive, announcing: "Hostilities may now be considered as commenced."

2 Polk now drafted a message to Congress: Mexico had "passed the boundary of the United States, had invaded our territory and shed American blood on American soil." In the bill accompanying the war message, Polk deceptively declared that "war exists by the act of Mexico itself" and summoned the nation to arms. Two days later, on May 13, the House recognized a state of war with Mexico by a vote of 174 to 14, and the Senate by 40 to 2, with numerous abstentions.* Some antislavery Whigs* had tried to oppose the war but were barely allowed to gain the floor of Congress to speak. Since Polk withheld key facts, the full reality of what had happened on the distant Rio Grande was not known. But the theory and practice of Manifest Destiny*

---

*abstentions: refusals to vote.
*Whigs: A nineteenth-century political group formed to oppose the Democratic party. The Whigs favored a loose interpretation of the Constitution.
*Manifest Destiny: The doctrine that the United States had not only the right but the duty to expand westward.

had launched the United States into its first war on foreign territory.

3   The war spawned an outpouring of poetry, song, drama, travel literature, and lithographs that captured the popular imagination and glorified the war. New lyrics to the tune "Yankee Doodle" proclaimed: "They attacked our men upon our land / and crossed our river too sir / now show them all with sword in hand / what Yankee boys can do sir." Most of the war-inspired flowering in the popular arts was patriotic. But not everyone cheered. The abolitionist James Russell Lowell considered the war a "national crime committed in behoof of slavery, our common sin." Ralph Waldo Emerson confided to his journals in 1847: "The United States will conquer Mexico, but it will be as the man swallows arsenic which brings him down in turn." (Adapted from Norton et al., *A People and a Nation,* pp. 3611–3662.)

Sharpening Your Skills

DIRECTIONS Answer the following questions by filling in the blanks or circling the letter of the correct response.

1. What's the first hint that the authors also believe Polk wanted to go to war with Mexico?

_____

2. On April 24, 1846, Mexican troops ambushed a U.S. cavalry unit. But what had the U.S. done to initiate hostilities?

_____

3. The authors do not explicitly define the term "expansionist strategy" in paragraph 1. But context suggests what meaning?

a. Polk wanted to expand U.S. boundaries.

b. Polk wanted to expand the power of the president.

c. Polk wanted to increase his own personal wealth.

4. In paragraph 2, the authors say that Polk "deceptively declared that 'war exists by the act of Mexico itself.'" What was deceptive about that statement?

_____

5. What's the main idea in paragraph 3?

   a. The war against Mexico unleashed a flood of patriotism in the United States.
   b. The war against Mexico was not popular with abolitionists.
   c. The war against Mexico aroused mixed emotions.

6. Paraphrase the last sentence of paragraph 2.

   _____

7. The quotations from Lowell and Emerson in paragraph 3 are there to illustrate what point?

   _____

8. How would you paraphrase Emerson's position on the war with Mexico?

   _____

9. What patterns of organization are at work in paragraphs 1 and 2?

   a. definition
   b. classification
   c. process
   d. sequence of dates and events
   e. comparison and contrast
   f. cause and effect

10. What pattern of organization is used in paragraph 3?

    a. definition
    b. classification
    c. process
    d. sequence of dates and events
    e. comparison and contrast
    f. cause and effect

WORD NOTES: WORDS AND MYTHS

Page 96 introduced the phrase "Pygmalion effect." The footnote, in turn, explained that the phrase was derived from the myth of Pygmalion, the king of Cyprus. As you may already know, a number of other words have also been derived from mythology. Here are just a few:

1. *Mentor.* Mentor was the trusted friend and teacher of Odysseus. While Odysseus was away, a goddess came down to earth to protect the family of Odysseus. To do so, she disguised herself as Mentor and took over his role as teacher and counselor. Today we use the word *mentor* to mean someone we consider a teacher and adviser.

Sample Sentence   My older brother has always been my *mentor* in life.

Definition   teacher, counselor, guide

2. *Atlas.* According to Greek mythology, Atlas was a Titan* who held up the world on his shoulders. Historically, the image of Atlas often appeared on the covers of map collections. Today when we talk about an *atlas,* we are usually referring to a bound collection of maps.

Sample Sentence   She studied the *atlas* with much fascination.

Definition   book of maps, book of tables and charts

3. *Herculean.* Hercules was a Greek hero who possessed extraordinary strength. It was said that he could perform fantastic feats. Today when we use the word *Herculean,* we are talking about something that demands a great deal of effort or strength.

Sample Sentence   Before she became vice president, she had to complete the *Herculean* task of reorganizing the entire office system.

Definition   difficult; demanding in mental or physical strength

---

*Titan: In Greek mythology, the Titans sought to rule heaven but were overthrown by other gods.

4. *Flora and fauna.* Flora was the Roman goddess of flowers, and Faunus was the Roman god of nature and fertility. Today we use the expression *flora and fauna* to mean the plants and animals of a particular region.

Sample Sentence   We spent three whole days studying the *flora and fauna* of New Zealand.

Definition   plants and animals of a particular region

Other Forms of the Word   florae *or* floras, faunae *or* faunas

5. *Narcissism.* Narcissus was a beautiful young man who loved no one until the day he saw his own reflection in a pool of water. From then on, he was in love with himself. Today when we talk about *narcissism,* we are talking about excessive love or admiration for oneself.

Sample Sentence   Only his incredible *narcissism* allowed him to ignore all the insulting remarks directed his way.

Definition   self-love, admiration for oneself

Other Forms of the Word   narcissist, narcissistic

Now fill in the blanks with one of the above words.

1. Most geography books contain a section listing the

   _____ of different regions.

2. Practically every library has several _____ as a part of the reference room.

3. She was more than a friend; she was my _____.

4. His excessive _____ endangered their marriage.

5. The champion weightlifter's _____ strength impressed the crowd.

Test 1: Reviewing the Key Points

DIRECTIONS Answer the following questions by filling in the blanks or circling the correct response.

1. _____ is the first step toward discovering the main idea of a paragraph.

2. *True* or *False*. You should always be able to express the topic in a single word.

3. To discover the main idea, you need to ask two questions. Those questions are _____ and _____.

4. The function of the topic sentence is to _____.

5. *True* or *False*. The first sentence of a paragraph is not necessarily the topic sentence.

6. Contrast transitions signal to the reader that _____ _____.

7. Major details serve to _____.

8. Minor details serve to _____.

9. *True* or *False*. Minor details are never important enough to be included in your notes.

10. Recognizing the organizational pattern underlying a reading can help you decide what to underline and what to include in your notes. It can also help you _____.

Test 2: Recognizing Topic Sentences

DIRECTIONS Write the number (or numbers) of the topic sentence in the accompanying blank.

1. ¹Throughout the 1950s, repeated attempts were made to unionize migrant farm workers, but because the workers had to follow the crops they picked, they were hard to organize. ²They were never in one place for very long. ³However, in the 1960s, a Mexican-American farm worker named Cesar Chavez succeeded against all odds at unionizing agricultural workers. ⁴Using the donations he had gathered from friends and supporters, Chavez traveled from farm to farm speaking to California's migrant workers, most of whom were Mexican Americans like himself. ⁵Used to union activists who came to their fields and talked down to them, the farm workers knew immediately that Chavez understood and respected them in a way other union organizers had not. ⁶One by one, they joined his organization, the National Farm Workers' Association. ⁷In 1965, recognizing the power in numbers, Chavez persuaded union members to take part in a strike initiated by Filipino grape pickers. ⁸Then he went to the media and told the country that no one should eat grapes because the people who picked them were paid starvation wages and denied the right to toilet facilities while working in the fields. ⁹To the amazement of the grape growers, millions of people listened. ¹⁰The boycott lasted until 1970, and cost the growers millions of dollars. ¹¹Cesar Chavez's National Farm Workers' Association had become a force to be reckoned with. ¹²Farm owners had to recognize the union, which was renamed the United Farm Workers.

Topic Sentence ———

2. ¹The sinking of the luxury liner *Lusitania* by a German submarine helped propel the United States into World War I. ²Although initially it was claimed that the ship had been torpedoed for no reason except German viciousness, later evidence contradicted that story. ³In fact, the boat's cargo was almost completely contraband.* ⁴It was carrying fifty-one tons of shrapnel shells and five thousand boxes of bullets. ⁵Within eighteen minutes of being hit at 2:10 P.M. on the afternoon of May 6, 1915, the *Lusitania* sank beneath three hundred feet of water. ⁶Because there weren't enough crew members to man the forty-eight lifeboats, panic reigned and hundreds

———

*contraband: goods prohibited by law or treaty from being imported.

of people died—1,195 to be exact. [7]Furious at what was perceived to be German treachery, the American public began to support the idea of going to war against Germany.

Topic Sentence _____

3. [1]In 1987, Brazilian labor leader and environmentalist Francisco "Chico" Mendes was awarded the United Nations Global 500 Prize, along with a medal from the Society for a Better World. [2]Sadly, medals couldn't save his life when he took on a group of cattle ranchers in Acre, Brazil. [3]Determined to drive out rubber workers like the ones Mendes represented, the ranchers openly used threats and violence to do it. [4]Mendes, who had a public name and the respect of his fellow workers, was a special thorn in the ranchers' side, and they threatened his life. [5]Mendes took their death threats seriously but refused to give up his labor activities. [6]On December 15, 1988, he told a friend, "I don't think I'm going to live." [7]One week later, Mendes was shot in the chest as he stepped out of his house.

Topic Sentence _____

4. [1]The Underground Railroad was an informal network of routes traveled by a few thousand American slaves escaping to freedom between 1840 and 1860. [2]These routes included paths through woods and fields; transportation such as boats, trains, and wagons; and homes where runaways hid from slave owners and law enforcement officials. [3]In keeping with the idea of a railroad, slaves were referred to as "passengers," homes that took them in were "stations," and the people who assisted them were known as "conductors." [4]These conductors were abolitionists and included both free blacks and many sympathetic whites, particularly those who practiced the Quaker faith. [5]Abolitionists defied fugitive slave laws to shelter and feed runaways and to guide them along the safest routes out of the South to free states in the North. [6]Harriet Tubman, for example, liberated at least 300 black slaves after she herself had used the Underground Railroad to escape.

Topic Sentence _____

Test 3: Recognizing and Paraphrasing Topic Sentences

DIRECTIONS Write the number (or numbers) of the topic sentence in the accompanying blank. Then paraphrase it on the lines that follow.

1. [1]The largest demographic* group in the United States, called "baby boomers," consists of those born between 1946 and 1964. [2]Because baby boomers are presently the segment with the greatest economic impact, they are the target for numerous products and services. [3]This includes cars, housing, foreign travel, and recreational equipment. [4]Boomers are also heavy consumers of banking and investment services. [5]They are the heaviest users of frozen dinners and are a growing market for movies, especially highly original ones with adult themes. [6]They are also the target of marketing efforts for children's products and services. (Hoyer and MacInnis, *Consumer Behavior*, p. 357.)

Topic Sentence _____

Paraphrase _____

_____

2. [1]Beavers, North America's largest rodents (they grow to more than two feet long), are delightful to watch for their industry and their family affection. [2]Yet few animals have been so relentlessly exploited as the beaver. [3]In the eighteenth and nineteenth centuries, beaver pelts were worth their weight in gold. [4]As a result, by 1896, at least fourteen American states—Massachusetts, Vermont, New Hampshire, New York, Rhode Island, Connecticut, Pennsylvania, New Jersey, Delaware, Maryland, Illinois, Indiana, West Virginia, and Ohio—had announced that all of their beavers had been killed. [5]By the beginning of the twentieth century, it looked as if the beaver was about to disappear from the face of the earth. [6]But thanks to a beaver recovery program, which included trapping and relocating to protected areas, beavers have made an impressive comeback throughout the country. (Adapted from Montgomery, *Nature's Everyday Mysteries*, p. 99.)

Topic Sentence _____

_____

*demographic: related to the characteristics of a population.

Paraphrase _____

_____

3. [1]Coral reefs are extremely important to the environment, and they perform many useful functions; above all, they provide a habitat for organisms that cannot survive elsewhere. [2]Yet coral reefs all over the world are being threatened by human activities. [3]Logging near the waters of Bascuit Bay in the Philippines has destroyed 5 percent of the coral reefs in the bay. [4]Dynamite fishing around the world has not only killed large numbers of fish, it has also blown apart a significant number of coral reefs in Kenya, Tanzania, and Mauritania. [5]Coral reefs have also fallen victim to the tourist industry. [6]Coral and shells are hot tourist commodities, and they have been collected in large quantities for sale to souvenir-hungry tourists. [7]Undoubtedly, the most violent assault on the reefs has come from nuclear testing. [8]France, for example, has detonated* more than 100 nuclear devices in Polynesian waters once rich with coral reefs that are rapidly disappearing.

Topic Sentence _____

Paraphrase _____

_____

4. [1]Where can you exchange messages with the president, find ten people interested in full-body tattoos, or assume an entirely new personality? [2]Yes, it's the Internet. [3]Unless you happen to have just emerged from a years-long stay in a cave, you have probably heard of this network of computers and their users, but you may not be aware of the wealth of information that it can provide *anyone*. [4]The most basic Internet service is electronic mail or **e-mail.** [5]This service allows you to contact other Internet users at their Internet address. [6]Next up the line in netdom is the **newsgroup,** a computerized discussion group. [7]The Internet is currently running over 5,000 newsgroups on just about every imaginable topic—from whale watching to kick boxing. [8]With a **browser,** a software program that allows you to view documents on the World Wide Web, you can find information about any topic that strikes your fancy just by typing keywords into a box labeled *search*. [9]Want to download, or copy onto your computer, the information you find? [10]No problem. [11]With **FTP,** file transfer protocol, you can load up on free data and soft-

_____
*detonated: set off, caused to explode.

ware. (Adapted from *Culturescope: Guide to an Informed Mind*, Ed. Staff of *Princeton Review*, p. 348.)

Topic Sentence _____

Paraphrase _____

_____

5. [1]Around 1950 agriculture in the United States underwent a profound change. [2]For one thing, agriculture became energy intensive, or, more specifically, fossil-fuel intensive. [3]In 1950, an amount of energy equal to less than half a barrel of oil was used to produce a ton of grain. [4]By 1985, the amount of energy needed to produce a ton of grain had more than doubled. [5]Searching for ways to increase the yield of the lands already in use, farmers also began to rely heavily on inputs of water, on inputs of chemical fertilizers and pesticides (many of which are petroleum-derived products), and on high-yield strains of crops. [6]In some areas, especially the drier regions of the Southwest, irrigation projects allowed dry lands to be cultivated. [7]In contrast to past agricultural practice, farmers began to concentrate on producing only one or two profitable crops as opposed to a variety of crops. (Adapted from Kaufman and Franz, *Biosphere 2000*, p. 182.)

Topic Sentence _____

Paraphrase _____

_____

Test 4: Topic Sentences and Supporting Details

DIRECTIONS Read each paragraph and write the number (or numbers) of the topic sentence in the blank. Then answer the questions that follow by circling the correct response or writing it in the blanks.

1. [1]The term **bilingual education** refers to programs designed to instruct nonnative speakers of English who have not yet mastered English as their second language. [2]For the most part, bilingual programs are considered purely transitional, providing support to students in their native language until they can speak English well enough to function in classrooms where only English is spoken. [3]A typical bilingual program begins by teaching kindergarten students in their primary language and translating key words into English. [4]However, by the end of first or second grade, English is the primary language, with words only occasionally being translated into the students' native tongue. [5]For a while now, bilingual education has been a controversial topic, with critics arguing that the native language should be eliminated from the classroom as early as possible because it interferes with the learning of English. [6]But research does not support this claim (Hakuta & Garcia, 1989). [7]On the contrary, bilingualism seems to improve the thinking abilities of children. (Adapted from Santrock, *Life-Span Development*, p. 301.)

   a. Topic sentence: _____

   b. What question or questions about the topic sentence do the major details help answer?

   _____

   _____

   c. *True* or *False:* Sentence 3 is a major detail.

   Explain your answer. _____

   _____

   d. *True* or *False:* Sentence 4 is a minor detail.

   Explain your answer. _____

   _____

2. [1]Analyses of non-Western cultures suggest that beliefs about maintaining ties with those who have died vary from culture to culture. [2]In contrast with Western beliefs, maintaining ties with the deceased

is accepted and sustained in the religious rituals of Japan. [3]Yet among the Hopi Indians of Arizona, the deceased are forgotten as quickly as possible and life is carried on as usual. [4]In fact, the Hopi funeral ritual concludes with a break-off between mortals and spirits. [5]The diversity of grieving is nowhere clearer than in two Muslim societies—one in Egypt, the other in Bali. [6]Among Muslims in Egypt, the bereaved* are encouraged to dwell at length on their grief, surrounded by others who relate similarly tragic accounts and express their own sorrow. [7]By contrast, in Bali, bereaved Muslims are encouraged to laugh and be joyful rather than be sad. (Santrock, *Life-Span Development*, p. 301.)

a. Topic sentence: _____

b. What question or questions about the topic sentence do the major details help answer?

_____

_____

c. *True* or *False:* Sentence 2 is a major detail.

   Explain your answer. _____

_____

d. *True* or *False:* Sentence 4 is a minor detail.

   Explain your answer. _____

_____

3. [1]Even more than had been the case with Vietnam, Operation Desert Storm*—thanks to time-zone difference and satellite relays, as well as around-the-clock reporting—was a televised "living room war" on American prime time. [2]But it was a far more *controlled* television war than Vietnam had been, the result of tight Pentagon* limits on media access to troops and events and of censorship. [3]Television showcased military successes, highlighting exotic hardware through the use of Pentagon-released videos and making widespread use of on-air expert commentators—many of them retired military officers. [4]There was little or no analysis or criticism of the military effort or of diplomatic efforts immediately before or after—

---

*bereaved: those suffering the loss of a loved one.
*Desert Storm: a 1990–1991 war waged to get Iraqi troops out of Kuwait.
*Pentagon: the United States military establishment.

instead, the emphasis was on live-action shots of American technological superiority. [5]Later, in mid-1991, television covered victory parades in Washington, New York, and elsewhere. [6]These programs projected an America throwing off old self-doubts that had lingered since the loss in Vietnam nearly two decades before. [7]Only months after the war was over did disquieting television reports about Iraqi civilian losses, allied soldiers killed by "friendly fire," and attempted cover-ups of other military mistakes become widely reported—but by then few were paying attention. (Head et al., *Broadcasting in America*, p. 434.)

a. Topic sentence: _____

b. What question or questions about the topic sentence do the major details help answer?

_____

_____

c. *True* or *False:* Sentence 3 is a major detail.

Explain your answer. _____

_____

d. *True* or *False:* Sentence 4 is also a major detail.

Explain your answer. _____

_____

4. [1]Research on attitude change suggests that people pay attention to messages that fit their established opinions and ignore those that don't. [2]Thus, media such as radio, television, and newspapers tend to reinforce existing views rather than changing them. [3]Faced with a message that challenges their beliefs, the listener, viewer, or reader often ignores anything that doesn't fit his or her existing world view; this kind of selective perception* also accounts for what's called the *boomerang effect*. [4]Experiments have shown that those with strong beliefs are likely to misinterpret messages that challenge their opinions. [5]In other words, people will ignore or distort evidence rather than be challenged by it. [6]The classic example of the boomerang effect was the popular television show *All in the Family*. [7]The show was meant—in the person of the lead character, Archie Bunker—to make bigotry* look laughable and silly. [8]Yet

_____
*perception: way of seeing.
*bigotry: prejudice.

viewer surveys consistently discovered that those who shared Archie Bunker's wide-ranging prejudices thought of the character as a role model who helped confirm the rightness of their opinions.

a. Topic sentence: _____

b. What question or questions about the topic sentence do the major details help answer?

_____

_____

c. *True* or *False:* Sentence 4 is a major detail.

Explain your answer. _____

_____

d. *True* or *False:* Sentence 5 is a minor detail.

Explain your answer. _____

_____

5. [1]**Trichotillomania** is a disorder characterized by an inability to resist the impulse to pull out one's own hair. [2]Although trichotillomania principally involves the hairs in the scalp, a person with this disorder may pull hair from other parts of the body, such as eyelashes, beard, or eyebrows. [3]The hair pulling is not provoked by skin inflammation, itch, or other physical conditions. [4]Rather, the person simply cannot resist the impulse, which begins with a feeling of tension that is replaced by a feeling of release or gratification* after the hair is pulled. [5]Initially, the hair pulling may not disturb the follicles, and new hair will grow. [6]In severe cases, new growth is compromised and permanent balding results. [7]One thirty-five-year-old woman entered therapy saying that she had a compulsion to pull the hairs from her head. [8]When asked to reveal the extent of her hair pulling, the woman took off her wig. [9]She was completely bald except for a few strands of hair at the back of her head. [10]There is no information on the prevalence of trichotillomania, although it is probably more common than currently believed and more common among women than men (Meyer, 1989). [11]About 1 to 2 percent of college students appear to have a past or current history of this disorder (American Psychiatric Association, 1994). (Sue et al., *Understanding Abnormal Behavior*, p. 247.)

_____

*gratification: pleasure.

a. Topic sentence: ____

b. What question or questions about the topic sentence do the major details help answer?

_____

_____

c. *True* or *False:* Sentence 3 is a minor detail.

Explain your answer. _____

_____

d. *True* or *False:* Sentence 4 is also a minor detail.

Explain your answer. _____

_____

Test 5: Recognizing Organizational Patterns

Circle the appropriate letter or letters to identify the organizational pattern or patterns in each paragraph.

1. A **cartel** is an organization of independent firms whose purpose is to control and limit production and maintain or increase prices and profits. A cartel can result from either formal or informal agreement among members. Like collusion,* cartels are illegal in the United States but occur in other countries. The cartel most people are familiar with is the Organization of Petroleum Exporting Countries (OPEC), a group of nations rather than a group of independent firms. During the 1970s, OPEC was able to coordinate oil production in such a way that it drove the market price of crude oil from $1.10 to $32.00 a barrel. For nearly eight years, each member of OPEC agreed to produce a certain limited amount of crude oil as designated by the OPEC production committee. Then in the early 1980s, the cartel began to fall apart as individual members began to cheat on the agreement. Members began to produce more than their allocation in an attempt to increase profit. As each member of the cartel did this, the price of oil fell, reaching $12 per barrel in 1988. Oil prices rose again in 1990 when Iraq invaded Kuwait, causing widespread damage to Kuwait's oil fields. But as repairs have been made to Kuwait's oil wells, Kuwait has increased production and oil prices have dropped. (Boyes and Melvin, *Fundamentals of Economics,* p. 109.)

   a. definition

   b. classification

   c. process

   d. sequence of dates and events

   e. comparison and contrast

   f. cause and effect

2. The Bermuda Triangle is, without a doubt, a strange and mysterious area of the Atlantic Ocean. During the last century, more than one hundred ships, boats, and airplanes have disappeared in this area. For example, the USS *Cyclops,* a Navy ship with 306 people aboard, disappeared there in 1918. Also lost without a trace was an entire squadron of five Navy torpedo bombers that took off from Fort Lauderdale, Florida, in 1945. In 1947, a United States C-54 bomber dis-

---

*collusion: a secret agreement between parties for the purpose of illegal activities.

appeared near Bermuda and was never seen again. One year later, the same thing happened to the British airliner *Star Tiger*. And in 1968, the *Scorpion*, a nuclear submarine, vanished only to be found after a long search. It was finally located in the waters on the fringes of the Triangle, but none of its crew members were on board.

a. definition

b. classification

c. process

d. sequence of dates and events

e. comparison and contrast

f. cause and effect

3. Instinctive behavior is caused by specific signals from the environment. For example, stalking behavior in cats may be initiated by the sight of prey. In male ring doves, the sight of an adult female triggers the bowing associated with courtship. The environmental signals that evoke, or release, instinctive behavior are called **releasers.** A releaser may be only a small part of any appropriate situation. For example, fighting behavior in territorial male European robins can be released not only by the sight of another male within their territories, but even by the sight of a tuft of red feathers at a certain height. Such a response usually "works" because red feathers at that height within the territory are normally on the breast of a competitor. The point is that the instinctive act can be triggered by only certain parts of the total environmental situation. (Adapted from Wallace, *Biology*, p. 450.)

a. definition

b. classification

c. process

d. sequence of dates and events

e. comparison and contrast

f. cause and effect

4. Eighteenth-century assemblies bore little resemblance to twentieth-century state legislatures. Much of their business would today be termed administrative; only on rare occasions did assemblies formulate new policies or pass laws of real importance. Members of the assemblies also saw their roles differently from that of modern legislators. Instead of believing that they should act positively to improve the lives of their constituents, eighteenth-century assem-

blymen saw themselves as acting defensively to prevent encroachments on the people's rights. In their minds, their primary function was, for example, to stop the governors or councils from enacting oppressive taxes, rather than to pass laws that would actively benefit their constituents. (Norton et al., *A People and a Nation*, vol. 1, p. 111.)

a. definition
b. classification
c. process
d. sequence of dates and events
e. comparison and contrast
f. cause and effect

5. Earth's atmosphere is divided into four regions of atmosphere classified by temperature. The *troposphere* is the lowest level of the atmosphere and is heated to an average of 59° F. In the *stratosphere*, the layer above the troposphere, temperatures range from −76° F to near 32° F, while the temperature maximum is called the "stratopause." Temperatures in the *mesosphere* can drop much lower. They range from 32° F to −212° F. The *thermosphere* is the highest layer of the atmosphere, and the temperature rises with altitude to extreme values of thousands of degrees. The meanings of these extreme temperatures, however, can be misleading. High thermosphere temperatures represent little heat. (Adapted from John Rennie, ed., *Scientific American Science Desk Reference*. New York: John Wiley & Sons, 1999, p. 266.)

a. definition
b. classification
c. process
d. sequence of dates and events
e. comparison and contrast
f. cause and effect

C H A P T E R 4

Understanding and Outlining Longer Readings

In this chapter, you'll learn

- **how to adapt what you know about paragraphs to longer, multiparagraph readings.**

- **how to recognize the *thesis statements* that put main ideas into words.**

- **how to locate major and minor supporting details.**

- **how to create informal outlines.**

In Chapter 4, you'll be using some of the same skills you polished in Chapter 3, "Reviewing Paragraph Essentials." Only this time, you'll apply those skills, with some modification, to readings a good deal longer than a paragraph.

Understanding Longer Readings

To thoroughly understand a paragraph, you need to answer three questions:

1. What's the topic?
2. What's the main idea?
3. Which supporting details are essential to understanding that main idea?

Fortunately, those same questions also apply to readings longer than a single paragraph. Still, that's not to say there are no differences between reading a single paragraph and reading longer selections. There are, in fact, six crucial differences you need to take into account.

The Main Idea Controls More Than a Paragraph

In longer readings, there is one main idea that unifies not just a single paragraph but all or most of the paragraphs in the selection. Because it controls the content of the other paragraphs, you can think of this main idea as the "controlling main idea." The controlling or central main idea gives all the other paragraphs a purpose. They exist to explain, clarify, and argue its meaning.

The Main Idea Might Well Be Expressed in Several Sentences

The main idea of an entire reading can often be summed up in a single sentence. But sometimes it requires several sentences, maybe even a paragraph. For that reason, many composition textbooks use the term **thesis statement** to talk about the stated main idea of a research paper or essay. Following that tradition, we'll use the same term here in order to emphasize that the main idea of a reading will not always be summed up in one single sentence.

Introductions Are Likely to Be Longer

In paragraphs, introductions are usually limited to only a sentence or two. However, in longer readings, introducing the main idea may require several paragraphs. While it's true that textbook authors are likely to present readers with the main idea in the first or second paragraph, don't assume that's the case with magazine or journal articles and essays. In these materials, writers sometimes include lengthy introductions in order to provide background or stimulate reader interest.

Thesis Statements Don't Wander Quite So Much

Topic sentences can appear anywhere in a paragraph—at the beginning, middle, or end. Thesis statements, in contrast, are more fixed in their location. Yes, an author will occasionally build up to the main idea and put the thesis statement at the very end of a reading. But that's not typical. Far more likely is the appearance of the thesis statement at the beginning of a reading. Thus, the opening paragraphs in an essay, article, or chapter section deserve particularly close attention.

Major Supporting Details Take Up More Space

In longer readings, one supporting detail essential to the main idea can take up an entire paragraph. Thus, longer readings require you to do a good deal more sifting and sorting of information as you decide which individual statements are essential to your understanding of a major detail.

Minor Details Can Also Occupy an Entire Paragraph

As they do in paragraphs, minor details in longer readings further explain major ones. They add colorful facts or supply repetition for emphasis. Like major details, minor details can also occupy an entire paragraph. And just as in paragraphs, minor details may or may not be important.

Sometimes minor supporting details supply the more specific examples or explanations necessary for a clear understanding of a major detail. When this is the case, the minor details should be considered essential. But if they simply offer a colorful or humorous anecdote or just provide repetition for emphasis, you need not store them away in your long-term memory. Nor should you make an effort to include them in your notes.

Now that you know how reading a paragraph is different from

reading a more extended piece of writing, it's time to put what you have learned into practice. Read the following selection.

Research on Leadership

1 In business, managers have to be leaders. Thus, it comes as no surprise that researchers have been studying the nature of leadership in business. *Thesis Statement* <u>At the University of Michigan, researchers have found that leadership behavior among managers can be divided into two categories. Whereas some managers are job-centered, others tend to be employee-centered.</u>

Topic Sentence 2 <u>Leaders who practice job-centered behavior closely supervise their employees in an effort to monitor and control their performance.</u> They are primarily concerned with getting a job done and less concerned with the feelings or attitudes of their employees—unless those attitudes and feelings affect the task at hand. In general, they don't encourage employees to express their opinions on how best to accomplish a task.

Topic Sentence 3 <u>In contrast, leaders who practice employee-centered behavior focus on reaching goals by building a sense of team spirit.</u> An employee-centered leader is concerned with subordinates' job satisfaction and group unity. Employee-centered leaders are also more willing to let employees have a voice in how they do their jobs.

Topic Sentence 4 <u>The Michigan researchers also investigated which kind of leadership is more effective.</u> They concluded that managers whose leadership was employee-centered were generally more effective than managers who were primarily job-centered. That is, their employees performed at higher levels and were more satisfied. (Adapted from Van Fleet and Peterson, *Contemporary Management*, p. 332.)

Having read "Research on Leadership," look closely at the two sentences that make up the thesis statement. Now look at the topic sentences of the remaining paragraphs. Can you see how those topic sentences serve to clarify the thesis statement? This reading illustrates how thesis statements and topic sentences work together. The thesis statement introduces the author's general point. Then the topic sentences of each paragraph serve as supporting details that flesh out and clarify that point. Within each paragraph, the major details should always clarify the topic sentence; however, they may or may not directly support the thesis statement.

The following diagram expresses the relationship between the thesis statement and the topic sentences within a reading or essay.

Thesis Statement

At the University of Michigan, researchers found that leadership behavior among managers can be divided into two categories. Whereas some managers are job-centered, others tend to be employee-centered.

Topic Sentence of Paragraph 2	Topic Sentence of Paragraph 3	Topic Sentence of Paragraph 4
Leaders who practice job-centered behavior closely supervise their employees in an effort to monitor and control their performance.	Leaders who practice employee-centered behavior focus on reaching goals by building team spirit.	Michigan researchers also investigated which kind of leadership is more effective.

Before going on to Exercise 1, read the following selection and underline the thesis statement. Remember, the thesis statement shouldn't unify just one paragraph. It should unify the entire reading.

Looking Back at the Death Penalty

1 Today the penalty of death is reserved for "serious" crimes such as murder, treason, espionage, and rape. And when it is actually carried out (as it is in only one of every thirty death sentencings in the United States), the means of execution in Western countries are by firing squad, hanging, gas chamber, electric chair, and lethal injection—all relatively fast ways to go.

2 In ancient and medieval times, however, death was handed out for many more offenses, some trivial by modern standards. In India, you could have been sentenced to death for spreading falsehoods, killing a cow, or stealing a royal elephant. In Egypt, during the peak of feline worship, death was the punishment for injuring a cat (even if it recovered). Judeans imposed the death penalty for cursing; the Babylonians for selling bad beer; the Assyrians for giving a bad haircut, since stylish coiffures were signs of class.

3 In parts of the Middle East, perjurers were executed by being

intravenously embalmed while still alive. The embalming solution replaced the victim's blood and quickly caused cardiac arrest, and in that regard the mode of execution was a forerunner of the modern lethal injection.

4   The oldest reference to a death sentence dates back to 1500 B.C. The criminal was a teenage male, and his crime was recorded simply as "magic." The mode of death was left to his choosing (poisoning or stabbing), and the executioner was to be himself.

5   In Rome during the same period, a citizen could be executed for many serious offenses, but also for trivial matters, as prescribed by law: for "publishing lies," for singing "insulting songs" about high-ranking officials, for "cheating by a patron of his client," and for "making disturbances in the city at night." (Adapted from Panati, *Extraordinary Endings*, pp. 136–137.)

Tempting as it might be to assume that the first paragraph of the reading contains the thesis statement, that assumption would lead you astray in this instance. None of the sentences in paragraph 1 is developed beyond the first paragraph. Thus, the first paragraph cannot possibly contain the thesis statement.

Look now at paragraph 2. The first sentence is the topic sentence. All of the sentences after the first one serve to illustrate the rather "trivial" offenses that once earned the death sentence. However, the topic sentence of paragraph 2 also expresses the main idea of the entire reading. As a matter of fact, the topic sentence in paragraph 2 is also the thesis statement of the entire reading. If you look at paragraphs 3, 4, and 5, you'll see that all three—like the individual sentences in paragraph 2—serve to identify the trivial offenses mentioned in paragraph 2.

CHECK YOUR UNDERSTANDING

Without looking back at the text, describe how single paragraphs differ from longer readings. When you finish, compare your list to the original explanation to see where you might need to review.

1. _____

_____

2. _____

_____

3. _____

_____

4. _____

_____

5. _____

_____

6. _____

_____

EXERCISE 1

DIRECTIONS Underline the thesis statement of each reading.

EXAMPLE

The Trail of Tears

*Thesis
Statement* 1 Throughout the nineteenth century, the Cherokee Indians proved themselves to be highly inventive and enterprising. They also showed a willingness to adapt and excel at whatever they learned from white settlers. Unfortunately, their success did not save them from being evicted from their tribal lands.

2 In 1820, the tribe established a system of government modeled on that of the United States. It elected a principal chief, a senate, and a house of representatives. In 1821, Sequoya, a Cherokee warrior who had been crippled in a hunting accident, produced a workable alphabet of Cherokee characters. The Cherokees studied the alphabet enthusiastically, and within months thousands could read and write the new alphabet. By 1828, the Cherokees were producing their own weekly newspaper, and the paper's readership was growing faster than the papers could be produced.

3 Unfortunately, in the same year, the Georgia legislature outlawed the Cherokee government. Gold had been discovered on tribal lands almost ten years before, and greedy land speculators* were determined to take control of those lands, even if it meant il-

---

*speculators: people who engage in risky financial dealings in order to gain high profits.

legally evicting the Cherokee people. In 1832, the U.S. Supreme Court ruled in favor of the Cherokees' right to their lands. But that decision was ignored by federal authorities, and, in 1838, federal troops drove about 20,000 Cherokees west on a forced march for three hundred miles. During the march so many Cherokees died from hunger, disease, and exposure that the route they followed came to be called the "Trail of Tears."

EXPLANATION In this reading, the thesis statement consists of three sentences rather than one. The thesis statement tells readers that the author intends to explore two related points: (1) The Cherokees were highly enterprising and inventive and (2) their achievements did not save them from being evicted from their tribal lands. Paragraphs 2 and 3 then provide the supporting details that clarify both parts of this thesis statement.

1. Altering Consciousness

1   People throughout history have sought ways to alter consciousness. A dramatic example is the sweat lodge ritual of the Sioux Indians. During the ritual, several men sit in total darkness inside a small chamber heated by a bed of coals. Cedar smoke, bursts of steam, and the aroma of sage fill the air. The men chant rhythmically. The heat builds. At last, they can stand it no more. The door is thrown open. Cooling night breezes rush in. And then? The cycle begins again—often to be repeated four or five times more. Among the Sioux, this ritual is viewed as a cleansing of mind and body. When the experience becomes especially intense, it brings altered awareness and personal revelation.*

2   Some altered states of consciousness are sought primarily for pleasure, as is often true of drug intoxication. Yet, as the Sioux example illustrates, many cultures regard changes in consciousness as pathways to enlightenment. Almost every known religion has accepted at least some altered states as a source of mystical experience. Accepted avenues have ranged from fasting, meditation, prayer, isolation, sleep loss, whirling, and chanting, to self-inflicted pain and mind-altering substances.

3   In many cultures, the special powers attributed to medicine men, shamans, or healers are believed to come from an ability to enter a trance and communicate with spirits. Often, rituals that help form tribal bonds among community members are accentuated by altered states of consciousness.

4   In short, all cultures recognize and accept some alterations of

---

*revelation: sudden insight or understanding.

consciousness. However, the meanings given various states vary greatly—from signs of "madness" and "possession" by spirits to life-enhancing breakthroughs. Thus, cultural conditioning greatly affects what altered states a person recognizes, seeks, considers normal, and attains (Ward, 1989). (Coon, *Essentials of Psychology*, p. 222.)

2. Our Oldest Enemy: The Locust

1   On July 28, 1962, radar operators at the Indian National Physical Laboratory in Delhi sounded the alarm. They had spotted a gigantic airborne invasion in progress, and the enemy was already only sixty miles south of the city.

2   Specialized emergency teams were instantly alerted. India and her traditionally hostile neighbor, Pakistan, joined forces: Aircraft from both countries roared into action, flying only sixty-five feet above the ground in a skillful counterattack. The initial battle raged for a week; sporadic fighting continued until December, when the two countries declared themselves victorious. The enemy dead numbered more than one-hundred *billion.*

3   It had been no human invasion but a far more fearsome and rapacious* threat: locusts. Using chemicals sprayed from aircraft, humans wreaked havoc on these prodigiously* destructive pests. Nevertheless, throughout most of history, the reverse has been true. When a plague of locusts arrives, it has been people who have suffered more than the locusts.

4   The earliest written record of a locust plague is probably in the Book of Exodus, which describes an attack that took place in Egypt in about 3500 B.C.: "They covered the face of the whole earth, so that the land was darkened . . . and there remained not any green in the trees, or in the herbs of the field, through all the land of Egypt." Another biblical account, in the Book of Job, describes trees "made white" as locusts even stripped the bark from the branches.

5   Locusts have always spelled disaster. In 125 B.C., they destroyed the grain crop in northern Africa; 80,000 people died of starvation. In A.D. 591, a plague of locusts in Italy caused the deaths of more than a million people and animals. In 1613, disaster struck the French region of La Camargue when locusts ate enough grass in a single day to feed 4,000 cattle for a year. The Nile Valley suffered in 1889 when locusts so thoroughly destroyed crops that even the mice starved in their wake. Between 1949

---

*rapacious: greedy.
*prodigiously: enormously.

and 1963 locust swarms in Africa caused an estimated $100 million worth of damage annually. In 1988, the Ethiopian cereal crop was laid waste, leaving a million people without food. (Adams and Riley, eds., "The Ravenous Millions," *Facts and Fallacies,* p. 50.)

3. Killer Bees

1   Although their name makes them sound like something out of a horror film, killer bees really do exist. And while they are not quite so terrifying as their name implies, they are definitely not an insect—like the ladybug—that one should invite into the garden. On the contrary, both animals and humans would do well to avoid these sometimes ferociously angry bees.

2   Killer bees (officially called Africanized honeybees) originated in Brazil in 1956 as an experiment in mating the African honeybee with local bees. The breeders were hoping to get bees that would produce more honey. Instead, they produced extremely aggressive bees that have attacked—and in some cases killed—both people and animals. Each year the bees move about 350 miles (563 kilometers) north; in 1990, they crossed the U.S. border into Hidalgo, Texas.

3   Similar to the rumors that surround sharks, myths about African bees abound.* For example, it's not true that they fly faster than domestic honeybees. On the contrary, both types of bees average between 12 and 15 miles per hour. Also, the sting of the African bee actually has less, not more, venom than that of domestic honeybees. African bees are also a good deal smaller than domestic honeybees, not gigantic in size as has been rumored.

4   Still, African bees do have some features that make them an insect to avoid. When an African bee's body is crushed—from a swat, for example—it releases an odor that incites nearby bees to attack. Also, African bees vigorously and aggressively protect their hives. About ten times as many African bees as European bees will sting when their colonies are invaded. The good news is that scientists believe the African bees' aggressiveness will eventually diminish as they interbreed with the more peaceful European bees to the north.

4. Eat Garlic for Your Health

1   The ancient Egyptians believed that garlic could cure a wide variety of ills. In fact, early writings on the medical uses of herbs record close to thirty uses for the plant that the Romans used to

---

*abound: exist in great supply.

call "the stinking rose." For example, it was claimed that garlic could heal wounds, cure stomach cramps, and chase away common colds. What's surprising about these claims is that modern science actually bears some of them out, and eating garlic seems to be remarkably good for your health.

2   In 1858 Louis Pasteur* discovered that garlic could kill bacteria. Since Pasteur's time, researchers have found that garlic also inhibits the growth of bacteria in the stomach. A diet rich in garlic actually inhibits the growth of the bacteria that cause ulcers. Some studies have also suggested that eating garlic can slow the growth of cancers in the colon, breast, and skin. Although research still needs to be done to prove conclusively* that garlic can help prevent or cure cancer, existing evidence does suggest it may well help us fight this deadly disease.

3   There are also indications that garlic can help prevent heart disease. A diet high in garlic consumption seems to reduce the chance of blood clots. In addition, garlic may reduce hardening of the arteries, another heavy contributor to heart problems.

4   Because garlic has such a powerful—some would even say unpleasant—smell, many people are loath* to eat it. Instead, they consume deodorized garlic pills. Unfortunately, though the pills do confer some health benefits, they aren't as effective as the raw garlic cloves. So if you want to eat garlic for your health, you might consider stocking up on breath mints as well.

 ## Major and Minor Details

Major details in longer readings directly explain the thesis statement. They answer potential questions readers might raise; further define any general words or terms; and, when necessary, offer proof of an author's claim. While major details in a paragraph consist of single sentences, in longer readings you may find that an entire paragraph is devoted to explaining one major detail. When this happens, you'll have to decide how much of the paragraph is essential to your understanding of that one detail.

As they do in paragraphs, minor details in longer readings further explain or flesh out major details; they also provide color or emphasis. But here again, you can't assume that minor details are auto-

---

*Louis Pasteur: (1822–1895) French microbiologist who invented pasteurization and developed a vaccine for rabies.
*conclusively: without a doubt.
*loath: unwilling.

matically not essential to your understanding of the thesis statement. It all depends on what they contribute to your understanding
of the major details they modify.

Read the following selection. As you do, think about which supporting details are essential to your understanding of the underlined
thesis statement.

Defining Love

1   What is love? No one knows for sure. However, researcher R. J.
Thesis Sternberg has a theory. <u>According to Sternberg, love consists of</u>
Statement <u>three separate ingredients, and each one is crucial either to fall-</u>
<u>ing in love or to staying in love.</u>

2   Passion is a feeling of heightened sexual arousal, and it's usually accompanied by a strong, romantic attraction. In the throes*
of passion, each lover feels that life is barely worth living unless
the other is present. Unfortunately, passionate feelings almost always diminish over time, although they are still essential to initiat-
ing the love relationship. Luckily, if there's a strong sense of intimacy between the partners, the loss or decrease of passion can
be accepted and the love maintained.

3   Intimacy—feelings of closeness, sharing, and affection—is essential to staying in love. Both partners need to feel that they
view the world in similar ways and can turn to one another in
times of great sadness or joy. If the one you love is not the one
you feel particularly close to, you may find that, over time, love
doesn't last. Typically in a relationship, intimacy grows steadily
at first and then levels off.

4   Commitment refers to a conscious decision to stay with a person both in good times and in bad. Like intimacy, a sense of commitment is essential to staying in love over time. But unlike intimacy, commitment frequently requires some hard work and
determination. It seldom comes without effort.

While reading the thesis statement in this selection, you probably
wondered what three ingredients the author had in mind. Anticipat-
ing that question, the author defines all three. Those definitions are
the major details that refer directly to the thesis statement. However,
the minor details that expand upon those major details cannot simply be ignored—not if you want to understand Sternberg's theory.
Minor detail or not, it is important to remember that if intimacy is

---

*throes: pangs, spasms.

lacking, love doesn't last—at least from R. J. Sternberg's point of view.

 # Thesis Statements and Major Details

In trying to differentiate between major and minor details, it's important to use any and all clues provided by the thesis statement. For example, the thesis statement in the reading about love on page 146 pointed out that love consisted of "three separate ingredients." This phrase is a tip-off to the major details. It practically guarantees that each major detail will describe one of the three ingredients.

Key Words in Thesis Statements

Anytime a thesis statement focuses on general words like *reasons, studies, groups, causes,* and *theories,* those words need to be further explained in order to be meaningful to readers. After all, if you know that there are three reasons for increased violence in the schools, this information doesn't help you much until you know what the reasons are. When you see words like *reasons, causes,* and so on in what you think is the thesis statement, check to see if the paragraphs that follow further explain those reasons or causes. If they do, you have won on two fronts: (1) you have confirmed your guess about the thesis statement and (2) you have discovered a key to the major details. Look now at the opening paragraph of a reading from a psychology text. Read it through and see if you can find a word or phrase that points the way to the major details.

> In everyday life, requests for compliance are common. A stranger asks you to yield a phone booth so she can make a call. A salesperson suggests you buy a more expensive watch than the one you first asked to see. Or a coworker asks to borrow fifty cents in order to buy a danish during coffee break. Have you ever wondered what determines whether or not you say yes? Although many different factors come into play when we agree to a request, there are three essential strategies for inducing compliance.

Based on that paragraph, do you have the strong sense that the major details will describe the three strategies that encourage compliance? If you do, you are right on the mark. That is precisely the function of the major details that follow the opening paragraph. See for yourself:

1   One way of encouraging compliance is to employ the *foot-in-the-door strategy.* The name comes from a technique long used in the days when salespeople went door to door to sell their wares. As the saying went at the time, "If you can get your foot in the door, the sale is almost a sure thing." In psychological terms, the foot-in-the-door strategy means that if someone can get you to comply with some small request, you are very likely to comply with a much larger demand. For example, if the committee to reelect your local mayor wants you to put a huge sign in your front window promoting her candidacy, members of the committee might first ask you to display a bumper sticker. Once you agreed to display the bumper sticker, they might ask you to wear a button. Once you had agreed to those two smaller requests, you would more than likely be ready to put that sign in your window.

2   Psychologists suspect that the foot-in-the-door strategy works because we observe our own behavior. Recognizing that we have agreed to a small request, we convince ourselves that the next, larger demand isn't all that different. Thus, we are ready to comply.

3   The *door-in-the-face strategy*—the name was coined by psychologist Robert Cialdini—is a variation on the foot-in-the-door, and it works like this: If you have flatly said no to a large and inconvenient request ("slammed the door in someone's face"), you are more likely to agree to a smaller bid for help. Say, for example, your neighbor comes by and asks you to pick up his daughter at school for the next week while he is working overtime. Chances are you will say no because it requires too big a chunk of your own time. But if he comes back the next day and says he got a friend to handle Monday, Wednesday, and Friday, you are likely to agree to take over on Tuesday and Thursday.

4   This strategy works because it seems as if the person making the request is being reasonable and making a concession. For that reason, the person doing the favor feels that it is only fair to comply with the smaller request.

5   If you or someone you know has ever purchased a car, you will recognize the *low-ball* technique of encouraging compliance. In the context of car buying, the salesperson offers a "low-ball" price that is significantly less than that of the competition. Once the customer seems interested, the salesperson begins to bump up the price step-by-step. In other words, the low-ball technique gets you to comply with a request that seems to cost little or nothing. Once you say yes, the person starts tacking on additional terms. For example, your roommate asks for a ride to the local ticket of-

fice, where she hopes to get tickets to a hot concert. Since the
ticket office is only five minutes away by car, you say, "Sure, no
problem." It's at that point that your roommate tells you she has
to be there by 5:00 in the morning because that's when the line
starts forming. If you agree, you've just succumbed to the
low-ball technique. (Source of information: Coon, *Essentials of
Psychology,* p. 625.)

Particularly in textbooks, thesis statements frequently offer clues
to major details in the form of phrases like "three common factors,"
"four major reasons," and "five different categories." Generally
speaking, every one of those factors, reasons, or categories is likely
to be a major detail. Keep that in mind while you are completing
your textbook assignments or doing research.

EXERCISE 2

DIRECTIONS Read each selection and look carefully at the underlined thesis statement. Then answer the questions that follow by
filling in the blanks or circling the correct letter.

EXAMPLE

The Ancient Roman Circus

*Thesis
Statement*

1 Although nowadays we think of the circus as an amusing entertainment for kids, originally it was not quite such a harmless
event. To be sure, the first circus, like its modern counterpart, included death-defying events. But there was one big difference. In
the early Roman circus, death was a very real possibility, and circus spectators were accustomed to—and expected—bloodshed.

2 The Roman Circus Maximus began under the rule of Julius
Caesar, and it specialized in two big events—brutal fights between gladiators (or between gladiators and animals) and equally
bloody chariot races. In most cases, both events ended in the
death of either a person or an animal. If nobody died, the audience was likely to be disappointed. Even worse, the emperor
would be displeased.

3 Not surprisingly, the circus event that was in fashion usually
reflected the taste of the man in power. Julius Caesar, for example, favored aggressive chariot races. Because the charioteers
were usually slaves racing to win their freedom, they drove
their horses unmercifully, and serious accidents were an exciting possibility. In the hopes of surviving, the charioteers wore

helmets and wrapped the chariot reins around their bodies. They also carried knives to cut themselves free if necessary. Spills occurred more often than not, and the charioteers would be thrown from the chariot and dragged repeatedly around the ring by runaway horses. Knives and helmets not withstanding, most did not survive, not that the screaming crowd cared.

4   During the reign of Augustus, from 27 B.C. to A.D. 14, a fight to the death between man and beast was the favored circus event, and more than 3,500 lions and tigers perished in the circus arena, taking with them hundreds of gladiators. Under the half-mad Emperor Nero, who ruled in the first century A.D., the most popular circus spectacle was lion versus Christian, with the Christians the guaranteed losers. Fortunately for both Christians and the slaves who followed in their wake, this savage circus practice was outlawed in A.D. 326 by the Emperor Constantine.

5   Although the pitting of Christians against lions was staged in a special arena, most of the circus events that took place in Rome were staged in the largest arena of them all—the Colosseum. The capacity of this great stadium, completed in A.D. 79, was enormous. It seated close to 50,000 people. In one Colosseum season alone, 2,000 gladiators went to their deaths, all in the name of circus fun.[1]

1. How would you paraphrase the thesis statement?

Unlike the modern circus, the ancient Roman circus was a good deal more deadly.

2. Which question about the thesis statement do the major supporting details help to answer?

   a. What are the similarities between ancient and modern circuses?

   b. How did early circus events all but guarantee death?

EXPLANATION As it should, the paraphrase restates the point of the thesis statement but alters the words. The most likely question raised by the thesis statement is *b*. The main idea of the entire read-

---

[1]Based on the figures cited by Charles Panati, *Browser's Book of Beginnings.* Boston: Houghton Mifflin, 1984, pp. 262–264.

ing is that ancient circuses were often deadly, and the reader needs to know why this was so.

1. The Police Personality

Thesis Statement

1 In *Justice Without Trial*, sociologist Jerome Skolnick argues that in the same way doctors, janitors, lawyers, and industrial workers develop unique ways of looking at, and responding to, their work environment, so too do police officers. This effect of work on a person's world outlook Skolnick calls the **working personality.** Not surprisingly, the working personality of the police officer is molded by the dangerous conditions in which police work.

2 Police work is potentially dangerous, so officers need to be constantly aware of what is happening around them. It's not surprising, then, that suspicion is a key element of the police officer's working personality. At the academy, trainees are warned about what happens to officers who are too trusting. They also learn about the many officers who have died in the line of duty because they did not exercise proper caution. On the street they need to stay alert for signals that crimes may be in progress: an unfamiliar noise, someone "checking into" an alleyway, a secret exchange of goods. Under these conditions, it would be surprising if officers did *not* become suspicious. As George Kirkham, police officer and professor, argues: "Chronic suspiciousness is something that a good cop cultivates in the interest of going home to his family each evening."

3 The environment in which they work demands that police officers gain immediate control of potentially dangerous situations. Because the police are routinely called upon to demonstrate authority, the need to be in authority also becomes a crucial element of the officer's working personality. However, that authority is often challenged by a hostile public, and in some cases the police have overreacted to what they perceive as challenges to their authority.

4 Public hostility, coupled with other factors—a belief that courts are too lenient on criminals; the realization that it is often wiser to "look the other way" if they become aware of corrupt practices by their peers; the part that favoritism may play in promotions—leads to yet another trait that characterizes the police officer's working personality: cynicism.*

5 In a study of 220 New York City police officers, Professor Arthur Niederhoffer, himself a former police officer, found that 80 percent of the new recruits believed that the department was a smoothly op-

---

*cynicism: a tendency to believe the worst.

erating, effective organization. Within a couple of months on the job, fewer than one-third still held that belief. They had become cynical about police work, supervisors, and the operating policies of the department. Moreover, cynicism increased with length of service and among the more highly educated who were not promoted. Researchers Robert Regoli and Eric Poole argue that cynicism increases police officers' desire to exert authority over ordinary citizens. As the use of authority increases, citizens become more hostile, making police feel even more threatened, and the cycle continues. (Adapted from Adler et al., *Criminal Justice*, p. 237.)

1. How would you paraphrase the thesis statement?

_____

_____

2. Which question about the thesis statement do the major supporting details help to answer?

    a. How is the working personality of police officers affected by the conditions in which they work?

    b. How does the working personality of the police officer differ from that of the doctor?

2. Taking Spam Off the Menu

1 Most computer users who have e-mail addresses are familiar with spam, unwanted e-mail messages advertising a product or service. Spam includes offers for everything from weight loss aids to get-rich-quick schemes. It's the electronic version of the "junk mail" delivered to post office boxes or the on-line equivalent of a telemarketing phone call. Experts estimate that one in every ten e-mail messages sent today is spam. The average Internet user received almost 1500 junk messages in 2001.

2   Spam is a cheap form of advertising. That's why it's attractive to businesses with products or services to market. A business can buy a list of consumers' e-mail addresses from another company or compile its own list by performing a sweep of the World Wide Web. Once the list is composed, e-mail messages can be sent out instantly to thousands of possible customers. Sending ten messages or ten million messages costs about the same.

3   Consumers, however, find spam extremely annoying. Determining which messages are spam and then deleting them is irritating and time-consuming. Spam is also leading many individuals to be more reluctant about using the Internet. They fear that going to

a chat room or signing up for a mailing list will lead to an ava-lanche of new junk mail. As a result, unwanted e-mail is one of the major complaints of subscribers to Internet service pro-viders.

4   Employers dislike spam, too. On the job, when workers spend even a few minutes a day dealing with spam, the labor costs can add up quickly. As a result, many companies are spending addi-tional money on filters to screen out spam altogether. These fil-ters sometimes cause more problems because they can block im-portant, necessary messages from getting through.

5   Companies who choose to filter messages often hire a firm that specializes in blocking unwanted spam. BrightMail is one success-ful anti-spam service. It maintains thousands of e-mail accounts that collect and identify sources of spam. Then, it installs soft-ware on its clients' e-mail gateways, including those of many of the largest Internet service providers. When a known spam mes-sage tries to get through the gateway, the software blocks it.

1. How would you paraphrase the thesis statement?

_____

_____

2. Which question about the thesis statement do the major sup-porting details help answer?

a. Why is spam unwanted?

b. How does spam compare to junk mail?

 ## Outlining Longer Readings

For reading assignments that cover fairly familiar or uncomplicated material, you can probably prepare for class discussions or exams simply by reviewing your underlining and your annotations. How-ever, if the material is at all complicated, you may want to take notes using an **informal outline.**

Like a formal outline, an informal outline signals relationships by aligning or indenting sentences, words, or phrases. However, with informal outlines you needn't worry about using *all* sentences or *all* phrases, and you don't have to fuss over capital or lowercase letters. You can also use whatever symbols seem appropriate to the mate-rial, combining letters, numbers, abbreviations, dashes, and so on, as you need them. In other words, informal outlines are not governed by a fixed set of rules. The main thing to keep in mind is the goal of your informal outline: to develop a clear blueprint of the author's ideas and their relationship to one another.

Here are some pointers for creating informal outlines that are clear, concise, and complete.

Start with the Title

The title of an essay, article, or chapter section usually identifies the topic being discussed. Sometimes it will identify the main idea of the entire reading. Thus, your outline should usually open with the title.

Follow with the Thesis Statement

After the title comes the paraphrase of the thesis statement. Because indenting to show relationships is crucial to outlining, put your paraphrase at the left-most margin of your notepaper.

List the Major Details

Now's the time to look over the supporting paragraphs and sift out the major details. At this point, keep in mind that the major details you select have to be carefully evaluated in relation to the thesis statement, and minor details in a paragraph should only be included if they are essential to the major ones. Outlining, like underlining, requires conscious and consistent selectivity. Here's an outline of the reading from pages 149–150.

The Ancient Roman Circus

The first circus began in ancient Rome, but it was much bloodier than the circus we know today.

1. The first circus, Circus Maximus, originated under Julius Caesar.
2. Ancient circuses specialized in bloody events; emperor and spectators were upset if no one died.
3. Which event was featured depended on the emperor in power.

    a. Julius Caesar liked chariot races: slaves raced for their freedom and risked their lives, often dying in the process.

    —dragged around the ring when they couldn't cut themselves free

    b. During reign of Augustus, hundreds of gladiators died, taking with them more than 3,500 lions and tigers.

    c. Under Nero, Christians were thrown to the lions.

4. Colosseum in Rome staged biggest circuses.

    a. It held 50,000 people.

    b. In one season, 2,000 gladiators went to their death.

Always Indent

As the sample outline illustrates, an outline is not the same as a list. When you make an outline, you have to indent to indicate whether different ideas carry equal weight. Major details, for example, should all be aligned underneath one another to indicate their equal relationship. Similarly, if you are summarizing several different chapter sections, then the main ideas of each section should be aligned one underneath the other.

Be Consistent

Letters, numbers, dashes (—), stars (☆☆☆), or asterisks (**) can help you separate major and minor details. Whichever symbols you use, be sure to use them consistently within the outline. Don't switch back and forth, sometimes using numbers for major details and sometimes using letters. In the long run, this kind of inconsistency will only confuse you.

Be Selective

When you outline, reduce the original text as much as possible, retaining essential details and eliminating nonessential details. When adding supporting details to your outline, always decide what you need to include and what you can safely leave out.

EXERCISE 3

DIRECTIONS Read the following selection. Underline and annotate it. Then make an outline that is both concise and complete.

EXAMPLE

World War II: Interning Japanese-Americans

1   Compared with previous wars, the nation's wartime civil liberties record during World War II showed some improvement, particularly where African-Americans and women were concerned. But there was one enormous exception: the internment* of 120,000 Japanese-Americans. The internment of Japanese-Americans was based not on suspicion or evidence of treason; their crime was solely their race—the fact that they were of Japanese descent.

2   Popular racial stereotypes used to fuel the war effort held that Japanese people abroad and at home were sneaky and evil, and the American people generally regarded Japan as the United States's chief enemy. Moreover, the feeling was widespread that the Japanese had to be repaid for Pearl Harbor. Thus, with a few notable exceptions, there was no public outcry over the relocation and internment of Japanese-Americans.

3   Yet there were two obvious reasons why the internment of Japanese-Americans was completely unnecessary. First and foremost, there was absolutely no evidence of any attempt by Japanese-Americans to hurt the American war effort. The government's own studies proved that fact beyond question. Thus it's not surprising that in places where racism was not a factor, in Hawaii for example, the public outcry for internment was much more muted.

4   Secondly, Japanese-American soldiers fought valiantly for the United States. The all Japanese-American 442nd Regimental Combat Team—heavily recruited from young men in internment camps— was the most decorated unit of its size in the armed forces. Suffering heavy casualties in Italy and France, members of the 442nd were awarded a Congressional Medal of Honor, several Distinguished Service Crosses, 350 Silver Stars, and more than 3,600 Purple Hearts. (Adapted from Norton et al., *A People and a Nation*, p. 795.)

Title <u>World War II: Interning Japanese-Americans</u>

Main Idea <u>In World War II, the imprisonment of Japanese-Americans spoiled an otherwise creditable civil rights record.</u>

————

*internment: imprisonment.

Supporting Details **1.** *Racial stereotypes used to power the war effort encouraged*
people to see Japanese-Americans as the enemy.

2. *There was also a general belief that the Japanese had to be*
paid back for bombing Pearl Harbor.

3. *Two reasons why internment unnecessary*

1) *Absolutely no evidence of wrongdoing, a fact proven*
by government studies

2) *Japanese-American soldiers fought bravely to defend the U.S.*
—The all Japanese-American combat team was recruited
largely from internment camps, and it was the most
decorated of its size.

EXPLANATION Your outline of the same reading might have used
letters instead of numbers and avoided dashes altogether. Still the
content would have been fairly similar. Given the thesis statement
in paragraph 1, you need to include the causes of internment as well
as the reasons why the authors consider it an "enormous exception"
to an otherwise creditable record on civil rights.

1. The Gains and Losses of Beauty

1 No doubt about it, extremely good-looking people have a significant social edge. They are less lonely, less socially anxious (especially about interactions with the opposite sex), more popular,
more sexually experienced, and, as we noted earlier, more socially
skilled (Feingold, 1992b). The social rewards for physical attractiveness appear to get off to an early start. Mothers of highly attractive newborns engage in more affectionate interactions with
their babies than do mothers of less attractive infants (Langlois et
al., 1995). Given such benefits, one would expect that the beautiful would also have a significant psychological advantage. But
they don't. Physical attractiveness (as rated by judges) has little if
any association with self-esteem, mental health, personality
traits, or intelligence (Feingold, 1992b).

2   One possible reason why beauty doesn't affect psychological
well-being is that *actual* physical attractiveness, as evaluated by
others, may have less impact than *self-perceived* physical attractiveness. People who view themselves as physically attractive do

report higher self-esteem and better mental health than those who believe they are unattractive (Feingold, 1992b). But judges' ratings of physical attractiveness are only modestly correlated* with self-perceived attractiveness. When real beauties do not see themselves as beautiful, their appearance may not be psychologically valuable.

3   Physically attractive individuals may also fail to benefit from the social bias for beauty because of pressures they experience to maintain their appearance. In contemporary American society, such pressures are particularly strong in regard to the body. Although both facial and bodily appearance contribute to perceived attractiveness, an unattractive body appears to be a greater liability than an unattractive face (Alicke et al., 1986). Such a "body bias" can produce a healthy emphasis on nutrition and exercise. But it can sometimes lead to distinctly unhealthy consequences. For example, men may pop steroids in order to build up impressive muscles. Among women, the desire for a beautiful body often takes a different form.

4   Women are more likely than men to suffer from what Janet Polivy and her colleagues (1986) call the "modern mania for slenderness." This zeal* for thinness is promoted by the mass media. Popular female characters in TV shows are more likely than popular male characters to be exceedingly thin; women's magazines stress the need to maintain a slender body more than do men's magazines (Silverstein et al., 1986b). (Brehm and Kassin, *Social Psychology*, p. 180.)

Title _____

Main Idea _____

_____

_____

Supporting Details _____

_____

_____

_____

_____

---

*correlated: related to.
*zeal: strong desire.

_____

_____

_____

_____

_____

_____

_____

_____

_____

_____

2. The Value of Social Diversity

1 Some groups are more diverse than others, with a greater number of members differing in ethnicity, gender, personality, skill, or other qualities. Generally, the more diverse a group, the more effective it is in achieving its goal. Research has found, for example, that athletic teams with a wide range of different skills among their members often outperform teams with less diverse skills, and that the more heterogeneous* the personnel of a bank, the more likely the bank will adopt innovative practices, make high-quality decisions, and become successful (Johnson and Johnson, 1997).

2 Why is diversity so useful? Because diverse groups have more ways of solving a problem than less diverse ones. Suppose each member of any group has only one way of solving a problem. Now, a group of, say, five people who think differently and see the world differently will come out with five different ways of solving a problem, while a group of five people who think alike and see the world the same may discover only one solution. A diverse group, then, can draw on an ample supply of ideas and data, but a homogeneous* group is more likely to suffer a shortage of ideas and data.

3 A diverse group is also unlikely to have the problems that a homogeneous group often has, such as the tendency to engage in groupthink and the difficulty in adapting to changing conditions

_____

*heterogeneous: varied, different.
*homogeneous: uniform, similar.

(Johnson and Johnson, 1997). Diversity can have problems, though, if people are prejudiced, intolerant, or closed-minded against fellow group members who are different. (Thio, *Sociology*, pp. 103–104.)

Title _____

Main Idea _____

_____

_____

Supporting Details _____

_____

_____

_____

_____

_____

_____

_____

_____

_____

_____

CHECK YOUR UNDERSTANDING
Describe the main goal of an effective informal outline.
_____
_____
_____

■ **DIGGING DEEPER**

LOOKING AHEAD The killer bees described on page 144 have gotten most of the attention, but according to the following article, there's a bug from south of the border that's even scarier.

THERE ARE WORSE THINGS THAN KILLER BEES

1 One painfully memorable day this spring Jack Reese did a crazy dance in the middle of a persimmon grove on his farm in Oktibbeha County, Mississippi. Flailing wildly, he tried to yank off his pants and swat his ankles at the same time. He had made one of the worst mistakes a Southern farmer can make: he forgot to watch the ground for a moment and thus tromped on a foot-high mound full of fire ants. Incensed by the intrusion, the insects promptly swarmed up Reese's legs, stinging him mercilessly over and over again. It felt like dozens of hot needles being plunged into his skin.

2 Killer bees, it turns out, are not the most menacing marauders to hail from South America. Their less publicized cousins the fire ants are more widespread in the U.S., more destructive and, so far, deadlier. The antagonistic ants have been harassing people, mostly in the South, for decades—ruining picnics, forcing the cancellation of high school football games, making small children afraid to venture into their backyards—and the threat is getting worse than ever. In some areas the rapidly spreading ants are crowding out (or killing) other insects, lizards, birds and small mammals, knocking natural ecosystems completely out of whack. Their mounds—up to hundreds of them per acre–have made many a farm field all but unplowable. And because the ants are strangely attracted to electric current, they have been known to chew through underground cables, disrupting everything from telephone service to airport runway lights and even starting fires.

3 While the minuscule monsters have traditionally attacked only people who stepped on their turf, they've recently brought their mayhem indoors as well. Says Marion Bernhardt, seventy-eight, of West Palm Beach, Florida, who last year survived an ant assault in a hospital bed: "I was stung all up and down my legs, and I had welts all over them and on my side. They burned for days. I never had such an experience in all my life." She was lucky. At least fifty people have died in recent years from allergic reactions to fire-ant stings.

4 Worst of all, fire ants are on the move. They are already established throughout the South, from Texas east to Florida and north to Tennessee, with isolated pockets even farther north— there's a colony, for example, in Virginia Beach, Virginia. Most of the West Coast, from Southern California up to Vancouver, British Columbia, would make fine fire-ant habitat as well. And while the moisture-loving insects can't spread westward through arid reaches of West Texas on their own, they don't have to. Fire ants have been known to hitch rides on truckloads of produce, nursery stock and even industrial chemicals. According to Richard Patterson, a U.S. Department of Agriculture entomologist* based at the University of Florida, infestations of fire ants have been found in Arizona, New Mexico, California, Oregon and Washington.

5 So far, the bugs' aversion to frost has kept them out of the Midwest and Northeast, but even that may change. Tim Lockley, an entomologist at the Agriculture Department's fire-ant lab in Gulfport, Mississippi, says the ants have now settled in the mountains of east Tennessee, where as much as 7 percent of the population survived the especially frigid winter of 1993–94. Says Lockley: "It's just amazing how adaptive they are."

6 The threat began in the 1930s, when the aggressive red fire ants came to Mobile, Alabama, perhaps on shiploads of lumber imported from the insects' home territory in South America (the milder-mannered black fire ant had arrived, also from the Southern Hemisphere, in 1918). In the 1950s and early '60s concerned government officials tried to eradicate the insects with such powerful chemicals as heptachlor and mirex. The program was later dubbed "the Vietnam of entomology" for both its destructiveness and its futility. The poisons killed not only their targets but also most other wildlife in the treated areas. By the late '70s the pesticides were banned.

7 Now the ants have grown so nasty that some folks argue for a return to chemical warfare. Says Republican Congressman Tom DeLay of Texas, the House majority whip and a former exterminator: "The scientific evidence doesn't justify the mirex ban."

8 Still worried about the pesticides' impact on the environment, government scientists think they may have a better answer to the fire-ant menace. Patterson's lab at the Agriculture Department is studying a tiny parasitic fly that lays its egg right on the fire ant's body. The fly maggots then eat their way into the ant's head and eventually sever the head from the body. Best of all, the fly seems to attack only fire ants. If laboratory and field tests show that the

---

*entomologist: person who studies insects.

fly is indeed safe to use, says Patterson, the natural ant killer could be available within a year—and Jack Reese will no longer have to be so careful about where he steps. (Michael D. Lemonick, David Bjerklie, and Scott Norvell, "Science: Ants in Our Pants," *Time,* June 5, 1995, © 1995 Time Inc. Reprinted by permission.)

Sharpening Your Skills

DIRECTIONS Answer the following questions by filling in the blanks or circling the letter of the correct response.

1. Based on the title, what question should a reader pose to focus concentration and attention? _____

   _____

2. What is the main idea of the entire reading? _____

   _____

3. The thesis statement appears in

   a. paragraph 1.
   b. paragraph 2.
   c. paragraph 3.

4. What's one of the questions answered by the supporting details?

   _____

   _____

5. How would you paraphrase the main idea of paragraph 3?

   _____

   _____

6. In paragraph 3, how is Marion Bernhardt's statement relevant, or related, to the main idea?

   _____

7. How would you paraphrase the main idea of paragraph 4?

   _____

   _____

8. The detail about the frigid winter of 1993–94 is used to illustrate what point?

   _____

9. What organizational pattern is at work in paragraph 6?

   a. cause and effect

   b. process

   c. sequence of dates and events

10. Paragraph 8 combines what two patterns?

    a. comparison and contrast with process

    b. cause and effect with process

    c. definition with comparison and contrast

WORD NOTES: TWO COMMONLY CONFUSED WORDS

Recall that on page 145 some people were loath, or reluctant, to eat garlic because of the effect on their breath. Now that you know the adjective *loath*, you should also learn the related and commonly misused verb *loathe*, meaning "to hate or dislike." Although both *loath* and *loathe* are based on an Old English root *lath*, meaning "hateful," the two words are different in meaning and function. To show that you understand those differences, fill in the blanks left in the following sentences. Then write two sentences of your own, using *loathe* or *loath*.

1. The people of Chile quickly learned to _____ the policies of the military government.

2. Although she detested his behavior, the secretary of health and human services was _____ to openly defy someone so powerful.

loathe: _____

_____

loath: _____

_____

Test 1: Reviewing the Key Points

DIRECTIONS Answer the following questions by filling in the blanks or circling the correct response.

1. To understand the difference between paragraphs and longer readings, how many crucial differences do you need to take into account? _____

2. *True* or *False.* In longer readings, the main idea is sometimes expressed in several sentences.

3. *True* or *False.* Thesis statements are more fixed in location than are topic sentences.

4. *True* or *False.* In multiparagraph readings, the introduction is usually limited to a sentence or two.

5. Words like _____, _____, and _____ are clues to major details.

6. Outlines are appropriate for material that is _____.

7. Formal and informal outlines signal relationships by _____.

8. The goal of an informal outline is to _____.

9. *True* or *False.* In outlines, you should start with the title and main idea.

10. *True* or *False.* In informal outlines, consistency of style is not important.

Test 2: Underlining Thesis Statements

DIRECTIONS Underline the thesis statement in each selection.

1. Marital Satisfaction in New Families

1 Almost all studies that measure marital satisfaction before and after the birth of the first child have found that the birth of a child is a mixed marital blessing (Cowan & Cowan, 1988). Jay Belsky and Michael Rovine (1990) found that couples who were least satisfied with their marriages before the birth were most likely to report decline in satisfaction after, since problems that existed before were likely to have been magnified by the additional stresses brought on by the birth.

2 Babies do not appear to create severe marital distress where none existed before; nor do they bring couples with distressed marriages closer together. Rather, the early postpartum* months bring on a period of disorganization and change. The leading conflict in these first months of parenthood is division of labor in the family. Couples may regain their sense of equilibrium in marriage by successfully negotiating how they will divide the new family responsibilities. Husbands' participation in child and home care seems to be positively related to marital satisfaction after the birth. One study found that the more the men shared in doing family tasks, the more satisfied were the wives at six and eighteen months postpartum and the husbands at eighteen months postpartum (Cowan & Cowan, 1988).

3 While many couples experience a difficult transition to parenthood, they also find it rewarding. Children affect parents in ways that lead to personal growth, enable reworking of childhood conflicts, build flexibility and empathy, and provide intimate, loving human connections. They also give a lot of pleasure. In follow-up interviews of new parents when their children were eighteen months old, Philip Cowan and Carolyn Cowan (1988) found that almost every man and woman spoke of the delight they felt from knowing their child and watching the child develop. They reported feeling pride for and closeness to their spouses, more adult with their own parents, and a renewed sense of purpose at work. (Adapted from Seifert et al., *Lifespan Development*, p. 488.)

---

*postpartum: following a birth.

2. **Partner Selection**

1 What characteristics do men and women look for in a potential romantic partner? According to the research of psychologist David Buss, men and women often look for similar characteristics, most importantly kindness, understanding, and intelligence.

2 Although we have all heard the old saying "opposites attract," this does not appear to be the case when it comes to selecting a romantic partner for a long-term committed relationship. In his research, Buss studied similarities and differences between spouses and found that the similarities were indeed striking. Couples in Buss's study were similar in age, race, religion, ethnic background, and socioeconomic status. They often grew up within driving distance of each other. Additionally, Buss also found that attitudes, opinions, and worldviews were also very much alike among the couples.

3 As couples live together, over time certain compatibilities become more important. Sharing values, a willingness to tolerate flaws and to make changes in response to each other, communicating effectively, and sharing religious beliefs seem to be especially important in the long run.

4 The results of a nationally representative study of sexual practices in the United States, reported in 1994, has confirmed Buss's findings. Robert Michael and his colleagues state that "on every measure except religion [including race/ethnicity, age, and educational level], people who are in any stage of a sexual relationship are remarkably similar to each other. And married people are even very likely to have the same religion." Michael and his colleagues point out that some individuals do have successful romantic relationships with people who are very different from themselves, but this is an exception—not the rule. Additionally, Michael and his colleagues believe the pattern of "like attracts like" holds true for homosexuals as well as heterosexuals.

5 Michael and his colleagues propose that it is easier for individuals in a romantic relationship to share their lives with each other when they have similar backgrounds and interests. Additionally, they believe that social networks, consisting of family, friends, and business associates, exert subtle and not so subtle influences on individuals to select a romantic partner that will fit into these social groups. (Mullen et al., *Connections for Health,* pp. 212–213.)

Test 3: Thesis Statements and Supporting Details

DIRECTIONS Underline the thesis statement. Then answer the questions by filling in the blanks or circling the correct response. Note: To decide if a detail is major or minor, you will probably need to look at the sentences in the context of the paragraphs where they appear.

1. Feminist Objections to Pornography

1   Beginning around 1978, some—though not all—feminists became very critical of pornography (e.g., Griffin, 1981; Lederer, 1980; Morgan, 1978). Why are feminists opposed to pornography? In general, there are three basic reasons for their objections.

2   First, they argue that pornography debases women. The milder, soft-core versions portray women as sex objects whose breasts, legs, and buttocks can be purchased and then ogled.* This scarcely represents a respectful attitude toward women. Second, pornography associates sex with violence toward women. As such, it contributes to rape and other forms of violence against women and girls. Robin Morgan put it bluntly: "Pornography is the theory and rape is the practice" (Morgan, 1980, p. 139). Third, pornography shows, indeed glamorizes, unequal power relationships between women and men. A common theme in pornography is that of men forcing women to have sex, and so the power of men and subordination of women is emphasized. Consistent with this point, feminists do not object to sexual materials that portray women and men in equal, humanized relationships—what we would term *erotica*.

3   Feminists also note the intimate relationship between pornography and traditional gender roles. They argue that pornography may serve to perpetuate traditional gender roles. By seeing or reading about dominant males and submissive,* dehumanized females, each new generation of adolescent boys is socialized to accept these roles. (Adapted from Hyde, *Understanding Human Sexuality*, p. 524.)

1. Based on the title, what question should you use to guide your reading?

_____

2. In your own words, what is the main idea?

_____

_____

*ogled: stared at.
*submissive: obedient.

3. Based on the thesis statement, how many major details should you be looking for? _____

4. Which of the following is *not* a major detail?

    a. Pornography associates sex with violence toward women.

    b. Feminists do not object to sexual materials that portray women and men in equal, humanized relationships.

5. Which of the following is a minor detail?

    a. Feminists argue that pornography debases women.

    b. Pornography glamorizes unequal power relationships.

    c. A common theme in pornography is that of men forcing women to have sex.

2. The Meaning of Touch

1 Touching and being touched is an essential part of being human. However, the amount and meaning of touch changes with age, purpose and location. Infants and their parents, for example, engage in extensive touching behavior, but this decreases during adolescence. The amount of touching behavior increases after adolescence as young people begin to establish romantic relationships. No matter how much we are touched, however, most of us want to be touched more than we are (Mosby, 1978).

2 Generally speaking, the meaning of touch varies with the situation, and there are five general categories of meaning. *Positive affective touches* transmit messages of support, appreciation, affection, or sexual intent. *Playful touches* lighten our interactions with others. *Control touches* are used to get other people's attention and to gain their compliance. *Ritualistic touches* are those we use during communication rituals such as greeting others and saying good-bye. *Task-related touches* are those that are necessary for us to complete tasks on which we are working. Touches also can fit into more than one category at a time. We can, for example, touch others as part of a ritual to express positive affection.

3 Age, sex, and region of the country also influence the amount people touch. To illustrate, people between eighteen and twenty-five and between thirty and forty report the most touching, while old people report the least (Mosby, 1978). Women find touching more pleasant than men do, as long as the other person is not a stranger (Heslin, 1978). Finally, people who live in the South touch more than people who live in the North (Howard, 1985).

4   The United States is generally a noncontact culture. People do not engage in a great deal of touching. There are, however, situations in which people are likely to touch (Henley, 1977). People are more likely to touch, for example, when giving information or advice than when receiving information or advice. People are more likely to touch others when giving orders than when receiving orders, when asking for a favor than when granting a favor, or when trying to persuade others than when being persuaded. (Adapted from Gudykunst et al., *Building Bridges,* pp. 319–320.)

1. Based on the title, what question would you use to guide your reading?

_____

2. In your own words, what is the main idea of the entire reading?

_____

_____

3. Which of the following is a major detail?
   a. People who live in the South touch more than do people who live in the North.
   b. Age, sex, and region influence the amount people touch.
   c. People are more likely to touch, for example, when giving information or advice.

4. Which of the following is a major detail?
   a. Generally speaking, the meaning of touch varies with the situation and there are five general categories of meaning.
   b. We can, for example, touch others as part of a ritual to express positive affection.
   c. People between eighteen and twenty-five and between thirty and forty report the most touching.

5. Which of the following is a minor detail?
   a. Women find touching more pleasant than men do as long as the other person is not a stranger.
   b. The amount and meaning of touch change with age, purpose, and location.
   c. The United States is generally a noncontact culture.

◢◗ Test 4: Outlining Longer Readings

DIRECTIONS Read the following selection. Then fill in the blanks left in the informal outline. *Note:* Whenever possible, paraphrase rather than copy word for word.

1. Forming a Union

1 The first step in forming a union is the *organizing campaign.* Its primary objective is to develop a widespread employee interest in having a union. To kick off the campaign, a national union may send organizers to the firm to stir this interest. Alternatively, the employees themselves may decide they want a union. Then they contact the appropriate national union and ask for organizing assistance.

2 The organizing campaign can be quite emotional, and it may lead to conflict between employees and management. On the one hand, the employees who want the union will be dedicated to its creation. On the other, management will be extremely sensitive to what it sees as a potential threat to its power and control.

3 At some point during the organizing campaign, employees are asked to sign *authorization cards* to indicate—in writing—their support for the union. Because of various NLRB* rules and regulations, both union organizers and company management must be very careful in their behavior during this authorization drive. For example, employees cannot be asked to sign the cards when they are supposed to be working. And management may not indicate in any way that employees' jobs or job security will be in jeopardy if they *do* sign the cards.

4 If at least 30 percent of the eligible employees sign authorization cards, the organizers generally request that the firm recognize the union as the employees' bargaining representative. Usually the firm rejects this request, and a *formal election* is held to decide whether to have a union. This election usually involves secret ballots and is conducted by the NLRB. The outcome of the election is determined by a simple majority of eligible employees who choose to vote.

5 If the union obtains a majority, it becomes the official bargaining agent for its members and the final step, *NLRB certification*, takes place. The union may immediately begin the process of negotiating a labor contract with management. If the union is voted down, the NLRB will not allow another election for one year.

6 Several factors can complicate the unionization process. For

———

*NLRB: National Labor Relations Board.

example, the **bargaining unit,** which is the specific group of employees that the union is to represent, must be defined. Union organizers may want to represent all hourly employees at a particular site (such as all workers at a manufacturing plant). Or they may wish to represent only a specific group of employees (such as electricians in a large manufacturing plant). (Pride et al., *Business*, p. 285.)

Title Forming a Union

Main Idea A union organizing campaign involves a fixed sequence of steps.

_____

Supporting Details **1.** Union may send organizers to stir up interest in unionizing or employees contact union.

    a. conflict may result

_____

    b. _____

_____

2. Employees asked to sign authorization cards to indicate support for union.

    a. NLRB rules and regulations are strict.

       1) Employees can't be asked to sign cards while at work.

_____

       2) _____

_____

3. If 30 percent of eligible employees do sign, organizers ask firm to recognize the union as bargaining representative.

    a. firm usually rejects request and formal election held

1) _____

_____

2) outcome determined by simple majority of eligible

employees who vote

4. If union gets a majority, it becomes bargaining agent and

NLRB certification takes place.

_____

a. If union voted down, NLRB prohibits new election for one

year.

b. _____

_____

5. _____

_____

_____

a. Bargaining unit must be defined.

1) Union organizers may represent all hourly workers or

only a specific group.

2. Psychological Pricing Strategies

1 Psychological pricing strategies encourage purchases based on emotional responses rather than on economically rational responses. These strategies are used primarily for consumer products rather than industrial products.

2 **Odd Pricing**   Many retailers believe that consumers respond more positively to odd-number prices like $4.99 than to whole-dollar prices like $5. **Odd pricing** is the strategy of setting prices using odd numbers that are slightly below whole dollar amounts. Nine and five are the most popular ending figures for prices.

3   Sellers who use this strategy believe odd prices increase sales. The strategy is not limited to low-priced items. Auto manufacturers may set the price of a car at $11,999 rather than $12,000. Odd pricing has been the subject of various psychological studies,

but the results have been inconclusive as to whether or not it encourages consumer buying.

4 **Multiple-Unit Pricing**   Many retailers (and especially supermarkets) practice **multiple-unit pricing,** setting a single price for two or more units, such as two cans for 99 cents rather than 50 cents per can. Especially for frequently purchased products, this strategy can increase sales. Customers who see the single price, and who expect eventually to use more than one unit of the product, regularly purchase multiple units to save money.

5 **Prestige Pricing   Prestige pricing** is the strategy of setting a high price to project an aura of quality and status. Because high-quality items are generally more expensive than those of average quality, many buyers believe that high price *means* high quality, especially for certain types of products such as cosmetics, perfumes, and jewelry. High-priced products like Rolex watches and high-priced stores like Neiman Marcus tend to attract quality- and prestige-conscious customers.

6 **Price Lining   Price lining** is the strategy of selling goods only at certain predetermined prices that reflect definite price breaks. For example, a shop may sell men's ties only at $22 and $37. This strategy is widely used in clothing and accessory stores. It eliminates minor price differences from the buying decision—both for customers and for managers who buy merchandise to sell in these stores. (Pride et al., *Business*, p. 353.)

Title Psychological Pricing Strategies

Main Idea "Psychological pricing strategies" rely on emotional appeals to encourage consumer buying.

Supporting Details **1.** _____

    a. 9 and 5 popular ending figure for price

    b. _____

    c. not limited to low-priced items

    d. psychological studies inconclusive about effectiveness of odd pricing

2. Multiple-unit pricing sets the same price for two or more items

    a. _____

     _____

    b. seems to work among product users _____

3. _____

    _____

    a. Based on consumer belief that high price means high quality

    b. Sellers of cosmetics, perfumes, jewelry employ this strategy.

4. _____

    _____

    a. sell ties at only two prices, $22 and $37 _____

    b. _____

    c. _____

C H A P T E R   5

Summarizing and Synthesizing: Two More Strategies for In-Depth Learning

> **In this chapter, you'll learn**
>
> - how to compose summaries.
>
> - how to adapt your summary to your purpose.
>
> - how to create synthesis statements for exam reviews.

At this point, you're ready to work on summarizing and synthesizing, two learning strategies that can markedly improve your mastery of college texts. To effectively summarize a chapter section or journal article, you have to reduce it to its bare-bone essentials, and that process pays off in two ways: (1) If you can't figure out what essentials should go in your summary, you need to reread the material. Thus, summarizing is a good way to check your comprehension. (2) While you are analyzing a text in order to summarize it, you are also giving your mind a chance to focus on the author's ideas and store them in long-term memory.

Synthesizing comes into play when you have two or more sources dealing with the same or a similar subject. When this happens—as it often does with textbook assignments and outside readings—you need to create synthesis statements that identify not just the authors' individual ideas but also the relationship they share. Again, this is the kind of mental activity that ensures both in-depth learning and long-term remembering.

 ## Writing Summaries

As the following pages illustrate, the requirements of summary writing can differ depending on your purpose. The summary you write purely for your own use will differ from the one you turn in to your instructor. Still, there are some general pointers that do apply to all summaries.

How to Write a Good Summary

1. Apply the One-Quarter Rule of Thumb

Generally speaking, try to reduce the original text to about one-quarter of its original length. You can usually accomplish this by including in your summary (1) the main idea of the entire reading and (2) the main idea of each supporting paragraph.

2. Make Distinctions Between the Essential and the Absolutely Essential

If the author uses the opening paragraph to describe the topic before introducing the main idea, don't summarize the introduction. Instead, start right off with the main idea. Similarly, if the author uses three separate examples to explain or prove a point, decide which of them best illustrates the main idea and answers any questions it might raise. That's the example to include in your summary.

However, if the author uses three reasons to support an argument or four categories to explain a system of classification, you need to include at least one sentence about each one. Personal anecdotes, quoted material, and clever comments to the reader are the writer's way of giving the material audience appeal, but none of these things needs to be included in your summary.

3. Underline and Annotate Before You Write

Thoroughly mark up your text before you write the summary. Circle important names and dates, underline keywords, and write the main idea along with several supporting details in the margins. In this way, by the time you start writing your summary, you will have already sifted out the nonessential material.

4. Paraphrase

Paraphrasing will help you significantly condense the original text. Just keep in mind the key rule of paraphrasing: Change the form but don't alter the meaning.

5. Don't Interpret or Evaluate

Even if you are convinced that a writer is spouting nonsense, don't let that opinion make its way into your summary. Restrict your opinions to the margins. That way, if you need to cite the ideas you have summarized later on—say, in an essay exam or a research paper—you won't mistakenly include a point of view the author never intended.

Writing Chapter Summaries

If you are working your way through a chapter that is dense with details, facts, and figures, you should probably not use summary writing as a method of note taking and review. However, if you are reading a psychology or sociology text where the subject matter is familiar and the ideas fairly general, you might consider summary writing in place of or in addition to reciting after reading. For an illustration, read the following excerpt and summary.

Role of Culture in Listening

Like brain dominance, a person's culture influences listening and learning abilities. Some cultures, such as many in Asia, stress good listening and the importance of receiving—rather than giving—messages. People in Japan, for example, are likely to spend less time talking on the job than do European Americans, stressing instead the listening aspect of communication. In addition, some cultures stress concentration, which results in longer attention spans. Buddhism, for instance, has a notion called "being mindful." This means giving whatever you are doing your complete and full attention. Training to have long attention spans starts in childhood. To those raised in a typical European American environment, these listening-enhancing concepts are not part of their background.

Cultures have been identified as low context and high context. In low-context cultures such as the United States and Canada, communicators expect to give and receive a great deal of information, since these cultures perceive that most message information is obtained in words. In high-context cultures such as Japan and Saudi Arabia, more of the information is situated in the communicators themselves and in the communication setting, so fewer words are necessary. "In high-context cultures, it is the responsibility of the listener to understand; in low context, it is the speaker who is responsible for making sure the listener comprehends all." (Berko et al., *Communicating,* p. 94.)

Now here's a summary of that chapter section:

> Our culture affects how we learn and listen. Not all cultures, for example, place as much emphasis on self-expression. Some cultures place more emphasis on listening. The Japanese, for instance, don't talk nearly as much as Americans do while they work. When it comes to listening, cultures can be labeled high or low context. In low-context cultures, words are considered essential to communication, and it is up to the speaker to get his or her message across to listeners. In high-context cultures, more responsibility lies with the listener, who is expected to pay close attention in order to understand.

The sample summary reduces the original text to two key points: (1) Culture affects how we listen and learn, and (2) cultures, in general, can be labeled high or low context, depending on which activity is emphasized, listening or speaking. The addition of one example helps illustrate how culture affects people's readiness to favor either speaking or listening.

 # Reviewing Through Summary Writing

If you decide to include summarizing in your arsenal of reading and study strategies, there are two ways you can do it.

Method 1 After you finish a chapter section that you thought fairly easy to understand, see if you can summarize in writing the overall main idea and a few essential details. Don't look back at the text itself. Write your summary from memory. The ease with which you can summarize will tell you how well you have understood the material. A summary you have to struggle over suggests that you need to give the text a slow and thorough second reading. A summary that you can quickly dash off, however, suggests you probably don't need to do a second reading. When it comes time for exam review, you can just do a quick rereading of the material you underlined.

Method 2 If you know that the chapter section you just completed was a bit hard to understand, write your summary with the text in front of you. That way you can evaluate each and every sentence. Pondering the material in this way will deepen your understanding. It will also ensure remembering and make it easier for you to grasp the main point of the chapter section that follows.

CHECK YOUR UNDERSTANDING

When is it a good idea to review through summary writing?

_____

When is it not a good idea to review through summary writing?

_____

EXERCISE 1

DIRECTIONS Read each selection, then choose the most effective summary.

EXAMPLE

Going West

1   In America in the nineteenth century, most migrants went West because opportunities there seemed to promise a better life. Railroad expansion made remote farming regions accessible, and the construction of grain elevators eased problems of shipping and storage. As a result of population growth, the demand for farm products grew rapidly, and the prospects for commercial agriculture—growing crops for profit—became more favorable than ever.

2   Life on the farm, however, was much harder than the advertisements and railroad agents suggested. Migrants often encountered scarcities of essentials they had once taken for granted. The open prairies contained little lumber for housing and fuel. Pioneer families were forced to build houses of sod and to burn manure for heat. Water was sometimes as scarce as timber. Few families were lucky or wealthy enough to buy land near a stream that did not dry up in summer and freeze in winter. Machinery for drilling wells was scarce until the 1880s, and even then it was very expensive.

3   Weather seldom followed predictable cycles. In summer, weeks of torrid* heat and parching winds suddenly gave way to violent storms that washed away crops and property. The wind and cold of winter blizzards piled up mountainous snowdrifts that halted all outdoor movement. During the Great Blizzard that struck Nebraska and the Dakota Territory in January 1888, the temperature plunged to 36 degrees below zero, and the wind blew at 56 miles per hour. The storm stranded schoolchildren and killed several parents who ventured out to rescue their children. In the spring, melting snow swelled streams, and floods threatened millions of acres. In the fall, a week without rain could turn dry grasslands into tinder, and the slightest spark could ignite a raging prairie fire.

4   Nature could be cruel even under good conditions. Weather that was favorable for crops was also good for breeding insects. Worms and flying pests ravaged corn and wheat. In the 1870s and 1880s swarms of grasshoppers virtually ate up entire farms. Heralded only by the din of buzzing wings, a mile-long cloud of insects would smother the land and devour everything: plants, tree

---

*torrid: intensely hot.

bark, and clothes. As one farmer lamented, the "hoppers left behind nothing but the mortgage." (Norton et al., *A People and a Nation*, pp. 492–493.)

Summary (a.) During the nineteenth century, countless men and women went west in the belief that farming was a way to make money and improve their lot in life. Life on the farm, however, proved to be much harder and more rigorous than most expected. Essentials like lumber and water were hard to come by. The weather was both harsh and unpredictable. In winter, the temperature might plunge as low as 36 degrees below zero while the wind could blow at 56 miles per hour. In summer, scorching heat and drought would suddenly be followed by slashing rain storms. Insects were an additional problem and plagues of insects could devour entire farms.

b. In the nineteenth century, the American West seemed to be the land of opportunity. Many were convinced that farming was the way to make a fortune, but they were deeply disappointed upon their arrival. Lumber and water were hard to obtain. People were forced to build their houses out of sod and burn manure to stay warm. Machinery was scarce and expensive, making farm labor backbreaking and discouraging. If that weren't enough, there was the weather to contend with, and the heat and cold were intolerable. During the Great Blizzard that struck Nebraska and the Dakota Territory in January of 1888, the temperature plunged to 36 degrees below zero and the wind blew at 56 miles per hour. The storm stranded schoolchildren and killed several parents who ventured out to rescue their children. And in the spring, when streams melted, there were floods to contend with. It was a no-win situation, and it is not surprising that so many people gave up and went back east.

c. Throughout the nineteenth century, thousands of men and women decided to make their way west and try their hand at farming in the hopes of earning a fortune. But those hopes were quickly dashed upon their arrival. Life was hard in the west and it was easy to get discouraged and give up, particularly given the weather, which alternated between torrid heat and freezing cold. As if the unpredictable weather were not bad enough, there were floods and fires to contend with, along with plagues of locusts and bees. And the sound of buzzing wings was a warning of disaster. People who migrated west in the nineteenth century were badly fooled by the railroad agents who promised a land of milk and honey in exchange for the price of a ticket.

EXPLANATION Summary *a* is the most effective of the three paragraphs for two reasons. First, *a* sticks to the author's original ideas. Summaries *b* and *c* do not. Summary *b*, for example, ends with the explanation that difficulties out West made people go back East. This may be true, but that point is not made in the original, which means it shouldn't appear in the summary either. The same kind of error turns up in summary *c*. It's probably accurate to say that railroad agents tricked more than one would-be pioneer. But if the original didn't make that point, neither should the summary.

Summary *a* is also the most effective because it includes only the most essential details. A good summary includes only those details critical to fleshing out the main idea. In a personal essay, a detail like the "sound of buzzing wings" gives the reader a wonderful sense of atmosphere. But in the context of a summary, this detail, which appears in summary *c*, breaks a basic rule of summarizing: Include only those details essential to clarifying or proving the main idea.

1. Kinds of Salespersons

1   Because most businesses employ different salespersons to perform different functions, marketing managers must select the kinds of sales personnel that will be most effective in selling the firm's products. Salespersons may be identified as order getters, order takers, and support personnel. A single individual can, and often does, perform all three functions.

2   An **order getter** is responsible for what is sometimes called creative selling: selling the firm's products to new customers and increasing sales to present customers. An order getter must perceive buyers' needs, supply customers with information about the firm's product, and persuade them to buy the product. Order-getting activities may be separated into two groups. In current-customer sales, salespeople concentrate on obtaining additional sales, or leads for prospective sales, from customers who have purchased the firm's products at least once. In new-business sales, sales personnel seek out new prospects and convince them to make an initial purchase of the firm's product. The real estate, insurance, appliance, heavy industrial machinery, and automobile industries in particular depend on new-business sales.

3   An **order taker** handles repeat sales in ways that maintain positive relationships with customers. An order taker sees that customers have products when and where they are needed and in the proper amounts. *Inside order takers* receive incoming mail and telephone orders in some businesses; salespersons in retail stores are also inside order takers. *Outside* (or *field*) *order takers*

travel to customers. Often the buyer and the field salesperson develop a mutually beneficial relationship of placing, receiving, and delivering orders. Both inside and outside order takers are active salespersons and often produce most of their companies' sales.

4 **Support Personnel** Support personnel aid in selling but are more involved in locating *prospects* (likely first-time customers), educating customers, building goodwill for the firm, and providing follow-up service. The most common categories of support personnel are missionary, trade, and technical salespersons.

5   A *missionary salesperson,* who usually works for a manufacturer, visits retailers to persuade them to buy the manufacturer's products. If the retailers agree, they buy the products from wholesalers, who are the manufacturer's actual customers. Missionary salespersons are often employed by producers of medical supplies and pharmaceuticals to promote these products to retail druggists, physicians, and hospitals.

6   A *trade salesperson,* who generally works for a food producer or processor, assists customers in promoting products, especially in retail stores. A trade salesperson may obtain additional shelf space for the products, restock shelves, set up displays, and distribute samples. Because trade salespersons are usually order takers as well, they are not strictly support personnel.

7   A *technical salesperson* assists the company's current customers in technical matters. He or she may explain how to use a product, how it is made, how to install it, or how a system is designed. A technical salesperson should be formally educated in science or engineering. Computers, steel, and chemicals are some of the products handled by technical salespeople. (Pride et al., *Business,* pp. 402–403.)

Summary a. Most businesses employ different salespeople to perform different functions. Some salespeople are order getters, whereas others are order takers. Businesses also need salespeople who can act as support personnel. In some cases, one person can fulfill all three functions.

  The order getter is responsible for what is called creative selling. The goal of creative selling is to get new customers or to increase the number of orders from old customers. Order getters accomplish this by figuring out a customer's needs and persuading that customer to fill those needs by buying products. Generally speaking, there are two kinds of order getting: (1) The salesperson convinces an existing customer to supply leads to new customers or to order more than the usual number of products, or (2) The salesperson seeks out new customers and writes up their orders for products. The second kind of order getting is especially important in the real estate, insurance, appliance, and automobile industries.

Order takers handle repeat sales and maintain positive relationships, whereas support personnel are more essential to locating prospects, educating customers, and building goodwill for the firm.

b. Sales personnel generally fall into three different groups: order getters, order takers, and support personnel. *Order getters* look for new customers and try to increase sales among existing customers. *Order takers* handle repeat sales and do their best to keep customers happy. An inside order taker handles calls in-house, whereas an outside order taker travels to the customer. *Support personnel* do sell, but they are more involved in finding customers or in maintaining the goodwill of existing customers.

Support personnel fall into three categories: (1) Missionary salespeople work for manufacturers and encourage retailers to buy products from wholesalers, who are the manufacturers' real customers. Medical and pharmaceutical companies often employ missionary salespeople. (2) Trade salespeople are most likely to work for food producers. Trade salespeople try to get more shelf space for a particular product, create displays of their products, and distribute samples. (3) As their name implies, technical salespeople show customers the technical ins and outs of a product. They are most likely to be employed by computer, steel, and chemical companies.

c. Sales personnel can be identified as order getters, order takers, and support personnel. Order getters are solely responsible for getting new customers. Order takers handle repeat sales, and support personnel are engaged in public relations.

2. Records and Students' Right to Privacy

1 In this information age, most of us probably have a history tucked away on computer disks. For students, the history may consist of school records, various test scores, and ratings by teachers on everything from citizenship to punctuality. Teachers and other staff members judge a student's character and potential, and others use those judgments to decide whether or not the student should go to this school or get that job. Certainly we need some system of exchanging information about one another; otherwise, we would hire only our friends or attend only those schools

where enough people knew us to vouch for us. However, the kind of information in school records may be very imperfect, and the danger that it will be misinterpreted or fall into the wrong hands is great.

2   In the early 1970s, a series of situations came to light in which information was poorly used or parents and students were denied access to records (for example, when a diagnosis was used to justify sending a child to a class for students with mental retardation). In response, Congress passed the Family Educational Rights and Privacy Act in 1974. The act, also known as the **Buckley amendment,** outlines who may and who may not see a student's record and under what conditions. A clear winner from this legislation is parents, who previously were kept from many of the officially recorded judgments that affected their children's futures. The amendment states that federal funds will be denied to a school if it prevents parents from exercising the right to inspect and review their children's educational records. Parents must receive an explanation or interpretation of the records if they so request.

3   However, the Buckley amendment does not give parents the right to see a teacher's or an administrator's unofficial records. For instance, a teacher's private diary of a class's progress or private notes about a particular child may not be inspected without the teacher's consent.

4   Although the Buckley amendment has undoubtedly reduced the potential for abuse of information, it has had a somewhat chilling effect on teacher's and others' willingness to be candid* in their judgments when writing student recommendations for jobs or colleges. Because students may elect to see a teacher's letter of recommendation, some teachers choose to play it safe and write a vague, general letter that lacks discriminating judgments, pro or con, about the student. In effect, some faculty members and other recommenders have adopted the attitude "Well, if a student doesn't trust me enough to let me write a confidential recommendation, I'll simply write an adequate, safe recommendation." (Ryan and Cooper, *Those Who Can, Teach,* pp. 434, 436.)

Summary a. In 1974, Congress passed the Family Educational Rights and Privacy Act, also known as the Buckley amendment. Although the Buckley amendment does not give parents the right to see unofficial records such as a teacher's diary, it does grant them access to all official records. In fact, any school that denies parents that right can lose federal funding.

---

*candid: open, straightforward.

For parents, the Family Educational Rights and Privacy Act has been a blessing because now they can see the educational records that can powerfully affect their children's future. Teachers feel themselves less blessed by the Buckley amendment because they are now nervous about what they can say in student recommendations. Some simply won't take the risk of writing a candid recommendation. They would rather write a safe one that can't get them into trouble.

b. A student's history consists of records, test scores, and student ratings. For years that history was used to decide a student's future. But prior to 1974, neither students nor parents could view that history.

   Then, in the early seventies, a number of situations involving poor use of student records made it clear that something had to change. At this time, for example, it was possible to assign a student to a class for the learning disabled without letting parents see the records on which such a decision was based. However, such assignments without full disclosure became impossible with the passage of the Family Educational Rights and Privacy Act in 1974. The act, also known as the Buckley amendment, outlines who may or may not view student records, and it allows parents to see all official records. It further states that federal funds will be denied any school that prevents parents from exercising their right to access their children's records.

   Parents have been understandably overjoyed at the act's passage, but teachers have been less so. Now when students ask for a recommendation, many instructors are fearful about making any comments that might be considered negative. To protect themselves, they are prone to writing safe recommendations that won't get them into trouble.

c. It's hard to imagine any piece of legislation that's done more harm than the Family Educational Rights and Privacy Act of 1974. Also known as the Buckley amendment, this legislation gives parents the right to view all student records. The result has been that teachers are now fearful of saying what they think in recommendations, and they say what's safe rather than what's true.

◼ EXERCISE 2

DIRECTIONS Read and summarize the following passages.

EXAMPLE The search for a cheap, quick, and long-lasting insecticide was finally successful in 1939, when a Swiss chemist, Paul

Müller, confirmed the bug-killing properties of dichlorodiphenyl-trichloroethane (DDT). Used on everything from the potato beetle to disease-bearing lice and fleas (as well as in World War II to fumigate troops' bedding and clothing), DDT was heralded as a huge success for twentieth-century agriculture. But within twenty years, many insects developed strains resistant to the poison. Meanwhile, it wreaked havoc on the food chain by killing off insects beneficial to the environment. In the end, DDT was not a boon to the human race. If anything, it proved a disaster, the proportions of which are still becoming known.

Summary   *When it was first introduced, DDT was considered a miracle chemical that could destroy pesky insects like lice, fleas, and beetles, but within twenty years it proved to be more disaster than miracle. Unfortunately, it killed off valuable insects as well as those that did harm.*

EXPLANATION As it should, this summary begins with the main idea of the original passage. In addition to the main idea, the sample summary also adds just enough supporting details to answer the potential question: How did the supposed miracle turn into a disaster?

1. The American family today is very different from a half century ago. In the fifties, husbands were usually considered the leaders of the family. They were the ones who made the major buying decisions and distributed income, in the form of an allowance, to their wives and children. The wife's main role was to take care of the home. But even here, she based her actions largely on what would please or help her husband. If, for example, he liked to eat dinner early so he could work in the evening, she would set the dinner hour accordingly. Nowadays, however, power and authority tend to be shared between husband and wife. Men have started taking responsibility for household chores. They also shop for groceries, toys, and cleaning products. Women today have a much greater voice in decisions about purchases and lifestyle. For instance, automakers have found that women constitute a large portion of their consumer market, and they have changed their car designs accordingly. Although changes in the family have been rightly attributed to feminist demands for equality, there is another source for the marked shift in power relations. In the current economy, it's usually essential that both spouses work full-time, and wives who bring in half the family's

income are far less willing to turn major decisions over to their husbands than were wives in the 1950s.

Summary _____

_____

_____

_____

2. Since 1928, the year penicillin was discovered, humans have significantly improved their health and longevity by using antibiotics to conquer infections. However, the misuse of antibiotics is reducing their effectiveness. Antibiotics are often prescribed and taken when they're not necessary. As a matter of fact, researchers estimate that as many as 50 percent of antibiotic prescriptions are inappropriate. Many people fail to take antibiotics correctly, and they often don't complete a full course of medication. When a course of medication is not finished, the bacteria that remain in the body can grow stronger. Antibiotics are also overused because they are injected into livestock and, thus, into our food. In addition, we put them into many soap products. Our overexposure tends to eliminate the weaker bacteria while encouraging the growing number of antibiotic-resistant strains. As a result, some infections that were once curable with antibiotics are becoming deadly.

Summary _____

_____

_____

_____

EXERCISE 3

DIRECTIONS Write a summary of each selection.

1. **Negative Aspects of Internet Use**

In spite of all its positive aspects, the Internet has its detractors. Some attack the use of the Internet as being time-consuming and addictive. In reality, research has shown that 90 percent of people who get on the Internet do what they need to do and then get off. It's the other 10 percent who are problem users. Early research stated that "although the new electronic media are frequently criticized for their so-called addictive qualities, little empirical evidence has been found to support the assertion that heavy media use is psychologically or physiologically addictive."

Newer findings indicate that **cyberaddiction**—compulsive pre-occupied usage of the Internet, chatrooms, and the World Wide Web—can be a major negative aspect of Net usage. (Cyberaddiction is also called computer addiction, impulse control disorder, and Internet addictive disorder.) It is now believed that an Internet user can become addicted to the point of neglecting personal and work responsibilities, and becoming socially isolated. A study of college students, for example, found that 73 percent of students accessed the Internet at least once a week, and 13 percent of students indicated that their computer use interfered with personal functioning. Typically, computer addicts are bright, creative individuals who also feel lonely and isolated. They also can be bored, depressed, angry, or frustrated. In one study, "about 71 percent were diagnosed as suffering from bipolar disorder, commonly called manic depression."

The results of cyberaddiction can include lost jobs, college expulsions, emotional breakdowns, pedophiles stalking youngsters, marriages destroyed, domestic violence, unchecked deepening depression, heightened anxiety, mounting debts, broken trust, lies, and cover-ups.

Symptoms of cyberaddiction include lying about or hiding the level of Internet usage, being preoccupied with using the Internet, and neglecting everything else in one's life. It's like a craving that you continue to satisfy despite the problems it's causing. On the other hand, spending time on-line may be more positive than excessive time in front of a television or playing video games. The key question to ask might be, "Is your on-line time disrupting your face-to-face relationships, allowing you to hide from participating in face-to-face interactions, or forcing you to put other elements of your life on hold?" If you are an addict or think you are overdoing cyberconnectedness, ask yourself what you would do instead of spending so much time on-line. Learn how to control the computer so it doesn't control you, and set definite time limits to your computer use. Some people who are addicted may need mental health therapy. (Berko et al., *Communicating*, pp. 135–136.)

Summary _____

_____

_____

_____

_____

_____

_____

_____

_____

_____

_____

_____

2. **Attitudes at General Motors**

Attitudes play a major role in all organizations. And at few places are they more critical today than at General Motors. GM is going through the painful process of closing plants and terminating thousands of workers. The attitudes of those workers, combined with those of managers involved in making critical decisions, are key to the potential success of GM's efforts.

Two plants in particular provide a marked contrast in workers' attitudes at GM. Workers at each plant know that they are working at a plant that may be closed and that they are fighting for job survival. One plant is the GM facility in Orion Township, in Michigan. Orion is one of GM's newest plants, built in the late 1980s. Most workers at Orion were transferred to the plant when older plants were shut down.

Orion workers take a very adversarial posture toward GM. Most are long-time members of the United Auto Workers, or UAW. Moreover, because they are primarily from Michigan and grew up in the auto industry, they are accustomed to the relatively high wages and benefits paid to UAW members.

The UAW leadership at Orion wants as little as possible to do with employee involvement. Some of the union leaders believe that product quality is something that should not concern them. They feel that their workers should follow orders but do nothing more, and that it's management's job to worry about quality and improvement.

There is also considerable hostility among the workers themselves at Orion. Fights are common, for example, and police investigations are routine. Company data suggests that Orion ranks twenty-second among GM's twenty-eight plants in terms of productivity, and a recent spot check found unacceptable defects in eighty-eight of one hundred cars.

The GM factory in Oklahoma City provides a sharp contrast to Orion. Most workers at this plant are in their first UAW-represented job. The wages and benefits they receive, while comparable to those in other auto plants, are somewhat higher than those of other Oklahoma workers in the manufacturing sector.

When the Oklahoma City workers realized that their jobs were endangered, they rallied behind management to help improve productivity and quality at the plant. For example, they have willingly adopted several popular Japanese management techniques, such as just-in-time and employee involvement. These and other changes have helped make the Oklahoma City plant one of the most productive facilities owned by GM.

Many of the workers there eagerly volunteer for the plant's various training programs. Between fifty and one hundred employees per day receive training in everything from equipment operation to computer manufacturing to preparation for high-school equivalency tests. In contrast to most GM facilities, the training at Oklahoma City is provided by union members rather than by management. (Van Fleet and Peterson, *Contemporary Management*, p. 360.)

Summary _____

_____

_____

_____

_____

_____

_____

_____

_____

_____

_____

_____

 # Writing Summaries of Assigned Readings

If you are assigned to write a summary that will be turned in to your instructor, all the pointers mentioned so far most certainly apply. However, you will need to consider some other requirements.

Don't Forget the Author and Title

If you are turning in your summary, make sure to add the author and title of the selection. Sometimes instructors want that information in a heading or a footnote, but often you'll be expected to weave it into the opening sentence. When you are assigned to write a summary, always check with your instructor to find out how he or she wants you to handle information about author and title.

Make Connections Between Sentences

Writing summaries requires you to combine information from different parts of the original text. As a result, the original connections between sentences can get lost. For that reason, it's important to read your summary aloud and check to hear how your sentences flow together. If you can't figure out why one sentence follows another, you may need to add some transitions to connect the ideas. As you know from Chapter 3, transitions are verbal bridges that help readers move easily from one thought to another. Here's a list of the most common transitions.

Common Transitional Signals

Transitions indicating an addition to the original train of thought:
also, in addition, further, furthermore, last, moreover, first, second, secondly,* too

Transitions indicating that the author is changing, challenging, or contradicting the original train of thought:
although, after all, but, by (in) contrast, however, nevertheless, on the contrary, yet, still, despite that fact, rather, on the other hand, regardless

Transitions signaling that the author is pointing out similarities:
similarly, likewise, by the same token, in the same vein

Transitions that introduce examples and illustrations:
for example, for instance, specifically, in other words, that is

Transitions that introduce the effects of some cause:
as a result, consequently, thus, therefore, hence, in response

---

*Many handbooks for college composition frown on the use of "secondly," so you should probably avoid using it. However, you will see it in print.

Transitions that help readers follow a sequence in time:
in the meantime, next, soon, after a while, in time, of late, thereafter, afterward, finally, then, before

Transitions that repeat a point already made:
in short, in brief, in conclusion, in other words, on the whole, in summary, to reiterate, to sum up, to repeat

Revise If Necessary

If the summary you're writing is to be handed in for an assignment, you should revise to double-check your word choice, grammar, and punctuation.

Synthesizing Different Sources on the Same Subject

Imagine you are assigned to read your history book's account of President John Adams's* tenure in the White House and that account emphasizes Adams's praiseworthy efforts to stop the country's undeclared war with the French. Now imagine as well that you are assigned an outside reading. The outside reading harshly criticizes Adams's role in bringing about passage of the Alien and Sedition Acts.* Having read about two different sides of the same subject, John Adams, how to you think you should proceed? Should you try to remember the main idea of each reading separately? Or should you look for a way to **synthesize,** or combine, the two different positions into one unified or connected piece of information?

If you said yes to the second choice, it may be because you already know a basic rule of memory: The human mind has an easier time storing connected pieces of information than unrelated ideas, theories, or facts. Thus, whenever you read different authors who talk about the same subject, it pays to see if you can combine their ideas into a synthesis statement. **Synthesis statements** identify and clarify relationships between different sources that discuss the same topic.

Take the two readings mentioned above. Each one focuses on a different aspect, or side, of Adams's career. One reading notes a pos-

---

*John Adams: (1735–1826) the second president of the United States (1797–1801).
*Alien and Sedition Acts: acts that discriminated against the foreign born and blurred the distinction between political discussion and attempts to overthrow the government.

itive accomplishment, the other focuses on a more negative achievement. A synthesis statement like the following links the two readings and would help you remember the ideas in both: "Fans of John Adams like to point to his abilities as a peacemaker during the conflict with the French, but his critics can't forget that the Alien and Sedition Acts came into being during his presidency."

Taking the time to create synthesis statements based on two or even three different sources of information does more than improve your memory. It also deepens your understanding of the individual viewpoints. To create a synthesis statement, you have to think long and hard about each reading and how it connects to the other reading or readings. This kind of prolonged processing of information is bound to improve your level of comprehension.

Useful Questions to Ask

When writers disagree, it's fairly easy to come up with a synthesis statement that emphasizes the authors' differences of opinion. Yet there will be times when the readings you want to synthesize are more similar than different. At those times, the following questions will prove useful. They will help you pinpoint the connection between or among the readings.

1. Do the authors express a similar point of view only in different forms, say poem and essay, fiction and nonfiction?

2. Does one author offer a general interpretation, whereas the other cites specific examples of the same interpretation?

3. Do the readings address the same topic or issue but from different time frames—say, past and present—or from the point of view of different groups—say, the elderly and the young, or the working person versus a corporation?

4. Does one author focus on the cause or causes of a problem while the other looks more closely at a solution?

5. Does one author zero in on the causes of an event while the other concentrates on the aftermath of that event?

6. Do the authors come from different schools of thought? Does one author, for example, concentrate on the psychological roots of an event while the other views it from an economic perspective?

7. Does one author offer an interpretation that is challenged by the other?

Adding a Third Source

Suppose that after reading two different accounts of John Adams's term as president, you were assigned an essay that focused on Adams's relationship to his wife, Abigail, and the essay stresses his readiness to accept her political counsel. You might then decide to revise your synthesis statement to include that additional information. Here, then, is a synthesis statement that sums up all three points of view: "Hardly anyone faults John Adams in his role as Abigail's husband, but when it comes to his presidency, the views are more varied. Fans like to point to his abilities as a peacemaker during the conflict with the French, but his critics can't forget that the Alien and Sedition Acts came into being during his presidency." This is the kind of synthesis statement that can be invaluable during exam reviews. It offers you the broad general outlines of ideas you've covered in your course work, leaving you to fill in the specifics. As you fill in those specific details, you'll be in a better position to determine which ideas are already clear in your mind and which ones need further study.

The Essential Steps

In the end, it doesn't matter whether you are synthesizing two or three different sources. The steps are the same:

1. Read each selection carefully to determine the main idea.

2. Write down the main idea of each selection.

3. Read over the main ideas. As you read, try to determine the relationship between the various points of view expressed in the readings. (Here's where you can use the questions on page 195.)

4. Write a synthesis statement that reveals how the different readings are connected.

5. Check your statement to make sure it doesn't contradict or misstate the ideas it links.

6. Add the statement to your review notes.

Synthesizing for a Purpose

Whatever you do, don't create synthesis statements and then forget about them. They should be the backbone of your exam reviews. If you can look at those statements and fill in the specific details that make them meaningful, you are ready to be tested. If you can't, you need to go back to the original readings or your notes and review what you've learned from each source.

CHECK YOUR UNDERSTANDING

What should a good synthesis statement accomplish?

_____

_____

How can synthesis statements help during exam reviews?

_____

_____

EXERCISE 4

DIRECTIONS Read each group of passages. Then circle the number of the statement that more effectively synthesizes all three passages. *Note:* Keep in mind that an effective synthesis statement should not in any way contradict the passages it combines.

EXAMPLE

a. John Steinbeck's *Grapes of Wrath* movingly conveys the misery facing the migrant workers who, throughout the depression, traveled Route 66 across the country, searching for work. Steinbeck writes, "Route 66 is the path of people in flight, refugees from dust and shrinking land, from the thunder of tractors and shrinking ownership, from the twisting winds that howl up out of Texas, from the foods that bring no richness to the land and steal what little richness is there."

b. Statistics suggest the magnitude of the Great Depression's effect on the business world. The stock market crash in October 1929 shocked investors and caused a financial panic. Between 1929 and 1933, one hundred thousand businesses failed; corporate profits fell from $10 billion to $1 billion; and the gross national product was cut in half. Banks failed by the thousands. (Adapted from Norton et al., *A People and a Nation*, p. 754.)

c. As unemployment soared during the Great Depression, both men and women suffered homelessness. In 1932, a squad of New York City police officers arrested twenty-five in "Hoover Valley," the village of tents and crates constructed in Central Park. All over the country, people were so poor they lived in miserable little camps called "Hoovervilles," named in sarcastic honor of President Herbert Hoover, whose policy on the Depression was to pretend it didn't exist.

Synthesis   1. During the Great Depression, no one suffered more than the men
Statement   and women who earned their living as migrant workers.

②. The Great Depression took a terrible toll on people from all walks of life.

EXPLANATION Passages *a*, *b*, and *c* all give specific examples of different groups that suffered as a result of the Great Depression. Statement 1 is incorrect because it puts the suffering of migrant workers above the suffering of the other groups, and none of the passages makes that point. Sentence 2 is a better synthesis statement because it combines the ideas in all three passages without adding any ideas that weren't there in the first place.

1. a. When World War II broke out in Europe on September 1, 1939, the United States was the only world power without a propaganda agency. Ever since World War I, Americans had been suspicious of the claim that propaganda could be used to good effect. Many believed that British propaganda had helped maneuver the United States into World War I. They had also not forgotten the bloody anti-German riots that had been touched off by movies like America's own *Beast of Berlin* (1919). To most Americans, *propaganda* was simply a dirty word, no matter what its purpose.

b. In 1939, as the world began to career into World War II, the president of the United States, Franklin Delano Roosevelt, applied pressure on Hollywood to make feature films that were little more than propaganda vehicles, but Hollywood producers were not so ready to give in. Committed to the doctrine of pure entertainment, pure profit, and above all to the need for America to stay out of the war, most balked at making films that reflected the horror engulfing Europe.

    c. The Japanese bombed Pearl Harbor on December 7, 1941. Astonished and outraged, the United States entered World War II. On December 17 of the same year, President Roosevelt appointed Lowell Mellett as head of the Hollywood propaganda office. Mellett's job was to make sure that Hollywood films aided the war effort, and for the most part, Hollywood was happy to cooperate by making films that celebrated the war effort and castigated* America's enemies.

Synthesis Statement 1. Up until the bombing of Pearl Harbor, the United States did not have an official propaganda office, a terrible mistake that produced unexpected and horrifying consequences.

    2. Before the bombing of Pearl Harbor, Hollywood, like most of America, mistrusted propaganda. But after the bombing, propaganda became an acceptable part of the war effort and Hollywood embraced it.

2. a. The Egyptians revered Maat as the goddess of justice who weighed the hearts of the dead on a scale. The right balance guaranteed a happy afterlife; the wrong one promised torment.

    b. The ancient Greeks worshipped Dike as the goddess of justice. When the Romans inherited her, they renamed her Justitia and represented her with a blindfold around her eyes to symbolize her lack of bias.*

    c. With the arrival of Christianity and the rejection of the ancient gods, the goddess of justice was demoted to a saint and people apparently became suspicious of her ability to fairly deal out justice. Santa Justitia was often depicted holding an unevenly balanced scale. The implication was that the rich got different justice than the poor.

Synthesis Statement 1. Whereas the ancient Greeks and Romans held the goddess of justice in great respect, the early Christians seem to have been a bit more suspicious of how justice was meted* out.

    2. The Christians refused to accept all of the ancient gods and goddesses, including Justitia, the goddess of justice.

---

*castigated: harshly criticized or punished.
*bias: prejudice in favor of one side or another (for more on this subject, see Chapter 10).
*meted: distributed.

3. a. In the 1992 election, political action committees (PACs) contributed over $50 million to the various campaigns. The 1996 election saw even greater amounts of PAC money pour into campaign coffers. This sort of funding of the presidency puts a price tag on democracy: Whoever contributes the most money has the most access to the president.

   b. In the name of campaign reform, there are those who would make illegal the contributions of political action committees (PACs). Yet these contributions, no matter how high the sums, are nothing more than a legitimate form of free speech. Any group who wants to contribute to a political campaign as a show of support should have the right to do so.

   c. Given the millions of dollars that were contributed to campaign funds in the 1992 and 1996 elections, it's not hard to understand why enthusiasm for campaign reform has never been higher. Yet, while outlawing all contributions by political action committees (PACs) seems extreme, it's clear that they have to be more closely monitored and accounted for.

Synthesis Statement 1. When it comes to the campaign contributions of political action committees, or PACs, there's a good deal of disagreement. But on one point, no one disagrees: PACs contributed huge sums to the presidential campaigns of 1992 and 1996.

2. Political action committees (PACs) and their contributions to political campaigns may be controversial, but there is no proof of the claim that has so often been made—that they weaken the democratic process.

4. a. In 1998, many people objected to President Clinton's proposed plan to bomb Iraq, and they made their feelings known by sending e-mails to the president.

   b. In the campaign against the elimination of land mines* around the world, computers played a key role. Those who supported the elimination of the mines kept in touch and up-to-date via e-mail.

   c. In 1998, activists fighting to make insurers extend hospital stays for breast cancer patients used the Internet to publicize their fight and collect signatures for petitions.

Synthesis Statement 1. Because of the Internet, people who never found the time to write letters are managing to stay in touch.

---

*land mines: explosive devices, usually laid below the surface of the ground, that explode if stepped on.

2. Thanks to the Internet, it's become easier for political activists around the world to stay in touch.

5. a. With its brilliant and innovative techniques, D. W. Griffith's *The Birth of a Nation* dramatically changed the face of American movies forever. Before Griffith, movies contained neither close-ups nor fade-outs. It was Griffith who brought those two techniques to the screen. With the exception of Orson Welles and the film *Citizen Kane*, no other director and no other film have been as influential as Griffith and *The Birth of a Nation.*

   b. By 1910, motion pictures had become an art form, thanks to creative directors like D. W. Griffith. Griffith's most famous work, *The Birth of a Nation* (1915), an epic film about the Civil War and Reconstruction, used innovative techniques—close-ups, fade-outs, and battle scenes—that gave viewers heightened drama and excitement. Unfortunately, the film fanned racial prejudice by depicting African-Americans as a threat to white moral values. An organized black protest against it was led by the infant National Association for the Advancement of Colored People (NAACP). (Norton et al., *A People and a Nation*, p. 583.)

   c. Despite the film's famed innovations, it's nearly impossible for moviegoers to take pleasure in D. W. Griffith's *The Birth of a Nation.* Powered by racism, the film enrages more than it entertains, and it's no wonder that the NAACP picketed the film when it first appeared. Members of the group correctly feared that Griffith's film would revitalize the Ku Klux Klan.

Synthesis Statement 1. D. W. Griffith was a famous film director who profoundly influenced the American film industry; in fact, Griffith changed the face of American film.

2. Although no one can deny the contribution that D. W. Griffith's *The Birth of a Nation* made to film history, many find it hard to overlook the racism that runs through the film.

◀ EXERCISE 5

DIRECTIONS Read each set of statements. Then write a synthesis statement that links them together.

EXAMPLE

a. Even before the war, Nazi officials had targeted Jews throughout Europe for extermination. By war's end, about 6 million Jews had been forced into concentration camps and had been systematically killed by firing squads, unspeakable tortures, and gas chambers. (Norton et al., *A People and a Nation*, p. 843.)

b. To protest Hitler's treatment of the Jews during World War II, the philosopher Simone Weil went on a prolonged hunger strike. In the end, Weil starved to death rather than take food while the prisoners of concentration camps were being reduced to walking skeletons.

c. Born to a wealthy Swedish family, Raoul Wallenberg could easily have ignored the horror Adolf Hitler unleashed on the world. But he chose not to. Using his considerable daring, charm, and brains, Wallenberg saved the lives of thousands of Jewish refugees who would have died a horrible death without his help.

Synthesis Statement   *During World War II, the tragic plight of the Jews stirred people like Simone Weil and Raoul Wallenberg to extraordinary acts of heroism.*

EXPLANATION All three passages focus on the plight of the Jews in World War II, and two of the passages describe how two people tried to stop or hinder what was happening. As you can see, the synthesis statement weaves together those two threads of thought.

1. a. Having studied the meditative states of monks and yogis,* researcher Elmer Green advocates and practices meditation. For him, it is a way of making the mind enter a deeper state of consciousness.

b. In the 1960s and 1970s, the Essalen Institute at Big Sur was the center of what was then called the "human potential movement." At the heart of Essalen and the movement in general was Michael Murphy, who had cofounded the institute with his former classmate Richard Price. Although Murphy eventually moved away from the anti-intellectualism of Essalen's teachers, he remains committed to the daily practice of meditation. For him, the meditative state is a way to unlock human creativity.

c. Although many exaggerated claims have been made for the benefits of meditation, the research supporting those claims has not always been forthcoming. Much of the existing research consists of personal anecdotes, or stories, and many of the studies

---

*yogis: people versed in meditation and focused more on the spirit than on the body.

designed to test the effects of meditation have been poorly designed.

Synthesis Statement

_____

_____

_____

2. a. Every society is concerned with the socialization of its children—that is, with making sure that children learn early on what is considered socially correct and morally ethical behavior.

   b. In Asian societies, the family is considered the most important agent of socialization.

   c. In the last decade, a number of studies have suggested that in the United States, a child's peer group may be overtaking the family as the most powerful agent of socialization.

Synthesis Statement

_____

_____

_____

3. a. No matter how far back in history we look, we find human beings making and listening to music. . . . At some point in our past, it was important enough that all human beings born, no matter whether Bengalese, Cruit, or Quechua, no matter whether blind, left-handed, or freckled, were not merely *capable* of making music; they *required* music to add meaning to their lives. (Diane Ackerman, *A Natural History of the Senses.* New York: Vintage Books, 1991, p. 210.)

   b. The little girl would take no notice of anyone who entered the room. She seemed locked inside her own private world, unable or unwilling to leave it. But if her uncle played the piano, she would sit next to the piano bench, listening raptly,* a smile playing around her lips. As far as anyone knew, the music of the piano was the only sound that reached her.

   c. Music doesn't just seem to soothe the spirit, it also appears to have a powerful effect on the body. In two different studies conducted at the University of Wisconsin, patients suffering from high blood pressure experienced a five- to ten-point decrease in

_____

*raptly: intently.

their blood pressure readings after listening to the music of Mozart for a half hour.

Synthesis
Statement

_____

_____

_____

4. a. Anne Frank was a German-Jewish girl who hid from the Nazis with her parents, their friends, and some other fugitives in an Amsterdam attic from 1942 to 1944. Her diary covering the years of hiding was found by friends and published in 1947. Against the background of the mass murder of European Jewry, the book presents an impressive picture of how a group of hunted people found a way to live together in almost intolerable proximity.* It is also a stirring portrait of a young girl whose youthful spirit triumphs over the misery of her surroundings.

   b. *The Diary of Anne Frank* has been read by millions. It has been both a successful play and film. People are drawn to the story of Anne and her family because it reminds us that the human spirit has enormous resiliency* even in the face of terrifying evil.

   c. In *Surviving and Other Essays,* psychologist and concentration camp survivor Bruno Bettelheim argued that the world had embraced Anne Frank's story too uncritically. For Bettelheim, Anne's fate demonstrated "how efforts at disregarding in private life what goes on around one in society can hasten one's destruction."

Synthesis
Statement

_____

_____

_____

---

*proximity: closeness.
*resiliency: the ability to respond or spring back.

■ **DIGGING DEEPER: READING 1**

LOOKING AHEAD A number of passages in this chapter focused on events that took place during World War II. The two readings that follow evaluate the event that ended it, President Harry Truman's decision to drop the atomic bomb. The reading, drawn from a current history text, expresses doubts about the necessity of Truman's decision.

REEXAMINING TRUMAN'S MOTIVES

1 What motivated President Harry Truman to order the dropping of the atomic bomb? Truman explained that he did it for only one reason: to end the war as soon as possible and thus prevent the loss of 1 million American casualties in an invasion of Japan. An earlier generation of historians, writing in the aftermath of the war, echoed President Truman's explanation. But more recently historians have revised this interpretation: They argue that Japan might have surrendered even if the atomic bombs had not been dropped, and they dispute Truman's high estimate of casualties as being pure fiction and several times the likely figure. These revisionists* have studied the Potsdam Conference of July 1945 attended by Truman, Joseph Stalin, and Winston Churchill. In their research, they have demonstrated the value of diaries as historical evidence by consulting those kept by certain participants, notably Secretary of War Henry Stimson and Truman himself.

2   Scholars cite Stimson's diary as evidence that Truman's chief motivations included not only ending the war but also impressing the Russians with America's military might and minimizing the USSR's* military participation in the final defeat and postwar occupation of Japan. On July 21 Stimson reported to Truman that the army had successfully tested an atomic device in New Mexico. Clearly emboldened by the news, Truman said that possession of the bomb "gave him an entirely new feeling of confidence. . . ." The next day, Stimson discussed the news with British prime minister Churchill. "Now I know what happened to Truman," Churchill responded. "When he got to the meeting after having read this report he was a changed man. He told the Russians just where they got off and generally bossed the whole meeting."

---

*revisionists: people who challenge a long-standing view or theory.
*USSR: Union of Soviet Socialist Republics.

3 A few historians contend that the decision to drop the atomic bomb was partly racist. As evidence, they point to Truman's handwritten diary entry in which he discussed using the bomb against "the Japs," whom he denounced as "savages, ruthless, merciless and fanatic." Others cite these words to claim that Truman desired to avenge the Japanese attack at Pearl Harbor. It is clear that while personal diaries can help to settle some historical disagreements, they can also generate new interpretive disputes.

4 The deeply emotional question about the necessity for dropping the atomic bomb has stirred debates among the public as well as among historians. In 1995, for example, the Smithsonian Institution provoked a furor with its plan for an exhibit prompted by the fiftieth anniversary of the decision to drop the bomb. Rather than incur the wrath of politicians, veterans' groups, and other Americans outraged by what they perceived to be an anti-American interpretation of events, the Smithsonian shelved most of the exhibit. (Norton et al., *A People and a Nation,* p. 766.)

Sharpening Your Skills

DIRECTIONS Answer the following questions by filling in the blanks or circling the letter of the correct response.

1. What's the main idea of this reading?

_____

2. According to the reading, why was Henry Stimson's diary important?

_____

3. In paragraph 2, the authors use the word *emboldened:* "Clearly emboldened by the news, Truman said that possession of the bomb 'gave him an entirely new feeling of confidence.'" Based on the context, how would you define the word *emboldened?*

_____

4. What pattern of organization is at work in paragraph 4?

_____

5. Write a summary of the reading.

Reexamining Truman's Motives

_____

_____

_____

_____

_____

_____

_____

_____

_____

_____

■ **DIGGING DEEPER: READING 2**

LOOKING AHEAD This excerpt was taken from a textbook published in 1965. As you read it, compare this author's perspective with the one expressed in the previous reading.

TRUMAN'S CHOICE

1 Although many Americans have expressed contrition over exploding the first atomic bombs, it is difficult to see how the Pacific war could otherwise have been concluded, except by a long and bitter invasion of Japan. . . . The explosion over Hiroshima caused fewer civilian casualties than the repeated B-29 bombings of Tokyo, and those big bombers would have had to wipe out one city after another if the war had not ended in August. Japan had enough military capability—more than 5000 planes with kamikaze*-trained pilots and at least 2 million ground troops—to have made our planned invasion of the Japanese home islands in the fall of 1945 an exceedingly bloody affair for both sides. And that would have been followed by a series of bitterly protracted battles on Japanese soil, the effects of which even time could hardly have healed. Moreover, as Russia would have been a full partner in these campaigns, the end result would have been partition of Japan, as happened to Germany.

2 Even after the two atomic bombs had been dropped, and the Potsdam declaration had been clarified to assure Japan that she could keep her emperor, the surrender was a very near thing. Hirohito* had to override his two chief military advisers and take the responsibility of accepting the Potsdam terms. That he did on 14 August, but even after that, a military coup d'état* to sequester* the emperor, kill his cabinet, and continue the war was narrowly averted. Hirohito showed great moral courage; and the promise to retain him in power despite the wishes of Russia (which wanted the war prolonged and Japan given over to anarchy*) was a very wise decision.

---

*kamikaze: related to a suicidal air attack.
*Hirohito: the emperor of Japan.
*coup d'état: the sudden overthrow of government by a small group of persons previously in positions of authority.
*sequester: isolate.
*anarchy: lawlessness.

3 After preliminary arrangements had been made at Manila with General MacArthur's and Admiral Nimitz's staffs, an advance party was flown into Atsugi airfield near Tokyo on 28 August. Scores of ships of the United States Pacific Fleet, and of the British Far Eastern Fleet, then entered Tokyo Bay. On 2 September 1945, General MacArthur, General Umezu, the Japanese foreign minister, and representatives of Great Britain, China, Russia, Australia, Canada, New Zealand, the Netherlands, and France signed the surrender documents on the deck of the battleship *Missouri*. (Samuel Eliot Morison, *The Oxford History of the American People.* New York: Oxford University Press, 1965, pp. 1044–1045.)

Sharpening Your Skills

DIRECTIONS Answer the following questions by filling in the blanks or circling the letter of the correct response.

1. What's the main idea of this reading?

   _____

   _____

2. Which of the following is *not* a supporting detail used to make the author's main idea convincing?

   a. The explosion over Hiroshima caused fewer deaths than bombing Japan would have caused.

   b. Long before the bombing of Nagasaki and Hiroshima, the Japanese were prepared to surrender.

   c. Russia would have been involved more and, therefore, been able to demand the right to control part of Japan.

3. Based on context, how would you define the word *contrition* in the first sentence of paragraph 1?

   _____

   _____

4. Write a synthesis statement that connects this reading to the previous one.

   _____

   _____

WORD NOTES: BORROWING FROM THE FRENCH

The reading on page 208 introduced the French term *coup d'état* (coo-day-tah) to describe the planned overthrow of the Japanese emperor Hirohito. Here are three more words with French origins that you can add to your vocabulary.

1. Blasé (blah-zay). A person described as blasé is considered sophisticated and worldly-wise, the kind of person who seems to have done and seen everything at least twice.

   Sample Sentence Born to parents of both wealth and taste, ten-year-old Seymour had traveled widely and already become a bit *blasé*.

2. Raison d'être (ray-zon det'ra). This French expression means "reason for being," and it refers to a person's main goal or purpose in life.

   Sample Sentence Now that his wife has left him, his young daughter has become his *raison d'être*.

3. Savoir faire (sav-wahr fair). This phrase describes the ability to get things done with skill, tact, and charm.

   Sample Sentence What the new CEO lacked in *savoir faire*, she made up for in determination and hard work.

Fill in the blanks with one of these words or phrases: *coup d'état, blasé, raison d'être, savoir faire.*

1. The generals were determined to regain their power even if it meant a _____.

2. Even at seventy, he had the kind of _____ that made him a sought-after companion.

3. Impressed by her surroundings but determined not to show it, the teenager tried to act as _____ as possible.

4. Even as a teenager, earning money and getting rich had been his _____.

Test 1: Reviewing the Key Points

DIRECTIONS Answer the following questions by filling in the blanks or circling the correct response.

1. Generally speaking, when you summarize, your goal is to reduce the original material to about _____.

2. *True* or *False*. Introductions, personal anecdotes, and quoted material are especially important in summaries.

3. *True* or *False*. It's a good idea to underline and annotate before you write your summary.

4. *True* or *False*. Your personal opinion should not make its way into a summary.

5. *True* or *False*. Whether you are summarizing a chapter section for yourself or writing a summary for your instructor, the same rules or principles always apply.

6. *True* or *False*. When you write a summary, you never have to fuss with transitions.

7. When you synthesize information from different sources that focus on the same topic, you need to create a statement that _____
   _____.

8. *True* or *False*. Synthesis statements always pinpoint the differences between authors.

9. During exam reviews, synthesis statements provide a _____
   _____, leaving you to _____.

10. *True* or *False*. Synthesis statements are not effective if you are dealing with more than two sources.

Test 2: Selecting the Better Summary

DIRECTIONS Read each selection. Then circle the letter of the summary that follows the pointers outlined in the box on pages 177–178.

1. The Triumph of American Movies

1 Moving pictures in America got their start in carnivals and side-shows. Cheap amusements, they were the poor person's substitute for live theater. Popular almost from the beginning, movies were still not considered quite legitimate in the early years between 1896 and 1910, and "nice" people didn't always admit to watching them. However, by the 1920s, the "picture shows" had become a popular and accepted form of entertainment. American movies had begun to take over the foreign market, and movies were America's fifth-biggest industry.

2 It was in the twenties that American director Mack Sennett brought the Keystone Cops to the silver screen. Wildly popular with audiences, the Keystone Cops specialized in endless chases, scantily clad young women, and slapstick comedy of the pie-in-your-face variety. The 1920s also saw the rise of screen idols such as Mary Pickford and Rudolph Valentino. While Pickford played roles that celebrated the power of little-girl innocence, Valentino specialized in Latin lovers, whose handsome face and burning eyes made women swoon. Actors like Pickford and Valentino were the first movie stars to be so popular they actually had fan clubs, a common enough occurrence now but not then.

3 However, it was the British-born Charlie Chaplin, in his role as "The Little Tramp," who truly won the world's heart. With his cane, bowler hat, and ragged, baggy pants, Chaplin breathed life into corny stories about a young man whose aspirations never matched his abilities and who rarely if ever won the heart of the girl he loved. Chaplin's genius was to make his audiences laugh and cry at the same time, and they loved him for it—not just in his adopted American home but abroad as well. Almost single-handedly, Chaplin won for the American movie industry an unrivaled mass audience that spanned the continents.

4 Only German moviemakers briefly competed with the Americans in the twenties. In films like *The Cabinet of Dr. Caligari,* German directors such as F. W. Murnau produced highly acclaimed Expressionist* dramas that specialized in heightened emotional states of horror and madness. But it wasn't long before American

*Expressionist: a movement in the arts that focused on extreme states of mind.

money had beckoned the Germans to Hollywood and consolidated America's domination of the picture industry.

Summary a. American movies started out in carnivals and sideshows. Movies were what poor people watched because they couldn't afford a ticket to the theater. But by the 1920s, the American movie industry was a virtual blockbuster: It was the fifth largest industry in the country. In the 1920s, America was also in heated competition with Germany for dominance over the world movie industry, but it wasn't long before the Germans were won over by American money, leaving the field clear for American domination. In addition, the Germans never produced movie stars as popular as Mary Pickford, Rudolph Valentino, and Charlie Chaplin. It was this trio that made the American film industry a powerhouse at home and abroad.

b. By the 1920s, the American movie industry was garnering huge profits both at home and abroad. While stars like Mary Pickford and Rudolph Valentino were widely popular at home, it was Charlie Chaplin who really captured the international market with his portrayal of "The Little Tramp." True, the German movie industry briefly rivaled the American, but that rivalry didn't last long as the more gifted German directors, like F. W. Murnau, were lured to Hollywood by the promise of huge salaries.

2. Disappearing Species

1 On several occasions in the earth's history, large numbers of species have become extinct, perhaps because of the impact of comets and asteroids. Ecologists believe that the earth is currently experiencing an extinction catastrophe as large as the ancient geological ones, but in this case, the catastrophe will not be the result of a comet or asteroid.

2   Instead, scientists point the accusing finger at our own human species: The problem is our success. From Africa, we have spread over Europe and Asia, then Australia, into the Americas (probably within the last 10,000 years or so), and, even more recently, across the remote islands of the Pacific. We are one of the most abundant species on the planet, and our numbers are rapidly increasing. Each year we consume about 40 percent of the world's total plant growth on land. (Some of this consumption is what we and our domestic animals eat; some is the wood we burn or use for other purposes.) In the oceans, we have repeatedly taken out more than the annual growth—the "interest" in our ecological savings account—and the balance has shrunken accordingly. Many

once-profitable fisheries, such as herring and cod, are now virtually depleted and dozens of species of birds are dying or are near
death. (Adapted from Stuart L. Pimm, *Triumph of Discovery*, New
York: Henry Holt, 1995, p. 39.)

Summary a. Thanks to the successful spread of the human race, the earth
may be experiencing an extinction catastrophe. Herring and cod
are almost extinct, and many species of birds are dead or dying,
because of humanity's march across the globe.

     b. Throughout history the earth has experienced large-scale spe-
cies extinction, and now is no exception. Herring and cod are
almost extinct, as are many species of birds. This is simply
what's known as survival of the fittest.

Test 3: Selecting the Better Summary

DIRECTIONS Read each selection. Then circle the letter of the summary that follows the pointers outlined in the box on pages 177–178.

1. Risk-Taking Behavior

1 Why are some individuals willing to take risks that can be a real threat to life and health whereas others prefer to play it safe? There are at least two reasons for the differences in risk-taking behavior. Although the risk of danger may be real, perceptions of that risk can vary from person to person, or from time to time. Two people, for example, may have very different ideas about a situation's risk potential. Whereas one person might conclude that there is very little risk involved, another might think that the risk to health or well-being is quite high. For example, how many among us would walk a tightrope strung one thousand feet above the ground? Yet some people do it on an almost daily basis and think nothing of it. Then, too, most people will not take the same risks at forty as they did at twenty. Age tends to convince most of us that death is a reality while the young are likely to think it will happen to someone else.

2 A second reason why we vary in our willingness to take risks is that the vision of future rewards can cloud our assessment of danger. Some people might be willing to work in very hazardous environments (e.g., the clean-up following a nuclear accident in a reactor) for a high salary, while others would not consider it at any price. Money, however, is only one form of reward that modifies our evaluation of risk. Taking risks in return for potential social admiration is another circumstance in which there is a potential for reward—one that is particularly prevalent among young adults. For example, driving a car very fast may be the result of a desire for social admiration.

3 In such a case, risk is evaluated by balancing the rewards and the potential dangers. When the potential rewards are larger than the perceived risk, some individuals may fail to take any actions that reduce the threat of injury. Eyes on the prize, they choose to ignore the threat of danger. (Adapted from Mullen et al., *Connections for Health*, p. 317.)

Summary a. Why are some individuals willing to take a risk that others would never even consider? There are two different answers to that one question. First of all, people evaluate risk in different ways. A twenty-year-old may well perceive little risk in driving too fast while under the influence of alcohol, whereas a forty-year-old may determine that the same situation is fraught* with danger. Then, too, some people place little value on a human life, even when it's their own.

b. Why are some people willing to take risks that endanger both life and limb? There are two different answers to that seemingly simple question. One answer is that we don't all define risk in the same way. Risky behavior for one person may not be considered risky for another. A second reason is that the promise of a reward can help disguise the threat of risk. Money and social admiration are powerful rewards that can cloud the amount of risk involved in a particular activity such as working in a hazardous environment or driving too fast.

2. Faces and First Impressions

1   People may not measure each other by bumps on the head, as phrenologists* used to do, but first impressions are influenced in subtle ways by a person's height, weight, skin color, hair color, eyeglasses, and other aspects of appearance (Alley, 1988; Bull & Rumsey, 1988; Herman et al., 1986). As social perceivers, we are even influenced by a person's name. For example, Robert Young and his colleagues (1993) found that fictional characters with "older generation" names such as Harry, Walter, Dorothy, and Edith are judged less popular and less intelligent than those with "younger generation" names such as Kevin, Michael, Lisa, and Michelle.

2   The human face in particular attracts more than its share of attention. For example, Diane Berry and Leslie Zebrowitz-McArthur (1986) have found that adults who have baby-faced features— large round eyes, high eyebrows, round cheeks, a large forehead, smooth skin, and a rounded chin—are seen as warm, kind, naive, weak, honest, and submissive. In contrast, adults with mature features—small eyes, low brows and a small forehead, wrinkled skin, and an angular chin—are seen as stronger, more dominant, and less naive. Thus, in small claims court, judges are more likely to favor baby-faced defendants accused of intentional wrong-doing, but they tend to rule against baby-faced defendants accused of negligence (Zebrowitz & McDonald, 1991). And in the workplace, baby-faced job applicants are more likely to be recommended for employment as daycare teachers, whereas mature-

---

*fraught: heavy, filled with.
*phrenologists: people who claim to analyze character by touching the bumps on their subjects' heads.

faced adults are considered to be better suited for work as bankers (Zebrowitz et al., 1991).

3   What accounts for these findings? There are three possible explanations. One is that human beings are genetically programmed to respond gently to infantile features so that real babies are treated with tender loving care. Another possibility is that we simply learn to associate infantile features with helplessness and then generalize this expectation to baby-faced adults. Third, maybe there is an actual link between appearance and behavior—a possibility suggested by the fact that subjects exposed only to photos or brief videotapes of strangers formed impressions that correlated with the self-descriptions of these same strangers (Berry, 1990; Kenny et al., 1992). Whatever the explanation, the perceived link between appearance and behavior may account for the shock that we sometimes experience when our expectations based on appearance are not confirmed. (Adapted from Brehm and Kassin, *Social Psychology,* pp. 83–84.)

Summary   a. Like our names, our faces play an important role in making a first impression. Researchers Diane Berry and Leslie Zebrowitz-McArthur have shown, for example, that people with baby faces are frequently perceived, at first sight, to be innocent, naive, and helpless. In contrast, people with sharper, more mature and more angular faces are often thought to be strong and domineering. No one really knows why this is so, but there are three theories. One theory is that human beings are genetically programmed to treat with care those who have childlike faces. Another theory says that we are used to treating babies in a certain way, and we then apply that same behavior to grownups who happen to have baby faces. And finally, there really may be a connection between how people look and how they behave.

    b. We may no longer try to determine people's character by the bumps on their head—the way phrenologists used to do—but we are still influenced, it turns out, by a person's name. In 1993, researcher Robert Young found that characters with old-fashioned names like Harry, Dorothy, and Edith were assumed to be less popular and less intelligent than characters with more modern names like Kevin, Lisa, and Michelle. Our sense that appearance and behavior must be a match is probably one reason why we are so shocked when a person's behavior doesn't fit his or her appearance. We never seem to expect, for example, someone with a baby face to commit a violent crime. That's the kind of thing we would expect of someone who had a more mature and more angular face.

Test 4: Writing Summaries

Read and summarize each selection.

1. **Interpreting Your Dreams**

   In an effort to understand and analyze dreams, Sigmund Freud identified four ways in which dreams disguised their meaning. According to Freud, the first disguise is **condensation.** Through condensation, a single character in a dream may represent several people at once. A character in a dream who looks like a teacher, acts like your father, talks like your mother, and is dressed like your employer might be a condensation of all the authority figures in your life. A second way of disguising dream content is **displacement.** Displacement may cause the most important emotions or actions of a dream to be redirected toward safe or seemingly unimportant targets. Thus, a student angry at his parents might dream of accidentally wrecking their car instead of directly attacking them. A third dream process is **symbolization.** Freud believed that dreams are often expressed in images that are symbolic rather than literal* in their meanings. To uncover the meaning of dreams, it helps to ask what feelings or ideas a dream image might symbolize. Let's say, for example, that a student dreams of coming to class naked. A literal interpretation would be that the student is an exhibitionist.* A more likely symbolic meaning might be that the student feels vulnerable in the class or is unprepared for a test. A process called **secondary elaboration** is the fourth method by which the meaning of dreams is disguised. Secondary elaboration is the tendency to make a dream more logical, and to add details when remembering it. (Adapted from Coon, *Essentials of Psychology,* p. 256.)

Summary _____

_____

_____

_____

_____

_____

_____

*literal: based on reality.
*exhibitionist: a person who will do anything for attention.

_____

_____

2. **Technology and Modern Warfare**

1 Technological innovations have changed the nature of warfare. For one thing, advances in technology have greatly increased the accuracy of bombs. During World War II, for instance, bomber crews were lucky to hit the right city, especially during night missions. Today, sophisticated radar, satellites, and spy planes can gather detailed information about intended targets. Strike aircraft with computer systems can then hit those targets with amazing precision. "Smart bombs," too, are guided by satellites or lasers to hit exact targets.

2 Technological advances in military communications have also had a profound effect on modern warfare. In twentieth-century conflicts, military commanders could never get enough information about their own troops' movements and activities, let alone those of the enemy. These days ground forces use satellite communications gear and laptop computers to talk directly and instantly to pilots overhead. They also use new Information Age technologies to monitor the enemy's communications.

3 These innovations in weapons and communications have led to changes in the role of the foot soldier. During twentieth-century wars, including World War I and the Vietnam War, the foot soldier's mission was to get close enough to the enemy to kill him with whatever weapon he was carrying. That weapon might be a bayonet, a gun, or a grenade. Most battles occurred when the opposing forces were less than 25 yards apart. Today, the foot soldier's main function is to gather information about ground targets, mark them, and then call in fire from aircraft and missiles.

4 Together, all of these changes are eliminating the "fog of war," the uncertain outcomes caused by lack of accurate information. These innovations have also reduced the risk of death or injury to military personnel. Errors such as misfires, civilian casualties, and "friendly fire"* accidents are far less common today.

Summary _____

_____

_____

_____
*friendly fire: the weapons fire of one's own side.

_____

_____

_____

_____

_____

Test 5: Synthesizing Sources

> **DIRECTIONS** Read each group of three passages. Then circle the
> number of the better synthesis statement.

1. a. Sigmund Freud, the founder of psychoanalysis,* insisted that a
child's relationship to his or her mother determined behavior
even in adult life. For Freudians, then, therapy needs to focus
on childhood patterns and their reemergence in adult life.

b. Initially a follower of Sigmund Freud, Carl Jung broke with Freud
over Jung's belief that the human psyche was deeply influenced
by unconscious *archetypes,* patterns of behavior that had been
part of humanity for centuries but were called forth only under
certain conditions. For Jung and those who followed him, understanding the effect of ancient archetypes on behavior was a crucial part of therapy—more important, in fact, than the analysis
of early childhood behavioral patterns.

c. For the philosopher Jean-Paul Sartre, behavior is not a product
of the past. Rather it is the end result of conscious choices on
the part of the individual. For the followers of Sartre—called *exis-
tentialists*—the individual is free to make and remake the pattern
of his or her own life.

Synthesis   1. Freud and Jung both believed that human behavior was the
Statement   product of the past. However, they disagreed profoundly about
what in the past most profoundly shapes human behavior.

2. In contrast to Freud and Jung, who believed that human behavior was fixed on patterns from the past, Jean-Paul Sartre believed
that each individual was responsible for the shape of his or her
existence.

2. a. Albert Einstein, the most influential scientist of the twentieth
century, was considered by his parents to be retarded. He spoke
slowly and haltingly and never answered questions quickly or
without thinking. Even in high school, he was considered one of
the slower students, and his teachers were unimpressed by his
performance.

b. Pablo Picasso, whom many consider the twentieth century's
greatest painter, was a failure at school. He did so badly that his

---

*psychoanalysis: a theory of the human mind and its ills.

father hired a special tutor for him, but the tutor quit because he considered Picasso a dunce.*

c. Early on, Wolfgang Amadeus Mozart was considered a musical prodigy,* and his father knew immediately that his son would accomplish great things. By the age of seven, Mozart was already writing and performing his own music, and his musical genius burned brightly until his death at the age of thirty-seven.

Synthesis Statement 1. Although some geniuses are like Mozart and reveal their talent as children, others are like Picasso and Einstein—slow to reveal their extraordinary gifts.

2. Already in childhood, it's usually clear which children are destined for genius. Mozart is a good example of this general rule.

3. a. For Freud, the father of psychoanalysis, therapy did not promise happiness. His patients, Freud said, could expect only to change "misery into common unhappiness." To ask for more was, in his opinion, a naive notion based on an unrealistic worldview.

b. From Freud's perspective, human nature would always be plagued by a death instinct that would undermine all attempts to live fully, productively, and happily. The best he could promise from therapy was that the patient would learn how to make unconscious and destructive desires more conscious and thereby control them, but the struggle to do so would never end.

c. Whereas Freud anchored his therapy firmly in the unconscious, the psychologist Carl Rogers, born when Freud was first formulating his theory of the unconscious in 1902, concentrated on the conscious. More optimistic than Freud ever dreamed of being, Rogers believed that clients—he disliked the term *patients*—could discover solutions to life's problems and become happier people.

Synthesis Statement 1. For the European temperament, Freudian psychology and its strain of pessimism may have been appropriate, particularly in the early part of the twentieth century when the world was racked by war. But Americans did not take kindly to Freud's bleak worldview.

2. Unlike Sigmund Freud, who considered unhappiness a natural and normal part of life, Carl Rogers insisted that successful ther-

---

*dunce: a person with no brains.
*prodigy: person, often a child, with exceptional talents or powers.

apy could solve life's problems and make happiness a realistic goal.

4. a. In the 1997 film *Gridlock'd,* the ill-fated rap singer Tupac Shakur combined a magnetic screen presence with the ability to create a believable and sympathetic film character. Up against one of the most gifted actors working today, Tim Roth, Shakur more than held his own. Whatever one might think of his music, there's no denying that Shakur could act.

   b. Tupac Shakur was a man who seemed to be beset by demons, and his music reflected his personal conflicts. At one moment, he could sing with tenderness and compassion about the strength and determination of women, as in "Brenda's Got a Baby" and "Keep Ya Head Up"; in the next, in songs like "Hit 'Em Up," he would switch to a mean-spirited gangster persona* who considered women little more than sexual prizes to be won or lost in brutal male rivalries.

   c. I don't know whether to mourn Tupac Shakur or to rail against all the terrible forces—including the artist's own self-destructive temperament—that have resulted in such a wasteful, unjustifiable end. I do know this, though: Whatever its causes, the murder of Shakur, at age twenty-four, has robbed us of one of the most talented and compelling voices of recent years. He embodied just as much for his audience as Kurt Cobain did for his. That is, Tupac Shakur spoke to and for many who had grown up within (and maybe never quite left) hard realities—realities that mainstream culture and media are loath to understand or respect—and his death has left his fans feeling a doubly-sharp pain. (Gilmore, "Tupac Shakur: Easy Target," *Night Beat.* New York: Doubleday, 1998, p. 386.)

Synthesis Statement 1. Like rapper Biggie Smalls, the violence of Tupac Shakur's music spilled over into his personal life and ultimately destroyed him.

2. Like his music, Tupac Shakur's personal life was filled with self-destructive violence, but there is no denying that he was a man of extraordinary gifts.

5. a. A significant change in the role of the first lady came with Lady Bird Johnson. Her predecessor, the youthful Jackie Kennedy, had captivated the American public with her beauty, charm, and elegance. Lady Bird Johnson shrewdly staked out her own terri-

---

*persona: mask.

tory, choosing an issue with which to identify herself (beautification of America) and playing a visible role in working for relevant policy changes. (Janda et al., *The Challenge of Democracy*, p. 416.)

b. During Johnson's tenure* in the White House, Lady Bird Johnson was always at his side offering him advice about how to conduct the presidency. Few people, however, realized the extent of Lady Bird's influence. When Lady Bird talked, Lyndon listened. Many believe that it was Lady Bird who convinced Johnson to drop out of the presidential race in 1968, a decision that stunned the nation.

c. Although her campaign to beautify America was often derided, Lady Bird Johnson should be viewed as one of America's first environmentalists. In her own gentle way, she made people realize that America the beautiful would never stay that way unless people took action to preserve it.

Synthesis
Statement
1. Few people recognized the fact that Lady Bird Johnson played a powerful role in influencing government policy while her husband, Lyndon Baines Johnson, was in the White House.

2. Lady Bird Johnson may not have had Jackie Kennedy's youthful beauty and charm, but in her role as presidential wife, she had an important and long-lasting effect on American society.

---

*tenure: the period of time during which something—usually an office—is held.

Test 6: Writing Synthesis Statements

Read each pair of passages. Then for each one, write a synthesis statement that links them together.

1. a. Eleanor Roosevelt (1884–1962) shattered the traditional, ceremonial role of the first lady and used her position and talents to make her own positive contributions to American society. She assisted her husband, Franklin D. Roosevelt, by traveling all over the country to gather information about the American people and their needs. However, she also took up her own causes. Eleanor worked hard to promote civil rights for African Americans, and it was she who convinced her husband to sign a series of executive orders that prevented discrimination in the administration of his New Deal projects. She also devoted her considerable energies to many different organizations devoted to social reforms. In particular, she argued for equal rights and equal opportunities for women. She advocated women's right to work outside their homes and secured government funds for building childcare centers. She also used her gifts for public speaking, writing, and organizing to work toward the elimination of child labor. Throughout her career, Eleanor managed to transcend society's stereotypical views of presidential wives to effect, in her own right, many significant improvements in social justice and equality.

   b. As first lady, Hillary Rodham Clinton (1947–) used her intelligence and talents to improve the lives of people across the United States and all over the globe. Before becoming first lady, she worked in Arkansas on issues affecting children and families. While in the White House, she published a book, *It Takes a Village,* in which she argued that all areas of society must work together to improve the lives of American children. Also during the two-term presidency of her husband, Bill Clinton, she headed a task force devoted to improving the health care system. In this position, she traveled all over the country, talking to health care professionals and American citizens about how the government could help improve access to high-quality, affordable medical care. In addition, she visited many countries all over the world, serving as a goodwill ambassador for the United States and supporting human rights, women's rights, and health care reform. At the end of her term as first lady, she managed to do what none of her predecessors had done before: She established her own independent political organization and successfully ran for the United States Senate.

Synthesis
Statement

_____

_____

_____

a. Somehow NASA* has convinced the world that it landed men on the moon. In reality, though, the entire Apollo space program was an elaborate hoax concocted by the U.S. government. Most people don't know it, but the government actually faked the whole series of landings. For one thing, NASA didn't possess the technical knowledge or equipment to get humans to the moon. In particular, there's no way the astronauts could have survived a trip through the Van Allen belt, a region of radiation trapped in Earth's magnetic field. This radiation would have penetrated the thin hulls of the spacecrafts and killed the men inside. NASA also can't explain the so-called landings themselves. The lunar landers' thrusters should have blasted craters into the moon's surface as the crafts descended. Yet, photographs of the landers show them sitting on undisturbed areas of what is supposedly the surface of the moon. Other photographs taken by the astronauts are just as suspicious. For instance, in photos, there are no stars in the background. NASA apparently forgot to add them when it staged the settings for the photographs. Also, the actual photographers must not have realized that their studio had a slight breeze that rippled the American flag in the photos. Because there is no air on the moon's surface, a flag could not have waved. These glaring inconsistencies, and many others, prove that the Apollo program's moon landing was faked from beginning to end.

b. Surprising as it may seem, many people seriously believe that NASA's Apollo space program never really landed men on the moon. On the contrary, they claim that the moon landings were nothing more than a huge conspiracy, perpetrated by a government desperately in competition with the Russians and fearful of losing face. According to the theory, the U.S. government knew it couldn't compete with Russia in the race to space, so it was forced to fake a series of successful moon landings. As the television program "Conspiracy Theory: Did We Land on the Moon?" revealed, conspiracy theorists believe they have several pieces of evidence proving unquestionably that there was a cover-up. First of all, they claim that astronauts could never have safely passed

*NASA: National Aeronautics and Space Administration.

through the Van Allen belt, a region of radiation trapped in Earth's magnetic field. If the astronauts had really gone through the Van Allen belt, they would be dead, say those crying fraud. Scientists, however, have a twofold response to this argument. They point out that the metal hulls of the spaceships were designed to block the radiation and that the spacecrafts passed so quickly through the belt, there wasn't time for the astronauts to be affected. Conspiracy theorists, however, are not impressed by this argument, preferring to believe their own version of events.

Conspiracy theorists also argue that the lunar lander should have blasted a crater in the moon's surface when it descended. Photographs of the lunar surface, however, reveal no such craters. For some, this is clear proof of NASA's deception. They discount NASA's claims that the lander was purposely designed to land gently, disturbing the moon's surface as little as possible.

Photographs of the landing are supposedly another piece of evidence supporting the theory of a faked moon landing. The photographs taken do not show any stars visible. Supporters of the conspiracy insist, therefore, that the photos are faked. They refuse to acknowledge NASA's argument that the cameras used were set to photograph bright objects like the astronauts' white suits. The faint light of the stars was not strong enough to register on the camera meters.

Proponents of a conspiracy also want to know why the U.S. flag planted on the moon is rippling when it should be still because there is no air on the moon. They don't seem to grasp scientists' explanation that a flag can ripple in a vacuum of space. They also flatly don't believe the more common-sense explanation: The cloth of the flag rippled because the astronaut in the photograph was adjusting the rod that held it. They seem to consider this explanation just too simple to be true.

In other words, despite all proof to the contrary, conspiracy theorists are determined to believe that a hoax has been perpetrated on the American public. From their point of view, only a few wise souls like themselves have been smart enough to spot it. If the rest of us would only open up our eyes to their "evidence," perhaps we would see the error of our ways. Yes, and if we would only let the scales drop from our eyes, we might also recognize the existence of the tooth fairy!

Synthesis
Statement

_____

_____

_____

Reading Between the Lines: Drawing the Right Inferences

In this chapter, you'll learn

- how to draw inferences about main ideas in paragraphs.
- how to infer the appropriate thesis statement for a longer reading.
- how to evaluate your inferences.
- how to infer supporting details.

Chapter 6 shows you how to put into words what the author suggests but never says outright. In short, it teaches you the art of drawing inferences. By the way, it's no accident that Chapter 6 bridges the gap between the comprehension and critical reading parts of this textbook. Essential

to understanding an author's meaning, drawing appropriate inferences also lies at the heart of critical reading.

Inferring Main Ideas in Paragraphs

Although many paragraphs contain topic sentences, not all of them do. Sometimes authors choose to imply, or suggest, the main idea. Instead of stating the point of the paragraph in a sentence, they offer specific statements meant to lead or guide readers to the appropriate inference, or conclusion. Here's an example:

> The philosopher Arthur Schopenhauer lived most of his life completely alone; separated from his family and distrustful of women, he had neither wife nor children. Irrationally afraid of thieves, he kept his belongings carefully locked away and was said to keep loaded pistols near him while he slept. His sole companion was a poodle called *Atma* (a word that means "world soul"), but even Atma occasionally disturbed his peace of mind. Whenever she was bothersome or barked too much, her master would grow irritated and call her *mensch*, the German word for "human being."

In this paragraph the author makes specific statements about Schopenhauer's character and behavior: (1) he lived most of his life alone, (2) he distrusted women, (3) he always thought he was going to be robbed, (4) his only companion was a dog, and (5) he would call his dog a "human being" if she irritated him. However, none of those statements sums up the point of the paragraph. That means the paragraph lacks a topic sentence.

Nevertheless, the paragraph implies a main idea like the following: "Schopenhauer did not care for his fellow human beings." Because this inference follows naturally from statements made in the paragraph, it qualifies as an appropriate inference.

Appropriate and Inappropriate Inferences

Experienced readers know that authors do not always state their main ideas in a sentence. Thus, if readers can't find a sentence that sums up the paragraph, they read between the lines and infer a main idea that fits the paragraph. However, they are always careful to draw an **appropriate inference,** which is solidly based on statements made by the author.

To recognize the difference between an appropriate and an inappropriate inference, imagine that we had inferred this main idea from the sample paragraph about Schopenhauer:

Schopenhauer's miserable childhood made it impossible for him to have a healthy relationship with other people.

Although the paragraph offers plenty of evidence that Schopenhauer did not have a healthy relationship with people, it doesn't discuss his childhood. Because our inference is not based on information drawn from the paragraph, it is inappropriate. It's likely to lead the reader in a direction the author never intended.

Although common sense suggests that an adult who has problems may have had a troubled childhood, we cannot rely mainly on common sense to draw inferences. To be useful, *inferences in reading must rely most heavily on what the author explicitly, or directly, says.* Inferences that lean in the direction of the reader's experience rather than the author's intent are often the cause of a communication breakdown between reader and writer.

Recognizing Appropriate and Inappropriate Inferences

To judge your ability to distinguish, or see the difference, between appropriate and inappropriate inferences, read the following paragraph. When you finish, look over the two inferences that follow and decide which one is appropriate and which one is not.

In the West, the Middle Eastern country of Kuwait has a reputation for being more liberal than other Middle Eastern countries, at least where women's rights are concerned. Yet the majority of female students are not permitted to study abroad, no matter how good their grades. Similarly, female students almost never receive funding for international athletic competitions. Although the Kuwaiti government promised to give women the right to vote once the Gulf War of 1990–91 was over, the women of Kuwait are still not allowed to participate in elections. Kuwaiti feminists, however, remain hopeful that the government will one day keep its promise.

Based on this paragraph, which of the following implied main ideas do you think is appropriate?

1. It's clear that the government of Kuwait will never honor its promise to let women vote.

2. Despite Kuwait's liberal reputation, women are not treated as the equals of men in many key areas.

If you chose inference 2, you've grasped the difference between appropriate and inappropriate inferences. Inference 2 is solidly backed by what the author says in the paragraph. The author's specific examples support the idea that women lack equality in key areas. Inference 2 is also not contradicted by anything said in the paragraph, and that's important. If you infer a main idea that is undermined or contradicted by any statements in the paragraph, you need to draw a new inference.

In contrast to inference 2, inference 1 is contradicted by the last sentence in the paragraph. If Kuwaiti feminists still have hope, there's no reason to infer that the Kuwaiti government will *never* honor its promise to give women the vote.

Another problem with inference 1 is that the paragraph does not focus solely on voting rights. The paragraph also addresses funding for female athletes and travel privileges for female students. None of the statements addressing these issues can be used as the basis for inference 1, making it clear that the inference is inappropriate.

Appropriate inferences are solidly based on—or follow from—statements made in the paragraph, and they are not contradicted by any of the author's statements.

Inappropriate inferences do not follow from statements made in the paragraph, and they are likely to be contradicted by the author's actual words. Overall, they tend to rely too heavily on the reader's personal experience or general knowledge rather than on the author's statements.

┅┇ **EXERCISE 1**

DIRECTIONS After reading each paragraph, circle the letter of the correct inference.

EXAMPLE Countless numbers of men and women have paid large sums of money for a treatment commonly known as *cell therapy*. Their reason was simple: They believed that the injection of cells taken from lambs could help them maintain their youth. They either did not know or did not choose to believe what any doctor would tell them: Animal cells, when injected into the body of a human being, are treated like any other foreign substance. The body gathers its defenses to reject the cells, and within three or four days they are destroyed.

Implied Main Idea (a.) Cell therapy is both expensive and useless.

    b. Cell therapy should be available for everyone, not just for the rich.

> **EXPLANATION** Nothing in the paragraph suggests that cell therapy should be made available to everyone. On the contrary, most of the statements in the paragraph suggest that cell therapy is useless against aging, making inference *a* the better choice for an implied main idea.

1. In all fifty states, the law protects the confidentiality of Catholics' confessions to their priests. Even when a person in confession reveals that he or she has physically harmed another person, priests are required to observe canon law* and withhold the information from law enforcement authorities. South Carolina and Oregon, for example, both protect the priest-penitent* privilege even when a confession reveals the sexual abuse of children. However, other states—including New Hampshire and Kentucky—do not permit priests to offer confidentiality to child abuse suspects, even when the suspects reveal their crime in the darkness of the confession box. Other states are distinguishing between conversations inside and outside of the confessional. While many states, such as New Jersey, still grant confidentiality to all priest-penitent conferences, regardless of their setting, others are ruling that conversations outside the confession box may not always qualify as privileged communications. In Idaho, for example, a court ruled that an abusive father's confession to a chaplain in a hospital was not protected by the law.

Implied Main Idea a. Some states are limiting priest-penitent confidentiality in the interest of protecting the welfare of those who may be in danger.

    b. All laws protecting the confidentiality of Catholic confessions should be stricken from the books.

2. According to Dr. Susan Love, women behave in a doctor's office much as they do in social settings. "Women want a relationship with their doctors," says Dr. Love. "They want the doctor to talk to them, to explain things."[1] Men, in contrast, aren't all that interested in a

---

*canon law: a code of laws established by a church council.
*penitent: person confessing his or her sins.
[1]Abigail Zieger, "What Doctors of Both Sexes Think of Patients of Both Sexes," *New York Times*, June 2, 1998, p. 20.

relationship with their physicians. When something is wrong, they want it fixed, and friendly chitchat is pretty irrelevant. Studies suggest, too, that men don't get as much routine health care as women do, and they generally try to escape the doctor's office as quickly as possible.

Implied Main Idea a. Men and women behave differently with their doctors.

        b. Physicians like their female patients more than they like their male ones.

3. On the one hand (if you can forgive the pun*), left-handers have often demonstrated special talents. Left-handers have been great painters (Leonardo da Vinci, Picasso), outstanding performers (Marilyn Monroe, Jimi Hendrix), and even presidents (Ronald Reagan, George Bush). (As these examples suggest, left-handedness is considerably more common among males than among females.) And left-handedness has been reported to be twice as common among children who are mathematical prodigies as it is in the overall population (Benbow, 1988). On the other hand, left-handers have often been viewed as clumsy and accident-prone. They "flounder about like seals out of water," wrote one British psychologist (Burt, 1937, p. 287). The very word for "left-handed" in French—*gauche*—also means "clumsy." Because of such negative attitudes toward left-handedness, in previous decades parents and teachers often encouraged children who showed signs of being left-handed to write with their right hands. (Rubin et al., *Psychology,* p. 59.)

Implied Main Idea a. Left-handed people tend to be more creative than right-handed people; nevertheless, the world has been organized to suit right-handers rather than left-handers.

        b. Although some very gifted people have been left-handers, left-handed people have a reputation for being clumsy or awkward.

4. The topaz, a yellow gemstone, is the birthstone of those born in November. It is said to be under the influence of the planets Saturn and Mars. In the twelfth century, the stone was used as a charm against evil spirits, and it was claimed that a person could drive off evil powers by hanging a topaz over his or her left arm. According to Hindu tradition, the stone is bitter and cold. If worn above the heart, it is said to keep away thirst. Christian tradition viewed the topaz as a symbol of honor, while the fifteenth-century Romans thought the stone could calm the winds and destroy evil spirits.

---

*pun: play on words.

Implied Main Idea a. There are many superstitions associated with the topaz.

      b. The superstitions surrounding the topaz are yet another example of human stupidity.

5. For the record, no mushroom has ever attacked a person, even when provoked. Touching mushrooms does not produce poisoning, rashes, or warts. And of the thousands of North American mushroom species, only six are known to be deadly. Many dozens are edible, and many thousands are strikingly beautiful. All are ecologically* important, giving back nutrients to the earth and enhancing the lives of trees, herbs, and flowers. (Montgomery, *Nature's Everyday Mysteries*, pp. 81–82.)

Implied Main Idea a. For the most part, mushrooms are both beautiful and beneficial.

      b. Most people are afraid of eating wild mushrooms, but they shouldn't be.

EXERCISE 2

DIRECTIONS Read each paragraph. Then write a sentence that sums up the implied main idea of the paragraph.

EXAMPLE The plant known as kudzu was introduced to the South in the 1920s. At the time, it promised to be a boon* to farmers who needed a cheap and abundant food crop for pigs, goats, and cattle. However, within half a century, kudzu had overrun seven million acres of land, and many patches of the plant had developed root systems weighing up to three hundred pounds. Currently, no one really knows how to keep kudzu under control, and it's creating problems for everyone from boaters to farmers.

Implied Main Idea *Intended to help farmers, kudzu has proven to be more harmful than beneficial.*

EXPLANATION At the beginning of the paragraph, the author tells readers that in the 1920s kudzu was viewed as a help to farmers. However, by the end of the paragraph, the author tells us what a pest the plant has become. Thus, it makes sense that the implied main idea unites these two different perspectives on kudzu.

---

*ecologically: having to do with the relationship between organisms and their environment.
*boon: benefit, favor.

1. For football and baseball players, the mid-twenties are usually the years of peak performance. Professional bowlers, however, are in their prime in their mid-thirties. Writers tend to do their best work in their forties and fifties, while philosophers and politicians seem to reach their peak even later, after their early sixties. (Adapted from Coon, *Essentials of Psychology,* p. 139.)

Implied Main Idea _____

_____

2. The webs of some spiders contain drops of glue that hold the spiders' prey fast. Other webs contain a kind of natural Velcro that tangles and grabs the legs of insects. Then, too, spiderwebs don't always function simply as traps. Some webs also act as lures. Garden spiders use a special silk that makes their intricate decorations stand out, and experiments have shown that the decorated parts attract more insects. Other kinds of spiders, like the spitting spider, use their webs as weapons. The web is pulled taut to snap shut when a fly enters.

Implied Main Idea _____

_____

3. The day you learned of your acceptance to college was probably filled with great excitement. No doubt you shared the good news and your future plans with family and friends. Your thoughts may have turned to being on your own, making new friends, and developing new skills. Indeed, most people view college as a major pathway to fulfilling their highest aspirations. However, getting accepted may have caused you to wonder: What will I study? How will I decide on a major? Will I do the amount of studying that college requires? Will I be able to earn acceptable grades? (Adapted from Williams and Long, *Manage Your Life,* p. 157.)

Implied Main Idea _____

_____

4. Every year the scene is so unchanging I could act it out in my sleep. In front of the Hayden Planetarium on a muggy Saturday morning, several dozen parents gather to wave goodbye to their boys as the bus ferries them off for eight weeks of camp. First-time campers are clutchy. Old-timers are cocky. My own sons fret at length about carsickness. Then the parents give the kids a final hug and shuffle sullenly back to their depopulated urban nests. But not this year. When the bus pushed out of the planetarium's circular driveway four Sat-

urdays ago, at last removing the waving boys at the tinted windows completely from our view, one parent interrupted the usual hush by very tentatively* starting to clap. Then other parents joined in, first clapping and finally laughing uproariously. (Frank Rich, "Back to Camp," *New York Times*, July 22, 1995, p. 19.)

Implied Main Idea _____

_____

5. In the nineteenth century, when white settlers moved into territory inhabited by Navajo and other tribal peoples, the settlers took much more than they needed simply to survive. They cut open the earth to remove tons of minerals, cut down forests for lumber to build homes, dammed the rivers, and plowed the soil to grow crops to sell at distant markets. The Navajo did not understand why white people urged them to adopt these practices and improve their lives by creating material wealth. When told he must grow crops for profit, a member of the Comanche tribe (who, like the Navajo, believed in the order of the natural environment) replied, "The earth is my mother. Do you give me an iron plow to wound my mother's breast? Shall I take a scythe* and cut my mother's hair?" (Norton et al., *A People and a Nation*, p. 499.)

Implied Main Idea _____

_____

CHECK YOUR UNDERSTANDING
Explain the difference between appropriate and inappropriate inferences. _____ _____ _____

 ## Inferring the Main Idea in Longer Readings

Longer readings, particularly those in textbooks, generally include thesis statements that express in words the main idea or thought of

---

*tentatively: hesitantly, shyly.
*scythe: a sharp curved knife used to cut wheat.

the entire reading. However, even writers of textbooks occasionally imply a thesis statement rather than explicitly stating it. When this happens, you need to respond much as you did to paragraphs without a topic sentence. Look at what the author actually says and ask what inference can be drawn from those statements. That inference is your *implied thesis statement.*

To illustrate, here's a reading that lacks a thesis statement, yet still suggests a main idea:

J. Edgar Hoover and the FBI

1 Established in 1908, the Federal Bureau of Investigation (FBI) was initially quite restricted in its ability to fight crime. It could investigate only a few offenses like bankruptcy fraud and antitrust violations, and it could not cross state lines in pursuit of felons. It was the passage of the Mann Act in 1910 that began the Bureau's rise to real power. According to the Mann Act, the Bureau could now cross state lines in pursuit of women being used for "immoral purposes" such as prostitution. Prior to the Mann Act, the Bureau had been powerless once a felon crossed a state line; now at least the FBI could pursue those engaged in immoral acts.

2 It was, however, the appointment of J. Edgar Hoover in 1924 that truly transformed the Bureau. Hoover insisted that all FBI agents had to have college degrees and undergo intensive training at a special school for FBI agents. He also lobbied* long and hard for legislation that would allow the Bureau to cross state lines in pursuit of all criminals. He got his wish in 1934 with the Fugitive Felon Act, which made it illegal for a felon to escape by crossing state lines. Thanks to Hoover's intensive efforts, the way was now open for the FBI to become a crack crime-fighting force with real power.

3 And fight crime the agency did. Its agents played key roles in the investigation and capture of notorious criminals from the thirties, among them John Dillinger, Clyde Barrow, Bonnie Parker, Baby Face Nelson, Pretty Boy Floyd, and the boss of all bosses— Al Capone.

4 In 1939, impressed by the FBI's performance under Hoover, President Franklin D. Roosevelt assigned the FBI full responsibility for investigating matters related to the possibility of espionage by the German government. In effect, Roosevelt gave Hoover a mandate* to investigate any groups he considered suspicious. This new

---

*lobbied: worked to influence government officials.
*mandate: legal right.

responsibility led to the investigation and arrest of several spies. Unfortunately, J. Edgar Hoover did not limit himself to wartime spying activities. Instead, he continued his investigations long after World War II had ended and Germany had been defeated.

5   Suspicious by nature, Hoover saw enemies of the United States everywhere, and his investigations cast a wide net. In secret, the agency went after the leaders of student and civil rights groups. Even esteemed civil rights leader Martin Luther King Jr. was under constant surveillance by the FBI. FBI investigation techniques during this period included forging documents, burglarizing offices, opening private mail, conducting illegal wire taps, and spreading false rumors about sexual or political misconduct. It wasn't until Hoover's death in 1972 that the FBI's secret files on America's supposed "enemies" were made public and these investigations shut down. (Source of information: Adler, *Criminal Justice*, pp. 146–147.)

Look for a sentence or group of sentences that sum up this reading, and you're not going to find them. There is no one thesis statement that sums up J. Edgar Hoover's positive *and* negative effect on the FBI. It's up to the reader to infer one like the following: "J. Edgar Hoover was a powerful influence on the FBI. Although he did some good, he also tarnished the agency's reputation and image." This implied thesis statement neatly fits the contents of the reading without relying on any outside information not supplied by the author. It is also not contradicted by anything said in the reading itself. In short, it meets the criteria of an appropriate inference.

◢ EXERCISE 3

DIRECTIONS Read the following selections. Then circle the letter of the statement that more effectively sums up the implied main idea of the entire reading.

The Hermits of Harlem

1   On March 21, 1947, a man called the 122nd Street police station in New York City and claimed that there was a dead body at 2078 Fifth Avenue. The police were familiar with the house, a decaying three-story brownstone in a run-down part of Harlem. It was the home of Langley and Homer Collyer, two lonely recluses* famous in the neighborhood for their odd but seemingly harmless ways.

2   Homer was blind and crippled by rheumatism. Distrustful of

---

*recluses: people who live alone, cut off from others.

doctors, he wouldn't let anybody but Langley come near him. Using his dead father's medical books, Langley devised a number of odd cures for his brother's ailments, including massive doses of orange juice and peanut butter. When he wasn't dabbling in medicine, Langley liked to invent things, like machines to clean the inside of pianos or intricately wired burglar alarms.

3   When the police responded to the call by breaking into the Collyers' home, they were astonished and horrified. The room was filled from floor to ceiling with objects of every shape, size, and kind. It took them several hours to cross the few feet to where the dead body of Homer lay, shrouded in an ancient checkered bathrobe. There was no sign of Langley, and the authorities began to search for him.

4   When they found him, he was wearing a strange collection of clothes that included an old jacket, a red flannel bathrobe, several pairs of trousers, and blue overalls. An onion sack was tied around his neck; another was draped over his shoulders. Langley had died some time *before* his brother. He had suffocated under a huge pile of garbage that had cascaded down upon him.

5   On several occasions, thieves had tried to break in to steal the fortune that was rumored to be kept in the house. Langley had responded by building booby traps, intricate systems of trip wires and ropes that would bring tons of rubbish crashing down on any unwary intruder. But in the dim light of his junk-filled home, he had sprung one of his own traps and died some days before his brother. Homer, blind, paralyzed, and totally dependent on Langley, had starved to death.[2]

Implied Main Idea (a.) In the end, the Collyer brothers' eccentric and reclusive ways led to their death.

b. The Collyer brothers' deaths were probably suicides.

EXPLANATION In this case, *a* is the more appropriate inference because statements in the reading suggest that the brothers' eccentricity contributed to their deaths. It was, for example, a trap of Langley's own devising that killed him. However, there is no evidence that either of the brothers chose to die.

1. Frustration

1 **External frustrations** are based on conditions outside of the individual that impede progress toward a goal. All of the following are

---

[2]Adams and Riley, "Hermits of Harlem," *Facts and Fallacies.* Pleasantville, N.Y.: Reader's Digest Association, 1988, p. 226.

external frustrations: getting stuck with a flat tire, having a marriage proposal rejected, finding the cupboard bare when you go to get your poor dog a bone, finding the refrigerator bare when you go to get your poor tummy a T-bone, finding the refrigerator gone when you return home, being chased out of the house by your starving dog. In other words, external frustrations are based on *delay, failure, rejection, loss,* and other direct blocking of motives.

2   **Personal frustrations** are based on personal characteristics. If you are four feet tall and aspire to be a professional basketball player, you very likely will be frustrated. If you want to go to medical school, but can earn only D grades, you will likewise be frustrated. In both examples, frustration is actually based on personal limitations. Yet, failure may be *perceived* as externally caused.

3   Whatever the type of frustration, if it persists over time, it's likely to lead to aggression. The frustration-aggression link is so common, in fact, that experiments are hardly necessary to show it. A glance at almost any newspaper will provide examples such as the following:

Justifiable Autocide

BURIEN, Washington (AP)—Barbara Smith committed the assault, but police aren't likely to press charges. Her victim was a 1964 Oldsmobile that failed to start once too often.

When Officer Jim Fuda arrived at the scene, he found one beat-up car, a broken baseball bat, and a satisfied 23-year-old Seattle woman.

"I feel good," Ms. Smith reportedly told the officer. "That car's been giving me misery for years and I killed it."

(As quoted in Coon, *Essentials of Psychology*, p. 419.)

Implied Main Idea   a. External frustration is the more painful type of frustration, and it frequently leads to aggressive feelings and actions.

b. Although there are two different types of frustration, both can, if they persist, lead to aggressive behavior.

2. Children Having Children

1   Like other sixteen-year-olds, Gail thinks about her clothes, her friends, and getting her homework done. But Gail has to think about something else that most sixteen-year-olds do not: her six-month-old daughter. Gail is one of more than a million teenagers in the United States who get pregnant each year. Many of these girls will raise their baby as a single parent (Children's Defense Fund, 1989).

2   Today, few pregnant teenagers opt for adoption, in part because of greater acceptance of single parents (Rickel, 1989). For a girl uncertain about her identity and future, a baby can seem a

"solution" to teenage dilemmas. "I want to have the baby," said one teenage mother. "It would be my own. Something that was mine and would love me" (Kaser, Kolb, & Shephard, 1988). The girls most likely to become single parents are those who are doing poorly in school, have low self-esteem and aspirations, and grow up in poor single-parent families (Furstenberg, Brooks-Gunn, & Chase-Lansdale, 1989).

3   The teen mother is thrust prematurely into adult responsibilities. "This is harder than I thought it would be," a fifteen-year-old confided. "My mother can't always take care of [the baby], and my friends don't want him around" (Kaser, Kolb, & Shephard, 1989). Compared to their peers who delay parenthood, teenage girls who become pregnant are more likely to drop out of school, to require public assistance, to have more children, and to have poor job prospects.

4   The children of the young single mothers often have problems in school, in their social relationships, and with the law (Furstenberg, Brooks-Gunn, & Chase-Lansdale, 1989). The mother's lack of education, low income, and inexperience as a parent can cause difficulties. For example, adolescent mothers tend to talk to their infants less than older mothers do—perhaps because they don't know that infants benefit from such stimulation.

5   For children to be successful parents, they must grow up a lot faster than their peers. Recently, social programs have been developed to help teenagers—and more are needed. Family-planning and sex-education programs aim at preventing pregnancy. Counseling programs help pregnant teenagers think about their options, which include adoption, abortion, and keeping the baby. Comprehensive programs help teenage mothers stay in school by providing daycare and teaching effective parenting skills. (Rubin et al., *Psychology,* p. 242.)

Implied Main Idea a. With the help of new social programs, most teenage mothers are avoiding the problems that plagued them in the past.

b. Most teenage mothers have a difficult time raising their children.

EXERCISE 4

DIRECTIONS Read each selection. Then write the implied main idea in the blanks that follow.

1. Defining the Government's Role in Health Care

1 The process of defining Washington's role in the U.S. health care

system began after the Civil War, when Congress authorized a network of hospitals for disabled Union veterans. The system of federally funded medical facilities steadily expanded in the twentieth century to serve veterans of World War I, World War II, and later conflicts.

2   Efforts to extend the government's health care role further met bitter opposition from the medical profession. The Sheppard-Towner Act of 1921 appropriated $1.2 million for rural prenatal and infant-care centers run by public-health nurses. However, the male-dominated American Medical Association (AMA) objected to this infringement on its monopoly, and Congress killed the program in 1929. Efforts to include health insurance in the Social Security Act of 1935 failed in the face of opposition from the AMA and private insurers. President Truman proposed a comprehensive medical-insurance plan to Congress in 1945, but the AMA again fought back, stigmatizing* the plan as an encroaching wedge of "socialized medicine."

3   Medicare and Medicaid (1965), which provide health insurance for the elderly, disabled, and poor, broke this logjam. Nevertheless, lobbyists for the AMA, hospitals, and private insurance companies succeeded in limiting Washington's function to that of bill payer, with no role in shaping the health care system or, most important, in containing costs. The new programs assured millions of Americans better health care, but they proved very expensive. From 1970 to 1990, Medicare costs ballooned from $7.6 billion to $111 billion, and Medicaid from $6.3 billion to $79 billion. As the population aged, long-term care for the elderly became an especially pricey component.

4   Rising costs made up only part of a larger tangle of problems. While America boasted the world's best health care, its benefits were unevenly distributed. Inner-city minorities and rural communities often lacked adequate care. Life expectancy, infant mortality, and other health indexes varied significantly along racial, regional, and income lines. The 1989 infant-mortality rate, for example, stood at 8.2 per 1,000 live births for whites and 17.7 for blacks. Although many workers belonged to prepaid health systems, millions of Americans lacked health insurance. (Boyer, *Promises to Keep*, p. 206.)

Implied Main Idea _____

_____

---

*stigmatizing: branding as disgraceful.

2. Classrooms Across Cultures

1 The average performance of U.S. students on tests of reading, math, and other basic academic skills has tended to fall short of that of youngsters in other countries, especially Asian countries (International Association for the Evaluation of Education Achievement, 1999). In one comparison study, Harold Stevenson (1992) followed a sample of pupils in Taiwan, Japan, and the United States from first grade, in 1980, to eleventh grade, in 1991. In the first grade, the Asian students scored no higher than their U.S. peers on tests of mathematical aptitude and skills, nor did they enjoy math more. However, by the fifth grade the U.S. students had fallen far behind. Corresponding differences were seen in reading skills.

2 Important potential causes of these differences were found in the classroom itself. In a typical U.S. classroom session, teachers talked to students as a group; then students worked at their desks independently. Reinforcement or other feedback about performance on their work was usually delayed until the next day or, often, not provided at all. In contrast, the typical Japanese classroom placed greater emphasis on cooperative work between students (Kristof, 1997). Teachers provided more immediate feedback on a one-to-one basis. And there was an emphasis on creating teams of students with varying abilities, an arrangement in which faster learners help teach slower ones.

3 However, before concluding that the differences in performance are the result of social factors alone, we must consider another important distinction: The Japanese children practiced more. They spent more days in school during the year and, on average, spent more hours doing homework. Interestingly, they were also given longer recesses than U.S. students and had more opportunities to get away from the classroom during a typical school day.

4 Although the significance of these cultural differences in learning and teaching is not yet clear, the educational community in the United States is paying attention to them. Indeed, psychologists and educators are considering how principles of learning can be applied to improve education (Bransford, Brown, & Cocking, 1999; Woolfolk-Hoy, 1999). For example, anecdotal and experimental evidence suggests that some of the most successful educational techniques are those that apply basic principles of operant conditioning,* offering frequent testing, positive reinforcement for correct performance and immediate corrective feedback following

---

*operant conditioning: process of behavior modification in which a specific behavior is increased or decreased through positive or negative reinforcement.

mistakes (Kass, 1999; Oppel, 2000; Walberg, 1987). (Bernstein and Nash, *Essentials of Psychology,* pp. 171–172.)

Implied Main Idea _____

_____

 # Inferring Details

In addition to inferring main ideas, writers also expect their readers to read between the lines and infer supporting details. For an illustration, read the following paragraph. Then decide which supporting detail is suggested but never explicitly stated.

> The bacteria that caused a fourteenth-century plague known as The Black Death appear to have started their deadly course in the Gobi desert in the 1320s and begun moving west along trade routes. By 1347 the plague had reached Italy, and by 1348 it had spread throughout Europe. Within two years, it had killed one-third of Europe's population and caused a devastating labor shortage. Throughout the remainder of the fourteenth century, the workers who were left rebelled against low wages and unfair treatment. As a result, the standard of living for those workers who had survived the plague improved.

Implied
Supporting Detail

1. The workers' rebellion was crushed immediately.

2. The workers' rebellion was successful.

Look at the paragraph and it's clear that detail 2—rather than detail 1—is the one implied. As a reader, you need to infer that the rebellion was successful if you are going to make any sense out of the last sentence of the paragraph. Without that implied detail, it's not clear how or why the standard of living improved.

EXERCISE 5

DIRECTIONS After reading each paragraph, circle the letter of the implied supporting detail that readers are expected to supply.

EXAMPLE The incidence* of melanoma, the most dangerous and the deadliest form of skin cancer, has nearly doubled in the past ten

---
*incidence: the extent, or frequency, of an occurrence.

years. That increase may be due to many factors, including lifestyle changes, migration to the Sunbelt, and better detection, but the depleted ozone layer may also be partly to blame. While it's not clear how much ozone depletion has been responsible for current melanoma cases, there's no doubt that the thinning ozone layer raises the future risk of skin cancer. (Adapted from *Consumer Reports,* 1991, p. 51.)

Supporting Detail (a.) It's generally believed that the ozone layer will continue to be depleted.

b. The use of pesticides and industrial pollution will further damage the ozone layer.

EXPLANATION The words *thinning* and *future risk* suggest that the decrease in the ozone layer is an ongoing process that will continue into the future, making *a* the better answer.

1. If we're really interested in saving the environment, and therefore ourselves, there are some not-so-easy things we can and must do. About population: On the personal level, we can stop at two, or one, or none—and learn to love other people's children. On the government level, we can give every couple the knowledge and technology to choose the number of their children, and then give them straight, honest reasons why they should choose no more than two. The U.S. government, which used to be foremost in this field, has essentially stopped funding family planning and population education both domestically and internationally. We need to lean hard on our leaders to reverse that policy. (Donella Meadows, "Four Not-So-Easy Things You Can Do to Save the Planet," *In Context,* No. 26, Summer 1990, p. 9.)

Supporting Detail a. Big families are no longer popular in America.

b. Earth is in danger of being overpopulated.

2. Dr. C. James Mahoney seemed incredulous* as he sat cuddling a four-month-old chimpanzee named Cory. But the reports were true: The highly regarded New York University primate research center* at which the veterinarian had worked for eighteen years was being taken over by a New Mexico foundation charged by federal officials with a long list of violations of animal-welfare laws. The primate center and its 225 chimpanzees were added last week to the holdings

---

*incredulous: stunned, disbelieving.
*primate research center: center that studies the behavior of animals closely related to humans.

of the Coulston Foundation, a research group that already owns or leases 540 other chimpanzees for medical tests. The foundation, based in Alamogordo, New Mexico, now has control of well over half of the chimpanzees used in medical research in the United States. Critics, including Dr. Jane Goodall, who pioneered studies of the endangered species in the wild, claim that the foundation, already cited for the deaths of at least five chimpanzees, cannot possibly care for more. (Andrew C. Revkin, "A Furor over Chimps," *New York Times,* August 13, 1995, p. 2.)

Supporting Detail a. Dr. C. James Mahoney was stunned at learning that he would soon be out of a job.

b. Dr. C. James Mahoney was stunned by the news that the chimps he had cared for would be turned over to the Coulston Foundation.

3. In the nineteenth century, questions about natural resources caught Americans between the desire for progress and the fear of spoiling the land. By the late 1870s and early 1880s, people eager to protect the natural landscape began to coalesce* into a conservation* movement. Prominent* among them was western naturalist John Muir, who helped establish Yosemite National Park in 1890. The next year, under pressure from Muir and others, Congress authorized President Benjamin Harrison to create forest reserves—public land protected from cutting by private interests. Such policies met with strong objections. Lumber companies, lumber dealers, and railroads were joined in their opposition by householders accustomed to cutting timber freely for fuel and building material. Public opinion on conservation also split along sectional lines. Most supporters of regulation came from the eastern states, where resources had already become less plentiful; opposition was loudest in the West, where people were still eager to take advantage of nature's bounty.* (Norton et al., *A People and a Nation,* p. 509.)

Supporting Detail a. Because the early conservation movement was led by Easterners, many Westerners did not support it.

b. In the East, the early conservation movement caught on quickly because people there had begun to see firsthand that the country's resources were not endless.

---

*coalesce: to come or grow together.
*conservation: the act of protecting or preserving.
*prominent: famous.
*bounty: goodness, riches.

4. Although his armies were all defeated by April of 1865, Jefferson Davis, the leader of the Southern Confederacy, remained in hiding and called for guerrilla* warfare and continued resistance. But one by one, the Confederate officers surrendered to their opponents. On May 10, Davis and the Confederate postmaster were captured near Irwinville, Georgia, and placed in prison. Andrew Johnson, who had assumed the presidency upon Lincoln's death, issued a statement to the American people that armed rebellion against legitimate authority could be considered "virtually at an end." The last Confederate general to lay down his arms was Cherokee leader Stand Watie, who surrendered on June 23, 1865. (Berkin et al., *Making America,* p. 439.)

Supporting Detail a. Because he did not know his armies were all defeated, Jefferson Davis continued to fight.

b. Even in the face of total defeat, Jefferson Davis refused to abandon the Confederate cause.

5. In Saudi Arabia, women cannot appear in public unless they are covered from head to toe in loose black scarves and robes. The Saudis interpret their Islam religion to mean that all women should be shielded from view. Women are also not allowed to drive. When they ride in a car, they must sit in the back seat. They cannot even travel without male permission. A wife has to obtain a permission slip from her husband before she can check into a hotel or leave the country. Women are not permitted to work or study alongside men. They are also forbidden from entering cemeteries because their mourning might distract men.

Supporting Detail a. Women in Saudi Arabia are covered from head to toe in public because the Saudis believe females should be shielded from the view of outsiders.

b. The women of Saudi Arabia do not mind the restrictions placed on their movements and behavior.

*guerrilla: used to characterize warfare waged by small, informal bands of soldiers.

■ DIGGING DEEPER

LOOKING AHEAD The passage on page 245 described a researcher so attached to the chimpanzees he studied, he was heartbroken at the thought of turning them over to a laboratory that he believed would not give them proper care. But if the researcher and his beloved chimps lived in New Zealand, he might not be heartbroken, and his charges might not be in danger.

HE'S NOT HAIRY, HE'S MY BROTHER

1 Humans and chimpanzees are 99 percent identical genetically, have similar blood groups and similar brain structures, and show near-identical behavior in their first three years of life. All five hominids* are unique in sharing humanlike characteristics that scientists group under the labels self-awareness, theory of mind, and incipient* moral awareness. "In other words, the special mental qualities that make human life so precious in our moral and legal systems are also shared by our closest cousins," said Rowan Taylor, a publicist for the Great Apes Project, an ape-advocacy group.

2 "It's actually an injustice to call chimpanzees and orangutans 'animals.'" he said. "It puts them in with rabbits and a whole variety of organisms that they are not close to. And it separates them from us. Apart from the hair and certain features of anatomy, you'd have a difficult time defining a significant difference."

3 Like Shylock,* these advocates cry, "If you prick them, do they not bleed? If you tickle them, do they not laugh?" Or, as Richard Wrangham, a chimpanzee behavior expert at Harvard University, once put it: "Like humans, they laugh, make up after a quarrel, support each other in times of trouble, medicate themselves with chemical and physical remedies, stop each other from eating poisonous foods, collaborate in the hunt, help each other over physical obstacles, raid neighboring groups, lose their tempers, get excited by dramatic weather, invent ways to show off, have family traditions and group traditions, make tools, devise plans, deceive, play tricks, grieve, are cruel and are kind." As research continues, long-held distinctions between the species continue to dissolve.

---

*hominids: primate members of the family to which humans also belong.
*incipient: beginning to exist or appear.
*Shylock: a reference to a character in Shakespeare's *The Merchant of Venice*.

4   The logical outcome, the advocates say, is human rights for apes. They quote the scientist Carl Sagan, from his book *The Dragons of Eden:* "If chimpanzees have consciousness, if they are capable of abstractions,* do they not have what until now has been described as 'human rights'? How smart does a chimpanzee have to be before killing him constitutes murder?"

5   Rights for apes, the advocates say, is simply the next step in the development of a moral society where no group is denied its fair place—whether it has a different skin color or ethnic background, whether it is disabled or mentally impaired, or whether it is covered in hair. "Think of it as a continuum," said David Penny, a theoretical biologist at Massey University in New Zealand. "As recently as 100 or 150 years ago, it wasn't accepted that all humans should be treated as equal. Torture was normal 300 or 400 years ago, even in Europe. Slavery was normal in many parts of the world. Ignoring children's education was standard in many places. Capital punishment is slowly disappearing."

6   The first rights the advocates are seeking for apes are: not to be deprived of life, not to be subjected to torture or cruel or degrading treatment, and not to be subjected to medical or scientific experimentation. In addition, there is a movement under way to recognize the other four great apes as "persons" under the law, rather than property. As with young or intellectually impaired humans, that lobby says, apes should be provided with guardians to safeguard their rights and, should the need arise, plead their cases in court.

7   Like the great civil rights leaders of the 1960s, these new advocates have a dream, and it is to persuade the United Nations to adopt a Declaration on Great Apes, a sort of updated version of the Universal Declaration on Human Rights.

8   Such a move may seem, if not impossible, then impossibly far off. But in the great continuum that is the law, the ape advocates have already won a victory. Two years ago, New Zealand became the first nation to adopt a law guaranteeing rights to great apes. They are now protected from scientific research or experimentation that is not explicitly in their own interests.

9   Granted, it was not a difficult place to start. There was no scientific experimentation on apes in New Zealand. Nevertheless, officials reacted with pride in what some might call their humanity. "This requirement recognizes the advanced cognitive and emotional capacity of great apes," said the agriculture minister, John

---

*abstractions: thinking in terms that are more theoretical than practical or concrete.

Luxton. "New Zealand is the first country in the world to legislate in this way. This is a small but nevertheless important step."

10   Once the world is seen through the prism* of five essentially equal hominid groups, everything begins to look different. Movies, for instance.

11   As "Planet of the Apes" prepared to open [in 2001], a chapter of the Great Ape Project issued a press release condemning the film for what it called a false depiction of our fellow hominids. It also described a preview at which a girl asked if that was a "monkey" on the screen. "The father replied, 'Yes. And someday they'll take over. So be good.'" "Perhaps said lightheartedly," the release went on, "this comment may have created a subconscious prejudice against real nonhuman great apes who are experiencing such trauma and abuse that they need our compassion and support. This mockery is reminiscent of racial jokes and films that, however far-fetched, may have created or perpetuated fear and intolerance."

12   Reality check. Not everybody sees through this prism. For most, the parallel to racism does not work. "I just don't believe argument by analogy* is a legitimate basis for the kind of proposals they are making," said Ronald D. Nadler, an animal behaviorist associated with the Yerkes Primate Center in Atlanta. Though scientists at the center believe in humane treatment of apes, Dr. Nadler said, "It doesn't make sense to me to say that because they are 99 percent similar in terms of certain biomeasures that that makes them sufficiently similar to change our view of how we think of them." . . . Yes, apes are like us . . . but that doesn't make them human.

13   So if you want to use logic, said Frans de Waal, primatologist at Yerkes who has explored similarities between apes and humans, it all seems to come down to this: "If being humanlike is the criterion, then of course we humans should always come first." (Excerpted from Seth Mydans, "He's Not Hairy, He's My Brother," *New York Times,* August 12, 2001, p. 5.)

Sharpening Your Skills

DIRECTIONS Answer the following questions by circling the letter of the correct response or filling in the blanks.

---

*prism: a glass or other transparent body that is used to reflect beams of light.
*analogy: a comparison, often used in arguments to imply that if two things agree in some aspects they will agree in all.

1. Which statement more effectively sums up the implied main idea of this reading?

   a. It won't be long before the United States follows in the footsteps of New Zealand.

   b. Advocates of human rights for apes are passionately committed to their cause.

   c. Although most people believe that apes should be treated humanely, they don't necessarily agree that apes should have human rights.

   d. New Zealand has taken an important step in the war against cruelty to animals, and for that reason, New Zealanders deserve a great deal of credit.

2. The quotation from Carl Sagan's book *Dragons of Eden* is a supporting detail used to bolster what idea?

   _____

   _____

3. In paragraph 5, David Penny says, "Think of it as a continuum." He then goes on to list some of the abuses once thought to be normal or acceptable. What is Penny implying?

   _____

   _____

4. In paragraph 9, what does the author imply by saying that New Zealand's decision to grant human rights to apes was not difficult?

   _____

   _____

5. In paragraph 12, Ronald D. Nadler says that he doesn't believe in "argument by analogy." Based on context, how would you define argument by analogy?

   a. People who argue by analogy rely heavily on logical reasoning to support their claims.

   b. People who argue by analogy use the process of elimination.

   c. People who argue by analogy claim that similarities in one area should also be applied to similarities in another area.

   d. People who argue by analogy rely heavily on appeals to emotion.

WORD NOTES: ANALYZING ANALOGIES

The previous reading introduced you to the word *analogy.* This is a word that deserves some serious attention. Writers and speakers often use analogies as a way of convincing an audience. That is, they use resemblance as a form of evidence, saying, in effect, these two things are alike; therefore, what is true of one will also be true of the other. (Analogies can also work in reverse, suggesting that what is not true for one will also not be true for the other.) Look, for example, at the following: "At the parent-teacher's meeting, one mother suggested the high school introduce a course on marriage so that kids wouldn't think that they were ready to choose a mate at eighteen. But marriage courses for teenagers are a waste of time. Trying to teach high school kids about marriage is like trying to teach them to swim without having them set foot in the water. It can't be done."[3]

Used as evidence in arguments, analogies are frequently on shaky ground. Because two things are similar in one way doesn't mean they are similar in all ways. And the differences do count. Take the above example. A marriage course for unwed teenagers does resemble teaching swimming without water in one sense. In both cases, a crucial ingredient is missing: The kids aren't really in a binding marriage, and the wannabe swimmers haven't set foot in the water.

However, in a marriage course you can have students role-play some of the problems likely to be raised in a marital relationship, and that role playing can provide some insight about married life. In contrast, teaching a swimming stroke without the presence of water is useless. Without your arms moving against the force of the water, it's impossible to even simulate the physical experience of swimming. There is, then, a real and relevant difference between teaching a marriage course to people who aren't married and teaching a swimming course to people who haven't entered the water. Marriage courses, even when the people attending aren't married, can effectively re-create some of the experiences that make up married life. Swimming courses without water can't possibly re-create the feeling of the physical movements involved in swimming.

---

[3]This is a variation on an argument by analogy appearing in M. Neil Browne and Stuart Kelley, *Asking the Right Questions.* Upper Saddle River, N.J.: Prentice Hall, 2001, p. 138.

Anytime someone offers you an analogy for evidence, consider whether or not the two things compared have some relevant differences that undermine the force of the analogy. In most cases, the differences will be as important as the similarities, and those differences will weaken the analogy's effectiveness as evidence.

Preparing for Analogy Tests

In abbreviated form, analogies often turn up on tests of general intelligence. Thus, when taking an employment test, you might run into a question like this one: Walk is to limp* as (a) swim : drown, (b) recite : forget, (c) speak : stutter, (d) draw : sketch. Questions like this one are asking you to select a pair of words that expresses the same relationship as the one set out in the phrase "walk is to limp." If you think about it a moment, you will see a relationship between the words *walk* and *limp*. When we limp, our walking is hindered or impeded. In the three pairs of words that follow, we are now looking for a relationship in which the second word interferes with the activity described in the first. The only one that fits is answer *c*, "speak : stutter." Here again, the first word (speak) identifies an activity that is impeded by the presence of the second word (stutter).

Here's another one. A beggar is to wealth as a (a) traveler : loyalty, (b) fool : wisdom, (c) hero : courage, or (d) leader : enthusiasm. The first step is to figure out the relationship between *beggar* and *wealth*. The most obvious one is that of lack or absence. In other words, a beggar lacks wealth. If you look at the four choices, the only one that fits is *b* because a fool, by definition, lacks wisdom.

Now it's your turn to select the correct answers.

1. A beach is to sand as a
   a. mountain : view
   b. meadow : grass
   c. lake : clear
   d. desert : cactus

2. A writer is to words as a
   a. dancer : tights
   b. actress : stage

---

*Often the tests will present the analogies with single and double colons, for example, walk : limp : : (a) swim : drown.

   c. piantist : fingers

   d. sculptor : stone

3. Sauce is to gravy as a

   a. potato : fries

   b. dinner : supper

   c. steak : cow

   d. dessert : pie

4. Can is to container as a

   a. box : bowl

   b. car : automobile

   c. newspaper : publication

   d. table : chair

Test 1: Reviewing the Key Points

DIRECTIONS Answer the following questions by circling the correct response or filling in the blanks.

1. Readers who cannot locate a sentence that sums up a passage or reading are always ready to do what?

_____

2. Appropriate inferences should be based on or follow from

_____. They are not _____

_____.

3. Inappropriate inferences tend to rely too heavily on _____

_____.

4. Why do readers need to avoid inappropriate inferences?

_____

5. *True* or *False.* Only main ideas need to be implied. All other essential information will appear on the page.

▱◉ Test 2: Recognizing the Appropriate Inference

DIRECTIONS Read each paragraph. Then circle the letter of the main idea implied by the paragraph.

1. Every year desperate, distraught cancer victims travel to the Philippines in the hopes of being cured by people who call themselves "psychic surgeons." These so-called surgeons claim to heal the sick without the use of a knife or anesthesia, and many victims of serious illness look to them for a cure. But curing the sick is not what these surgeons are about. When they operate, they palm* bits of chicken and goat hearts; then they pretend to pull a piece of disease-ridden tissue out of the patient's body. If a crowd is present, and it usually is, the surgeons briefly display the lump of animal tissue and pronounce the poor patient cured. Not surprisingly, psychic surgeons cannot point to many real cures; nevertheless, the desperate and dying still seek them out.

Implied Main Idea a. More people than ever before are flocking to psychic surgeons.

b. Psychic surgeons are complete frauds.

2. Do you like to watch colorful birds? Then keep your eyes peeled for the gorgeous indigo bunting, with its marbled mix of green, yellow, and blue feathers. Well, at least the male is a fabulous creature; the female is a rather drab brown. If your tastes run to splashes of pure brilliant color, then scan the woods for the scarlet tanager, whose fire-engine-red color is interrupted only by pure black wings. Unless, of course, you're looking at a female, who's a bit on the dowdy side. If you prefer your birds even more flamboyant,* then keep your eyes peeled for the Halloween-colored Baltimore oriole, who likes to hang out around swampy areas. The female is a bit bolder and more inclined to appear at bird feeders. Unfortunately, she's—you guessed it—a drab brown.

Implied Main Idea a. Bird watching has become a more popular hobby than ever before, but unfortunately, it still has a nerdy image.

b. Among certain birds, only the males are colorful.

3. For a long time, scientists have speculated that birds might actually be descended from dinosaurs; but they haven't had any proof, at least not until recently. In 1998, diggers in China's fossil-rich earth

---

*palm: conceal in one's hand.
*flamboyant: showy, outrageous.

found dinosaur bones bearing what appeared to be featherlike markings. According to paleontologist Philip Currie, the fossils are the evidence needed to prove the dinosaur-bird connection. However, Larry Martin, a paleontologist at the University of Kansas, is less convinced that the impressions on the bones came from feathers. Still, he, like almost everyone else who tries to reconstruct the past, is anxious to see the new fossils when they go on display. From his point of view, seeing just may be believing.

Implied Main Idea   a. Although not everyone is convinced, there is now some real evidence suggesting that birds descended from dinosaurs.

b. Thanks to the discovery of dinosaur bones in China, it's now definite that birds descended from dinosaurs.

4. Writer and feminist Gloria Steinem became a Playboy Bunny to give readers an inside look at what female employees of the Playboy Clubs had to go through to please the boss as well as the customers. The journalist Carol Lynn Mithers posed as a man to get a job on a sports magazine and published the results in a *Village Voice* article called "My Life as a Man." Anchorman Walter Cronkite voted under false names twice in the same election to expose election fraud. *Miami Herald* reporters went undercover to expose housing discrimination. CBS's "60 Minutes" set up a bar called the Mirage, staffed it with undercover journalists, and watched as various city officials demanded bribes for their services. The *Chicago Sun-Times* sent female journalists into clinics in downtown Chicago that performed costly abortions on women who were not pregnant. And in 1992, ABC News's "Prime Time Live" used undercover reporters and hidden cameras to document charges that some Food Lion grocery stores sold tainted meat and spoiled fish. (Source of information: Joe Saltzman, "A Chill Settles Over Investigative Journalism," *USA Today*, July 1997, p. 29.)

Implied Main Idea   a. Investigative journalists of the past have used deception to expose corruption.

b. Since Food Lion sued and won its case against the newspaper that exposed some unsafe practices in Food Lion stores, investigative journalism has been on the decline.

5. Between 1845 and 1846, Ireland was hit by a blight that attacked its staple crop, potatoes. As the potatoes rotted in the fields, close to one million people died from starvation, malnutrition, and disease, and an additional million were forced to flee their starving country. Between 1847 and 1854, the United States opened its

doors to 1.2 million Irish immigrants. Yet, fearful of this large, new population, many Americans looked on the suffering Irish arrivals with suspicion. All too often, Irish immigrants were confronted by signs that read "No Irish Need Apply," and many wondered if they hadn't made a terrible mistake.

Implied Main Idea   a. When Irish immigrants arrived in America between 1847 and 1854, they were blamed for everything from poverty to unemployment.

b. Fleeing the catastrophic effects of the potato blight of 1845, many Irish immigrants fled to the United States, but they did not receive an especially warm welcome.

Test 3: Recognizing the Appropriate Inference

DIRECTIONS Read each paragraph. Then circle the letter of the main idea implied by the paragraph.

1. In one study, done in the early 1970s when young people tended to dress in either "hippie" or "straight" fashion, experimenters donned hippie or straight attire and asked college students on campus for a dime to make a phone call. When the experimenter was dressed in the same way as the student, the request was granted in more than two-thirds of the instances; when the student and requester were dissimilarly dressed, the dime was provided less than half the time (Emswiller, Deaux, & Willits, 1971). In another experiment, marchers in an antiwar demonstration were found to be more likely to sign the petition of a similarly dressed requester *and* to do so without bothering to read it first. (Cialdini, *Influence*, p. 164.)

Implied Main Idea a. The results of two different studies suggest that people respond positively to those who wear conventional clothing.

b. The results of two different studies suggest that we are more likely to respond positively to those who dress the way we do.

2. Some people choose to handle conflict by engaging in **avoidance**, or not confronting the conflict at all. They simply put up with the situation, no matter how unpleasant it may be. While seemingly unproductive, avoidance may actually be useful if the situation is short-term or of minor importance. If, however, the problem is really bothering you or is persistent, then it should be dealt with. Avoiding the issue often uses up a great deal of energy without resolving the aggravating situation. Very seldom do avoiders feel that they have been in a win-win situation. Avoiders usually lose a chunk of their self-respect since they so clearly downplay their own concerns in favor of the other person's. (Berko et al., *Communicating*, p. 248.)

Implied Main Idea a. Avoiding conflict is a bad strategy for dealing with life's problems; it's often better to meet problems head-on.

b. Although avoiding conflict can be effective in some situations, it's an ineffective strategy when the problem is persistent.

3. For generations, Smokey the Bear has warned Americans that forest fires are tragic and should be prevented, and it's true that fires often destroy large areas of natural vegetation. However, fires also produce new growth. The ash that results from a fire enriches the soil.

Fire also stimulates the release of new seeds. Lodgepole pine cones, for instance, release new seeds only when temperatures greater than 113 degrees Fahrenheit melt the waxy coating that encases them. Fire also burns away trees' leaves and branches, allowing sunlight, which is necessary for seed growth, to reach the forest floor. In addition, wildfires strengthen existing growth. They eliminate dead material that accumulates around live growth. Wildfires also help weed out smaller plants. This removal of both live and dead vegetation reduces the remaining plants' competition for water, sunlight, nutrients, and space, allowing them to grow stronger.

Implied Main Idea a. Wildfires are certainly hazardous, but they are also beneficial.

        b. The National Park Service should do more to promote fires in our national forests.

4. According to the National Alliance for Youth, 15 percent of youth sports events involve some kind of verbal or physical abuse from competitive parents or coaches. To combat increasing instances of "sideline rage," some youth sports leagues require parents to attend classes or workshops on appropriate fan behavior. Some leagues even insist that parents sign a pledge of good conduct. If parents fail to attend the workshop or sign the pledge, their children cannot play on the team. The Positive Coaching Alliance holds similar workshops all over the country to teach coaches how to handle players' parents or referees. Other youth sports leagues are simply creating new rules that prohibit spectators from yelling from the stands at participants. Some of these leagues even fine anyone who shouts out criticism of coaches, players, or referees. In addition, many state legislatures have recently passed or are now considering bills that impose more severe punishments on anyone who attacks a referee at a sporting event. The Illinois legislature, for example, mandated a minimum $1,000 fine for battery* of a sports official.

Implied Main Idea a. Parents who live through their children are likely to interfere if their children are not on the winning side in competitive games.

        b. A number of measures are now being aimed at curbing the parental "sideline rage" that has become a serious problem at sports events for kids.

*battery: physical abuse.

Test 4: Drawing the Appropriate Inference

DIRECTIONS Read each paragraph. Then write what you think is the implied main idea.

1. When the Barbie doll first appeared in prefeminist 1959, she had large breasts, a tiny waist, rounded hips, shapely legs, and little feet in high-heeled shoes. She wore heavy make-up, and her gaze was shy and downcast. She was available in only two career options: airline stewardess or nurse. In the 1960s era of women's liberation, though, Barbie had her own car and her own house, and a Barbie Goes to College play set became available. In 1967, her face was updated to sport a more youthful, model-like appearance with a direct gaze. In the 1970s, Barbie's career options expanded to include doctor and Olympic medalist, and in 1977, she got another facelift that left her with a softer, friendlier look, a wide smile and bright eyes. During the 1980s and 1990s, when girls were encouraged to grow up to be independent wage earners, Barbie's options increased even more to include professions such as business executive, aerobics instructor, and firefighter. Today, Barbie has a thicker waist, slimmer hips, and smaller breasts, and she comes in black, Asian, and Latino versions.

Implied Main Idea _____

_____

2. Doctors are treating some leukemia patients by giving them small, intravenous doses of arsenic, a deadly poison. Other patients are ingesting mercury and platinum, two metals that seem to demonstrate cancer-fighting properties. A successful new drug that combats breast cancer comes from the bark of the Pacific yew tree. Some volunteer patients are trying to cure their cancers with high doses of vitamin D, and still others are experimenting with high doses of vitamin C. Yet another experimental group of patients is testing the cancer-fighting abilities of green tea.

Implied Main Idea _____

_____

3. Over billions of years, the human body has evolved to function and to thrive in a gravitational environment. When astronauts spend extended periods of time in outer space, where there is no gravity, they

lose muscle mass. That's because weightlessness allows many muscles in the body to go unused. Without the constant pull of gravity to work against, the muscles become very weak. Astronauts who spend months aboard a space station can barely stand when they return to Earth. Their heart muscles deteriorate, too. They also lose bone mass, so their skeletal system is weakened. The redistribution of fluids in zero-gravity environment also results in fluid loss. In addition, the immune system does not function as effectively.

Implied Main Idea _____

_____

4. Yoga, a series of deep-breathing and stretching movements, relaxes the body by slowing heartbeat and respiration, and by lowering blood pressure. Yoga also massages the lymph system. This stimulates the elimination of waste products from the body. Yoga seems to improve cardiovascular circulation in cardiac patients, too. It relieves the insomnia and mood swings of menopausal women and often reduces the pain of many people who suffer from backaches. In addition, the stretches and poses of yoga improve balance, flexibility, strength, and endurance. As a result, more and more athletes and exercise buffs are adding yoga to their fitness routines.

Implied Main Idea _____

_____

5. Most scientists would agree that animals experience fear. Many mammals, for example, exhibit the "fight or flight" response when confronted by a predator. More and more scientists are also now claiming that many mammals feel grief as well. Elephants, for instance, seem to mourn over dead or dying family members for days. Chimpanzees who lose a relative sometimes exhibit signs of depression and even refuse to eat. Scientists have also found evidence that animals might be capable of love and affection. Two whales that mate, for example, stroke each other with their flippers and swim slowly side by side. In addition, many creatures are clearly capable of feeling playful happiness. Mammals such as dolphins frolic and chase each other, especially when they're young. Scientists claim that young dolphins are not just developing adult skills. They are displaying feelings of joy in the fun they're having.

Implied Main Idea _____

_____

Test 5: Inferring Supporting Details

> **DIRECTIONS** Read each paragraph. Then answer the questions about supporting details by filling in the blanks.

1. Next time you hear complaints about how long it takes the Food and Drug Administration to approve a new drug, you might want to remind the person who's complaining about the thalidomide scandal of the 1950s. Thalidomide was produced by a small German pharmaceutical firm called Chemie Grunenthal, and the drug appeared on the market around 1957. Sold as a tranquilizer and a treatment for morning sickness, thalidomide had not been adequately tested. Yet assured by the drug's makers that it was safe, doctors prescribed it and thousands of patients, most of them pregnant women, dutifully ingested it. Then in the early 1960s, hospitals in Germany, the United States, Canada, Great Britain, and the Scandinavian countries began to report the birth of babies with horrifying deformities. The infants had hands but no arms, feet but no legs. However, it wasn't until Dr. William McBride, a physician in Australia, made the connection between thalidomide and the babies' deformities that the drug was finally removed from the market. But that was in 1961. By that time, twelve thousand deformed infants had already been born. Astonishing as it might seem in light of its tragic past, thalidomide actually made a comeback in the 1990s when it was discovered that the drug might be useful in the treatment of leprosy and AIDS.

Implied Supporting Detail The author does not say what caused twelve thousand deformed infants to be born. Instead she expects readers to infer that _____

_____.

2. In 1963, Martin Luther King Jr. sought to increase the support of the movement for civil rights. In May, he helped organize demonstrations for the end of segregation in Birmingham, Alabama. The protesters found the perfect enemy in Birmingham's police commissioner, Eugene "Bull" Connor, whose beefy features and snarling demeanor made him a living symbol of everything evil. Connor's police used clubs, dogs, and fire hoses to chase and arrest the demonstrators. President John F. Kennedy watched the police dogs in action on television with the rest of the country and confessed that the brutality made him sick. He later observed that "the civil rights movement should thank God for Bull Connor. He's helped it as

much as Abraham Lincoln." As a result of the demonstrations, the president sent the head of the Justice Department's civil rights division to Birmingham to try to work out an arrangement that would permit desegregation of lunch counters, drinking fountains, and bathrooms. The president also made several calls to business leaders himself, and they finally agreed to his terms. (Schaller et al., *Present Tense*, p. 235.)

Implied The authors never explain why President Kennedy thought Bull
Supporting Detail Connor actually helped the civil rights movement. Instead, they ex-

pect you to infer that Connor helped the movement by _____

_____.

3. During a national address focusing on civil rights, President John F. Kennedy acknowledged that the nation faced a moral crisis. He rejected the notion that the United States could be the land of the free "except for the Negroes." Reversing his earlier reluctance to request civil rights legislation, he announced that he would send Congress a major civil rights bill. The law would guarantee service to all Americans regardless of race in public accommodations—hotels, restaurants, theaters, retail stores, and similar establishments. Moreover, it would grant the federal government greater authority to pursue lawsuits against segregation in public education and increase the Justice Department's powers to protect the voting rights of racial minorities. (Schaller et al., *Present Tense*, p. 236.)

Implied The authors do not specifically define the moral crisis facing the na-
Supporting Detail tion. Instead they expect readers to infer that _____

_____

was the cause of a moral crisis in America.

4. On Christmas Day, 1859, the ship HMS *Lightning* arrived at Melbourne, Australia, with about a dozen wild European rabbits bound for an estate in western Victoria. Within three years, the rabbits had started to spread, after a bushfire destroyed the fences enclosing one colony. From a slow start at first, the spread of the rabbits picked up speed during the 1870s, and by 1900 the rabbit was the most serious agricultural pest ever known in Australia. Rabbits eat grass, the same grass used by sheep and cattle, and so quickly the cry went up: "Get rid of the rabbit!" The subsequent history of control attempts in Australia is a sad tale of ecological ignorance. Mil-

lions of rabbits were poisoned and shot at great expense with absolutely no effect on their numbers. Nowhere else has the introduction of an exotic species had such an enormous impact and spotlighted the folly of such introduction experiments. (Adapted from Krebs, *The Message of Ecology*, p. 8.)

Implied
Supporting Detail Although the author does not specifically say how the rabbits got off the estate, he expects readers to infer that they ＿＿＿＿＿＿＿＿＿

＿＿＿＿＿＿＿＿＿＿＿＿＿＿＿＿＿＿＿＿＿＿＿＿＿＿＿.

Test 6: Recognizing the Implied Main Idea in Longer Readings

DIRECTIONS Circle the letter of the statement that sums up the implied main idea.

1. Explaining the Growth of the Bureaucracy*

1 What accounts for the growth of bureaucracies and bureaucrats since the late 1800s? Was all this growth the result of bureaucratic incompetence and unresponsiveness? Many observers believe that the growth can be attributed directly to the expansion of the nation itself. There are a great many more of us—more than 248 million in 1990, compared with fewer than 5 million in the 1790s—and we are living closer together. Not only do the residents of cities and suburbs require many more services than did the predominantly rural dwellers of the early 1800s, but the challenges of urban and industrial life have intensified and outstripped the capacity of families or local and state governments to cope with them. Thus the American people have increasingly turned to their national government for help.

2   There is considerable evidence that the growth of bureaucracies is "of our own making." Public opinion polls indicate widespread public support for expanding federal involvement in a variety of areas. Even when public support for new programs is low, pollsters find Americans unwilling to eliminate or reduce existing programs. Furthermore, the public's expectations about the quality of service it should receive are constantly rising. The public wants government to be more responsive, responsible, and compassionate in administering public programs. Officials have reacted to these pressures by establishing new programs and maintaining and improving existing ones.

3   The federal bureaucracy has also expanded in response to sudden changes in economic, social, cultural, and political conditions. During the Great Depression and World War II, for example, the federal bureaucracy grew to meet the challenges these situations created. Washington became more and more involved in programs providing financial aid and employment to the poor. It increased its regulation of important industries and during the war imposed controls over much of the American economy. As part of the general war effort, the federal government also built roads and hospitals and mobilized the entire population. When these crises ended,

---

*bureaucracy: management of a government through bureaus or departments staffed by nonelected officials.

the public was reluctant to give up many of the federal welfare and economic programs implemented during the time of emergency. (Gitelson et al., *American Government*, p. 358.)

Implied Main Idea   a. Bureaucracies are simply a fact of modern life, and there is no escaping them.

b. At least three different factors account for the growth of bureaucracies.

2. Holiday Cheer

1   The observance of public school holidays began at the end of the nineteenth century. The goal of school holidays, at that time at least, was to bring people together. Holiday celebrations in the schools—particularly Christmas—were meant to unite a nation of immigrants. But as Bob Dylan would say, "The Times They Are a-Changin'."

2   In Chicago, the principal of the Walt Disney Magnet School saw his attempt at holiday harmony backfire. This elementary school has a mix of students, including black, Asian, Muslim, Hispanic, Yugoslavian, Romanian, and Jewish children, so the principal tried to tone down Christmas by issuing a ban on Santa Claus and any other symbols or activities associated with "a specific religious tradition." Teachers protested—one gave the principal a copy of *How the Grinch Stole Christmas*—and the head of the school board overturned the ban. With Christmas parties, decorations, and carols in full swing throughout the school, Essam Ammar, a Muslim parent, asked, "How am I going to raise my children as proud Muslims with all this going on?"

3   As passions intensify over how to celebrate the holiday season, some parents are demanding that a wide variety of other religious and ethnic holidays, including the Hindu Diwali festival, Hanukkah, and Kwanzaa, get equal time with Christmas. Others protest any diminution* of Christmas traditions, such as bans on trees and Santa Claus in some communities. At the moment, there seems to be no resolution in sight.

Implied Main Idea   a. Celebrating the holiday season in public schools began as an effort to bring together people who might otherwise stay separated.

b. Observing the holidays in public shools has become far more complicated than it once was as different ethnic groups compete to celebrate their particular holiday.

---

*diminution: act of decreasing.

◢◣◗ Test 7: Inferring the Implied Main Idea in Longer Readings

DIRECTIONS Read the selection and then write the implied main idea on the blanks.

1. **Improving Your Memory**

1 Do you, like just about everyone else, want to improve your memory? Well, the good news is that you can. All you have to do is put the following advice into practice, and you'll see immediate results.

2   For example, remembering when Christopher Columbus discovered America is easy enough if you use visualization. You could, for example, imagine Columbus standing on the beach with his ships in the harbor in the background. Fortunately, unrealistic images work just as well or better, and you could imagine Columbus's boat having the large numerals *1492* printed on its side, or Columbus reviewing his account books after the trip and seeing in dismay that the trip cost him $1,492. You could even envisage something still more fanciful: Since 1492 sounds like the phrase "for tea, nightie two," you might imagine Columbus serving tea in his nightie to two Indians on the beach. A weird image like this is often easier to remember than a realistic one because its silliness makes it more distinct (Levin, 1985).

3   Visual imagery also works well for remembering single terms, such as unfamiliar words in a foreign language. The French word for snail, *l'escargot,* can be remembered easily if you form an image of what the word sounds like in English—"less cargo"—and picture an event related to this English equivalent, such as workmen dumping snails overboard to achieve "less cargo" on a boat. The biological term *mitosis* (which refers to cell division) sounds like the phrase "my toes itch," so it is easier to remember if you picture a single cell dividing while scratching its imaginary toes.

4   Another device for memory improvement is called the method of loci, or locations. With this method, you purposely associate objects or terms with a highly familiar place or building. Suppose you have to remember the names of all of the instruments in a standard symphony orchestra. Using the method of loci, choose a familiar place, such as the neighborhood in which you live, and imagine leaving one of the instruments at the doorstep of each house or business in the neighborhood. To remember the instruments, simply take an imaginary walk through the neighborhood, mentally picking up each instrument as you come upon it.

5   Research on loci has found the method effective for remembering a wide variety of information (Christen and Bjork, 1976). The
same loci, or locations, can work repeatedly on many sets of
terms or objects without one set interfering with another. After
memorizing the musical instruments in the above example, you
could still use your neighborhood to remember the names of exotic fruit, without fear of accidentally "seeing" a musical instrument by mistake. Loci can also help in recalling terms that are
not physical objects, such as scientific concepts. Simply imagine
the terms in some visual form, such as written on cards, or, better yet, visualize concrete objects that rhyme with each term and
leave these around the mental neighborhood.

6   Imagery and visual loci work for two reasons (Pressley and
McDaniel, 1988). First, they force you to organize new information, even if the organization is self-imposed. Second, they encourage you to elaborate mentally on new information. In "placing"
musical instruments around the neighborhood, you have to think
about what each instrument looks like and how it relates to the
others in a symphony. These mental processes are essential for
moving information into long-term memory. (Adapted from Seifert,
Educational Psychology, pp. 199–201.)

Implied Main Idea _____

_____

2. Remembrance of Things Past

1   A whiff of perfume, the top of a baby's head, freshly cut grass, a
locker room, the musty odor of a basement, the floury aroma of a
bakery, the smell of mothballs in the attic, and the leathery scent
of a new car—each may trigger what Diane Ackerman (1990) has
called "aromatic memories." Frank Schab (1990) tested this theory in a series of experiments. In one, subjects were given a list of
adjectives and instructed to write an antonym, or word opposite
in meaning, for each adjective. In half of the sessions, the sweet
smell of chocolate was blown into the room. The next day, subjects were asked to list as many of the antonyms as they could—
again, in the presence or absence of the chocolate aroma. As it
turned out, the most words were recalled when the smell of chocolate was present at both the learning and the recall sessions. The
reason? The smell was stored in the memory right along with the
words, so it later served as a retrieval cue.

2   The retrieval of memories is influenced by factors other than
smell. In an unusual study, Duncan Godden and Alan Baddeley

(1975) presented deep-sea divers with a list of words in one of two settings: fifteen feet underwater or on the beach. Then they tested the divers' recall in the same or another setting. Illustrating what is called *context-dependent memory*, the divers recalled 40 percent more words when the material was learned and retrieved in the same context. The practical implications are intriguing. For example, recall may be improved if material is retrieved in the same room in which it was initially learned (Smith, 1979).

3   Indeed, context seems to activate memory even in three-month-old infants. In a series of studies, Carolyn Rovee-Collier and her colleagues (1992) trained infants to shake an overhead mobile equipped with colorful blocks and bells by kicking a leg that was attached to the mobile by a ribbon. The infants were later more likely to recall what they learned (in other words, to kick) when tested in the same crib and looking at the same visual cues than when there were differences. Apparently, it is possible to jog one's memory by reinstating the initial context of an experience. This explains why I will often march into my secretary's office for something, go blank, forget why I was there, return in defeat to my office, look around, and ZAP!, suddenly recall what it was I needed.

4   Studies also reveal that it is often easier to recall something when our state of mind is the same at testing as it was while we were learning. If information is acquired when you are happy, sad, drunk, sober, calm, or aroused, that information is more likely to be retrieved under the same conditions (Bower, 1981; Eich, 1980; Eich et al., 1994). The one key complicating factor is that the mood we're in leads us to evoke memories that fit our current mood. When we are happy, the good times are most easy to recall; but when we feel depressed or anxious, our minds become flooded with negative events of the past (Blaney, 1986; Ucros, 1989). (Adapted from Kassin, *Social Psychology*, p. 231.)

Implied Main Idea _____

_____

C H A P T E R   7

Defining the Terms *Fact* and *Opinion*

In this chapter you'll learn

- **how to tell the difference between *fact* and *opinion*.**

- **how to recognize statements that mix opinion with fact.**

- **how to distinguish between *informed* and *uninformed* opinions.**

- **how to identify opinions backed by *circular reasoning* and *irrelevant facts*.**

- **how to determine the right balance of fact and opinion in textbooks.**

The goal of Chapter 7 is to ensure that you have a clear understanding of the terms *fact* and *opinion*. Once you understand exactly what these two terms mean, you'll be in

a better position to evaluate how well or poorly an author uses facts to buttress, or support, opinions readers might question.

 # Distinguishing Between Fact and Opinion

Statements of **fact** provide information about people, places, events, and ideas that can be **verified,** or checked, for accuracy. Facts do not reveal the author's personal **perspective,** or point of view. The following are all statements of fact:

- American Samoa consists of seven islands in the South Pacific.
- The Treaty of Versailles ended World War I.
- For his work on atomic structure, scientist Niels Bohr was awarded the Nobel Prize in physics in 1922.
- John Wilkes Booth assassinated Abraham Lincoln on April 14, 1865.

These facts can be checked in encyclopedias or other reference books in libraries anywhere in the world and they will always be the same. Facts do not vary with place or person. Whether you live in Dayton, Ohio, or Fairbanks, Alaska, if you look up Martin Luther King Jr.'s date of birth, it will always be the same: January 15, 1929.

Troubling Facts

Because facts can be checked, they are generally not subject to question or argument. However, statements of fact can be questioned if they are not widely known. For example, it's a fact that the Native-American leader Black Elk publicly criticized the book bearing his name, *Black Elk Speaks.* But that fact is not generally known and therefore could be questioned, particularly by those who admired the book.

Then, too, facts can and do change over a period of time as new discoveries or methods of research come to light. This is especially true in fields like science, history, and medicine, where information is considered factual only insofar as it is based on existing levels of knowledge. As scientists and historians gain a more precise knowledge of the world, the facts on which they base their theories sometimes undergo a dramatic change.

For example, it was once considered a fact that the Sun revolved around Earth. But in the sixteenth century, a Polish astronomer named Nicolaus Copernicus used the laws of planetary motion to challenge that "fact." Copernicus proved that, *in fact*, Earth revolves around the Sun.

Generally, however, facts are fixed pieces of information. They often consist of dates, names, and statistics, and thus cannot be affected by the writer's background or training. Facts can be **verified,** or checked, and *proved* accurate or inaccurate, true or false, to the satisfaction of most people. Thus, unless they are newly discovered, they are not often the subject of disagreement.

Statements of Fact

- can be checked for accuracy or correctness.
- can be proved true or false.
- are not affected by the writer's background or training.
- rely heavily on names, dates, and statistics.
- are not usually the subject of argument.

Calling It a Fact Doesn't Necessarily Make It One

Because people tend to accept facts without giving them too much thought, some writers and speakers preface opinions with the phrase "the fact is," as in the following sentence: "*The fact is* that Richard Nixon, had he not resigned, would have been impeached." Despite the opening phrase, this statement really is an opinion, and not everyone would agree with it. In effect, what the author tries to do is bully you into agreeing that the statement is an indisputable, or unquestionable, fact when it's anything but. Similarly, beware of the phrase "it's a fact that." This phrase is often used to discourage readers or listeners from thinking critically about a writer's or speaker's claims.

Opinions

Statements of **opinion** reflect the writer's perspective on the subject discussed. Shaped by an author's personal experience, training, and background, opinions on the same subject can vary from person to person, group to group, and place to place. For an illustration, ask a group of teenagers how they feel about high school dress codes. Then ask their parents. Don't be surprised if you uncover a marked difference of opinion.

Unlike facts, opinions cannot be verified with outside sources. They are too **subjective**—too personal—to be checked in reference books or historical records. The following are all statements of opinion:

- Jennifer Lopez is an artist of extraordinary talent.
- Thanks to cellist Yo-Yo Ma, the glorious music of Argentinian Astor Piazzolla is now more widely known.
- Pet owners deserve legal punishment if their animals do someone harm.
- This country needs stricter gun control laws.

Because opinions are so heavily influenced by one's training, knowledge, and experience, it's impossible to talk about them as accurate or inaccurate, right or wrong. For example, if you own a dog and firmly believe that dogs are more desirable pets than cats, no cat lover can prove you wrong. That's your opinion, and you have a right to express it.

Evaluating Opinions

Saying that everyone has the right to an opinion doesn't mean that opinions can't be judged or evaluated. They most certainly can. Critical readers want and need to distinguish between informed and uninformed opinions. **Informed opinions** are backed by evidence; **uninformed opinions** lack adequate evidence. Once you can distinguish between the two, you'll be surprised at how often writers give their opinions without bothering to support them. So yes, the old saying is true: Everyone has the right to an opinion. But it's also true that every opinion does not deserve the same consideration or respect. (For more on informed and uninformed opinions, see pp. 279–282.)

Statements of Opinion

- can be evaluated but cannot be verified for accuracy or correctness.
- cannot be proved true or false.
- are shaped by the writer's background or training.
- often communicate value judgments, indicating that the author thinks something is right or wrong, good or bad.

In addition to the characteristics listed in the box, the language a writer uses is another important clue to the presence of opinions.

The Language of Opinions

- Statements of opinion often include verbs or adverbs such as *appears, seems, possibly, probably, likely,* and *presumably.*
- Statements of opinion often make comparisons using words such as *more, most, better, best, greatest,* and *finest.*
- Statements of opinion include words that make value judgments: *beautiful, perfect, significant, interesting,* and *crucial.*
- Opinions are frequently prefaced, or introduced, with phrases like *one interpretation of, another possibility is, this study suggests, in all likelihood,* and *it would seem.*

CHECK YOUR UNDERSTANDING

What's the essential difference between facts and opinions?

_____

_____

_____

EXERCISE 1

DIRECTIONS Label each statement *F* for fact or *O* for opinion.

_____ 1. All this uproar about animal rights is nonsense. Animals don't have rights.

_____ 2. In 1909, Ernest Rutherford showed that atoms were mostly space.

_____ 3. When it was under Spanish control, the city of Los Angeles was called *El Pueblo de Nuestra Señora la Reina de Los Angeles del Río Porciúncula,* which means "The Town of Our Lady the Queen of the Angels by the Little Portion River."[1]

_____ 4. People who refuse to believe in alien abduction* are simply afraid to face the truth.

_____ 5. Martin Luther King Jr.'s "Letter from Birmingham Jail" was published in 1963 by the American Friends Service Committee, a Quaker organization.

_____ 6. Teenagers today are obsessed with money and success. They don't care about making the world a better place.

_____ 7. The atomic weight of carbon is closer to 12 than to 14.

_____ 8. Women's stomachs are less effective than men's when it comes to absorbing alcohol and neutralizing* its effects.

_____ 9. Rap music is here to stay.

_____ 10. Queen Victoria of England died on January 22, 1901; at her death, she had been queen for almost sixty-four years.

Blending Fact and Opinion

Reading critically would probably be a good deal easier if authors kept statements of fact and opinion neatly divided. But they don't. Whether consciously or unconsciously, writers of all kinds—and textbook authors are no exception—can't always avoid coloring a fact with an opinion. Your job as a critical reader is to make sure you recognize when and where fact and opinion blend together. Then you won't mistakenly accept as fact an opinion you haven't consciously thought through or considered. Take, for example, the following sentence:

> At least thirty-eight states have sensibly decided to give terminally ill patients the right to refuse medical treatment.

---

[1]Bill Bryson, *Made in America.* New York: William Morrow and Company, 1994, p. 106.
*abduction: kidnapping.
*neutralizing: making harmless or without effect.

At a quick glance, this sentence might appear to be a statement of fact. After all, it's easy enough to verify how many states have given terminally ill patients the right to reject medical treatment. But think again about the author's use of the word *sensibly*. This is a word with positive **connotations,** or associations. Use it to describe someone, and chances are he or she would be pleased. What the author has done in the above sentence is to include her opinion of the action taken by those thirty-eight states. That makes the statement a blend of both fact and opinion.

Now what about the next sentence? How would you label it—fact, opinion, or a blend of both?

> In 1944, Russian troops entered eastern Czechoslovakia, and the nightmare of life under Communist rule began.

The first part of this sentence is a fairly obvious statement of fact. Any encyclopedia can tell you when Russian troops entered Czechoslovakia. But what about the phrase *nightmare of life under Communist rule?* Do you detect any trace of opinion in those words? If you said yes, you're well on your way to being a critical reader. People who took part in or supported the Communist regime in Czechoslovakia would probably not agree that life under Communist rule was a nightmare. What we have here is another example of a statement that blends fact and opinion.

To discover when writers have mixed a pinch of opinion in with their facts, you'll need to be alert to **charged,** or **connotative, language**—language that carries with it strong positive or negative associations. Writers dealing in pure fact tend to rely heavily on **denotative language.** They employ words that suggest little more than their **denotation,** or dictionary definitions. Words like *table, chair,* and *rock,* for example, carry little or no emotional impact. Thus, they are considered far more denotative than connotative.

Changing the Connotation with the Context

Change the **context,** or setting, of a word, and it can become more connotative than denotative. For example, the word *stories* in the following sentence evokes little more than its denotation.

> *Aesop's Fables* is a collection of *stories* written by a Greek story-teller.

However, look what happens when the context of the word *stories* changes:

In an effort to deny Jean a promotion, a jealous coworker spread *stories* about her character.

With this change in context, the word *stories* no longer refers to "an account of events"; instead, it becomes a synonym for *lies* and takes on a negative connotation. This example illustrates a key point about labeling language connotative or denotative: *Context is crucial.* Don't assume that a word which is denotative in one sentence is always lacking an emotional charge. A word can be connotative or denotative, depending on the setting in which it appears.

CHECK YOUR UNDERSTANDING

Explain how an author can mix an opinion in with a fact.

_____

_____

EXERCISE 2

DIRECTIONS Read each sentence and look carefully at the italicized word or words. Then fill in the blank with one of the following letters:

D for dictionary meaning only
C+ for positive connotation
C− for negative connotation

D   **EXAMPLE** Gertrude Stein was a *twentieth-century author* who spent most of her life in France.

EXPLANATION The phrase *twentieth-century author* does not carry with it any positive or negative associations. It simply identifies the time in which Stein lived.

_____ 1. Displaying his usual blend of *stamina, strength,* and *determination,* Lance Armstrong won his third Tour de France bicycle race in 2001.

_____ 2. "Zulu" is a *general name* for some 2.5 million Bantu-speaking peoples who live in South Africa.

_____ 3. The Amazon River is the *second longest river* after the Nile.

_____ 4. Nuclear weapons are the *plague of this century.*

_____ 5. In the nineteenth century, Marshall "Wild Bill" Hickok was *fearless* in his pursuit of outlaws.

_____ 6. *Famed revolutionary hero* Emiliano Zapata was *beloved* by the poor of Mexico.

_____ 7. Gospel music is the kind of *intense joyful music* that *makes the spirit sing.*

_____ 8. Francisco Goya was a Spanish painter of the *late eighteenth and early nineteenth centuries.*

_____ 9. John James Audubon was a nineteenth-century *painter and naturalist.**

_____ 10. John D. Rockefeller, founder of the Standard Oil Company, was famous for his charity work, but he was also known as a *robber baron* whose business methods were remarkably *ruthless.*

EXERCISE 3

DIRECTIONS Some of the following statements are purely factual. Others blend fact and opinion. Label the statements that are pure fact with an *F*. For the statements that blend fact and opinion, put a *B* in the blanks. For those sentences you mark with a *B*, underline the word or words that led you to your conclusion.

B **EXAMPLE** Leslie Marmon Silko's *Ceremony* is the <u>deeply moving</u> story of a young Native American held prisoner during World War II.

EXPLANATION In this statement, the author provides factual information about the book's plot. The words *deeply moving* convey the author's opinion of the book.

_____ 1. According to the Television Advertising Bureau, an extraordinary 98.2 percent of all American households have a television set.

_____ 2. Psychiatrist Bruno Bettelheim spent decades studying fairy tales and their effect on children.

_____ 3. An astounding number of people have tattoos covering 98 percent of their body.

_____ 4. Amazingly, Diane Nash was only twenty-two years old when she led the campaign to desegregate the lunch counters in Nashville, Tennessee.

_____ 5. Jerry Garcia, the long-time lead singer for the Grateful Dead, died on August 5, 1995.

*naturalist: person who studies nature.

——— 6. Juan Rodríguez Cabrillo explored the coast of California in 1542.

——— 7. After World War I, victorious Britain and France greedily divided up the Turkish Empire.

——— 8. Surprisingly, Muhammad, the founder of Islam, devoted a number of his sermons to the subject of women's rights.

——— 9. After World War II, Great Britain turned Palestine over to the United Nations, which in November 1947 voted to create the State of Israel.

——— 10. In 1908, the phenomenal Jack Johnson became the first African American to win the world heavyweight championship.

 ## Informed vs. Uninformed Opinions

While everybody has a right to an opinion, it doesn't follow that every opinion deserves the same degree of attention or respect. Imagine, for example, that a friend saw you taking an aspirin for a headache and told you that chewing a clove of garlic was a far better remedy. When you asked why, he shrugged and said: "I don't know. I heard it someplace." Given this lack of explanation, not to speak of evidence, it's unlikely that you would start chewing garlic cloves to rid yourself of headaches. Uninformed opinions—opinions lacking sufficient reasons or evidence—usually do fail to persuade.

More likely to convince are informed opinions backed by logic or evidence. For an example, look at this paragraph, which opens by expressing an opinion about the Internet's darker side.

> Although the Internet provides us with a convenient way to conduct research and to shop, it also has a darker side. Every day, hundreds of people report that they are victims of online stalking. In 2000, police arrested John Edward Robinson, the first Internet serial killer, who murdered at least five women he met and corresponded with online. In 1999, the FBI investigated 1500 online child solicitation* cases, a number more than double that of the previous year. Criminals are also using the Internet to steal credit card numbers, thereby costing card holders and issuers hundreds of millions of dollars per year. Online identity theft is a growing problem, too. Law enforcement officials say that it's the fastest-growing financial crime; in 1999, the Social Security Administration received more than 30,000 complaints of misused social secu-

———

*solicitation: approaching someone for sexual purposes.

rity numbers, which can be bought and sold via the Internet. Still other criminals are using the Internet for adoption fraud. For example, Internet adoption broker Tina Johnson caused much heartache and created an international dispute in 2001 when she took money from two couples in two different countries for the adoption of the same infant twin girls.

In this example, the author opens with an opinion—that the Internet, whatever its advantages, also has a "darker side." Aware, however, that not everyone might agree, she adds a significant number of facts and reasons designed to make her opinion convincing. Among other things, we learn that on a daily basis hundreds of people report they are the victims of online stalkers. We also hear about an Internet serial killer and about criminals' use of the Internet to steal credit card and Social Security numbers. All of these supporting details are factual. In one way or another, they can be verified. By the end of the passage, it's clear that we are dealing with an informed opinion, one worthy of serious consideration.

Recognizing Circular Reasoning

The paragraph about the Internet offers a good example of an informed opinion. Would you say the same about the next passage?

We Americans like to brag about progress, but, in fact, life was better in the nineteenth century than it is now. People were happier and more at peace with themselves. There just wasn't the same kind of anxiety and tension that there is today. If we had a chance, we would probably all get into a time machine and go backward, rather than forward. All of our highly touted technological progress has not brought us an increased measure of contentment.

The author of this paragraph believes life was better a century ago. However, she—like our friend who prescribes garlic for headaches—offers no solid evidence to back up that opinion. The author could have quoted from journals, letters, or interviews; cited statistics; or even mentioned that there was hardly any divorce a century ago. But instead of offering support that might justify her opinion, the author simply makes the same claim over and over again in different words. This tactic, called **circular reasoning,** is typical of writers given to promoting uninformed opinions. Lacking evidence, they rely on repetition. In response to circular reasoning, critical readers rightly become skeptical, or suspicious, of the opinion expressed.

CHECK YOUR UNDERSTANDING

Explain and give an example of circular reasoning.

_____

_____

_____

Identifying Irrelevant Facts

Authors who haven't completely thought out the basis for their opinions are also given to supplying **irrelevant,** or unrelated, facts. Look, for example, at the following example.

> Health care workers must be tested for the virus that causes AIDS. To date, more than 100,000 people have died from AIDS-related illnesses. In addition, current figures from the national Centers for Disease Control show that thousands more are already infected with HIV, the virus that causes AIDS, and will probably develop full-blown AIDS.

To make her opinion about AIDS testing convincing, the author needs factual statements that support a cause and effect connection between infected health care workers and the spread of the virus that causes AIDS. Those facts would be relevant and would help justify her opinion.

But those are not the facts the author supplies. Instead, she offers two facts proving that AIDS is a serious epidemic. Unfortunately, these facts are irrelevant to her opinion about mandatory testing. Critical readers would not be convinced.

Looking for Relevant Facts

In judging opinions, critical readers are always on the lookout for **relevant facts** that have a direct connection to the opinion being expressed. Consider, for example, the following passage.

> The Italian government takes excellent care of Italy's mothers. Pregnant women in Italy are guaranteed paid leaves, combined with free medical care. According to a 1971 law, pregnant women must be allowed to stay at home during the last two months of

pregnancy, and new mothers can stay at home for the first three months following their baby's birth. During this five-month period, the government guarantees women who worked before their pregnancy 80 percent of their former salary.

In this passage, the author offers readers an opinion about how the Italian government treats mothers. (Note the connotations of the word *excellent*.) In support of this point of view, the passage supplies specific facts describing the financial and medical aid offered to mothers by the Italian government. Unlike the facts in the earlier paragraph on testing health care workers, the facts in this passage are relevant, or related, to the author's claim.

CHECK YOUR UNDERSTANDING

Explain the difference between relevant and irrelevant facts.

_____

_____

EXERCISE 4

DIRECTIONS Read each statement of opinion. Then look carefully at the two statements meant to provide support. Only one will be relevant; the other will be either irrelevant or circular. Put an *R* in the blank following the relevant statement. Mark the remaining statement with either a *C* (circular) or an *I* (irrelevant).

Opinion **EXAMPLE** Radon gas is a serious health hazard, one that can no longer be ignored.

Support a. A 1997 study by the federal government confirmed what other studies have found: there is a connection between radon gas in the home and the occurrence of lung cancer.

    R

b. When it comes to radon gas, Americans are like ostriches. They refuse to acknowledge the threat, preferring to stick their heads in the sand and pretend it doesn't exist.

    C

EXPLANATION Statement *a* is relevant because it cites a study supporting the author's claim that radon gas is a serious threat that must be recognized. Statement *b*, however, goes around in circles, repeating the opening opinion in different words.

Opinion **1.** All too often, doctors aren't sensitive to their patients' emotional needs.

Support   a. When Francine Vogler suffered a neck injury, her physician told her she might die or become a quadriplegic. Then he walked out of the room.[2]

_____

b. A bedside manner is crucial to being an effective physician, but many doctors today lack the skills to provide their patient with the emotional comfort so essential to healing.

_____

Opinion **2.** Canadian health care is a far cry from what it used to be.

Support   a. Historically, Canadians have been proud of their health care system. But currently that system is undergoing some profound changes, and few of those changes are improvements.

_____

b. The Canadian government has reduced its contributions to the health care system by 30 percent, and doctors have begun refusing to see patients if they think they will not be paid.

_____

Opinion **3.** Internet Web sites are a terrific source of information for news-hungry Americans.

Support   a. One house in five relies on the Internet for news.

_____

b. At the Web site called Newshub, the leading headline stories are updated every fifteen minutes, so that Web users can get a quick update in a minimal amount of time.

_____

Opinion **4.** The past decade has seen some amazing archaeological discoveries.

Support   a. Archaeologists have found the cave where the Greek playwright Euripides wrote at least one of his plays more than 2500 years ago.

_____

_____

[2]Thio, *Sociology*, p. 466.

b. Euripides is believed to have written at least ninety-two plays; among the most famous are *Medea* and *The Bacchants*.

———

Opinion **5.** It's becoming increasingly clear that there must be life on Jupiter.

Support a. According to new images of Jupiter, there appears to be a warm sea in which heat and moisture may well have encouraged the formation of life.

———

b. Skeptics may doubt it, but all the signs lead to one conclusion: life exists on Jupiter.

———

Opinion **6.** Currently, trampolines are popular toys for kids, but they shouldn't be. Trampolines are dangerous.

Support a. Every year, trampoline jumping produces more than sixty thousand injuries, including fractures and dislocations.[3]

———

b. Trampolines are not toys, and they shouldn't be treated as such.

———

Opinion **7.** On June 23, 1972, President Richard Nixon signed Title IX into law, making gender discrimination in education illegal. Thanks to Title IX, women's sports would never be the same.

Support a. When Title IX was enacted, little more than 30,000 women participated in college athletics; today there are more than 120,000 female athletes on college campuses.

———

b. When Richard Nixon signed Title IX into law, neither he nor anyone else realized what a profound impact it would have on women's sports.

———

Opinion **8.** Vitamin E just may be the most beneficial vitamin a person can take in an effort to ensure a healthy old age.

Support a. Recent reports in the *New England Journal of Medicine* show that

———

[3]*Time,* March 16, 1998, p. 22.

the mental deterioration caused by Alzheimer's disease can be dramatically slowed by taking vitamin E.

_____

b. High doses of a mineral called selegiline also appear to slow down the mental deterioration caused by Alzheimer's disease.

_____

Opinion   9. Read Sebastian Junger's *The Perfect Storm,* and you may never set foot on a boat again.

Support   a. *The Perfect Storm* describes in terrifying detail the destruction of the *Andrea Gail,* a fishing boat that sank during a 1991 storm, taking with it all six crew members.

_____

b. Sebastian Junger's *The Perfect Storm* stayed on the bestseller list for months, earning him a good deal of money and several lawsuits.

_____

Opinion   10. At present, English dominates on the Internet, but it may not dominate for long.

Support   a. Usenet, the bulletin board system for the Internet, is where one can find messages on just about any topic.

_____

b. Many non-English-speaking people are creating Web sites in their own languages, and efforts are under way to develop software that provides immediate translations.

_____

EXERCISE 5

DIRECTIONS Read each passage. Then in the blank at the end, label each passage either *U* for uninformed or *I* for informed. If you label the passage uninformed, circle the appropriate letter to indicate if the author relied on circular reasoning or irrelevant facts.

EXAMPLE It's time for schools and sports teams like the Atlanta Braves and the Washington Redskins to end their use of Native-American names and symbols. These symbols are often historically inaccurate. For instance, the Plains Indians never wore the feathered headdresses so often used to symbolize the Native-American experience. Also, schools that portray Indians as fierce, tomahawk-wielding warriors misrepresent tribal life both past and present. In addition, these names and symbols are insensitive and offensive. All too often, the cartoonish images reflected by logos* and mascots stereotype Native American life. Not surprisingly, many Native-American leaders object to these unflattering symbols for fear that they will encourage children to disrespect Indian culture. Some also claim that the use of these symbols leads to poor self-image among Native-American children.

<u> *I* </u>

a. Circular reasoning

b. Irrelevant facts

EXPLANATION This is an informed opinion because the author supplies both relevant facts and reasons to make her opinion convincing to her readers.

1. Professional-wrestling television shows are not appropriate for children. These programs are not intended for younger viewers. Yet, about one million kids under the age of twelve are watching TV wrestling. Parents who let their young children watch these shows don't realize the harm they are causing. They need to think about the long-term damage their kids could suffer and to be more cautious about the potential risks. Kids must be encouraged to choose among the many other TV shows that are more appropriate for young children.

<u>   </u>

a. Circular reasoning

b. Irrelevant facts

2. Every American should seriously consider buying one of the new hybrid gasoline-electric cars. Thousands of people have already bought a Honda Insight or a Toyota Prius, both of which cost around $20,000. The demand for these cars, which combine a small gasoline engine with an electric motor, already exceeds production. Within the next two years, various auto manufacturers plan to introduce a hybrid sport utility vehicle, a hybrid mini-van, and a hybrid truck. It's clear that hybrid vehicles are a growing trend, and one day in the near future, there should be one in

*logos: symbols representing institutions.

every American garage. Fortunately, there are signs that hybrid autos are catching on and becoming trendy among celebrities. Anxious to imitate their idols, ordinary Americans will probably follow suit.

_____

a. Circular reasoning

b. Irrelevant facts

3. The career of legendary queen of salsa Celia Cruz has been both long and influential. In her half-century career, Cruz has recorded more than seventy albums and has traveled all over the world, entertaining four generations of fans with her extraordinary voice and flamboyant performances. More than anything else, she helped define salsa, an Afro-Cuban musical style characterized by Latin rhythms. Cruz has also received numerous awards and honors—including the prestigious National Medal of Arts, a Grammy Award, and an honorary doctorate degree from Yale University—all in recognition of her contributions. Perhaps most important, Cruz is credited with breaking down racial and cultural barriers by winning a mainstream audience over to Latin music. Twenty of her albums went gold, selling more than 500,000 copies each. Because her music appeals to a wide range of people and because she takes pride and joy in her Cuban heritage, she has served as a passionate ambassador of Hispanic culture. Aware of her accomplishments, Cruz has credited them to her father: "In a sense, I have fulfilled my father's wish to be a teacher as, through my music, I teach generations of people about my culture."

_____

a. Circular reasoning

b. Irrelevant facts

4. Although the so-called Mozart effect has been widely accepted by educators, parents, legislators, and music marketers, new evidence indicates that it may not exist after all. In 1993, researchers at the University of Wisconsin claimed that college students who listened to ten minutes of a Mozart sonata prior to taking a spatial-reasoning test significantly improved their ability to perform tasks such as cutting and folding paper. This study gave birth to the belief that listening to Mozart's music helps increase intelligence. However, researchers have not been able to duplicate the results of this first experiment. As a matter of fact, a Harvard University graduate analyzed the conclusions of sixteen similar studies and found no scientific proof that music increased IQ or improved academic performance. Researchers at Appalachian State University and two Canadian universities have come to the same conclusion.

———

a. Circular reasoning

b. Irrelevant facts

5. When the threat of bioterrorism came to seem very real in the fall of 2001, some companies began to market home-testing kits for the detection of anthrax, a deadly respiratory disease spread by bacteria. Costing from twenty to twenty-five dollars, the kits were available primarily over the Internet. Alarmed by the public's positive response to the kits, members of several different consumer groups issued warnings against the purchase of such kits, and for good reason. Testing for anthrax should not be done by individuals. Even when the government tested buildings for the presence of anthrax, the results of those tests were not always accurate. In the case of a test performed at one site, for example, the test came back negative at first. But later tests showed that there were actually anthrax spores present. The government has the capability to test and retest, using a variety of different and more refined methods in order to double- and even triple-check for accuracy. Average householders, however, do not have such resources at their disposal. Ordinary people are likely to perform the test and take the results as accurate. Yet there is always the possibility of a false positive that indicates anthrax is present when it isn't; or, even worse, a false negative, suggesting the house is safe from disease when it's really not. Performing the same test two or three different times is probably not the solution. Often what's needed is a more sophisticated screening device, precisely the kind available in laboratories but not available to the ordinary consumer.

———

a. Circular reasoning

b. Irrelevant facts

Fact and Opinion in Textbooks

Many students assume that textbook writers restrict themselves to facts and avoid presenting opinions. Although that may be true for some science texts, it's not true for textbooks in general, particularly in the areas of psychology, history, and government. Look, for example, at the following passage. Do you detect the presence of an opinion?

> Presidents are not just celebrities, they are the American version of royalty. Lacking a royal family, Americans look to the president to symbolize the uniqueness of their government. (Gitelson et al., *American Government*, p. 311.)

If you said the entire passage was an opinion, you'd be right. There's no way to verify how *all* Americans feel about the role of the president. And a good many may have no use for the notion of royalty, so why would they look for a substitute?

As the excerpt illustrates, textbooks do, indeed, offer opinions along with facts. However, that's not a failing as long as the authors offer support for the opinions they convey in their writing.

Here, for example, is another textbook excerpt. The authors open with an opinion about the American military's attempt to manage news during the Gulf War. Note, however, that the opinion is not left unsupported. On the contrary, a specific example follows right on its heels.

Opinion

Example offered as support

> Part of the strategy [during the Gulf War] was to "spin" the news, so that U.S. successes were emphasized and losses minimized. When announcing that eleven marines had been killed in action, for example, the military first showed twenty minutes of footage on Iraqi bridges and buildings being blown up, and the American deaths were treated virtually as an afterthought. The strategy, which worked, was to force nightly news programs to divide their attention between the bad news—eleven killed at the outset of a potentially difficult ground war—and the good news—visually spectacular footage of a truck traveling across a bridge seconds before the bridge blew up. (Johnson et al., *American Government*, p. 354.)

The two examples cited here should make it clear that you can't reserve critical reading skills for newspapers and magazines. You also have to apply them to textbooks. In short, be on the alert for the presence of personal opinions in your textbooks and check to see that those opinions are followed by relevant supporting details.

■ **DIGGING DEEPER**

LOOKING AHEAD The passage on page 286 claimed that letting your kids watch wrestling was a very bad idea. Read the following selection to see if the author supports or contradicts that point of view.

SUBURBAN SMACKDOWN

1   In a leafy suburban backyard about an hour's drive south of Manhattan, a tableau* of choreographed violence is taking shape. A dozen boys have gathered on a miserably hot Saturday afternoon. They've set up a video camera, loudspeakers and a wrestling ring. Steve Toth, sixteen, provided the yard. But his mom, Colleen, has retreated indoors. She'd rather not watch as the teenagers punch, kick and insult one another, as they do most Saturdays.

2   It may not be Rock vs. the Undertaker on prime-time TV, but the high school boys of the Extreme Wrestling Federation of Sayreville, New Jersey, try hard to make their contests look just as "real." They organize weekly bouts featuring costumed characters, intricate plot lines and the inevitable black eyes and scratches. In the EWF, as in the big leagues, fighters are assigned roles: lowdown "jobbers" routinely get beaten up; superstars vie for championship titles. The boys know who will get slammed with a metal chair or smashed on a table. During the interview portions, characters accuse one another of cheating. The referee is jeered and mauled.

3   Inspired by television wrestling, similar matches are staged weekly in hundreds of backyards across the country. In South Euclid, Ohio, you can watch a show mounted by the teenage Alliance of Violence. In Poinciana, Florida, the federation calls itself Insane Violent Hardcore Extreme Wrestling. More than 400 leagues have websites. And kids trade bootleg* videotapes of their antics. Just harmless roughhousing? Not according to critics, including many from the pro-wrestling industry. "If I had a kid doing it, I'd lock him in his bedroom," says Verne Langdon, a trainer and owner of Slammers Wrestling Gym in Studio City, California. "Pros don't always set a good example."

4   Among the images on a Best of Backyard Wrestling video: kids jumping onto barbed wire, setting opponents on fire and diving

---

*tableau: picture or image.
*bootleg: illegally obtained.

onto mattresses studded with thumbtacks. And the violence seems to be trickling down from teenagers to tots. Last year in Dallas, a three-year-old boy was killed when his seven-year-old brother stiff-armed him in the throat, copying a move he'd seen on TV. Emergency rooms report a rise in injuries among backyard wrestlers. "It's scary," says Colleen Toth. "But my son does everything to make it safe. If he's going to do it, I'd rather it be in my backyard."

5   The two major pro-wrestling outfits, World Championship Wrestling and the World Wrestling Federation, now run don't-try-this-at-home ads during their bouts. But to the boys in Sayreville, the warnings seem silly. "I wear kneepads," says Donnie Deleto, sixteen. "We don't crack light bulbs on each other. We don't use cheese graters. We get a bad rap because idiots do that. We're putting on a show." Just like on TV. (Daren Fonda, "Sport: Suburban Smackdown," *Time*, June 26, 2000, p. 53, © 2000 Time Inc. Reprinted by permission.)

Sharpening Your Skills

DIRECTIONS Answer the following questions.

1. The author opens by saying that the mother of the boy who wrestles doesn't like to watch her son and his friends. What does her reluctance imply? _____

    _____

2. In paragraph 3, the author poses a question: "Just harmless roughhousing?" What answer is implied by the reading as a whole? _____

    What in the reading led you to draw this inference? _____

    _____

3. In paragraph 4, the author offers the opinion that violence in wrestling "seems to be trickling down from teenagers to tots." What evidence does the author offer for this opinion?

    _____

    Would you call this opinion informed or uninformed? _____

    _____

4. Would you say that the title uses emotionally charged or emotionally

neutral language? _____

Explain your answer. _____

_____

WORD NOTES: SEARCHING FOR TRUTH

The discussion of fact and opinion on page 271 introduced a form of the verb *verify*, meaning to prove true. *Verify* is an important word to add to your vocabulary. However, you should also consider learning some of its synonyms. Learning groups of words related in meaning is a good way to rapidly enlarge your vocabulary.

1. **Confirm:** to remove all doubts, as in "Can you *confirm* the receipt of my proposal?"

2. **Corroborate:** to strengthen through statements supplied by another, as in "No one was alive to *corroborate* the testimony of the accused."

3. **Substantiate:** to establish something by means of factual evidence, as in "The historian's position had now been firmly *substantiated* by the discovery of both diaries and letters."

4. **Authenticate:** to prove genuine, as in "The museum was swindled when it paid for the sculpture before it was *authenticated*."

Now fill in the blanks with one of the four words defined above.

1. Because the professor's long-time assistant was able to

_____ his statements, the police were willing to let him go.

2. The art historian was unable to _____ the painting as a genuine Picasso.

3. The secretary called to _____ the arrival of the package.

4. Researchers have been able to _____ long-standing rumors about Thomas Jefferson's affair with his slave, Sally Hemmings.

Test 1: Reviewing the Key Points

DIRECTIONS Answer the following questions by circling the correct response or filling in the blanks.

1. The true test of a fact is whether or not it can be _____.

2. Opinions can't be _____, but they can be _____.

3. Critical readers need to distinguish between _____ and _____ opinions.

4. *True* or *False*. Writers always keep their facts and opinions separate from one another.

5. Connotative language carries with it strong _____.

6. Denotative language relies strictly on the _____.

7. *True* or *False*. Changing the context of a word can make it more denotative or connotative.

8. *True* or *False*. Textbooks report facts; they do not include opinions.

9. Facts or reasons offered in support of an opinion need to be

   _____.

10. When writers use circular reasoning, they usually lack _____

    so they rely instead on _____.

Test 2: Distinguishing Between Fact and Opinion

DIRECTIONS Label each of the following statements *F* for fact, *O* for opinion, or *B* for both.

_____ 1. As George Orwell so correctly said, "The greatest enemy of clear language is insincerity."

_____ 2. Among people suffering from depression, one portion of the brain is significantly smaller than the other.

_____ 3. The planet Neptune was discovered in 1846 by the German astronomer Johann G. Galle.

_____ 4. The murder in Dallas, Texas, of John Fitzgerald Kennedy, the thirty-fifth president of the United States, proved to be one of the most profound acts of the twentieth century. (David Wallechinsky, *The Twentieth Century.* Boston: Little, Brown, 1995, p. 147.)

_____ 5. The Mexican revolutionary Emilio Zapata (1879–1919) had a profound influence on modern Mexico.

_____ 6. Louise Brown, the world's first test-tube baby, was born on July 25, 1978.

_____ 7. We should return to the days when films were made in black and white rather than color.

_____ 8. For decades, it's been painfully clear that our water resources are limited, and we must pay more attention to water conservation.

_____ 9. Physical competence produces psychological competence. (M. Burch Tracy Ford, head of Miss Porter's School in Farmington, Conn.)

_____ 10. Eggs contaminated by salmonella bacteria are the number one cause of food poisoning outbreaks in the United States.

Test 3: Recognizing Informed and Uninformed Opinions

DIRECTIONS Label each passage with either an *I* for informed opinion or a *U* for uninformed opinion.

1. Although most people over the age of three love firework displays, they probably don't realize that fireworks are big business, and a highly creative and competitive one at that. A few family-owned companies, such as Zambelli International, Sunset Fireworks, and Pyro Spectacular, compete fiercely for a chance at the big Fourth of July displays. To make sure they have an edge, each company closely guards its recipes for spectacular effects. No one really knows, for example, how Zambelli International creates its gorgeous floral bouquet of red camellias and gold chrysanthemums. And if it's up to the owners, no one ever will.

   _____

2. Even though Elvis Presley died on August 6, 1977, he is certainly not forgotten. On the contrary, the legend of Elvis lives on. To honor the twentieth anniversary of his death, RCA released a four-volume CD, *Elvis Presley Platinum: A Life in Music.* It was so popular that record stores couldn't keep it on the shelves. In honor of that same anniversary, more than fifty thousand fans descended on Graceland, Elvis's former home in Tennessee. In 1997 and 1998, the San Jose Ballet toured the country performing a ballet in the singer's honor. It was called *Blue Suede Shoes.*

   _____

3. It shouldn't have taken the murder of a tiny beauty queen to make parents question the value of beauty pageants for children. These pageants were always a disgrace. They do nothing but harm to both parents and children alike. Beauty pageants for grown-up women are bad enough, but beauty pageants for children are simply disgusting. They should be sharply criticized by the media and, if possible, banned by state legislatures.

   _____

4. Hunters like to claim that they were among the first environmentalists, but nothing could be further from the truth. Hunting benefits only those men and women who like to kill living creatures for sport. Oddly enough, environmental groups like the National Audubon Society and the Sierra Club support hunting, but that should not en-

courage anyone else to do so. The only way animals should be hunted is with a camera, never with a gun.

———

5. The label *organic* doesn't necessarily mean that food has been grown or raised without pesticides and man-made fertilizers. Currently, what's considered organic in one state may not be in another. Some states' certification programs allow organic produce to be grown with certain fertilizers and insecticides that other states specifically prohibit. Moreover, twenty states have no rules whatsoever governing organic food. "As it now stands, in an unregulated state there's nothing to stop some farmers from just sticking an organic label on their tomatoes, say, and putting them out for sale without ever having followed any organic principles," observes Katherine DiMatteo, executive director of the national Organic Trade Association. (Adapted from Jennifer Reid Holman, "Can You Trust Organic?" *Self*, November 1997, p. 163.)

———

Test 4: Recognizing Circular Reasoning and Irrelevant Facts

DIRECTIONS Label each supporting statement with one of these three letters: *R* (relevant), *I* (irrelevant), or *C* (circular).

Opinion **1.** The Internet certainly can't replace the family doctor, but, now more than ever, it is possible to get accurate medical information online.

Support   a. To ensure that citizens get accurate medical information, the U.S. government has created the Healthfinder Web site (www.healthfinder.gov), which evaluates all health-related Web sites for accuracy.

         ———

    b. More and more Americans are becoming dissatisfied with traditional medical care and are turning to alternative medical treatments like acupuncture and herbal remedies; in fact, one out of three Americans now seeks medical care from a person not in possession of a conventional medical degree.

         ———

Opinion **2.** Almost single-handedly, Roger Tory Peterson (1908–1996) made bird watching a hobby anyone could pursue.

Support   a. Before Peterson, there was no pocket-size guidebook that birders could use for identifying the birds they saw. Peterson's guidebook was the first that could be carried in a pocket for ease of identification.

         ———

    b. Birds are more than beautiful; they are early indicators of what's right or wrong with the planet.

         ———

Opinion **3.** Although many historians have portrayed Aaron Burr as the villain in his duel with Alexander Hamilton, the facts do not appear to support that interpretation.

Support   a. Rather than rejoicing when his bullet found its target, Burr by all accounts seems to have been shocked by Hamilton's collapse and rushed forward to speak to him.

         ———

       b. Given the way in which history has portrayed Aaron Burr, one might assume that Burr murdered Hamilton in cold blood, but the evidence does not support the claim.

       _____

Opinion **4.** Astronomers taking part in Project Phoenix are looking for extraterrestrial intelligence in the universe.

Support   a. Project Phoenix scientists hope to discover life on other planets.

       _____

       b. Project Phoenix is funded entirely by private donations.

       _____

Opinion **5.** The Brady Law, which requires background checks of potential gun buyers, has been very effective.

Support   a. Congress did the right thing when it passed the Brady Law.

       _____

       b. James Brady, for whom the law is named, was wounded by gunfire and is now confined to a wheelchair.

       _____

Test 5: Recognizing Circular Reasoning and Irrelevant Facts

DIRECTIONS Circle the appropriate letter to indicate if the passage expresses an informed opinion, uses circular reasoning, or cites an irrelevant fact (or facts).

1. NASCAR should mandate that all drivers wear head-and-neck restraint devices during races. Dale Earnhardt, who died in a crash during a Daytona 500 race in February 2001, was one of the all-time great stockcar drivers. Earnhardt began racing cars on dirt-track speedways in the 1970s and made a name for himself in 1979 by winning a major race in Bristol, Tennessee. During a career that spanned twenty-six years, he won the Winston Cup Series championship seven times. Earnhardt is credited with helping stockcar racing evolve into a mainstream American sport. Tragically, he was only forty-nine years old when he died.

   a. The passage expresses an informed opinion.

   b. The passage relies on circular reasoning.

   c. The passage cites an irrelevant fact or facts.

2. The one-cent penny still serves several necessary roles, so Americans should not eliminate this coin. First of all, rendering the penny obsolete would hurt the poor. Because merchants usually round up to the nearest nickel on cash purchases, lower-income Americans, who conduct most of their business using cash, would wind up paying more. The nonprofit organization Americans for Common Cents claims that rounding will cost consumers an additional $600 million a year. Those who advocate keeping the penny also say that eliminating it would hurt charities because they collect millions of dollars in donated pennies. Finally, the penny should remain in circulation because Americans are fond of it. According to Americans for Common Cents, polls consistently show that up to 65 percent of Americans oppose getting rid of this coin.

   a. The passage expresses an informed opinion.

   b. The passage relies on circular reasoning.

   c. The passage cites an irrelevant fact or facts.

3. Local, state, and federal governments violate citizens' right to privacy when they post public records on the Internet. Easy access to the personal information contained in voter registration records, property tax rolls, and court records should alarm every American. Putting such data online simply makes public records *too* public.

It's become much too easy to obtain personal information that should be kept private. Web sites that post such information are a disservice to the people of this country. That's why governments should not improve the public's access to sensitive records by putting them online.

a. The passage expresses an informed opinion.

b. The passage relies on circular reasoning.

c. The passage cites an irrelevant fact or facts.

4. In the United States, not being able to speak Spanish handicaps an individual personally and professionally. The Hispanic population is growing rapidly. Currently, 3.5 million Hispanics reside in this country. In many communities, their numbers have doubled in the last decade, and in many cities and counties, even in states like Kansas, Hispanics now account for almost half of the population. Thirty-two percent of all California residents are now Hispanic. With this many Spanish-speaking neighbors, English-speaking citizens will see the Spanish language entering more and more into pop culture like television commercials and music. The ability to speak Spanish will also be a tremendous asset in the workplace as increasing numbers of businesses seek to hire bilingual employees who can communicate with their Hispanic customers. In particular, professionals who interact with the public on a daily basis—such as law enforcement officers and nurses—will need to be able to speak Spanish in order to do their jobs effectively.

a. The passage expresses an informed opinion.

b. The passage relies on circular reasoning.

c. The passage cites an irrelevant fact or facts.

5. The underpaid and underappreciated officials who referee National Football League (NFL) games deserve a raise in salary. Referees see to it that the rules and regulations of the game are enforced. Without them, the game could turn into a dangerous free-for-all. Yet, in general, their job is a thankless one that earns them insults and worse from the players and boos from the crowd. A bit more money in referees' paychecks seems necessary to offset the drawbacks of their thankless job. This seems only fair since 41 percent of Americans, according to a Peter Harris Research Group survey, say that their favorite leisure activity is watching football.

a. The passage expresses an informed opinion.

b. The passage relies on circular reasoning.

c. The passage cites an irrelevant fact or facts.

C H A P T E R   8

Identifying Purpose and Tone

 In this chapter, you'll learn

- how *informative* and *persuasive* writing differ.

- why discovering the author's purpose is essential to critical reading.

- how the title and source of a reading help you predict the writer's purpose.

- how thesis statements help you confirm or revise your prediction.

- how tone relates to purpose.

- how to recognize an ironic tone.

Most writing falls into three categories: (1) writing meant to inform, (2) writing designed to persuade, and

(3) writing intended purely to entertain. Because we're focusing on critical reading issues, such as evaluating evidence and separating fact from opinion, this chapter is solely concerned with writing meant to inform or persuade. Determining whether a writer intends to inform or persuade can sometimes be difficult. However, writing bent on entertaining is pretty easy to recognize. The only possible complication or difficulty might be that you don't share the author's sense of humor.

 # Understanding the Difference Between Informative and Persuasive Writing

To be a good critical reader, you need a clear understanding of how informative and persuasive writing differ.

Informative Writing

The goal of **informative writing** is to make the audience more knowledgeable about a particular subject. Informative writing usually leans heavily on factual information and doesn't promote any one opinion. If anything, informative writing is likely to offer competing opinions on the same subject while the author remains objective, or impartial, refusing to champion one opinion over another.

Here's a good example of writing meant primarily to inform:

Two factors in the development of obesity in children are beyond human control. These two factors are heredity and age. Like it or not, thinness and fatness do run in families. Overweight children tend to have overweight parents and underweight parents tend to have underweight children (LeBow, 1984). In addition, most people inevitably put on fat more during certain periods of life than during others. Late childhood and early puberty form one of these periods; at this time, most children gain fat tissue out of proportion to increases in other tissues, such as muscle and bone. (Adapted from Seifert and Hoffnung, *Child and Adolescent Development*, p. 390.)

In this example, the topic is obesity in children, and the authors briefly describe two of its causes: heredity and age. Notice, however, that they themselves do not express a point of view about their subject. Nor do the authors suggest that readers should adopt a particular point of view. Their primary purpose is dispensing information. It is not persuasion.

Persuasive Writing

Persuasive writing promotes one particular opinion. Its goal is to make readers share or at least seriously consider the author's point of view. Although writers intent on persuasion certainly use facts, those facts are carefully chosen to make their case convincing. And when they present opposing points of view, it is only to disprove them. Unlike authors of informative writing, authors of persuasive writing are not objective. Even if they try to keep an open mind, they remain *subjective.* That means they are committed to their point of view and hope you will share it. Here, to illustrate, is a passage written with a persuasive intent.

> The notion that strangers must be feared is not only lamentable* but also wrong. The media have documented the crimes of psychopathic rapists, kidnappers, child snatchers, and criminals. Such monsters exist. But the harsh truth is that more people are hurt by those they know than they are by those whom they don't. Women are more likely to be battered by their husbands and lovers than by strangers. They are more likely to be raped by someone they know. Social workers and physicians frequently find that when the elderly are neglected and abused, the perpetrators are spouses and children and not paid caretakers. And when children are abducted, sexually molested, and/or abused, the culprit is most often a parent, a stepparent, or a trusted relative. (Joan Retsinas, "Don't Speak to Strangers," *Newsweek*, October 31, 1988, p. 10.)

In this case the author has a definite point of view she wants readers to share: Encouraging the notion that strangers are automatically dangerous is a mistake. She then goes on to offer evidence for her position in the hope that readers will share it.

---

*lamentable: sad.

CHECK YOUR UNDERSTANDING

See how well you can sum up the differences between informative and persuasive writing.

Informative Writing	Persuasive Writing

The Importance of Purpose

Identifying an author's primary **purpose,** or reason for writing, is important because the author's purpose determines how critically you need to read. After all, your time is limited. You can't possibly check every source or ponder everything you read. With informational writing, you can relax and read to understand the author's message. You can safely assume that the writer is objectively describing events or ideas without telling you how to interpret or view them. In fact, a writer whose primary purpose is to inform is very likely to give you different explanations of the same events so that you can develop your own opinions.

However, the more an author leans toward persuasion, the more you must *evaluate* what you read, considering the amount and kind of evidence offered. Because persuasive writing tries to affect how you think, feel, and behave, you need to look for reasons, check facts, and consider the effect of word choice before you let yourself be influenced.

In a very real way, the author's purpose shapes or determines your reading response. The clearer it becomes that an author is intent on persuasion, the more willing you must be to do a close and critical reading.

Determining the Primary Purpose

To be sure, a good deal of writing blends information and persuasion. For example, a writer who wants to inform her readers about changes that have taken place in Berlin, Germany, since the Berlin Wall* came down also needs to persuade her readers that her account is accurate and trustworthy. Similarly, an author may wish to convince his readers that they should give more money to AIDS research. But to make that position persuasive, he will probably inform them about current funding.

As a critical reader, you should always try to determine an author's primary, or major, purpose. Be aware, however, that it's not always possible to claim with absolute certainty whether a writer meant to inform *or* persuade. Some writers inform and persuade in equal measure.

CHECK YOUR UNDERSTANDING
In your own words, why is knowing the author's purpose important?

◢▱▭◉ Predicting Purpose

The only way to truly identify an author's purpose is to read what he or she has to say. However, even before you begin reading, there are two very important clues you can use to predict the author's purpose—the source of the reading and the author's background.

The Source Is a Clue to Purpose

The source or location of a reading is often a solid clue to purpose. Technical manuals, guidebooks, science texts and journals, refer-

---

*Berlin Wall: the wall that divided East and West Berlin. It was erected by the Communist government to keep East Germans from fleeing to democratic West Germany.

ence books, dictionaries, reports of scientific experiments, and newspaper accounts of current events are usually written primarily to inform. Writing drawn from these sources usually does not promote any one particular point of view, but instead offers an *objective,* or impersonal, account of both people and events.

Unlike the above sources, editorials, opinion pieces, letters to the editor, and book, movie, and theater reviews in both newspapers and magazines are all likely to promote one particular point of view over other, competing points of view. The same applies to pamphlets published by political parties or special interest groups, books and articles challenging or revising commonly held beliefs or theories, biographies of famous people, and journals promoting particular causes. All of these sources are likely to feature persuasive writing.

Check the Author's Background

Information about the author's background is not always available to you. But when it is, it can be a useful clue to purpose. For example, a government official who represents the U.S. Department of Health and Human Services and reports on the use of antibiotics in poultry raising is less likely to have a persuasive intent than the president of the New England Poultry Association. If a writer represents a group that could benefit from what he or she claims, then you should suspect a persuasive purpose. You might be wrong, but the chances are good that you will be right.

EXERCISE 1

DIRECTIONS What follows is a list of possible sources for written material. Next to each item on the list is a blank. Put a *P* in the blank if you think the source is likely to contain persuasive writing. If you think it's likely to contain informative writing, put an *I* in the blank.

P   EXAMPLE A letter to the editor on the subject of gun control, taken from the *Pittsburgh Post-Gazette*

EXPLANATION In contrast to other newspaper writing, letters to the editor—like editorials—are likely to feature persuasive writing.

_____   **1.** An article about Cuban leader Fidel Castro appearing in the *Encyclopaedia Britannica*

_____ **2.** An article about Fidel Castro appearing on the front page of the *New York Times*

_____ **3.** A biography of Fidel Castro titled *The Man Who Destroyed Cuba*

_____ **4.** A book titled *A Field Guide to American Houses*

_____ **5.** A government pamphlet titled *Historic Buildings in the Southern States*

_____ **6.** A book review of a work titled *The Triumph of American Architecture*

_____ **7.** A government report on global warming

_____ **8.** A letter about global warming written to the editor of the *Atlanta Times*

_____ **9.** A book titled *The Field Guide to North American Birds*

_____ **10.** An article about the disappearance of songbirds appearing in a journal titled *Save the Earth Now*

Titles Also Provide Clues

Another clue to purpose is the title of a reading. Titles that simply describe a state of affairs—"Teamwork Used to Teach Math"—usually signal that the writer simply wants to inform readers without necessarily persuading them. Titles that express an opinion are quite a different matter. A title like "Teamwork and Mathematics Don't Mix" should immediately suggest to you that the author's primary purpose is persuasion.

Sometimes, of course, the title is no help whatsoever in determining the author's purpose. For example, titles like "A Look at the Nation" or "Family Affairs" don't reveal the author's purpose.

EXERCISE 2

DIRECTIONS Read each pair of titles. If the title suggests the writer wants mainly to inform, put an *I* in the blank. If it suggests persuasion, fill in the blank with a *P*.

EXAMPLE

a. Bilingual Education Is on the Rise ___*I*___

b. Congress Should Pass "English Only" Legislation ___*P*___

EXPLANATION The first title simply describes a state of affairs without passing any judgment. The second title takes a definite stand, indicating that the writer wants readers to be persuaded.

1. a. Against Assisted Death _____

   b. Assisted Death in the Netherlands _____

2. a. Support for Same-Sex Schools Is Increasing _____

   b. It Will Take More Than Same-Sex Schools to Get Rid of Gender Bias _____

3. a. Women Don't Belong in the Military _____

   b. Women in the Military _____

4. a. Astrology: The Science of Crackpots* _____

   b. Understanding Astrology _____

5. a. The Science of Cloning _____

   b. Let's Be Cautious About Cloning _____

EXERCISE 3

DIRECTIONS Try your hand at creating titles that express your intent. Make title *a* a statement that suggests your purpose is to inform. Title *b* should reveal your intention to persuade.

EXAMPLE

Topic Animal Rights

a. _The History of the Animal Rights Movement in America_

b. _Animals Don't Have Rights; People Do_

EXPLANATION Title *a* suggests the writer is intent on describing the animal rights movement whereas title *b* suggests the author wants to discourage support for the movement.

1. **Topic** The Super Bowl

   a. _____

   b. _____

---

*crackpots: persons with odd ideas.

2. **Topic**   School Prayer

   a. _____

   b. _____

3. **Topic**   Internet Courtships

   a. _____

   b. _____

4. **Topic**   Divorce

   a. _____

   b. _____

5. **Topic**   Cloning

   a. _____

   b. _____

 # The Main Idea Is the Clincher

The title, source, and any available information about the author's background can frequently suggest the author's purpose. But it's the author's stated or implied main idea that is the clincher, or deciding factor. It will tell you whether your initial prediction about purpose is accurate or in need of revision.

Main Ideas in Informative Writing

In writing meant to inform, authors describe, but they do not judge or evaluate, events, people, or ideas. Here, for example, the writer describes an author's beliefs about Greek culture.

> In *Black Athena*, Charles Bernal argues that the Greeks were deeply indebted to the Egyptians for almost every aspect of their culture.

Based on this thesis statement, which does not in any way evaluate Bernal's work, experienced critical readers would assume the author intends to describe Charles Bernal's book without making any claims about its value. While the remainder of the reading could prove them wrong—critical readers continuously test and revise their expectations—it's more than likely that their first response will prove correct.

Main Ideas in Persuasive Writing

Writers intent on persuasion will usually state or imply a main idea that identifies some action which needs to be taken, some belief that should be held, or some value judgment that should be shared. Here is an example.

> Charles Bernal has expended enormous energy on *Black Athena*, but he is absolutely wrong to assert, as he does, that he has rewritten the history of the eastern Mediterranean. (Emily Vermeale, "The World Turned Upside Down," *New York Review of Books*, March 26, 1992, p. 43.)

Faced with this thesis statement, most critical readers would correctly assume that the author wants readers to share her opinion of *Black Athena.*

Look now at the next two thesis statements. Which one do you think suggests that the author's goal is to persuade? Put a *P* in the blank next to that statement.

_____ **1.** A number of factors cause children to become obese, or seriously overweight.

_____ **2.** Because obesity is a serious health problem, parents need to pay close attention to what their children eat.

If you filled in the blank next to statement 2, you correctly recognized that the first statement did not encourage readers to pass any judgment or take any action. Statement 2, in contrast, strongly suggests that readers should share the author's feelings about obesity in children—it's a serious health problem. It also encourages parents to act on those feelings by keeping a close watch on their children's diet. This is the kind of thesis statement that tells readers to look for and evaluate the author's evidence for such a claim.

■ EXERCISE 4

DIRECTIONS Read each pair of thesis statements. Write an *I* in the blank if the writer intends mainly to inform. Write a *P* if the statement encourages readers to share the writer's point of view.

EXAMPLE

a. In 1998, five U.S. sites were listed among the one hundred most endangered historic spots in the world; all are threatened by housing developments, industry, or simple neglect.

   I

b. In 1998, Mesa Verde National Park in Colorado landed on the list of one hundred most endangered historic spots. Mesa Verde is the site of eight-hundred-year-old cliff dwellings built by the Anasazi, Native Americans who inhabited Colorado and Utah about A.D. 100. Given its historical significance, we must do everything possible to save the park.

   P

EXPLANATION Statement *a* simply identifies an existing state of affairs, while statement *b* calls readers to action.

1. a. Nothing could be more wrong-headed than San Francisco's decision to make smoking marijuana legal for medical purposes.

   ___

   b. In 1991, San Franciscans approved the use of marijuana for medical purposes.

   ___

2. a. In 1996, Buck and Luther, two Atlantic bottlenose dolphins, were retired from Navy service with full honors. To prepare them for a return to the sea, the Navy sent them to a retraining center in Florida. But some person or group set the dolphins free before retraining was completed, and the two dolphins barely survived their punishing first few weeks at sea.

   ___

   b. It's sad but true that we humans often hurt wild animals in our attempts to help them. When two Atlantic bottlenose dolphins, Buck and Luther, were retired from Navy service, they were sent to a retraining center in preparation for their return to the ocean and life on their own. Unfortunately, some misguided animal lovers decided to speed up the process and liberated the dolphins before they were ready. As a result, Buck and Luther barely survived their newfound freedom.

   ___

3. a. The Tuskegee Study of Untreated Syphilis in the Negro Male was begun in 1932, when the United States Public Health Service began tracking 399 black men with syphilis. The study's stated purpose was to chart the natural history of the disease without recourse to any treatment, but the men recruited for the study were never told its true purpose.

──────

b. In May of 1997, President Clinton apologized on behalf of the nation to the survivors of the Tuskegee Study of Untreated Syphilis in the Negro Male. But his apology can never erase the horrible stain that experiment left on America's history.

──────

4. a. The research of sociologists Elaine Wethington and Ronald Kessler is too flawed to be taken seriously. It brings little or nothing to the debate about women and work.

──────

b. Sociologists Elaine Wethington of Cornell University and Ronald Kessler of the University of Michigan found that women who worked at low-wage, part-time jobs were more stressed than women who worked full time.

──────

5. a. Radon, particularly in combination with smoking, poses an important public health risk and it should be recognized as such.

──────

b. Research strongly suggests that radon, a naturally occurring radioactive gas, which collects in many homes, is linked to more than 20,000 deaths from lung cancer.[1]

──────

6. a. Now that scientists have found the hormone that triggers hunger, they need to take the next step and discover how this hormone can be controlled. Such a discovery would be an enormous advance in the war against obesity.

──────

───────────

[1]"Researcher Links Radon to 21,000 Deaths a Year," *New Haven Register,* February 20, 1998, p. F1.

b. Based on research at the University of Texas Southwestern Medical Center, scientists believe they have found the hormone that triggers feelings of hunger.

_____

7. a. On any given day at least ten Americans will die waiting for an organ transplant.

_____

b. We need a strong public relations campaign that encourages people to become organ donors.

_____

8. a. Scientists have found seven fossil ants encased in chunks of amber that are almost one hundred million years old.

_____

b. The seven fossil ants encased in amber millions of years old prove that ants had a complex social system of behavior much earlier than anyone previously realized.

_____

9. a. Those of us who rely on e-mail need to pay more attention to grammatical correctness.

_____

b. A quick glance at almost any electronic bulletin board reveals a marked lack of interest in grammatical correctness.

_____

10. a. The bald eagle, a scavenger* and carrion* eater, is not fit to be America's national emblem.

_____

b. Once an endangered species, the bald eagle is making a comeback, and it has been sighted in several locations around the country.

_____

_____

*scavenger: one who feeds on dead or decaying material.
*carrion: dead and decaying flesh.

EXERCISE 5

DIRECTIONS Write two paired thesis statements about the same topic. Statement *a* should suggest you want to inform; statement *b* that you want to persuade. *Note:* If possible, write statements that are factually accurate. But if you don't have the facts, you can, for the sake of this exercise, invent them.

EXAMPLE

Topic   Beta-Carotene Pills and Cancer

a. *In the fight against cancer, the World Health Organization recommends eating fresh fruit and vegetables rather than relying on beta-carotene pills, which have been promoted as a nutritional weapon against the war on cancer.*

b. *Thanks to the stand taken by the World Health Organization, it's now abundantly clear that beta-carotene pills are useless in the fight against cancer.*

EXPLANATION As it should, statement *a* simply describes a state of affairs—the World Health Organization's stand on beta-carotene pills. Statement *b*, however, uses the World Health Organization's position to make a value judgment about beta-carotene pills: They're useless in the war against cancer.

1. **Topic**   Body Piercing

a. _____

_____

_____

b. _____

_____

_____

2. **Topic** Children Who Commit Violent Crimes

a. _____

_____

_____

b. _____

_____

_____

3. **Topic** School Uniforms

a. _____

_____

_____

b. _____

_____

_____

4. **Topic** Fertility Treatments

a. _____

_____

_____

b. _____

_____

_____

Purpose Affects Tone

Tone in writing is much like tone of voice in speech. It's the emotion or attitude that emerges from the author's choice of both language and content. For an illustration of how tone can vary from author to author, read the following excerpts.

I am a lawyer. I have practiced law for more than thirty years. I think it is an honorable profession. And yet lawyers are the target of the most demeaning* (and immensely popular) jokes in our society. At a time when ethnic, gender, and racial jokes are considered politically incorrect, lawyer bashing has become the great American pastime. (Gerald D. Skoning, "Lawyer Jokes Are No Joke," *Chicago Tribune*, March 6, 1998, p. 23.)

As a lawyer myself, I would like to say just how annoyed and insulted I am by the current popularity of lawyer jokes. I think I do a good job for my clients and that I am appropriately paid for the long hours I put in service to their interests. But somehow being well paid for work well done is considered bad form, and I and other members of my profession would apparently be better liked if we were willing to work for nothing. Fortunately, all those lawyer bashers out there (who can't resist a cheap shot) have not made me hate myself or my profession.

Both of these passages are about lawyer bashing, and both express resentment that it exists. Note, however, the difference in tone. While the first author uses a reasonable tone that expresses his dislike of lawyer jokes without anger, the second author employs an insulted tone that makes his annoyance hard to miss.

The ability to create tone is an important writing skill. However, it's just as important for readers to recognize how tone can help identify purpose.

Tone in Informative Writing

Critical readers are alert to the relationship between tone and purpose. They know, for example, that informative writing is likely to have a cool, unemotional, neutral tone. A neutral tone relies heavily on denotative language and doesn't try to affect readers' emotions. In informative writing, the tone is unlikely to betray the author's personal feelings about the topic discussed.

Look, for example, at the following passage from pages 302–303, written solely to inform. Note the absence of charged language. Note, too, that the authors' personal feelings are not revealed.

Two factors in the development of obesity in children are beyond human control. These two factors are heredity and age. Like it or not, thinness and fatness do run in families. Overweight children tend to have overweight parents, and underweight children tend to

---

*demeaning: undignified, humiliating.

have underweight parents (LeBow, 1984). And most people inevitably put on fat more during some periods of life than others. Late childhood and early puberty form one of these periods; at this time, most children gain fat tissue out of proportion to increases in other tissues, such as muscle and bone. (Seifert and Hoffnung, *Child and Adolescent Development,* p. 390.)

In the passage above, the authors simply want to tell readers about the two factors in obesity that are beyond human control, and their tone matches their purpose—objective and direct.

Tone in Persuasive Writing

In persuasive writing, tone can vary enormously. Although it can be cool and reserved, it's more likely to express some kind of emotion. The tone in persuasive writing can be coaxing, admiring, enthusiastic, rude, even sarcastic. How, for example, would you describe the tone of the following passage?

I have been fat all of my life and I am thoroughly sick of apologizing for it. This is my declaration of independence from all you skinny people out there who have insisted how much better off I would be if I lost a few pounds. Tragically, we live in a culture that celebrates the thin and denigrates* the fat. This state of affairs leads to the kind of desperate and dangerous dieting I have engaged in for most of my adult life. And I am not alone in this obsession with losing weight. At some time in their lives, at least 80 percent of the American population has dieted to lose weight, even though studies show the majority of diets fail (Fett and Dick, 91). We would probably all be a lot better off if we spent time improving our souls instead of our bodies. No matter what we do, our bodies will decay; our souls will not.

At the beginning of the paragraph, judging by the words alone, it appears that the author wants only to inform readers about his own miserable dieting experience. He seems to focus solely on himself. He doesn't express any wish to affect other people's lives. But the passionate and angry tone is a dead giveaway to the author's real purpose, which is more persuasive than informative. By the end of the passage, it's clear the author wants us to believe that we should stop thinking so much about dieting and instead spend more time concentrating on our souls.

Checking the match between tone and purpose is important. In-

*denigrates: criticizes, demeans.

formative writing that suddenly becomes angry and emotional in tone may be more persuasive in intent than you initially realized. Or, it may be that the writer honestly intends to inform, but his or her bias interferes with the writer's ability to stay fair and balanced. Whatever you do, *don't think of tone as verbal decoration.* For writers, it's a tool to create meaning. For readers, it's a crucial clue to the author's primary purpose. Tone also tells you how willing the author might be to at least acknowledge another point of view.

Words Useful for Describing Tone

admiring	humorous
amused	insulted
annoyed	insulting
angry	ironic (saying the opposite of
appalled	what is intended)
astonished	joyful
awed (filled with wonder)	nostalgic (looking fondly to-
cautious	ward the past)
confident	outraged
critical	passionate
disgusted	regretful
disrespectful	sad
dumbfounded (very sur-	sarcastic
prised)	shocked
embarrassed	solemn
engaged (deeply involved)	sorrowful
enthusiastic	sure
horrified	surprised

EXERCISE 6

DIRECTIONS After reading each selection, identify the author's purpose. Then circle the letter of the word or phrase that best fits the author's tone.

EXAMPLE Jazz singer Ella Fitzgerald was a quiet and humble woman who experienced little of the love she sang about so exquisitely for more than fifty years. Her voice, even in later years when she suffered from crippling arthritis, was always filled with a clear, light energy that could set the toes of even the stodgiest* listeners

---
*stodgiest: lacking in life, without energy.

tapping. Although Fitzgerald, an African American, came of age in an era when racism was rampant, whatever bitterness she felt never spilled over into her music. She sang the lyrics of a white Cole Porter or a black Duke Ellington with the same impossible-to-imitate ease and grace, earning every one of the awards that were heaped upon her in her later years. When she performed with Duke Ellington at Carnegie Hall in 1958, critics called Fitzgerald "The First Lady of Jazz." Although she died in 1996, no one has come along to challenge her title, and Ella Fitzgerald is still jazz's First Lady.

Purpose a. to inform
(b.) to persuade

Tone a. coolly annoyed
(b.) enthusiastic and admiring
c. emotionally neutral

EXPLANATION Throughout the passage, the author describes Ella Fitzgerald in strong, positively charged language, thereby creating an enthusiastic and admiring tone that encourages readers to share the admiration. The purpose is therefore persuasive.

1. As a mail carrier for more than twenty years, I can tell you firsthand that we are much maligned members of the population. Customers see only the flaws in mail delivery. They never appreciate the huge effort that makes service both speedy and efficient. For an absurdly small price, you can send mail anywhere in the country, from Hawaii to Alaska. You'd think this would impress most people, but no. Instead of thanking us for services rendered, they whine and complain about the few times mail gets lost. And just because a few members of the postal service have engaged in violent behavior, people now use the insulting expression *going postal* to refer to unexpected outbreaks of violence brought on by stress. This phrase unfairly insults the rest of us hardworking employees who do our jobs without complaint day in and day out.

Purpose a. to inform
b. to persuade

Tone a. comical
b. insulted
c. emotionally neutral

2. In his book *An Anthropologist on Mars,* the renowned neurologist* Dr. Oliver Sacks gives readers an important and insightful perspective on injuries and disorders of the brain. According to Dr. Sacks, some injuries and disorders result in greater creativity and achievement. With compassionate insight, Dr. Sacks describes, for example, a painter who becomes colorblind through a car accident. Initially in despair, the painter eventually started painting stunning black-and-white canvases that won him more critical acclaim than he had received before his mishap.

   As in his previous works, Dr. Sacks gives readers an unexpected perspective on disease and injury. In *An Anthropologist on Mars,* he once again makes us rethink and reconsider our most cherished beliefs about health and illness. His book should be required reading for anyone interested in the power of human beings to adapt to and ultimately overcome loss.

Purpose a. to inform

   b. to persuade

Tone a. admiring

   b. cautious

   c. emotionally neutral

3. Deep processing, which is effective for many kinds of learning, involves analyzing information in terms of its meaning. If, for example, you want to learn a new word, it frequently helps to break the word down into meaningful parts. For example, to remember the meaning of *taciturn* ("inclined to silence; not liking to speak"), you might think about it as being partially made up of the more common word *tacit*, meaning "unspoken." Or, perhaps you've never quite managed to remember the difference between *libel* and *slander.* If you think about the fact that *libel* appears to contain the same word-root found in *library*, that will make it easier to remember that *libel* means "making false statements harmful to a person's reputation" *in writing* while *slander* refers to making those kinds of statements *orally.* (Adapted from Gamon and Bragdon, *Learn Faster & Remember More,* p. 159.)

Purpose a. to inform

   b. to persuade

---

*neurologist: a doctor who specializes in the workings and diseases of the nervous system.

Tone a. outraged

 b. relaxed and friendly

 c. emotionally neutral

4. Jazz pianist Michel Petrucciani, who died in 1999 at the age of thirty-one, was only about four feet tall. But he was a giant when he sat in front of a piano. The childhood victim of a disease that turned his bones so brittle they could barely support his tiny body, Petrucciani couldn't go out and play like other kids. Instead, he stayed home, playing the piano, and listening to the music of jazz and swing greats like Dexter Gordon, Benny Goodman, and Miles Davis. For Petrucciani—who remained upbeat, determined, and feisty* until the day of his death—disease had forced him to turn to music. Ironically, he was grateful for that. The world, in turn, should be grateful for the music this young man produced. Although Petrucciani's music never quite loses its jazz edge, it's also lush and lyrical, filled with a sense of passionate longing. Michel Petrucciani died with a small but loyal following, yet if there is any justice in the world, that following will grow. One only has to listen to the artist play songs like "Miles Davis Licks" and "Bimini" to know immediately that his talent was both rare and great.

Purpose a. to inform

 b. to persuade

Tone a. solemn and serious

 b. emotionally neutral

 c. enthusiastic and admiring

5. Owners of sport utility vehicles (SUVs) should show their patriotism, not by waving flags, but by getting rid of their gas-guzzling cars. SUV ownership contributes to this country's unhealthy dependence upon foreign oil. Just look at the Ford Excursion, a nine-foot-long, four-ton monster that gobbles up an entire gallon of gas to travel a mere twelve miles. SUV owners use more than their fair share of oil and keep America beholden to the Middle East for fuel. SUVs also contribute to the destruction of our planet's environment. Over its lifetime, the Ford Excursion spews 70 tons of carbon dioxide—the main cause of global warming—into the atmosphere. As a result, enviormental groups like the Sierra Club have nicknamed the Ex-

---

*feisty: combative.

cursion the "Ford Valdez" after the *Exxon Valdez*, an oil tanker that dumped 11 million gallons of oil into the ocean.

Purpose   a. to inform

b. to persuade

Tone   a. irritated

b. casual

c. emotionally neutral

CHECK YOUR UNDERSTANDING
Define the term *tone* and explain its relationship to purpose.

 ## Learning to Recognize Irony

No discussion of tone would be complete without some mention of **irony**—the practice of saying one thing while implying exactly the opposite. This might sound confusing at first, but like most of us, you've probably used irony more than once in your life. Haven't you ever had a really horrible day and said to someone, "Boy, what a great day this was!" Or, seeing a friend wearing a sad expression, maybe you said, "Gee, you look happy."

If either of these examples sounds familiar, then you know more about irony than you think, and you're prepared for writers who assume an ironic tone like the one used in the following example:

> The school board has decided to reduce the school budget once again. But why take half measures? Why not eliminate the budget altogether and close our schools? After all, a little learning is a dangerous thing. Better to keep our children totally ignorant and out of harm's way.

The author of this paragraph doesn't want his readers to take what he says *literally*, or at face value. After all, who would seriously suggest that keeping children ignorant is a good idea? The author's point is just the opposite of what he actually says. He doesn't want the school budget further reduced. But instead of saying that directly, he makes an outrageous suggestion that draws attention to where the cuts could lead.

When writers present what seems to be an outrageous or impossible opinion as if it were obvious common sense, critical readers assume the writer is being ironic, and they respond by inferring a message directly opposed to the author's actual words. As you might expect, *an ironic tone is a good indicator of a persuasive purpose.*

CHECK YOUR UNDERSTANDING

What is irony?

_____

_____

_____

EXERCISE 7

DIRECTIONS Read each passage and circle the letter that best identifies the author's tone.

1. According to the American Association of Furriers, wearing fur coats is once again back in fashion. Well, isn't that good news for the thousands of mink, rabbits, foxes, and raccoons that are brutally slaughtered so that fashionable men and women can sport a trendy fur coat or hat. No doubt these animals are honored to suffer and die for the sake of human vanity.

Tone a. ironic

   b. comical

   c. emotionally neutral

2. When the voters of Michigan sent Charles Diggs Jr. to the United States House of Representatives in 1954, he became the first black congressman in the state's history. He was not, however, the first black congressman in the United States. During the period of Reconstruction, from 1865 to 1877, the United States government tried to rebuild the South after the political and economic devastation of the Civil War. Black citizens held prominent government positions throughout the nation, including the posts of mayor, governor, lieutenant governor, state supreme court justice, U.S. senator,

and U.S. congressman. (Juan Williams, *Eyes on the Prize.* New York: Penguin, 1987, p. 49.)

Tone a. outraged

b. lighthearted

c. emotionally neutral

3. It is refreshing to note that many right-thinking citizens are calling for a ban on the celebration of Halloween because the holiday encourages devil worship. Hallelujah? It doesn't take the intellect of a TV evangelist to see that the wearing of "Casper the Friendly Ghost" costumes leads children to the wanton embrace of Beelzebub.* And it is a known fact that candy corn is the first step toward addiction. Only the devil (or an underemployed dentist) would knowingly offer popcorn balls to innocent children. But why stop at Halloween? Many other holidays conceal wickedness behind a vicious veil of greeting cards and Bob Hope TV specials. (Steve Ruebal, "Toss Out Halloween? Let's Not Stop There," *USA Today,* October 29, 1991, p. 11A.)

Tone a. confident

b. ironic

c. emotionally neutral

4. According to one of your readers, insufficient attention has been paid to the possibility that men are also victims of domestic violence. It is his opinion that men are, in fact, just as likely to be victimized by women as women are by men. The difference is that men, for fear of looking unmasculine, fail to report it. Well, I'm just all broken up at the thought of this new social problem. I can imagine how horrible it is for a 220-pound male to be terrorized by a 120-pound female. The poor thing must live in terror at the thought of her menacing approach. A man like that is certainly as much in need of our sympathy as are the women who end up hospitalized or worse in the wake of a domestic dispute.

Tone a. ironic

b. friendly

c. emotionally neutral

5. On December 1, 1955, Rosa Parks left the Montgomery Fair department store late in the afternoon for her regular bus ride home. All

---

*Beelzebub: another name for the devil.

thirty-six seats of the bus she boarded were soon filled, with twenty-two Negroes seated from the rear and fourteen whites from the front. Driver J. P. Blake, seeing a white man standing in the front of the bus, called out for the four passengers on the row just behind the whites to stand up and move to the back. Nothing happened. Blake finally had to get out of the driver's seat to speak more firmly to the four Negroes. "You better make it light on yourselves and let me have those seats," he said. At this, three of the Negroes moved to stand in the back of the bus, but Parks responded that she was not in the white section and didn't think she ought to move. She was in no-man's-land. Blake said that the white section was where he said it was, and he was telling Parks that she was in it. As he saw the law, the whole idea of no-man's-land was to give the driver some discretion* to keep the races out of each other's way. He was doing just that. When Parks refused again, he advised her that the same city law that allowed him to regulate no-man's-land also gave him emergency police power to enforce the segregation codes. He would arrest Parks himself if he had to. Parks replied that he should do what he had to do; she was not moving. She spoke so softly that Blake would not have been able to hear her above the drone of normal bus noise. But the bus was silent. Blake notified Parks that she was officially under arrest. (Taylor Branch, *Parting the Waters.* New York: Simon & Schuster, 1988, p. 128.)

Tone a. ironic

b. admiring

c. emotionally neutral

Clues to Purpose

Informative Writing

- appears in textbooks, newspapers, lab reports, research findings, case studies, and reference works.
- employs a title that simply names or describes a topic.
- states or suggests a main idea that describes a situation, an event, a person, a concept, or an experience without making any judgment.
- relies more on denotative than connotative language.
- employs more statements of fact than statements of opinion.

---

*discretion: ability or power to decide.

- takes an emotionally neutral tone.
- remains objective and reveals little or nothing about the author's personal feelings.
- includes pros and cons of the same issue.

Persuasive Writing

- appears in newspaper editorials, political pamphlets, opinion pieces, and articles or books written to explain the author's position on current or past events.
- employs a title that suggests a point of view.
- states or suggests a main idea identifying an action that needs to be taken or a belief that should be held—or at the very least considered.
- often leans heavily on connotative language.
- relies a good deal on opinion and uses facts mainly to serve opinions.
- often expresses a strong emotional tone that reveals the author's personal feelings.
- includes only the reasons for taking action or explains why arguments against are not sound.
- can employ irony.

■ **DIGGING DEEPER**

LOOKING AHEAD The following reading introduces a topic briefly referred to in the chapter—bilingual education. The authors of this selection, however, will provide you with a good deal more information about bilingual education and the controversies surrounding it.

BILINGUAL EDUCATION

1 Congress passed the Bilingual Education Act in 1968, and subsequently amended it five times, to provide federal funds to develop bilingual programs. Much of the expansion of bilingual programs in the 1970s can be attributed to a series of court cases, the most notable of which was the 1974 U.S. Supreme Court case of *Lau* v. *Nichols*. The case involved a class action suit on behalf of Chinese-speaking students in San Francisco, but it had implications for all of the nation's non-English-speaking children. The Court found that "there is not equality of treatment merely by providing students with the same facilities, textbooks, teachers, and curriculum; for students who do not understand English are effectively foreclosed from any meaningful education." Basing its ruling on the Civil Rights Act of 1964, the Court held that the San Francisco school system unlawfully discriminated on the basis of national origin when it failed to cope with the children's language problems.

2 Although the *Lau* case did not mandate bilingual education as the means to solve the problem, subsequent state cases did order bilingual programs. With the advice of an expert panel, the U.S. Office of Civil Rights suggested guidelines for school districts to follow, the so-called Lau Remedies. The guidelines "specified that language-minority students should be taught academics in their primary home language until they could effectively benefit from English language instruction."

Bilingual Education Models

3 Several types or models of **bilingual education** programs exist. In the *immersion model*, students learn everything in English. Teachers using immersion programs generally strive to deliver lessons in simple and understandable language that allows students to internalize English while learning academic subjects. The extreme case of immersion is called *submersion*, wherein students must "sink or swim" until they learn English.

4   The *transitional* model provides intensive English-language instruction, but students get some portion of their academic instruction in their native language. The goal is to prepare students for regular classes in English without letting them fall behind in subject areas. In theory, students transition out of these programs within a few years.

5   *Maintenance* or *developmental* bilingual education aims to preserve and build on students' native-language skills as they continue to acquire English as a second language.

Controversies

6 Students with a native language other than English have two goals in school: learning English and mastering content. But the debate over how students can best reach those goals has become a divisive political battle.

7   While some educators believe students who use English as a second language should be educated in their native language as well, critics insist such an approach doesn't work. The critics believe the best path to academic achievement for language-minority students in most cases is to learn English and learn it quickly. Too many bilingual programs, they say, place LEP* students into slower learning tracks where they rarely learn sufficient English and from which they may never emerge. These critics basically support an immersion model of bilingual education but oppose the transitional and maintenance models. But supporters of transitional and maintenance models argue that students can best keep up academically with their English-speaking peers if they are taught at least partly in their native languages while learning English.

8   The transitional and maintenance models of bilingual education are in growing jeopardy, as first California and now other states threaten these bilingual programs. In 1998, California voters passed Proposition 227, which called for LEP students to be taught in a special English-immersion program in which nearly all instruction is in English, in most cases for no more than a year, before moving into mainstream English classrooms. Proposition 227 basically ended transitional and maintenance models of bilingual education in California, except when sufficient numbers of parents specifically request that their children continue in them. Many parents, administrators, and teachers are concerned that all children, not just LEP students, will be affected as main-

---

*limited English proficient.

stream teachers grapple with students who may be unprepared to deal with grade-level work in English after one year in immersion. The legality of Proposition 227 is also being challenged in the courts. One year after voters approved Proposition 227, it appears that bilingual education continues to flourish in pockets across the state, but overall only about 20 percent of the students who were previously enrolled in such programs have requested to continue in bilingual education.

9   Whereas in the early 1970s language-minority speakers and their advocates fought for bilingual education as their right, today many of them are expressing doubts about the effectiveness of bilingual programs. Civil rights and cultural issues are giving way to concerns that non-native English speakers are just not sufficiently mastering the English language. But advocates say it is not fair to blame bilingual education for the slow progress some students are making. They cite research indicating that instruction in the native language concurrent with English instruction actually enhances the acquisition of English. The problem is not bilingual education, they say, it's that becoming proficient in any second language takes longer than just one or two years. And they point out that there is a shortage of well-qualified, fully bilingual teachers, so that in many cases the problem with bilingual classes is not the curriculum but the quality of instruction.

10   Despite this controversy, many school districts are in desperate need of bilingual teachers, particularly those who speak Spanish and Asian languages. If you speak a second language or still have time to include learning a language in your college program, you could help meet a serious educational need and at the same time greatly enhance your employment opportunities. Speaking a foreign language, especially Spanish, is also an asset for the regular classroom teacher who may have Spanish-speaking students in class. (Ryan and Cooper, *Those Who Can, Teach,* pp. 119–121.)

Sharpening Your Skills

DIRECTIONS Answer the following questions by circling the letter of the correct response or filling in the blanks.

1. Which statement more effectively sums up the main idea of the entire reading?

    a. The 1974 U.S. Supreme Court case *Lau* v. *Nichols* changed the face of American education, and the controversy surrounding that case continues to this day; in fact, there are signs that the controversy is heating up rather than cooling down.

b. Congress passed the Bilingual Education Act in 1968, but it was the *Lau* v. *Nichols* case that had the most profound effect on bilingual education.

c. Research suggests that students from other countries learn English more quickly through the immersion method.

d. The problem with bilingual instruction is not the curriculum but the quality of instruction.

2. Although the author does not say it directly, you can infer that the students in the *Lau* case filed their suit against the

a. federal government.

b. San Francisco school system.

c. U.S. Office of Civil Rights.

3. Which of the following statements more effectively paraphrases the Supreme Court's view on equality of treatment?

a. Students who have not mastered English are required by law to attend bilingual classes until they pass an exam that indicates their English mastery.

b. If students have not mastered English, giving them the same books, classrooms, teachers, and course work cannot be considered equal treatment.

4. In paragraph 3, which sentence is the topic sentence?

a. sentence 1

b. sentence 2

c. sentence 3

5. What pattern of organization can you see at work in paragraph 3?

a. cause and effect

b. classification

c. process

6. How many times was the Bilingual Education Act amended?

a. twice

b. three times

c. five times

7. If you were to take an exam based on this reading, which two of the following would you *not* expect to appear on the exam?

   a. Describe the effect of *Lau* v. *Nichols* on American education.

   b. What does the existing research tells us about the effects of speaking two languages?

   c. Name and describe each of the models for bilingual education.

   d. Take a stand either for or against Proposition 227. Then argue your position with sound evidence drawn from the reading.

8. The Lau Remedies are

   a. court cases that followed in the wake of *Lau* v. *Nichols*.

   b. guidelines for school districts to follow.

   c. countersuits that challenged the ruling in *Lau* v. *Nichols*.

9. How would you describe the purpose of this reading?

   a. to inform

   b. to persuade

10. How would you describe the author's tone?

<hr/>

WORD NOTES: THREE KINDS OF IRONY

The word *irony*, defined on page 322 as the practice of "saying one thing while implying exactly the opposite," is a widely used term and like so many other words, its meaning can vary with context. For an example, take a look at the word *ironic* in the following sentence: "Isn't it a bit *ironic* for you to simultaneously imitate and criticize your best friend's behavior?" In this sentence, the word *ironic* indicates that a particular action is exactly the opposite of what one would expect under the circumstances. This is another common meaning for the words *irony* or *ironic*.

You also need to know that the word *irony* is closely related in meaning to *sarcasm*. In both irony and sarcasm, what is said is actually the opposite of what is meant. The difference is that *irony* is used to make a point whereas *sarcasm* is used strictly to insult or hurt (which may be one good reason why sarcastic people don't have a lot of friends).

In your literature or drama classes, you may have also been

introduced to the phrase *dramatic irony.* The phrase refers to a device playwrights use when they create characters who know less than their audience. All through the famous play *Oedipus Rex,* for example, the audience knows that disaster will strike when King Oedipus finds out the truth about his birth, but the king himself remains completely unaware of his doom until it's too late.

Take a philosophy course and you could also be introduced to the term *Socratic irony.* According to the Greek philosopher Plato, his teacher, Socrates, would first claim ignorance and then ask a series of questions that led his students to the point he wanted to make: "I know nothing of it, but I wonder 'what is the nature of love?'" This method is called Socratic irony, in part because it is based—like irony in general—on a contradiction. Socrates always claimed not to know anything but was, in fact, leading his students toward the very conclusion he had in mind.

Test 1: Reviewing the Key Points

DIRECTIONS Answer the following questions by filling in the blanks.

1. The goal of informative writing is to _____.

2. Informative writing is likely to offer _____ on the same subject.

3. The goal of persuasive writing is to _____.

4. Identifying an author's primary purpose is important because the author's purpose determines _____.

5, Even before you begin reading, you can use two clues to predict the author's purpose. These two clues are _____ and _____.

6. When trying to determine purpose, the _____ is the clincher, or deciding factor.

7. In informative writing, the author _____ but does not _____ people, events, or ideas.

8. Informative writing relies more on _____ language, whereas persuasive writing relies more on _____ language.

9. Tone is the _____ an author expresses through words.

10. In informative writing, the tone is likely to be _____, but in persuasive writing, it's likely to _____.

Test 2: Identifying Purpose and Tone

DIRECTIONS Circle the appropriate letters to identify the author's purpose and tone.

1. President George W. Bush has talked about granting amnesty to millions of illegal Mexican immigrants now living in the United States, and he is right to do so. These people are already living and working here, and the vast majority are productive, law-abiding men and women, who simply want a better life for themselves and their families. Many left their native country and endured severe hardship in hopes of being able to better themselves by working in the United States. President Bush's plan to give these illegal immigrants a chance is both compassionate and humane, and it should not be abandoned in the face of protest. Nor should it be forgotten as America wages war on terrorism. The problem of illegal immigrants working for low wages and in poor conditions because they do not have legal status is a long-standing one. It needs to be resolved as soon as possible.

The author's purpose is

a. to inform.

b. to persuade.

The author's tone is

a. emotionally neutral.

b. casual.

c. engaged.

2. The media has completely exaggerated the threat of shark attacks at popular vacation beaches. During the summer of 2001, when "real" news was scarce, magazines, newspapers, and television news shows gave a lot of coverage to several instances of sharks biting human swimmers and surfers. These few attacks, combined with dramatic video footage of swarms of migrating sharks off the coast near Tampa, Florida, helped the media create unnecessary worries for American beachgoers. Even *Time* magazine devoted most of one of its issues to sharks and proclaimed that summer to be "The Season of the Shark." In reality, though, the number of shark attacks in 2001 was actually only average. According to George Burgess, director of the International Shark Attack File at the University of Florida, that average is fewer than one hundred attacks per year worldwide. In 2000, for example, seventy-nine shark attacks oc-

curred worldwide, with fifty-one of them in the United States (thirty-four of those in Florida). Fatalities due to shark bites average only eight per year worldwide. In 2001, the media's implication that there were an unusually large number of sharks in the water was false. Furthermore, contrary to media suggestion, sharks were not any more interested in humans than usual. As a matter of fact, sharks never intentionally target humans because they don't like the taste of human flesh. In general, most shark attacks on humans are due to the shark's mistaking a person for a fish or a seal. Unfortunately, the "hysterical" media stories failed to mention that people actually have a better chance of being struck by lightning than being bitten by a shark.

The author's purpose is

a. to inform.

b. to persuade.

The author's tone is

a. emotionally neutral.

b. critical.

c. solemn.

3. Oregon and Washington have proven that voting by mail is superior to the old method of voting in a polling place. First of all, surveys clearly show that voting by mail is an option people want. Seventy percent of Oregonians and 65 percent of Washingtonians prefer voting by mail. They like the convenience of a mail-in ballot that allows them to integrate voting more easily into their busy lives. Furthermore, voters feel that voting by mail allows them to make more informed choices. For example, one survey of Washington residents revealed that residents believe they make better decisions because they can take more time with their ballot at home rather than rushing to complete it in a voting booth. Not surprisingly, the benefits of voting by mail have produced a dramatic increase in voter turnout during elections. For instance, almost 80 percent of registered voters in Oregon submitted a ballot in the 2000 presidential election, compared to a nationwide average of 51 percent voter turnout. Other states should follow the footsteps of Washington and Oregon.

The author's purpose is

a. to inform.

b. to persuade.

The author's tone is

a. anxious.

b. emotionally neutral.

c. confident.

4. The United States had been fighting Japan in World War II for almost four years when President Harry Truman decided to use the brand-new atomic bomb to end the war. In July 1945, he called for Japan's surrender, promising the Japanese "prompt and utter destruction" if they refused. Japan ignored the threat. So, on Monday, August 6, 1945, at approximately 8:11 A.M., an American B-29 bomber named the *Enola Gay* dropped an atomic bomb over the southwestern Japanese port of Hiroshima at an altitude of 31,600 feet. At 2,000 feet, the bomb exploded, producing first a blinding fireball and then a huge mushroom cloud that billowed miles into the sky. The explosion obliterated everything in a one-mile radius, killing 75,000 people instantly. About 25,000 more people would die later from the effects of the radiation. Still Japan did not surrender. So, three days later, on August 9, 1945, at 11:00 A.M., the United States dropped a second atomic bomb on Nagasaki, a Japanese city 186 miles southwest of Hiroshima. More than 35,000 Japanese perished immediately in the blast. On August 14, the Japanese accepted America's terms for surrender, and President Truman announced the end of the Second World War.

The author's purpose is

a. to inform.

b. to persuade.

The author's tone is

a. emotionally neutral.

b. fearful.

c. furious.

5. The Apollo Space Program of the 1960s and 1970s was responsible for man's series of lunar landings. In 1967, the project got off to a tragic start when fire killed three astronauts during a preflight test on the launch pad. In 1968 and 1969, however, a series of successful missions took astronauts into space for six to ten days at a time. Apollo missions 7, 8, 9, and 10 tested the equipment and operations necessary for putting men onto the moon's surface. On July 20, 1969, the Apollo 11 mission fulfilled its objective when astronauts

Neil Armstrong and Buzz Aldrin became the first humans to set foot on the moon. A second lunar landing occurred that same year as part of the Apollo 12 mission. In 1970, Apollo 13 was supposed to result in a third landing. However, damage to the spacecraft caused the mission to be aborted, and the astronauts barely made it safely back to Earth. In 1971 and 1972, though, four more Apollo flights produced four more lunar landings. Apollo 14, 15, 16, and 17 astronauts walked on the moon, performed scientific experiments, collected samples of moon rocks, and took photographs. On December 14, 1972, during the Apollo 17 mission, humans walked on the moon for the last time, and no one has been back since.

The author's purpose is

a. to inform.

b. to persuade.

The author's tone is

a. emotionally neutral.

b. skeptical.

c. admiring.

Test 3: Recognizing Purpose and Tone

DIRECTIONS Read each passage. Then answer the accompanying questions by circling the appropriate letter or letters.

1. **Navajo Skinwalkers**

1 Among the Navajo of the southwestern United States, it is said that no human being is all good or all evil. In the Navajo view, human beings have both qualities or, more accurately, the capacity to do both good and evil. According to Witherspoon (1977), the goal of Navajo life is to bring one's impulses under control so that one grows and develops through a complete life in a condition of *hozho*—the state of beauty, harmony, good, and happiness—and then dies naturally of old age and becomes one with the universal beauty, harmony, and happiness that make up the ideal positive environment.

2 A person's *ch'indi*, or potential for evil, can be controlled by rituals that restore one to a state of *hozho*. Although the state of inward beauty achieved through living in outward harmony with the ideal environment can be disrupted by contact with dangerous (*bahadzid*) things or by the sorcery* of others, perhaps leading to illness or death, such states can be countered by a traditional ritual chant, or "sing," of which there are over sixty. Rituals channel supernatural power by reenacting the Navajo creation myths, which relate the deeds of the gods, both good and evil. (Crapo, *Cultural Anthropology*, p. 211.)

1. What is the primary purpose of this reading?

   a. to inform

   b. to persuade

2. Which of the following helped you determine the author's purpose?

   a. title

   b. thesis statement or implied main idea

   c. source of the selection

   d. tone

   e. all of the above

3. How would you describe the author's tone?

   a. admiring

   b. critical

   c. emotionally neutral

*sorcery: witchcraft.

2. **You Either Have Free Speech or You Don't**

1 A controversial issue for many Americans is whether people who are known to be racist or to have other destructive views should be allowed to speak at public places like state universities. Even those who cherish the American Constitution and its guarantee of free speech have difficulty supporting free speech for bigots.* However, painful as it may be to accept, freedom of speech is an all-or-nothing proposition.* You can't have freedom of speech for some people and not for others. If you ban unpopular people from speaking, you no longer have freedom of speech. In short, you no longer have a democracy.

2 As the A.C.L.U. has correctly argued, the best way to respond to hatred and bigotry is to have more speech, not less. How this principle works in practice can be illustrated by an incident involving David Duke, a man who was once a grand wizard of the Ku Klux Klan.

3 In 1996, Duke was invited to the University of California in order to debate affirmative action.* The invitation caused an uproar in both the university and the community. One local editorial labeled Duke's views beyond the limits of legitimate discussion. Even the governor of the state agreed that Duke's invitation should be withdrawn. In short, there were people who wanted to deny Duke the right to free speech. The president of the university, however, correctly argued that public institutions must be places where *all* ideas can be explored. In addition to the president, members of African-American and gay organizations argued that Duke should be allowed to speak because they wanted the opportunity to challenge him in person.

4 As a result of those arguments, the debate took place. Even more important, it took place peacefully, with only a few incidents involving protesters outside the auditorium. The president of the university courageously held her ground in refusing to interfere with the students' decision to invite Duke to speak and thus refusing to limit one of the most precious rights we Americans possess. After all, once the first speaker is banned, it becomes a little too easy to ban the second. Hard as it is to accept, it's still true that "you either have free speech or you don't."

1. What is the primary purpose of this reading?

    a. to inform

    b. to persuade

---

*bigots: people who consider other people to be inferior because of their race, gender, religion, or sexual orientation.
*proposition: a statement put forth for acceptance.
*affirmative action: a federally supported plan to make sure that women and minorities have access to jobs and education.

2. Which of the following helped you determine the author's purpose?

    a. title

    b. thesis statement or implied main idea

    c. source of the selection

    d. tone

    e. all of the above

3. How would you describe the author's tone?

    a. deeply concerned

    b. light-hearted and humorous

    c. emotionally neutral

3. New Ideas in Education

1 In the early 1800s, school curricula had consisted chiefly of moralistic pieties.* *McGuffey's Reader,* used throughout the nation, taught homilies* such as "By virtue we secure happiness" and "One deed of shame is succeeded by years of penitence." But in the late nineteenth century, psychologist G. Stanley Hall and educational philosopher John Dewey asserted that modern education ought to prepare children differently. They insisted that personal development, not subject matter, should be the focus of the curriculum. Education, argued Dewey, must relate directly to experience; children should be encouraged to discover knowledge for themselves. Learning relevant to students' lives should replace rote memorization and outdated subjects.

2 Progressive education, based on Dewey's *The School and Society* (1899) and *Democracy and Education* (1916), was a uniquely American phenomenon. Dewey believed that learning should focus on real-life problems and that children should be taught to use their intelligence and ingenuity as instruments for controlling their environment. From kindergarten through high school, Dewey asserted, children should learn through direct experience. Dewey and his wife Alice put these ideas into practice in the Laboratory School that they directed at the University of Chicago.

3 Personal growth became the driving principle behind higher education as well. Previously, the purpose of American colleges and universities had been that of their European counterparts: to train a select few for the professions of law, medicine, teaching,

---

*pieties: statements designed to teach the value of virtuous behavior.
*homilies: statements with a moral message.

and religion. But in the late 1800s, institutions of higher education multiplied, aided by land grants and by an increase in the number of people who could afford tuition. Between 1870 and 1910 the number of colleges and universities in the United States grew from 563 to nearly 1,000. Curricula expanded as educators sought to make learning more appealing and to keep up with technological and social changes. (Norton et al., *A People and a Nation*, pp. 609–610.)

1. What is the primary purpose of this reading?

   a. to inform

   b. to persuade

2. Which of the following helped you determine the author's purpose?

   a. title

   b. thesis statement or implied idea

   c. source of the selection

   d. tone

   e. all of the above

3. How would you describe the author's tone?

   a. sarcastic

   b. lighthearted

   c. emotionally neutral

4. *Juku*, Japanese for "Cram School"

1   On a brisk Saturday morning, while most of their friends were relaxing at home, sixteen-year-old Jerry Lee and eight other Asian teenagers huddled over their notebooks and calculators for a full day of math and English lessons.

2   During the week they all attend public schools in the city. But every Saturday, they go to a Korean *hagwon,* or cram school, to spend up to seven hours immersed in the finer points of linear algebra or Raymond Chandler.*

3   "I complain, but my mom says I have to go," said Jerry, a Stuyvesant High School student from Sunnyside, Queens, who has already scored a 1520 on the Scholastic Aptitude Test for college but is shooting for a perfect 1600. "It's like a habit now."

---

*Raymond Chandler (1888–1959): considered by many to be the finest mystery writer of all time; the creator of fictional detective Philip Marlowe.

4   Long a tradition in the Far East, where the competition to get into a top university borders on the fanatic, the cram schools of Asia have begun to appear in this country too, in Queens and New Jersey and Los Angeles and elsewhere, following the migration of many Koreans, Japanese, and Chinese over the last two decades.

5   In the last ten years, the cram schools—called *juku* in Japanese and *buxiban* in Chinese—have become a flourishing industry, thriving on immigrant parents' determination to have their children succeed. Only a handful of cram schools existed here when the *hagwon* that Jerry attends, the Elite Academy, opened in 1986. Today, the Korean-language yellow pages list about three dozen Asian cram schools in the New York area. In Los Angeles, the Chinese yellow pages list about forty.

6   While the pressure to get into a good school is not nearly so extreme in the United States, the cram schools, such as the ambitiously named Nobel Education Institute in Arcadia, a heavily Asian suburb of Los Angeles, have nonetheless found a burgeoning niche in Asian communities. Chinese and Korean newspapers bulge with cram school advertisements. Some schools simply print lists of their graduates who have been accepted to New York City's specialized high schools, as well as to Harvard, Stanford, and MIT.

7   For many busy parents, the schools have become a kind of academic baby-sitting service. But most see them as a way of ensuring that their children excel in spite of the public schools that they perceive as lax* and unchallenging compared with those in Asia. (Ashley Dunn, "Cram Schools: Immigrants' Tools for Success," *New York Times,* January 28, 1995, p. 1.)

1. What is the primary purpose of this reading?

    a. to inform

    b. to persuade

2. Which of the following helped you determine the author's purpose?

    a. title

    b. thesis statement or implied main idea

    c. source of the selection

    d. tone

    e. all of the above

---

*lax: lacking in strictness or firmness.

3. How would you describe the author's tone?

    a. admiring

    b. critical

    c. emotionally neutral

5. **And They Call This Mercy?**

1 The word *euthanasia* means "good death" or "mercy killing." But the name does not fit the act. When one person assumes the right to take the life of another, there is no goodness or mercy involved. No one has the right to decide when a life should end.

2   Life is our most precious gift and we cannot fling that gift away when it suits us. Refusing to accept assistance from machinery that maintains respiration is one thing, but asking to die is another. That's why the book *Final Exit* is such a disgrace to the publishing industry. The book suggests that we as individuals have the right to plan our own death; to decide, in effect, that we are tired of living. Yet that decision—to decide when life ends—lies in God's hands, not in ours.

3   Jack Kevorkian, the man who has championed an individual's right to take his or her own life, has not done the public a service by making headlines aiding and abetting suicide. Instead, he has encouraged others to believe that they too can choose when to die. That choice, however, is not ours to make. (Dale Matthews, "And They Call This Mercy?" *Moral Matters,* April 12, 1999, p. 20.)

1. What is the primary purpose of this reading?

    a. to inform

    b. to persuade

2. Which of the following helped you determine the author's purpose?

    a. title

    b. thesis statement or implied main idea

    c. source of the selection

    d. tone

    e. all of the above

3. How would you describe the author's tone?

    a. outraged

    b. astonished

    c. emotionally neutral

Test 4: Recognizing Purpose and Tone

DIRECTIONS Read each passage. Then answer the accompanying questions by circling the correct letter or letters.

1. **The Ritual Slaves of Ghana**

   1 Just twelve years old, with a shy smile, bare feet, and simple printed cloth that serves as her only clothing, Abla Kotor has begun a life of servitude* and atonement* for a crime she did not commit.

   2   For now her duties mostly involve sweeping the dirt courtyard of a local fetish* priest, a spiritual intermediary* between worshippers and deities of the area's traditional religion, juju.* But her responsibilities will grow to include providing sexual favors to the priest who has become her master. In the meantime, she must learn to cook and to farm, serving long hours weeding fields where there are crops of yam, manioc, and corn. And servants like her are typically denied the fruits of their hard labor. Instead, their families, often wretchedly poor, are expected to send food to feed them.

   3   Miss Kotor has little idea of why she was sent to the shrine here by her family four months ago, or, for that matter, what the future holds. Without even knowing it, she has joined a community of several thousand female ritual slaves in the corner of southeastern Ghana. Here, girls known as *trocosi*, or slaves of the gods, are routinely given by their families to work as slaves in religious shrines as a way of appeasing the gods for crimes committed by relatives.

   4   Once given to a priest, a girl is considered his property, and can be freed only by the priest, in which case her family must replace her with a new young girl. To ensure that the gods remain appeased, this process is repeated for a serious crime, with families giving up generation after generation of girls in perpetual atonement. (Excerpted from Howard W. French, "The Ritual Slaves of Ghana: Young and Female," *New York Times*, January 20, 1997, pp. A1, A4.)

   1. How would you describe the author's primary purpose?

   a. to inform

   b. to persuade

---

*servitude: slavery.
*atonement: repayment for a crime.
*fetish: something believed to have magical powers.
*intermediary: person in the middle; a go-between.
*juju: the giving of supernatural powers to an object.

2. Which of the following helped you determine the author's purpose?

    a. title

    b. thesis statement or implied main idea

    c. source of the selection

    d. tone

    e. all of the above

3. How would you describe the author's tone?

    a. sad

    b. disgusted

    c. emotionally neutral

2. Vaccinations, Pros and Cons

1 A vaccine is a medication, given either orally or by injection, that prevents or reduces the risk of contracting a particular disease. Vaccines are also known as *immunizations* because they stimulate the natural disease-fighting abilities of the body. They work by giving the body practice in fighting off a disease. A vaccine contains a small amount of bacteria or virus that causes a certain infection. When that bacteria or virus is introduced into the body, the immune system recognizes it as an intruder and manufactures specific antibodies that will fight infection if the body comes under attack.

2   Immunizations for children continue to be the subject of heated debate because they do have some negative side effects. Mild, short-term side effects include pain or tenderness at the point of injection, mild fever, irritability, sleepiness, and decreased appetite. More serious side effects, though rare, include an increased risk of seizures. In addition, a very small number of children have had a severe allergic reaction, called anaphylaxis, to some vaccines. This reaction includes hives, breathing difficulties, and a drop in blood pressure. Such consequences have led some people to create anti-vaccine groups. Convinced that vaccines can cause problems such as autism, diabetes, learning disabilities, and asthma, members of these groups refuse to immunize their own children. They also fight against laws that require children to be vaccinated in order to attend public schools.

3   The positive effects of vaccinations, however, are simply undeniable. As a matter of fact, vaccines were on the Centers for Disease Control's list of top ten public health achievements in the twenti-

eth century. Immunizations have eliminated altogether diseases that killed or severely disabled thousands every year. For example, vaccines have completely eliminated polio. They also wiped out smallpox, which 10 million people used to contract every year as late as the 1960s. Vaccines have also significantly reduced the occurrence of a number of other diseases. Measles used to infect about 4 million children per year, but in 1997, there were only 138 cases of measles in the United States. Vaccines have also reduced the number of cases of diphtheria, meningitis, and pertussis (whooping cough), which used to kill or cause brain damage in thousands of children each year. Consequently, the vast majority of healthcare professionals believe that the benefits of immunization far outweigh their few risks.

1. How would you describe the author's primary purpose?
   a. to inform
   b. to persuade

2. Which of the following helped you determine the author's purpose?
   a. title
   b. thesis statement or implied main idea
   c. source of the selection
   d. tone
   e. all of the above

3. How would you describe the author's tone?
   a. sure and confident
   b. sad and solemn
   c. emotionally neutral

3. Make It Illegal to Be a Bad Samaritan*

1 On May 25, 1997, twenty-two-year-old Jeremy Strohmeyer chased seven-year-old Sherrice Iverson into the stall of a public bathroom, where he molested and then strangled her. At one point, his friend David Cash looked over the door of the stall and saw Strohmeyer struggling with the little girl. Cash, however, didn't intervene to help Sherrice. Instead, he told his friend they had to get going and left the little girl alone with her killer.

---

*Samaritan: Someone from Samaria. In the Bible, the Good Samaritan selflessly helps someone who has been hurt.

2   Although Jeremy Strohmeyer is now serving a life sentence without parole, David Cash is a free man. In Las Vegas, where the crime was committed, there's no law saying a bystander has to come to the aid of a crime victim, even if the victim is in danger of being murdered. Yet as the case of Sherrice Iverson suggests, we need a Good Samaritan law. We need a law that says bystanders can't simply watch or walk away while someone is being brutally attacked. They don't have to intervene physically, but they must call for help. If they don't, they should be fined and sentenced to spend some time in jail. In states where they already have a Good Samaritan law, the penalties for breaking that law should be made much, much tougher. In Vermont, for example, failure to help someone being attacked only results in a hundred-dollar fine. The fine should be a hundred times that amount.

3   Although many European countries do have Good Samaritan laws, American individualism seems to have interfered with the court's willingness to make protecting others part of our legal code. According to UCLA law professor Peter Arnella, "The criminal law in this country tends to overvalue the notion of individual rights . . . even when the person is risking a serious social harm."

4   A famous turn-of-the-century case often cited by legal scholars certainly supports Arnella's position. During a couple's weekend vacation, one member fell into a drug-induced coma. The man's partner responded by going home and leaving him to die. The case ultimately went all the way to the Michigan Supreme Court, where the court found that the partner who left had no legal duty to intervene and offer aid.

5   Legal or not, most people would argue that there was a moral duty at stake in the Michigan case and certainly in the case of Sherrice Iverson. We need a Good Samaritan law on the books, and we need it now. (Helen Robeson, "Make It Illegal to Be a Bad Samaritan," *Modern Moral Choices*, June 1, 1999, p. 25.)

1. How would you describe the author's primary purpose?

   a. to inform

   b. to persuade

2. Which of the following helped you determine the author's purpose?

   a. title

   b. thesis statement or implied main idea

   c. source of the selection

   d. tone

   e. all of the above

3. How would you describe the author's tone?

  a. confident

  b. angry

  c. emotionally neutral

4. **Hyphenated America**

1 In the nineteenth century, most **old-stock Americans*** assumed
that immigrants should quickly learn English, become citizens,
and restructure their lives and values to resemble those of old-
stock Americans. Immigrants from Britain were often rapid assimilators,* for they already spoke English and their religious values
were similar to those of major old-stock Protestant denominations.* Most immigrants, however, resisted rapid assimilation.

2 For most immigrants, assimilation took place over a lifetime or
over generations. Most held fast to customs in their own culture
at the same time that they took up a new life in America. Their
sense of identity drew on two elements: where they came from
and where they were now. Being conscious of their new identity
as a German in America, or an Italian in America, they often
came to think of themselves as **hyphenated Americans:** German-
American, Italian-American, Polish-American.

3 On arriving in America, with its strange language and unfamiliar customs, many immigrants reacted by seeking out people
who shared their cultural values, practiced their religion, and,
especially, spoke their language. Ethnic communities emerged
throughout regions with large numbers of immigrants. These communities played significant roles in newcomers' transition from
the old country to America. They gave immigrants a chance to
learn about their new home with the assistance of those who had
come before. At the same time, they could retain the values and
behavior from their old country that they found most important.

4 Hyphenated America developed a unique blend of ethnic institutions, often unlike anything in the old country but also
unlike those of old-stock America. Fraternal lodges based on
ethnicity sprang up, and often provided not only social ties but
also benefits in case of illness or death. Among these lodges were
the Ancient Order of Hibernians (Irish), the Sons of Hermann
(German), and the Sons of Italy. Social groups often included
singing societies devoted to the music of the old country. Foreign-

---

*old-stock Americans: term used by the Census Bureau to describe people who
were born in the United States.
*assimilators: people who readily fit into a new way of life.
*denominations: religious groups.

language newspapers were vital in developing a sense of identity that connected the old country to the new, for they provided news from the old country as well as from other similar communities in the United States. (Berkin et al., *Making America,* p. 557.)

1. How would you describe the author's purpose?

    a. to inform

    b. to persuade

2. Which of the following helped you determine the author's purpose?

    a. title

    b. thesis statement or implied main idea

    c. source of the selection

    d. tone

    e. all of the above

3. How would you describe the author's tone?

    a. disgusted

    b. astonished

    c. emotionally neutral

5. We Need Less Hysteria and More Common Sense

1 In the fall of 1997, a young man named Ross Vollbrecht from Nashville, Indiana, was barred from playing in his school's final game of football. What did the young man do to merit such a punishment? Surely he must have stolen from a classmate, sworn at a teacher, or cheated on an exam. These are the kinds of student infractions* one expects to hear about if a boy or girl is forbidden to participate in a crucial high school ritual. Ross Vollbrecht, however, did none of these things. His mistake was to take up chewing tobacco and get caught with the tobacco on his person. Yes, Ross was eighteen and had a legal right to chew tobacco if he wanted to, but school policy forbids the use of drugs, and tobacco is, after all, a drug. The young man had to be punished and punished severely.

2   When I read Ross's story, my first response was, "Well, coffee's a drug, too. Why didn't they penalize every player who had a cup of java during the semester?" Does this make me sound unsympa-

———————

*infractions: violations of rules.

thetic to the school's position? If so, good; I am unsympathetic. Actually, I am outraged because this case reminds me of an earlier one, where a young girl almost got suspended for bringing Advil on campus. It, too, is a drug, you see. And while we are citing the sins of today's youth, let's not forget the seven-year-old boy who got suspended from school for stealing a kiss from one of his female classmates. We'll teach him to harass helpless females.

3   Now I know full well that we need to have our young people follow rules and regulations, but the application of those rules and regulations needs to be tempered by common sense. Schools do need to guard against drug use and sexual harassment, but school administrators need not go on witch hunts looking for these twin evils where they don't exist. If a drug is legal off of school grounds, then the administration has to think twice before penalizing a student for its possession. And come on, a seven-year-old who steals a kiss from a classmate is not exactly in the same position as the owner of a computer company who thinks his or her secretary should pay for a promotion with sexual favors. Again, each case has to be considered in its proper context. Above all, the people in charge of our schools need to apply more reason and less hysteria when monitoring the behavior of their young charges. (A letter to the editor of the *Carson City Flyer* from Ellen Niemand, a high school teacher.)

1. How would you describe the author's primary purpose?

   a. to inform

   b. to persuade

2. Which of the following helped you determine the author's purpose?

   a. title

   b. thesis statement or implied main idea

   c. source of the selection

   d. tone

   e. all of the above

3. How would you describe the author's tone?

   a. angry and ironic

   b. amused and humorous

   c. emotionally neutral

C H A P T E R 9

Understanding Figurative Language

> **In this chapter, you'll learn**
>
> - **the meaning of figurative language.**
>
> - **how to recognize and make sense out of similes.**
>
> - **how to recognize and interpret metaphors.**
>
> - **how to recognize and respond to allusions.**

Like understanding the difference between fact and opinion, knowing how to interpret *figurative language*—language that makes sense in imaginative rather than realistic terms—is essential to reading in general and critical reading in particular. Once you become familiar with the three kinds of figurative language introduced in this chapter, you

351

will be in a better position to determine meaning, identify tone, and even detect bias.

 ## What Is Figurative Language?

Figurative language encourages the comparison or association of two seemingly unlike things or ideas. Although figurative language works in imaginative terms, it makes little sense in literal, or real, terms. For example, if a friend tells you that his uncle is "a bear of a man," you don't—if introduced—expect to see a grizzly with a human head. You know right off that your friend is making an imaginative comparison between his uncle and a creature similar in stature and strength, maybe even in temperament. Your friend is speaking figuratively, not literally.

CHECK YOUR UNDERSTANDING
Define the term *figurative language*.
_____
_____

 ## Types of Figurative Language

Figurative language can be broken down into different **figures of speech.** These are special types of verbal expression, all of which employ some kind of comparison or association between people, events, objects, or ideas. The following pages introduce three of the most important figures of speech used in writing: similes, metaphors, and allusions.

Similes

Similes are comparisons that use the words *like* or *as* to create meaning by revealing an unexpected connection or likeness. For example, in his famous "Letter from Birmingham Jail," Martin Luther

King Jr. argued that racial tension was "like a boil that can never be cured as long as it is covered up." The purpose of this simile was to help readers vividly imagine how dangerous it was for racial tension to fester without ever being acknowledged. The simile also helped create the intensely serious tone of King's letter.

Now look at the next simile, drawn from a book review. What does it tell you and what kind of tone does it help create?

> Reading Alice Mattison's novel *Hilda and Pearl* is like eating a DoveBar. It's so rich and delicious, one can't help wishing it would never end.

In this instance, the simile tells you that reading Mattison's novel is a delightful experience; it also helps create the author's admiring tone.

Similes can also use the word *as*. For example, Raymond Chandler, a mystery writer whose mastery of clever similes contributed to his fame, described one character with an unforgettable simile. In Chandler's words, the man was "as crazy as two waltzing mice"—a phrase that perfectly expressed the character's oddball disposition and at the same time contributed to the smart-alecky tone Chandler used for his crime stories.

CHECK YOUR UNDERSTANDING

What is a simile?

_____

_____

Create a simile that describes a friend, family member, or classmate.

_____

_____

EXERCISE 1

DIRECTIONS Read each passage. Then identify and explain the simile.

EXAMPLE Talking to General Dunlop is always an unsettling experience. To me, it's like hitting a tennis ball over the net only to have a pineapple lobbed back at you. The only thing you know for sure is that you'd better expect the unexpected.

a. According to the author, talking to General Dunlop is like

playing tennis with someone who returns a pineapple instead of a tennis ball.

b. What point does that comparison help to make?

When you talk to General Dunlop, you never know what to expect.

EXPLANATION The simile in this passage illustrates just how unsettling conversations with General Dunlop really are. When talking to the general, you can expect a response as surprising as a pineapple being returned to you in a tennis game.

1. When he was a Harvard professor, the philosopher and psychologist William James would think aloud in front of his students, letting his ideas flow like a "rambling, sparkling stream." (David S. Reynolds, "Radical Pragmatist," *New York Times Book Review*, March 15, 1998, p. 11.)

   a. In this passage, James's thought process is compared to

   _____

   _____.

   b. What point does that simile help to make?

   _____

   _____

2. Many parents complain that bringing home their first baby is like walking around with a dozen eggs on their head. They're afraid to make one false move for fear of disaster.

   a. In this passage, the author compares bringing home a new

   baby to _____

   _____.

   b. What point does that simile help to make?

   _____

   _____

3. Jazz singer Billie Holiday lived a rough-and-tumble life that left her a legacy of despair. But when she went on stage before an audience, the past was forgotten. She was like a queen totally in command of her awestruck subjects, none of whom dared make a sound.

    a. In this passage, Holiday's appearance on stage is compared to

    _____

    _____ .

    b. What point does that simile help to make?

    _____

    _____

4. Writing about a computer hacker who invaded his privacy, author Joshua Quittner claimed, "I remember feeling as powerless as a minnow in a flash flood. Someone was invading my private space— my family's private space—and there was nothing I or the authorities could do."[1]

    a. In this passage, Quittner's feelings of powerlessness are compared to _____ .

    b. What point does that simile help to make?

    _____

    _____

5. Cornering the governor on the question of campaign financing was like cornering a colt in an open field. Move in one direction and he'd quickly move to the other.

    a. In this passage, the governor's behavior is compared to _____

    _____

    _____ .

    b. What point does that simile help to make?

    _____

    _____

---

[1]Joshua Quittner, "Invasion of Privacy," *Time*, August 25, 1997, p. 30.

Metaphors

Metaphors also make unexpected comparisons that contribute to both meaning and tone. They aren't, however, as easy to spot as similes because they don't use the words *like* or *as*. Note the absence of either word in the following passage, where the author compares family conversations to volcanic eruptions in order to emphasize the extreme explosiveness of family discussions.

> The voices of my world were seldom tender and unquestioning. Conversations, especially among members of my mother's family, were choleric* eruptions. (W. S. DiPiero, "Gots Is What You Got," in *The Best American Essays 1995*, ed. Jamaica Kincaid. Boston: Houghton Mifflin, 1995, p. 84.)

When the passage is presented in a more expanded form, you can see even more clearly how the author's use of metaphor contributes to his angry, bitter tone.

> The voices of my world were seldom tender and unquestioning. Conversations, especially among members of my mother's family, were choleric eruptions. If by some accident a rational argument took place, defeat was registered not by words or acknowledgment but by a sardonic,* defiant sneer. Anger, impatience, and dismissive ridicule of the unfamiliar were the most familiar moods. Everyone around me, it seemed, except for my father's side of the family, spoke in brittle, pugnacious* tones that I still hear when my own voice comes snarling out of its vinegary corner. (W. S. DiPiero, "Gots Is What You Got," in *The Best American Essays 1995,* p. 84.)

Did you spot the other metaphors in the passage? Did you notice, for example, that by using the word *snarling,* the author compares himself to an angry animal. Or perhaps you noticed the word *vinegary,* which implies that the author's corner of the room was sour and bitter, like the taste of vinegar.

If you picked up on either one of these metaphors, you are well on your way to understanding the power of figurative language. Now look at the next passage. The author uses a metaphor to express the degree of her pain. Can you find that metaphor?

> Twenty years ago, when I was nine and living in America, I came home from school one day with a toothache. Several weeks

---

*choleric: excitable, easily ignited or set off.
*sardonic: mocking, scornful.
*pugnacious: ready to fight.

and misdiagnoses later, surgeons removed most of the right side of my jaw in an attempt to prevent the cancer they found there from spreading. No one properly explained the operation to me, and I awoke in a cocoon of pain that prevented me from moving or speaking. (Lucy Grealy, "Mirrorings," in *The Best American Essays 1994,* ed. Tracy Kidder. Boston: Houghton Mifflin, 1994, p. 183.)

Up until the last sentence, the language is more or less denotative (see page 276). But in the last sentence the author compares herself to an infant moth or butterfly wrapped in a cocoon, only her cocoon is made out of pain, not silk.* By means of that comparison, the author helps readers imagine the extent of her pain: It covered her entire body and allowed her no escape. The cocoon image also reinforces the author's helpless and bewildered tone.

Be Aware of Submerged Metaphors

In your reading, you are bound to notice that some metaphors are more explicit, or more obviously expressed, than others. "A bear of a man," for example, is a pretty clear-cut metaphor. But some metaphors have been in use for so long it's easy to forget that a comparison is implied; that's why some people refer to them as *submerged.* Consider the expression "to round everybody up," as in the following sentence: "Make sure you round everybody up before the meeting." In this case, gathering people together is implicitly compared to a cattle roundup. Yet, because the phrase has been used so often, it's easy to forget its metaphorical basis. Still, it is critical to be alert to submerged metaphors rather than letting them influence your thinking without your realizing it. Consider, for example, the following:

> Our troops have gone into the infested area. With enough firepower, exterminating the enemy will not be difficult.

The submerged, or underlying, metaphor used here suggests that the enemy forces are bugs rather than people and helps to cover up the reality of what's being discussed—killing human beings, not bugs. Critical readers would "think through" the metaphor to decide if they actually support the action described.

---

*The cocoons of some moths and butterflies are spun from silk.

CHECK YOUR UNDERSTANDING

Explain the difference between a metaphor and a simile.

_____

_____

You have already used a simile to describe a friend or class-mate. Now use a metaphor to describe the same person.

_____

_____

EXERCISE 2

DIRECTIONS Underline the submerged metaphor in each sentence.

EXAMPLE "Don't tell me what to do," she <u>shot</u> back.

EXPLANATION We have been comparing a harsh verbal retort to shooting a gun off for so long, it's easy to forget that there is actually a metaphor in play in that expression.

1. That kind of monotonous work grinds you down after a while.
2. When the World Trade Center was destroyed by terrorists, grief counselors flooded New York City in the hopes of consoling those who had lost friends and relatives in the terrible tragedy.
3. They had just met, but he was already head over heels in love.
4. Her spiteful attitude poisoned the atmosphere of the meeting.
5. After working the night shift, he fell into a dead sleep.

EXERCISE 3

DIRECTIONS Identify and explain each metaphor.

EXAMPLE The wrestler's mountainous body belied* his gentle and somewhat shy nature.

_____

*belied: contradicted.

a. In this passage, the author uses a metaphor to compare *the wrestler's body* to *a mountain range.*

b. That comparison helps to make what point?
The man's physical presence was extremely imposing because of his size.

EXPLANATION The word *mountainous* is meant to make readers imagine a huge body that hides the wrestler's true personality.

1. During the second round, Gogarty caught the 135-pound Martin flush on the nose, opening a spigot of blood. After the round as cornermen tried to stop the flow, Jim asked Christy if she wanted to continue. "I was concerned because she's my wife first, my fighter second," he says. "She told me, 'Don't you dare stop this fight!'" (Steve Wulf, "Belle of the Brawl," *Time*, April 1, 1996, p. 20.)

a. In this passage, the author uses a metaphor to compare

_____ to _____ .

b. That comparison helps to make what point?

_____

_____

2. The Olympics present America's racial mosaic* as the great gift it is. . . . When Derek Parra, the first Mexican-American to win gold at the Winter games, and Vonetta Flowers, the first black person to do so, stood on the podium with tears running down their faces, as the American flag was raised above them, it was hard not to feel that a tiny piece of the American promise had been fulfilled. (Gary Kamiya, Oh yes! Oh no! *Salon*, 2/21/02. www.salon.com/news/sports)

a. In this passage, the author uses a metaphor to compare

_____ to _____ .

b. That comparison helps to make what point?

_____

_____

3. By the time Elvis Presley died, he had become a beloved national ruin. (The metaphor is derived from Julie Baumgold, "Midnight in

---

*mosaic: a picture made of tiny colored stones or tiles.

the Garden of Good and Elvis," in *The Best American Essays 1995*, pp. 50–51.)

a. In this passage, the author uses a metaphor to compare

_____ to _____.

b. That comparison helps to make what point?

_____

_____

4. If your sentences are carelessly formed, not only will the summary be unreadable, you will also lose the connection among the pieces of information in the summary. You could simply wind up with tossed word salad. (Bazerman, *The Informed Writer*, p. 79.)

a. In this passage, the author uses a metaphor to compare

_____ to _____.

b. That comparison helps to make what point?

_____

_____

5. When Arturo (Chico) O'Farrill died in a New York hospital on June 27, 2001, some Latin music old-timers and connoisseurs* mourned his death. Yet most Latinos failed to recognize they had lost one of the gardeners who planted their musical roots here. (Adapted from Miguel Perez, "Farewell to 'Duke Ellington of Latin Jazz,'" *The Record* [Bergen County, NJ], July 13, 2001, p. 11.)

a. In this passage, the author uses a metaphor to compare

_____ to _____.

b. That comparison helps to make what point?

_____

_____

Allusions

Allusions are brief references to historical events, mythological figures, and famous people—both real and fictional. In an earlier time,

---

*connoisseurs: experts.

allusions functioned mainly to display a writer's learning, but nowadays their role is more complex. Allusions are a form of verbal shorthand meant to call up a whole chain of associations in readers. They help writers explain or prove a point; they also contribute to tone and reveal bias. For an illustration, look at the following example. Do you recognize the allusion?

> Undoubtedly, an increasing number of men have rejected the traditional male-role imperatives.* "Be the breadwinner," "Push your way to the top," "Stick in there and fight," "Men don't cry." Indeed, there is a life after Rambo. (Thio, *Sociology*, p. 292.)

Did you recognize the allusion to Rambo, the fictional character created by actor Sylvester Stallone in a series of highly successful action films? In these films, the character of Rambo is icily independent. With much bloodshed, he single-handedly lays to rest his many enemies, apparently without remorse or anxiety. Relying on readers to recognize the allusion, the author uses it to define the phrase "male-role imperatives"—to be tough, strong, and unemotional. At the same time, the allusion helps maintain the relaxed, informal tone of his writing.

Note how the same passage, with a different allusion, takes on a slightly more formal, more academic tone.

> Undoubtedly, an increasing number of men have rejected the traditional male-role imperatives. "Be the breadwinner," "Push your way to the top," "Stick in there and fight," "Men don't cry." As the poet Robert Bly has suggested, men are exhausted by the effort of trying to be the invincible warrior.

What about the next passage? Can you find an allusion that helps the author define for readers the power of gossip columnist Walter Winchell?

> In the thirties and forties, the slogan on Walter Winchell's newspaper column read: "He sees all, he knows all." No wonder Winchell was known as the Big Brother of gossip columnists.

If you've read George Orwell's book *1984*, you know already that the allusion in the above passage is to Big Brother, a character in that famous novel. In the novel, Big Brother uses a network of spies to gather information about the populace under his control. No wonder Winchell was once widely feared. If his name could be linked to Big Brother, he too must have had access to even the best-kept secrets.

---

*imperatives: commands.

Enlarging Your Store of Allusions

Allusions can help you determine meaning and identify tone. But they are only useful if you recognize them when you see them. Consider, for example, the following italicized allusion to a famous female character.

> Following in the tragic footsteps of Tolstoy's *Anna Karenina*, too many women still seem to believe that sacrificing all for love is a worthwhile choice to make. It appears, in fact, that on the romance front, feminists have not made much progress. Women, unlike men, still seem to believe that romance is what gives life meaning.

If you know that Anna Karenina, the heroine of Tolstoy's novel by the same name, gave up her marriage, her children, and ultimately her life for the love of a man who abandoned her, you immediately grasp the author's point. But if you don't, your understanding of the passage is probably a little vague.

This is just one instance in which an allusion is central to the author's meaning. But it's not atypical. The more you read, the more likely you are to encounter numerous allusions from science, the arts, and popular culture. While popular culture references, like the one to Rambo, will be readily at your disposal, you may have to work at developing a vocabulary of allusions that extend beyond those from TV and movies. Anytime you encounter an allusion you don't know, make a note of it and look it up when you get a chance. Paperback dictionaries don't usually include names of people and places, but hardbound desk dictionaries often do. In addition, there are some very good reference works that have compiled long lists of our culture's common allusions. *Merriam Webster's Dictionary of Allusions*, *The Dictionary of Cultural Literacy*, *The Dictionary of Global Culture*, and the *Oxford Dictionary of Phrase and Fable* are four very good ones.

CHECK YOUR UNDERSTANDING

When they were first used, what was the purpose of allusions? _____

What is their purpose now? _____

_____

EXERCISE 4

Copyright © Laraine Flemming. All rights reserved.

DIRECTIONS Read each sentence or passage and look at the italicized allusion. Then read the explanation of that allusion. When you finish, circle the letter of the statement that best explains the purpose of the allusion.

EXAMPLE America has finally found its *Homer* in Ken Burns, creator of the highly acclaimed Public Broadcasting series *The Civil War*, which will be watched and talked about for generations.

> Homer was an ancient Greek poet said to have written *The Iliad*, a long poem that recorded the events of the Trojan War. Homer's description of the war between the Greeks and the Trojans ramains so powerful that translations of *The Iliad* are still read and discussed to this day.

The author alludes to Homer in order to

a. suggest that Ken Burns is also a great poet who will be read for centuries.

b. suggest the extraordinary nature of Ken Burns's achievement.

EXPLANATION Since Homer was a famous poet who made the ancient Trojan War live on in history, using his name in reference to Ken Burns is a great compliment. Through this allusion, the writer praises the filmmaker's ability to make the Civil War seem vivid and alive, so much so that the series will survive the test of time.

1. I was thirty years old when I had my right nostril pierced, and back home friends fell speechless at the news, lapsing into long telephone pauses of the sort that *June Cleaver* would employ if the *Beave* had ever called to report, "Mom, I'm married. His name's Eddie." (Natalie Kusz, "Ring Leader," in *The Best American Essays 1997*, pp. 70–71.)

> June Cleaver was a character in a famous situation comedy called *Leave It to Beaver*. On the show, she was the perfect mother who never had a hair out of place, never raised her voice, and never ever made a mistake. To many, she was the symbol of the perfect suburban mom. "The Beave" was a nickname for her mischievous young son.

The author alludes to June Cleaver and the Beave to suggest

a. that her friends admired her daring and were envious of it.

b. the degree of shock her friends experienced at her news.

2. Waiting for the judge to arrive, I had the feeling that I was a character in Beckett's *Waiting for Godot*, and messages from the bailiff that the judge was on her way did little to cheer me up.

> *Waiting for Godot* is a play about two tramps, Vladimir and Estragon, who wait for a man called Godot. Each day a boy comes to tell them Godot will be there tomorrow, but as the play ends, Vladimir and Estragon are still waiting.

The author alludes to *Waiting for Godot* to suggest that

a. she no longer believes the judge will appear.

b. she is too bored to pay attention to the bailiff's words.

3. When it comes to talent, the young dancer is another *Nijinsky*. Yet given the young man's odd behavior, even his most devoted admirers fear that he has more in common with Nijinsky that just talent.

> Vaslav Nijinsky (1890–1950) was a Russian ballet dancer whose phenomenal talent made him a world-famous star. In 1919 Nijinsky was diagnosed with schizophrenia and spent the rest of his life in treatment for the devastating disease.

The author alludes to Nijinsky to suggest that

a. the young dancer will eventually alienate all of his admirers because he is so demanding and ill-tempered.

b. the young dancer is extremely talented but may also be suffering from a serious psychological disorder.

4. Watching the couple as they eyed the menu suspiciously, I couldn't help but think of Grant Wood's *American Gothic*. The two seemed a throwback to another, sterner time, when dinner out was not part of the weekly—or for that matter, the yearly—routine. For these two, dinner out seemed to be another chore to be finished as quickly as possible.

> The painting *American Gothic* (1930) by Grant Wood shows an unsmiling, middle-aged couple from the nineteenth century. The man holds a pitchfork and looks solemn. The woman, dressed in black, stares into space with pursed lips and a pinched face.

The author alludes to *American Gothic* to suggest that

a. the two people are quarreling with one another.

b. the two people don't appear to be enjoying themselves.

5. Even as a young man, the president had had his eye on the political prize, and to get where he wanted to go, he wasn't above taking pointers from Machiavelli's *The Prince*.

> Niccolo Machiavelli was a Renaissance political philosopher whose book *The Prince* advised rulers to be ruthless and cunning if they wanted to hold on to their power.

The author alludes to Machiavelli to suggest that

a. the president behaved like a man from another century.

b. the president was, at a young age, wily* and determined in pursuit of his goals.

---

*wily: clever, tricky.

■ **DIGGING DEEPER**

LOOKING AHEAD Page 358 of this chapter referred to the grief counselors who traveled to New York on September 11, 2001, in an effort to aid those stricken by the collapse of the World Trade Center. While the authors of the following reading do not question the good intentions of such counselors, they do raise doubts about the usefulness of grief counseling.

WHEN TRAGEDY STRIKES, GRIEF COUNSELORS GIVE AID

1 When the lord of the underworld snatched away her beloved daughter, Demeter was inconsolable. She wandered through the world and in her misery allowed the fields to lie barren. In modern parlance, she was "in trauma." Today the Greek goddess of agriculture might have talked about her loss, vented her frustration, and worked through her grief. Certainly, she would not have been left alone with her sorrow.

2 Tragedy is immemorial, but we have grown less tolerant of its psychic consequences. In Littleton, Colorado, where Hades visited us in the guise of two teenage boys, counselors spent 1,500 hours talking to students in the first week after the April 20 shooting. "The trauma is astronomical throughout this community," says Steve Poos-Benson, pastor of a church near Columbine High School. "It has affected even those who casually drive by." Oklahoma City, riven* by catastrophes twice in the past four years, has settled into painful routine. At the Community Counseling Center, counselors who helped after the 1995 bombing of the Alfred P. Murrah Federal Building were called on again following last week's tornadoes. The American Red Cross, which has more than 80 counselors in the area, put its 2,000 mental-health officials on alert.

3 Where there is no consolation, there is now counseling. But is it necessarily helpful? The huge growth in such on-the-scene therapy has raised questions about the value of pouring out one's grief to the social workers, psychologists, psychiatrists, and clergy who are invariably on hand at disasters to lend empathic support. If local resources feel the strain, the Red Cross, Salvation Army, National Organization for Victim Assistance, and a host of other nonprofit organizations send in volunteers. During presiden

---

*riven: torn apart.

tially declared disasters, the Center for Mental Health Services contributes federal funds for counseling. It spent $10 million last year.

4   The notion of talking through trauma gained currency during World War II, when soldiers were "debriefed" on the beaches of Normandy, In the 1970s, Jeffrey Mitchell, then a paramedic and now president of the International Critical Incident Stress Foundation, developed one of the most popular debriefing models. Intended to be used in conjunction with other services, such as one-on-one counseling and on-scene support, Critical Incident Stress Debriefing is conducted in groups a couple of days after a disaster. Typical questions include "What were the first thoughts that raced through your mind at the time of the crisis?" and "What was the worst moment for you?"

5   After the Columbine High School shooting, school psychologists employed a similar approach, not only with students from Columbine but with those at twelve nearby schools. "Debriefing is a therapeutic opportunity to get people to open up, ask questions, and unburden the psychic pain they are carrying round," says Theodore Feinberg, a New York–based psychologist who flew to Littleton as part of a team sent by the National Association of School Psychologists.

6   But others wonder whether talk is truly the best remedy. British psychologist Simon Wessely reviewed half a dozen studies of debriefing last year and found that it had no effect. "People race into disaster areas, but there is no research that says people benefit from trauma counseling," according to Tana Dineen, a psychologist who wrote *Manufacturing Victims: What the Psychology Industry Is Doing to People.* "These counselors get people to talk about how upset they are, but they may be doing damage."

7   The trauma experts handle the immediate aftershocks of disaster. Once they leave, grief counselors take over, providing longer-term help for those who have suffered a loss. The discipline of grief counseling was virtually unknown three decades ago. Today there's a national organization—the Association for Death Education and Counseling—that certifies grief counselors.

8   Most grief counselors rely on the seminal teachings of J. William Worden, a Harvard psychologist who published *Grief Counseling and Grief Therapy: A Handbook for the Mental Health Practitioner* in 1982. Worden identified four basic tasks of mourning: (1) to accept the reality of the loss, (2) to experience emotions connected to that loss, (3) to adjust to life without the deceased, and (4) to relocate the deceased in one's mind so that progress is possible. Though Worden hoped to inform mental-health counselors

about bereavement, he didn't anticipate that his theories would give rise to a veritable industry of professional grief counselors. "I didn't know what I've spawned," he says ruefully.

9   One such counselor is Alan Wolfelt, founder of the Center for Loss and Life Transition in Colorado, who describes himself as "a person who creates safe places for people to mourn." He argues that as life expectancy has increased, Americans have lost the "art" of grieving. "Our culture is full of buck-up therapists who want to move people away from grief," he says. "But you have to feel it to heal it. You have to go through the wilderness."

10   That kind of sound bite appeals to a generation raised on *Oprah*, but some psychologists are skeptical. George Bonanno, assistant professor of psychology at the Catholic University of America, studied bereaved individuals over twenty-five months. He found that those who focused on their pain, either by talking about it or displaying it in their facial expressions, tended to have more trouble sleeping and maintaining everyday functions. In other words, there may be benefits to the discredited practice of keeping a stiff upper lip.

11   Such misgivings should not cast doubt on the sincere goodwill of people who lend their help to survivors of tragedy. Even as many victims of last week's tornadoes declined help, counselors handed out leaflets and toll-free numbers "just in case." And some of those victims may need it. At nearly 140 schools in the Denver area, students have reported problems ranging from instances of regression (such as bed-wetting and wanting to share a bed with parents) to anxiety and depression. In Oklahoma City, victims of the 1995 bombing still undergo counseling (the Red Cross has forty cases open), and at least six people closely linked to the carnage have committed suicide. Moved by Demeter's anguish, Zeus intervened so that Persephone could return to her mother for part of the year. Modern tragedies are not so easily repaired. (Nadya Labi, Richard Woodbury, and Maggie Sieger, "Behavior: The Grief Brigade," *Time*, May 17, 1999, pp. 69+, © 1999 Time Inc. Reprinted by permission.)

Sharpening Your Skills

DIRECTIONS Answer the following questions by circling the letter of the correct response or filling in the blanks.

1. What's the main idea of the entire reading?

   _____

   _____

2. What is the allusion to Demeter, goddess of agriculture (paragraph 1), meant to illustrate?

   a. It illustrates that talking about one's grief was also a therapy familiar to the ancient world.

   b. It illustrates the dangers of remaining silent about one's deepest and most painful feelings.

   c. It illustrates the difference between how grief was handled in ancient times and how it is handled today.

   d. It illustrates how much the Greeks liked to dramatize their emotions.

3. What patterns of organization are at work in the opening paragraph?

   a. process and cause and effect

   b. comparison and contrast with process

   c. comparison and contrast with cause and effect

4. What pattern is at work in paragraph 8?

   _____

5. The word *parlance* in paragraph 7 is based on the Latin root *parler*, meaning "to speak." Based on this information and the use of context, what is a synonym for *parlance*?

   _____

6. In paragraph 6, the authors quote two psychologists: Simon Wessely and Tana Dineen. The questions are meant to illustrate what main idea?

   _____

7. In paragraph 8, J. William Worden, who had a profound influence on grief counselors, says, "I didn't know what I've spawned." Worden's quote, along with the word *ruefully*, implies that he _____

   _____.

8. In paragraph 9, grief counselor Alan Wolfert says, "You have to go through the wilderness." In this instance, Wolfert is speaking

   a. figuratively.

   b. literally.

9. In paragraph 10, the authors say that "there may be benefits to the discredited practice of keeping a stiff upper lip." What evidence do they offer in support of that opinion?

_____

10. In paragraph 10, the authors refer to the quotation from grief counselor Alan Wolfelt as a "sound bite." A "sound bite" is a brief broadcast meant to reduce complex issues to their simplest form. What do the authors imply by using the phrase "sound bite" to describe Mr. Wolfelt's statement?

_____

WORD NOTES: DEAD METAPHORS

Now that you are skilled at recognizing and interpreting metaphors, you might choose to use them more in your own writing, as well you should. However, if you do, take care to avoid "worn out" or "dead" metaphors. These are metaphors that have been used so often they no longer work to make ideas clear and vivid. If anything, dead metaphors make even fresh ideas seem stale and old. Three such metaphors appear in the following sentences. Put a circle around each one.

1. Those old conflicts are all water over the dam.

2. The attorney decided to burn her bridges and abandon the firm.

3. He turned out to be such a scoundrel; it's really true that you can't tell a book by its cover.

Cliché is another word for dead metaphor, and you can use the two terms interchangeably. We all use clichés, or dead metaphors, in conversation. In general we don't have the time to ponder every word for originality. But for the most part, writers do have the time, and dead metaphors like those shown above should be avoided.

Give three examples of dead metaphors:

_____

_____

_____

Test 1: Reviewing the Key Points

DIRECTIONS Answer the following questions by filling in the blanks.

1. Figurative language makes sense in _____ rather than _____ terms.

2. Figurative language can be broken down into three different _____.

3. Similes are _____ that _____ _____.

4. Like similes, metaphors make _____, but they don't _____.

5. What are submerged metaphors? _____ _____.

6. It's critical to be alert to submerged metaphors rather than letting them _____.

7. Allusions are _____.

8. In earlier times, allusions functioned mainly _____ _____.

9. Now writers use allusions to _____.

10. Once you can recognize and interpret figurative language, you will be in a better position to determine _____, identify _____, and detect _____.

Test 2: Understanding Similes, Metaphors, and Allusions

DIRECTIONS Answer the following questions by filling in the blanks, underlining the appropriate word, or circling the letter of the correct response.

1. Explain the simile used in the following sentence: "Propaganda is a bit like pornography—hard to define but most people think they will know it when they see it." (Koppes and Black, *Hollywood Goes to War*, p. 49.)

   a. In this sentence, the authors use a simile that compares

   _____ to _____.

   b. What point does that simile help to make?

   _____

   _____

2. In 1997, Susan Charlé of the *New York Times* wrote an article about bear thievery in Yosemite. Charlé described how the bears, lusting for cookies and such, broke into hundreds of cars to steal food. She titled the article "To the Bears of Yosemite, Cars Are Like Cookie Jars." Explain the simile at work in that title.

   Cars are like cookie jars because _____

   _____.

3. Underline the submerged metaphor used in the following sentence: "The committee's members are trying to bulldoze the president into signing the bill, but they will not succeed."

4. Explain the metaphor in the following passage:

   Unfortunately for Alexander Hamilton, Thomas Jefferson was an elusive target in debates. Every time Hamilton thought he laid Jefferson's logic to rest, Jefferson came up with yet another powerful argument against Hamilton's plan for a powerful federal government.

   a. In this passage, Thomas Jefferson is compared to

   _____.

   b. What does the metaphor suggest about Jefferson's debating style?

   _____

5. Identify the metaphor in the following passage:

> In North Korea, starvation is everywhere, and, as usual, the hardest hit are the children. They sit quietly, speaking little and playing not at all. Their arms and legs are twigs. The U.S. government should put politics aside and offer North Korea aid immediately.

In this passage, what metaphor does the author use to bring home to readers the suffering of starving children?

_____

6. Identify the metaphor in the following sentence: "Time is the worst kind of thief, greedy and invisible." (Christina Garcia, "Thou Shalt Not Steal," *Self*, December 1997, p. 140.)

In this sentence, the author uses a metaphor that compares

_____ to _____.

7. Identify the metaphor in the following passage:

> The poet Carl Sandburg said that slang "rolls up its sleeves, spits on its hands and goes to work."

Sandburg's metaphor compares slang to _____.

The point of the comparison is to show

   a. how sophisticated and elegant slang can be when used in the right context.

   b. that slang can get right to the point without a lot of fancy words.

   c. that slang is never appropriate in polite conversation.

8. Explain the allusion in the following sentence: "It was a *Gone With the Wind* type of romance. Because their timing had always been off, none of their friends was surprised when the couple finally split up."

> *Gone With the Wind* is a famous novel that became an even more famous movie. By the time the novel's heroine, Scarlett O'Hara, finally decides she loves its hero, Rhett Butler, he is no longer in love with her.

What does the allusion in this passage say about the couple's romance?

_____

_____

9. Explain the allusion in the following sentence: "That newspaper is a piece of trash, and the editor makes William Randolph Hearst seem scrupulous* by comparison."

> William Randolph Hearst was a newspaper publisher in the late nineteenth and early twentieth centuries. In the 1890s, his newspapers whipped up public hostility toward Spain and helped lead America into the Spanish-American war. Hearst even printed false stories about Spanish mistreatment of Cuban citizens. But Hearst didn't care as long as newspaper sales increased.

In the above sentence, the allusion to William Randolph Hearst says what about the newspaper editor?

_____

_____

10. Explain the allusion in the following passage:

> For decades, we felt free to ignore the threat of once deadly diseases like pneumonia and tuberculosis. After all, we had antibiotics. With them on hand, we believed ourselves safe, like the French behind the Maginot Line.

> The Maginot Line was a chain of fortifications built to protect France's eastern border with Germany. During World War II, it was considered foolproof protection against German invasion. The Germans, however, invaded successfully by going around the Maginot Line.

The allusion to the Maginot Line makes what point?

_____

_____

_____
*scrupulous: conscientious and exact.

Test 3: Understanding Similes, Metaphors, and Allusions

DIRECTIONS Answer the following questions by filling in the blanks or underlining the appropriate word.

1. The Dutch scholar Erasmus said that a good memory should be like a fish net. It should keep all the big fish and let the little ones escape. What point about memory was Erasmus trying to make by means of this simile?

   _____

   _____

2. Identify the metaphor in the following passage.

   The Japanese health care system is remarkably democratic. Thanks to a national health insurance system, few are left outside the umbrella.

   a. In this passage, the author compares _____

      to _____.

   b. What is the point of the metaphor?

      _____

3. Identify the metaphors in the following passage.

   Unexpectedly, I turned inward. I encircled myself in solitude. I didn't know it at the time, but it was kind of a cloak around me. (Mary Morris, *Nothing to Declare*. New York: Penguin Books, 1988, p. 180.)

   a. In this passage, the author compares solitude to _____

      and to _____.

   b. What is the point of those metaphors?

      _____

4. Identify the simile in the following sentence: The point you are making is about as useful as a pair of high heels at a relay race.

   a. In this passage, the author compares _____

      to _____.

b. What is the point of the simile? _____

_____

5. Identify and explain the following metaphor: Currently the debate over how the U.S. government should handle China is at high boil.

a. In this sentence, the author compares _____

to _____.

b. The use of this metaphor helps make what point? _____

_____

6. Explain the italicized allusion in the following passage.

Feminism didn't start in the factory. It started in wood-paneled salons, spread to suburban living rooms, with their consciousness-raising sessions,* and eventually ended up with *Norma Rae.* (Gina Bellafante, "It's All About Me," *Time,* June 29, 1998, p. 5.)

Norma Rae was a 1979 movie starring Sally Field in the title role. As Norma Rae, Field plays a working-class woman who successfully brings a union into her factory.

What point does the allusion in this passage help to make?

_____

_____

7. Underline the simile in the following sentence:

The lights went down and the curtains opened like a huge chenille bathrobe. (Shirley Abbott, *Love's Apprentice.* New York: Houghton Mifflin, 1998, p. 8.)

8. What point does the author want to make through the allusion to Moby Dick?

For the senator, national health care had become his Moby Dick. He was determined, no matter what the cost, to make the issue come to a vote in the Senate, and he didn't care if he offended both his friends and his enemies to do it.

_____

*consciousness-raising sessions: group meetings in which women got together to discuss their concerns. Such meetings were popular in the 1960s and 1970s.

> *Moby Dick, or The Whale* (1851) is a book by American writer Herman Melville. In it the main character, the one-legged Captain Ahab, is intent on finding and killing Moby Dick, the great white whale who cost him his leg. To that end, he sacrifices his life and the lives of most of his crew.

What point does the allusion in this passage help to make?

_____

_____

9. Identify and explain the simile in the following sentence.

   Day after day, the heat in Dallas seems to build like a Gulf hurricane growing in force. (National Public Radio, *Morning Edition*, July 16, 1998.)

   a. In this simile, the author compares _____

      to _____.

   b. The point of the simile is that _____

      _____.

10. What point does the author want to make through the allusion to Spike Lee's first film?

    Native-American writer Sherman Alexie is hoping that his first movie, *Smoke Signals*, which he wrote and directed, will do for him what *She's Gotta Have It* did for director Spike Lee.

    > Spike Lee made his commercial film debut with *She's Gotta Have It* in 1986, when he was twenty-nine years old. The movie, made on a shoestring budget, was a surprise hit, and it launched Lee's career as a filmmaker.

    What point does the allusion in this passage help to make?

    _____

    _____

Test 4: Understanding Similes, Metaphors, and Allusions

DIRECTIONS Answer the following questions by filling in the blanks or underlining the correct response.

1. Read the following passage and identify the simile:

   Marilyn Volker, sex therapist and codependency expert, is conducting a workshop on "childhood messages about sexuality." Like a talk show host, sleek in purple silk, she works the room, seeking testimony, accosting us with her microphone. When it is my turn, when her microphone is in my face, I politely ask her to move back. Later, when the workshop is over, several women compliment me on my "assertiveness." (Wendy Kaminer, *I'm Dysfunctional, You're Dysfunctional.* New York: Vintage Books, 1992, p. 87.)

   a. The author uses a simile to compare _____

   to _____.

   b. What do you think is the point of the simile? What does the author want to say about her subject? _____

   _____

2. Read the following sentence and underline the submerged metaphor: "The limping economy was quickly becoming a cause for alarm."

3. Read the following passage and identify the simile:

   When corporate lobbyists realized that the federal government was going to bail out those industries hardest hit by the terrorist attack, they descended on Washington like flies on road kill. The lobbyists were determined to see that the companies they represented got their fair share of federal money, regardless of whether those companies had suffered any damage as a result of the tragedy.

   a. The author uses a simile to compare _____

   to _____.

   b. What does the author want to say about her subject? _____

   _____

4. In the following passage, author Mark Twain describes his feelings about New York City:

I have at last, after several months' experience made up my mind that it [New York] is a splendid desert . . . where the stranger is lonely in the midst of a million of his race. A man walks his tedious miles through the same interminable street every day, elbowing his way through a buzzing multitude of men, yet never seeing a familiar face, and never seeing a strange one the second time. (Karl Meyer, ed., *Pundits, Poets, and Wits,* New York: Oxford University Press, 1990, p. 80.)

a. Underline the metaphor Twain uses to describe the city.

b. The passage also contains an implied comparison between the

people of New York and _____ .

5. In the following excerpt, writer H. L. Mencken imagines the kind of audience likely to applaud the speeches of then-president Warren G. Harding.

They do not want ideas—that is, new ideas, ideas that are unfamiliar that challenge the attention. . . . They like phrases which thunder like salvos* of artillery. Let that thunder sound, and they take all the rest on trust. (H. L. Mencken, "Gamalielese," *Pundits, Poets, and Wits,* p. 160.)

a. Underline the simile Mencken uses to describe the language favored by Harding's admirers.

b. What is the point of Mencken's simile? What does he want to communicate to his readers about Harding's fans?

_____

6. Read the following passage and identify the simile:

The man stood in the checkout line, holding onto the new bicycle as if it were a prize horse. From time to time, he caressed the blue machine gently, stroking the handlebars, patting the seat, running his fingers across the red reflectors on the pedals. (Ellen Goodman, "A Gift to Remember," *Boston Globe,* December 19, 1980, p. 15.)

a. The author uses a simile to compare _____

to _____ .

_____

*salvos: discharges of firearms.

b. What is the point of the simile? What is it supposed to convey to

readers? _____

_____

7. Identify the metaphor writer Andrew Sullivan uses to express his feelings about romantic love:

> The love celebrated on Valentine's Day conquers nothing. It contains neither the friendship nor civility that makes marriage successful. It fulfills the way a drug fulfills—requiring new infusions* to sustain the high. (Andrew Sullivan, "The Love Bloat," *New York Times Magazine*, February 11, 2001, p. 24.)

a. Sullivan's metaphor compares _____

to _____.

b. The point of the metaphor is that neither one _____

_____.

8. Explain the allusion to Sigmund Freud in the following sentence:

> You don't have to be Sigmund Freud to know that denial can be an effective defense against disappointment.

> Sigmund Freud was a Viennese doctor who devoted himself to understanding the workings of the human mind.

The allusion to Freud makes what point? _____

_____

9. In describing the decades-long civil war that raged in Afghanistan prior to 2001, the journalist Anthony Lloyd wrote, "In Afghanistan's twenty-two-year-old struggle, loyalty, allegiance, even fear and hate have become . . . commodities available for barter." (Anthony Lloyd, "The Defectors," *New York Times Magazine*, November 4, 2001, p. 53.)

a. Lloyd's metaphor compares _____

to _____.

b. The point of the metaphor is that _____

_____.

_____
*infusions: injections.

10. At thirty-two the boxer was past his prime and flat broke. He wasn't about to let his fresh-faced opponent become his Waterloo. He couldn't afford it.

> In 1815, Waterloo, located nine miles from Brussels, Belgium, was the scene of Napoleon Bonaparte's greatest and final defeat in battle. The defeat at Waterloo finished Napoleon's chances to regain political power in France. After Waterloo, he was exiled to the island of St. Helena, where he died in 1821.

The allusion to Waterloo says what about the boxer's need to win?

_____

C H A P T E R   1 0

Recognizing and Evaluating Bias

> **In this chapter, you'll learn**
> - how to spot bias in informative writing.
> - how to evaluate the degree of bias in persuasive writing.

Chapter 10 returns to the subject of *bias.* You'll learn how a writer's personal feelings can find their way into informative writing despite a writer's best efforts to remain emotionally uninvolved or objective. You'll also learn how to recognize when bias in persuasive writing has gone too far. While bias is a natural part of persuasive writing, it can sometimes interfere with an author's ability to treat opposing points of view fairly. When that happens, critical readers take note and reserve judgment.

Bias Isn't Necessarily Bad

The word *bias* has a bad reputation. We frequently use it to suggest that someone has a closed mind and cannot or will not listen to opposing points of view. But *bias* merely refers to a point of view or personal leaning. In other words, expressing a bias isn't necessarily bad.

Because of our background, experience, and training, most of us have personal opinions that influence how we see and interpret the world around us. Thus, how critical readers react to or evaluate an expression of bias depends a good deal on context, on where that bias appears, and on the degree, or strength, of the bias expressed.

For example, unless they are writing for the editorial page, newspaper reporters are expected to describe events as objectively as possible. If reporters describe those events in highly connotative or emotionally charged language that reveals their personal point of view, they are doing readers a disservice, and their biases are inappropriate in that context.

In contrast, newspaper editorials are supposed to express a personal bias. That's one of the reasons we read them. We want, for example, to get columnists Maureen Dowd's and Bob Herbert's perspectives on some current issue or event. However, even writers determined to persuade should offer readers a fair and reasonable argument. If a writer is so committed to one point of view that he or she can't be logical or fair, then the degree of bias is excessive, and we need to be wary of accepting that writer's point of view.

In sum, then, all writers have biases, and there's nothing wrong with revealing them in the appropriate context. What's important is that writers not let bias interfere with their ability to be logical and fair.

 ## Recognizing Bias in Informative Writing

Writers whose primary goal is to inform rather than persuade usually work hard to keep their biases to themselves. For example, the author of a textbook on modern American history might be a long-time Republican who considers Democrat Lyndon Baines Johnson one of history's worst presidents. Yet, in writing a chapter that covers Johnson's presidency, he should control his inclination to criticize Johnson's record. Like writers of reference works, authors of textbooks are expected to provide an impersonal and objective account of events and allow students to form their own opinions.

Still, writers are only human. Try as they might, they can't always eliminate every shred of personal bias from their writing. Although the overall tone of a passage may be emotionally neutral, the connotations of individual words or phrases can still suggest a personal bias or leaning. Note, for example, the italicized words in the following paragraph. These words have negative connotations and suggest that the authors do not admire the way former president Harry Truman handled foreign policy.

> President Truman . . . had a personality that tended to increase international tensions. Whereas Roosevelt had been *ingratiating,** patient, and evasive, Truman was *brash,* impatient,* and direct. *He seldom displayed the appreciation of subtleties so essential to successful diplomacy.* In his first meeting with V. M. Molotov, the Soviet commissar of foreign affairs, Truman sharply *berated** the Soviet Union* for violating the Yalta accords,* a charge Molotov denied. When Truman *shot back* that the Soviets should honor their agreements, Molotov stormed out of the room. The president was pleased with his "tough method." "I gave it to him straight 'one-two to the jaw.'" This *simplistic display of toughness* became a trademark of American Cold War* diplomacy.* (Norton et al., *A People and a Nation,* p. 488.)

The authors of this textbook passage don't seem to be fans of Harry Truman. But would you say the same about the author of the next passage?

> On his first day in office, Harry Truman remarked to a newspaperman, "Did you ever have a bull or a load of hay fall on you? If you ever did, you know how I felt last night." Yet President Truman's *native intelligence enabled him to grasp quickly the situation into which he was so suddenly thrown,* and on which he had not been briefed by Roosevelt. He had to have a few boon* companions

---

*ingratiating: eager to please.
*brash: hasty and unthinking.
*berated: criticized harshly at length.
*Soviet Union: the former name of fifteen separate republics governed by the Communist party, also called "Soviet Russia."
*Yalta accords: agreements made at the end of World War II in the city of Yalta, located near the Black Sea.
*Cold War: a period of hostile rivalry between the United States and Communist Russia.
*diplomacy: the conduct by government officials of relations between nations.
*boon: in this context, good-natured, jolly.

from Missouri around the White House for relaxation, but *he won the friendship and respect of gentlemen in politics* such as Dean Acheson, soldiers such as General Marshall, and foreign statesmen such as Clement Attlee. He made good cabinet, judicial, and ambassadorial appointments; *he kept a firm hand* on the new Department of Defense and the foreign service; and, *with more fateful decisions than almost any president in our time, he made the fewest mistakes.* Truman was always folksy, always the politician, *but nobody can reasonably deny that he attained the stature of a statesman.* (Samuel Eliot Morison, *The Oxford History of the American People.* New York: Oxford University Press, 1965, p. 1051.)

Unlike the authors of the first passage, the author of this passage admires Harry Truman's record as president, and his choice of words encourages readers to do the same.

When they recognize bias in writing meant to inform, critical readers don't throw up their hands in horror and refuse to read further. Instead, they try to identify the author's particular leaning and make sure that they don't absorb it right along with the author's description of events or ideas.

What's Left Out *Is* Significant

Sometimes the intrusion of bias in informative writing is obvious in the author's choice of words. But bias can also be more subtle. Sometimes writers reveal bias not by what they say but by what they leave out. For instance, a history writer who records only the successful or praiseworthy actions of President Franklin Delano Roosevelt but leaves out Roosevelt's order to intern, or imprison, Japanese Americans during World War II reveals a bias in favor of Roosevelt. Anytime an author describes a person or position where opposing points of view are possible without mentioning—or just barely acknowledging—the opposition, your critical antennae should go up. The writer's purpose may be informative, but you, the reader, are still not getting the whole story.

CHECK YOUR UNDERSTANDING

Explain why bias isn't all bad.

_____

_____

Rhetorical Questions Can Reveal a Hidden Bias

As you may know from composition class, rhetoric is the art of using language to persuade. Thus it probably comes as no surprise that **rhetorical questions**—questions that do not require or expect a reply—are a signal of both persuasive intent and personal bias. You can certainly expect rhetorical questions to turn up in persuasive writing, but they can also appear in writing that is meant to inform. They are a tip-off to the unexpected presence of bias. Here's an example:

> Given that more teenagers than ever before are grappling with problems such as depression, alcoholism, and drug abuse, desperate parents are looking for help in raising their children. Many parents are turning to wilderness programs, which promise to change the attitude and behavior of the young people who attend by exposing them to and training them for life in the outdoors. Most of these programs are in western states like Idaho and Utah. Some of them are on farms or in deserts. Almost all of them share the same premise—that sustained exposure to a natural world where kids have to fend for themselves can provide troubled young boys and girls with new skills and increased self-confidence. Yet promising as these programs may sound, they raise a crucial question: Is the wilderness—with its inherent, overwhelming, and often uncontrollable dangers—really the place to heal the psyche of troubled children?

Up until the last sentence, this passage is mainly informative. The author describes the purpose, location, and theory behind wilderness programs. But in the final sentence, she uses a rhetorical question that reveals her bias. The question, with its emphasis on nature's dangers, is phrased in a way that ensures only one answer—a definite no. Because it doesn't really expect any answer except the one suggested, the rhetorical question reveals a persuasive purpose and personal bias not apparent in the other sentences.

When authors ask questions that don't require an answer, those questions are rhetorical, and you need to be aware of the bias such questions reveal.

Informative Writing Lacking in Bias

- employs an emotionally neutral tone throughout.
- describes both sides of an issue equally without evaluating or judging either side.

- includes no personal opinions or value judgments from the author.
- includes little or no connotative language.

Informative Writing That Reflects a Bias

- may use charged language that interrupts an emotionally neutral tone.
- gives the author's personal opinion.
- emphasizes either positive *or* negative views of a subject but doesn't give equal space to both sides.
- uses rhetorical questions.

EXERCISE 1

DIRECTIONS Each of the following passages comes from a source where one would expect the author to eliminate any evidence of bias. Read each passage. Then circle the appropriate letters to indicate whether or not the author or authors have eliminated all evidence of bias.

EXAMPLE

Trial Elements

1 A trial is often compared to a boxing match. Both are contests between *adversaries,* persons who oppose or fight one another. In a trial, the adversaries are called **litigants** and, rather than hitting each other, they challenge each other's evidence and testimony. For this reason, an American trial is often labeled an **adversary proceeding.** The judge acts as a referee and interprets the rules of the "match."

2 The person who files suit in a civil case is called a **plaintiff.** In a criminal trial, the prosecution brings the charges. The United States attorney is the prosecutor in federal cases. In state trials, the prosecutor may be known as the state's attorney, county prosecutor, or district attorney. The person being sued or charged with the crime is the **defendant.**

3 Every trial has two purposes: to establish the facts of the case, and to find the law that applies. The role of the jury is to decide questions of fact. (Adapted from Hardy, *Government in America,* p. 502.)

Presence of Bias   a. The author is describing the elements of a trial and clearly favors our legal system.

b. The author is describing the elements of a trial and is clearly critical of our system.

(c.) It's impossible to determine the author's personal feelings.

> **EXPLANATION** Drawn from a textbook, this selection does not reveal any bias for or against our legal system. The language remains almost completely denotative, and there is no evidence whatsoever of the author's personal opinion.

1. The Presidency of John F. Kennedy

1 John F. Kennedy's ambitious social program, the New Frontier, promised more than Kennedy could deliver: an end to racial discrimination, federal aid to education, medical care for the elderly, and government action to halt the recession* the country was suffering. Only eight months into his first year, it was evident that Kennedy lacked the ability to move Congress, which was dominated by conservative Republicans and southern Democrats. Long-time members of Congress saw him and his administration as publicity hungry. Some feared the president would seek federal aid to parochial schools. The result was the defeat of federal aid to education and of a Kennedy-sponsored boost in the minimum wage.

2 Still struggling to appease conservative members of Congress, the new president pursued civil rights with a notable lack of vigor. Kennedy did establish the President's Committee on Equal Employment Opportunity to eliminate racial discrimination in government hiring. But he waited until late 1962 before honoring a 1960 campaign pledge to issue an executive order forbidding segregation in federally subsidized housing. Meanwhile, he appointed five die-hard segregationists to the federal bench in the Deep South. The struggle for racial equality was the most important domestic issue of the time, and Kennedy's performance disheartened* civil rights advocates. (Adapted from Norton et al., *A People and a Nation,* p. 991.)

Presence of Bias   a. The authors are admirers of John F. Kennedy.

b. The authors are critical of John F. Kennedy.

c. It's impossible to determine the authors' personal feelings.

_____
*recession: economic downturn.
*disheartened: disappointed.

2. **The Civil Rights Act of 1964**

1 In 1961, a new administration, headed by President John F. Kennedy, came to power. At first Kennedy did not seem to be committed to civil rights. His stance changed as the movement gained momentum and as more and more whites became aware of the abuse being heaped on sit-in demonstrators, freedom riders (who tested unlawful segregation on interstate bus routes), and those who were trying to help blacks register to vote in southern states. Volunteers were being jailed, beaten, and killed for advocating activities among blacks that whites took for granted.

2 In late 1962, President Kennedy ordered federal troops to ensure the safety of James Meredith, the first black to attend the University of Mississippi. In early 1963, Kennedy enforced the desegregation of the University of Alabama. In April 1963, television viewers were shocked to see civil rights marchers in Birmingham, Alabama, attacked with dogs, fire hoses, and cattle prods. (The idea of the Birmingham march was to provoke confrontations with white officials in an effort to compel the national government to intervene on behalf of blacks.) Finally, in June 1963, Kennedy asked Congress for legislation that would outlaw segregation in public accommodations.

3 Two months later, Martin Luther King Jr. joined in a march on Washington, D.C. The organizers called the protest "A March for Jobs and Freedom," signaling the economic goals of black America. More than 250,000 people, black and white, gathered peaceably at the Lincoln Memorial to hear King speak. "I have a dream," the great preacher extemporized,* "that my four little children will one day live in a nation where they will not be judged by the color of their skin but by the content of their character."

4 Congress had not yet enacted Kennedy's public accommodations bill when he was assassinated on November 22, 1963. His successor, Lyndon B. Johnson, considered civil rights his top legislative priority. Within months, Congress enacted the Civil Rights Act of 1964, which included a vital provision barring segregation in most public accommodations. This congressional action was, in part, a reaction to Kennedy's death. But it was also almost certainly a response to the brutal treatment of blacks throughout the South. (Janda et al., *The Challenge of Democracy*, pp. 549–550.)

Presence of Bias   a. The authors are admirers of John F. Kennedy.

b. The authors are critical of John F. Kennedy.

c. It's impossible to determine the authors' personal feelings.

_____

*extemporized: spoke without practice or preparation.

3. **Lowell, Robert** (1917–1977) American poet from a famous aristocratic American family; regarded by most critics as the best English language poet of his generation and by certain readers as beyond criticism altogether. For better or for worse, Lowell was the modern poet-as-film-star: his private affairs were apparently carried out mainly in public (this is miscalled "confessionalism"): his themes included the personalities and behavior of his relatives, his various marriages and liaisons,* the (presumably) affective disorder* which landed him in hospital many times, and so on. Lowell was extremely gifted but the conventional view of his development, even where it judges the most recent poems as failures, is not quite correct, for it mistakes potential for achievement, and overrates him. (Adapted from Martin Seymour-Smith, *Who's Who in Twentieth Century Literature.* New York: McGraw-Hill, 1976, p. 216.)

Presence of Bias   a. The author admires Robert Lowell.

b. The author is critical of Robert Lowell.

c. It's impossible to determine the author's personal feelings.

4. **The Animal Rights Movement**

1 Opposition to animal research has a long history, going back at least as far as the antivivisectionist movement of the nineteenth century. In recent years the growth of the animal rights movement was spurred by a book called *Animal Liberation* (1975), by Australian philosopher Peter Singer. Singer argued that many uses of animals by humans—for food, for clothing, and as captive research subjects—reflected "speciesism": the exploitation of certain species (nonhuman animals) for the benefit of another (humans). Because animals, like humans, can feel pain, Singer argued, they are entitled to just as much consideration as humans are.

2   In Singer's view, speciesism is a form of discrimination that is just as evil as racism and sexism. "Would the experimenter be prepared to perform his experiment on a human infant?" Singer asks. "If not, then his readiness to use nonhumans is simple discrimination" (Singer, 1976, p. 156).

3   Many animal rights supporters have advanced their views in books and articles and have worked for laws and regulations that would ensure the humane treatment of animals. Others have resorted to acts of terrorism in the name of animal rights (Jasper &

---

*liaisons: love affairs.
*affective disorder: a disorder that involves extreme shifts in emotion, in Lowell's case from great enthusiasm to deep depression.

Nelkin, 1992). Some activists have invaded animal laboratories, destroyed equipment, stolen data, and let the animals out of their cages. Animal rights activists have also staged dramatic demonstrations . . . in an attempt to convince the public of what they see as the cruelty of animal research.

4   The animal rights movement has been accused by researchers of painting a distorted picture of animal research. In fact, most animal research is neither cruel nor painful, and the large majority of animal researchers are concerned about animal welfare (Novak, 1991). When researchers employ surgical procedures with animals, they almost always use anesthesia to eliminate pain. Many animal rights supporters acknowledge such humane practices but believe that animal research remains unnecessarily intrusive. But the moral fervor of other animal rights advocates has led them to engage in misleading portrayals of scientists as sadists and laboratories as torture chambers. (Rubin et al., *Psychology,* pp. 68–69.)

Presence of Bias   a. The authors support the animal rights movement.

b. The authors are critical of the animal rights movement.

c. It's impossible to determine the authors' personal feelings.

5. **Frida Kahlo**

1 The Mexican artist Frida Kahlo (1907–1954) was born Magdalena Carmen Frida Kahlo Calderónin Coyoacán, Although she began her education intending to be a physician, she was forced to change her mind when she suffered a terrible accident at the age of eighteen. The accident left her so debilitated that a life devoted to medicine would have been far too strenuous for her to pursue.

2   While she was recovering from the accident, Kahlo began painting. In 1928, she approached famed muralist Diego Rivera (1866–1957) and asked for his opinion of her work. Rivera thought she had talent and encouraged her. One year later, the two were married. Their relationship, however, was stormy, and they were divorced in 1939, only to remarry the following year.

3   Kahlo's first public exhibition took place in 1938. In 1939, her work was exhibited in a Paris exhibition called "Mexique." As a result of the exhibition, one of her works, a self-portrait, was purchased for the famed French museum the Louvre. Although her problems with Rivera and her constant physical pain—her body had never completely recovered from the accident—encouraged Kahlo's growing dependency on alcohol, Kahlo continued to paint,

further developing her brand of colorful, personalized surrealism.*
However, she did not have a major exhibition in her own country
until 1953, one year before her death. Overshadowed in her lifetime by her famous husband, Kahlo overtook him in death, so
much so that her name has become better known than his. Yet in
comparing the works of the two artists, a key question emerges.
Does Kahlo's fame rest on the quality of her work or on the current tendency to celebrate women artists whatever their degree of
talent? (Christopher Fresa, *Modern Painters.* Cleveland: Bogus
Publications, 1999, p. 200.)

Presence of Bias   a. The author admires Kahlo's work.

b. The author thinks Kahlo's work is overrated.

c. It's impossible to determine the author's bias.

 # Responding to Bias in Persuasive Writing

We don't expect to find bias in informative writing, so encountering
it usually comes as a surprise. Persuasive writing, in contrast, raises
different expectations. We expect writers to be personally engaged—
to tell us about the personal reasons, experiences, or feelings that
led them to their point of view. In short, we expect persuasive writing
to express a bias. What we don't expect, even in persuasive writing,
is that writers be imprisoned or blinded by their biases. Despite their
personal feelings, we expect them to acknowledge opposing points
of view and to treat those points of view fairly. A writer who fails
to acknowledge opposing points of view or, even worse, ridicules or
insults them should not be completely trusted. Yes, the writer may
sound confident and convincing. Still, you need to know a bit more
before deciding to support or share the writer's point of view.

Appropriate and Inappropriate Bias

To understand the difference between appropriate and inappropriate bias in persuasive writing, compare the following passages.

---

*surrealism: a movement in art and literature emphasizing the expression of the
imagination as it might appear in dreams, with the emphasis on free association
rather than logic and reason.

After reading about courses teaching television literacy,* I must say I am appalled by the sheer idiocy that abounds on so many college campuses today. What should instructors do if they discover that students have trouble reading their textbooks because they have spent too much time watching television? What else? Give those same students more television to watch. That way, teachers can avoid making demands on students *and* avoid doing their job. All they need to do is flip on the television set and call themselves "media specialists."

The author of this passage expresses a strong bias against courses in television literacy. But the problem with the passage is not the author's bias. The problem is that the author doesn't explain or defend those feelings. Instead, in a tone of outraged irony, he ridicules the opposing point of view. In this case, the author's bias interferes with his ability to be persuasive.

To see how an author can express a bias and still be persuasive, read the following passage. Although the author freely admits her bias, she still keeps an open mind and points out not just what's wrong about opposing points of view, but what's right as well.

I must admit to being troubled by courses that make commercials and soap operas the focus of study. Although I agree that television programming plays a powerful role in most people's lives and that its influence over our minds and imaginations should be critically examined, I'm not sure courses in television literacy are the answer. A better alternative would be to make television viewing a small portion of a course on critical reading and thinking. Then students could apply their critical skills to both television scripts and images. This approach would eliminate what seems to be a legitimate objection to courses in television literacy—that they encourage students to do more of what they already do: Watch too much TV.

In this passage, the author expresses a definite bias: She is not in favor of courses "that make commercials and soap operas the focus of study." Still, that bias does not prevent her from giving the opposing point of view its due. She admits that the influence of television "should be critically examined," and she suggests an alternative to courses in television literacy: critical thinking or reading courses that would allot a small portion of time to analyzing scripts and images.

To evaluate bias in persuasive writing, look over the following list.

---

*television literacy: the condition of being educated or knowledgeable on the subject of television.

Anytime you encounter a writer intent on persuasion, make sure you can say no to these five questions.

Questions to Help Evaluate Bias in Persuasive Writing

1. Does the author use a tone that drips sarcasm or erupts in anger?
2. Does the author ignore the possibility that opposing points of view might exist?
3. Does the author rely more on insulting the opposition than on explaining the merits of his or her point of view or position?
4. Does the author insist that opposing points of view have no value or merit *without* explaining why those opposing points of view are mistaken or inaccurate?
5. Does the author make use of circular reasoning or irrelevant facts? (See Chapter 7.)

If you answer "yes" to even one of the above five questions, you need to find a more balanced discussion of the issue at hand before taking sides.

EXERCISE 2

DIRECTIONS Each selection expresses a bias, but only one expresses such a strong bias that critical readers would be suspicious of the author's ability to fairly evaluate opposing points of view. Put a check (√) in the blank if you think the author is biased but fair. Put a *B* in the blank if you think the author is too biased to be fair.

EXAMPLE

Jefferson's Bible

1 While serving as third president of the United States, Thomas Jefferson began a project to revise the Bible. Jefferson studied the Scriptures every day and selected what he considered to be the Bible's best and most authentic material. Concentrating on the New Testament—specifically the Gospels of Matthew, Mark, and Luke—Jefferson literally cut out his favorite

passages (which he said were like "diamonds in a dunghill") with a razor and pasted them together to create his own version. In doing so, he censored out any mention of Jesus as God or the Son of God. He also eliminated all miracles and supernatural events.

2   For example, his version does not include any reference to Mary's immaculate conception,* the miracles attributed to Jesus, or the Resurrection. Jefferson's version ends with Jesus's burial. Jefferson told one correspondent that the material he discarded was all "ignorance . . . , superstitions, fanaticism, and fabrications." The material he chose is mainly composed of parables and sayings that focus on the morals and ethics Jesus preached and demonstrated. According to one scholar, Jefferson "made a Socrates out of Jesus."

3   Jefferson never intended for anyone to see this new version. However, it was discovered in 1886 and published by the Government Printing Office from 1904 to 1957. The book was distributed to all new congressional members during that time. In 2001, the book was reissued by Beacon Press as *The Jefferson Bible: The Life and Morals of Jesus of Nazareth.* Since its publication, some scholars and religious leaders have denounced Thomas Jefferson's revision of the New Testament as "sheer audacity." These critics object to Jefferson's project of cutting and pasting together what he considered to be the best and most authentic passages of Scripture. They say his tampering with a sacred work mocks the Christian faith.

4   Although understandable, this criticism of Jefferson is not really fair. Jefferson did not rewrite the Bible; he merely selected those passages that were, to him, most meaningful. What Jefferson did was no different from highlighting, underlining, or annotating the Bible to mark favorite passages, something many Christians have done for years with their own personal copies. Furthermore, Jefferson did not intend for his version of the Bible to be published. He intended to keep it to himself for his own private study and reflection. Remember it was discovered and printed only after his death.

5   The point is that Jefferson did not try to convince anyone else to accept his personal beliefs. Throughout his career Jefferson fought for religious freedom for all Americans, and we still possess this freedom today. Therefore, it's not fair to attack Jefferson for exercising the same right we ourselves enjoy. On the contrary,

*immaculate conception: the Catholic doctrine that says the Virgin Mary was conceived without the stain of original sin.

we should view his version of the Bible as an important historical document, one that helps us better understand this very important and influential founding father.

___√___

EXPLANATION The author of this reading openly expresses her support of Jefferson's project to create his own version of the Bible. However, her bias in favor of Jefferson's Bible does not render her unable to treat opposing points of view with respect.

1. ## Hunters Are Wildlife's Best Friends

1 I am a hunter. I feed my family with the game I kill. All Americans eat dead stuff, but our meat is better, and it is harvested with a responsible connection to the earth. This is true conservation— the wise use.

2 Our time-honored tradition continues because, in the face of global habitat destruction, those of us who cherish wildlife have demanded restrictions on its harvest, based on a sound and proven scientific equation of sustained-yield management.

3 We save and guard habitat and manage wildlife not for our freezers or shooting opportunities but rather for the future of this most valuable resource. The condition of wildlife and the ground that supports it are a barometer by which the quality of our lives is based.

4 Read this very carefully, because these game laws and restrictions are self-imposed, insisted upon, policed and financed by us hunters to the tune of billions of dollars a year.

5 The lies of the animal-rights freaks are perpetrated for the single cause of greed. They are to animals what Jim Bakker* was to religion. After deceiving millions of Americans out of millions of dollars, they have yet to save any animals.

6 Look closely at their shameful agenda and track record. These zealots* hate Americans who eat turkey on Thanksgiving. They are also extremely dangerous, having bombed medical-testing labs, destroyed family-run farms, and even been convicted of animal abuse on occasion, grandstanding their lies at the expense of real animals' welfare. They recently committed their most repulsive act yet when one group proclaimed that the heinous crimes charged to accused mass murderer Jeffrey Dahmer were the exact same crimes as the preparation of a chicken for the grill. No clear-thinking American could possibly stand behind such statements.

_____

*Jim Bakker: a television evangelist who served time in prison for improper use of funds collected for religious purposes.
*zealots: people so committed to a cause they lack all reason or compassion.

7   If you truly appreciate wild animals, these people must be stopped and hunters' dedicated efforts must be supported. Sure, we have bad guys. But those who conduct legal banking businesses should never be lumped together with bank robbers. Poachers are the bad guys, and hunters despise them as our number one enemy.

8   When responsible citizens are genuinely concerned about the well-being and future of wildlife, they do their homework and discover the truth. Our Ted Nugent World Bowhunters organization is dedicated to this truth and to sharing the wonderment of the great out-of-doors with our families and friends. (Ted Nugent, "Hunters Are Wildlife's Best Friends," *USA Today*, October 3, 1991.)

——

2. **Living with Wildlife**

1   Hunters tend to think of themselves as friends of wildlife. But I find the position hard to accept when I consider the harm hunting does to animals. The stress hunting inflicts on animals—the noise, the fear and the constant chase—severely restricts the ability to eat properly and store the fat and energy they need to survive the winter.

2   Hunting also disrupts migration and hibernation; and the campfires, recreational vehicles, trash, and other hunting side effects endanger the wildlife and the environment. For animals like wolves who mate for life and have close family units, hunting can severely harm entire animal communities.

3   Hunters claim that they pay for "conservation" by buying hunting licenses, duck stamps, etc., but the relatively small amount each hunter pays does not cover the cost of hunting programs or game warden services. The public lands many hunters use are supported by taxpayers, and the U.S. Fish and Wildlife service programs, which benefit hunters, get as much as 90 percent of their funds from fees. Funds benefiting "nongame" species are scarce.

4   Hunters kill more animals than recorded tallies indicate. It is estimated that for every animal a hunter kills and recovers, at least two wounded but unrecovered animals die slowly and painfully of blood loss, infection, or starvation. Those who don't die often suffer from disabling injuries. Because of carelessness, or the effects of alcohol, scores of horses, cows, dogs, cats, hikers and others are wounded or killed each year by hunters.

5   Before you support a "wildlife" or "conservation" group, ask if it supports hunting. Such groups as the National Wildlife Federation, The National Audubon Society, The Sierra Club, the Izaak Walton League, The Wilderness Society and many others are prohunting.

6   To combat hunting in your area, post "No Hunting" signs on your land, join or form a local antihunting organization, protest organized hunts, play loud radios and spread deer repellant or human hair (from barber shops) near hunting areas, tell others the facts about hunting, and encourage your legislators to enact or enforce wildlife protection laws.

7   As the actor Jimmy Stewart put it, "Animals give me more pleasure through the viewfinder of a camera than they ever did in the cross hairs of a shotgun. And after I've finished 'shooting,' my unharmed victims are still around for others to enjoy." (Excerpted from "People for the Ethical Treatment of Animals," PETA.)

 ## Bias and Careless Thinking

Writers whose bias keeps them from considering opposing points of view are inclined to use circular reasoning and irrelevant facts (see pages 280–282). They don't do this because they're dishonest. They are just so certain of their own rightness they don't always think about convincing others. Sure that they—and only they—are right, they fail to thoroughly explain their position.

In addition to using circular reasoning and irrelevant facts, writers blinded by bias also tend to engage in two other kinds of careless thinking—*slippery slope* and *personal attack.*

Slippery Slope

Writers who engage in *slippery slope* thinking insist that taking even one step in a particular direction will invariably lead to another series of steps that will end in disaster. Here's an example:

> If we ban handguns, the next step will be the banning of rifles, and then people who hunt for food will no longer be able to feed their families.

Writers who use slippery slope thinking assume that events similar in nature follow one another without reference to any specific context or conditions. They ignore the fact that events usually arise in response to or as a result of particular circumstances. For example, many people want to ban handguns because statistics show a connection between handguns in the home and violent crime, both in and outside the home. That same connection does not exist between hunting rifles and crime. Thus, it makes no sense to claim that banning handguns will automatically lead to banning rifles. Handguns and rifles are similar kinds of weapons, but they are used in very different ways and in very different circumstances.

Personal Attacks

Be wary of writers who respond to opposing points of view by personally attacking the opposition. In the following passage, note how the author attacks her opponent's character rather than his point of view.

> Once again, David DeGrecco, columnist for the *New Jersey Sun*, has presented his tired old case for gun control. As usual, De-Grecco serves up the argument that gun control laws can help eliminate some of the violence plaguing city streets across the country. Outspoken as usual, DeGrecco is curiously silent about his own recent bout with criminal behavior. Less than two weeks ago, he and several others were arrested for demonstrating at the opening of a nuclear power plant. For one so determined to bring law and order to our streets, DeGrecco does not seem to mind breaking a few laws himself.

Here the author is obviously biased against the gun control laws championed by David DeGrecco. That's certainly her right. Still, to be persuasive, she needs to challenge what the columnist claims— that gun control laws can help eliminate violence. But instead of doing that, she attacks the man personally, pointing out that he was recently jailed. Yet DeGrecco's position on nuclear power has nothing to do with the issue at hand—gun control. This, then, is another instance of bias clouding the writer's ability to respond fairly and respectfully to opposing points of view.

EXERCISE 3

DIRECTIONS Each of the following readings expresses a strong bias for or against a particular position. But in some cases the author has fallen victim to the two errors in reasoning described above. Identify those errors by putting an *S* (for slippery slope) or a *P* (for personal attack) in the blank. If the passage does not contain either error, put a check (✓) in the blank.

1. No Sexual Harassment Equals No Soldiers

1 Over the years, there's been a good deal of attention focused on sexual harassment in the military, and rightly so. No one wants to see officers in charge of young female recruits abuse their power by sexually harassing those in their charge. However, supporters of women in the military are making a crucial mistake when they try to eliminate sexism in the military and at the same time insist that women should go into combat right alongside men.

2   To be a warrior means that a soldier has to revert to a more primitive mode of behavior and thought. It means that one has to assume a kill-or-be-killed mentality that allows little room for compassion or thought. It is very hard, perhaps impossible, to encourage this mindset in men and at the same time expect them to fight side by side with women without reverting to a more primitive mode of behavior. As Fred C. Ikle, an undersecretary of defense in the Reagan administration, expressed it, "You can't cultivate the necessary commitment to physical violence and fully protect against the risk of harassment. Military life may . . . foster the attitudes that tend toward rape, such as aggression and single-minded assertion."[1]

3   Viewed from this perspective, efforts to eliminate sexual harassment could have disastrous consequences during wartime, particularly if women are allowed into combat. Committed to being respectful toward women, male soldiers will also feel that they must rein in their aggression in the presence of women. As a result, they will hold back during combat training and eventually during combat itself. Our country will lose its military strength and its position as a world power.

------

2. Egg Donation May Not Be Such a Miracle for Donors

1 Because so many couples desperately want a child and can't have one, the search for women willing to donate their eggs for in vitro fertilization* has become a big business. Although many people consider in vitro fertilization a wondrous miracle, I must admit to being skeptical about the use of egg donors. The couple who gains a child, thanks to a donor, may be rightly jubilant; the donor, however, may be taking more risks than she realizes.

2   For starters, the egg donation process is not particularly pleas-

------

[1]Richard Raynor, "The Warrior Besieged," *New York Times*, June 22, 1997, p. 29.
*in vitro fertilization: *in vitro* literally means "in glass"; the term refers to the process of creating life in an artificial setting outside the human body.

ant. To prepare, women take daily hormone injections which force the maturation of ten to twenty eggs instead of the normal one or two. As a result of the injections, donors often suffer cramping and mood swings. Sometimes their ovaries become dangerously enlarged. At this time, there have been no signs of long-term side effects on donors, but it is possible that the injections may increase the possibility of ovarian cancer. No one really knows for sure what the long-term effects are mainly because in vitro fertilization hasn't been around for very long.

3   Those who favor the use of egg donors argue that the women are being well paid for the risks they take. Unfortunately, the issue of payment only points to another objection. Clinics and hospitals pay donors as much as five thousand dollars for their eggs. In the face of such a sum, women who are young or poor—or in many cases both—can be lured by the money into ignoring the risks. As Diana Aronson, the executive director of Resolve, the national support group for infertile couples, points out, the large sums of money offered donors can lead to what she calls "inappropriate assessment of risk. If you're a college student, four cycles at $5,000 each may pay for . . . college"[2] and if you're a poor, unmarried mother, $5,000 will pay the rent for months.

4   Yes, egg donation may well provide infertile couples with the baby they so desperately desire, but someone else may be paying a terrible price for their joy. Couples desiring the use of egg donation should ask themselves if they are willing to let another human being take serious health risks so they can become parents.

———

3. Attica Still Haunts Us

1   The worst prison insurrection in U.S. history occurred at the Attica Correctional Facility near Buffalo, New York, in September 1971. The atmosphere at the prison had been tense due to overcrowded and deteriorating conditions. Then, on September 9, a guard broke up a scuffle between two inmates, who were put into isolation cells as a result. A rumor that the inmates were being tortured spread throughout the facility. The next day, a group of inmates armed with baseball bats, pipes, chairs, and knives seized control of an exercise yard and took forty guards hostage.

———

[2]Marie McCullough, "Life for Sale: Market for Women's Eggs Is Heating Up," *Philadelphia Inquirer,* March 8, 1998, pp. A-1 and 19.

They demanded, among other things, better conditions and amnesty for crimes committed during the revolt. They also insisted that New York's governor, Nelson Rockefeller, come to the prison to address the problem. Governor Rockefeller refused. Three days after the riot began, he authorized state police to regain control of the facility by force if necessary.

2   On September 13, police armed with tear gas and shotguns stormed the prison, firing more than 2,000 rounds of ammunition in a total of six minutes. Eleven hostages and thirty-two inmates were killed as a direct result of the police attack, although initially it was thought that the deaths were a result of prisoners' violence. When the prison's guards were again in control, they stripped, beat, and tortured the inmates. They were especially brutal with the riot's leaders. In the first hours after regaining control of the prison, police also denied medical care to the wounded. As a result, in 1974, lawyers filed a class-action lawsuit on behalf of the 1,280 prisoners who were harassed during the attack.

3   But it wasn't until August of 2000 that the State of New York finally settled the suit filed on behalf of the 1,280 prisoners incarcerated at the Attica Correctional Facility during the riot. Those men still alive received a group settlement of $8 million for the suffering they endured as a result of the prison insurrection. And make no mistake, they deserve every penny of that settlement and a good deal more. Prior to the revolt, inmates had endured appallingly inhumane conditions at this facility. They had been permitted a shower just once a week and given a roll of toilet paper just once a month. Their food was poor in quality and badly prepared. Requests for meals reflecting religious preferences were routinely denied. Because the prison's capacity had been exceeded by more than 40 percent, prisoners were also subjected to terrible overcrowding. When the inmates finally seized control of an exercise yard and took the guards hostage, Nelson Rockefeller flatly refused to address what were very legitimate grievances. Determined to present himself as tough on crime and criminals, Rockefeller ordered a poorly executed assault on the prison, which left over forty people dead.

4   Given the circumstances, it's hard to understand critics who claim the Attica settlement was unjust. Clearly, those opposing the $8 million award for damages have no compassion for prisoners, who apparently don't deserve to be treated like human beings. For critics of the Attica award there is no such thing as rehabilitation in prison. Their motto is: "Lock 'em up and throw away the key."

4. Do We Really Need Single-Sex Schools?

1 In 1992, the American Association of University Women published the report *How Schools Shortchange Girls.* As the title indicates, the study strongly suggested that public schools were not doing enough to ensure that boys and girls were treated equally. The report made a great deal of the fact that teachers tend to call on boys more than on girls. Ever since that AAUW report, many educators have begun to sing the praises of single-sex schools. In fact, the pages of this newspaper recently featured letters from several who had gone to all-girl schools and were convinced that they were better off as a result. Still, no matter how trendy it may be to applaud same-sex schools, I beg to disagree.

2 Girls need to have boys in the classroom. If they don't learn how to work with and compete against boys while they are in school and the stakes aren't so high, how will they compete after graduation when they enter the world of work? Imagine, for example, that a young woman who has never been in intellectual competition with men enters a management meeting where only men are present. Is she going to hold her own, or is she going to become anxious and tongue-tied because her male colleagues don't use the "nurturing" style purportedly employed more by women than by men?

3 Then, too, where does this isolation by gender end? Can we expect women who have gone to same-sex schools to demand that the workplace also be segregated?* Probably. Once we agree that women should study only with one another, the segregated workplace can't be far behind.

CHECK YOUR UNDERSTANDING

Explain slippery slope thinking.

_____

_____

---

*segregated: divided by sex or race.

■ **DIGGING DEEPER**

LOOKING AHEAD The authors of the passages on pages 392–393 questioned the value of making television the subject of serious study. The author of this next selection, however, clearly thinks that television talk shows merit serious attention. Although talk shows may give ordinary people a chance at the fifteen minutes of fame artist Andy Warhol claimed everyone gets sooner or later, that fame can sometimes come at a price.

THE ETHICS OF TELEVISION TALK SHOWS

1   Television talk shows differ in significant ways from radio talk shows. The most important difference is that television talk shows have a visual component that is lacking in radio. The television shows are usually taped before a live audience, members of which are often allowed to participate in the program. After the program's guests are presented on stage and after their problems are exposed or their stories told, the program host often seizes a microphone and gallops into the audience. Individuals are singled out here and there for their comments about what they have just seen and heard. Two key ethical issues raised by these talk shows are *content* and *procedures.*

Content
2   Geraldo Rivera, Sally Jessy Raphael, Montel Williams, Rikki Lake, Maury Povich, Jenny Jones, and Jerry Springer are among those who have television talk shows available via syndication in almost every major market. Among the topics discussed on these programs on a typical autumn Friday in 1997 were the following: gossip, plastic-surgery woes, crime stories on television news, hair makeovers, and paternity tests. As long as the gossip isn't malicious, an ethicist could not find much to strenuously object to in this collection of programs. However, on Tuesday of the following week, the overall nature of the program content had changed. Viewers were able to tune in programs on serial killers, drugs, former lovers, a sex survey, erotomania, dangerous teens, unfulfilled wishes, and lovers. Talk show critics argue that this latter list of program topics more accurately reflects the overall nature of these programs.

3   As is the case with radio talk shows, the television "talk culture is spectacularly ill-suited to dealing with complicated subjects." Therefore, "the plot is always the same. People with problems—

'husband says she looks like a cow,' 'pressured to lose her virginity or else,' 'mate wants more sex than I do,' 'boy crazy,' 'dresses like a tramp'"—are subjected to relentless preaching by the host and the studio audience." With few exceptions, the guests are often poor and have little education. The subjects under discussion are often lurid,* if not bizarre. Some critics feel that this sort of public humiliation of guests borders on class exploitation and has important ethical implications. Should these programs be capitalizing on people who are "so needy—of social support, of education, of material resources and self-esteem—that they mistake being the center of attention for being actually loved and respected?" Rousseau's* philosophy advocates treating others with compassion and seeking to promote harmony among all those involved. Do television talk shows of the sort described promote that goal?

4   As theater, these talk shows are fairly entertaining, but as serious program material—and they are taken seriously by many viewers—they fail to provide much positive benefit to either participants or audience. Although television talk show guests have more on-air time than radio call-in participants, there is still precious little time to present a problem in its full context before advice is shouted to the guests by audience members, all of whom are strangers and none of whom is a qualified advice giver. On television talk shows, on-stage guests do get Andy Warhol's 15 minutes of fame, but selected audience members get only about 15 seconds. What positive outcomes can result from such exchanges?

5   A Pennsylvania State University researcher who studied daytime talk shows concluded that they "do more harm than good." Most of these shows "are simply mouthing mantras* of pop-therapy. . . . Strangers get to give advice without being responsible for its effect. The central distortion that these shows propound is that they give useful therapy to guests and useful advice to the audience." St. Thomas Aquinas* reminds us that the best actions are those guided by prudence,* justice, temperance,* and courage. Can any of these virtues be said to be at work on television talk shows?

6   The content of these television talk shows, then, is an important ethical issue. Why must private lives be made public? Of what use are these programs to participants if no sound, reason-

---

*lurid: marked by sensationalism.
*Jean Jacques Rousseau (1712–1778): French philosopher who believed that humanity, although basically good, was corrupted by society.
*mantras: commonly repeated words or phrases.
*St. Thomas Aquinas (1225–1274): Italian philosopher and theologian whose teachings combined reason and faith.
*prudence: good judgment.
*temperance: moderation.

able, problem solution is offered them? Why are commercial breaks inserted at precisely the moment someone in the audience begins to question the whole process or takes the issue in a direction not approved of by the host? It is not difficult to see how "the national conversation has been coarsened, cheapened, reduced to name-calling and finger-pointing, and bumper-sticker sloganeering" by television talk shows.

Procedures

7 If the content of television talk shows were not troubling enough, the way some of these shows "ambush" their guests raises additional ethical concerns. A 1995 study by the Kaiser Family Foundation found that "America's television talk show hosts score an average of sixteen 'ambush disclosures' an hour on guests. . . . Often guests have little or no control about the disclosure." The study analyzed 200 videotapes of daytime talk shows and found what most already know: "Hosts and guests talk mostly about family, personal relationships, and sex." The study found that "the most common disclosures per hour were: five of a sexual nature, four about a personal attribute such as addiction, three about abuse, two about an embarrassing situation, and two about criminal activity."

8   Ambush disclosures can sometimes have decidedly negative consequences. One legendary talk show moment featured a brawl between white skinheads and the black civil rights activist Roy Innis. On another show, this one about domestic violence, chairs were thrown, and the host, Geraldo Rivera, suffered a broken nose. Another famous talk show moment came when a male guest on the *Jenny Jones Show* was told he would meet a secret admirer. The guest "was humiliated when the admirer turned out to be a homosexual man. The guest was charged with murdering the admirer following the taping."

9   Clearly, the "ambush" nature of these program raises serious ethical concerns. Lawrence Kohlberg's moral development philosophy notes that the most mature level of ethical decision making is one where all involved are treated with dignity and are recognized as having certain rights, especially when actions involve them as individuals and concern personal matters. Do television talk shows operate on Kohlberg's highest level of ethical decision making? Is the dignity of each guest respected? Are guests properly informed about what might happen on the show?

10   For his part, Geraldo Rivera* took steps in early 1998 to clean

---

*Geraldo Rivera has, for the moment at least, abandoned television talk shows for more serious work as a war correspondent.

up his journalistic image. After 11 seasons of serving up "daily dosages of urban blight and occasional fisticuffs," the *Geraldo Rivera Show* was scheduled to leave the air. Rivera struck a deal with NBC that was reportedly worth $40 million. He planned to return to the mainstream of network news, but, as of early 1999, had not done so. Before his syndicated talk show, he spent some time as a journalist with ABC News, but was fired in 1985.

11   Jenny Jones remained unrepentant. In her autobiography, *Jenny Jones, My Story*, published in 1997, she was unapologetic for her syndicated talk show, "a favored target of critics, part of the . . . trash TV trend where family feuds, makeovers . . . dominate daytime." Jones says her detractors "never want to write about how the show, and she personally, helps many people." Critics often take an elitist view of her show, she says, noting that she does not exploit her guests or look down on them. "They're the same people I run into when I go shop at Kmart, which I do," she says. (Leslie, *Mass Communication Ethics*, pp. 263–266.)

Sharpening Your Skills

DIRECTIONS Answer the following questions by filling in the blanks or circling the letter of the correct response.

1. What's the main idea of this reading?
    a. Television talk shows differ from radio talk shows.
    b. Television has a visual component lacking in radio.
    c. The context and precedures of television talk shows raise some crucial ethical issues.
    d. Television talk shows exploit people who lack money and education.

2. The author does not specifically define "ambush disclosures." However, you can infer a definition. Write that definition below.

    _____

    _____

3. According to the author, which of the following is *not* one of the ethical issues raised by television talk shows?
    a. Television talk shows exploit people who are poor and lacking in education.
    b. Television talk shows only pretend to solve serious and complicated problems.

    c. Television talk shows insult the intelligence of viewers.

    d. The "ambush" methods of television talk shows can have violent consequences.

4. The author alludes to the ideas of two famous philosophers, Jean Jacques Rousseau and St. Thomas Aquinas. What is the purpose of the allusions?

    a. To show how television talk shows do not fulfill the teachings of these philosophers.

    b. To show how television talk shows fulfill the teachings of these philosophers.

    c. To show the superiority of radio talk show hosts when it comes to commonsense solutions to life's problems.

    d. To illustrate how the world has changed since these philosophers were alive.

5. Which of the following is *not* a rhetorical question?

    a. What positive outcomes can result from such exchanges? (paragraph 4)

    b. Can any of these virtues be said to be at work on television talk shows? (paragraph 6)

    c. Why must private lives be made public? (paragraph 6)

6. How do you think the author feels about former talk show host Geraldo Rivera?

    _____

    What statements from the author helped you draw your inference? (Please paraphrase.)

    _____

    _____

    _____

    _____

7. In her autobiography, why does Jenny Jones mention that she shops at Kmart?

    _____

8. How would you describe the author's tone?

   a. neutral

   b. heated

   c. light-hearted

   d. skeptical

9. Which statement more effectively describes the author's bias?

   a. The author is in favor of television talk shows because they put the spotlight on people whose lives are often ignored.

   b. The author is very critical of television talk shows.

   c. It's impossible to determine the author's bias.

10. What do you think is the author's purpose?

   a. to inform

   b. to persuade

   Explain the basis for your answer.

   _____

   _____

   _____

   _____

WORD NOTES: BERATING SYNONYMS

On page 384, you learned the meaning of the word *berate*—to criticize harshly and at length. This is yet another word with some useful synonyms that you should add to your vocabulary.

1. **Upbraid:** to criticize or reproach with good reason, as in "The court *upbraided* her for fleeing the country after she had been allowed to go free on bail."

2. **Revile:** to criticize or reproach using abusive language, as in "Those who had collaborated with the Nazis were *reviled* by their neighbors after the war ended."

3. **Rail:** to criticize or reproach with language that is harsh but not necessarily abusive, as in "It does not pay to *rail* at one's fate; a better strategy is to do something that will change it."

4. **Vituperate:** to criticize with abusive language. *Note:* The word *vituperate* appears more frequently as a noun or an adjective than a verb, as in (1) "The king was not touched by the *vituperation* heaped on him by his hungry subjects" and (2) "In arguments, she tends to use the kind of *vituperative* language that only makes matters worse."

Pay attention to the subtle differences among these four words as you use them to fill in the blanks. *Note:* You will have to change the endings.

1. The young mother _____ her tiny daughter for running into the street.

2. There's really no point in _____ at the Internal Revenue Service. Taxes are like death; they are simply part of life.

3. When his neighbors found out he had been a member of

   the Ku Klux Klan, he was _____ for it.

4. The level of _____ in his speech was terrifying; it was hard to believe that one human being could be filled with so much hate.

Now it's your turn to use them in sentences.

1. **upbraid:** _____

   _____

2. **revile:** _____

   _____

3. **rail:** _____

   _____

4. **vituperation:** _____

   _____

Test 1: Reviewing the Key Points

DIRECTIONS Answer the following questions by filling in the blanks or circling the correct response.

1. *True* or *False*. Writers whose primary purpose is to inform never allow themselves to reveal a personal bias or leaning.

2. Sometimes writers reveal bias not by what they say but by

   _____.

3. Bias in persuasive writing is bad or excessive when the writers are

   unable to _____.

4. *True* or *False*. There is no point to looking for evidence of bias in a textbook. Textbooks don't express a bias.

5. Rhetorical questions are _____.

6. If you spot one or more rhetorical questions in informative writing,

   there is a good chance that the author _____.

7. Which of the following statements does *not* describe informative writing?
   a. Informative writing uses mostly connotative language.
   b. Informative writing presents both sides of an issue.
   c. Informative writing avoids presenting the author's personal opinions on the subject.
   d. Informative writing doesn't often ask rhetorical questions.

8. Even writers who openly express a bias should not be

   _____ by their biases. They should still be able to

   _____ opposing points of view.

9. Writers who engage in slippery slope thinking insist that

   _____.

10. A writer who can't make a logical argument against an opposing point

    of view often attacks _____ instead of the position.

Test 2: Recognizing Bias

DIRECTIONS Each of the following passages appears in a source where one would expect to find no evidence of bias. However, some of the passages do reveal a bias. Read each one. Then circle the appropriate letter to indicate what the passage does or does not reveal about the author's bias.

1. **Donoso, José (1924–)** Born in Santiago, Chile, to a prominent family, José Donoso quit school at age nineteen and traveled in South America, where he worked on sheep farms and as a dockhand. Later, he went to school in the United States and received a B.A. from Princeton University in 1951. Donoso spent the next decade working as a teacher and journalist in Chile, writing profusely. In 1955, Donoso published his first book, *Veraneo y otros cuentos* (*Summer Vacation and Other Stories*), which received the Municipal Literary Prize; one year later, he published *Dos cuentos* (1956; *Two Short Stories*), and in 1957 his first novel, *Coronación* (*Coronation*), appeared to much critical acclaim. *Coronación* describes the moral collapse of an aristocratic family, a recurrent theme in Donoso's work. Marrying Maria Pilar Serrano, a Bolivian painter, in 1961, Donoso began writing what is often considered his masterpiece, *El obsceno pájaro de la noche* (1970; *The Obscene Bird of Night*). He also renewed his friendship with Mexican novelist Carlos Fuentes, whom he had met in grade school. While spending some time at Fuentes's home, he completed *El lugar sin límites* (1966; *Hell Has No Limits*) and *Este Domingo* (1966; *This Sunday*), grim novels of psychological desolation and anguish. (Kwame Anthony Appiah and Henry Louis Gates Jr., *The Dictionary of Global Culture*. New York: Alfred Knopf, 1997, p. 185.)

   a. The authors admire Donoso's work.

   b. The authors are critical of Donoso's work.

   c. It's impossible to determine the author's personal feelings.

2. **Christoph Gottwald (1960–),** German Novelist and Poet.   Because he got his start writing mysteries popular with everyone but the critics, Gottwald's emergence as a serious novelist has been shamefully ignored. Yet his 1997 novel *End Station Palma*, reminiscent of Heinrich Böll's early work, is worthy of serious critical attention. Using themes he probed previously in novels like *Cologne Crackup* (1980) and *Lifelong Pizza* (1994),

Gottwald again explores the inability of language to communicate our deepest needs, often with tragic results. Abandoning the comic detachment he used so brilliantly in his first two books, the novelist now assumes the voice of a man passionately committed to his subject and tortured by the strength of his own emotions. A conservative voice in a literary world desperate to be trendy, Gottwald may not get the audience he deserves, either in Germany or America. However, his fiction— in contrast to the work of his more highly praised and less talented contemporaries—will be read by future generations, long after more acclaimed novelists have been properly consigned to the trashbin of history. (Lawrence Wordsmith, *Twentieth Century Comparative Literature.* Nanuet, NY: Bushwhacked Press, 1999, p. 20.)

a. The author admires Gottwald's work.

b. The author is critical of Gottwald's work.

c. It's impossible to determine the author's personal feelings.

3. **Magnet Schools**

1 One alternative approach to school integration has gained some advocates in recent years: *magnet schools.* These are schools, usually located in inner cities, with special academic programs.

2   The first magnet schools appeared in the early 1970s. By the 1980s, they were often used as the chief tool for achieving school integration: Dallas, Houston, Los Angeles, Milwaukee, and San Diego received court orders to found them; Chicago, Cincinnati, Indianapolis, and Seattle set them up hoping to sidetrack legal trouble; a few cities, including Cambridge, Massachusetts, even set them up without threat of court order.

3   Despite the proliferation* of magnet schools across the country, they have their critics. One criticism is that they deliberately skim off the brightest students and teachers in each district. Moreover, they often cost more money to set up and run than ordinary schools do. In addition, some magnet schools are apparently special in name only. In the mid-seventies, an investigation of twenty magnet schools in Berkeley, California, seemed to show that all the schools were pretty much the same. And in Boston most principals of magnet schools were reported to "admit privately that their magnet theme is grossly underdeveloped—or non-

---

*proliferation: spread, increase.

existent" (Barr, 1982; see also U.S. Department of Education, 1984). (Popanoe, *Sociology*, p. 400.)

   a. The author is a supporter of magnet schools.

   b. The author is critical of magnet schools.

   c. It's impossible to determine the author's personal feelings.

4. Sigmund Freud

1   Sigmund Freud (1885–1939), the father of psychoanalytic theory, grew up in a middle-class Jewish family in Vienna, Austria, where he spent most of his life. As a young man, Freud received a medical degree and opened a practice as a neurologist. Among his patients were many cases of *hysteria*, an emotional disorder characterized by physical symptoms such as twitches, paralysis, and even blindness without any discernible* physical basis. Freud's work with these patients gradually led him to conclude that repressed memories and wishes underlie emotional disorders and that personality involves a perpetual conflict among forces within ourselves.

2   Freud's early writings were denounced by other scientists. In his later years, however, Freud began to receive the recognition he deserved for his courageous exploration of the human mind. When the Nazis invaded Austria in 1938, Freud was persuaded to move to England. He died a year later. (Rubin et al., *Psychology*, p. 395.)

   a. The authors admire the work of Sigmund Freud.

   b. The authors are critical of Freud's work.

   c. It's impossible to determine the authors' personal feelings about Freud's work.

5. Jewish Refugees from the Holocaust

By World War II's end, about six million Jews had been forced into concentration camps and had been systematically killed by firing squads, unspeakable tortures, and gas chambers. The Nazis also exterminated as many as 250,000 gypsies and about 60,000 gay men. During the depression, the United States and other nations had refused to relax their immigration restrictions to save Jews fleeing persecution. The American Federation of Labor and Senator William Borah of Idaho, among others, argued that new immigrants would compete with American workers for

*discernible: visible to the eye.

scarce jobs, and public opinion polls supported their position. This fear of economic competition was fed by anti-Semitism. Bureaucrats applied the rules so strictly—requiring legal documents that fleeing Jews could not possibly provide—that otherwise-qualified refugees were kept out of the country. From 1933 to 1945, less than 40 percent of the German-Austrian immigration quota was filled. (Norton et al., *A People and a Nation,* p. 543.)

a. The authors believe that World War II immigration restrictions were necessary at the time.

b. The authors are highly critical of World War II immigration restrictions.

c. It's impossible to determine the authors' personal feelings.

Test 3: Recognizing Excessive Bias

DIRECTIONS Each of the following passages expresses a bias, but only two express a bias so strongly that readers should be wary of the author's ability to be fair. Put a check (√) in the blank if the author is biased but fair. Put a *B* in the blank if you think the author's bias has clouded his or her judgment.

1. Movie critics, like politicians, should have a limited term in office. Over time, they become cynical, stupid, and self-serving. Keep in mind, after all, that movie critics loved Quentin Tarantino's movie *Pulp Fiction* and hated Kevin Costner's film *Waterworld*. Yet I really loved *Waterworld* and hated *Pulp Fiction*. The former had no foul language and no sex. It also had a happy ending. The latter, in contrast, had nothing but foul language, perverted sex, and gruesome violence. If so-called "respected" critics can favor *Pulp Fiction* over *Waterworld*, then there's something wrong somewhere, and we need to get rid of all the old-timers and replace them with people who know how to tell a good movie from a bad one.

_____

2. Without doubt, most of the people who favor assisted suicide are motivated by compassion and pity for those in pain. Still, those who support assisted suicide are making a false assumption. They assume that the men and women contemplating suicide are determined to die because life has become too hard, too difficult, and too pain-ridden for them. Yet, workers at suicide hotlines report that, apart from fearing unbearable pain, what the terminally ill fear most is being a burden to their families.[3] Hence, their so-called choice is motivated more by a desire to help others than it is by a desire to help themselves. Before deciding that someone has the legal right to assist in a suicide, we need to know a good deal more about why a person chooses to die.

_____

3. The school day and the school year are quite long enough already and should not be extended as some state legislatures have suggested. A 185-day year with an 8:30 A.M. to 3:00 P.M. schedule is altogether sufficient. After all, school is not the only important thing in kids' lives. Kids learn a great many things while partici-

---

[3]"Against Assisted Death," *Wall Street Journal*, April 1, 1997, p. A-18.

pating in extracurricular activities like basketball, baseball, or band. They also learn a lot about life in the time they spend with friends and family or even in the time they spend alone. Reducing children's chances to enjoy these activities so they can spend more time in school will not create healthy, happy, well-rounded individuals. Then, too, extending the time children spend in school may actually *reduce* the quality of their education. Teachers in the United States already spend more time instructing and less time preparing than teachers in other nations. Extending the school day or year would reduce teacher preparation time even further, making it difficult for teachers to plan the kind of creative and informative lessons children need for effective learning.

———

4. In the 1970s, President Jimmy Carter and his Army chief of staff asked that women be included in Selective Service registration so they, too, could serve their country during times of war. At the time, Congress and the Supreme Court disagreed, blocking the request because women had always been forbidden to serve in combat positions. However, it's time to reverse this outdated thinking and require women to register for the draft. One reason why both genders should register is that women have proven to be as capable as men, even in combat positions. For example, 40,000 women participated in the Persian Gulf War in the 1990s. They performed so well that since then, the armed forces have assigned them combat roles in the Balkans, the Middle East, and Afghanistan, where female fighter pilots blew up enemy targets. The second reason women should be asked to serve is in order to fully acknowledge their equality to men. Caroline Forell, a law professor and expert on women's legal rights, says that "failure to require [Selective Service registration] of women makes us lesser citizens." It is insulting to women not to ask them to serve their country in a time of national crisis. It implies that they do not have equal responsibilities as Americans.

———

5. Museum directors should resist the latest crassly commercial trend to exhibit common objects such as motorcycles, guitars, and clothing. This junk is not art. It may bring more crowds to money-hungry museums, but it appeals to the lowest common denominator, the uncultured masses who have no idea of what art really is. Furthermore, "dumbing down" the museum's collections

does nothing to enlighten the public. As a result, the museum is not serving its primary purposes: to educate, to encourage scholarship, and to promote appreciation of true art. Instead, it swindles the misguided by taking their money in exchange for an empty aesthetic* experience.

———

———
*aesthetic: related to the arts.

Test 4: Spotting the Slippery Slope and Personal Attack

> **DIRECTIONS** Circle the appropriate letter to indicate if the passage is based on a sound argument or employs either slippery slope logic or personal attack in order to convince readers.

1. A growing number of parents, educators, and politicians have expressed an interest in posting the biblical Ten Commandments on the walls of America's public schools. This is a dangerous idea. Allowing it will open the floodgates to a torrent of other religious practices in the classroom. It will be only a matter of time before our children are required to participate in daily Bible study. And it won't be long before the separation between church and state on which our country is based will disappear entirely.

   a. The author's reasoning is sound.

   b. The author employs slippery slope reasoning to convince readers.

   c. The author attacks the person rather than the position.

2. Schools that institute stricter dress codes are doing what's right for students. Tight, skimpy, skin-baring clothes that reveal underwear are a distraction. Dress codes that ban such attire ensure that students' attention will not be distracted by what their peers are wearing. In this way, dress codes will create an environment more conducive to learning. Dress codes can also promote students' self-respect. When young people are dressed neatly and more professionally, they feel better about themselves and their abilities. One 1995 study by the Connecticut Work Force Board, for example, revealed that high school dress codes result in improved academic achievement and better attendance. Finally, dress codes seem to improve students' behavior. Educators have reported that when students dress more conservatively, they are more respectful of teachers and engage in fewer fights with one another.

   a. The author's reasoning is sound.

   b. The author employs slippery slope reasoning to convince readers.

   c. The author attacks the person rather than the position.

3. Pharmaceutical companies have recently begun advertising drugs for the treatment of attention deficit and hyperactivity disorder

(ADHD). These ads are appearing in magazines and on television. In a break with tradition, they are now being aimed directly at parents rather than physicians. These ads, however, should be banned. For thirty years, pharmaceutical companies have had an agreement with the U.S. Drug Enforcement Agency. The pharmaceutical companies agreed to refrain from advertising controlled substances with a high potential for abuse. Drugs used to treat ADHD—which include Ritalin, Adderall, Concerta, and Metadate CD—are in this addictive-but-legal category. Yet these drugs are the very ones being heavily advertised in popular magazines. The DEA correctly claims that such advertising is pushing the limit of the existing agreement. In addition to the legal problems involved, the ads also oversimplify ADHD by suggesting that the drugs alone will cure kids' attention problems. Most ads make no mention of nonmedical solutions that might be just as effective. Finally, it's very possible that the new onslaught of drug advertising will encourage the misuse of ADHD drugs. Frustrated parents with unruly but non-ADHD children may find it tempting to put their kids on medication in order to control inappropriate behavior more easily. Because the ads imply that kids on these drugs learn how to behave and perform better in school, parents are more likely to ask for a prescription even if a child doesn't really need it.

a. The author's reasoning is sound.

b. The author employs slippery slope reasoning to convince readers.

c. The author attacks the person rather than the position.

4. A Swiss gynecologist has administered fertility treatments to fifty women over the age of fifty. One of his patients, a French woman, recently gave birth at the age of sixty-two, and for some, this was cause for celebration. Postmenopausal women, however, should not be having babies, and there are a number of reasons why fertility clinics should refuse to treat them. For one thing, the health risks are greater for pregnant women over fifty. An older woman is prone to experience more complications than a younger woman might. A woman in middle age who seeks fertility treatment is thinking only of herself and not of her child's welfare. That's why her doctor must be the voice of reason. The Swiss doctor's judgment was obviously clouded by his love of the media spotlight. He cared more about his own fame than about his patients and their children.

a. The author's reasoning is sound.

b. The author employs slippery slope reasoning to convince readers.

c. The author attacks the person rather than the position.

5. More and more American workers, such as grocery store cashiers and shelf stockers, are claiming to suffer from repetitive-motion, on-the-job injuries. It's not fair, though, for the federal government to force companies to alter their employees' work stations or work rules. Companies should not have to make major changes just to accommodate a few employees. In point of fact, an individual should not work a particular job if his or her body cannot handle the physical demands of the job. Because many employers won't be able to afford the high cost of making all the required changes, as well as compensating employees for their aches and pains, they might be forced to go out of business. Then workers would lose their jobs altogether. This kind of massive unemployment can lead us right into an economic depression.

a. The author's reasoning is sound.

b. The author employs slippery slope reasoning to convince readers.

c. The author attacks the person rather than the position.

C H A P T E R   1 1

Understanding and Evaluating Arguments

In this chapter, you'll learn

- why the ability to analyze arguments is a key critical reading skill.

- how to identify the essential elements of an argument.

- how to recognize some common errors that undermine or weaken an argument.

You may not realize it, but arguments are everywhere. The candidate who says "vote for me" offers an argument explaining why. The salesperson who wants to sell you a new DVD player is quick to describe the advantages of the latest models. Even a neighbor who wants to sell you her used car will try to convince you that you're getting a real bargain.

The point of these examples is simple: You need to be in a position to analyze and evaluate the competing arguments that confront you practically every day. Once you are able to do that, you can make informed decisions about which arguments are convincing and which ones are not. Then you can decide with confidence whether you want to share—or at least consider—the other person's point of view.

 # What's the Point of the Argument?

The starting point of an argument is the opinion, belief, or claim the author of the argument wants readers to accept or at least seriously consider. Whenever you encounter an argument in your reading, the first thing to do is decide what opinion, belief, or claim the author thinks you should share. In other words, you need to discover the main idea or central point of the author's argument. Discovering that point will be easier once you are familiar with the three kinds of statements—condition, value, and policy—likely to be at the heart of written arguments. What follows are the three types of statements, along with a description of the evidence they usually require.

Statements of Condition

These statements assert that a particular condition or state of affairs exists or existed. Although these statements are based more on fact than opinion, they usually identify a state of affairs not likely to be well known by readers and thus in need of proof. The following would all be considered statements of condition.

1. Most of the great classical novels have not been turned into financially successful movies.
2. The family as we know it has not been in existence for very long.
3. Although Henry David Thoreau celebrated solitude in his now classic book, *Walden,* he actually spent very little time alone.
4. Romantic love is an altogether modern invention.

Although reasons are essential in any argument, statements of condition usually rely heavily on sound factual evidence.

Statements of Value

Statements of value express approval or disapproval. Frequently, they contrast two people, ideas, or objects and suggest that one is better or worse than the other. The following are all statements of value.

1. Among all the sports, boxing is the most dehumanizing.
2. Cats are smarter than dogs.
3. The American educational system is in a serious state of decline.
4. The current crop of movies relies too much on action and not enough on dialogue.

Although statements of value can and do require facts, they typically need examples and reasons as well. For example, to talk about the "state of decline" in American education, a writer would probably have to offer statistics proving an earlier superiority and more statistics or examples illustrating the current decline.

Statements of Policy

Statements of policy insist that a particular action should or should not be taken in response to a specific condition or situation. These opinion statements often include words like *must, need, should, would,* or *ought.* The following are all statements of policy.

1. The Internet needs to be censored so that children do not have access to pornographic material.
2. Shoeless Joe Jackson* should be admitted to the National Baseball Hall of Fame.
3. College athletes who do not maintain a B average should be prohibited from playing any team sports.
4. Consumers should have the right to take legal action against HMOs that provide inadequate medical care.

With statements of policy, factual evidence is important, but sound reasons that answer the question *why* are also essential.

Can different types of argument statements be combined? The answer is most definitely yes. Here's an example: "Despite the cloud of shame surrounding his name, Shoeless Joe Jackson was never convicted of any crime. As one of the most talented players in the

---

*Shoeless Joe Jackson: a famous baseball player who many think was unfairly implicated in the Black Sox baseball scandal of 1919.

history of baseball, he should be admitted to the Baseball Hall of Fame." In this case, we have a statement of condition (Jackson was never convicted of a crime). But we also have a statement of value (he was one of the most talented players in the history of baseball), and a statement of policy (he should be admitted to the Baseball Hall of Fame).

When you analyze an argument, be on the lookout for statements that describe an existing condition, assign value, or urge a policy or action. Such statements, separately or combined, are usually central to an author's argument.

CHECK YOUR UNDERSTANDING

Describe the three types of statements likely to be at the center of an argument.

1. Statements of Condition: _____

_____

2. Statements of Value: _____

_____

3. Statements of Policy: _____

_____

EXERCISE 1

DIRECTIONS Read each statement. In the blank that follows, identify the type of statement by circling the correct letter or letters.

EXAMPLE

1. Every survey course in American literature should include several of the authors who emerged during the Harlem Renaissance.*

    a. statement of condition

    b. statement of value

    c. statement of policy

---

*Harlem Renaissance: a period during the 1920s when Harlem was an intellectual and cultural capital.

2. Legalized gambling threatens community stability; therefore, it should be banned from our state.

    a. statement of condition

    (b.) statement of value

    (c.) statement of policy

EXPLANATION Sentence 1 is a statement of policy. It clearly announces an action that *should* be taken. Sentence 2 combines a statement of value—legalized gambling threatens the community—with a statement of policy—it should be banned.

1. Because pesticides are endangering our food supply, more should be done to increase public awareness concerning the dangers posed by pesticides.

    a. statement of condition

    b. statement of value

    c. statement of policy

2. Eating garlic may not do a lot for your breath, but it can do wonders for your health.

    a. statement of condition

    b. statement of value

    c. statement of policy

3. People who use marijuana solely for medicinal purposes should not be subject to prosecution.

    a. statement of condition

    b. statement of value

    c. statement of policy

4. Those of us who truly care about animals need to make a commitment to vegetarianism.

    a. statement of condition

    b. statement of value

    c. statement of policy

5. Poet and philosopher Ralph Waldo Emerson had a gift for friendship: He brought out the best in everyone he met.

    a. statement of condition

    b. statement of value

    c. statement of policy

6. Listening to music can sharpen and enhance a person's creative powers. Instead of being eliminated, music appreciation should be part of our elementary curriculum.

   a. statement of condition

   b. statement of value

   c. statement of policy

7. Snowboarding does not deserve to be an Olympic sport.

   a. statement of condition

   b. statement of value

   c. statement of policy

8. Mark Twain was a humorist whose writing had a serious social message.

   a. statement of condition

   b. statement of value

   c. statement of policy

9. Online magazines like *Salon* and *Feed* have an energy and bite not found in print magazines like *The Atlantic Monthly* and *The New Yorker*.

   a. statement of condition

   b. statement of value

   c. statement of policy

10. Parents should limit the amount of television preschool children are allowed to see.

    a. statement of condition

    b. statement of value

    c. statement of policy

EXERCISE 2

DIRECTIONS Make up three different statements you think you could effectively argue. One should be a statement of value; the other two should be statements of policy and condition.

Statement of value: _____

_____

Statement of policy: _____

_____

Statement of condition: _____

_____

_____

EXERCISE 3

DIRECTIONS Read each passage. At the end, paraphrase the main idea or point of the argument and identify it as a statement of policy, value, or condition.

EXAMPLE

Banning Bathing Suits

1 After far too many years, critical attention has finally been paid to the portion of the Miss America pageant called the swimsuit competition. Thankfully, people are beginning to complain about this event. In 1999, a telephone poll was conducted on the night of the pageant to determine if the swimsuit competition should remain. Although the majority of callers voted to retain it, a good portion were critical and argued that the swimsuit segment should be eliminated. The question will undoubtedly be raised again and again, and in time the answer may well be different. Let's hope so, because this portion of the pageant serves only to demean the women who participate in it.

2   It should be clear to everyone that there are women whose appearance and intellect make them likely candidates for the crown. Yet these same women might well be eliminated from the competition for some minor physical flaw, like bulging thighs. A woman who has the appropriate appearance and intellect should not be eliminated because she shows a few bulges in a bathing suit. Beauty and brains are infinitely more important criteria for choosing Miss America than are a few extra pounds of body fat.

a. What is the author's point?

The swimsuit competition should be eliminated.

_____

b. That point is expressed in a statement of

   a. condition.

   b. value.

   (c.) policy.

EXPLANATION Because the author supports a particular action—the eliminating of the swimsuit competition—"statement of policy" is the correct answer.

1. The Supreme Court has ruled that disabled professional golfer Casey Martin should be allowed to ride in a golf cart while participating in tournaments. That decision is a sound one. It is very much in accord with the Americans with Diabilities Act. The act requires "reasonable modification" so that those with a disability can enter the same places and enjoy the same activities as the nondisabled. Casey Martin can play golf; however, a degenerative leg condition prevents him from walking the course. Allowing him to ride in a cart is exactly the kind of modification the ADA was designed to ensure. Some critics argue that using a golf cart gives Martin an unfair advantage over his competitors, but the majority of the Supreme Court justices disagreed. Justice John Paul Stevens, who wrote the majority opinion, said that the Professional Golf Association is wrong to ban carts from tournaments because walking the course has no effect on a golfer's performance.

   a. What is the author's point?

   _____

   _____

   b. That point is expressed in a statement of
      a. condition.
      b. value.
      c. policy.

2. Some students, parents, and civil liberties organizations object to school administrators searching students' lockers. Despite these objections, it's clear that locker searches are essential to our children's safety and school administrators should perform them on a regular basis if they think necessary. Schools most certainly have the right to enforce rules that prohibit students from bringing guns, bombs, or other weapons onto the campus. Searching lockers is a valid method of ensuring compliance with those rules, and school administrators are wise to use every method at their disposal to guarantee the safety of all students. Some argue that by performing locker searches, school personnel foster a climate of suspicion and paranoia among the student body. That point is well taken. Nevertheless, these searches often expose potentially dangerous weapons that should not be on school grounds. Clearly, the positive consequences of such searches outweigh the negative ones.

    a. What is the author's point?

    _____

    _____

    b. That point is expressed in a statement of

       a. condition.

       b. value.

       c. policy.

3. Parents with a computer in the house should purchase software that filters, or blocks out, objectionable Web sites. Although most parents do not turn their kids loose in front of a computer and let them surf the Web on their own, even the most devoted of parents cannot be with their children all of the time. What this means is that impressionable children can find their way to inappropriate and dangerous Web sites. Kids can, for example, access Web sites that feature pornographic pictures and text. Children with access to the Web can also come into contact with people who want to seduce and abuse them. To avoid these very real dangers, parents need to purchase one of the many brands of software that effectively puts a lock on all sexually explicit Web sites. There is also software that blocks access to Web sites that are expressly racist or anti-Semitic.* Parents might think about purchasing this type of software as well. While such Web sites may not endanger children's bodies, they can certainly cause harm to children's minds.

    a. What is the author's point?

    _____

    _____

    b. That point is expressed in a statement of

       a. condition.

       b. value.

       c. policy.

4. In far too many cases, student grades have become so inflated they're virtually meaningless. A whopping 83 percent of high school seniors who took the Scholastic Aptitude Test (SAT) in 1993 claimed to be A or B students, while only 28 percent of their 1972 counterparts made the same claim. We could hope that the nation's kids are just getting smarter. However, we'd have to overlook the fact that

_____

*anti-Semitic: discriminating against people of the Jewish faith.

during the same period, the average SAT score actually *fell* from 937 to 902. And what happens to all of these stellar* students when they get to college? Well, they are likely to receive more inflated grades. The old "gentleman's C"* earned by those who put forth only minimum effort has become the "average person's B." Even elite, demanding schools like Harvard are doling out A's and B's to those who do little more than show up for class. The C grade no longer seems to exist. That's why graduate schools and employers have begun interpreting applicants' grade point averages much differently. Nowadays, they know that A can sometimes mean "average."

a. What is the author's point?

_____

_____

b. That point is expressed in a statement of
   a. condition.
   b. value.
   c. policy.

5. Most of us know about Rosa Parks and her decision, on December 1, 1955, not to move to the back of the bus. Parks's bravery sparked the historic bus boycott in Montgomery, Alabama, and her name entered the history books. What fewer people know is that more than ten years before, in 1944, a young black woman named Irene Morgan boarded a Greyhound bus to Gloucester County, Virginia. Weak from recent surgery, Morgan also refused to move to the back of the bus when told to do so. The police were called and she was placed under arrest. Convicted of her "crime," Morgan appealed her decision and made legal history when Thurgood Marshall argued her case before the Supreme Court and won.

a. What is the author's point?

_____

_____

b. That point is expressed in a statement of
   a. condition.
   b. value.
   c. policy.

*stellar: brilliant, excellent.
*gentleman's C: an old expression indicating that the sons of the wealthy or well-placed need not worry about achieving high grades, since they had money and position to back them up.

Four Common Types of Support

Writers who want their arguments to be taken seriously know they have to do more than state their position. They also have to provide support. In response, critical readers need to recognize and evaluate that support, deciding if it is both relevant and up-to-date. Four common types of support are likely to be used in an argument: reasons, examples and illustrations, expert opinions, and research results.

Reasons

Reasons are probably the most common method of support used by authors who want to argue a point. In the following passage, the author hopes to convince readers that cockfighting should be outlawed in the three states that still permit it.

> Cockfighting has been outlawed in forty-seven states. In the three remaining states—New Mexico, Louisiana, and Oklahoma—people can still legally participate in this violent pastime. It's high time that those states, too, end the brutality by passing laws to make cockfighting a crime. Cockfighting is one of the worst forms of animal cruelty. Participants strap razor-sharp spurs to two roosters' legs, feed the birds stimulants, and then toss the birds into a pit, where they tear each other apart until one of them dies a bloody death.
>
> Besides being cruel to animals, cockfights encourage illegal and violent behavior. They are notorious arenas of illegal gambling and drug trafficking, firearms dealing, and fighting. Shootings have even occurred when the violence in the ring spills over into the crowd. Raids of cockfights often result in many arrests. In a very real way, cockfights reinforce the idea that violence is a source of amusement. Perhaps worst of all, they send that very same message to children whose parents allow them to witness these fights. The parents apparently consider them nothing more than good, clean fun.

To persuade readers to share her point of view, the author of the above passage provides four specific reasons: (1) cockfighting is cruel to animals, (2) it encourages illegal and even violent behavior, (3) it reinforces the idea that violence is a source of amusement, and (4) it sends that message to children. By means of these four reasons, the author hopes that readers will begin to share, or at least to seriously consider, her point of view.

Examples and Illustrations

Particularly when arguing general statements of value—for example, boxing is dangerous, pesticides cause health problems, or Isaac Newton was an eccentric* genius—writers are likely to cite examples, illustrations, or even personal experience as proof of their point. Look at how the following author uses examples to persuade readers that plastic litter is not just unsightly, but also deadly.

> As litter, plastic is unsightly and deadly. Birds and small animals die after getting stuck in plastic six-pack beverage rings. Pelicans accidentally hang themselves with discarded plastic fishing line. Turtles choke on plastic bags or starve when their stomachs become clogged with hard-to-excrete crumbled plastic. Sea lions poke their heads into plastic rings and have their jaws locked permanently shut. Authorities estimate that plastic refuse annually kills up to two million birds and at least 100,000 mammals. (Gary Turbak, "Plastic: 60 Million Pounds of Trouble," *American Legion Magazine.*[1])

Here's a case where the author piles example upon example in an effort to convince readers that plastic can be lethal.

Expert Opinions

In an effort to be persuasive, writers will also call upon one or more experts to support their position. In the following passage, for instance, the author suggests that cloning geniuses may not be a good idea. To make her point, she gives a reason *and* cites an expert.

> With the birth of Dolly, the first successfully cloned sheep, some have suggested that we can now consider the human gene pool a natural resource. We can clone a Nobel Prize–winning writer like Toni Morrison or a star athlete like Michael Jordan and thereby create a population of gifted and talented people. What could be wrong with that? Well, in the long run, probably a lot.
>
> There's simply no guarantee that the cloned copies would be everything the originals were. After all, genes don't tell the whole story, and the clone of a prizewinning scientist, if neglected as a child, might well end up a disturbed genius, no matter what the original gene source. As John Paris, professor of bioethics at Boston College, so correctly says on the subject of cloning, "Choosing personal characteristics as if they were the options on a car is an invitation to misadventure."[2]

*eccentric: odd, weird.
[1]Also used in Rosen and Behrens, *The Allyn and Bacon Handbook.*
[2]Jeffrey Kluger, "Will We Follow the Sheep?" *Time,* March 10, 1997, p. 71.

In this case, the author doesn't just let her argument rest solely on her own reasoning. She also makes it clear that at least one knowledgeable expert is very much on her side.

Research Results

In the same way they use experts, writers who want to persuade are likely to use the results of research—studies, polls, questionnaires, and surveys—to argue a point. In the following passage, for example, the author uses an expert and a study to support a statement of condition: There's a quiet revolution taking place among Amish women.

> In a tiny shop built on the side of a farmhouse in Pennsylvania's Lancaster County, Katie Stoltzfus sells Amish* dolls, wooden toys, and quilts. Does she ever. Her shop had "a couple of hundred thousand" dollars in sales last year, says the forty-four-year-old Amish entrepreneur and mother of nine. Mrs. Stoltzfus's success underscores a quiet revolution taking place among the Amish. Amish women, despite their image as shy farm wives, now run about 20 percent of the one thousand businesses in Lancaster County, according to a study by Donald B. Kraybill, a professor of sociology at Elizabethtown College in Elizabethtown, Pennsylvania. "These women are interacting more with outsiders, assuming managerial functions they never had before, and gaining more power within their community because of their access to money," says Professor Kraybill, who recently wrote a book about Amish enterprises. (Timothy Aeppel, "More Amish Women Are Tending to Business," *Wall Street Journal*, February 8, 1996, p. B1.)

To make sure that readers seriously consider his position, the author cites a study and identifies the person who conducted the study, making it clear that his opinion is grounded in solid research.

CHECK YOUR UNDERSTANDING

Name the four types of support common to written arguments.

1. _____   3. _____

2. _____   4. _____

---

*Amish: a religious group that generally avoids contact with the modern world and its modern machinery.

EXERCISE 4

DIRECTIONS Each group of statements opens with an opinion or a claim that needs to be argued. Circle the letters of the two sentences that help argue that point.

EXAMPLE

Eyewitness testimony is far from reliable.

(a.) The testimony of eyewitnesses can often be influenced by the desire to please those in authority.

(b.) Studies of eyewitness testimony reveal an astonishingly high number of errors.

c. Eyewitness testimony carries a great deal of weight with most juries.

EXPLANATION Statements *a* and *b* both undermine the reliability of eyewitnesses and thereby provide reasons why eyewitness testimony cannot always be considered reliable. Statement *c*, however, is not relevant, or related, to the claim made about eyewitness testimony.

1. Uniforms should be mandatory* for all high school students.

   a. Most students hate the idea of wearing a uniform.

   b. Parents on a strict budget would no longer have to worry about being able to provide expensive back-to-school wardrobes.

   c. If uniforms were mandatory in high school, students would not waste precious time worrying about something as unessential as fashion.

2. All zoos should be abolished.

   a. Zoos only encourage the notion that animals are on Earth for the amusement of humans.

   b. If all zoos were closed, no one has any idea what would happen to the animals now living in them.

   c. Although many zoos have improved the living conditions for the animals they possess, those animals still lack the freedom they have in the wild.

3. Because the deer population is sky-high, hunters should be allowed to shoot more deer per season.

   a. Desperate for food, deer are foraging by the roadside, where many are hit by cars, another indication that their population has to be reduced.

   ---

   *mandatory: required or commanded by authority.

b. With the exception of hunting, there doesn't seem to be any practical way to slow down the growth in the deer population.

c. Most hunters have a great respect for the animals they kill.

4. Parents need to limit the amount of television their children watch.

a. Unlike reading, watching television does not encourage a child to think imaginatively.

b. Children who watch a lot of television are consistently exposed to violence and can easily become too accepting of it.

c. Programs for children dominate Saturday morning television.

⊟ EXERCISE 5

DIRECTIONS Read each passage. Then answer the questions that follow.

EXAMPLE Unfortunately, some people still believe that African Americans endured slavery without protest. But nothing could be further from the truth. In 1800, for example, Gabriel Prosser organized an army of a thousand slaves to march on Richmond. However, a state militia had been alerted by a spy, and the rebellion was put down. Prosser was ultimately executed for refusing to give evidence against his co-conspirators. In 1822, Denmark Vesey plotted to march on Charleston, but he, too, was betrayed by an informer. Probably the most serious revolt occurred in 1831 under Nat Turner. It resulted in the execution of Turner and more than a hundred black rebels.

a. What is the point of the author's argument?

It's simply not true that African Americans endured slavery without protest.

b. Paraphrase the examples used to support that claim.

1. In 1800, Gabriel Prosser organized an army of slaves to march on Richmond.

2. In 1822, Denmark Vesey plotted to take over Charleston.

3. In 1831, Nat Turner and 100 rebels revolted.

EXPLANATION In this case, the author uses three examples to make her point: African Americans did not endure slavery without protest.

1. The fact that more women are lawfully arming themselves should be good news for everyone concerned with violence against women.

Since the publication of Betty Friedan's *The Feminine Mystique,* feminists have been urging women to be independent and self-sufficient. What better evidence that women have "arrived" than that they no longer have to rely exclusively on police (still mostly male) for protection? Feminists should applaud every woman who is skilled in handgun use. (Talk about controlling your own body.) Liberation from fear when walking on a dark street, driving on a country road late at night, or withdrawing cash from a bank machine is more important on a daily basis to most women than smashing any glass ceiling in the workplace. (Laura Ingraham, "Armed and Empowered," *Pittsburgh Post-Gazette,* May 19, 1998, p. E-3.)

a. What is the point of the author's argument?

_____

_____

b. Paraphrase the reason she uses to support that claim.

_____

_____

2. Alfred Nobel, born in 1833, was the inventor of dynamite, but, ironically, he was also a committed promoter of peace. When a newspaper mistakenly printed the Swedish businessman's obituary, calling him a "merchant of death," Nobel grew obsessed with leaving behind a peaceful legacy that would help improve society. When he died in 1896, his relatives were outraged by his will: Ninety-four percent of his vast fortune was to be used for an annual award to a handful of people around the globe whose work—in physics, chemistry, medicine, literature, and peacemaking (the economics category was added in 1969)—had "conferred the greatest benefit on mankind." The will's wording was so vague, however, that its executors spent five years quarreling over what it meant. Thus, the first Nobel Prizes were not awarded until the fifth anniversary of Nobel's death.

a. What is the point of the author's argument?

_____

_____

b. How does the author illustrate that point?

_____

_____

_____

3. It's never too late to get physically fit. As a matter of fact, a 1999 study published in the *New England Journal of Medicine* showed that taking up weight training can reverse some of the effects of aging. In the experiment, nursing home residents ranging in age from eighty-six to ninety-five participated in a supervised, eight-week weight-training program. All of these elderly people increased their strength and improved their balance. Another recent study conducted by the University of Pennsylvania Medical School has shown that elderly people who take up weight training can improve their bone density and reduce arthritis pain.

a. What is the point of the author's argument?

_____

_____

b. Paraphrase the results of the studies used to support the author's point.

_____

_____

_____

_____

4. Almost every college student has experienced prefinals terror—the horrible anxiety that puts your stomach on a roller coaster and your brain in a blender. Few escape those final-exam jitters because everyone knows just how much is riding on that one exam, often more than half of the course grade. Yet therein lies the crux* of the problem. Infrequent high-stakes exams don't encourage students to do their best work. More frequent tests—given, say, every two or three weeks—would be a much more effective method of discovering how well students are or are not mastering course concepts. With more frequent testing, students would be less anxious when they take exams; thus anxiety would no longer interfere with exam performance. More frequent testing also encourages students to review on a regular basis, something that a one-shot final exam does not do. Lots of tests also mean lots of feedback, and students would know early on in the course what terms or concepts required additional explanation and review. They wouldn't have to wait until the end of the semester to find out that they had misunderstood, or missed altogether, a critical point or theory.

_____

*crux: core, heart, key point.

a. What is the point of the author's argument?

_____

_____

b. Paraphrase the reasons the author uses to support that claim.

_____

_____

_____

_____

_____

_____

_____

 Flawed Arguments

The previous section of this chapter introduced four common types of support that are likely to appear in an argument. In this section, you'll learn about the flaws or errors you should check for in each one.

Irrelevant Reasons

In their haste to prove a point, authors sometimes include reasons that aren't truly relevant, or related, to their claim. Here, for example, is an argument flawed by an irrelevant reason.

> The 1996 tragedy on Mount Everest in which eight people died in a single day is proof enough that amateurs should not be scaling the world's highest mountain. Even with the most skillful and reliable guides, amateurs with little or no mountaineering experience cannot possibly know how to respond to the sudden storms that strike the mountain without warning. Dependent upon their guides for every move they make, amateur climbers can easily lose sight of the guides when a heavy storm hits. Left to their own devices, they are more than likely to make a mistake, one that will harm themselves or others. Besides, rich people—the climb can cost anywhere from $30,000 to $60,000—shouldn't be encouraged to think that money buys everything. As F. Scott Fitzgerald so powerfully illustrated in *The Great Gatsby*, it's precisely that attitude that often leads to tragedy and death.

The point of this passage is clear-cut: Amateurs should not be climbing Mount Everest. In support of that claim, the author does offer a relevant reason. Mount Everest can be the scene of sudden storms that leave amateur climbers stranded, separated from their guides, and likely to harm themselves or others. But tucked away in the passage is a far less relevant reason: Rich people should not be allowed to think money buys everything. Well, maybe they shouldn't. Yet that particular reason, along with the allusion to *The Great Gatsby,* is not related to the author's claim. Neither one clarifies why amateurs and the world's tallest mountain don't mix. This is the point that needs to be argued.

Circular Reasoning

As you know from Chapter 7, writers sometimes engage in circular reasoning. They offer an opinion and follow it with a reason that says the same thing in different words. Unfortunately, circular reasoning is not that unusual—particularly when an author is utterly convinced of his or her own rightness. In the following passage, for example, the writer believes that health care workers should be tested for AIDS. He's so convinced he's right, he's forgotten to give his readers a reason why the testing should be done. Instead, he repeats his opening point as if it were a reason for his claim.

> Health care workers, from hospital technicians to doctors, should be forced to undergo AIDS testing, and the results should be published. Although there has been much talk about this subject, too little has been done, and the public has suffered because of it. We need to institute a program of mandatory testing as soon as possible.

Hasty Generalizations

Generalizations, or broad general statements, by definition cover a lot of territory. They are used to sum up and express a wide variety of individual events or experiences. When generalizations appear in arguments, the rule of thumb is simple: The broader and more wide ranging the generalization, the more examples writers need to supply in order to make their point convincing. If an author generalizes about a large group on the basis of one or even two examples, you need to—metaphorically speaking—prick up your ears. Something is definitely wrong.

In the following passage, the author makes a general statement about all HMOs. Unfortunately, that statement is based on one lone example, a fact that seriously weakens his argument.

> HMOs are not giving consumers adequate health care. Instead, budgeting considerations are consistently allowed to outweigh the patients' need for treatment. In one case, a child with a horribly deformed cleft palate was denied adequate cosmetic surgery because the child's HMO considered the surgery unnecessary, yet the child had trouble eating and drinking.[3]

Unidentified or Inappropriate Experts

In the passage about cloning on page 433, it makes sense for the author to quote a bioethicist in support of her opinion. After all, a bioethicist specializes in the study of moral and ethical issues that result from biological discoveries and applications. However, critical readers are rightly suspicious of allusions to unidentified experts, who may or may not be qualified to offer an opinion. Consider, for example, the "expert" cited in the following passage:

> Despite the doom-and-gloom sayers who constantly worry about the state of the environment, the earth is actually in pretty good shape. As Dr. Paul Benjamin recently pointed out, "Nature is perfectly capable of taking care of herself; she's been doing it for hundreds of years."

The author uses Dr. Paul Benjamin to support her claim that environmentalists anxious about the earth's future are dead wrong. Yet for all we know, Dr. Benjamin might be a dentist, and a dental degree does not qualify him as an environmental expert. Without some knowledge of Dr. Benjamin's **credentials,** or qualifications, we shouldn't be swayed by his opinion. It also wouldn't hurt to know more about Dr. Benjamin's personal background and biases. If, for example, he's worked for a company cited for abuses to the environment, his ability to stay objective, or neutral, is suspect.

Occasionally, a writer might also attempt to support an argument by citing a famous person who doesn't truly qualify as an expert in the area under discussion.

> We should abolish NATO and end foreign aid. After all, didn't George Washington tell us to avoid entangling ourselves in the affairs of other nations? Even today, we should let his wisdom be our guide and steer clear of foreign involvements that drain our energy and our resources.

---

[3]Howard Fineman, "HMOs Under the Knife," *Newsweek*, July 27, 1998, p. 21.

In the eighteenth century, George Washington may well have qualified as an expert in foreign affairs. But to cite him as an authority on modern problems is a mistake. It is doubtful that Washington could have imagined America's current status as an international power. Because his opinion could not be considered adequately informed, critical readers would not be impressed by references to his name and authority.

Unidentified or Dated Research

In the following passage, the author relies on some "studies" to prove a statement of policy: Pornography should be more strictly censored. But to be convincing as support, scientific research needs **attribution;** in short, readers need to know who conducted it. References to unnamed studies like the one in the following passage would arouse skepticism in critical readers.

> Pornography must be more strictly censored. It does, in fact, offer a clear and present danger to the lives of women. Studies have shown again and again that pornography is directly related to the number of rapes and assaults on women. As if that weren't enough, by repeatedly presenting women as sexual objects, pornography encourages sexual discrimination, a cause-and-effect relationship noted by several prominent researchers.

Authors may identify a study in the text itself or in a footnote that refers readers to a list of sources in the back of the book. Where a study is identified doesn't matter. What matters is that the author provides readers with enough information to check the source of the supposed evidence.

It also helps to know *when* the study was conducted; a writer who uses out-of-date studies rightfully runs the risk of losing readers' confidence. Take, for example, the following passage.

> The threat of radon gas is not as serious as we have been led to believe. In 1954, a team of government researchers studying the effects of radon in the home found no relationship between high levels of the gas in private dwellings and the incidence of lung cancer.

Here we have an author trying to prove a point about radon gas with a study almost a half-century old. To be considered effective evidence for an opinion, scientific research should be considerably more up-to-date.

CHECK YOUR UNDERSTANDING

Complete the following chart by explaining each type of error that can occur in an argument.

Type of Support	Possible Error	Definition of Error
Reasons	Irrelevant Reasons	
	Circular Reasoning	
Examples and Illustrations	Hasty Generalizations	
Expert Opinion	Unidentified Experts	
	Inappropriate Experts	
Research Results	Unidentified Research	
	Dated Research	

EXERCISE 6

DIRECTIONS Identify the error in reasoning by circling the appropriate letter.

1. If you have a grass lawn surrounding your house, you are probably contributing to this country's environmental problems. For one thing, you could be using fertilizers and pesticides that can damage the soil structure, pollute wells, and kill wildlife. Homeowners with lawns actually use more fertilizers annually than the entire country of India puts on its crops. They also apply up to ten times more pesticides than U.S. farmers do. Unfortunately, research has proven that these chemicals wash off from yards and pollute water supplies, thus contaminating the food chain. Lawn mowers cause another environmental problem. They produce as much air pollution in one hour as a car produces in a 350-mile drive. In addition, grass clippings are choking already-overflowing landfills. Yard waste, most

of which is composed of cut grass, is the second largest component of the 160 million tons of solid waste we dump into landfills every year. If that weren't enough, your lawn may be contributing to the destruction of plant and animal species. When developers building new houses bulldoze complex habitats and replace them with houses and grass, many plants and animals are killed or starved out.

a. irrelevant reasons

b. circular reasoning

c. hasty generalizations

d. unidentified or inappropriate experts

e. unidentified or dated research

2. The United States government needs to invest more money to improve and expand this country's rail service. In particular, Congress should commit to developing a national intercity network of high-speed trains. An intermodal transportation system (one that includes rail along with highways and airlines) is essential to keeping America moving in the event of a crisis. During a national emergency that disrupts one mode of transportation, the others should be able to absorb the traffic and allow people to continue to travel. For example, when airplanes were grounded for several days following terrorist attacks in September 2001, people relied on Amtrak passenger trains to get them where they needed to be. Without the trains, our nation would have been paralyzed. Furthermore, we need a rail system like those in European countries such as France and Germany. Railroad transportation is an important public service, and it needs to be kept efficient and up-to-date.

a. irrelevant reasons

b. circular reasoning

c. hasty generalizations

d. unidentified or inappropriate experts

e. unidentified or dated research

3. The publication of autopsy photos is not, as has been claimed, an invasion of privacy, and newspapers have a right to publish them. First of all, interested readers should have access to these images. If people are curious about autopsy photographs, then newspapers should make them available. Also, the public has a right to be informed about legal matters. If a crime or an accident caused an indi-

vidual's death, the public should be able to review all information—
including the autopsy photographs—related to the case. Finally, the
publication of these photographs could act as a deterrent to would-
be criminals or thrill seekers. Because such pictures depict the cold,
stark reality of death, they might cause readers to think twice about
harming themselves or others.

a. irrelevant reasons

b. circular reasoning

c. hasty generalizations

d. unidentified or inappropriate experts

e. unidentified or dated research

4. It just may be nature itself—not humans burning fossil fuels—that
is causing global warming. Naturally occurring gases such as water
vapor, methane, nitrous oxide, and ozone contribute to the so-called
greenhouse effect that has raised Earth's temperature 30 degrees
since the last "Little Ice Age" of the seventeenth and eighteenth
centuries. The oceans, too, seem to be partly responsible for this
overall increase in our planet's temperature. From 1958 to 1978,
Dane Chang and his colleagues at Hill Laboratories carefully
studied the correlation between ocean temperatures and levels of
carbon dioxide, the gas that causes global warming. These researchers found that increases in ocean temperatures are followed by a
rise in the atmosphere's carbon dioxide levels. Such studies would
seem to indicate that natural factors are producing our warmer climate.

a. irrelevant reasons

b. circular reasoning

c. hasty generalizations

d. unidentified or inappropriate experts

e. unidentified or dated research

5. A growing number of school districts are rightly banning the childhood game of dodge ball from physical education classes. The game
is simply too aggressive and can cause serious harm. In one California incident, a child was knocked to the ground by the impact of a
ball. Dodge ball is also not especially good exercise, particularly for
those who are overweight. The children who are the slowest or the
heaviest usually get knocked out of the game quickly. They then
spend the rest of the game watching while the more athletic kids
keep playing. It doesn't take a highly trained psychologist to realize

that this experience cannot be good for an overweight child's self-esteem or self-image.

a. irrelevant reasons

b. circular reasoning

c. hasty generalizations

d. unidentified or inappropriate experts

e. unidentified or dated research

EXERCISE 7

DIRECTIONS Read each selection and answer the questions by circling the appropriate letters or filling in the blanks.

EXAMPLE

The Scopes Trial Revisited

1   The 1925 Scopes trial, also known as the Monkey Trial, got its name from John Scopes, a Tennessee high school teacher who was tried and found guilty of breaking Tennessee's newly created Butler Act. The act forbade the teaching of Darwin's* evolutionary theory, which argued that fossil evidence showed how humans had evolved from lower forms of animal life—an idea that directly challenged the Christian view of creation. Ultimately, Scopes was charged with teaching theories that denied the biblical version of human creation.

2   Scopes's conviction was eventually overturned by the Supreme Court. Yet even before his conviction was struck down, his trial had done what seemed to be irreparable damage to the creationist notion that humans, unlike animals, were created by God. Scopes's defense attorney was the brilliant, witty, and eloquent Clarence Darrow, who mercilessly grilled his client's accusers. Darrow was particularly hard on the leading prosecutor, William Jennings Bryan, repeatedly posing questions that left Bryan embarrassed and stumbling for answers.

3   Regardless of the outcome of the Scopes trial, the controversy over how to teach human origins in the schools has never really gone away. Periodically it is stirred up again, as it was in Kansas in 1999, when the state school board removed the theory of evolution from the high school curriculum. It was reinstated in 2001,

---

*Charles Darwin (1809–1882): the naturalist whose books *Origin of Species* and *The Descent of Man* scandalized the public by insisting there was concrete evidence to support the notion of humans' evolution from lower species.

leaving some parents irate and determined to pull their children out of school and teach them at home. It would seem, then, that no school board's decision about how to teach the origins of humanity can leave everyone satisfied. Still, there is another possibility to consider: Schools could teach both theories so that neither group, creationist or evolutionist, feels slighted.

4   And there does seem to be some support for this more flexible position. A 1999 Gallup poll, for example, found that 68 percent of American adults believe children should learn both theories. A more recent poll came up with similar results. Then, too, don't parents have the right to determine what their children learn in school? Parents who want their kids to learn about creationism should not have their wishes denied; nor, for that matter, should parents who want their kids to learn about evolution. Both sides can be made happy if schools would present the evidence for both theories and let students decide which makes more sense to them.

5   An essential goal of education is to teach students to think critically. We want, that is, for them to know how to evaluate evidence and arrive at an informed decision. What better way to encourage critical thinking than to lay all the evidence for both sides of this controversy before students. Then they can decide which theory of human origins they choose to believe.

1. What is the author's point?

   Schools should teach both evolution and creationism.

2. What three reasons does the author offer in support of her point of view?

   a. *Polls suggest that a majority of parents want their children to learn both theories.*

   b. *Parents should have the right to decide what their children are taught.*

   c. *Teaching both theories would encourage critical thinking.*

3. In addition to these three reasons, which of the following does the author offer in support of her conclusion?

   a. specific illustration
   b. results of research
   c. expert opinion

4. Which error in reasoning can you detect in paragraph 4?

a. irrelevant reason

b. circular reasoning

c. hasty generalization

d. unidentified or inappropriate expert

e. unidentified or dated research

EXPLANATION In this example the author presents readers with a statement of policy. To convince them, she identifies three reasons why her proposal makes sense. Her evidence, however, is a bit shaky. You can tell that by the presence of a rhetorical question in paragraph 4, where she doesn't allow for the suggestion that maybe parents shouldn't be permitted to determine and select curriculum. Even less convincing is her claim (paragraph 4) that "a more recent poll" also found that a majority of adults want both theories taught. Unfortunately, who conducted the poll remains a mystery, and this is a good example of unidentified research.

1. Who Really Benefits from the Lottery?

1 In a recent editorial published in this newspaper, an argument was put forth in favor of a state-run lottery. According to the author of the editorial, there are many benefits to a state-run lottery and apparently no drawbacks. Now, the writer may honestly believe that a lottery would be a boon to everyone in the state, but I would argue that legalized gambling is a disaster waiting to happen.

2 Knowingly or unknowingly—and it doesn't matter which—state governments encourage addictive gambling when they promote lotteries. According to the American Psychiatric Association, addictive, or problem, gambling is a mental illness. Although treatable, it's still an illness, and it can lead to a host of social problems such as bankruptcy, theft, domestic violence, and job loss. Needless to say, these social problems can, in the end, prove costly to states hoping to benefit from lottery revenues. In promoting lotteries, the state, in essence, collects money from gambling with one hand and pays out double that amount in social services with the other. Advocates of state-run lotteries should consider that fact when they justify the lotteries by claiming they are a source of revenue for social programs. That logic may seem sound, but it doesn't add up on paper when the costs of addictive gambling are taken into account.

3 For example, a 1995 study by the Wisconsin Policy Research Institute estimated that each problem gambler cost the state

around $9,500 per year in social services and business losses. The total loss to the state was about $307 million per year.[4] Another study indicates that around one in four problem gamblers has a history of substance abuse. This is yet another reason why state governments should not encourage gambling.

4   As Dr. Benjamin Martino has pointed out, legalized gambling blurs an important moral distinction: the distinction between honestly earned money and "ill-gotten" gains. Money from gambling is ill-gotten because it is not connected with any honest labor that benefits society. When we sanction* legalized gambling, we approve of bestowing wealth on people who have not worked for it. Given the number of ways in which legalized gambling hurts a society, how can any state government see fit to promote it?

1. What is the author's point?

   _____

   _____

2. Identify the four reasons the author gives in support of that point?

   a. _____

   _____

   b. _____

   _____

   c. _____

   _____

   d. _____

   _____

3. In addition to these four reasons, which of the following does the author offer in support of his conclusions?

   a. specific illustration

   b. results of research

   c. expert opinion

---

[4]Chester Hartman, "Lotteries Victimize the Poor and Minorities," *New Haven Register*, August 3, 1998, p. 17.
*sanction: approve.

4. Which error or errors in reasoning can you detect in paragraphs 3 and 4?

   a. irrelevant reason

   b. circular reasoning

   c. hasty generalization

   d. unidentified or inappropriate expert

   e. unidentified or dated research

2. Speed-Cams: More for Profit Than Safety

1 In more than sixty cities across the United States, law enforcement officials are installing traffic cameras that photograph drivers who speed or violate other rules of the road. These devices, also known as "speed-cams" and "red-light cameras," are controlled by a computer and a companion metal detector installed under the pavement. When the metal detector calculates that a car is moving too fast, it signals the camera to snap a photo of the vehicle's license plate. A police officer then reviews these records and issues a citation to the driver. Many Americans are rightly outraged by these "robocops" on our roads. In fact, seven states have decided *not* to implement this technology. States currently using these cameras should follow suit and remove the devices immediately.

2 First of all, these cameras don't really deter speeders. Unless it's dark enough so that you see a flash in your rearview mirror, odds are you won't know you've been caught by a speed-cam. If you don't realize you've been caught, you're not likely to slow down. Then, too, there have to be other, less intrusive ways of ensuring motorists' safety. While some states photograph only the rear of the car, other states—including Arizona, California, and Colorado—photograph the driver, too. This type of electronic monitoring should concern every citizen of this country, and we should not allow our government to take pictures of us without our consent.

3 Their unreliability is another reason to scrap these cameras. These technological marvels can, in fact, malfunction and fail. In San Diego, speed-cam sensors clocked drivers going much faster than they really were. As a result, the city disconnected the cameras in July 2001. This example proves once and for all that these machines cannot be counted on to take accurate measurements and create error-free records.

4 Finally, opponents of speed-cams object to them because private companies handle the picture-taking with only a mini-

mum of police involvement. More to the point, these companies earn a profit on the number of tickets issued. Sometimes
the profit amounts to as much as $70 per ticket. Cities, too,
are raking in increased revenues from fines paid by violators.
Since August 1999, for example, Washington has pulled in
$12.8 million. This increase in revenue without a corresponding
increase in human resources is certainly one of the technology's
most attractive features, causing some critics to argue that city
governments are more interested in money than in public
safety.

5   In September 2001, a California Superior Court judge in
San Diego rejected traffic camera evidence as inadmissible
evidence. Perhaps this sensible decision will spark a chain
reaction. With any luck, it will result in the removal of these
devices from our country's streets. (Source of information:
Anita Hamilton, "Speeders Say Cheese," *Time*, September 17,
2001, p. 32.)

1. What is the author's point?

   _____

   _____

2. Identify the four reasons the author gives in support of that
   point.

   a. _____

   _____

   b. _____

   _____

   c. _____

   _____

   d. _____

   _____

3. In addition to these four reasons, which of the following does the
   author use as support?

   a. specific illustration

   b. results of research

   c. expert opinion

4. Which error or errors in reasoning can you detect in paragraph 3?

   a. irrelevant reason

   b. circular reasoning

   c. hasty generalization

   d. unidentified or inappropriate expert

   e. unidentified or dated research

3. **Grooming Counts or Does It?**

1 Many companies have established rigid grooming standards for their employees. Walt Disney World, for example, insists that employees follow established guidelines for hairstyle, jewelry, makeup, and facial hair. Airlines also require flight attendants to meet certain weight restrictions. Federal Express (FedEx) and United Parcel Service (UPS), too, impose grooming standards that limit the length of men's hair. Currently, however, some of these policies are being justifiably challenged in the courts by workers who claim that the standards infringe upon their religious rights. At issue is whether or not employers have a right to enforce rigid grooming rules on workers whose appearance expresses their religious belief or their cultural heritage.

2 According to the Equal Employment Opportunity Commission (EEOC), no company is allowed to prevent its employees from expressing religious beliefs through their appearance. The EEOC claims that forbidding such expressions of religious belief violates the Civil Rights Act. Both FedEx and UPS, for example, have fired drivers who refused to cut off their dreadlocks—long, thick strands of knotted or braided hair associated with Rastafarianism.* Similarly, several police officers employed by the Dallas Police Department were reprimanded or fired for wearing dreadlocks. In these cases and others, the EEOC and the Justice Department's Civil Rights Division have interceded on behalf of the employees.

3 The question of civil rights aside, employers also need to keep in mind that an employee's appearance seldom interferes with his or her ability to do the job. In other words, employers can afford to be more tolerant. Chris Warden, for example, was terminated from his job as a FedEx driver for wearing dreadlocks even though his manager's evaluations called him a superior employee. Warden's case proves that wearing dreadlocks does not affect an individual's job performance and therefore should not be a cause of dismissal.

*Rastafarianism: a religious and political movement originating in the 1930s in Jamaica.

4   As the multicultural population of the United States continues to grow, companies will be challenged more often for their insistence on homogeneous grooming policies. It's high time employers embraced diversity and redefined outdated notions about what is "reasonable" and "acceptable." (Source of information: David France, "Law: The Dreadlock Deadlock," *Newsweek*, September 10, 2001, p. 54.)

1. What is the author's point?

   _____

   _____

2. Identify the two reasons the author gives in support of that point.

   a. _____

   _____

   b. _____

   _____

3. In addition to these two reasons, which of the following does the author use as support?

   a. specific illustration

   b. results of research

   c. expert opinion

4. Which error or errors in reasoning can you detect in paragraph 3?

   a. irrelevant reason

   b. circular reasoning

   c. hasty generalization

   d. unidentified or inappropriate expert

   e. unidentified or dated research

4. Could El Al Be a Model?

1 Officials of Israel's El Al Airline say that the four suicide hijackings that occurred in the United States on September 11, 2001, could never have occurred on their airplanes. They may be right. El Al has the most elaborate, thorough, and successful security system in the entire airline industry.

2   El Al's rigorous system of luggage screening prevents bombs and weapons from getting on board an airplane. Before being loaded onto an aircraft, all suitcases and bags are put into a pres-

surized box that will recognize and detonate any explosives inside. Bags transferring from flights are subjected to the same screening, and bags that cannot be matched to a passenger are not permitted on board. El Al also subjects passengers themselves to a time-consuming and controversial* screening process, used to ensure that potential terrorists will not board the plane. Even before a traveler arrives at the airport, his or her name has already been compared to a computerized list of terrorist suspects compiled by law enforcement agencies around the world.

3   If a would-be hijacker manages to foil this system and board the plane, he or she faces still another security measure: undercover agents who travel on every flight. These armed agents, who look and behave like ordinary travelers, are stationed in aisle seats, where they watch for trouble. They are ready to defend passengers and protect the plane from a terrorist takeover. In addition to the presence of undercover agents, most of El Al's pilots are well educated and have advanced degrees.

4   El Al is based in a country torn for years by conflict and violence, yet it keeps travelers safe. In fact, the sole hijacking of an El Al plane occurred in 1968, at a time when the current security measures were not in place. (Source of information: Vivienne Walt, "Unfriendly Skies Are No Match for El Al," *USA Today*, October 1, 2001, p. ID.)

1. What is the author's point?

   _____

   _____

2. Identify the three reasons the author offers in support of that point?

   a. _____

   _____

   b. _____

   _____

   c. _____

   _____

---

*Critics of El Al's policies have complained that the screening process smacks of racial profiling.

3. In addition to these three reasons, which of the following does the author use as support?

    a. specific illustration

    b. results of research

    c. expert opinion

4. Which error or errors in reasoning can you detect in paragraph 3?

    a. irrelevant reason

    b. circular reasoning

    c. hasty generalization

    d. unidentified or inappropriate expert

    e. unidentified or dated research

Are There Any Objections?

By definition, an argument is guaranteed to include a point of view or position and some type of support. Many arguments, however, contain an additional element. They include an objection or opposing point of view, often followed by the author's response. Look, for example, at the following reading from page 428. In the original reading, the author argued against the inclusion of a swimsuit segment in the Miss America contest. But now, she has extended her argument to include her answer to what could be a major objection.

Banning Bathing Suits

1   After far too many years, critical attention has finally been paid to the portion of the Miss America pageant called the swimsuit competition. Thankfully, people are beginning to complain about this event. In 1999, a telephone poll was conducted on the night of the pageant to determine if the swimsuit competition should remain. Although the majority of callers voted to retain it, a good portion were critical and argued that the swimsuit segment should be eliminated. The question will undoubtedly be raised again and again, and in time the answer may well be different. Let's hope so, because the swimsuit competition serves only to demean the women who participate in it.

2   It should be clear to everyone that there are women whose appearance and intellect make them likely candidates for the crown. Yet these same women might well be eliminated from the competi-

tion for some minor physical flaw, like bulging thighs. A woman who has the appropriate appearance and intellect should not be eliminated because she shows a few bulges in a bathing suit. Beauty and brains are infinitely more important criteria for choosing Miss America than are a few extra pounds of body fat.

3   Many who insist on retaining the swimsuit competition will argue that it is an established tradition. Yet, as everyone knows, traditions change with the times. Nowadays, who really believes it's improper for women to play sports with men? But in the nineteenth century, a woman who did so would have challenged the traditional view of femininity. Once again, the times are ripe for a change.

In this case, the author challenges those who believe traditions are sacred and not subject to change. Her answer is that traditions have changed before and they need to do so again.

EXERCISE 8

DIRECTIONS Read each argument. Then answer the questions that follow.

EXAMPLE

Home Schooling Just Isn't School

1 As a teacher in a public school, I have to admit I cringe every time I hear the phrase "home schooling." I know that many parents believe they are helping their children by teaching them at home. But in my experience, home schooling may do more harm than good.

2   Children who enter my class after a long period of home schooling usually have huge gaps in their education. True, they often read and write better than the average fifth grader, and their spelling is good. But they know very little about the social sciences, and science itself seems to be a foreign word.

3   In addition, children who have gone to school at home frequently have difficulty working with other children. Unused to the give-and-take of group interactions, they are quick to show their discomfort or displeasure. Their response is understandable since they have spent years being schooled at home in a class of one or two at most.

4   I know that many parents believe that home schooling protects their children from dangerous or corrupting ideas and experiences. They are probably correct in that assumption. Unfortunately, the protection home schooling provides may cost a heavy

intellectual price. Most parents simply do not have the necessary training or background to give their children the wide-ranging and up-to-date education they need. And certainly parents alone cannot provide the kind of socialization found in schools outside the home.

1. What is the point of the author's argument?

   Home schooling may do more harm than good.

2. What two reasons does the author give in support of that point?

   a. *Children can end up with huge gaps in their education.*

   b. *Children schooled at home usually have difficulty working in groups.*

3. Identify the opposing point of view mentioned in the reading.

   Parents believe that they are protecting their children from bad experiences and inappropriate ideas.

4. Paraphrase the author's response.

   The protection costs too much socially and intellectually.

EXPLANATION As is often the case, the author states the point of the argument at the beginning of the reading—home schooling can do more harm than good—and then follows with two reasons for that position. Although the answer to a possible objection appears at the end, this is not necessarily standard. Answers to objections can just as easily be sprinkled throughout.

1. The Benefits of Home Schooling

1 Although it has been harshly criticized by many—often by those who have a vested interest* in supporting the status quo*—home schooling just may be the answer to our current educational crisis.

2 At home, children learn one-on-one or in small groups. If they need some additional explanation or instruction, the home tutor

---

*vested interest: having a special reason to promote or protect that which gives one a personal advantage.
*status quo: existing state of affairs.

can readily supply it. In public schools, however, children often sit in classrooms with twenty or thirty other students. Such class numbers make it almost impossible for teachers to give students the individual attention they so frequently need. There are so many competing voices and questions, a teacher can't possibly respond to all of them. Someone has to go consciously unattended or unconsciously ignored.

3   Another advantage of home schooling is that it allows children to learn in a comforting, familiar environment, lacking in distractions. Any parent who has ever delivered a weeping child to the door of his or her classroom knows full well how terrifying some children find the classroom atmosphere with its noisy hubbub. Children who learn at home aren't distracted by their surroundings, nor are they inhibited by the presence of other children who might unthinkingly laugh at their mistakes.

4   Critics who claim that home schooling can't provide children with the breadth of knowledge they need always assume that the parents don't have the necessary qualifications. Yet, of the parents I know personally who teach their children at home, two have a master's degree in physics, another a doctorate in psychology, and still another is a former elementary teacher with ten years of teaching experience to her credit. Parents who take on the responsibility of home schooling do not do so lightly. They know full well that they must provide their children with an education that prepares them for the world they will eventually enter.

1. What is the point of the author's argument?

    _____

    _____

2. What two reasons does the author give in support of that point?

    a. _____

    _____

    b. _____

    _____

3. Identify the opposing point of view mentioned in the reading.

    _____

    _____

4. Paraphrase the author's response.

_____

_____

2. **Community Service and Graduation**

1   In 1997, the Chicago public schools made community service a condition of graduation for high school seniors. In order to get their diploma, students will now have to complete sixty hours of volunteer work in the community. Among other duties, they may help children learn to read, assist patients at a local hospital, or spend time with the elderly in a nursing home. They will be able to choose from a variety of social programs. What they won't be able to choose is _not_ to participate—not if they want to graduate.

2   As one might expect, some students are grumbling that they won't learn anything from doing community service. But is that even possible? After all, if you teach a child how to read, you have to learn a good deal about effective teaching and learning, and that is not exactly useless information. Spend time with the elderly and you are bound to learn about aging and what it entails, physically, mentally, and financially. In fact, students who feel that life is forever, that doors never close, and that choices will always be available could probably benefit mightily from time spent with people who know for sure that choices made or not made in youth often have lasting consequences. Put another way, community service can teach students lessons they need to learn about life's limits.

3   It can also give students career ideas. A young person who spends some time working in a hospital might decide to be an X-ray technician or a cardiologist. For that matter, a student who volunteers to work in the library might become a researcher or a librarian. Volunteering to work in the community puts students in contact with career choices they never knew they had.

4   Then, too, in a society where the word "values" is constantly bandied about, why shouldn't schools teach the young that giving something back to the community is an essential part of community membership. It's a straightforward lesson in civics.* Sometimes your community helps you; sometimes you help the community. This is the kind of lesson textbooks don't teach, but it's one that needs to be learned. The Chicago public schools are doing

_____

*civics: the branch of political science that deals with the rights and duties of citizens.

the right thing by making community service a graduation requirement.

1. What is the point of the author's argument?

   _____

   _____

2. What three reasons does the author give in support of that point?

   a. _____

   _____

   b. _____

   _____

   c. _____

   _____

3. Identify the opposing point of view mentioned in the reading.

   _____

   _____

4. Paraphrase the author's response.

   _____

   _____

3. Reducing the Deer Population

1 According to the National Forest Service, there are currently around 27 million deer roaming the woodlands of the United States. They damage seedlings in new growth forests, destroy habitats of smaller animals, and ravage suburban gardens. In 1996, more than one hundred people were killed when their cars collided with deer. Clearly, the deer population must be reduced in order to avoid the continuation of these problems.

2 However, lengthening the hunting season, as some have suggested, is not the answer. After all, deer often roam in highly populated areas, and how could we guarantee that a family pet or, even worse, a child wouldn't be hit by a hunter's bullet? Clearly, a safer, more humane method of reducing the deer population must be found.

3   An experiment at Fire Island National Seashore suggests that a safer solution to deer overpopulation is already in existence. Since 1993, female deer on Fire Island have been injected with what amounts to a birth control pill. The injection is given either after the animal has been tranquilized or by means of a blow dart. A few weeks after the first injection, the doe gets a booster shot, and from then on, she is revaccinated once a year.

4   This experiment proves that the problem of deer overpopulation can be solved. We just need to expand the Fire Island experiment to include woodland areas all across the nation.

1. What is the point of the author's argument?

_____

_____

2. What reason does the author give in support of that point?

_____

_____

3. Identify the opposing point of view mentioned in the reading.

_____

_____

4. Paraphrase the author's response.

_____

_____

4. Sex Selection Is a Bad Idea

1 Many fertility clinics all over the United States now offer prospective parents the controversial option of selecting their baby's sex. Scientists can segregate sperm carrying Y chromosomes (which result in boys) from X chromosomes (which result in girls), and the mother can then be inseminated with the sperm of her choice. One recent study published in *Fertility and Sterility* showed that the procedure is about 75 percent effective for conceiving boys and 69 percent effective for girls. Yet, effective or not, society should reject technology that allows human beings to tamper with reproduction. Sex selection of babies will, in the long run, cause serious problems.

2   Sex selection could seriously upset the natural population balance. When left alone, nature has a way of maintaining similar numbers of male and females. If people are given the ability to tamper with those numbers, the result is likely to be a disproportionate number of males. For example, gender preference studies conducted at Cleveland State University found that 94 percent of people who said they would use sex selection technology would do so in order to have a son first. It's worth noting here that such research firmly contradicts claims by supporters of reproductive technology, who insist that parents interested in choosing their baby's sex want solely to ensure gender variety in their families. Supporters of sex selection may take comfort in this belief, but the research doesn't back them up.

3   An even more dangerous outcome of gender selection could be discrimination against and devaluation of women. If enough couples ended up with first-born sons as only children, the resulting disproportionate number of males could relegate women to permanent second-class status and erase their gains in equal rights and opportunities. The consequences could be even more dire in other cultures, such as India and China, where women are already the subject of significant discrimination. Arthur Caplan, director of the Center for Biomedical Ethics at the University of Minnesota, warns that gender selection will worsen the plight of women in countries where infanticide and abortion of female children already exist.

4   Couples who are considering choosing the sex of their unborn child should reconsider. The negative biological and social outcomes of this technology are too risky. A child's sex is still better left to chance.

1. What is the author's point?

   _____

   _____

2. What two reasons does the author give in support of that point?

   a. _____

   _____

   b. _____

   _____

3. Identify the opposing point of view mentioned in the reading.

_____

_____

4. Paraphrase the author's response.

_____

_____

■ **DIGGING DEEPER**

LOOKING AHEAD   The author of the reading on pages 450–451 has no faith in the use of photo radar to stop speeding. As the title below announces, the author of the following reading fully agrees, but he takes the argument a step further and suggests an alternative.

WHY PHOTO RADAR JUST DOES NOT WORK

1   The recent flap in Calgary over three teens being issued tickets for the alleged crime of holding up signs warning motorists about a photo radar trap has once again exposed the hypocrisy over the insidious* machines. Because if the real purpose of photo radar is, as the police claim, to slow motorists down, then anything that slows motorists down should be a good thing, including kids warning speeding drivers of radar traps ahead. After all, what real difference is there between some kids standing on the side of the road with a "radar ahead" sign, and the local radio station offering all the radar locations in their regular traffic reports?

Photo Radar Isn't About Speeding

2   But, of course, photo radar isn't about speeding, it's about revenue. And we didn't need this sorry episode in Calgary to prove that. Just go for a drive along a major thoroughfare. Do the speed limit. At least half of the cars on the road will pass you, many of them at blistering speeds. Don't be surprised, either, if some of those speed demons happen to be driving marked police patrol cars. I had the experience a couple of weeks ago of having a patrol car constantly speed up ahead of me on 170th Street. I'd catch up to him at the light, and he'd take off again when it turned green. We'd meet at the next light, and on it went all the way to 69th Avenue before he turned off. There was no emergency (or else he wouldn't have stopped for the red lights) but he sure seemed to be ignoring the speed limit. Not exactly setting the best example for the rest of us.

3   Beyond that, photo radar is useless for getting people to slow down. Because unless you're driving at night and you see the flash in the rear-view mirror, chances are you won't even realize you've been caught by the camera. In other words, photo radar does nothing to stop you from speeding at that point in time. And you'll keep speeding until you get the ticket in the mail, at which point you'll still keep speeding.

─────────────
*insidious: harmful.

4 We've had photo radar for years here in Edmonton, and the vast majority of drivers still ignore the speed limit. So how can photo radar be a deterrent? In my experience, there's only one surefire way to get people to maintain the speed limit, and that's to blanket the road with police cruisers nailing people for going too fast. Case in point: a road trip earlier this summer to Tacoma, Washington. During the long drive from Edmonton to Vancouver, we passed maybe two RCMP* cruisers, and neither one seemed to be particularly interested in catching speeders. Needless to say, virtually every driver on the highway was ignoring the speed limit. And why not? It's not like it was being enforced.

5 But we hadn't been in Washington State for three minutes before a state trooper roared out of his hiding spot in the bushes, raced down the interstate past everyone, pulled over some poor guy ahead of us, and wrote him a ticket. Naturally, after the state trooper went blazing past us, most of the traffic going south on I-5 slowed to the speed limit. And pretty much every driver stayed close to the speed limit for the rest of the way. Why? Because there were Washington state troopers everywhere—in marked cruisers, unmarked minivans, pickup trucks, and even one VW Bug—picking off speeders left, right, and center.

6 We saw more police enforcing the speed limit in the short drive from the border to Tacoma than we saw from Edmonton to Vancouver or during our return trip through Canada. In fact, once we were back in Canada, I don't recall running into a police vehicle again until Calgary. During the final stretch run along Highway 2 from Cowtown to Edmonton, the lone RCMP cruiser we encountered along the way seemed as oblivious to the speeders as the lead foots were of the posted limit. The Washington state police had the right idea. Lots of real police officers in real cars pulling over real speeders is a far better deterrent than a robotic camera parked on the side of the road. (Mike Jenkinson, "Why Photo Radar Just Does Not Work," *The Edmonton Sun*, August 13, 2001, p. 11.)

Sharpening Your Skills

DIRECTIONS Answer the following questions by filling in the blanks, underlining the appropriate word, or circling the letter of the correct response.

---

*RCMP: Royal Canadian Mounted Police.

1. The question at the end of paragraph 1 is
   a. a question in need of an answer.
   b. a rhetorical question that requires no answer.

2. What alternative to photo radar does the author suggest?

   _____

3. What kind of evidence does the author offer in support of his alternative?
   a. illustrations
   b. reasons
   c. expert opinion
   d. research

4. What error in reasoning can you spot in the evidence?
   a. hasty generalization
   b. slippery slope
   c. irrelevant reason

5. Underline the two submerged metaphors in the following sentence:

   > In my experience, there's only one surefire way to get people to maintain the speed limit, and that's to blanket the road with police cruisers nailing people for going too fast.

6. Underline the submerged metaphor in the following sentence:

   > At least half of the cars on the road will pass you, many of them at blistering speeds.

7. How would you describe the author's purpose?
   a. to inform
   b. to persuade

8. Which of the following helped you identify the author's purpose?
   a. the title
   b. the main idea
   c. the source of the reading
   d. the author's language
   e. all of the above

9. How would you describe the author's tone?

    a. angry

    b. comical

    c. skeptical

    d. neutral

10. What's your opinion of photo radar?

_____

_____

Now give one or two reasons that support your opinion.

_____

_____

_____

_____

WORD NOTES: SPEAKING OF SANCTIONS

Page 449 introduced the verb *sanction,* meaning "to approve." Similarly, the noun *sanction* can mean "permission" or "approval." However, the noun *sanction* has an additional definition, one you should be aware of because it often turns up in the news. In its plural form, the word refers to penalties or actions used to bring about a change in a nation's behavior. For example, there are economic *sanctions* in place against the country of Iraq; the goal of those penalties is to exact more responsible behavior from Iraqi leader Saddam Hussein.

    The following sentences use the word *sanction* in different ways. For each sentence, give the correct meaning.

1. How can you *sanction* such obviously unethical practices?

_____

2. The economic *sanctions* against the government of South Africa were harshly criticized by the corporations who had a vested interest in free trade.

_____

Now it's your turn to create two different sentences, each one illustrating a different use of the word *sanction.*

1. _____

   _____

2. _____

   _____

◢◣● Test 1: Reviewing the Key Points

DIRECTIONS Answer the following questions by filling in the blanks or circling the letter of the correct response.

1. The starting point of an argument is the _____.

2. Which one of the following statements is *not* likely to be at the heart of an argument?

   a. statement of negation

   b. statement of condition

   c. statement of value

   d. statement of policy

3. Writers who want their arguments to be seriously considered know they have to provide the appropriate support. Critical readers, in turn, know that they have to _____ and

   _____ that support.

4. In addition to reasons and examples or illustrations, writers will often use _____ and _____ to support their claims.

5. In their haste to prove a point, writers sometimes include reasons that are not _____ to their claim.

6. A writer who offers an opinion and supports it by saying the same thing in different words is guilty of using _____.

7. Writers who offer one example to prove a broad general claim are guilty of drawing _____.

8. A writer who uses expert opinion should give readers an idea of the expert's _____.

9. Writers who use research to support their claims need to provide some form of _____, so that readers know who conducted it.

10. Writers who use research also need to make sure that the research cited is not so _____ it may no longer be applicable.

Test 2: Analyzing Arguments

DIRECTIONS Read each argument and answer the questions that follow. *Note:* The author may or may not respond to opposition and the argument may or may not include an error.

1. TV Coverage Leaves Opening for the Internet

1 By the time the Olympics roll around again, those who want to watch the games may be spending more time on the Internet than they do in front of the television set. After all, why would viewers choose to watch hours-old videos of athletes winning the gold, when they can watch them winning live on the Internet? Sure, they won't have the pleasure of listening to highly paid anchors shoot the breeze. And yes, they will be denied the dubious delight of all those biographical short features the networks are so fond of running. You know the ones I mean. They have lots of close-ups of the athletes doing the fun things they enjoy in their every-day lives like going on family picnics and dancing in nightclubs. Yet does it really matter to anyone that skater Michelle Kwan is a diehard shopper or avid photographer when she is not on the ice?

2 Although the networks don't seem to know it, most fans of the Olympics don't care about getting up close and personal with the athletes. What they care about is seeing the people they root for win gold—silver or bronze will do, too—medals. And they want to see them win live. They don't want to see them triumph a day later, after the results of the games have already been announced in the newspaper.

3 In the Atlanta games in 1996, a camera was set up at every venue. It was called the Sneak Peak Cam, and every 15 seconds it took a picture of a sports event and sent it to the Olympic Internet site. In this way, fans of the high jump, for example, could get a stop-and-go version of what was happening in Atlanta almost at the very moment that the athletes sprang into the air. Now that's entertainment. It's also precisely what television cannot, and in some cases will not, provide.

4 Armando Garcia of IBM, who was involved in creating an Internet site for the Olympics, says there is no reason why the Internet won't be able to bring "near-TV" quality viewing to a mass audience. According to Garcia, "there are debates about when it will happen, but it will happen."[5]

5 Let's hope it happens soon, so that those of us who are diehard fans of the Olympics, summer or winter, will never again have to en-

---

[5]Kevin Maney, "Olympics TV Coverage Leaves Opening for the Internet." *USA Today*, February 12, 1998, p. 2B.

dure boring commercials, newscaster chatter, or those tedious, often saccharine,* biographical sketches that are inflicted upon us before we are allowed to see our favorite athlete go for the gold.

1. What is the author's point?

   _____

   _____

2. What two reasons does the author give to support his point of view?

   a. _____

   _____

   b. _____

   _____

3. Does the author include any of the following?

   a. examples or illustrations

   b. research results

   c. expert opinion

4. Does the author respond to any opposing point of view? _____ If so, fill in the blanks that follow.

   Opposition   _____

   _____

   Response   _____

   _____

5. Circle one or more of the appropriate letters to indicate the presence or absence of errors in the author's argument.

   a. irrelevant reason

   b. circular reasoning

   c. hasty generalization

   d. unidentified or inappropriate expert

   e. unidentified or dated research

   f. no errors

   _____

   *saccharine: overly sweet and sentimental.

2. **Kids and Sports**

1 For many parents, competitive team sports like Little League Baseball and Peewee Football are an essential part of childhood. Thus, they are anxious for their kids to try out and "make the team." Supposedly, competitive sports build physical strength. Even more important—or so the argument goes—playing competitive sports early on in childhood builds character. Still, parents intent on making sure their kids learn how to compete might want to rethink the notion that sports in which somebody has to win or lose are important to a young child's development. Competitive sports for preteen kids have some important disadvantages; these disadvantages need to be considered before parents push kids onto a playing field where the winner takes all.

2 Here's one thing that should be considered: Competitive sports can unduly stress a child's still developing body. Football, basketball, baseball, and even tennis are physically demanding. They put a very heavy strain on the body. This is particulary true if muscles or bones are still developing. Now, a ten-year-old who is just playing for the fun of it will probably not repeat a movement or motion that hurts, but what if that same child is playing for a trophy? Is he or she going to stop throwing that tough-to-hit curve ball just because there is a little pain involved? It's not likely. Unfortunately, the end result can be lifelong damage to a shoulder or an arm. Thomas Tutko, author of the book *Winning Is Everything and Other Myths*, argues that kids should not be playing physically demanding sports before the age of fourteen. From Tutko's perspective, playing demanding competitive sports before that age is simply too "traumatic," both physically and psychologically.

3 In his book *No Contest: The Case Against Competition*, author and researcher Alfie Kohn emphasizes that the psychological effects of competitive sports on those still too young to play them may be worse than the physical injuries that can ensue. Kohn's book summarizes the results of several hundred studies focusing on the effects of competition both on and off the playing field. Whether in the context of sports or the classroom, Kohn contends that competition "undermines self esteem, poisons our relationships, and holds us back from doing our best."[6] Clearly, Kohn would not support the notion of competition as a character builder for children. If anything, he sees it as a character destroyer, even if those competing are grownups.

4 To be fair to those who insist there's no point to playing basket-

---

[6]A. Kohn, "No Win Situations," *Women's Sports and Fitness*, July/August 1990, pp. 56–58.

ball, football, or baseball unless you keep score, these are games where the score counts. However, the position argued here is not that competitive sports should be abandoned; rather, they should be postponed until the child is ready to be not just a winner, but a loser as well. A fifteen-year-old is probably able to accept the simple fact that, at some time in life, everyone loses at something. But does a nine-year-old have to learn this lesson? In their early years, kids should concentrate on achieving their personal best. Are they running faster, jumping higher, or throwing faster than they did the last time around? Those are the questions they should be asking themselves, not who won and who lost.

1. What is the author's point?

   _____

   _____

2. What two reasons does the author give in support of that point?

   a. _____

   _____

   b. _____

   _____

3. Does the author include any of the following?

   a. examples or illustrations

   b. research results

   c. expert opinion

4. Does the author respond to any opposing point of view? _____
   If so, fill in the blanks that follow.

   Opposition   _____

   _____

   Response   _____

   _____

5. Circle one or more of the appropriate letters to indicate the presence or absence of errors in the author's argument.

   a. irrelevant reason

   b. circular reasoning

   c. hasty generalization

    d. unidentified or inappropriate expert

    e. unidentified or dated research

    f. no errors

3. Opening Adoption Files

1 In some states, people who have been adopted are not allowed access to their adoption files. Consequently, they have no idea who their real parents are or why they were put up for adoption, and all attempts to discover this information are met with firm bureaucratic resistance. Simply put, most adoption officials will tell them nothing.

2   However, in the past decade, many adoptees have publicly protested this situation, causing some states to change their policies. What I want to argue here is that such changes in policy need to happen nationwide. Adopted children need to know about their parents and their past. Those adoptees who do not care can simply refuse access to their files.

3   Although restricting access to adoption files makes the search much harder, it does not necessarily deter adoptees in search of their biological parents. Those men and women desperate to find their biological parents will, if they can afford it, hire a detective to find out what they want to know. If they cannot afford the service of detectives, some adoptees devote all their time and energy to discovering their origins. This shows how important it is for adoptees to recover their past. Thus the state should not place obstacles in their path.

4   Many adoptees feel guilty about being put up for adoption. They assume that they did something wrong, something that made them so unlovable their parents were forced to give them up. These men and women need to know the real causes for their adoption. It helps an adoptee to know, for example, that his mother gave him up for adoption because she was too young to support him, not because she didn't love him. Such knowledge helps relieve the burden of guilt some adoptees carry around their entire lives.

5   There are also physical—rather than psychological—reasons why adoptees need access to their files. To take proper care of their health, they need to know what diseases they might be likely to inherit. In more extreme cases, knowledge about the biological parents can mean the difference between life and death. Sometimes adoptees are in need of an organ transplant, and they require an organ that comes from a natural relative. If all their relatives are unknown, these adopted men and women

are at a terrible disadvantage—one that could cost them their lives.

6   Many parents who have given up their children for adoption resent the idea of opening up adoption files. They feel that their right to privacy will be threatened. Yet this objection is based on the assumption that adopted children want to hunt down their parents and intrude on their lives. But, as study after study shows, adoptees only want to know who their biological parents are. In some cases, they may even want to meet them, but they do not want to push their way into the lives of people who will not accept them. Giving the adopted person access to files does not mean that the parent or parents forsake all rights to privacy. It only means that the adopted child can attempt to make contact if he or she wishes, and the parents can refuse or accept as they see fit.

1. What is the author's point?

   _____

   _____

2. What three reasons does the author give in support of that point?

   a. _____

   _____

   b. _____

   _____

   c. _____

   _____

3. Does the author include any of the following?

   a. examples or illustrations

   b. research results

   c. expert opinion

4. Does the author respond to any opposing point of view? _____
   If so, fill in the blanks that follow.

   Opposition   _____

   _____

Response _____

_____

5. Circle one or more of the appropriate letters to indicate the presence or absence of errors in the author's argument.

   a. irrelevant reason

   b. circular reasoning

   c. hasty generalization

   d. unidentified or inappropriate expert

   e. unidentified or dated research

   f. no errors

4. **The Death Penalty: Legal Murder**

1 I am opposed to the death penalty, and current state efforts to reinstate it across the country sadden and anger me. The death penalty should be abolished, not reinstated. It is not just morally reprehensible*; it is also not even an effective deterrent* to murder.

2   When we support the death penalty we support the very act we claim to abhor*—the taking of human life. We stoop to the level of the killers we mean to punish and make it even harder for them to understand why what they have done was morally wrong. If, as a society, we truly believe in the value of human life, then the taking of it—whether justified by law or not—is an immoral act. Legalized murder is still just that—murder.

3   To those who claim that the death penalty acts as a deterrent to crime, I can only say that the research is not on your side. When William Bowers analyzed the murder rate in New York State from 1907 to 1973, he found that the number of murders rose by an average of two following an execution. As a result of his research, Bowers argued that executions only encourage acts of murder by legitimizing violence. His research results and his conclusions have been reaffirmed by similar state-funded studies in Utah and California. After more than a century of international research, the American Civil Liberties Union has also come to the conclusion that the death penalty does not act as a deterrent to murder.

---

*reprehensible: wrong.
*deterrent: means of discouragement.
*abhor: hate, detest.

1. What is the author's point?

   _____

   _____

2. What two reasons does the author give in support of that point?

   a. _____

   _____

   b. _____

   _____

3. Does the author include any of the following?
   a. examples or illustrations
   b. research results
   c. expert opinion

4. Does the author respond to any opposing point of view? _____
   If so, fill in the blanks that follow.

   Opposition   _____

   _____

   Response   _____

   _____

5. Circle one or more of the appropriate letters to indicate the presence or absence of errors in the author's argument.
   a. irrelevant reason
   b. circular reasoning
   c. hasty generalization
   d. unidentified or inappropriate expert
   e. unidentified or dated research
   f. no errors

Test 3: Analyzing Arguments

Read each argument and answer the questions that follow. *Note:* The author may or may not respond to opposition and the argument may or may not include an error.

1. Banning Peanuts

1 There was a time when the peanut butter and jelly sandwich was a staple of the school lunchbox. Often it was the one food that fussy children would willingly eat, and parents were grateful it existed, even if they personally found the combination distasteful. The popularity of peanut butter and jelly sandwiches, however, is a thing of the past as schools from New York to California have stopped serving them in the cafeteria. Many school officials have also asked parents not to put peanut products of any kind into their kids' lunches.

2 If the ban on peanuts sounds silly to you, then you obviously don't know an important fact: Around 5 percent of children under the age of six have food allergies, and many of those same children are violently allergic to peanuts in any form. The ban on peanuts in the school may sound trivial, but it's not. On the contrary, it's a matter of life or death, particularly since studies show that allergies to peanuts are on the rise.

3 In November of 1998, seventeen-year-old Mariya Spektor of Niskayuna, New York, died after she unknowingly ate some cereal that had peanut oil in it. In the very same month, twelve-year-old Kristine Kastner of Mercer Island, Washington, died after she ate a chocolate chip cookie that had finely minced peanuts in it. The reality is that children can and do die if they unwittingly ingest peanut products, and neither parents nor educators can afford to take the chance that this might happen.

4 Opponents of the ban, among them members of The Food Allergy Network, an advocacy group for people with allergies, argue that it pits parents against parents and avoids the real issue: teaching children with allergies how to manage them. As a spokesperson for the group has pointed out, no medical studies indicate that sitting next to someone else eating peanuts can cause an allergic reaction, so why tell parents they can't put peanut products into school lunches?

5 This criticism, however, seems to miss a crucial point. Kids sit together at lunch and trade food all the time. Thus if schools allow kids to bring peanut products from home to school, there's every possibility that a child with an allergy will ingest a snack

that might prove deadly. Naturally, a child allergic to peanuts is not going to bite into a peanut butter and jelly sandwich, but that same child might well munch on a chocolate chip cookie containing peanuts, not realizing that nuts are in the cookie.

6   Parents of children allergic to peanuts are aware that many do not want peanut products banned from schools. One of those parents is Mark LoPresti of Grand Island, New York. LoPresti has a three-year-old son who is severely allergic to peanuts, and the father acknowledges the ban can create problems. Still he is fiercely determined that peanuts must be banned when his son is ready to go to school. As LoPresti puts it, "I'm not going to sacrifice my son's life for the right to have a peanut butter sandwich."[7] It's hard not to sympathize with LoPresti's point of view. When it comes to the ban on peanut products in schools, an old adage seems to apply: "It's better to be safe than sorry." (Source of information: Carrie Hodges, "Peanut Ban Spreads to Cafeteria." *USA Today*, December 3, 1998, p. 17a.)

1. What is the author's point?

    _____

    _____

2. What reason does the author give in support of that point?

    _____

    _____

3. Does the author include any of the following?
    a. examples or illustrations
    b. research results
    c. expert opinion

4. Does the author respond to any opposing point of view? _____ If so, fill in the blanks that follow.

    Opposition   _____

                    _____

    Response   _____

                    _____

5. Circle one or more of the appropriate letters to indicate the presence or absence of errors in the author's argument.

   a. irrelevant reason

   b. circular reasoning

   c. hasty generalization

   d. unidentified or inappropriate expert

   e. unidentified or dated research

   f. no errors

2. **Keep Our Libraries Free of Pornography**

1 The Child Online Protection Act of 2000 requires public libraries to install software that will "protect against" access to materials harmful to minors. Libraries that do not have such software in place by July of 2002 will lose federal subsidies for their online facilities. This law seems eminently sensible, yet already there is opposition to it from groups like the American Civil Liberties Union and the American Library Association. However, as long as libraries attract underage patrons—and may they always do so—computer access to X-rated sites needs to be strictly censored. And why not employ censorship where children are involved? By blocking children's access to sexually explicitly Web sites, we protect both their minds and their bodies. Who could object to that?

2   More than 75 percent of the nation's public libraries offer Internet access. Thanks to that access, any twelve-year-old—unless filters are in place—can reach Web sites featuring hard-core sex scenes. Even worse, kids can get into chat rooms where they might make contact with sex offenders or child molesters. Children should not be exposed to such Web sites or chat rooms. As Dr. Melanie Powers has pointed out, even one experience with a pornographic Web site can do irreparable damage to a child's psyche.

3   Opponents of filters claim that it's the job of parents, not libraries, to control what children view on the Internet. But parents can't rely on even the most obedient children to censor themselves. After all they are children; they don't realize the consequences of their actions. Since parents can't accompany their children on every visit to the library, it is up to the libraries to control what their younger patrons can view.

4   Libraries routinely enact the role of censor when they refuse to stock their shelves with pornographic books, magazines, or videos, and you won't find copies of *Hustler* or *Penthouse* tucked away in

the magazine rack of your local library. Nor for that matter will you find a copy of *Deep Throat* in the video department. Yet no one claims that this act of censorship infringes on the right to free speech. Why shouldn't the same principle apply to the Internet? Libraries don't stock pornography; therefore, why shouldn't they exclude pornographic sites from their offerings to the public.

5   Our libraries need to be open to everyone. But as long as children can get onto X-rated sites simply by typing in the word *sex*, they can't be. By allowing children access to any Web site available on the Internet, we are turning our libraries into adult bookstores and doing what real adult bookstores cannot do for fear of legal retribution. Libraries that don't use software filters are exposing vulnerable children to pornographic material that might well do them terrible, even lethal, harm.

1. What is the author's point?

     _____

     _____

2. What three reasons does the author give in support of that point?

     a. _____

     _____

     b. _____

     _____

     c. _____

     _____

3. Does the author include any of the following?

     a. examples or illustrations

     b. research results

     c. expert opinion

4. Does the author respond to any opposing point of view? _____
     If so, fill in the blanks that follow.

Opposition   _____

                 _____

Response _____

_____

5. Circle one or more of the appropriate letters to indicate the presence or absence of errors in the author's argument.

   a. irrelevant reason

   b. circular reasoning

   c. hasty generalization

   d. unidentified or inappropriate expert

   e. unidentified or dated research

   f. no errors

3. Dangerous Self-Esteem

1 For years now, we have heard that high self-esteem is a prerequisite for achievement. As a result, many students work in classrooms where posters proclaim "we applaud ourselves." Exactly for what isn't always made clear. In elementary school, students complete sentences that begin "I am special because. . . ."[8] According to what has become established educational wisdom, children who are praised, even for their mistakes, will become confident, successful adults. In response to that wisdom, some states (California for one) have established educational task forces on—you guessed it—promoting self-esteem. Yet now there is some evidence that self-esteem, if it's not backed by real achievements, might be dangerous.

2 As psychologist Brad Bushman of Iowa State University puts it, kids who develop unrealistically high opinions of themselves can, when brought face to face with a more realistic version of who they are, become "potentially dangerous."[9] Bushman, along with Ray Baumeister of Case Western Reserve University, conducted a study of unrealistic self-esteem and found that students inflated by self-esteem not based on real achievement were likely to react with hostility or aggression when confronted by a world that fails to mirror their sense of importance.

3 The findings of Bushman and Baumeister have also been echoed by James Gilligan of Howard Medical School. Gilligan,

---

[8]Sharon Begley, "You're OK, I'm Terrific," *Newsweek*, July 13, 1998, p. 69.
[9]Begley, p. 69.

a long-time researcher into the causes of violence, agrees that inflated self-esteem with no basis in fact can be dangerous. Clinical psychologist Robert Brooks of Harvard concurs as well. According to Brooks, if teaching self-esteem is done inappropriately, "you can raise a generation of kids who cannot tolerate frustration."[10]

4   Those who argue that the failure to teach self-esteem can cause a generation of children to grow up feeling worthless are missing the point. Schools and parents should continue to praise children for a job or task well done. No one is saying that they shouldn't. But self-esteem has to be based on real achievement, not on empty praise that encourages a child to believe everything he or she does is perfect, despite all evidence to the contrary.

5   In the end, inflated self-esteem not based on any real accomplishment may well do more harm than good. Unfortunately, this tendency for some young people to become aggressive whenever the world does not reflect their own inflated sense of self-importance is proof positive that an entire generation of young people will never amount to anything. Raised by self-indulgent parents who threw traditional values out the window because they had to "do their own thing," these kids never had a chance to become responsible adults. One can only fear for our society once it is in their hands.

1. What is the author's point?

_____

_____

2. What reason does the author give in support of that point?

_____

_____

3. Does the author include any of the following?
    a. examples or illustrations
    b. research results
    c. expert opinion

4. Does the author respond to any opposing point of view? _____
    If so, fill in the blanks that follow.

_____

[10]Begley, p. 69.

Opposition _____

_____

Response _____

_____

5. Circle one or more of the appropriate letters to indicate the presence or absence of errors in the author's argument.

   a. irrelevant reason

   b. circular reasoning

   c. hasty generalization

   d. unidentified or inappropriate expert

   e. unidentified or dated research

   f. no errors

4. In Praise of Bilingualism

1 Lack of English skills is the main reason why minority students fall behind in school. For those who care about the education of America's young people, that should be reason enough to promote bilingual education. But for those who are still not convinced, let me offer the results of some significant research and lay to rest commonly expressed worries about the effect of bilingual education on the acquisition of English.

2 Research on the effects of bilingual education shows that bilingualism does not interfere with performance in either language (Hakata & Garera, 1989). Thus, it makes no sense to argue that non-native speakers should not have bilingual instruction because it will interfere with their acquisition of English. This claim is not grounded in any factual evidence.

3 Instead of discouraging bilingual education by trying to eliminate funding for it, we should encourage it because research suggests that the ability to speak two languages improves cognitive flexibility* and the ability to think creatively (Diaz, 1983). This may be one reason why most other industrialized countries insist that their students master *at least* one other language. They know what we in the United States ignore: Bilingualism enlarges a person's capacity for understanding the world by giving him or her two different languages of interpretation. As linguist Benja-

---

*cognitive flexibility: ease and quickness of thinking.

min Whorf established decades ago in his now classic article "Science and Linguistics," "We dissect nature along lines laid down by one native language. . . . The world's presented in a kaleidoscopic* flux* of impression which has to be organized by our minds—and this means largely by the linguistic systems in our minds."[11]

4   The child—or for that matter, the adult—who can speak two languages has more tools for understanding the world than we who are limited solely to English.

1. What is the author's point?

   _____

   _____

2. What two reasons does the author give in support of that point?

   a. _____

   _____

   b. _____

   _____

3. Does the author include any of the following?

   a. examples or illustrations

   b. research results

   c. expert opinion

4. Does the author respond to any opposing point of view? _____ If so, fill in the blanks that follow.

   Opposition _____

   _____

   Response _____

   _____

---

*kaleidoscopic: like a child's toy that constantly changes patterns and colors.
*flux: change, movement.
[11]Edward T. Hall, *The Silent Language.* New York: Anchor Books, 1973, p. 123.

5. Circle one or more of the appropriate letters to indicate the presence or absence of errors in the author's argument.

    a. irrelevant reason

    b. circular reasoning

    c. hasty generalization

    d. unidentified or inappropriate expert

    e. unidentified or dated research

    f. no errors

Test 4: Analyzing Arguments

DIRECTIONS Read each argument and answer the questions that follow. *Note:* The author may or may not respond to opposition and the argument may or may not include an error.

1. Why Punish Needy Students Twice?

1 About 39 percent of college students receive some form of federal financial aid. However, that figure is bound to decrease due to a new question on the financial aid application: Have you ever been convicted of possessing or selling illegal drugs? The 35,000 people so far who have answered yes or left the question blank have found their request for aid was automatically denied. Yet this new law, which will prevent thousands of students from attending college, is seriously flawed. A previous drug conviction should not prevent an otherwise-deserving citizen from receiving financial aid, and this question should be removed from the application for financial aid.

2 For one thing, federal financial aid is not denied to people who commit far more serious crimes. The form does not ask about the applicant's overall criminal record, so those people who have been convicted of non-drug-related crimes can still receive financial aid. As one expert put it, "You can murder your grandmother and get financial aid, but you can't smoke a joint. You are denied aid even if you are convicted of a [drug] misdemeanor with no jail time. It is inequitable."

3 Furthermore, the criminal justice system has already punished the prospective student as a result of his or her conviction. Michael Cunningham, for example, was convicted of possessing a gram of marijuana. He paid the fine, completed his community service sentence, and now lives with the consequences of having a criminal record. It's not fair that he was also forced to quit school because he was denied the $3,000 he needed for his tuition. Mr. Cunningham's example is proof enough that this new legislation only serves to further penalize those who have already paid their debt to society.

4 Supporters of the law argue that it's a tough but necessary component of the war on drugs. They claim that the prospect of being denied financial aid will deter young people from getting involved with drugs. However, the law ignores the fact that people make mistakes but can still repent and change. Besides, most young people who experiment with drugs are just not thinking ahead three or four years to when they might need funds for college. Chances are that the law's ability to deter people from drug use is being overestimated.

3   Finally, this law is not even what its sponsor wanted. U.S. Representative Mark Souder, a Republican from Indiana, said, "It hasn't worked out at all the way I intended." He meant for the financial aid denial to apply only to those who were convicted of drug use while either applying for or actually receiving assistance. He says he did not mean to penalize those who honestly admitted to a prior conviction.

6   Obviously, this law robs students of much-needed aid and should be eliminated. The war on drugs will not be won by throwing extra obstacles in the paths of people who seek to better themselves by attending college. (Source of information: Michael Kranish, "Truth and Its Consequences," *Boston Sunday Globe*, September 9, 2001, pp. E1–E2.)

1. What is the author's point?

   _____

   _____

2. What four reasons does the author give in support of that point?

   a. _____

   _____

   b. _____

   _____

   c. _____

   _____

   d. _____

   _____

3. Does the author include any of the following?

   a. examples or illustrations

   b. research results

   c. expert opinion

4. Does the author respond to any opposing point of view? _____
   If so, fill in the blanks that follow.

Opposition   _____

   _____

Response _____

_____

5. Circle one or more of the appropriate letters to indicate the presence or absence of errors in the author's argument.

a. irrelevant reason

b. circular reasoning

c. hasty generalization

d. unidentified or inappropriate expert

e. unidentified or dated research

f. no errors

2. More Homework May Not Pave the Road to Success

1   Local communities across the nation are pressuring schools to boost test scores so kids can get into and do well in college. In response to that pressure, teachers are piling on the homework, starting in elementary school. A University of Michigan study found that in 1997, children ages nine to eleven were averaging three and a half hours of homework a week—a figure that is steadily increasing. At Farmland Elementary School in Rockville, fifth graders are being assigned up to an hour and a half of homework every day. Even six-year-olds are getting nightly homework assignments. Fortunately, more parents and education professionals are beginning to question the value of homework for younger children in an effort to stop a trend that has gotten out of control.

2   First of all, it's clear that homework assignments for elementary school children do not improve academic performance. A 1999 study conducted by Sandra Hofferth, a scientist at the University of Michigan's Institute for Social Research, found no link between heavy homework assignments and improved grades. Harris Cooper, Ph.D., the chairman of the Psychological Sciences Department at the University of Missouri at Columbia, is one of the top authorities on homework. Cooper claims that for kids in elementary school, "The effect of homework on achievement is trivial, if it exists at all."

3   While it's true that many parents and educators consider assignments that encourage creative thinking to be valuable, these are not the assignments children are getting for homework. Instead, they are being asked to complete dull textbook assignments that do not develop imagination or creativity.

4   Too much homework is also likely to generate angry, tearful battles at home because children dislike their dull assignments

and try to avoid doing them. Parents, in turn, must force their kids to sit down and do the work, all of which creates a tension-filled home environment. In the long run, children will only begin to dislike school and schoolwork even more. Furthermore, Boston school board president General Francis A. Walker pointed out in 1900 that homework harms children's health. Around the same time, many educators believed that homework caused tuberculosis, nervous conditions, and heart disease in youth.

5   Excessive homework also interferes with extracurricular activities, which are just as important as academic studies. Many children today are involved in sports, hobbies, and music lessons. After-school assignments make it difficult for kids to engage in these activities, which teach valuable life skills that are just as important as formal academic knowledge. Children also need time just to be kids. They need to play with their friends and have leisure time with their families. As child psychiatrist Stanley I. Greenspan, M.D., has pointed out, in his book *The Irreducible Needs of Children*, a child needs a variety of nonacademic activities to grow into a whole person. That's why school districts should follow the lead of the East Porter Country School Board in Indiana. In 1998, the board adopted a policy requiring school personnel to coordinate assignments so that students do not have to devote their entire evening to homework.

6   The drawbacks to homework outweigh the benefits. Let's stop pretending that it's helping kids achieve and keep schoolwork in the schools.

1. What is the author's point?

    _____

    _____

2. What four reasons does the author give to support his point of view?

    a. _____

    _____

    b. _____

    _____

    c. _____

    _____

d. _____

_____

3. Does the author include any of the following?

   a. examples or illustrations

   b. research results

   c. expert opinion

4. Does the author respond to any opposing point of view? _____
   If so, fill in the blanks that follow.

Opposition _____

_____

Response _____

_____

5. Circle one or more of the appropriate letters to indicate the presence or absence of errors in the author's argument.

   a. irrelevant reason

   b. circular reasoning

   c. hasty generalization

   d. unidentified or inappropriate expert

   e. unidentified or dated research

   f. no errors

3. Serving the Nation: A Universal Call

1 Israel requires all of its young men to serve three years of mandatory military service. The Israeli Defense Force drafts women, too, but not for combat positions. Sweden does not have a professional army. Instead, all of its younger men train for military service and then remain in the reserves until age forty-seven. The United States would do well to follow suit and require all of its young men and women to serve in the military for one or two years after leaving high school.

2 Opponents of compulsory service object that universal conscription* would cost too much. They argue that Americans won't permit an increase in taxes to fund a significantly larger

_____

*conscription: drafting for military service.

military. However, these critics forget that freedom is not free. All Americans should have the opportunity to serve their country. Also, learning to defend one's homeland is a patriotic obligation. Therefore, young people should be proud to devote a short time of their lives to fulfill an important civic responsibility.

3   This country needs compulsory military service in order to train its citizens to combat terrorism and to give them the skills to respond to threats and attacks of any kind. After World War II in 1945, President Truman noted that America's "geographic security is gone—gone with the advent of the atomic bomb, the rocket, and modern airborne armies." Yet fewer than 6 percent of Americans under the age of sixty-five know anything about military service. The rest of the population relies on a relatively small number of servicemen and women to protect them. This is a dangerous state of affairs given that the twenty-first century has ushered in a new age of warfare, one that often takes the form of attacks on innocent civilians. Americans can no longer be complacent or expect others to guard their safety. All citizens need to learn the specialized communication, emergency response, and civil defense skills necessary for combating various kinds of threats to the nation's security.

4   Mandatory military service would also help close the social gap that currently divides Americans from one another. According to journalism professor and naval reservist Philip Meyer, "One of the unplanned consequences of the military draft was a great leveling effect, where social-class distinctions were set aside." Unfortunately, once World War II came to an end, that leveling effect was no longer so powerful, and the country began to divide into separate and often unequal social groups. If all young men and women were once again required to serve together as equals, democratic ideals would be reinforced, and divisions between people of different classes would be narrowed.

5   In an era when America is threatened by suicide bombers and bioterrorism, it makes sense for all citizens to participate in basic military training. One to two years of service is a small price to pay for a stronger defense and greater national unity.

1. What is the author's point?

    _____

    _____

2. What two reasons does the author give to support his point of view?

    a. _____

    _____

    b. _____

    _____

3. Does the author include any of the following?

    a. examples or illustrations

    b. research results

    c. expert opinion

4. Does the author respond to any opposing point of view? _____ If so, fill in the blanks that follow.

Opposition   _____

   _____

Response   _____

   _____

5. Circle one or more of the appropriate letters to indicate the presence or absence of errors in the author's argument.

    a. irrelevant reason

    b. circular reasoning

    c. hasty generalization

    d. unidentified or inappropriate expert

    e. unidentified or dated research

    f. no errors

4. **Information About Anthrax Helps Calm Panic**

1 In the autumn of 2001, a wave of anthrax contaminations raised the possibility that America might be subjected to biological warfare. And it's certainly true that disease-causing microorganisms can be used as instruments of terror. Yet despite constant media speculation that our country's enemies might drop deadly anthrax bacteria from the skies or dump it into our waters, this particular biological weapon could probably not be used on a

massive scale. No matter what the media hype, there are three reasons why large-scale bioterrorism with anthrax would be difficult to achieve.

2   First of all, infecting large numbers of people would require specific types and large amounts of the deadly anthrax microorganism. Killer forms of anthrax, for example, must be manufactured in a laboratory by people who know which strains can be developed into lethal weapons. Then, once a fatal strain is actually produced, it must still be delivered in large enough quantities to infect a person. A toxic dose of anthrax is defined as 8,000 to 10,000 spores. Also, this quantity must be inhaled in order to fatally infect an individual. It has to be inhaled because anthrax-induced infections of the skin are fatal in only about 25 percent of cases.

3   Distributing anthrax on a large scale is another problem terrorists would face. For example, lethal anthrax spores would have to be ground finely enough to be inhaled. Each spore would have to be no larger than five microns. If the spores were dropped from airplanes, the wind would disperse the spores. This would make it unlikely that one individual could inhale enough of them to cause a fatal infection. Indoors, filters in buildings' ventilation systems would cleanse the majority of spores from the air.

4   Third, health care professionals can treat anthrax infections, with an arsenal of antibiotics. As talk show host Oprah Winfrey has assured the public, "There are plenty of drugs that can be used safely and effectively." So far, she claims, no anthrax strains have shown any resistance to antibiotics like penicillin and the tetracyclines. According to America's secretary of health and human services, Tommy Thompson, eight staging areas around the country are each stocked with 50 tons of medical supplies, including vaccines, antibiotics, gas masks, and ventilators. These supplies can be moved within hours to the site of a bioterrorist attack.

5   Yes, the American public should stay informed about the possible dangers of a bioterrorist attack. But people should not panic or let fear restrict their movements. Biological weapons are a reality, yet the likelihood of a successful large-scale attack is very slight.

1. What is the author's point?

_____

_____

2. What three reasons does the author give to support his point of view?

   a. _____

   _____

   b. _____

   _____

   c. _____

   _____

3. Does the author include any of the following?

   a. examples or illustrations

   b. research results

   c. expert opinion

4. Does the author respond to any opposing point of view? _____ If so, fill in the blanks that follow.

   Opposition _____

   _____

   Response _____

   _____

5. Circle one or more of the appropriate letters to indicate the presence or absence of errors in the author's argument.

   a. irrelevant reason

   b. circular reasoning

   c. hasty generalization

   d. unidentified or inappropriate expert

   e. unidentified or dated research

   f. no errors

C H A P T E R   1 2

Reading and Responding to Essay Questions

In this chapter, you'll learn

- **how to analyze essay questions.**
- **how to recognize key words in essay questions.**
- **how to write focused and complete answers.**

Like many students, you're probably anxious about essay exams. You may assume that you have a fighting chance with multiple-choice questions, but essay questions strike real fear into your heart. If that's how you feel, take a deep breath and relax. In working your way through *Reading for Thinking,* you've already mastered the skills you need to do well on essay exams. You already know how to identify topics, draw inferences, distinguish between fact and opinion,

and evaluate arguments. Chapter 12 shows you how to put together all these skills and use them to take and pass essay exams.

 ## The Three *Rs* of Passing Exams: Review, Review, Review

Chapter 1 encouraged you to review a chapter section right after you finish reading it. Chapter 2 talked about reviewing for exams by answering potential test questions you jotted in the margins. Chapter 5 suggested you summarize and synthesize your notes until you had only a few pages to review the night before the exam. Got the message? The reading and writing strategies outlined here will definitely help you do well on essay exams, but even they can't take the place of systematic reviews before the test.

 ## Reading Essay Questions

Nervous about the exam and anxious to get started, many inexperienced test takers skim the question and plunge into writing the answer. That's a mistake. Essay questions demand the kind of close and careful reading described in the pages that follow.

Identifying the Topic and Requirements

Your goal in analyzing an essay question is to discover the two essential elements of every essay question: the topic and the requirement or requirements. The topic of an essay question is like the topic of a paragraph. It's the subject you need to discuss. The requirements tell you how to approach or handle the topic.

Defining the Topic

Look at the following essay question. As you read it, ask yourself "What word or phrase most effectively sums up the topic?"

On occasion, Mark Twain's novel *Huckleberry Finn* has been criticized for its supposed racism. Yet according to Twain expert Mark

Fischer, Twain's novel is actually an attack on the institution of slavery, and the true hero of the novel is *not* Huck, but Jim. Begin your essay by summarizing Professor Fischer's argument. Then explain why you do or do not agree with it. Be sure to use evidence from the text to argue your position.

What is the topic of the question: (1) Mark Twain's novel *Huckleberry Finn*, (2) Mark Fischer's view of *Huckleberry Finn*, or (3) racism in the work of Mark Twain? If you chose topic 2, you're absolutely right. The sample essay question does not ask for a general discussion of the novel—its setting, characters, and themes. Nor does it ask you to go beyond *Huckleberry Finn* and look for evidence of racism in Twain's other works. The topic of the question is narrower than that. It focuses on Mark Fischer's defense of *Huckleberry Finn*. Your answer to the question should do the same.

Understanding the Requirements

Every essay question has one or more requirements, or tasks, that your answer must fulfill. Let's look again at that sample essay question about Mark Twain. How many requirements does it have? In other words, how many tasks must you complete in your answer in order to get full credit: one, two, or three?

On occasion, Mark Twain's novel *Huckleberry Finn* has been criticized for its supposed racism. Yet according to Twain expert Mark Fischer, Twain's novel is actually an attack on the institution of slavery, and the true hero of the novel is *not* Huck, but Jim. Begin your essay by summarizing Professor Fischer's argument. Then explain why you do or do not agree with it. Be sure to use evidence from the text to argue your position.

This essay question has three requirements: (1) summarize Professor Fischer's position, (2) explain why you agree or disagree, and (3) use evidence from the text. If you failed to do any one of these, your exam score would suffer. That's why reading closely to determine all the requirements of an essay question is so important.

Key Words Help Identify Requirements

To determine exactly how many requirements you need to fulfill, pay close attention to words like *who, where, why, when, which,* and *how.* They frequently introduce a specific requirement of the essay question, often one that asks you to recall an important fact before you express an opinion or take a stand.

However, you should also familiarize yourself with the words listed below. Words like *argue, describe,* and *summarize* frequently introduce the individual requirements in an essay question.

Key Words on Essay Exams

Analyze	Divide or break a large whole into parts and comment on one or more of the parts, showing how it relates to the whole or reveals an underlying meaning.	*Analyze* the following excerpt from James Madison's *Federalist Papers* and show how it reveals his bias in favor of the wealthy.
Apply	Show how a principle or theory is illustrated in a particular instance or process.	*Apply* the Doppler effect to the behavior of light and sound waves.
Argue	Express a definite point of view and make it convincing through specific reasons, illustrations, and studies.	*Argue* the positive or negative effect of the *Miranda* decision on the American legal system.
Compare and Contrast	Describe how two topics are both similar and different. *Note:* Some essay questions may only use the word *compare,* but that almost always means point out similarities *and* differences.	*Compare and contrast* the leadership roles played by Grant and Lee during the Civil War.
Criticize	Explain the positive and negative effects of a particular decision, argument, or stand. *Note:* Sometimes instructors use the word *criticize* to ask for a summation of negative effects. If the meaning is not clear from the context, clarify it with your instructor.	*Criticize* the current regulations governing the use of pesticides in agriculture.
Define	Give a full and complete meaning, preferably one that includes an example or two and some history of how the term came into being.	*Define* "Manifest Destiny" and explain its effect on the American West.

Describe	Tell how something looks or happens. Supply specific details.	*Describe* how Benjamin Franklin came to develop his theory of positive and negative charges.
Discuss	Give the details of a situation, stand, or decision. Then explain the consequences.	*Discuss* the role of California governor Earl Warren in the government's decision to intern Japanese Americans during World War II.
Evaluate	Explain the pros and cons of a situation or point of view and take a stand based on your evaluation.	*Evaluate* Richard Nixon's role in the shaping of U.S. policy toward China.
Illustrate	Give examples that clarify a point or show how something works.	*Illustrate* the different ways in which lasers have revolutionized the treatment of heart disease.
Interpret	Explain the meaning of a statement and give examples.	*Interpret* Edward L. Bernays's claim that "propaganda is only another word for education."
Show	Give examples. *Note:* This verb is usually used in combination with one of the other words listed here.	*Trace* the highlights of Lenny Bruce's career and *show* how he affected the next generation of American comedians.
Summarize	Cover the most essential points of a theory, discovery, or event.	*Summarize* the results of the Kefauver hearings on organized crime.
Trace	Step-by-step, explain how something happened (or happens) over a period of time.	*Trace* the chain of events that led to the Clean Air and Water Act.

What If the Question's Not a Question?

In the best of all possible worlds, essay requirements would always be neatly and clearly stated, as they are in the following example.

> Define the term "republicanism"* and explain why the framers of the Constitution chose it over "direct democracy."

*republicanism: form of government in which decisions are made by elected officials.

This question asks you to do two things: (1) define the term "republicanism" and (2) explain why the framers of the Constitution chose republicanism over "direct democracy." For an essay question, the requirements are pretty clear-cut. But what about this next question: Does it also neatly spell out its requirements?

> Compare the use of participant and nonparticipant observation in sociological research.[1]

This kind of vaguely formulated essay question really benefits from a critical reading that teases out its hidden questions: (1) What do the terms *participant* and *nonparticipant observation* mean? (2) In what ways are they different or similar?

If an essay question is vague, don't just run with it and hope for the best. Instead, do a critical reading to infer the question or questions it implies.

CHECK YOUR UNDERSTANDING

What two key elements should you look for in every essay question?

_____

_____

◄─ EXERCISE 1

DIRECTIONS Read each essay question. When you finish, answer the questions by filling in the blanks or circling the correct response.

EXAMPLE In the 1952 election, Dwight D. Eisenhower was the first presidential candidate to make effective use of television as part of his campaign. In your essay, identify the media adviser Ike relied upon and explain how and why he needed television to promote his candidacy.

1. The topic of this essay question is
   a. Dwight D. Eisenhower.
   b. Dwight D. Eisenhower's use of television in the 1952 presidential campaign.
   c. the media's role in the shaping of presidential candidates.

---

[1]Example comes from Gregory S. Galica, *The Blue Book*. New York: Harcourt, Brace, 1991, p. 40.

2. How many requirements are there? __3__

3. List each one separately.

   a. *Identify Ike's media adviser.* _____

   b. *Explain how Ike used television.* _____

   c. *Explain why Ike needed television.* _____

   _____

EXPLANATION In this case, you are not being asked to discuss the life and times of Dwight D. Eisenhower or the role of the media in presenting candidates to the public. The focus of the question is a good deal more specific. You're being asked to discuss Dwight D. Eisenhower's use of television in the 1952 presidential campaign—topic *b.*

1. Identify the historical event that provoked the internment of Japanese Americans and describe the arguments used to justify that policy. Outline the Supreme Court decisions that first justified and then criticized the policy of internment.

   1. The topic of this essay question is

      a. the role of Japanese Americans during World War II.

      b. hysteria during World War II.

      c. the internment of Japanese Americans during World War II.

   2. How many requirements are there? _____

   3. List each one separately.

      _____

      _____

      _____

      _____

2. Name and describe the four theories of motivation commonly used to explain behavior.

   1. The topic of this essay question is

      a. studies of motivation.

      b. the four theories of motivation.

      c. behavior modification.

2. How many requirements are there? _____

3. List each one separately.

_____

_____

_____

_____

3. Writer Gabriel García Márquez has been called a *magical realist.* Define that term and provide at least three examples of it from García Márquez's most famous work, *One Hundred Years of Solitude.*

1. The topic of this essay question is

   a. Gabriel García Márquez's effect on Latin American literature.

   b. Latin American literature in the twentieth century.

   c. magical realism in the work of Gabriel García Márquez.

2. How many requirements are there? _____

3. List each one separately.

_____

_____

_____

_____

4. Identify and define the five different styles of responding to conflict. Give a brief illustration of each one and explain both the advantages and disadvantages of each response.

1. The topic of this essay question is

   a. conflict.

   b. styles of conflict.

   c. response theory.

2. How many requirements are there? _____

3. List each one separately.

_____

_____

_____

_____

5. Describe William James's theory of the emotions. Then compare and contrast it with Cannon's theory of emotional response.

1. The topic of this essay question is

   a. William James.

   b. William James's theory of emotions.

   c. Cannon's theory of emotional response.

2. How many requirements are there? _____

3. List each one separately.

_____

_____

_____

_____

EXERCISE 2

DIRECTIONS Read the following excerpts. For each one, write an essay question that you think would test a reader's understanding of the material.

EXAMPLE

Developing an Ego Ideal

1 In his book _Fire in the Belly,_ author and activist Sam Keen offers an intriguing theory of how men and women develop their _ego ideal,_ the heroic being they aspire to be even if they never quite achieve their goal. For Keen, the mind of each person contains a mental Hall of Fame in which live the heroes and heroines of the moment. Our personal Hall of Fame may contain people in the news because of heroic achievements, but it can also contain people we know personally and admire because of their talent, wit, beauty, or character. One's internal Hall of Fame might include figures as diverse as the singer Queen Latifah, the runner Jesse Owens, and the director John Sayles, lined up right alongside your mother and favorite aunt. In his own Hall of Fame, Keen includes people such as the philosopher Soren Kierkegaard and Keen's wife, Jan.

2   But our ego ideal is not based solely on who lives in our Hall of Fame. According to Keen, we also compile, as the years go on, an internal Hall of Exemplars.* The people in this hall do not necessarily have anything to do with current events. Nor are they there because of some personal relationship to us. The Hall of Exemplars contains men and women who have been or will be honored throughout the ages because of their contributions to humanity. In Keen's case, the Hall of Exemplars contains figures like Jesus, Gandhi, Buddha, and Mother Teresa.

3   From Keen's point of view, the Hall of Exemplars and the Hall of Fame work together to help shape who we are and what we hope to be. The internalized* images living in the Hall of Fame help guide particular aspects of behavior. We decide, for example, that we want to be talented like Queen Latifah and determined like Aunt Betty, and we strive as much as possible to be like them. Members of the Hall of Exemplars, in contrast, act as our moral compass. They tell us what we could or should do to make the world a better place. They remind us that there is, indeed, a world beyond the self, one that deserves and requires our attention.

Essay Question   *Summarize Sam Keen's theory of how we define our ego ideal, making sure to explain the difference between the Hall of Fame and the Hall of Exemplars.*

EXPLANATION This is a good essay question because it tests the reader's understanding of Keen's theory. If you can summarize Keen's theory, then you've understood it. The question also picks up on and reflects a key point of the passage: the difference between the Hall of Fame and the Hall of Exemplars.

1. The Advent of Polio as an Epidemic

1   Poliomyelitis, more commonly known as polio, is an infectious disease caused by a virus that usually enters through the mouth and takes up residence in the throat and intestinal tract. Actually, there are three different forms of polio, each caused by a separate virus. However, only one of those three viruses can destroy nerve cells and cause lasting paralysis. Tragically, this was the virus that spread through the United States in the 1940s and '50s, leaving in its wake around 650,000 paralyzed children.

2   Ironically, the advent of polio as a treacherous, and sometimes deadly, disease was caused by advances in hygiene. Prior to the

---

*exemplars: people worthy of imitation, role models.
*internalized: taken within, made part of the self.

turn of the century, open sewers were everywhere and children were exposed to the polio viruses early on. As a result, they developed an immunity to the disease, usually by the age of six. Once the sewers were closed, the early exposure was gone and so was the childhood immunity. In 1916, the first polio epidemic hit the United States, and after that, not a year went by without another epidemic. By 1957, a vaccine was finally available—thanks to the work of Jonas Salk—and the threat of polio, while it didn't disappear altogether, was seriously diminished. In 1952, the disease had taken its toll on 52,000 victims, most of them children. By 1960, there were only 3,000 reported cases.

Essay Question _____

_____

_____

2. Three Types of Conversations

1   There are three types of conversations we have with others: monologues, technical dialogues, and dialogues (Buber, 1958). *Monologues* are self-centered conversations in which other people are treated as objects. When we engage in monologues, we do *not* see others as unique people or take their needs into consideration. We are engaging in monologues any time we focus on ourselves and do *not* take the other person into consideration or adjust what we say and do to what the other person says and does.

2   Often when we engage in monologues we are being conversational narcissists. *Conversational narcissism* is the "way conversationalists turn the topics of ordinary conversations to themselves without sustained interest in others' topics" (Derber, 1979, p. 5).

3   Narcissistic communication occurs when we emphasize our self-importance by boasting or using terms others do not understand, when we exploit others by shifting responses to ourselves or talking for long periods, when we engage in exhibitionism by using exaggerated facial expressions or making ourselves the focal point of conversations, and when we are nonresponsive to others by "glazing over" or being impatient when they are talking (Vangelisti, Knapp, & Daly, 1990).

4   *Technical dialogues* are information-centered conversations. The purpose of the conversation is to exchange information with the other person, *not* make a connection with the other person. Monologues and technical dialogues are necessary and appropriate at times, but problems emerge when they are used too frequently, because this leads to a lack of connection between the participants.

5   In *dialogues*, other people are not treated as objects. Rather, they are seen as unique humans. The goal of dialogue is *not* to use or change other people, but to understand them. In a dialogue, there is a search for mutuality (Buber, 1958). Goals and expectations do not come between the two people. Rather, what goes on between the two people is the focus. Participants in a dialogue adjust their goals and messages depending on what is taking place in the conversation. Each participant's feeling of control and ownership is minimized. Each participant confirms the other, even when conflict occurs. It is this mutual confirmation that allows us to be human (Buber, 1958). (Gudykunst et al., *Building Bridges*, pp. 96–97.)

Essay Question _____

_____

_____

 # Responding to Essay Questions: Getting Organized

Once you've analyzed and paraphrased the question, technically you're ready to start writing. But hold on a moment; this is the time to take a minute and get your thoughts organized.

Start with an Outline

Making a rough outline is one of the best ways to make sure your answer is complete and focused. Remember the question about Dwight D. Eisenhower's use of television in the 1952 campaign? Here's an informal outline listing the *absolutely essential* points—the ones that need to be fleshed out in the answer. Notice how each part of the outline is labeled to indicate which part of the question it answers. Annotations like these are a good way to get your thoughts organized before you begin writing.

who—1. Rosser Reeves was Ike's main media consultant.

why—2. Everyone horrified by how old and bland Eisenhower was coming across in campaign

how—3. Television spots with USP (Unique Selling Proposition)—based on Rosser's commercial experience

4. Reeves polled *Reader's Digest* for best image—Ike "Man of Peace" won

5. Flooded states where Eisenhower not doing well with TV spots

6. Transformed Ike into a statesman and he won the election

With an outline like the one above to guide you, you can be assured that you'll write an essay that focuses on the question and doesn't ramble away from the topic.

Watch the Time

Essential as it is to outline your answer, don't let it take up too much time. Your outline should take no more than a few minutes, so keep an eye on the clock.

EXERCISE 3

DIRECTIONS Take one of the essay questions you created for Exercise 2 and make a rough outline of the key points a good answer would cover. To illustrate, here's a rough outline for an answer to the sample essay question on page 505.

EXAMPLE

1. *We are defined by the people we admire.*
   —who you admire says who you want to be

2. *"Hall of Fame": people who are heroes for the moment.*
   —leaders, friends, achievers, heroes of the moment

3. *"Hall of Exemplars": people who expand our sense of what it means to be human, like Jesus and Gandhi.*

Writing to the Point

With some modification, you can apply to essay exams everything you've learned about writing to inform or persuade. Only this time, you're the writer who has to take your instructor-reader into account, making sure that you present your information effectively and argue your point convincingly.

Skip the Introduction

In your writing courses, you may have been encouraged to write creative introductions designed to stimulate your reader's interest. That instruction, however, does not apply to essay exams where you need to get right to the point and show your instructor that you have mastered the material on the exam.

Open with a General Answer to the Essay Question

The first sentence or two of your answer should generally outline how you intend to answer the question. To make sure your teacher understands that your answer will address the question asked, try to restate a portion of the question at the very beginning of your essay. Imagine, for example, that you were answering this question: "Describe the methods television news programs utilize in an effort to make current events visually exciting." Your answer could begin with a statement like this:

> Television news programs use three different methods to make their news coverage visually exciting: staging, tape doctoring, and ambush interviewing.

In effect, this is the thesis statement of your essay answer, and it does two things. First, by restating the topic—"methods used to make current events visually exciting"—it tells your instructor that you've understood the focus of the question and are going to respond appropriately. Second, it gives your instructor a mental blueprint to follow. That blueprint says your answer will have three parts to it. It also says that each of the three parts will be addressed according to the order indicated in your opening thesis statement.

◼ EXERCISE 4

DIRECTIONS Read each essay question. Then look at the opening statements that follow. Circle the letter of the statement that seems to respond most directly to the essay question.

EXAMPLE

Essay Question The view that "news" is simply what happens doesn't fit the reality. No form of mass media can carry every newsworthy event. It's up to reporters, editors, and publishers to decide what is news. In your essay, describe and illustrate the criteria used to select newsworthy stories.

Opening Statements

a. Unfortunately, most local news programs are committed to the old saying, "If it bleeds, it leads." In other words, if there's a lot of blood and gore in a local story, that story will get the most air time. The sad truth, then, is that local news programs spend less and less time on political issues. Politics, unless there's a scandal involved, isn't bloody enough.

(b.) Reporters, editors, and publishers are the ones who decide what is news because they decide which events are worthy of being reported, and they make their decisions on the basis of how these three questions are answered: (1) Is it timely or novel? (2) Is there any violence, conflict, or scandal? and (3) Are the people involved familiar to the public?

EXPLANATION Answer *b* is correct because it restates part of the essay question and lays out in general terms what the answer will accomplish. Answer *a* goes off in the wrong direction, focusing strictly on local news when the question addresses news on a broader scale.

Essay Question

1. By the 1920s, the Ku Klux Klan, formerly restricted to rural areas, had made inroads into several of America's biggest cities. What city was the exception to the Klan's invasion and why did it escape Klan influence?

Opening Statements

a. In the 1920s, New York City was the only racially diverse metropolis* to escape the influence of the Ku Klux Klan. Klan groups, called "Klaverns," were founded in New York City, but the opposition to them—from both the media and the local government— was so strong that the Klan eventually gave up hope of taking hold in New York City.

b. How did the Ku Klux Klan become an urban phenomenon?* According to Kenneth Jackson, the author of *The Ku Klux Klan in the City, 1915–1930*, the Klan claimed two to five million members in the 1920s, and many of these members lived in big cities. The Klan found a foothold in the cities because it had expanded its circle of hatred to include immigrants as well as African Americans.

Essay Question

2. The American mass media are relatively free of government restrictions. Nevertheless, the government does exercise some control over radio and television. In your essay, identify and describe the two ways in which the government regulates and, to some degree, controls these two media.

---

*metropolis: big city.
*phenomenon: an occurrence or event that is observable to the senses.

Opening
Statements

a. In 1934, Congress created the Federal Communications Commission (FCC); that agency has the power to monitor and regulate the use of the airwaves. For that very reason, the FCC has often been the target of lobbyists who want the FCC to exercise greater or lesser control.

b. Government licensing and the equal time rule are the two primary ways in which the Federal Communications Commission, founded by Congress in 1934, regulates both radio and television.

 ## Don't Skimp on Details

When you take an essay exam, you need to keep in mind your relationship to your instructor-reader. Of course, your instructor already knows the answer to the question posed on the exam, but that doesn't mean you are free to skimp on supporting details. Instructors give exams to test *your* knowledge of the subject matter they teach. Therefore, you need to answer exam questions as fully and completely as possible. A detailed answer is your way of saying, "I have mastered and am in command of the material covered by this question."

 ## Give Partial Answers When Necessary

Unfortunately, there may well be a time or two when you look at an essay question and just aren't sure how to answer all of the parts. If that should happen, don't freeze and give up. Instead, figure out what parts of the question you can answer and concentrate on those. When it comes to an essay exam, a partial answer is always better than none. In fact, if you run out of time while you're answering an essay question, include your outline when you turn in your test booklet. The purpose of turning in the outline is to show your instructor that you do know the answer, even if you didn't have time to get it down on paper.

 ## Become a Critical Reader

Imagine that you've finished writing your answer and that you've still got ten or fifteen minutes before the exam comes to an end. Do you get up, turn in your blue book, and trot out the door, happy the exam is over? Not on your life. This is the time to assume the role of critical reader—someone who objectively evaluates both content and style. The key word is *objectively*. The fact that it's your own writing you are evaluating does not mean you should relax your critical standards. If you think the opinion you expressed comes up short on evidence, spend a few minutes thinking about another example or study you might add. Because you may need to make some last-minute changes to your answer, it's always a good idea to write on every other line of your exam booklet. When you have to add something, there's space available.

In evaluating your essay answer, the key word is *clarity*. Check your sentences to make sure they say what you want them to. If you need to, add transitions to make sure that your reader can move smoothly from one sentence to the next. Here again, don't rely on the instructor to fill in the gaps. That task is yours, not your instructor's.

In the last minute or two, check for errors in punctuation and grammar. Make sure, too, that your writing is legible. Cross out any words that are scribbled or scrawled and rewrite them right over the space where you have crossed them out.

◼ EXERCISE 5

DIRECTIONS After studying the example below, read the selections and essay questions that appear on pages 514–519. Look over the two possible answers for each essay question and decide which one best fits the guidelines outlined in this chapter. Indicate your choice by circling the appropriate letter.

EXAMPLE

Silence on the Supreme Court

1 Often the cases that the Supreme Court doesn't decide are just as important as the ones it does decide. Here are some cases involving claims of religious freedom that were decided by lower courts. Since the Supreme Court refused to hear an appeal of these decisions, the lower court decisions, at least for now, are the law.

2 **Reading the Bible** In a Colorado public school, classrooms occasionally have a silent reading period during which the students and teachers can read various books. One teacher silently read his Bible during this period. There is no evidence his students knew what he was reading; however, the principal of the school told the teacher he could not read the Bible because *if* the students found out it might influence them to read the Bible also. A federal court upheld the principal.

3   **Mentioning God**   A professor of physiology at the University of Alabama occasionally mentioned in class the importance to him of his Christian faith. He also gave an after-class lecture on "Evidences of God in Human Physiology." Attendance was optional. The university ordered him not to present any comments from a Christian perspective in class. A federal court upheld the university.

4   **Spouse Abuse and Religion**   The New Orleans Baptist Theological Seminary expelled a student when it learned from the police that he had abused his wife. The state courts ordered him reinstated because spouse abuse did not bear on his academic qualifications for a degree. The seminary argued that giving him a degree would entitle him to be a Baptist minister, and that spouse abuse was incompatible with a religious vocation. The seminary lost. (Source of information: Michael McConnell, "Freedom from Religion?" *The American Enterprise*, January/February 1993, pp. 32–43. In Wilson and DiIulio Jr., *American Government*, p. 558.)

Essay Question

> According to the authors of your textbook, some of the cases that the Supreme Court does *not* decide are as important as those they do. Summarize three cases that the Supreme Court refused to hear and identify the issue or topic that connected all three.

Answers   a.   Over the years, the Supreme Court has been confronted by numerous church-state issues. In one key case, the New Orleans Baptist Theological Seminary expelled a student when it learned of the student's arrest for domestic violence. According to the seminary administration, spousal abuse was incompatible with the life and work of a minister.

The Louisiana state courts disagreed, arguing that abusing his wife had nothing to do with the man's academic qualifications. When the seminary appealed the courts' decision, the Supreme Court refused to hear the appeal.

In my opinion, this was a grave mistake on the part of the Supreme Court. Domestic violence is a crime, and a criminal should not be allowed to become a minister. The Louisiana courts were wrong to reinstate him, and the Supreme Court should have taken a stand and rectified that injustice. This is clearly a case where the Supreme Court's silence spoke loud and clear on the place of women in the legal system.

b.   In at least three separate cases involving religious freedom, the Supreme Court has let stand the decisions of lower courts. In one case, for example, a teacher in a Colorado public school read his Bible during a silent reading period. However, he was forbidden to do so by the principal on the grounds that the teacher might influence his students to do the same. A federal court sided with the principal and the Supreme Court refused to hear an appeal.

In a second instance, a professor of physiology at the University of Alabama mentioned in class how important his Christian faith was to his life. He also lectured after class on the "Evidence of God in Human Physiology" and invited his students to attend. In response, the university forbade him to comment on Christianity in the classroom, and the university's decision was upheld by a federal court. Here again the Supreme Court did not intervene.

In a third case, the New Orleans Theological Seminary expelled a student who had abused his wife. The seminary administration insisted that a man who abused his wife should not be allowed to become a minister. The State of Louisiana, however, disagreed. According to the state, spousal abuse had no bearing on the man's academic performance and ordered him reinstated. The Supreme Court refused to hear an appeal, and the seminary had to abide by the state's ruling.

EXPLANATION Answer *b* is a better answer because it stays focused on the question, which has two requirements: (1) summarize three cases rejected by the Supreme Court and (2) identify the issue that connects them. Answer *a* summarizes only one case and therefore can't possibly identify the connecting thread asked for in the question.

Answer *a* also assumes information not specified in either the reading or the question—that the man was convicted of domestic violence against his wife and could, therefore, be legally considered a criminal. The writer of the answer has, in short, drawn an inappropriate inference.

1. The Rights of the Disabled

1 In 1990 the federal government passed the Americans with Disabilities Act (ADA), a sweeping law that extended many of the protections enjoyed by women and racial minorities to disabled persons.

Who Is a Disabled Person?

2 Anyone who *has* a physical or mental impairment that substantially limits one or more major life activities (for example, holding a job), anyone who has a *record* of such impairment, or anyone who is *regarded* as having such an impairment is considered disabled.

What Rights Do the Disabled Have?

3   *Employment*   The disabled may not be denied employment or promotion if, with "reasonable accommodation,"* they can perform the duties of that job. (Excluded from this protection are people who currently use illegal drugs, gamble compulsively, or are homosexual or bisexual.) Reasonable accommodation need not be made if this would cause "undue hardship" on the employer.

4   *Government Programs and Transportation*   Disabled persons may not be denied access to government programs or benefits. New buses, taxis, and trains must be accessible to disabled persons, including those in wheelchairs.

5   *Public Accommodations*   The disabled must enjoy "full and equal" access to hotels, restaurants, stores, schools, parks, museums, auditoriums, and the like. To achieve equal access, owners of existing facilities must alter them "to the maximum extent feasible"; builders of new facilities must ensure that they are readily accessible to disabled persons, unless this is structurally impossible.

6   *Telephones*   The ADA directs the Federal Communications Commission to issue regulations to ensure that telecommunications devices for hearing- and speech-impaired people are available "to the extent possible and in the most efficient manner."

7   *Congress*   The rights under this law apply to employees of Congress.

8   *Rights Compared*   The ADA does not enforce the rights of the disabled in the same way as the Civil Rights Act enforces the rights of blacks and women. Racial or gender discrimination must end *regardless of cost;* denial of access to the disabled must end unless "undue hardship" or excessive costs would result. (Wilson and DiIulio Jr., *American Government,* p. 598.)

Essay Question   The 1990 Americans with Disabilities Act guaranteed certain rights to disabled Americans. In your essay, describe who would benefit from this act and summarize the rights they would be accorded.

Answers   a. The 1990 Americans with Disabilities Act guaranteed certain rights to disabled Americans. This group was defined as people who possessed a physical or mental impairment serious enough to limit a major life activity, such as holding a job, as well as those who had a record of such an impairment and those regarded as having such an impairment.

---

*accommodation: consideration.

Anyone who fell into one of these three categories was guaranteed the following rights. They could, for example, not be denied either employment or a promotion if, "with reasonable accommodation," they could do the job. Disabled persons could also not be denied access to government programs or benefits, and new buses, trains, and taxis had to be wheelchair accessible.

In the realm of public accommodations like hotels, parks, schools, and restaurants, access for the disabled had to be made available. This meant old buildings had to be altered to make them accessible to the disabled, while new buildings had to be created with the disabled in mind.

According to the ADA, the Federal Communications Commission had to make sure that telecommunications devices for hearing- and speech-impaired people were available "to the extent possible."

Modeled on civil rights legislation, the ADA still took the cost of change into account. Whereas the law says that racial and gender discrimination must end no matter what the cost, the ADA applied the yardstick of "undue hardship" in demanding change. Thus, for example, an employer could deny employment to a disabled person who could do the job only if very special and very expensive provisions were made.

b. In 1973, Congress passed the Rehabilitation Act, which forbids discrimination against disabled persons in any program receiving federal aid. A disabled person is defined as anyone who has a physical or mental impairment that substantially limits one or more of life's major activities.

Once the act passed, federal agencies, under pressure from organizations representing the disabled, decided on a broad interpretation that would bring about sweeping changes. For example, city transit systems receiving federal aid had to make sure that buses and subways were accessible to the disabled. While disabled people were pleased with this interpretation of the act, some state and city officials took a dim view of it.

New York City's mayor at the time, Edward Koch, protested that the expenses would be too great. Koch estimated that making all buses and subways accessible was going to cost the city billions, but his protests were ignored until 1981, when the Reagan administration relaxed the requirements that buses be able to lift wheelchairs aboard.

2. Problems Facing Women in Organizations

1 When women pursue nontraditional jobs or are selected for management-level positions, they usually face two challenges: the

wage gap and the glass ceiling. At the same time, many employers are gearing up for the predicted rise in the number of women available for work by offering working women and mothers alternatives that allow them to reach their full potential. Although these alternatives offer tremendous opportunities, they also require tough choices.

The Wage Gap

2 The gap between women's and men's earnings has been shrinking in recent years, but wage inequality continues. The Bureau of Labor Statistics reports that women earn about 75 cents for every dollar men earn. This figure is somewhat misleading because the Bureau does not compare similar jobs held by men and women; it lumps together all jobs that women hold and all jobs that men hold. When surveys focus on specific fields such as engineering, banking, or accounting, women earn 85 to 95 percent of what men in similar jobs get. Wage inequality is most apparent when you compare the earnings of men and women managers. For every dollar male managers earn, women earn about 60 cents.

3 Many organizations are taking steps to deal with the problem of wage inequality. Some have adopted a comparable-worth policy, which requires that women and men be paid equally not only for the same jobs but also for jobs that require the same level of skill, effort, and responsibility, and the same working conditions. Employers who are searching for workers with specific skills have found that other characteristics such as gender or race no longer matter as much as they once did. Employers who fail to adjust unequal pay scales can be sued under the Equal Pay Act of 1963.

The Glass Ceiling

4 There is a condition in the workplace that gives women a view of top management jobs but blocks their ascent. It is often referred to as the glass ceiling. The Glass Ceiling Commission, created by the U.S. Labor Department, has documented widespread limits on career advancement for women. Its research shows that about 95 percent of senior-level managers in the largest American companies are males. Although we are seeing some positive change, especially among the middle-management ranks, women are still being held back by some widely held misconceptions. Top male executives say the major barrier for women is a lack of significant general management and life experience and less time in the "pipeline." Women in senior management positions say the *real* problems are (1) stereotyping and preconceptions of women held by men and (2) exclusion of women from informal networks of communication.

5 Many companies are helping women break through the glass ceiling. Officials at Deloitte & Touche LLP, a large Wilton, Connecticut, accounting firm, were disappointed that too few women advanced to the level of partner and many talented women were leaving the company. Officials had mistakenly assumed that women were leaving only to start families. To help women move up in the company, they launched the "Advancement of Women" initiative. All of the organization's 4,700 managers and partners were sent to a two-day workshop where they could explore work-related gender differences. The company also set up a mentoring program, made sure women received career-advancing experience, and developed more family-friendly policies. The result after three years was a 30 percent increase in women partners and reduced turnover among women. Allstate Insurance, J. C. Penney Company, and Dow Chemical Company are some other companies that have taken specific steps to make sure women move to the top.

6 Some employers mistakenly believe that women will not relocate or stick around long enough to be groomed for top-level positions. They argue that most women will get married and move as their husbands' job assignments dictate or will leave to devote themselves full-time to raising their families. These assumptions are incorrect! Studies indicate that a majority of women who quit working for large companies moved on to other companies that were more female-friendly.

7 Women who find their advancement to the top blocked, or get tired of inflexible work schedules, often start their own business. Women today own one-third of all businesses and are starting businesses at twice the rate of men. We are seeing women start companies in industries such as manufacturing and construction, areas that were virtually closed to them in the past. (Adapted from Reece and Brandt, *Effective Human Relations in Organizations*, pp. 428–430.)

Essay Question Summarize the two challenges facing women in nontraditional jobs or management positions, and identify some ways these challenges are being addressed.

Answers a. Two challenges that face women in nontraditional jobs or management positions are the wage gap and the glass ceiling. The wage gap is the discrepancy between men's and women's salaries. For example, in fields such as engineering, banking, and accounting, women earn only 85 to 95 percent of their male counterparts' salaries. The Equal Pay Act of 1963 was designed to correct the problem; this law makes it possible to sue an employer who refuses to pay men and women according to the same scale. In addition, many companies have created internal policies to ensure that men and women received equal pay for comparable work.

Even if they receive equal pay, however, women face a second challenge: the glass ceiling. This term refers to limited career advancement for women. In other words, women are blocked from attaining the higher levels of management, which has resulted in 95 percent of males filling the top senior management positions at the largest American companies. Male executives argue that women's lack of management experience causes this barrier. However, women who have managed to break through the glass ceiling maintain that women are held back by men's stereotypes and by the exclusion of women from informal networks of communication. In response to these complaints, many companies are launching initiatives to eliminate the glass ceiling. For example, organizations such as accounting firm Deloitte & Touche, LLP, Allstate Insurance, J. C. Penney Company, and Dow Chemical Company are holding workshops, setting up mentoring programs, and instituting family-friendly policies that have helped women advance into higher positions.

b. It's hard to believe, but women still don't fare as well as men in the workplace. The Bureau of Labor Statistics reports that women earn only about 75 cents for every dollar men earn. It's worse if you look at management positions. In that field, women are earning only 60 cents for every dollar their male counterparts earn. Besides lower salaries, women are also not being promoted to the top positions in companies. As a matter of fact, 95 percent of senior-level managers in the largest American companies are males.

The men blame the women for their own lack of advancement. They say that women don't have enough experience yet and that women will only leave to move with their husbands or to have children. The women blame the men for stereotyping them and for keeping them out of informal communication networks.

So the battle of the sexes rages on, and women continue to suffer as a result. Many smart, capable women have chosen to get out of corporate America altogether to start their own business. Small business ownership is still one way for women to put their talents to good use. Women business owners can rest assured that they will not be subjected to discriminatory policies and they will never hit a glass ceiling. The only limits they will face will be the ones they put on themselves.

■ DIGGING DEEPER

LOOKING AHEAD The passage on page 510 stated that the government exercises "some" control over radio and television news reporting. The following reading identifies some specific instances in which the government has needed to control the flow of information not just on radio and television, but in newspapers as well.

THE MEDIA AND GOVERNMENT SECRECY DURING WARTIME

1 Although the press often engages in voluntary censorship, there are many examples of conflict when the media dispute the government's right to censor the news. Because a shared belief in the need for freedom of the press became such a tradition very early in the life of the nation, any effort by the government to limit that freedom has always met with hostility. During the Civil War, for example, the 57th Article of War stipulated a court martial and possible death sentence for anyone, civilian and military alike, who gave military information to the enemy. However, newspapers were an indirect source of military information, and Confederate leaders went to great lengths to obtain copies of major Northern papers because they often revealed the whereabouts of military units and naval vessels. As a result, the U.S. War Department tried to prevent newspapers from publishing any stories that described the movements of troops or ships. Editors generally ignored these orders. Even after the war, General Sherman refused to shake hands with Horace Greeley, publisher of the *New York Tribune,* maintaining that Greeley's paper had caused a heavy loss of life by revealing troop movements to the enemy.

2   Thus, even in wartime Americans have questioned censorship, asking what kinds of controls should be imposed and by whom. Clearly, the government has the need to protect itself and a duty to protect the nation. However, the press claims a right to inform the public of what government is doing, and the news media maintain that the public has the right to know. Therefore, an inherent conflict exists between the right to a free press and the need to control information that would be damaging to the government.

3   The conflict between government and the press has grown in recent decades, as the government itself has increased in size.

Since World War II we have supported a giant defense establishment, a complex network of foreign relationships, and a uniquely powerful nuclear arsenal. Government secrecy grew with all of these developments. The majority of editors and publishers cooperate with the government in maintaining secrecy when national security is clearly at stake. However, as a host of government bureaucrats classify thousands and thousands of secret documents each year, the press—and the public—often wondered how many of these secrets protected national security and how many protected the government from embarrassment. It is often difficult to determine what is being protected, or at what point a secret becomes so damaging to the national interest that the constitutional guarantee of free speech should be overruled. The historic case of the Pentagon Papers illustrates these questions dramatically.

4   During the Johnson administration, the Defense Department put together a forty-seven-volume history of American involvement in Vietnam from 1945 to 1967, including secret cables, memos, and other documents. The history, which came to be known as the "Pentagon Papers," was classified as *top secret*. In 1971, Daniel Ellsberg, who had worked on the papers but later opposed the war, leaked them to the *New York Times*, hoping that their release would turn public opinion against the war and help bring about its end. Although the papers were both stolen and classified, the *Times* began publishing a series of articles summarizing the contents and some of the documents themselves.

5   The Nixon administration went to court to stop the *Times* (and later other newspapers) from printing additional articles on the papers, arguing that their publication would endanger national security. In response, the courts issued a temporary restraining order stopping the *Times* from continuing its planned series on the papers.

6   Eventually, the case went to the Supreme Court, which ruled against the government. The government had failed to convince the Court that publication of the Pentagon Papers constituted a danger severe enough to warrant suspending freedom of the press. Relieved and triumphant, the newspapers resumed their articles. (Ellsberg was later tried for stealing the documents.) Yet the Court's decision in the Pentagon Papers case is still regarded as controversial and it resolved little of the debate between government and the press. Conflict continues over the press's right to publish, the public's right to know, and the government's need to protect the secrecy of some activities. (DeFleur and Dennis, *Understanding Mass Communication*, 1998, pp. 512–514.)

Sharpening Your Skills

DIRECTIONS Answer the following questions by filling in the blanks or circling the letter of the correct response.

1. Which statement most effectively expresses the main idea of the reading?

   a. The Supreme Court's decision on the Pentagon Papers remains controversial to this day.

   b. The press and the government do not always agree on the subject of censorship.

   c. Censorship of the press was at its highest during the Johnson administration.

   d. During wartime, most journalists will voluntarily censor themselves.

2. During the Civil War, the U.S. government tried to prevent newspapers from publishing any stories about ship or troop movements. Why did the government take this position?

   _____

3. How would you paraphrase the government's argument in favor of press censorship?

   _____

   _____

4. How would you paraphrase the press's argument against censorship during wartime?

   _____

   _____

5. Why does the author spend so much time describing the Pentagon Papers?

   a. The Pentagon Papers illustrate how one man can bring down a government.

   b. The Pentagon Papers illustrate the conflict between the press's right to publish and the government's need to keep some activities secret.

   c. The case of the Pentagon Papers illustrates how deeply Richard Nixon hated the *New York Times*.

   d. The Pentagon Papers offered concrete proof of the government's dishonesty during the Vietnam War.

6. In terms of personal bias, how would you describe this reading?

    a. The authors are inclined to favor freedom of the press even during wartime.

    b. The authors are in favor of the government's need for secrecy particularly during wartime.

    c. It's impossible to determine the authors' personal bias.

Please explain how you arrived at your answer.

_____

_____

7. How would you describe the author's tone? _____

8. Is the following statement a fact or an opinion? "An inherent conflict exists between the right to a free press and the need to control information that would be damaging to the government." _____

Explain your answer.

_____

9. Read the following test question carefully. Then identify the topic of the question and the number of requirements.

Essay Question

> Describe the inherent conflict between the government's need to control information and the press's duty to inform the public. Explain why the Pentagon Papers are a good illustration of this conflict.

    a. The topic of this question is _____.

    b. The question has _____ requirements.

10. Give your personal opinion about the government's need to censor the press during times of war. Should the press be censored or not? Then give two reasons for your position.

Opinion _____

_____

Reasons _____

_____

WORD NOTES: PHENOMENA OR PHENOMENONS?

Page 510 introduced the word *phenomenon*, meaning "an occurrence or event observable to the senses." But like many other words, this word has more than one meaning. The word *phenomenon* can refer to "an unusual or unaccountable fact," as in "The comet was a once-in-a-century phenomenon." It can also refer to a person who is remarkable or outstanding, as in "He was already a musical phenomenon at the age of nine." When *phenomenon* is used to identify someone or something remarkable, its plural form is *phenomenons.* However, if the word is used to describe something observable by the senses, then the plural form is *phenomena.*

Use the correct plural form of *phenomenon* to fill in the blanks.

1. The brothers were literary _____; they had both published first novels at the age of twenty.

2. Shooting stars are natural _____ in this part of the country.

Now it's your turn to use each plural in a sentence.

1. phenomena: _____

_____

_____

2. phenomenons: _____

_____

_____

Test 1: Reviewing the Key Points

DIRECTIONS Answer the following questions by filling in the blanks or circling the letter of the correct response.

1. Test takers need to read questions carefully in order to discover the _____ and the _____ of the question.

2. Which of the following words is not common in essay questions?
   a. trace
   b. define
   c. summarize
   d. vary

3. When an essay question is vague, test takers need to

   _____.

4. Creating an informal outline for the answer to an essay question should take no more than _____.

5. *True* or *False.* In essays written for tests, a smooth introduction is important.

6. To make sure your teacher understands that your answer addresses the question try to

   _____.

7. *True* or *False.* If you don't have a complete answer to an essay question, don't bother submitting a partial one.

8. *True* or *False.* If you've completed your answer to an essay question and still have ten or fifteen minutes left, don't change a thing. Your first response is almost always the best.

9. In evaluating your essay answer, you need to assume the role of a _____ who _____.

10. *True* or *False.* Because your instructor knows the material covered on the test, you don't need to be fussy about how sentences connect. Your instructor can always fill in the gaps.

Test 2: Analyzing Essay Questions

DIRECTIONS Circle the letter of the correct answer.

1. In 1535, English scholar and statesman Sir Thomas More was beheaded for refusing to comply with the Act of Supremacy. What was the Act of Supremacy, and why was More willing to die rather than uphold it?

   The topic of this question is

   a. political controversy in sixteenth-century England.

   b. Thomas More's refusal to comply with the Act of Supremacy.

   c. Thomas More's political career in the court of Henry VIII.

   The question has

   a. one requirement.

   b. two requirements.

   c. three requirements.

   d. four requirements.

2. Writer Budd Schulberg has called boxer Muhammad Ali "America's Paul Bunyan." Summarize the myth of Paul Bunyan. Then trace the highlights of Ali's career and show why the allusion to Paul Bunyan is an appropriate one.

   The topic of this question is

   a. Budd Schulberg's career as a critic of boxing.

   b. Paul Bunyan.

   c. Paul Bunyan and Muhammad Ali.

   The question has

   a. one requirement.

   b. two requirements.

   c. three requirements.

   d. four requirements.

3. What three antitrust acts were passed between 1890 and 1914,* and what specific effects did they have on existing business practices?

   _____
   *The Sherman Act (1890), the Federal Trade Commission Act (1914), and the Clayton Act (1914).

The topic of this question is

a. American corporations in the late nineteenth century.

b. antitrust legislation in the late nineteenth and early twentieth centuries.

c. antitrust legislation in the late nineteenth century.

The question has

a. one requirement.

b. two requirements.

c. three requirements.

d. four requirements.

4. Describe the Supreme Court controversy known as *Marbury v. Madison,* making sure to explain the roles of John Marshall and James Madison. How was this case resolved, and what effect did it have on the government of Thomas Jefferson?

The topic of this question is

a. James Madison.

b. *Marbury v. Madison.*

c. Thomas Jefferson.

The question has

a. one requirement.

b. two requirements.

c. three requirements.

d. four requirements.

5. Who was Charles Katz, and how did the case *Katz v. United States* affect the role of privacy in search and seizure cases?

The topic of this question is

a. the American justice system.

b. *Katz v. United States.*

c. the role of private property in search and seizure cases.

The question has

a. one requirement.

b. two requirements.

c. three requirements.

d. four requirements.

Test 3: Analyzing Essay Questions

DIRECTIONS Circle the letter of the correct answer.

1. Summarize both sides of the controversy over the use of animals in scientific research. Then state your own position on this topic and give specific reasons for your point of view.

The topic of this question is

a. the animal rights movement.

b. the role of animals in scientific research.

c. the controversy over the use of animals in research.

The question has

a. one requirement.

b. two requirements.

c. three requirements.

d. four requirements.

2. In her book *Without Lying Down*, author Cari Beauchamp argues that Hollywood between 1915 and 1925 was a place where women were equal in power to men; women flourished* not just as actresses but as writers, directors, producers, and editors. In your essay, identify at least three of the women Beauchamp uses to make her point. Be sure to explain not just who they were but what they accomplished as well. Then describe the changes in studio management that pushed these same women into the background and deprived them of their former power.

The topic of this question is

a. Cari Beauchamp.

b. Hollywood's failure to enlarge the role of women.

c. the role of women in Hollywood between 1915 and 1925.

The question has

a. one requirement.

b. two requirements.

*flourished: did well, were successful.

    c. three requirements.

    d. four requirements.

3. Since its discovery, Antarctica has been the source of competing national claims, but only once has there been actual fighting over the territory. What nations were involved in that fight, and what was the outcome?

The topic of this question is

    a. the Arctic circle.

    b. the fight over claims to Antarctica.

    c. the riches of Antarctica and the greed those riches inspire.

The question has

    a. one requirement.

    b. two requirements.

    c. three requirements.

    d. four requirements.

4. Throughout the 1970s, the Mexican-American group *La Raza Unida* was a powerful force in the Southwest. Who were the leaders of this group, and what were its goals? Once you have outlined the goals of the group, evaluate the group's success as a political force in the Southwest.

The topic of this question is

    a. Mexican Americans in the Southwest.

    b. Southwestern politics.

    c. *La Raza Unida.*

The question has

    a. one requirement.

    b. two requirements.

    c. three requirements.

    d. four requirements.

5. Summarize the reasons for the United States's withdrawal from Vietnam, and describe the public's reaction to that withdrawal.

The topic of this question is

a. the causes of the Vietnam War.

b. reasons for the U.S. withdrawal from Vietnam.

c. American foreign policy in Southeast Asia.

The question has

a. one requirement.

b. two requirements.

c. three requirements.

d. four requirements.

Putting It All Together

This section of *Reading for Thinking* lets you bring together everything you have learned about comprehension and critical reading. It also offers you the opportunity to deepen your understanding of several topics introduced in previous chapters. You'll revisit, for example, William James's theory of emotions and consider again the pros and cons of home schooling.

The readings that follow are accompanied by discussion questions and writing assignments, which ask you to do what up till now you've seen others do—argue a point of view. These questions and assignments are important because *Reading for Thinking* is not concerned solely with teaching you to understand and evaluate the ideas of others. Ultimately, its goal is to encourage you to express and argue with confidence your own particular point of view.

■ **READING 1**

THE PATERSON PUBLIC LIBRARY,
Judith Ortiz Cofer

LOOKING AHEAD Almost all of the readings in this section are linked to specific topics already introduced in previous chapters. The reading that follows is a definite exception. It's connected to *Reading for Thinking* less by topic and more by point of view. Like the author of "The Paterson Public Library," I also believe that reading is a way to both escape and discover the world.

FOCUS STRATEGIES While you read, underline or circle any figures of speech you think are particularly effective at conveying the author's meaning or experience. Above all, try to put yourself in the author's childhood shoes.

WORD WATCH Some of the more difficult words in the reading are defined below. Watch for these words as you read. They are marked with an asterisk.

---

archeological site: place where digging is done in an effort to locate remnants of the past

incongruous: not fitting; inappropriate to the setting

façade: outer surface of a building

astigmatism: a problem with the lens of the eye

supplicants: people who are worshipping or pleading

fait accompli: an accomplished fact

sanctuary: place of safety

organic: growing naturally out of the earth

internalized: accepted as true

insatiable: incapable of being satisfied

adept: skillful

obsessiveness: state of being totally focused on one idea or activity

---

1 IT WAS A GREEK TEMPLE IN THE RUINS OF AN AMERICAN CITY. To get to it I had to walk through neighborhoods where not even the carcasses of rusted cars on blocks or the death traps of discarded appliances were parted with, so that the yards of the borderline poor, people who lived not in a huge building, as I did, but in their own decrepit little houses, looked like a reversed archeo-

logical site,* incongruous* next to the pillared palace of the Paterson Public Library.

2   The library must have been built during Paterson, New Jersey's, boom years as the model industrial city of the North. Enough marble was used in its construction to have kept several Michelangelos[1] busily satisfied for a lifetime. Two roaring lions, taller than a grammar school girl, greeted those brave enough to seek answers there. Another memorable detail about the façade* of this most important place to me were the phrases carved deeply into the walls—perhaps the immortal words of Greek philosophers—I could not tell since I was developing an astigmatism* at that time and could only make out the lovely geometric designs they made.

3   All during the school week I both anticipated and feared the long walk to the library because it took me through enemy territory. The black girl Lorraine, who had chosen me to hate and terrorize with threats at school, lived in one of the gloomy little houses that circled the library like sackclothed supplicants.* Lorraine would eventually carry out her violence against me by beating me up in a confrontation formally announced through the school grapevine so that for days I lived with a panic that has rarely been equaled in my adult life, since now I can get grownups to listen to me, and at that time disasters had to be a fait accompli* for a teacher or a parent to get involved.

4   Why did Lorraine hate me? For reasons neither one of us fully understood at the time. All I remember was that our sixth-grade teacher seemed to favor me, and her way of showing it was by having me tutor "slow" students in spelling and grammar. Lorraine, older and bigger than myself since she was repeating the grade, was subjected to this ritual humiliation, which involved sitting in the hallway, obviously separated from the class—one of us for being smart, the other for the opposite reason. Lorraine resisted my efforts to teach her the basic rules of spelling. She would hiss her threats at me, addressing me as "*You little Spic.*" Her hostility sent shudders through me. But baffling as it was, I also accepted it as inevitable. She would beat me up. I told my mother and the teacher, and they both reassured me in vague adult terms that a girl like Lorraine would not dare get in trouble again. She had a history of problems that made her a likely candidate for reform school. But Lorraine and I knew that the violence she harbored had found a target: me—the skinny Puerto Rican girl whose father was away with the navy most of

---

[1]Michelangelo (1475–1564): Italian painter, sculptor, and architect.

the time and whose mother did not speak English; I was the perfect choice.

5   Thoughts like these occupied my mind as I walked to the library on Saturday mornings. But my need for books was strong enough to propel me down the dreary streets with their slush-covered sidewalks and the skinny trees of winter looking like dark figures from a distance: angry black girls waiting to attack me.

6   But the sight of the building was enough to reassure me that sanctuary* was within reach. Inside the glass doors was the inexhaustible treasure of books, and I made my way through the stacks like the beggar invited to the wedding feast. I remember the musty, organic* smell of the library, so different from the air outside. It was the smell of an ancient forest, and since the first books that I read for pleasure were fairy tales, the aroma of transforming wood suited me as a prop.

7   With my pink library card I was allowed to check out two books from the first floor—the children's section. I would take the full hour my mother had given me (generously adding fifteen minutes to get home before she sent my brother after me) to choose the books I would take home for the week. I made my way first through the world's fairy tales. Here I discovered that there is a Cinderella in every culture, that she didn't necessarily have the white skin and rosy cheeks Walt Disney had given her, and that the prince they all waited for could appear in any color, shape, or form. The prince didn't even have to be a man.

8   It was the way I absorbed fantasy in those days that gave me the sense of inner freedom, a feeling of power and the ability to fly that is the main reward of the writer. As I read those stories I became not only the characters but their creator. I am still fascinated by the idea that fairy tales and fables are part of humankind's collective unconscious—a familiar theory that acquires concreteness in my own writing today, when I discover over and over that the character I create or the themes that recur in my poems and in my fiction are my own versions of the "types" I learned to recognize very early in my life in fairy tales.

9   There was also violence in these stories: villains decapitated in honorable battle, goblins and witches pursued, beaten, and burned at the stake by heroes with magic weapons possessing the supernatural strength granted to the self-righteous in folklore. I understood those black-and-white duels between evil and justice. But Lorraine's blind hatred of my person and my knee-liquefying fear of her were not so clear to me at that time. It would be many years before I learned about the politics of race, before I internal-

ized* the awful reality of the struggle for territory that under-scored the lives of blacks and Puerto Ricans in Paterson during my childhood.

10   Each job given to a light-skinned Hispanic was one less job for a black man; every apartment leased to a Puerto Rican family was one less place available to them. Worst of all, though the Puerto Rican children had to master a new language in the schools and were often subjected to the scorn and impatience of teachers burdened with too many students making too many demands in a classroom, the blacks were obviously the ones singled out for "special" treatment. In other words, whenever possible they were assigned to special education classes in order to relieve the teacher's workload, mainly because their black English dialect sounded "ungrammatical" and "illiterate" to our white Seton Hall University and City College–educated instructors.

11   I have on occasion become angry at being treated like I'm men-tally deficient by persons who make that prejudgment upon hear-ing an unfamiliar accent. I can only imagine what it must have been like for children like Lorraine, whose skin color alone put her in a pigeonhole she felt she had to fight her way out of every day of her life.

12   I was one of the lucky ones; as an insatiable* reader I quickly became more than adept* at the use of the English language. My life as a navy brat, moving with my family from Paterson to Puerto Rico every few months as my father's tours of duty demanded, taught me to depend on knowledge as my main source of security. What I learned from books borrowed from the Greek temple among the ruins of the city, I carried with me as the lightest of carry-on luggage. My teachers in both countries treated me well in general. The easiest way to become a teacher's pet, or *la favorita,* is to ask the teacher for books to read—and I was always looking for reading material; even my mother's roman-tic novels by Corin Tellado and her *Buenhogar* (Spanish *Good Housekeeping* magazine) were not safe from my insatiable word hunger.

13   Since the days when I was stalked by Lorraine, libraries have always been an adventure for me. Fear of an ambush is no longer the reason why I feel my pulse quicken a little when I approach a library building, when I enter the stacks and inhale the familiar smell of old leather and paper. It may be the memory of the dan-ger that heightens my senses, but it is really the expectation that I felt then and that I still feel now about books.

14   I gained confidence in my intelligence by reading books. They

contained most of the information I needed to survive in two languages and in two worlds. When adults were too busy to answer my endless questions, I could always look it up; when I felt unbearably lonely, as I often did during those early gypsy years traveling with my family, I read to escape, and also to connect: You can come back to a book as you cannot always to a person or place you miss. I read and reread favorite books until the characters seemed like relatives or friends I could see when I wanted or needed to see them.

15   I still feel that way about books. They represent my spiritual life. A library is my sanctuary, and I am always at home in one. It is not surprising that in recalling my first library, the Paterson Public Library, I have always described it as a temple.

16   Lorraine carried out her threat. One day after school, as several of our classmates, Puerto Rican and black, circled us to watch, Lorraine grabbed a handful of my long hair and forced me to my knees. Then she slapped my face hard enough that the sound echoed off the brick walls of the school building and ran off while I screamed at the sight of blood on my white knee socks and felt the throbbing on my scalp where I would have a bald spot advertising my shame for weeks to come.

17   No one intervened. To this crowd, it was one of many such violent scenes taking place among the adults and the children of people fighting over a rapidly shrinking territory. It happens in the jungle and it happens in the city. But another course of action other than "fight or flight" is open to those of us lucky enough to discover it and that is channeling one's anger and energy into the development of a mental life. It requires something like obsessiveness* for a young person growing up in an environment where physical labor and physical endurance are the marks of a survivor—as is the case with minority peoples living in large cities. But many of us do manage to discover books. In my case, it may have been what anthropologists call a *cultural adaptation*. Being physically small, non-English-speaking, and always the new kid on the block, I was forced to look for an alternate mode of survival in Paterson. Reading books empowered me.

18   Even now, a visit to the library recharges the batteries in my brain. Looking through the card catalog reassures me that there is no subject I cannot investigate, no world I cannot explore. Everything that is, is mine for the asking. Because I can read about it.

Judith Ortiz Cofer, "The Paterson Public Library,"
from *The Latin Deli: Prose & Poetry* by Judith Ortiz
Cofer. The University of Georgia Press, pp. 28–33.

PUTTING IT ALL TOGETHER Answer the following questions by circling the letter of the correct response or filling in the blanks.

Main Idea 1. Which statement most effectively paraphrases the main idea of the entire reading?

   a. Throughout her life, the author has relied on books to provide her with knowledge, companionship, safety, and even escape.

   b. Despite her success as a writer, the author still carries with her the psychic wounds she suffered as a child who never quite fit in because of her small size and ethnic background.

   c. It was her discovery of libraries and the books they contained that made the author dream of becoming a writer.

   d. Writing about her life has given the author a socially acceptable place to vent her anger.

Patterns of Organization 2. Which pattern of organization is at work in paragraph 12?

   a. cause and effect

   b. comparison and contrast

   c. process

Inferences 3. Based on the reading, which inference do you think is appropriate?

   a. The author firmly believes in the importance of bilingual education programs.

   b. The author firmly believes that children should be introduced to books and reading.

   c. The author has never gotten over what she suffered as a child.

4. Why do you think that asking teachers for books to read is a direct path to becoming *la favorita* (paragraph 12)?

   _____

5. In paragraph 12, the author refers to what she learned from books as the "lightest of carry-on luggage." What does the author imply by that metaphor?

   a. The books she read didn't weigh much.

   b. The books she read became a part of her.

   c. The books she read were lightweight fiction, not serious literature.

Connotative and Denotative Language

6. How would you describe the author's use of language?

    a. She relies mainly on words that are more denotative than connotative.

    b. She relies heavily on connotative language to make her ideas clear and compelling.

Figurative Language

7. In paragraph 6, the author says, "I made my way through the stacks like the beggar invited to the wedding feast." That figure of speech is a

    a. simile.

    b. metaphor.

The figure of speech about the beggar and the wedding feast helps the author make what point?

_____

8. In paragraph 9, the author talks about her "knee-liquefying fear." That phrase illustrates which figure of speech?

    a. metaphor

    b. allusion

    c. simile

What does the author hope to communicate through the phrase "knee-liquefying fear"?

_____

_____

Purpose

9. Which statement most effectively describes the author's purpose?

    a. The author wants to tell her readers about the Paterson Public Library.

    b. The author wants to describe the racism she encountered as a child.

    c. The author wants to tell her readers about the role that reading played in her life.

Tone

10. How would you describe the author's tone?

    a. emotionally neutral

    b. arrogant and angry

    c. strong and passionate

■ **DRAWING**
YOUR OWN
CONCLUSIONS

1. Do you think the author does a good job making readers feel the power of books? Why or why not?

2. What do you think the author has in mind when she talks about the "politics of race" (paragraph 9)?

■ **THINKING**
THROUGH
WRITING

Describe your first experience being read to or learning to read. In either the introduction or the conclusion of your paper, be sure to tell your readers how the experience has affected you as an adult. Like the author of "The Paterson Public Library," re-create your experience with vivid, concrete detail and figurative language.

■ **READING 2**

JAMES'S THEORY OF EMOTIONS,
Douglas A. Bernstein and Peggy Nash

LOOKING AHEAD You already know the name of William James from Chapter 2 (p. 61). The following reading will familiarize you with his theory of emotional response. From James's point of view, emotions have no life of their own. They are simply the body's physical response to external experience.

FOCUS STRATEGIES Read with the intention of understanding James's theory so thoroughly that you can explain it to someone else without looking back a the text. To that end, use the margins of your text to summarize the theory and list the stages of response outlined in paragraph 3. Compare and contrast James's theory with the one offered by Walter Cannon, whose theory of the emotions is also discussed in the following pages.

WORD WATCH Some of the more difficult words in the reading are defined below. Watch for these words as you read. They are marked with an asterisk.

---

physiological: relating to the body, physical

perception: the act of recognizing an event

cerebrel cortex: the outer layer of the brain; responsible for reasoning, sensations, memory, and movement

neurons: impulse-conducting cells in the brain

autonomic: related to involuntary physical reactions

variant: variation

hypothesis: theory that's not yet been proven

---

1 SUPPOSE YOU ARE CAMPING IN THE WOODS WHEN A HUGE BEAR approaches your tent in the middle of the night. Scared to death, you run for dear life. Do you run because you are afraid, or are you afraid because you run? The example and the question come from William James, one of the first psychologists to offer a formal ac-

count of how physiological* responses relate to emotional experience. He argued that you are afraid *because* you run.

2   As first glance, James's theory sounds ridiculous. It defies common sense, which says it would be silly to run from something unless you already feared it. James concluded otherwise after examining his own mental processes. He decided that once all physiological responses are stripped away, nothing remains of the experience of an emotion (James, 1890). Emotion, he reasoned, is simply the result of experiencing a particular set of physiological responses. Without these responses, you would feel no fear, or any other emotion. The idea that emotions depend on experiencing physiological responses was also suggested by Carle Lange, a Danish physician, so James's view is sometimes called the *James-Lange theory* of emotions.

Observing Responses

3   Figure 1 on page 544 outlines James's theory of emotional experience. First, perception* affects the cerebral cortex.* The brain interprets a situation and automatically directs a particular set of physiological changes, such as increased heart rate, sinking stomach, perspiration, and certain patterns of blood flow. It is when we become *aware* of these physiological changes, said James, that we experience an emotion. According to this view, each particular emotion is created by a particular pattern of physiological responses.

4   Notice that according to James's theory, there is no special "emotion center" in the brain where the firing of neurons* creates a direct experience of emotion. If this theory is accurate, it might account for the difficulty we sometimes have in knowing our true feelings: We must figure out what emotions we feel by perceiving small differences in specific physiological response patterns.

Evaluating James's Theory

5   Research shows that certain emotional states are indeed associated with particular patterns of autonomic* changes (Damasio et al., 2000; Kelter & Buswell, 1996; R. Sinha & Parsons, 1996). For example, blood flow to the hands and feet increases in association with anger and declines in association with fear (Levenson, Ekman, & Friesen, 1990). Thus, fear involves "cold feet"; anger does not. A pattern of activity associated with disgust includes increased muscle activity but no change in heart rate. And when people mentally relive different kinds of emotional experiences, they show different patterns of autonomic activity (Ekman, Leven-

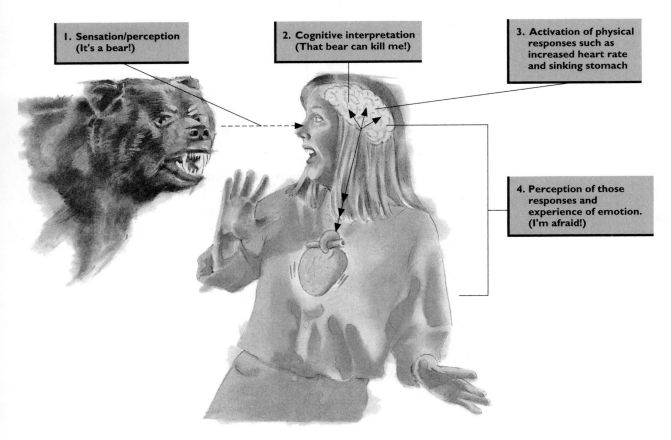

Figure 1 The Components of James's Theory of Emotions

son, & Friesen, 1983). These emotion-specific patterns of physiological activity have been found in widely different cultures (Levenson et al., 1992).

6   Furthermore, different patterns of autonomic activity are closely tied to specific emotional facial expressions, and vice versa. When research participants were asked to make various facial movements (Ekman, Levenson, & Friesen, 1983), these movements led to autonomic changes resembling those normally accompanying emotion. In addition, almost all of the participants reported *feeling the emotion* associated with the expression they had created, even though they could not see their own expressions and did not realize that a specific emotion was being portrayed.

7   To get an idea of how facial expressions can alter, as well as express, emotion, take careful note of another person's facial

expression, and try your best to imitate it. Doing this may elicit in you the same feelings and autonomic responses that the other person is experiencing. Research suggests that people do best at describing another person's emotions when their own physiological responses match those of the other person (Levenson & Ruef, 1992). Edgar Allan Poe noted the relationship between facial expressions and feelings more than a hundred years ago:

> When I wish to find out how wise or how stupid or how good or how wicked is anyone, or what are his thoughts at the moment, I fashion the expression of my face, as accurately as possible, in accordance with the expression of his, and then wait to see what thoughts or sentiments arise in my mind or heart, as if to match or correspond with the expression. (quoted in Levenson, Ekman, & Friesen, 1990)

8   A variant* of James's theory, the *facial feedback hypothesis,** maintains that involuntary facial movements provide enough information about the body to drive emotional experience (Ekman & Davidson, 1993). This hypothesis predicts that feeling yourself smile should make you feel happy. It also helps to explain the results mentioned earlier suggesting that voluntarily posed facial expressions create the emotions normally associated with them. (The next time you want to cheer yourself up, it might help to smile—even though you don't feel like it!)

Lie Detection

9   James's view that different patterns of physiological activity are associated with different emotions forms the basis for the lie-detection industry. If people experience anxiety or guilt when they lie, specific patterns of physiological activity accompanying these emotions should be detectable on instruments, called *polygraphs,* that record heart rate, breathing rate, perspiration, and other autonomic responses.

Cannon's Theory

10   James's theory assumes that the experience of emotion depends on facial movements and other bodily responses outside the brain. However, Walter Cannon believed that emotion can result from brain activity alone (W. B. Cannon, 1927/1987). He argued that you feel fear at the sight of a bear even before you run away from it. Emotional experience, he said, begins in the brain. Specifically, it starts in the thalamus, the brain structure that relays information from most sense organs to the cortex.

11   According to Cannon's theory of emotion (called the *Cannon-Bard theory*, in recognition of Philip Bard's contribution), sensory information about emotional situations first reaches the thalamus. The thalamus then sends signals *simultaneously* to the autonomic nervous system and to the cerebral cortex, where the emotion becomes conscious. So when you see a bear, the brain receives sensory information about it, interprets that information as a bear, and *directly* creates the experience of fear while at the same time sending messages to the heart, lungs, and legs to get you out of the situation. According to Cannon's theory, then, there is a direct, central nervous system experience of emotion, with or without feedback about bodily responses.

Updating Cannon's Theory

12   Subsequent research indicates that the thalamus is not the "seat" of emotion, as Cannon had suggested. Still, the thalamus does participate in some aspects of emotional processing (Lang, 1995). For example, studies in animals and humans show that the emotion of fear is generated by connections from the thalamus to the amygdala (A. K. Anderson & Phelps, 2000; LeDoux, 1995). The implication is that strong emotions can sometimes bypass the cortex without requiring conscious thought to activate them—thus possibly explaining why people find it so difficult to overcome an intense fear, or phobia, even though they may consciously know the fear is irrational.

13   An updated version of Cannon's theory suggests that specific brain areas produce the feelings of pleasure or discomfort associated with emotion. This idea arose from studies showing that electrical stimulation of certain parts of the brain is rewarding. Researchers found that rats kept returning to the place in their cage where they received stimulation through electrodes in their brains. When these animals were allowed to control delivery of the stimulation by pressing a lever, they pressed it until they were physically exhausted, ignoring even food and water (Olds & Milner, 1954). The brain areas in which stimulation is experienced as especially pleasurable include the dopamine systems, which are activated by cocaine and other psychoactive drugs (Bardo, 1998). In contrast, stimulation of other brain regions is so unpleasant that animals work hard to avoid it.

Adapted from Douglas A. Bernstein and
Peggy W. Nash, *Essentials of Psychology*.
Boston: Houghton Mifflin, 2002, pp. 284–288.

PUTTING IT ALL TOGETHER Answer the following questions by filling in the blanks or circling the letter of the correct response.

Main Idea

1. Which statement most effectively paraphrases James's theory?

    a. James argued that our emotions shape our experiences and distort their meaning.

    b. James argued that our emotions are nothing more than the body's physical responses to experiences.

    c. James argued that emotions need to be under strict control lest they cause us to overreact to experiences.

    d. James argued that during times of stress, the body reacts with a fight-or-flight response that produces changes in breathing, heart rate, and blood flow.

Supporting Details

2. Why do the authors mention that blood flow to the hands and feet increases in response to anger (paragraph 5)? What main idea does that detail support?

    _____

    _____

3. Explain how James's theory provided the basis for the lie detector industry.

    _____

    _____

4. The quotation from Edgar Allan Poe is used to support what main idea?

    _____

Inference

5. Based on the section titled "Evaluating James's Theory" (pp. 543–544) you can infer that

    a. James's theory is no longer taken seriously by modern scientists.

    b. there is some evidence that lends support to his theory.

    c. current research has proven William James's theory of emotions to be completely correct.

Patterns of Organization

6. What *two* patterns of organization can you detect in paragraph 3?

    a. classification

    b. cause and effect

    c. definition

    d. process

Summarizing **7.** Write a brief (no more than two sentences) summary of James's theory.

_____

_____

_____

_____

Synthesis Statement **8.** Which synthesis statement better combines the theories of James and Cannon?

    a. William James insisted that the emotions we feel are the brain's recognition of bodily processes. Walter Cannon, however, argued that emotional states correspond to specialized activity in the brain.

    b. William James's research suggested that the body's physical responses to a specific situation stimulate an emotional response in the brain. Walter Cannon, however, argued that the brain has nothing to do with our emotions. What we experience as emotions are nothing more than physiological changes in the body.

Purpose **9.** What would you say is the authors' primary purpose?

    a. to inform

    b. to persuade

What clues led you to your answer?

_____

Bias **10.** With which of the following statements do you agree?

    a. The authors favor James's theory of the emotions.

    b. The authors agree more with Cannon than with James.

    c. It's impossible to determine the authors' personal feelings.

■ **DRAWING YOUR OWN CONCLUSIONS** Which theory, James's or Cannon's, makes more sense to you and why?

■ **THINKING THROUGH WRITING** Write a paper that compares and contrasts the theories of James and Cannon.

■ **READING 3**

FIVE APPROACHES TO DEALING WITH CONFLICT,
**Roy Berko, Andrew D. Wolvin, and
Darlyn R. Wolvin**

LOOKING AHEAD — The essay question on page 503 indicated that there are several different ways to respond to conflict. The reading that follows describes five different methods of responding. As you read, see if you recognize yourself in any of the descriptions.

FOCUS STRATEGIES — When you finish, you'll be asked to write a summary of the reading. In preparation, use the margins of your text to identify and describe each of the five approaches to dealing with conflict. As often as you can, link the descriptions of a particular conflict style to the behavior of people you know.

WORD WATCH — Some of the more difficult words in the reading are defined below. Watch for these words as you read. They are marked with an asterisk.

---

ramifications: consequences   **status quo:** existing situation

habitual: regular, automatic   **equitable:** fair

---

1 PEOPLE REACT DIFFERENTLY IN DEALING WITH CONFLICT. SOME people pull back, some attack, and others take responsibility for themselves and their needs. Most of us use a primary style for confronting conflict. Knowing your style and its ramifications* can be helpful in determining whether you are pleased with your conflict style. If you are not, you may need to acquire the skills to make a change in your habitual* pattern. The styles of conflict management are (1) avoidance, (2) accommodation/smoothing over, (3) compromise, (4) competition/aggression, and (5) integration.

Avoidance

2 Some people choose to confront conflict by engaging in **conflict avoidance**—not confronting the conflict. They sidestep, postpone, or ignore the issue. They simply put up with the status quo,* no matter how unpleasant. While seemingly unproductive, avoidance

may actually be a good style if the situation is a short-term one or of minor importance. If, however, the problem is really bothering you or is persistent, then it should be dealt with. Avoiding the issue often uses up a great deal of energy without resolving the aggravating situation. Very seldom do avoiders feel that they have been in a win-win situation. Avoiders usually lose a chunk of their self-respect since they so clearly downplay their own concerns in favor of the other person's. Avoiders frequently were brought up in environments in which they were told to be nice and not to argue, and eventually bad things would go away. Or they were brought up in homes where verbal or physical abuse was present, and to avoid these types of reactions, they hid from conflict.

Accommodation/Smoothing Over

3   People who attempt to manage conflict through **conflict accommodation** put the needs of others ahead of their own, thereby giving in. Accommodators meet the needs of others and don't assert their own. In this situation, the accommodator often feels like the "good person" for having given the other person his own way. This is perfectly acceptable if the other person's needs really are more important. But unfortunately, accommodators tend to follow the pattern no matter what the situation. Thus, they often are taken advantage of, and they seldom get their needs met. Accommodators commonly come from backgrounds where they were exposed to a martyr who gave and gave and got little but put on a happy face. They also tend to be people who have little self-respect and try to earn praise by being nice to everyone.

4   A form of accommodation known as **conflict smoothing over** seeks above all else to preserve the image that everything is okay. Through smoothing over, people sometimes get what they want, but just as often they do not. Usually they feel they have more to say and have not totally satisfied themselves.

5   As with avoidance and accommodation, smoothing over occasionally can be useful. If, for example, the relationship between two people is more important than the subject they happen to be disagreeing about, then smoothing over may be the best approach. Keep in mind, however, that smoothing over does not solve the conflict; it just pushes it aside. It may very well recur in the future.

6   Those who use this technique as their normal means of confronting conflict often come from backgrounds in which the idea was stressed that being nice was the best way to be liked and pop-

ular. And being liked and popular was more important than satisfying their needs.

Compromise

7 **Conflict compromise** brings concerns out into the open in an attempt to satisfy the needs of both parties. It usually means "trading some of what you want for some of what I want. It's meeting each other half way." The definition of the word *compromise*, however, indicates the potential weakness of this approach, for it means that both individuals give in at least to some degree to reach a solution. As a result, neither usually completely achieves what she or he wants. This is not to say that compromise is an inherently poor method of conflict management. It is not, but it can lead to frustration unless both participants are willing to continue to work until both of their needs are being met. Those who are effective compromisers normally have had experience with negotiations and know that you have to give to get, but you don't have to give until it hurts. Those who tend to be weak in working toward a fair and equitable* compromise believe that getting something is better than getting nothing at all. Therefore, they are willing to settle for anything, no matter how little.

Competition/Aggression

8 The main element in **conflict competition** is power. Its purpose is to "get another person to comply with or accept your point of view, or to do something that person may not want to do." Someone has to win, and someone has to lose. This forcing mode, unfortunately, has been the European-American way of operation in many situations—in athletic events, business deals, and interpersonal relations. Indeed, many people do not seem to be happy unless they are clear winners. Realize that if someone wins, someone else must lose. The overaggressive driver must force the other car off the road.

9 The value of winning at all costs is debatable. Sometimes, even though we win, we lose in the long run. The hatred of a child for a parent caused by continuous losing, or the negative work environment resulting from a supervisor who must always be on top, may be much worse than the occasional loss of a battle. In dealing with persons from other cultures, European Americans sometimes are perceived as being pushy and aggressive. Many sales, friendships, and relationships have been lost based on the win-at-all-costs philosophy. Many of the aggressive behaviors in the personal lives of professional athletes are directly credited to their

not being able to leave their win-at-all-costs attitude on the athletic field.

Integration

10 Communicators who handle their conflicts through **conflict integration** are concerned about their own needs as well as those of the other person. But unlike compromisers, they will not settle for only a partially satisfying solution. Integrators keep in mind that both parties can participate in a win-win resolution and are willing to collaborate. Thus, the most important aspect of integration is the realization that the relationship, the value of self-worth, and the issue are important. For this reason, integrative solutions often take a good deal of time and energy.

11   People who are competitive, who are communication-apprehensive, or who are nonassertive find it nearly impossible to use an integrative style of negotiation. They feel that they must win, or that they cannot stand up for their rights, or that they have no right to negotiate. In contrast, people who tend to have assertiveness skills and value the nature of relationships usually attempt to work toward integration.

12   Avoidance, accommodation, and smoothing over are all nonassertive acts; the person's needs are not met. Competition is an aggressive act in that the person gets his needs met at the expense of another person. Integration is assertive since the objective is to get one's needs met without taking away the rights of someone else. Compromise, depending on how it is acted out, can be either nonassertive or assertive.

Roy Berko, Andrew D. Wolvin, and Darlyn R. Wolvin, *Communicating.* Boston: Houghton Mifflin, 2001, pp. 156–158.

PUTTING IT ALL TOGETHER Answer the following questions by filling in the blanks or circling the letter of the correct response.

Surveying 1. What crucial piece of information in the title should have guided your reading of the selection?

_____

Main Idea 2. Sum up the main idea of this reading in one brief sentence.

_____

_____

Paraphrasing 3. Paraphrase the authors' explanation of conflict avoidance.

_____

_____

4. In your own words, what's the drawback commonly associated with compromise as a response to conflict?

_____

_____

Supporting Details 5. Would you call the detail about professional athletes (paragraph 9)

a major or minor detail? _____

Explain:

_____

_____

Pattern of Organization 6. What overall pattern organizes the information in the reading?

_____

Inference 7. Make up your own example of someone engaging in conflict accommodation.

_____

_____

_____

_____

Purpose 8. How would you describe the authors' purpose?
   a. to inform
   b. to persuade

Connotation and Denotation 9. In which direction does the authors' language lean?
   a. The authors' language leans toward the highly connotative.
   b. The authors' language leans toward the highly denotative.
   c. The authors strike a balance between connotative and denotative language.

Bias **10.** Do the authors seem to favor any one style of conflict management over the other? ____

Explain why you answered yes or no.

_____

_____

■ **DRAWING YOUR OWN CONCLUSIONS** How would you describe you own style of dealing with conflict? How does your style match the authors' descriptions? Does it fit right in, or do you need a new category?

■ **THINKING THROUGH WRITING** Summarize the reading, reducing it to no more than ten or fifteen sentences, without eliminating either the definitions for each style or the advantages and disadvantages of each. Those are, after all, the essential elements of the reading.

■ **READING 4**

PORN USE A CATALYST FOR VIOLENCE,
Charlton Wimberly

LOOKING AHEAD Whether or not the consumption of pornography can be directly linked to violence against women is the subject of hot debate, but not for the author of this reading. As proof of his position, he points out that some of the most dangerous sexual predators started out reading pornography and progressed to sexual assault and murder.

FOCUS STRATEGIES The author expresses a strong opinion about pornography. As you read, evaluate the quantity and quality of the evidence he provides. Just as important, try to determine how you feel about pornography and the need for stricter censorship.

WORD WATCH Some of the more difficult words in the reading are defined below. Watch for these words as you read. They are marked with an asterisk.

---

captivated: fascinated

anomaly: abnormality

gratifying: satisfying

catalyst: stimulus, source of action

---

1 PORNOGRAPHY IS ABOUT AS HARD TO FIND AT TEXAS A&M University as beer and pizza. It's everywhere: in dorm rooms, at Blockbuster, on computers, even the Corps of Cadets has a rolling file of porn magazines that each year gets passed into the safekeeping of a freshman cadet. Many people treat porn with a "boys will be boys" mentality. They think it is natural for guys to look at "dirty magazines" and that no one is hurt in the process. This is a dangerous misconception. Pornography devalues human life, and it is a direct contributor to violence against women.

2 In an interview given the day before his execution in 1989, serial killer Ted Bundy explained how pornography set him on the path to murder. At the age of thirteen, he came across some pornographic magazines in a dump near his home. He was captivated* by those magazines, and as time went by he gradually began con-

suming more explicitly sexual—and eventually violent—pornography. There finally came a point when pornography could not stimulate him any further. Bundy said, "Once you become addicted to it . . . you reach the point where the pornography only goes so far—that jumping-off point where you begin to think maybe actually doing it will give you that which is just beyond reading about it and looking at it." Bundy did more than just think about doing it. After years of consuming pornographic images, he began luring women into his car, sexually assaulting them and then murdering them. Bundy was finally apprehended after killing a twelve-year-old girl and dumping her body in a pig sty. By that time he had murdered more than twenty-eight women.

3   Ted Bundy is not an anomaly.* Of thirty-six sex murderers interviewed by the FBI in 1985, twenty-nine admitted to extensively using pornography. Numerous other statistics show that pornography plays a major role in many violent offenses—particularly those that are sex-related.

4   In a laboratory study, sociologist Diana Russell showed the desensitizing effect pornography had on Bundy is common. Russell found that male college students "were more prone to accept commonly held conceptions like 'a woman really wants to be raped,' and 'yes means no,'" after being exposed to pornography in which women were depicted as enjoying rape. After repeated exposure for only two weeks, the college males "found the violent pornography to be less and less violent," and some subjects became increasingly aroused by the images.

5   Pornography leads to violence because it strips women of their human characteristics. What remains is nothing more than a two-dimensional object whose sole purpose is gratifying* its user. Men who use pornography stop seeing the women in pornographic images as human. In this way, pornography works as a catalyst* in propelling sexual and violent fantasies into reality. As women become less human, they become easier to use and easier to violate. In this way, pornography works to propel the sexual and violent fantasies of some porn users into reality.

6   Obviously, every guy who opens a *Playboy* magazine is not going to become a murderer. The danger is that those who use relatively mild porn, like *Playboy*, will eventually move on to more explicit pornography. This progression is common because of pornography's addictive nature.

7   The National Council on Sexual Addiction and Compulsivity has estimated there are 2 million sexually-addicted Internet users, many of whom spend fifteen to twenty-five hours per week viewing pornographic Web sites. Addicts spend such large quanti-

ties of time on these sites because the videos and images never satisfy them—their use of pornography only leaves them wanting something more stimulating. And it has already been shown what some of them will eventually do to achieve that stimulation.

8 Pornography has pervaded our society. It is a $10 billion industry, and it is more accessible than at any other time in history. The introduction of the Internet has made it possible for anyone with a computer to view limitless numbers of sexually and violently explicit images at any time, in any place, at no cost and with total anonymity. We as a nation need to wake up and recognize the dangers that pornography poses to our country. Drunk on our own freedoms, we are more concerned with our perceived right to look at what we choose than with the men rotting in addiction and the women suffering violence because of porn. Pornography devalues human life. If we do not take steps to remove it from our communities, we will all pay the price for it together.

Charlton Wimberly, "Porn Use a Catalyst for Violence," *The Battalion* (Texas A&M University), September 21, 2001.

PUTTING IT ALL TOGETHER Answer the following questions by filling in the blanks or circling the letter of the correct response.

Analyzing Arguments

1. In your own words, what's the point of the author's argument?

_____

_____

2. How would you label that point?

a. statement of policy

b. statement of value

c. statement of condition

3. Why does the author mention serial killer Ted Bundy? Why is Bundy central to the author's argument?

_____

_____

4. Why does the author mention Diana Russell in paragraph 4? How does Russell's work contribute to his argument?

_____

_____

Fact and
Opinion

5. In paragraph 5, the author says, "men who use pornography stop seeing the women in pornographic images as human."

Is this a factual statement? _____

Explain your answer. _____

_____

6. According to the author, "the National Council on Sexual Addiction and Compulsivity has estimated there are 2 million sexually-addicted Internet users."

Is this a factual statement? _____

Explain your answer. _____

_____

7. The author says that the "progression" from mild porn to hard core porn is "common." What is the evidence for that claim?

_____

_____

8. In paragraph 6, the author talks about pornography's "addictive nature." Is it a fact that pornography is "addictive"? _____

Explain your answer. _____

_____

Tone

9. How would you describe the author's tone?

a. passionate

b. relaxed

c. emotionally neutral

Similes

10. In the first sentence of the opening paragraph, the author uses a

simile that compares _____ to _____.

What's the point of the simile? What does he want to communicate to readers?

_____

_____

■   **DRAWING**   Look back at the title of the reading. Would you say that the author
   YOUR OWN   has or has not proven that pornography is a "catalyst for violence"?
   CONCLUSIONS

■   **THINKING**   Write an essay that opens with a clear statement of how you feel
   THROUGH   about the censorship of pornography. Does it, for example, require
   WRITING   greater censorship because it endangers life? Or do you consider it
protected by the constitutional right to free speech? Whatever your
position, present at least two reasons that are fully fleshed out by
supporting details.

■ **READING 5**

RESEARCHING THE EFFECTS OF PORNOGRAPHY,
Albert Richard Allgeier and Elizabeth Allgeier

LOOKING AHEAD The author of the previous reading had some very definite ideas about the effects of pornography. The authors of this next reading, in contrast, aren't quite so interested in telling you what they think. They are more interested in explaining what they learned from looking over some research that focuses on how pornography affects both men and women.

FOCUS STRATEGIES Read the first and last paragraphs. Then read the first sentence of each remaining paragraph and all the words in **Word Watch.** Based on your survey, how do you think the authors will answer this question: Does reading or viewing pornography contribute to violence against women?

_____

_____

This is rather technical reading, so don't rush through it. Take your time. If you need to, read the more difficult paragraphs twice. The more technical a reading, the slower your reading rate should be. As you read, ask yourself if the authors would or would not support the position expressed in the previous reading.

WORD WATCH Some of the more difficult words in the reading are defined below. Watch for these words as you read. They are marked with an asterisk.

coercive: characterized by the use of force or might

consensual: agreed upon by all parties

hypothesis: theory

confederate: companion, colleague

simulated: pretended

erotica: sexually explicit material

debriefed: questioned and instructed

replicated: repeated

depictions: descriptions

eroticized: arousing sexual love and desire

1   To EXAMINE THE EFFECT OF EXPOSURE TO VIOLENT POR-
nography, two of the most active researchers on the topic, Malamuth and Donnerstein (1984), exposed men to a series of slides
and tapes that included either coercive* or consensual* sexual interaction. Before participating in the studies, volunteers were
asked to indicate the likelihood that they would commit rape, if
they could be sure of not getting caught. Those who revealed that
they thought they might engage in coercive sexual acts were classified as *force oriented.*

2   Although the designs of these studies varied, the stimuli usually consisted of a story of an attractive woman wandering along a
deserted road. A man finds her there, but when he approaches
her, she faints. He carries her to his car, and when she awakens
they engage in sex. In one version of this basic story, the woman
is tied up and forced to have sex in the car. In other variations,
she clearly consents to the act. In both its variations, the story
was arousing for male volunteers. . . . This finding is consistent
with others showing that certain rape portrayals elicit relatively
high sexual arousal in nonrapists (Malamuth, 1984; Malamuth &
Check, 1983).

3   What about the kind of violent pornography that depicts a positive reaction on the part of the victim? As Donnerstein (1984)
pointed out, pornographic media quite often portray victims of assault as responding favorably to a rape. Further, in real life, convicted rapists often fail to perceive their assaults as coercive, believing that their victims desired intercourse and enjoyed their
sexual attentions (Gage & Schurr, 1976). Because exposure to violent pornography has been shown to heighten sexual arousal, promote acceptance of rape-supportive attitudes, and foster negative
attitudes toward women (Donnerstein & Linz, 1986; Malamuth,
1984), Donnerstein reasoned that such exposure would also increase aggressive behavior against women, particularly when a
woman is depicted as having a positive reaction to sexual assault.

4   To test this hypothesis,* each male volunteer was paired with a
female confederate,* who either angered the man or treated him
in a neutral manner. Each man then watched one of four films—
a neutral version, a variation that involved consensual sexual interaction, a version in which the victim had a negative reaction to
forced sex, or a variation in which the victim's reaction to forced
sex was positive.

5   After viewing one of these films, the volunteer was given an opportunity to administer simulated* electric shocks to his female
confederate. Of the volunteers who had been angered prior to
watching the movie, those who had viewed either of the forced-sex

films chose to give higher levels of electric shock to the female confederate than did those who viewed either of the other films. Even the nonangered men, however, became more aggressive (as measured by electric-shock level) following exposure to the version of the film showing a positive reaction to forced sex. It's worth noting, however, that even when a male confederate angered a male volunteer prior to the latter's exposure to the film, the forced-sex versions of the film did not affect aggression toward the male confederate (Donnerstein, 1984).

6   It also appears that a rape portrayal emphasizing the victim's pain and distress may, under certain conditions, stimulate high levels of sexual arousal in viewers. But this effect appears to vary as a function of whether the viewer describes himself as force oriented or not (Malamuth, 1981). Force-oriented volunteers reported having more arousal fantasies after exposure to the rape version than after exposure to the mutual-consent version. Non–force-oriented men, however, reported having more arousing fantasies in response to the variations of the story involving mutual consent than in response to the rape variation. . . .

7   One criticism of laboratory-based studies of aggressive behavior in response to portrayals of erotica* is that subjects are allowed only a limited number of responses (Fisher & Grenier, 1994). To determine if the limited range of responses provided by previous experimenters had affected the findings, Fisher and Grenier provided a broader range of alternatives for volunteers. For example, after being angered by a female confederate and then shown sexual material containing violence, men in Fisher and Grenier's research had three choices. They could administer shock; give verbal feedback; or simply be debriefed*, receive experimental credit, and terminate their participation in the study.

8   Almost all participants selected the last alternative. This research is preliminary and needs to be replicated* by other researchers to see if the findings hold up, but by providing the option of allowing participants to leave without displaying aggression against the confederate, Fisher and Grenier (1994) provided a more realistic range of responses in the well-controlled environment of the laboratory.

9   What is the effect of violent pornography on women's arousal? To investigate this question, Stock (1982) presented college women with variations in rape depictions* while measuring their . . . responses and their subjective reports of arousal. Stock also compared the effect on their arousal levels of highly eroticized versus more realistic rape depictions because Malamuth and

Check's depictions had focused on erotic aspects of the interaction rather than on the victims' negative response.

10   Accordingly, Stock's volunteers were exposed to either eroticized* or realistic rape depictions, as well as to other variations. Based on the women's responses, Stock concluded that "women are not aroused by rape when described in a realistic manner, but only by a distorted misrepresentation of rape in which the victim does not suffer and no harm is done. This is far from the experience of victims of rape" (1982, p. 9).

11   In their investigations of the effects of violent pornography, it is the romanticized portrayals of rape that concern Malamuth and his colleagues. Stock's finding that women, too, can be aroused by such eroticized rape depictions, but not by realistic rape depictions, also adds to our knowledge about the effects of violent pornography. The belief of some rapists and members of the general public that women secretly enjoy rape is not supported by Stock's conclusions, and her work suggests that society should be concerned about rape representations that lead viewers to perceive sexual assault as an erotic experience. In the context of films and videos portraying sexual assault, how would you work in the message that rape is a frightening and traumatizing experience for its victims?

12   Further research is needed on the effects of violent pornography. . . . Our present knowledge does not permit us to determine whether men who report strong arousal to rape depictions and who are aroused by their own rape fantasies will actually commit rape.

Adapted from Albert Richard Allgeier
and Elizabeth Rice Allgeier,
Sexual Interactions. Boston:
Houghton Mifflin, 1995, pp. 534–536.

PUTTING IT ALL TOGETHER Answer the following questions by filling in the blanks or circling the letter of the correct response.

Main Idea **1.** Which of these statements do you think most effectively sums up the contents of the reading?

    a. Studies on the effects of pornography all show the same results: Men who read or watch pornography are more likely to commit acts of violence against women, and there is a clear cause and effect relationship.

    b. Although some studies suggest a connection between violent pornography and violence against women, there is still not enough evidence to be absolutely sure, particularly given the artificial nature of the laboratory setting.

    c. The consumption of pornography does not lead to violence unless the person doing the consuming is already "force oriented."

    d. Exposure to pornography leads to heightened sexual arousal in both men and women.

2. Which sentence more effectively paraphrases the two-step topic sentence in paragraph 6?

    a. The effect of rape portrayals emphasizing the victim's pain and humiliation varies with the viewer.

    b. Rape portrayals emphasizing the pain and humiliation suffered by victims stimulate sexual arousal in viewers.

3. Which of the following statements more effectively synthesizes readings 4 and 5?

    a. While Charlton Wimberly sees a direct connection between pornography and violence against women, Albert and Elizabeth Allgeier argue that only hard core pornography leads to violence against women.

    b. For Charlton Wimberly, there is no doubt: pornography is a threat because it dehumanizes and potentially endangers the lives of women. The Allgeiers, however, are far more cautious. For them, research on the connection between pornography and rape is still inconclusive.

Inference 4. What inference can be drawn from the research cited in paragraph 6?

    a. It's not that easy to generalize about the effects of pornography on men.

    b. Force-oriented individuals are likely to commit rape if they watch violent pornography.

5. Do you think the authors of this reading would support laws forbidding the sale of pornography?

_____

Explain your answer: _____

_____

Fact and **6.** Label the following statement *F* (fact), *O* (opinion), or *B* (both).
Opinion

Force-oriented volunteers reported having more arousal fantasies after exposure to the rape version than after exposure to the mutual-consent version (paragraph 6). _____

Explain the basis for your answer: _____

_____

7. Label the following statement *F* (fact), *O* (opinion), or *B* (both).

Further research is needed on the effects of violent pornography (paragraph 12).

_____

Explain the basis of your answer: _____

_____

8. The 1994 study by Fisher and Grenier lends support to what opinion?

a. There is a direct link between watching violent pornography and violence against women.

b. A direct link between watching violent pornography and violence against women has not yet been firmly established.

Purpose **9.** Which statement more effectively describes the authors' purpose?

a. The authors want to inform their readers about current research on the connection between viewing violent pornography and carrying out acts of violence against women.

b. The authors want to persuade readers that there is no solid connection between viewing violent pornography and carrying out acts of violence against women.

Tone **10.** How would you describe the authors' tone?

_____

■ **DRAWING** What do you think: Does pornography lead to violence? Explain the
YOUR OWN basis for your opinion.
CONCLUSIONS

■ **THINKING** Write a paper describing what you would do and why if a store selling
THROUGH pornographic materials opened up in your neighborhood.
WRITING

■ **READING 6**

HARLEM IN THE TWENTIES,
Paul Boyer et al.

LOOKING AHEAD An earlier footnote already introduced you to the Harlem Renaissance. Yet this extraordinary artistic explosion deserves more than a footnote. In the reading that follows, the authors offer a vivid picture of Harlem in the twenties, when it was a cultural center that drew artists like a magnet. Through their music, painting, and above all, their stories, black artists vowed to make white America finally recognize what it meant to be black.

FOCUS STRATEGIES As you read, try to get a clear sense of who the black artists were that made Harlem such a cultural draw in the twenties. Write their names in the margins of your text. But don't limit yourself to names. Whenever possible, indicate titles of works as well, noting ideas and themes that the artists were trying to explore. Pay special attention to those passages that focus on the conflicted relationships shared by black artists and their white patrons.

WORD WATCH Some of the more difficult words in the reading are defined below. Watch for these words as you read. They are marked with an asterisk.

---

entrepreneurs: people who start their own businesses

avant-garde: modern, ahead of its time

pulsating: vibrating

prosaic: ordinary, everyday

cabarets: nightclubs that provide entertainment

arid: dry

marginal: at the edges, not central

naïveté: state of innocence or inexperience

motif: theme

---

1 BRAVING CHILLY BREEZES, NEW YORKERS CHEERED WARMLY ON February 17, 1919, as the all-black 15th Infantry Regiment, back from France, paraded up Fifth Avenue. Led by Lieutenant James Europe's band, thousands of black troops marched in formation. Banners blazed: "OUR HEROES—WELCOME HOME." When the parade reached Harlem, north of Central Park, discipline col-

lapsed amid joyous reunions. A new day seemed at hand for black America, and Harlem stood at its center.

2   The part of Manhattan Island that the early Dutch settlers had called Nieuw Haarlem was in transition by 1920. An elite suburb in the late nineteenth century, Harlem evolved rapidly during the First World War as its black population swelled. Some 400,000 southern blacks in search of wartime work migrated northward from 1914 to 1918, and the influx continued in the 1920s. That decade, New York City's black community surged from 152,000 to 327,000. Most of the newcomers settled in Harlem, where handsome old brownstone apartments were subdivided to house them. But racism and lack of education took their toll. Black Harlem had a small middle class of entrepreneurs,* ministers, and funeral directors, but most Harlemites held low-paying, unskilled jobs. Many found no work at all. Overcrowding and the population spurt gave rise to social problems and high rates of tuberculosis, infant mortality, and venereal disease.

3   But Harlem also became a vibrant center of black cultural activity in the twenties. On the musical-comedy stage, the 1921 hit *Shuffle Along* launched a series of popular all-black reviews. The 1923 show *Runnin' Wild* sparked the Charleston dance craze. The Cotton Club and other Harlem cabarets featured such jazz geniuses as Duke Ellington, Fletcher Henderson, and Jelly Roll Morton. Muralist Aaron Douglas, concert tenor Roland Hayes, and singer-actor Paul Robeson contributed to the cultural ferment.

4   Above all, the Harlem Renaissance was a literary movement. The poet Langston Hughes drew upon the oral traditions of transplanted southern blacks in *The Weary Blues* (1926). The Jamaican writer Claude McKay evoked Harlem's throbbing, sometimes sinister nightlife in *Home to Harlem* (1928). In his avant-garde* work *Cane* (1923), Jean Toomer used poems, drama, and short stories to convey the thwarted efforts of a young northern mulatto to penetrate the mysterious, sensual world of the black South. In her novel *Quicksand* (1928), Nella Larsen, a native of the Danish West Indies, told of a mulatto woman's struggle with her own sexuality and with the divergent cultural worlds of Denmark, the West Indies, the American South, and Harlem.

5   In essays and conversations at late-night parties, talented young blacks explored the challenge of finding a distinct cultural voice in white America. The gentle philosopher Alain Locke, a former Rhodes scholar who taught at Howard University in Washington, D.C., assembled essays, poems, and short stories in *The New Negro* (1925), a landmark work that hailed the Harlem Renaissance as black America's "spiritual coming of age." Wrote Locke:

"Harlem, I grant you, isn't typical, but it is significant. It is prophetic."

6   White America quickly took notice. Book publishers courted black authors. Charlotte Mason, a wealthy Park Avenue matron, funded the aspiring writers Langston Hughes and Zora Neale Hurston. The novelist and photographer Carl Van Vechten introduced black artists and writers to editors, publishers, and producers. White writers discovered and sometimes distorted black life. Eugene O'Neill's play *The Emperor Jones,* produced in 1921, starred Charles Gilpin as a fear-crazed West Indian tyrant. King Vidor's 1929 movie *Hallelujah,* featuring an all-black cast, romanticized plantation life and warned of the city's dangers. The 1925 novel *Porgy,* by Dubose and Dorothy Heyward, offered a sympathetic but sentimentalized picture of Charleston's black community. Reworked as a drama, *Porgy* won the Pulitzer Prize in 1927; George Gershwin's musical adaptation, *Porgy and Bess,* appeared in 1935.

7   In a decade of prohibition and shifting sexual mores, Harlem seemed to offer sensuality, eroticism, and escape from taboos. Prostitutes, speakeasies, and cocaine were indeed readily available. The whites who packed the late-night jazz clubs and the pulsating* dance reviews and who patronized black writers and artists widely praised black culture for its "spontaneous," "primitive," or "spiritual" qualities. Harlem, writes historian Nathan Huggins, offered the hope of recovering "that essential self one somehow lost on the way to civility." Few whites bothered to examine the more prosaic* realities of Harlem life. The Cotton Club, controlled by gangsters, featured black performers but barred most blacks from the audience. Observed black writer Rudolph Fisher in 1927: "White people [once] went to Negro cabarets* to see how Negroes acted; now Negroes go to these same cabarets to see how white people act."

8   And with patronage came subtle attempts at control. When Langston Hughes in the 1930s began to write about urban poverty rather than Africa or black spirituality, Charlotte Mason angrily withdrew her support. Wrote Hughes later, "Concerning Negroes, she felt that they were America's great link with the primitive. . . . But unfortunately I did not feel the rhythms of the primitive surging through me . . . I was only an American Negro. I was not Africa. I was Chicago and Kansas City and Broadway and Harlem."

9   The Harlem Renaissance lacked a political framework or organic ties to the larger African-American experience. Indeed, Alain Locke in *The New Negro* urged talented blacks to shift from "the arid* fields of controversy and debate to the productive fields of

creative expression." The writers and artists of the Renaissance ignored the racism, discrimination, and economic troubles faced by most African-Americans in the 1920s. They reacted with hostility to Marcus Garvey[1] and his efforts to mobilize the urban black masses.

10   With the stock market crash in 1929 and the onset of the Great Depression, the Harlem Renaissance ended. In the 1930s, a new generation of writers led by Richard Wright would launch a more politically engaged black cultural movement. Looking back in 1935, Alain Locke would write sadly: "The rosy enthusiasm and hopes of 1925 were cruelly deceptive mirages. [The Depression] revealed a Harlem that the social worker knew all along, but had not been able to dramatize. There is no cure or saving magic in poetry and art for precarious marginal* employment, high mortality rates, and civic neglect." Langston Hughes tersely assessed the movement in his 1940 autobiography: "The ordinary Negroes hadn't heard of the Negro Renaissance. And if they had, it hadn't raised their wages any."

11   But for all its naïveté,* the Harlem Renaissance left an important legacy. The post–World War II literary flowering that began with Ralph Ellison's *Invisible Man* (1952) and continued with the works of James Baldwin, Toni Morrison, Alice Walker, and others owed a substantial debt to the Harlem Renaissance. Walker, in particular, would pay generous tribute to Zora Neale Hurston. For black writers in the West Indies and in French West Africa, "Harlem" would become a core motif,* a symbol of both racial oppression and racial achievement. A fragile flower battered by the cold winds of the depression, the Harlem Renaissance nevertheless stands as a monument to African-American cultural creativity even under difficult circumstances.

Paul Boyer et al., *Enduring Vision.* Boston: Houghton Mifflin, 2000, pp. 695a–695b.

PUTTING IT ALL TOGETHER   Answer the following questions by circling the letter of the correct response or filling in the blanks.

Main Idea   1. What is the main idea of the entire reading?

   a. Harlem in the twenties was the setting for an extraordinary cultural explosion that unfortunately fizzled when the stock market collapsed.

   b. Of all the writers who became famous during the Harlem Renaissance, none was more important than Langston Hughes.

[1]Marcus Garvey (1887–1940): a black nationalist who believed African Americans had to dedicate themselves to economic self-determination.

    c. Unfortunately, the cultural richness of the Harlem Renaissance drew the attention of white writers, who badly misrepresented its content and meaning.

    d. Harlem in the twenties was the setting for an extraordinary cultural explosion that may have been short-lived yet still left behind a lasting legacy.

2. In paragraph 3, the names Duke Ellington,[2] Fletcher Henderson,[3] and Paul Robeson[4] are all mentioned to illustrate what main idea?

_____

Supporting Details **3.** In paragraph 6, the names Charlotte Mason and Carl Van Vechten are used to illustrate what main idea?

_____

4. In paragraph 8, the quotation from Langston Hughes concerning Charlotte Mason illustrates what main idea?

_____

Patterns of Organization **5.** Which two patterns are central to this reading?

    a. classification and comparison and contrast

    b. sequence of dates and events and cause and effect

    c. cause and effect and process

    d. comparison and contrast and process

Inferences **6.** In paragraph 5, what do you think Alain Locke meant when he said in reference to the Harlem Renaissance, "Harlem, I grant you, isn't typical, but it is significant. It is prophetic."

_____

7. Explain what you think Langston Hughes meant when he wrote, long after the Harlem Renaissance had passed, that "the ordinary Negroes hadn't heard of the Negro Renaissance. And if they had, it hadn't raised their wages any."

_____

_____

_____

[2]Edward Kennedy "Duke" Ellington (1899–1974): jazz composer, pianist and bandleader.
[3]Fletcher Henderson (1897–1952): jazz pianist, bandleader, and composer.
[4]Paul Robeson (1898–1976): an actor, singer, and political activist whose career was destroyed by cold war anti-communism.

Metaphor 8. In paragraph 11, the Harlem Renaissance is compared to

_____.

What's the point of the metaphor?

_____

Purpose 9. How would you describe the authors' purpose?

    a. to inform

    b. to persuade

Tone 10. How would you describe the authors' tone?

    a. emotionally neutral

    b. critical

    c. admiring

■ **DRAWING YOUR OWN CONCLUSIONS** Many of the figures in the Harlem Renaissance believed that the arts—literature, music, theater, and painting—could transform society for the better. Do you think that the arts in general or one art in particular, say music, can effect social change? Whatever your answer, please explain how you arrived at your position.

■ **THINKING THROUGH WRITING** Describe some creative work—a novel, movie, poem, drama, or song—that had a powerful effect on you. Start the paper by briefly describing the context in which you encountered the work: Were you a child or an adult? Were you generally in good spirits or feeling a bit low? Then generally describe the work. Save the most vivid details for the last part of the paper, in which you explain the work's effect on you. Here again, see if you can employ figurative language to communicate your experience to your readers.

■ **READING 7**

THE TRAGEDY OF JAPANESE INTERNMENT

LOOKING AHEAD In 1942, Franklin Delano Roosevelt—over the protests of his wife, Eleanor—signed Executive Order 9066. The selection that follows describes the misery and suffering Roosevelt's decision inflicted on Japanese Americans. They were rounded up, forced to sell their possessions, and herded into miserable makeshift camps, where they were confined for the duration of the war, despite the fact that there was no evidence of any wrongdoing on their part.

FOCUS STRATEGIES Read the first and last paragraphs along with the headings. What event would you predict played a key role in the creation of the internment camps?

As you read, ask yourself how it was possible that innocent people could be so badly treated without any public outcry. Look, too, for any passages that describe how Japanese Americans responded to internment.

WORD WATCH Some of the more difficult words in the reading are defined below. Watch for these words as you read. They are marked with an asterisk.

---

euphemisms: words that hide a harsh or disturbing reality

refuge: place of safety

unscrupulous: lacking any moral or ethical sense

affiliation: connection

foremost: most important

fervor: intense emotional feelings

dereliction: neglect, abandonment

reticent: shy, withdrawn

rebuff: rejection

unsubstantiated: unproven, lacking in evidence

reparations: repayments for injury

---

1 ON THE MORNING OF DECEMBER 7, 1941, JAPANESE SUBmarines and carrier planes launched an attack on the U.S. Pacific

Fleet at Pearl Harbor. Two hundred American aircraft were destroyed, eight battleships were sunk, and approximately eight thousand naval and military personnel were killed or wounded. This savage attack and its horrifying consequences propelled the United States into World War II.

2 For people of Japanese descent living in the United States—both the American-born *Nissei* and the Japanese-born *Issei*—the attack on Pearl Harbor was doubly catastrophic. It was tragic enough that their adopted country was going to war with the land of their ancestors. But the attack on Pearl Harbor also unleashed a storm of fury and outrage against America's Japanese citizens. The result was *Executive Order 9066,* issued in February 1942. Signed by the president of the United States, Franklin Delano Roosevelt, the order condemned 120,000 Japanese Americans—two-thirds of them native born—to be evacuated from their homes and interned in camps for the duration of the war. Even some Japanese Americans who had volunteered to fight for the United States were viewed as potential spies. They were stripped of their uniforms and sent to relocation camps because they were considered too dangerous to go free.

The Reality of the Camps

3 In discussing the camps, government administrators favored euphemisms.* The camps were temporary "resettlement communities"—"havens of refuge"* designed to protect the Japanese Americans from those who did not trust them (Weglyn, 89). Comforted by words like *community* and *refuge,* few Americans were confronted by the reality of camp life. If they had been, there probably would have been a groundswell of public outrage.

4 Erected at breakneck speed, the camps were crude and flimsy. The "family apartments," as they were called, were tarpaper shacks surrounded by barbed wire. They usually measured twenty by twenty-four feet and housed anywhere from five to eight people. Furniture, except for that brought by residents, was almost nonexistent. The apartments contained cots, blankets, mattresses, and a light fixture—nothing more.

5 Because the buildings were shoddy, the weather created hardships. In the summer, residents of the Manazar Camp in California sweltered. The sun beating down on tarpaper roofs turned rooms into ovens. Occasionally, the asphalt floors melted (Weglyn, 80). Those living in colder climates like the Gila Relocation Center in Arizona or the Granada Center in Colorado fared little better. They were exposed to freezing temperatures that turned their "homes" into iceboxes.

6   There were other hardships as well. Because walls would have added to building expenses, there were few of them. Camp residents had almost no privacy. They ate and showered together. Even the toilet facilities were communal. There was no way to be alone.

Economic Losses

7 Japanese Americans also suffered terrible economic losses. Forced by the government to settle their affairs in a matter of days, they fell victim to the unscrupulous,* who bought their property at the lowest possible prices. The property and possessions that couldn't be sold were stored, but no one seemed concerned with protecting what the Japanese Americans left behind. Much of it was stolen or vandalized (Conrat, 22). In the end, the Japanese who were interned lost property valued at more than $500 million; they lost as well their leading position in the truck-garden, floral, and fishing industries.

Psychological Loss

8 But the tragedy of relocation was not limited to physical hardship and economic loss. For Japanese Americans, the worst hardship was psychological. They had lost face in their adopted country. They had suffered the embarrassment and humiliation of being herded together and forced to live in poverty. For a proud people, it was a spiritual death sentence (Girdner and Loftis, 238). Their family life was disrupted, and they felt themselves powerless. Although the young were able to bear up under such indignity, some of the old could not. One elderly man committed suicide and was found holding an Honorary Citizenship Certificate in his hand (Weglyn, 78).

No Evidence of Espionage

9 Although many people seemed convinced that only a network of Japanese-American spies could account for the success of Japan's attack on Pearl Harbor, there was no evidence of such spying. On the contrary, there was a great deal of evidence affirming the loyalty of America's Japanese residents.

10   Two months prior to the attack on Pearl Harbor, Curtis B. Munson, a special representative of the U.S. State Department, conducted a study of Japanese Americans. His objective was to find the degree of their loyalty to America. The results of Munson's research suggested that Japanese Americans were deeply loyal to their adopted country. Their deepest affiliation* was to America

rather than to the land of their birth. From Munson's perspective, they showed a "patriotic eagerness" to be Americans. There was, in fact, no Japanese-American threat: "There is no Japanese problem on the coast. There will be no armed uprising of Japanese" (Weglyn, 47).

11   Unfortunately, the Munson report became one of the war's best-kept secrets. As Eugene Rostow, one of America's foremost* authorities on constitutional law, expressed it, "One hundred thousand persons were sent to concentration camps on a record which wouldn't support a conviction for stealing a dog" (Weglyn, 53).

How Could It Happen Here?

12   Given the lack of evidence against Japanese Americans, given the suffering they endured, the question must be raised: How could it happen? How could a country famous for its democratic fervor* allow loyal citizens to be imprisoned?

13   *The Humiliation of Pearl Harbor.*   Japan's attack on Pearl Harbor was extraordinarily swift and successful. Later investigations laid most of the blame at the feet of the two men in charge of the area, Rear Admiral Husband E. Kimmel and General Walter C. Short.[1] They were found guilty of errors in judgment and dereliction* of duty. Initially, however, Americans found it hard to blame their own military commanders. It was easier to believe rumors about a network of Japanese-American spies operating on the West Coast of the United States.

14   *A History of Prejudice.*   Then, too, as historians Donald Pike and Roger Olmstead point out, "a century of anti-Orientalism stood back of the relocation order" (Conrat, 16). Prejudice against Asians had first been ignited when the Chinese arrived during the gold rush of the 1850s. As the number of gold seekers increased, it was clear that there simply wasn't enough gold to go around. American miners retaliated by demanding restrictions on Chinese miners, who were labeled intruders on American soil. When the Japanese began arriving in the 1890s, they inherited the anger and distrust originally directed at the Chinese.

15   Throughout the beginning of the twentieth century, anti-

---

[1]The subject of who was to blame for Japan's success is still being debated today. Some historians believe Kimmel and Short were forced to take all the blame even though others were at fault as well.

Japanese sentiment tended to swell and ebb with the economy. In times of economic expansion, evidence of prejudice diminished. But in times of recession, the Japanese were singled out for restriction and ostracism. Prevented by labor unions from working in the city, they moved to agricultural areas, where they became successful farmers. Their thrift and industry made them significant competitors, able to purchase several hundred thousand acres of land. But their success backfired when California passed the Alien Land Law preventing Japanese from purchasing land or leasing it for more than three years.

16   Japan's entry into World War I on the side of the United States temporarily curbed anti-Japanese sentiment in America. But it flared up again following the war, when Japan invaded Manchuria and China, withdrew from the League of Nations, and refused to limit naval arms. A threat to her neighbors, Japan was also perceived as a threat to America. As a result, the United States passed the Japanese Exclusion Act of 1924, which specifically limited Japanese immigration. By the time Pearl Harbor exploded, the country was psychologically prepared to mistrust Japanese Americans.

17   *Fear of the Unknown.*   Following their internment, Japanese Americans tended to take the blame for their misfortunes. They blamed themselves for being too clannish, for trying to preserve Japanese customs, for being reticent* and reclusive when they should have been forward and open. Tragically, they had a point. "Because little was known about the minority which had long kept itself withdrawn from the larger community in fear of rebuff,* it was possible to make the public believe anything" (Weglyn, 36). Fed on vicious stereotypes about Oriental cunning and largely ignorant of Japanese customs, far too many Americans found it easy to believe the myth of Japanese conspiracy and sabotage.

18   *Government Secrecy.*   The decision to relocate the Japanese Americans was hardly a public one. It was made by a few government officials who justified their actions in various ways. When General John L. DeWitt was questioned about evidence of Japanese-American treachery, he offered this logic: "The very fact that no sabotage has taken place to date is a disturbing and confirming indication that such action will take place" (Weglyn, 39). According to this argument, Japanese Americans had to be imprisoned because they hadn't *yet* done anything wrong. From

DeWitt's perspective, their failure to engage in any spying activities was proof that they would do so any day. From DeWitt's peculiar angle of vision, internment was a form of preventive medicine.

19   When members of humanitarian, religious, and civil liberties groups protested the internment, they were given another explanation. They were told that the camps were nothing more than "protective custody." The government allegedly needed to protect its Japanese-American citizens because Pearl Harbor had aroused so much anti-Japanese sentiment.

20   If friends and neighbors of Japanese-American citizens protested the relocation policy, yet another reason was proposed. Military officials insisted that Japanese Americans were in possession of evidence that made internment a necessity. What this evidence was, however, had to be kept top secret—government security was involved.

The Final Verdict

21 Initially, the U.S. Supreme Court upheld the government's internment policy. In 1943 (*Hirabayashi v. U.S.*), the Court claimed that "residents having ethnic affiliations with an invading enemy may be a greater source of danger than those of different ancestry" (Norton et al., 801). Similarly, in the 1944 *Korematsu* case, the Court approved the removal of Japanese Americans from the West Coast. However, Justice Frank Murphy called the decision the "legalization of racism." In his anger, he echoed Circuit Court Judge William Denman, who had compared Japanese-American internment to the policies of the Nazis: "The identity of this doctrine with that of the Hitler generals . . . justifying the gas chambers of Dachau is unmistakable" (Norton et al., 802).

22   Thirty-eight years after these Supreme Court decisions, the government formed a special Commission on Wartime Relocation and Internment of Civilians. Not surprisingly, that commission did not share the earlier view of the Supreme Court justices. On the contrary, it recommended that victims of the internment policy be compensated for their suffering. In the view of the commission, they had been victimized by "race prejudice, war hysteria, and a failure of political leadership" (Norton et al., 802).

23   A year later, in 1983, the *Korematsu* case was overturned in a federal district court. The court ruled that Fred Korematsu had been the victim of "unsubstantiated* facts, distortions, and misrepresentations" (Norton et al., 802). In clearing Fred Korematsu, the court also implicitly cleared the other men, women, and children who had shared his fate.

24   Reparations* have been paid to Japanese Americans who suffered from the policy of internment. Although money can never make up for the humiliation and hardship they suffered, the reparations are a much needed form of public apology.

Sources of Information

Conrat, Maisie, and Richard Conrat. *Executive Order 9066.* California: Historical Society, 1972.

Girdner, Audrie, and Anne Loftis. *The Great Betrayal.* London: Collier-Macmillan, 1969.

Norton, Mary Beth, et al. *A People and a Nation.* Boston: Houghton Mifflin, 1986, pp. 801–802.

Weglyn, Michi. *Years of Infamy.* New York: William Morrow, 1976.

PUTTING IT ALL TOGETHER   Answer the following questions by filling in the blanks or circling the letter of the correct response.

Main Idea   **1.** Which of the following most accurately paraphrases the main idea of the entire reading?

a. The attack on Pearl Harbor shocked the United States and ended any indecision about the country's entry into World War II.

b. The attack on Pearl Harbor caused a storm of outrage against people of Japanese descent living in the United States, and that outrage paved the way for Executive Order 9066.

c. Initially the Supreme Court did the unthinkable: It upheld the government's right to place Japanese Americans in internment camps, but the court eventually reversed its decision.

d. For Japanese Americans, the psychological suffering was worse than their material losses.

2. In paragraph 7, which sentence is the topic sentence?

a. sentence 1

b. sentence 2

c. sentence 3

3. What's the main idea of paragraph 13?

a. Because Americans were reluctant to blame the bombing of Pearl Harbor on their own commanders, they found it easier to believe rumors about a Japanese-American spy ring.

b. Even today, no one really knows for sure how the Japanese were able to launch their surprise attack on Pearl Harbor.

Paraphrasing **4.** Which sentence more effectively paraphrases the topic sentence in paragraph 5?

    a. During the summer months, residents of the camps in California suffered terribly from the heat.

    b. Because the buildings in the camps were cheaply built, the weather added to the suffering of the camp's residents.

    c. Sweltering weather was just one of the miseries that confronted Japanese Americans upon their arrival in the camps.

Inference **5.** What's the implied main idea of paragraph 21?

    a. Most Americans believed that the U.S. Supreme Court's decision to uphold the policy of internment was unjust.

    b. Although initially the U.S. Supreme Court upheld the policy of internment, there were those who strongly criticized the judges' decision.

    c. Ruled by wartime hysteria, the Supreme Court found in favor of internment policies for Japanese Americans.

Patterns of Organization **6.** Paragraphs 14 through 16 rely on which *two* patterns of organization?

    a. classification

    b. cause and effect

    c. process

    d. sequence of dates and events

Purpose **7.** The title of the reading suggests that the author's purpose is

    a. to inform readers about the internment of Japanese Americans.

    b. to persuade readers that Japanese Americans were badly treated during the years of internment.

Forming an Opinion **8.** In paragraph 3, the author describes some of the euphemisms government administrators used to describe the camps. Why do you think these officials favored euphemisms?

    _____

    _____

    _____

Summarizing and Analyzing Arguments

9. Summarize the argument offered by General John L. DeWitt.

_____

_____

_____

_____

What key element is missing from DeWitt's argument?

_____

Bias **10.** In paragraph 17, the author describes the stereotypes that fed anti-Japanese sentiment. How do you think the author views those stereotypes?

_____

_____

What words reveal her personal bias?

_____

■ **DRAWING YOUR OWN CONCLUSIONS** Television was in its infancy during World War II, and certainly there was no televised coverage of what happened. Could television have made a difference in how Japanese Americans were treated? Why or why not? Do you think that something similar could ever happen again in the United States during time of war? Why or why not?

■ **THINKING THROUGH WRITING** Write a paper arguing that Americans do or do not need to know about such shameful incidents in the past as the internment of Japanese Americans. While some believe that we as a nation have to know about past injustices in order to avoid repeating them, others argue that there is no point in raking up a past better left forgotten. Begin your paper by stating your position and giving reasons for it. Then show how that position would be put into practice in a high school history course.

■ **READING 8**

HUNKS AND HANDMAIDENS,
Victoria Register-Freeman

LOOKING AHEAD Reading 8 revisits a topic introduced in Chapter 6, where one writer suggested that Britney Spears probably has more of an impact on young women today than does an earlier generation of feminists like Gloria Steinem and bell hooks. In "Hunks and Handmaidens," author Victoria Register-Freeman suggests that her brand of feminism doesn't seem to have made much of an impression on the girls of her son's generation.

FOCUS STRATEGIES As you read, underline the similes, metaphors, and allusions the author uses to describe the young women in her sons' lives. Think about what these figures of speech convey about the women. Ask yourself if the author's description of them seems true to life or exaggerated.

WORD WATCH Some of the more difficult words in the reading are defined below. Watch for these words as you read. They are marked with an asterisk.

---

flaxen-haired: having light yellow hair

metamorphosis: change, transformation

spawned: produced

manifesto: statement of rights or beliefs

atrophied: died, lost strength

en masse: in a large group

cum laude: with honors

disorient: confuse

cohorts: companions

subterranean: underground

---

1 RHETT, MY NINETEEN-YEAR-OLD SON, WENT FROM TOM SAW-yer to Tom Cruise around fifteen, about the time his voice changed. Suddenly, the family phone recorder began to fill up with breathless messages from what his older brother referred to as "Rhett's Gidgets," flaxen-haired* surfer girls from a nearby beach. Like fruit flies they appeared in dense buzzing masses with exotic names like Shaunna, Tiffany, Kendra, and Kimberly.

2   I was prepared for this metamorphosis* because it had happened to Rhett's older brother Robert at about the same age. My first inkling of the change came in a pizza parlor during a post-basketball-game dinner. Since I could not decide between black olives and anchovies, Robert gave his order first. The waitress, an attractive Madonna clone, went into great detail with him concerning salad dressings, crust types, cheese consistencies, toppings, whether he wanted ice with his Coke, did he live in the neighborhood, was there *anything* else he might want. When he smiled and shook his head, she floated off toward the kitchen, totally forgetting to take my order. Next to my son, I had become invisible.

3   I was stunned. Like most American moms, I had been so blinded by the sight of my offspring in ripped jeans and SAVE THE MANATEE T-shirts, and so deafened by numerous arguments over the acceptable decibel level of Beastie Boys CDs, that I was slow to recognize my firstborn had become heartthrob material.

4   Nevertheless, it was true, and it became equally true for his younger brother. Through some quirks of DNA, my ex-husband and I—two average-appearing adults—spawned* genetic celebrities: square-jawed, pearly-toothed, mahogany-haired, six-foot-five-inch slabs of guy flesh whose casual glance seems to turn many otherwise articulate young women into babbling Barbies.

5   I'm not proud of this. Wasn't the motherhood manifesto* for women of my generation to abolish stereotypes? Weren't . . . men supposed to be fully functioning members of a newly designed home team, a mutually supportive, multiskilled unit? I thought so. Many of my friends thought so too. We've done our part to raise our sons as full-fledged "new" team members—competent, caring individuals who can do more around the house than crush cans for the recycling bin and put a new plastic liner in the garbage pail. Both of my sons learned early to make an edible lasagna, toss a salad, sew on buttons, grocery-shop, and separate the whites from the darks at laundry time. They could iron a shirt as well as rebound a basketball or kick a soccer goal. Growing up in a single-mom household for much of their lives, they really had to carry their weight domestically. And they did—for a while.

6   Then came puberty and hunkhood. Over the last few years, the boys' domestic skills have atrophied* because handmaidens have appeared en masse.* The damsels have driven by, beeped, phoned, and faxed. Some appeared so frequently outside the front door they began to remind me of the suction-footed Garfields spread-eagled on car windows. While the girls varied according to height, hair color, and basic body type, they shared one characteristic. They were ever eager to help the guys out.

7   For example, Robert's freshman year at college, I arrived home from work one day to hear the sound of a vacuum. The sound intrigued me because Robert, home on spring break, was sprawled on the sofa reading the swimsuit edition of *Sports Illustrated* and Rhett was at crew practice. I daydreamed briefly that my fantasy had been realized and the dust wads under the bed had generated a cleaning lady. I strode back to the bedroom, briefcase in hand, but there was no one there but Bonnie, Robert's current girlfriend. Yes, it was cum laude* Bonnie of the Titian curls and the Always on Time Term Paper. Bonnie was vacuuming Robert's room—known in our family as The Room From Hell. This meant she had been on this project for most of the afternoon, because there hadn't been any visible floor in Robert's room for more than a year.

8   I pulled the plug on the Kenmore. "What are you doing, Bonnie?" I inquired gently. She replied that she was cleaning Robert's room for him. She did not see the broader implications. I sat down slowly on the unwrinkled bed, my entire life as a postmodern woman passing before my eyes. It was a psychic near-death experience; I felt I was on the Disorient* Express for good this time. I explained to her that Robert held the high school record for rebounds in a single basketball game. His motor skills were intact. He could clean his own room. It was his choice. He chose not to do so. He chose instead to lounge in the living room and undress Kathy Ireland with his eyes.

9   Bonnie, despite her 140 IQ, seemed perplexed. Her green eyes widened. Her brow furrowed. After all, Robert had mentioned his room was a mess and it seemed so natural to . . . This is the frightening thing I've noticed about my homegrown hunks. Females don't require enough "real" help from them. My sons do not have to employ many of the skills I've so painstakingly taught them during our time together. Young women take one look at the guys and stand in line to become the chosen one to clean rooms, pick up laundry, fry chicken, lend money, drop dates with girlfriends, rent videos, treat for drinks.

10   This is not the way it was supposed to be—the reason I read fifty books on raising males in the new world order. This is not the payoff I would like for spending years in a support group for single moms with sons. But I'm realistic. I've done my part. It's up to the others—the girlfriends, cohabitants, main squeezes, or wives—to insist that the hunks carry their fair share of the domestic load. Despite catchy commercials to the contrary, bringing home the bacon *and* frying it can get irksome. Besides, the hunks—like many of their cohorts*—have seen their moms work hard to survive economically. They know what women can do;

they respect that ability and—at some subterranean* level—
they're hard-wired to help. We, the Elvis-era moms, have done the
best we can. It's now up to Tiffany, Kendra, and Kimberly.

Victoria Register-Freeman, "Hunks
and Handmaidens," *Newsweek,*
November 4, 1996, p. 16.

PUTTING IT ALL Answer the following questions by circling the letter of the correct
TOGETHER response or filling in the blanks.

Main Idea **1.** Which statement most effectively paraphrases the main idea of the
entire reading?

    a. Now that my sons have grown up, they are following in the foot-
steps of their father and leaving housework to the women in their
lives.

    b. My sons have been trained to do their fair share of housework,
but the girls in their lives encourage them to treat housework as
women's work.

    c. Without my noticing, it seems my two sons turned into the kind
of men whom women adore.

    d. Like their father, my sons have learned how to exploit women.

2. In paragraph 2, the topic sentence is

    a. sentence 1.

    b. sentence 2.

    c. sentence 3.

Pattern of **3.** What pattern of organization do you recognize in paragraph 6?
Organization
    a. comparison and contrast

    b. cause and effect

    c. process

Inference **4.** When the author visits a pizza parlor and the waitress treats her as
if she were invisible, the author correctly infers that

    a. the young girl doesn't like her.

    b. her young son has turned into a handsome man.

    c. the young girl is too busy to pay her any attention.

Purpose **5.** Which statement more effectively describes the author's purpose?

    a. She wants to tell readers about her experience as a feminist
whose efforts to raise sons with a feminist consciousness have
been stymied, not by them, but by the girls in their lives.

b. She wants to convince her younger female readers that they should stop volunteering to do housework for her handsome sons.

Similes 6. In the opening paragraph, the author compares the girls to fruit flies. What is the point of that simile?

_____

Connotation and Denotation 7. Which statement more effectively describes the author's use of language?

a. The author's language is factual and denotative.

b. The author's language is highly connotative and rich in opinion.

Allusions 8. In the opening, the author says that her son went from Tom Sawyer to Tom Cruise at the age of fifteen. What does she mean to express by means of these two allusions?

_____

9. According to the author, her sons' casual glances turned many young women into "babbling Barbies." What does she imply with her allusion to the famed Barbie doll?

_____

Tone 10. How would you describe the author's tone?

a. angry and annoyed

b. humorously serious

c. emotionally neutral

■ **DRAWING YOUR OWN CONCLUSIONS** Have you seen young women behave as the author describes? Does her description ring true to you? Why or why not? Generally speaking, do you think most husbands and wives share the housework equally? What's your evidence for that generalization?

■ **THINKING THROUGH WRITING** Write a paper that summarizes and responds to the reading by Victoria Register-Freeman. Begin by briefly summarizing—no more than two or three sentences—the article; then explain why the author's description does or does not fit your experience. Do most of the young men you know refuse to let women clean up after them or do they prefer it? Similarly, do you think women behaving like "babbling Barbies" is a thing of the past or very much part of the present?

■ **READING 9**

Raoul Wallenberg: A Lost Hero

Looking Ahead Earlier in this text, you read about people who turned their backs on European Jewry during World War II. Raoul Wallenberg was most certainly not one of those. Unfortunately, his heroism could not save him from what most believe was a miserable death in a Russian prison camp.

Focus Strategies Read the first paragraph, all the headings, and the first sentence of each remaining paragraph. When you finish, see if you can predict what Wallenberg did to become one of the great heroes of World War II.

_____

_____

_____

As you read, imagine yourself in Wallenberg's place. Would you have been willing to do what he did for people who were neither friends nor family?

Word Watch Some of the more difficult words in the reading are defined below. Watch for these words as you read. They are marked with an asterisk.

> **cultivated:** refined by training and education
>
> **atrocities:** acts of cruelty and violence
>
> **callously:** without feeling or pity
>
> **unorthodox:** untraditional
>
> **dismantled:** taken apart

1 IN 1937, RAOUL WALLENBERG WAS A YOUNG MAN WHO SEEMED to have everything. Born into one of Sweden's richest and most respected families, he was cultivated,* handsome, and charming. His future seemed assured. After a few years spent learning the family business, he would follow in his grandfather's footsteps and become a banker.

2   But the young Wallenberg was not content. In a letter to his grandfather, he made it clear that something was missing: "To tell the truth, I don't feel especially bankish. . . . I think it is more in my nature to work positively for something" (Lester, 26).

3   Wallenberg's words were prophetic. By 1944, he was indeed working positively for something. He was risking his life to save the Jews of Budapest, Hungary. Members of the last large Jewish community in Europe, the Jews of Budapest had been targeted for extinction. Without their death, Nazi Germany could not claim that the "Final Solution," their plan to eliminate all the Jews in Europe, was a success. And, as the world now tragically knows, the Nazis were determined to be successful.

4   Adolf Eichmann, one of the architects of Hitler's Final Solution, openly proclaimed his enthusiasm for the Hungarian "project." He personally organized the transportation of Jews to Auschwitz and insisted that the job be completed as swiftly as possible (Lester, 69). But Eichmann had reckoned without the arrival of Raoul Wallenberg. Almost single-handedly, Wallenberg saved more than 100,000 Hungarian Jews. Then, in one of the great mysteries of all time, he vanished. To this day, his disappearance remains shrouded in mystery and his whereabouts, alive or dead, are still in question.

Wallenberg's American Connection

5   By late 1942, most of the world's leaders knew that the German government was determined to make all of Europe *judenrein,* or free of Jews. Although reports of atrocities* had been circulating for months, government officials had viewed them as isolated events. As 1942 drew to a close, however, both the American State Department and the British Foreign Office had to confront the terrible truth hidden behind the euphemism *Final Solution.* The Nazis were systematically killing, or, in their words "exterminating," the Jews of Europe.

6   By 1944, the American government had decided to organize the War Refugee Board. Its goal was to block "Nazi plans to exterminate all the Jews" (Lester, 61). This goal clearly required intervention in Hungarian affairs, because Hungary was the only remaining country with a large Jewish population. The country was also under German occupation.

7   As a result, Iver C. Olsen, a member of the U.S. Treasury Department, was sent to neutral Sweden. His task was to find a Swedish representative who could enter Hungary and somehow stop deportations to the concentration camps. Within days of meeting Olsen, Raoul Wallenberg was ready to travel.

A Powerful Piece of Paper

8 Raoul Wallenberg arrived in Budapest on July 9, 1944. When he entered the Swedish embassy, he saw a long line of people wearing the yellow Star of David that proclaimed their status as Jews. Word had gotten out that the Swedes were giving travel documents or citizenship papers to Hungarian Jews who were planning to become Swedish citizens or residents. In several previous cases, those documents had offered protection against deportation and death.

9 One Jewish businessman had even gone to court, claiming his Swedish citizenship protected him from deportation. To everyone's surprise, he had won his case. Another man had escaped deportation to Auschwitz, the most dreaded of all concentration camps, by showing a Swedish document. The German officer in charge had simply let him go, obviously intimidated by the sight of an official document.

10 Quick to infer a valuable lesson from these incidents, Wallenberg realized immediately that the same people who could callously* inflict suffering and death could also be intimidated by a piece of paper. Inhumanity did not disturb them, but failure to follow the rules did. Inspired by that knowledge, Wallenberg designed an impressive-looking document, bearing the symbol of the Swedish government. More important, it announced that anyone carrying the document was under the protection, or *Schutz*, of the Swedish government. The document was signed by Raoul Wallenberg.

11 Wallenberg's next step was to set up a small network for the distribution of the *Schutz* passes. He then visited members of the Hungarian government and showed them a letter from King Gustav of Sweden. He made it clear to all present that Sweden was committed to protecting the Jews against further aggression. Other Swedish diplomats were a bit taken aback by Wallenberg's unorthodox* efforts, citing questions of procedure and legality. But Wallenberg managed to brush all such considerations aside with one answer: "It will save lives" (Lester, 89).

12 By October of 1944, Wallenberg had been in Budapest just three short months. During that time, he had purchased a number of houses with the money provided by Olsen. Draping them with Swedish flags, Wallenberg claimed the houses were Swedish property and therefore not subject to German or Hungarian law. In effect, they became "safe houses," places of sanctuary for Jewish refugees.

13 When, on one occasion, Hungarian troops tried to force their way into one of Wallenberg's safe houses, he blocked their way,

saying, "No one leaves this place as long as I live" (Stanglin et al., 36). The troops withdrew.

14   On October 15, 1944, Hungarian radio announced that the war was lost, and the announcer openly blamed the Germans for dragging Hungary into a losing battle. In the Jewish quarter, there was dancing in the streets. Unfortunately, the dancing was premature. Shortly after the first announcement came another more ominous broadcast. The Hungarian Nazi Party, the hated and feared Arrow Cross, had taken over. Along with the German Nazis still in Hungary, members of the Arrow Cross would continue to be loyal to Adolf Hitler. Above all, they would continue to work toward the Final Solution.

The Arrow Cross's Reign of Terror

15   The notorious Adolf Eichmann was again in Budapest, and fifteen members of the Arrow Cross roamed the streets hunting down and shooting Jews on sight. At one point, a small band of Jewish laborers and a handful of Communists got hold of arms, and they fought back. Immediately the German SS[1] and the Hungarian police were at the scene of the fighting. They rounded up hundreds of suspected sympathizers and executed them where they stood (Lester, 105). A nightmare world prior to October 15, Budapest had now become a living hell.

16   As Soviet tanks drew closer, the Nazis became more violent and more vicious. They barged into Wallenberg's "safe" houses and dragged out the "protected" Jews. They tortured their victims, shot them, and then threw their bodies into the Danube River.

17   Eichmann, however, was furious that his plans for exterminating the Hungarian Jews were being interrupted. Nazi officials had become anxious about what was going to happen when the war ended. With good reason, they were afraid of being tried as war criminals. Auschwitz was being dismantled,* and orders had been given to stop the extermination program. But Eichmann was not to be stopped; he devised yet another scheme.

18   Jews now were to be rounded up to work on the "East Wall" in Vienna. The wall would supposedly be protection against the advance of the Russians. But, more important, Eichmann knew that most of the Jews who would be marched on foot to Vienna would not survive. The cold and hunger would do their work.

---

[1]SS: *Schutzstaffel* (protective units); the elite guard of the Nazi party, notorious for their brutal tactics.

19   Wallenberg also knew that the "labor march," as it was called, was bound to be a death march. He tried to have the march postponed but succeeded only in getting exemptions for those Jews bearing *Schutz* passes. On November 9, the march began.

20   Shivering for lack of clothing and starving for food, the Jews were marched toward the Austrian border. Anyone who stumbled or fell out of line was shot. The marchers were without hope. But then Wallenberg miraculously began to turn up at points along the way. Susan Tabor, a survivor of the march, described lying on the floor of a shed so crowded she could neither stand up nor move. Suddenly she saw Wallenberg stride in, carrying a briefcase. Through a megaphone he announced that food and medical supplies would soon arrive. When he left, the marchers had new hope. As Susan Tabor was to say long after the march was over, "He made me feel human again. For the first time I had hope" (Werbell & Clarke, 91).

21   As always, true to his word, Wallenberg returned the next day with food and medicine. He also brought a stack of protective passes. Within minutes, he had created chaos by telling the marchers to assemble in various lines:

> The Jews ran helter-skelter around the brick factory. They changed lines and jostled one another to get a good place as Wallenberg backed his trucks into the yard. The *Arrow Cross* guards lost control. . . . In the confusion many Jews simply walked away or bribed individual guards to let them escape. (Werbell & Clarke, 91)

This scene was repeated many times as Wallenberg worked tirelessly to save as many Jews as he could.

The Russians Arrive

22 By January of 1945, the Russians were closing in on Budapest, and it was clear to everyone that the war was truly coming to an end. On January 13, 1945, a small group of Russian soldiers broke through the wall of a house where Wallenberg was staying. He explained who he was, and the soldiers examined his documents. But something about Wallenberg or his papers seemed to make them suspicious. A few hours later, some high-ranking Soviet officials arrived to question him, in the first of several interrogations by the Russian secret police. Nevertheless, Wallenberg was permitted to move freely through the now-liberated city of Budapest.

23   On January 17, Wallenberg dropped in on friends before leaving to visit Soviet headquarters. He was in high spirits, convinced

that the Soviets wanted his advice on postwar relief and reconstruction: "The Russians are certain to respect the suggestions of a Swedish diplomat" (Werbell & Clarke, 157).

24   Shortly after the visit, Wallenberg left Budapest under Russian escort. As he looked at the soldiers who were to accompany him, he made a cruelly prophetic joke: "I still don't know if they're coming along to protect me or guard me. Am I a guest, or a prisoner?" (Werbell & Clarke, 158).

25   Even today, no one is really sure what happened to Raoul Wallenberg after he left with his Soviet escorts. When he failed to return to Budapest as planned, the Swedish Foreign Office sent the Russians a series of messages asking for an investigation. There was no reply. After repeated refusals of requests for information, the Soviets claimed to have no knowledge of his whereabouts. Then, in 1957, Andrei Gromyko, the Soviet deputy foreign minister, claimed Wallenberg had died in 1947. According to Gromyko, Wallenberg had suffered a heart attack at the age of thirty-four. Despite Soviet claims, however, rumors persist to this day that Raoul Wallenberg is still alive.

26   Whatever Wallenberg's fate, his name must be remembered and honored. As Frederick E. Werbell and Thurston Clarke have pointed out, Wallenberg's life is an important source of inspiration: "If the Holocaust is to be taken as evidence that human nature is essentially evil, then Wallenberg's life must be considered as evidence that it is not" (p. 256).

Sources of Information

Lester, Elenore. *Wallenberg: The Man in the Iron Web.* Englewood Cliffs, N.J.: Prentice-Hall, 1982.

Stanglin, Douglas, Mortimer B. Zuckerman, Jeff Trimble, and David Bartal. "A Lost Prisoner of the Gulag Still Holds Moscow Hostage." *U.S. News and World Report,* June 26, 1989, pp. 34–36.

"Wallenberg Reported Shot in '47." *New York Times,* October 18, 1990, A14.

Werbell, Frederick E., and Thurston Clarke. *Lost Hero: The Mystery of Raoul Wallenberg.* New York: McGraw-Hill, 1982.

PUTTING IT ALL TOGETHER   Answer the following questions by circling the letter of the correct response or filling in the blanks.

Main Idea and Paraphrasing   1. Which of the following most effectively paraphrases the main idea of the entire reading?

a. To this day, no one knows for sure what happened to Raoul Wallenberg.

b. After risking his life to save thousands of Hungarian Jews, Raoul Wallenberg mysteriously vanished, and, to this day, no one knows what happened to him.

c. If the life of Raoul Wallenberg illustrates everything that is good in humanity, the life of Adolf Eichmann reveals all that is evil.

d. Embarrassed by his wealth, Raoul Wallenberg wanted to give something back to the world.

Supporting
Details

2. Which of the following is a minor detail?

a. "In 1937, Raoul Wallenberg was a young man who seemed to have everything." (paragraph 1)

b. "His future seemed assured." (paragraph 1)

c. "Raoul Wallenberg arrived in Budapest on July 9, 1944." (paragraph 8)

d. "Wallenberg's next step was to set up a small network for the distribution of *Schutz* passes." (paragraph 11)

Inference and
Supporting
Details

3. What inference did Wallenberg draw from the stories about people who had escaped deportation and death?

a. People willing to commit murder could still be frightened by the sight of an official-looking document.

b. The Germans really were determined to kill all the Jews in Europe.

c. The Germans might not follow orders themselves, but they expected everyone else to do so.

d. The Nazis were none too bright.

4. Based on paragraph 11, which inference is appropriate?

a. Wallenberg held other Swedish diplomats in contempt.

b. Wallenberg was impatient with questions of procedure and legality when they concerned human lives.

c. Wallenberg was thoroughly disliked by other diplomats.

d. Hero or not, Wallenberg was often rude to subordinates.

5. In paragraph 13, which inference does the author expect readers to supply?

a. The troops withdrew because they had been called back to combat.

      b. The troops withdrew because they were intimidated by Wallenberg.

Irony **6.** Which of the following statements illustrates a type of irony discussed on pages 331–332?

      a. "If the Holocaust is to be taken as evidence that human nature is essentially evil, then Wallenberg's life must be considered as evidence that it is not."

      b. "The Russians are certain to respect the suggestions of a Swedish diplomat."

Explain your answer. _____

_____

7. In paragraph 16, why does the author use quotation marks for the words "safe" and "protected"?

_____

_____

Connotation **8.** During World War II, the followers of Adolf Hitler openly proclaimed
and their hatred and contempt for Jews. Yet they still used a euphe-
Denotation mism, "the Final Solution," to describe their plans for murdering all the Jews in Europe. What does that suggest to you?

_____

_____

_____

Tone **9.** How would you describe the author's tone?

      a. angry

      b. admiring

      c. emotionally neutral

Analyzing **10.** The author insists that Wallenberg must be remembered and hon-
Arguments ored. What reason does she give for her opinion?

_____

_____

_____

■   **DRAWING**   Why do you think Raoul Wallenberg was willing to risk his life for
   YOUR OWN   people he did not know? What do you think motivated him? Do you
   CONCLUSIONS   think you could be capable of that kind of heroism?

■   **THINKING**   It has been said that the Holocaust has become a symbol for the
   THROUGH   best and the worst in humanity. Write a paper explaining what you
   WRITING   think is meant by this claim, making sure to illustrate its meaning
   with specific examples.

■ **READING 10**

LEARNING AT HOME: DOES IT PASS THE TEST?
Barbara Kantrowitz and Pat Winger

LOOKING AHEAD Chapter 11 debated the subject of home schooling. The following reading suggests that home schooling, despite some controversy, is here to stay.

FOCUS STRATEGIES Read the first and last paragraphs. Then read the first sentence of the remaining paragraphs. When you finish, predict how you think the authors will answer the question posed in the title.

_____

_____

As you read, consider how you feel about home schooling. Would you consider taking your children out of school and teaching them at home?

WORD WATCH Some of the more difficult words in the reading are defined below. Watch for these words as you read. They are marked with an asterisk.

---

habitat: the place in which a person, plant, or creature is most likely to be found

province: area or location of control

fundamentalists: people who insist on extremely strict and rigid adherence to religious principles

unsavory: disagreeable, morally offensive

inundated: flooded

statutes: laws, rules

advocates: supporters

Pollyanna: a person who is foolishly optimistic; from the main character of the novel by the same name

---

1 THIS FALL, AS MOST KIDS MADE THEIR ANNUAL TREK BACK TO the classroom, a small but growing army of parents just said no to school. Some, like Jean Forbes of Alexandria, Virginia, thought their children needed extra attention. Forbes is a former actress

whose current career is teaching her two sons, Aaron, fourteen, and Jesse, seven, and running a theater group for forty other kids who are taught in their homes. She and her husband, Jan, pulled Aaron, who is dyslexic, out of public school six years ago because they felt teachers weren't helping him enough. Other parents want to give their kids the chance to follow their interests rather than a textbook. Outside Los Angeles, Marcy Kinsey, a mother of three kids—ages eleven, nine, and seven—calls herself an "un-schooler." Right now her kids are studying bats, everything from their diet to their wingspan to the specifics of their natural habi-tat.* They've even built a bat house in the backyard, which re-quired many hours of practical math problems.

2   Still other parents pull their kids out of school to solve what they think is a short-term problem—and find long-term chal-lenges. Eric and Joyce Burges, who live outside Baton Rouge, Lou-isiana, began home schooling nearly a decade ago after their old-est son, Eric Jr., had a disastrous year at a selective magnet high school. It was a struggle at first; neither is a professional teacher. But as Eric Jr.'s confidence rose at home, so did Joyce's, and she now teaches her four other kids, ages fifteen to three, at home as well. School begins every morning at 7 and lasts until lunch. Joyce says home schooling has been a test of her strengths and weaknesses. Accepting the latter, she hired music and algebra tu-tors. "I know what I want them to learn, and I know what they want to learn," she says. "I don't have to do it all."

3   Just a few years ago, home schooling was the province* of re-ligious fundamentalists* who wanted to instill their values in their children and back-to-the-earth types who rejected the insti-tutional nature of public schools. Now it's edging ever closer to the mainstream. In 1993—after years of court battles—it became legal in all fifty states for parents to take charge of their kids' edu-cation from kindergarten to college. While there are no national statistics, researchers who study home schooling estimate that as many as 1.5 million youngsters are currently being taught primar-ily by their mothers or fathers. That's five times the estimated number of home schoolers just a decade ago and bigger than the nation's largest public-school system, New York City's. The in-crease is especially remarkable in an era of two-income families, since it pretty much requires one parent to stay home (generally the mother), at some financial sacrifice. In a recent *Newsweek* poll, 59 percent of those surveyed said home-schooled kids were at least as well educated as students in traditional schools. "Home schoolers' image is not wacko, fringe, lunatic-type people anymore," says Brian Ray, president of the Home Education Research Insti-

tute in Salem, Oregon, a nonprofit group. "Today almost everyone knows a home schooler, so it's more socially acceptable."

4   Some of the new home-schooling parents are looking for a way to reclaim family closeness in an increasingly fast-paced society. Others have kids with special needs, perhaps because they're highly gifted or have learning disabilities or emotional problems. Still other parents worry about unsavory* influences in school—drugs, alcohol, sex, violence. Florida education officials report that in the last few years, the number one reason parents gave for home schooling was "safety." Some intend to teach at home all the way through twelfth grade. Others see home schooling as a way to get through a bad patch in a kid's school life.

5   Their lesson plans are as diverse as their reasons for dropping out of the system, but what unites all these parents is a belief that they can do a better job at home than trained educators in a conventional school. That would have been an outrageous notion a generation ago, when far fewer parents had college degrees and most people regarded teachers and schools with more respect and even awe. Today parents are much better educated, hooked up to a world of information via the Internet and inundated* with headlines about problems plaguing public schools. They see home schooling as one more step in the evolution of parent power that has given birth to school-choice programs, vouchers, and charter schools. "Americans are becoming fussy consumers rather than trusting captives of a state monopoly," says Chester Finn, a senior fellow at the Hudson Institute, a Washington, D.C., think tank. "They've declared their independence and are taking matters into their own hands."

6   But while home schooling is winning converts, it still has plenty of critics who worry that millions of youngsters will grow up without adequate academic or social skills. "Kids need to be successful in three overlapping spheres—at home, at school, and with peers," says Phoenix pediatrician Daniel Kessler, a member of the American Academy of Pediatrics developmental-behavior group. "Home schooling compresses all that into a single setting that can be very difficult for kids." The National Education Association, the nation's biggest teachers' union, backs much more rigorous regulation.

7   Only thirty-seven states now have statutes* that set standards for home schooling, says Christopher Klicka, executive director of the National Center for Home Education, an advocacy group. About half of those demand some kind of annual testing or evaluation; the rest require only that certain subjects be covered within a specified time frame. Many educators say it's the government's responsibility to make sure kids get what they need to become

productive citizens. "After all, if home schooling fails," says Ronald Areglado of the National Association of Elementary School Principals, "we pay the freight" when a person ends up on public assistance or in jail. Areglado has good reason for his concern; as a principal, he saw a home-schooled kid who got no instruction at all from his parents.

8   But home-schooling parents say they are better equipped than ever before to give kids what they need. "What they're doing is reinventing the idea of school," says Patricia Lines, a senior research analyst for the U.S. Department of Education. The Internet and sophisticated new educational software help fill in academic gaps. If they need more inspiration, they can browse through bookstore shelves filled with how-to books and subscribe to dozens of newsletters and magazines with titles like *Growing Without Schooling* that are packed with ads for home-schooling textbooks, videos and software, and seminars. "There are much better, more sophisticated curriculum materials available," says Kathi Kearney, an expert in the home schooling of gifted students at Iowa State University.

9   These tools have transformed the conventional image of a home-schooling family: a couple of kids with workbooks open on the kitchen table under the supervision of Mom or Dad. Not only have the new generation of home schoolers moved beyond workbooks, they've also moved well out of the kitchen and often join home-schooling cooperatives, where parents take turns teaching different subjects and get together for group field trips. Jean Forbes's home-schooling theater group in Virginia is more than just a chance for kids to enjoy center stage. History and even science lessons are part of the program. When the girls put on hoop skirts for *Little Women*, they talked about how children played a century ago. When they used dry ice onstage in a play, they talked about the science behind the special effects.

10   Home-schooling parents are also turning to a surprising source for help: public schools. In the wake of lawsuits in many states by home-schooling parents, more communities are opening the doors to school libraries or computer rooms. Some districts have "part time" options that allow kids to sign up for a few courses or participate in extracurricular activities like the football team or the band. Oregon even allows students to register for courses at different schools, so that a teenager could take advanced biology at one high school and art at another. Almost every state now has a home-schooling coordinator, and some, such as Washington and Iowa, have established resource centers for parents—giving families a chance to get something in return for their taxes.

11   In California—where the troubled public schools have pushed thousands of parents into home schooling—many families sign up for the independent study program at their local public schools to get books and other materials. A teacher monitors the child's progress, usually through monthly visits. Jon Shemitz, a computer-programming consultant, enrolled his son, Sam, ten, in independent study through his district near Santa Cruz. During the teacher's monthly visits, Shemitz says, she "fills out the paperwork, sits around and chats, and allows us to participate in a few programs like field trips."

12   Despite these new resources, no one really knows how this new generation of home schoolers will turn out. There are no reliable long-term studies, but advocates* say home schoolers generally do as well as other kids on standardized tests, and some are accepted into the most elite colleges. Harvard has even assigned an admissions officer, David Illingsworth, to review applications from home schoolers. "Ten years ago, if you didn't have a diploma we didn't want you," he says. "Today we're always willing to look at different kinds of credentials." Other colleges have mixed views of home-schooled students. In one recent survey of admissions officers, only 20 percent thought that parents were better able to motivate their children than teachers. But 83 percent agreed that high school students could be adequately taught at home.

13   At every age, a strong parent-child relationship is far more important than any particular curriculum, experts say. Those bonds can be stretched when the whole family is together 24-7. Kids have to respect parents as teachers and still love them as Mom and Dad—a difficult task. Parents don't even have the luxury of time off while their children are in the classroom; they are always on duty. It's so tough that some parents give up after only a year or two. "I've seen it tear families apart," says William Coleman, associate professor of pediatrics at the University of North Carolina.

14   Kids with special needs—gifted or learning disabled—are more likely than most to benefit from home schooling, researchers say, but only if their parents have the right training and resources. Ryan Abradi, a ten-year-old who lives in central Maine, started multiplying when he was just two and a half, and even then understood the concept of negative numbers. "From the beginning, he seemed hard-wired for math," says his mother, Valerie, a mechanical engineer. When he reached school age, she checked out the local gifted program and could tell right away that Ryan was already well beyond it. "He had no patience," she says. "He was intolerant of the questions other kids would ask." Ryan is now hap-

pily at home, working his way through second-semester college calculus.

15   Home-schooling parents reject critics' claims that their kids aren't well socialized. Many of them say they've overcome the isolation by getting kids involved in Scouts, 4-H, or sports teams. "Ninety percent of these kids play with people outside their families," says Brian Ray of the National Home Education Research Institute. But home-schooled kids themselves say they are different—in both good and bad ways. They're probably more likely to be independent and self-motivated, but group activities can be a struggle. Eighteen-year-old Jon Williams of Missoula, Montana, is clearly outgoing and confident: he's a Republican candidate for his state's legislature. But Williams, who has been home schooled since ninth grade, credits the eight years he spent in Christian school with helping him hone his basic social skills. . . .

16   Social isolation can be especially damaging in the middle-school years, says Coleman of the University of North Carolina. "Parents have this Pollyanna* view that they're going to keep their kids away from bad influences," he says, "when kids biologically and psychosocially are going to want to push away" from their families.

17   At some point, of course, home-schooled kids will move out on their own. What lessons will serve them best? The ultimate goal of any educational path is to inspire love of learning, a passion that lasts a lifetime.

Barbara Kantrowitz and Pat Winger,
"Learning at Home: Does It Pass the Test?"
Newsweek, October 5, 1998, pp. 66–70.

PUTTING IT ALL TOGETHER   Answer the following questions by circling the letter of the correct response or filling in the blanks.

Main Idea   **1.** Which statement more effectively sums up the main idea of the entire reading?

   a. Despite controversy, home schooling is becoming part of the mainstream with more and more parents teaching their kids at home.

   b. Home schooling, once the province of religious fundamentalists, has become so successful that children are leaving public schools in droves and threatening the future of public education.

   c. Academically, home schooling may offer kids advantages, but it will keep them socially inept.

   d. Home schooling is most appropriate for kids with special needs or special gifts.

2. What's the implied main idea of paragraph 4?

   a. Parents who choose home schooling are hoping that it will encourage family unity.

   b. There are several different reasons why parents choose to school their children at home.

   c. Parents who choose home schooling are worried about their children's safety.

Supporting Details

3. Paragraph 3 ends with which type of supporting detail?

   a. major

   b. minor

Predicting Test Questions

4. On the basis of the reading, which test question is likely to turn up on an exam?

   a. Identify at least three famous people who were taught at home.

   b. Write an essay explaining why some parents are teaching their children at home.

   c. Trace the history of home schooling from the nineteenth century until now.

Fact and Opinion

5. Label the following statement *F* (fact), *O* (opinion), or *B* (both).

   In 1993 . . . it became legal in all fifty states for parents to take charge of their kids' education from kindergarten to college.

   _____

   Explain your answer. _____

   _____

   _____

Purpose

6. Which statement more accurately expresses the purpose of this reading?

   a. The authors want to describe for their readers the current status of the home-schooling movement.

   b. The authors want to convince their readers that home schooling is a wise choice.

   How did you determine the author's purpose? What clues did you use?

   _____

   _____

Bias **7.** In paragraph 3, Brian Ray is quoted in support of home schooling. With what organization is he affiliated?

_____

What does that organization suggest to you about Mr. Ray's possible bias?

_____

8. In paragraph 6, Daniel Kessler criticizes the home schooling movement. What are his qualifications as a source of expert opinion?

_____

What do those qualifications suggest about Mr. Kessler's possible bias?

_____

_____

9. Based on how the authors describe Ronald Areglado in paragraph 7, would you expect Mr. Areglado to be biased in favor of or against home schooling?

_____

Explain your answer. _____

_____

Analyzing **10.** In paragraph 8, the author tells us that Kathi Kearney is an "expert." *Arguments* In response, what question might critical readers pose about her qualifications?

_____

■ **DRAWING YOUR OWN CONCLUSIONS** In the reading you just finished, both sides of the home-schooling debate argue their positions. Which side do you think offered the more effective argument and why?

■ **THINKING THROUGH WRITING** Write a paper in which you argue for or against home schooling. Give at least two reasons for your position, and be sure to respond to at least one objection.

Acknowledgments

Simon Adams and Lesley Riley, reprinted from *Facts & Fallacies,* copyright © 1988 by The Reader's Digest Association, Inc., Pleasantville, New York, www.rd.com. **Freda Adler, Gerhard O. W. Mueller, and William S. Laufer,** from *Criminal Justice,* 1994, pp. 237, 349, 352-353. Copyright © 1994. Reproduced with permission of The McGraw-Hill Companies. **Albert Richard Allgeier and Elizabeth Rice Allgeier,** *Sexual Interactions,* 5/e. © 1995 Houghton Mifflin Company. Reprinted by permission. **Carol Berkin et al.,** from *Making America: A History of the United States.* Copyright © 1995 by Houghton Mifflin Company. Used by permission. **Roy Berko, Andrew D. Wolvin, and Darlyn W. Wolvin,** from *Communicating.* Used by permission of Houghton Mifflin Company. **Douglas H. Bernstein and Peggy W. Nash et al.,** adapted from *Essentials of Psychology.* Copyright © 2002 by Houghton Mifflin Company. Used by permission. **Paul Boyer et al.,** from *Enduring Vision,* pp. 695a-695b. Copyright © 2000 by Houghton Mifflin Company. Used by permission. **Paul Boyer,** from *Promises to Keep.* Copyright © 1999 by Houghton Mifflin Company. Used by permission. **Sharon S. Brehm and Saul M. Kassin,** from *Social Psychology.* Copyright © 1997 by Houghton Mifflin Company. Used by permission. **Judith Ortiz Cofer,** from *The Latin Deli: Prose & Poetry,* pp. 28-33. Reprinted by permission of The University of Georgia Press. **Dennis Coon,** from *Essentials of Psychology: Exploration and Application,* 6/e, © 1994. Reprinted with permission of Brooks/Cole, an imprint of the Wadsworth Group, a division of Thomson Learning. Fax 800-730-2215. **Andrew J. DuBrin,** adapted from *Leadership.* Copyright © 1998 by Houghton Mifflin Company. Used by permission. **Ashley Dunn,** from "Cram Schools: Immigrants' Tools for Success," *New York Times,* 1/28/95, p. 1. Copyright © 1995 by the New York Times Co. Reprinted by permission. **Mike Eskenazi/FAIRFAX CITY,** from "Education/Special Report: The New Case for Latin. Some schools find that kids learn more about English by studying the language of ancient Rome," *Time,* 12/11/00, p. 61. © 2000 Time Inc. Reprinted by permission. **Daren Fonda/SAYREVILLE,** from "Sport: Suburban Smackdown. Wrestling fans, grab your lawn chairs. Teenage boys are brawling in a backyard near you," *Time,* 6/26/00, p. 53. © 2000 Time Inc. Reprinted by permission. **Howard W. French,** from "The Ritual Slaves of Ghana: Young and Female," *New York Times,* 1/20/97, pp. A1, A4. Copyright © 1997 by the New York Times Co. Reprinted by permission. **Alan Gitelson, Robert L. Dudley, and Melvin J. Dubrick,** from *American Government,* 5/e. © 1998 by Houghton Mifflin Company. Reprinted by permission. **William B. Gudykunst et al.,** from *Building Bridges: Personal Skills for a Changing World,* © 1995 by Houghton Mifflin Company. Reprinted by permission. **Janet Sibley Hyde,** from *Understanding Human Sexuality,* p. 524. Copyright © 1994. Reproduced with permission of the publisher, The McGraw-Hill Companies. **Kenneth Janda, Jeffrey M. Berry, and Jerry Goldman,** from *The Challenge of Democracy.* Copyright © 1995 by Houghton Mifflin Company. Used by permission. **Mike Jenkinson,** from "Why Photo Radar Just Does Not Work," *The Edmonton Sun,* 8/13/01, p. 11. Reprinted by permission of the author. **Barbara Kantrowitz and Pat Winger,** from *Newsweek,* October 5, 1998 © 1998 Newsweek Inc. All rights reserved. Reprinted by permission. **Saul Kassin,** from *Psychology.* Copyright © 1995 by Houghton Mifflin Company. Used by permission. **Nadya Labi,** "When Tragedy Strikes, Grief Counselors Give Aid," with reporting by Richard Woodbury/Littleton and Maggie Sieger/Oklahoma City, "Behavior: The Grief Brigade. When tragedy strikes, the counselors rush in. They offer succor, but their methods are up for debate," *Time,* 5/17/99, pp. 69+. © 1999 Time Inc. Reprinted by permission. **Michael D. Lemonick,** from "Science: Ants in Our Pants" reported by David Bjerklie/New York and Scott Norvell/Atlanta, 6/5/95. © 1995 Time Inc. Reprinted by permission. **Larry Z. Leslie,** from *Mass Communication.* Copyright © 2000 by Houghton Mifflin Company. Used by permission. **Michael McConnell,** information drawn from "Freedom from Religion?," *The American Enterprise,* Jan./Feb. 1993, pp. 32-43. Reprinted with permission of The American Enterprise, a magazine of Politics, Business, and Culture. **Samuel Eliot Morison,** from *The Oxford History Of The American People,* copyright © 1965 by Samuel Eliot Morison. Used by permission of Oxford University Press, Inc. **K. Mullen, R. McDermott, R. Gold, and P. Beleastro,** from *Connections for Health,* 4/e, pp. 211-213, 317, 380, 476. Copyright © 1996. Published by McGraw-Hill, Inc. Reprinted by permission of the authors. **S. Mydans,** "He's Not Hairy, He's My Brother," *New York Times,* 8/12/01. Copyright © 2001 by the New York Times Co. Reprinted by permission. **Mary Beth Norton et al.,** from *A People and a Nation.* Copyright © 1986, 1993, 1994, 1998, 2001 by Houghton Mifflin Company. Used by permission. **Ted Nugent,** from "Hunters Are Wildlife's Best Friends," *USA Today,* October 3, 1991. Reprinted by permission of the author. **Charles Panati,** reprinted by permission of Ellen Levine Literary Agency, Inc. Copyright © 1989 by Charles Panati. **PETA,** from fact sheet from "People for the Ethical Treatment of Animals." Used by permission of PETA. **William M. Pride, Robert J. Hughes, and Jack R. Kapoor,** from *Business.* Copyright © 2000, 1999 by Houghton Mifflin Company. Used by permission. **Kathleen Kelley Reardon,** copyright © 1995. First published in *They Don't Get It, Do They?* Reprinted by permission of Curtis Brown, Ltd. **Barry L. Reece and Rhonda Brandt,** from *Effective Human Relations in Organizations.* Copyright © 1999 by Houghton Mifflin Company. Used by permission. **Victoria Register-Freeman,** from *Newsweek,* November 4, 1996 © 1996 Newsweek Inc. All rights reserved. Reprinted by permission. **Zick Rubin, Letita Anne Peplau, and Peter Salovey,** from *Psychology.* Copyright © 1993, 1990 by Houghton Mifflin Company. Used by permission. **Kevin Ryan and James M. Cooper,** from *Those Who Can, Teach.* Copyright © 2000 by Houghton Mifflin Company. Used by permission. **Kelvin L. Seifert,** from *Educational Psychology.* Copyright © 1991 by Houghton Mifflin Company. Used by permission. **Kelvin L. Seifert, Robert Hoffnung, and Michele Hoffnung,** from *Lifespan Development.* Copyright © 2000 by Houghton Mifflin Company. Used by permission. **Alex Thio,** from *Sociology,* pp. 103-104, 174, 299. Copyright © 1997 by Allyn & Bacon. Reprinted/adapted by permission. **Van Fleet and Peterson,** adapted from *Contemporary Management.* Used by permission of Houghton Mifflin Company. **James Q. Wilson and John DiIulio, Jr.,** from *American Government,* 7/e. © 1998 by Houghton Mifflin Company. Reprinted by permission. **Charlton Wimberly,** "Porn Use a Catalyst for Violence," *University Wire,* 9/21/01. Reprinted by permission of the author.

INDEX